ISBN: 9781314513332

Published by:
HardPress Publishing
8345 NW 66TH ST #2561
MIAMI FL 33166-2626

Email: info@hardpress.net
Web: http://www.hardpress.net

Hunolt's Sermons.

Sermons by the Rev. Francis Hunolt, Priest of the Society of Jesus and Preacher in the Cathedral of Treves. Translated from the original German edition of Cologne, 1740, by the REV. J. ALLEN, D.D., Chaplain of the Dominican Convent of the Sacred Heart, King Williamstown, and of the Dominican Convent, East London, South Africa.

────── ▸◆◂ ──────

Vols. 1 & 2: The Christian State of Life;

Or, Sermons on the Principal Duties of Christians in general and of different States in particular, namely: Of young people towards God, their parents, and themselves, as far as the care of their souls and the selection of a state of life are concerned; of those who intend embracing the married state; of married people towards each other; of parents towards their children, in what concerns both the temporal and spiritual welfare of the latter; of heads of families towards their servants; of servants towards their masters; of subjects towards the spiritual and temporal authorities; of lay-people towards priests; of the rich towards God and the poor; on the state, dignity, and happiness of the poor; on the use of time, and making up for lost time; on the good and bad use of the morning and evening time, etc., etc. In **seventy-six Sermons**, adapted to all the Sundays and Holy-days of the Year. With a Full Index of all the Sermons, an Alphabetical Index of the Principal Subjects treated, and **Copious Marginal Notes.** 2 vols., 8vo, cloth, - - - - - - *net*, $5.00

Vols. 3 & 4: The Bad Christian;

Or, Sermons on the Seven Deadly Sins, and the different Sins against God and our Neighbor which flow therefrom. In **seventy-six Sermons**, adapted to all the Sundays and Holy-days of the Year. With a Full Index of all the Sermons, an Alphabetical Index of the Principal Subjects treated, and **Copious Marginal Notes.** 2 vols., 8vo, cloth, - - *net*, $5.00

BENZIGER BROTHERS, New York, Cincinnati, Chicago.

Hunolt's Sermons.

Vols. 5 & 6: The Penitent Christian;

Or, Sermons on the Virtue and the Sacrament of Penance, and on all that belongs to Repentance and the Amendment of one's life: including also special instructions on Penance during the time of a Jubilee and during Public Calamities. In **seventy-six Sermons**, adapted to all the Sundays and Holy-days of the Year. With a Full Index of all the Sermons, an Alphabetical Index of the Principal Subjects treated, and **Copious Marginal Notes**. 2 vols., 8vo, cloth, - *net*, $5.00

Vols. 7 & 8: The Good Christian;

Or, Sermons on the Chief Christian Virtues. In **seventy-six Sermons**, adapted to all the Sundays and Holy-days of the Year. With a Full Index of all the Sermons, an Alphabetical Index of the Principal Subjects treated, and **Copious Marginal Notes**. 2 vols., 8vo, cloth, - - - - - - *net*, $5.00

Vols. 9 & 10: The Christian's Last End;

Or, Sermons on the Four Last Things: Death, Judgment, Hell, and Heaven. In **seventy-six Sermons**, adapted to all the Sundays and Holy-days of the Year. With a Full Index of all the Sermons, an Alphabetical Index of the Principal Subjects treated, and **Copious Marginal Notes**. 2 vols., 8vo, cloth. *In preparation*, - - - - - - *net*, $5.00

Vols. 11 & 12: The Christian's Model;

Or, Panegyrics and Moral Discourses on the Life and Death of Our Lord Jesus Christ, and on the Example and Virtues of the Blessed Virgin Mary, and some of the great Saints. In **seventy-four Sermons**, adapted to all the Sundays and Holy-days of the Year. With a Full Index of all the Sermons, an Alphabetical Index of the Principal Subjects treated, and **Copious Marginal Notes**. 2 vols., 8vo, cloth. *In preparation*, *net*, $5.00

BENZIGER BROTHERS, New York, Cincinnati, Chicago.

Hunolt's Sermons.
Vol. VIII.

The Good Christian;

OR,

Sermons on the Chief Christian Virtues.

IN SEVENTY-SIX SERMONS.

ADAPTED TO ALL THE SUNDAYS AND MOST OF THE HOLY-DAYS OF THE YEAR.
WITH A FULL INDEX OF ALL THE SERMONS, AN ALPHABETICAL INDEX
OF THE PRINCIPAL SUBJECTS TREATED, AND

COPIOUS MARGINAL NOTES.

BY THE

REV. FATHER FRANCIS HUNOLT,

Priest of the Society of Jesus, and Preacher in the Cathedral of Treves.

Translated from the Original German Edition of Cologne, 1740,

BY THE

REV. J. ALLEN, D.D.,

*Chaplain of the Dominican Convent of the Sacred Heart, King Williamstown, and of
the Dominican Convent, East London, South Africa.*

VOLUME II.

NEW YORK, CINCINNATI, CHICAGO:

BENZIGER BROTHERS,

PRINTERS TO THE HOLY APOSTOLIC SEE.

1891.

Imprimatur.

† JAMES D. RICARDS,

*Bishop of Retimo and Vicar-Apostolic of the
Eastern Vicariate of the Cape Colony.*

CONTENTS OF VOL. VIII.

THIRTY-NINTH SERMON.

ON CONFIDENCE IN PRAYER.

Subject.

1. Confident prayer is that which is most pleasing to God, for He wishes us to pray to Him with confidence. 2. It is the most efficacious kind of prayer, to which God can refuse nothing.—*Preached on the Sunday within the Octave of the Nativity.*

Text.

Quæ non discedebat de templo, jejuniis et obsecrationibus serviens nocte ac die.—Luke ii. 37.

" Who departed not from the temple, by fastings and prayers serving night and day. "

Introduction.

Simeon, an old priest, comes into the temple; Anna, a widow eighty-four years of age, comes also at the same time. The former was urged to come by the Spirit of God: " And he came by the Spirit into the temple." [1] The latter came accidentally: " Now she at the same hour coming in confessed to the Lord." [2] They were both ignorant of what was to happen to them there, and both had the great joy and glory in their old age, before the end of their lives, to see and know Jesus, the Saviour of the world. Why were they so exceptionally favored? Of Simeon the Gospel says that he " was just, and devout, waiting for the consolation of Israel," [3] and of Anna, that she " departed not from the temple, by fastings and prayers serving night and day." Mark this, my dear brethren; both were anxiously looking out for the redemption of Israel, that is, the advent of the promised Messias. Simeon was " waiting for the consolation of Israel," and Anna " spoke of Him," that is, Christ, " to all that looked

---

[1] Et venit in spiritu in templum.—Luke ii. 27.
[2] Et hæc ipsa hora superveniens confitebatur Domino.—Ibid. 38.
[3] Justus et timoratus, exspectans consolationem Israel.—Ibid. 25.

7

for the redemption of Israel." [1] Both were equally confident in the prayers they offered up in the temple for this end. Therefore both had the happiness and great joy to see their Saviour. He who trusts in God shall not be disappointed, as I explained last Advent. But now, if besides constancy we also have confidence in prayer, what may we not obtain from the Divine Generosity? To answer that question in a word, I say, everything—everything that it is possible for us to obtain. For it is once for all certain that no prayer is more agreeable or efficacious in the sight of God than that which is offered to Him with confidence. This is the subject of this sermon.

Plan of Discourse.

God wishes us to have confidence in prayer; therefore confident prayer is that which pleases Him best. This I shall show in the first part. Confident prayer is the only one to which God can refuse nothing; therefore it is the most efficacious, as we shall see in the second part.

Give us all, O Lord, by Thy powerful grace, that confidence in prayer; we ask this of Thee through the intercession of Mary and of our holy guardian angels.

God wishes us to pray to Him as children to a father.

That the Lord wishes us to call upon Him with an assured confidence is evident enough from the first two words of that chief and most powerful of all prayers which Jesus Christ Himself taught us and exhorts us to say daily, " Our Father." Mark this well, my dear brethren, as the foundation of what I am about to say; God wishes us to pray to Him as children to a father. And He calls Himself by this name " Father" almost exclusively when speaking of prayer. He admonishes all men by the wise Ecclesiastes to think of Him and serve Him truly from their earliest years: " Remember thy Creator in the days of thy youth." [2] Thus He wishes us in our earliest years to think of our last end, so that we may serve Him all the days of our lives and be happy with Him forever in heaven. When He reproves His people for ingratitude, or reminds them of the benefits bestowed on them, He generally calls Himself their Saviour and Redeemer: " For I am the Lord thy God, the Holy One of Israel, thy Saviour; I have given Egypt for thy atonement, Ethiopia and Saba for thee." [3] And elsewhere He says: " I am the Lord, and there

---

[1] Loquebatur de illo omnibus qui exspectabant redemptionem Israel.—Luke ii. 38.

[2] Memento Creatoris tui in diebus juventutis tuae.—Eccles. xii. 1.

[3] Quia ego Dominus Deus tuus, Sanctus Israel, Salvator tuus ; dedi propitiationem tuam Ægyptum, Æthiopiam et Sabam pro te.—Is. xliii. 3.

is no saviour beside Me;"[1] for am I not your God and Saviour who brought you out of Egypt, and saved you from the yoke of your enemies? Why have you, then, been so ungrateful as to rebel against Me? Whenever He commands or forbids anything to be done, He generally uses the expression: "Thus saith the Lord;" go, O Prophet and tell the people in My name what I wish; "thus saith the Lord Almighty;" His object in speaking thus of Himself being to add weight to His commands, and let the people see that they must do what such a Sovereign Majesty orders. So, also, when He threatens to visit His people with scourges, He says, I will visit you with famine, war, and pestilence, and "you shall know that I am the Lord." But when speaking of prayer He lays aside all His glory and majesty, as it were, and takes that most meek and loving name of Father. So shall you pray and make known your wants to Me: Our Father who art in heaven. Do you wish to pray? says Christ in the Gospel of St. Matthew. Then go into your room alone, and there call on your Father: "But thou, when thou shalt pray, enter into thy chamber, and having shut the door, pray to thy Father in secret; and thy Father, who seeth in secret, will repay thee."[2] "Amen, amen I say to you, if you ask the Father anything in My name, He will give it you."[3] When two or three of you are gathered together in My name, whatever you ask shall be done to you by My Father. Thus, whenever mention is made of prayer, God does not speak of Himself as the Lord, or Almighty, or as Creator, or Saviour, but as Father.

But what is the meaning of that, unless that we are to pray to Him as children to a father, that is, with child-like love and confidence, with the assurance of receiving from Him whatever is good for us? For the name father, according to its proper signification, is one of goodness, affection, tender love, mercy, and generosity. "Father is a name of affection," says Cardinal Hugo. [4] If the name *pater* comes from *pati*, which means to suffer, then it signifies that a father suffers anything with readiness for the sake of his children. If it comes from the word *portare*, to carry, it signifies the love with which the father carries his child on his arm to keep it from evil. If it comes from

Hence He wishes us to pray with confidence. That is shown by the name of Father.

---

[1] Ego sum Dominus, et non est absque me salvator.—Is. xliii. 11.

[2] Tu autem cum oraveris, intra in cubiculum tuum, et clauso ostio ora Patrem tuum in abscondito; et Pater tuus, qui videt in abscondito, reddet tibi.—Matt. vi. 6.

[3] Amen, amen dico vobis, si quid petieritis Patrem in nomine meo, dabit vobis. John xvi. 23.   [4] Pater est nomen affectus.

patefacere, to open, it means that the father opens his heart to his children. And, finally, if it comes from *pascere,* to feed, it signifies the loving care with which the father provides his children with everything necessary for their support. All this tends to nothing else than to give children the utmost confidence in their fathers. "O great dignity of all who pray," exclaims Cajetan, "to have a Father in heaven!"[1] Rejoice, he continues; you are told to present your petition to God, not as a servant to a master, nor a subject to a sovereign, nor a criminal to a judge, "but as a son to a father, with filial affection, confidence, nay, certainty,"[2] that you will not be refused. St. Paul writes in the same strain to the Romans who were converted to the true faith. My dear brethren, he says, "you have not received the spirit of bondage again in fear, but you have received the spirit of adoption of sons, whereby we cry: Abba (Father),"[3] like little children, as St. Athanasius beautifully remarks, who clap their hands and cry out, Father, a word which inspires the utmost love and confidence.

Which should be enough to inspire us with child-like confidence.

And truly it must be a stupid or wicked child who has no confidence in its father. If you asked something of importance from your prince, and the latter referred the whole matter to your father, could you doubt that your request would be granted? Could the prince give you a more desirable answer than to say to you: Go to your father; I will agree to everything he says, and will at once grant your petition? Oh, what a good Saviour we have, Christians! When we want anything, He refers us to our heavenly Father, who is goodness, mercy, generosity, and love itself. To Him we must make known our wants, and cry out Abba, Father! And what an impression will not those words make on such a fatherly heart, in which love and mercy have their abode!

Shown by examples from Script-ure.

When the Patriarch Abraham was climbing the mountain with his son Isaac, whom he was about to sacrifice, Isaac said to him: "My father, behold fire and wood; where is the victim for the holocaust?"[4] I see you have the sword, I am carrying the wood for the fire, but I cannot see a victim. St. John Chrysostom considers those words of Isaac, "my father." Ah, what a cruel

[1] O magna dignitas cujuslibet orantis, habere Patrem in cœlo.
[2] Sed ut filius ad patrem, filiali affectu, filiali fiducia, imo securitate.
[3] Non accepistis spiritum servitutis iterum in timore, sed accepistis spiritum adoptionis filiorum, in quo clamamus : Abba (Pater).—Rom. viii. 15.
[4] Pater mi, ecce ignis et ligna, ubi est victima holocausti ?—Gen. xxii. 7.

wound those loving words of the child must have inflicted on the father's heart! And God allowed it, so that, Abraham's most tender affection for his son being aroused, his obedience might be put to a still greater proof; for the name of father pronounced by the lips of a child has a most powerful effect on the heart. Absalom was an undutiful son and a rebel against his father David, and yet how bitterly his father deplored his death! "The king therefore being much moved, went up to the high chamber over the gate, and wept. And as he went he spoke in this manner: My son Absalom, Absalom my son; would God that I might die for thee." [1] But, holy king, why dost thou weep? Dost thou mourn for a rebel who tried to deprive thee of thy throne? He is now out of thy way, and thou hast nothing more to fear from him; thou shouldst therefore rather rejoice. Ah, says St. Gregory in the person of David, you know not what it is to be a father. Although Absalom was an undutiful child, yet he was my son, and I am inconsolable, now that he is taken away from me by death. The prodigal was, as it appears, well aware of the force of fatherly love, for he said with the utmost confidence, in spite of his misdeeds: "I will arise and will go to my father, and say to him: Father, I have sinned against heaven and before thee." [2] What? says St. Peter Chrysologus; what? undutiful son that you are, will you dare to go to your father, whom you have so grievously offended? What hope or confidence can you have in approaching him? And he answers in the person of the prodigal: What hope? what confidence? That which I have in the fact that he is my father. If I have not behaved as his son, he has not therefore lost the quality of a father. [3] His heart and affection will plead for me far more powerfully than my words; and if I only say "father" to him, he must forgive me. Therefore I will go to him without hesitation; "I will arise and will go to my father."

If that is the case, my dear brethren, with what confidence should we not go to our heavenly father and pray to Him, of whom Tertullian says: "There is no one so loving, no one so fatherly." [4] He says of Himself by the Prophet Isaias: "Can a woman forget her infant, so as not to have pity on the son of

We should have much more confidence in our heavenly Father.

---

[1] Contristatus itaque rex ascendit cœnaculum portæ et flevit. Et sic loquebatur vadens: Fili mi Absalom, Absalom fili mi, quis mihi tribuat ut ego moriar pro te.— II. Kings xviii. 33.

[2] Surgam, et ibo ad patrem meum, et dicam ei: Pater, peccavi in cœlum et coram te.— Luke xv. 18.

[3] Ille quod patris est non amisit.

[4] Tam pius nemo; tam pater nemo.

her womb? And if she should forget, yet will not I forget thee; behold, I have graven thee in My hands."[1]   And Christ assures us in the Gospel of St. John: "I say not to you that I will ask the Father for you;" that is not necessary, "for the Father Himself loveth you;"[2] and He is already inclined and most desirous to bestow on you all the graces you wish.

And all the more since God wishes us to pray to Him in the name of His Son.

But if this title of loving Father is not powerful enough to inspire us with a child-like confidence in Him, God is pleased that we should pray to Him in the name of His only-begotten Son. When a suppliant has been fortunate enough to render some service to the lord to whom he presents his petition, he is far more likely to have that petition granted; for the lord will be moved to show his liberality to one who has been so useful to him. Thus the Jews, in order to urge Our Lord to hear the centurion's prayer and restore his servant to health, said: "He is worthy that Thou shouldst do this for him; for he loveth our nation."[3] Thus, too, the poor widows, in order to move St. Peter to raise Tabitha to life, showed him the clothes she gave them: "And all the widows stood about him weeping, and showing him the coats and garments which Dorcas made them."[4]   Now, my dear brethren, if the confidence we must have that God will hear our prayers had to be founded on our own merits, then indeed we might despair of obtaining the least thing from Him; but it is built on the merits of Jesus Christ, the Son of God, in whose name we offer our prayers to our heavenly Father, and whose merits far surpass all the graces that we can ever desire, and are accepted by the almighty Father with the assurance that they will be useful to us. Hence, although our prayers of themselves are worth nothing, yet, since they are offered in the name of Jesus Christ, who helps them with His infinite merits, they can obtain everything. Suppose that a prince agrees, in case you perform a certain service for him, to grant you, besides other rewards, the freedom of two men who are sentenced to death. You perform the service. The two criminals beg the prince to free them, mentioning your name, and you help their petition.

---

[1] Numquid oblivisci potest mulier infantem suum, ut non misereatur filio uteri sui? Et si illa oblita fuerit, ego tamen non obliviscar tui; ecce in manibus meis descripsi te.—Isa. xlix. 15, 16.

[2] Non dico vobis quia ego rogabo Patrem de vobis; ipse enim Pater amat vos.—John xvi. 26, 27.

[3] Quia dignus est ut hoc illi praestes; diliget enim gentem nostram.—Luke vii. 4, 5.

[4] Circumsteterunt illum omnes viduae flentes, et ostendentes ei tunicas et vestes, quas faciebat illis Dorcas.—Acts ix. 39.

Their prayers of themselves have no effect on the prince, but since they are coupled with your name, and on account of the service rendered him by you, the freedom which they do not deserve is granted to the malefactors. Amongst the other favors promised the sacred humanity of Our Lord by His heavenly Father, is the assurance that He would give Him all He might ask for us. God can refuse us; but when our intercessor Jesus Christ comes forward, and, as He has promised, speaks to His Father for us—"who is at the right hand of God, who also maketh intercession for us"[1]—there is then an almost infallible certainty, nay, an obligation of justice on the part of Christ that our prayers will be heard. "He exacts the right due to His merits," says St. Ambrose, speaking of this passage, "and obtains the concession of the reward which He had already asked the Father for us."[2] Therefore the Catholic Church usually concludes her prayers with the words "through Christ, Our Lord."

My dear brethren, if God had not given us such magnificent promises that He would hear our prayers—"Ask and you shall receive," He says—could He give more emphatic expression to His desire that we should address Him with child-like confidence and certainty in prayer than His wish that we should pray to Him as to a father, and that, too, in the name of His well-beloved Son? And yet we hesitate to trust to such a God! And we are afraid to approach Him with a joyful countenance, lest He should take it in bad part! Nay, we tremble when we think of Him, and dare not allow ourselves to believe that He means well towards us. We are filled with anguish when we remember the eternity to which we are hastening, and have not courage enough to claim a share in God and in the happiness He has promised in the next life. In a word, we almost despair of ever getting to heaven. O ye of little faith, I must say to such people, in the words of Our Lord to St. Peter when the latter was on the point of sinking into the water, why do you doubt? Let those who do not serve their God give way to despair and want of confidence; but you who try to serve God and do His will, hope in the Lord. Have confidence in your heavenly Father; if there is anything you require to help you on the road to heaven, ask Him for it, and that, too, with child-like confidence, for it is the will of God that we should put that confidence in Him. Nay,

Therefore we can and should pray to God with an assured confidence.

---

[1] Qui est ad dexteram Dei, qui etiam interpellat pro nobis.—Rom. viii. 34.

[2] Exigit jus suis meritis debitum, et præmium jam ante a Patre impetratum, quod nobis applicari petit et concedi.

prayer of this kind is the only one to which He can refuse nothing, as we shall see in the

Second Part.

God has promised everything to prayer, provided it is confident.

It seems to me that I have already proved this part of my subject when I said that God, besides pledging His own word, has also given us His Son as a proof that He is willing to grant us all we ask from Him. For according to the received saying, every promise makes an obligation. What we promise we are bound to fulfil. Hence He who is infinitely faithful, and cannot deceive, must of necessity keep His promise. And truly He will do so; but mark well that He has not bound Himself to hear the prayer that is, as it were, carelessly thrown down before Him. No; we cannot claim the fulfilment of His promise unless our prayers have, besides other qualities, that of assured faith and child-like confidence. In the first chapter of the Epistle of St. James you will find these words: "If any of you want wisdom, let him ask of God, who giveth to all men abundantly, and upbraideth not; and it shall be given him." But how is he to ask? "Let him ask in faith, nothing wavering; for he that wavereth is like a wave of the sea, which is moved and carried about by the wind; therefore let not that man think that he shall receive anything of the Lord." [1]   Hence we must pray in faith and without hesitation, which words St. Thomas Aquinas thus explains: "In faith, that is, with the confidence of being heard; nothing wavering, that is, not doubting of being heard." [2]   Such, too, is the meaning Our Lord gives to the word *faith* when He uses it speaking of prayer: "I say unto you, all things, whatsoever you ask when ye pray, believe that you shall receive, and they shall come unto you." [3]   "If thou canst believe," said He to the father who asked Him to free his son from the dumb spirit, "all things are possible to him that believeth." [4]   "Go, and as thou hast believed, so be it done to thee," [5] said He to the centurion in the Gospel of St. Matthew.

[1] Si quis autem vestrum indiget sapientia, postulet a Deo, qui dat omnibus affluenter, et non improperat, et dabitur ei. Postulet autem in fide, nihil hæsitans ; qui enim hæsitat similis est fluctui maris, qui a vento movetur et circumfertur. Non ergo æstimet homo ille quod accipiat aliquid a Domino.—James i. 5, 6, 7.

[2] In fide, hoc est in fiducia obtinendi ; nihil hæsitans, hoc est, de impetratione non diffidens.

[3] Dico vobis, omnia quæcunque orantes petitis, credite quia accipietis, et evenient vobis. —Mark xi. 24.

[4] Si potes credere, omnia possibilia sunt credenti.—Ibid. ix. 22.

[5] Vade, et sicut credidisti fiat tibi.—Matt. viii. 13.

"Do you believe that I can do this unto you?" He asked the blind men. "Yea, Lord," they answered. "Then He touched their eyes, saying: According to your faith be it done unto you."[1] "All things whatsoever you shall ask in prayer believing, you shall receive,"[2] He assures us by St. Matthew. "Amen I say to you, that whosoever shall say to this mountain, Be thou removed and be cast into the sea, and shall not stagger in his heart, but believe that whatsoever he saith shall be done, it shall be done unto him."[3]

From that, my dear brethren, you can see that the measure according to which God will hear our prayers is the confidence and steadfast faith with which they are offered to Him. We read of Anna, the wife of Elcana, that, after having prayed with many tears for a male heir, "the woman went on her way, and ate, and her countenance was no more changed,"[4] as if she were quite certain that her prayer would be heard. Speaking of this passage, St. John Chrysostom says: See the faith of that woman; before receiving what she asked for she was just as satisfied as if it were already in her possession. In the same way should you, too, O Christian, trust in God. Do you want something that is necessary or advantageous for your salvation? then betake yourself to prayer, and believe firmly that you will be heard: believe it as firmly as if an angel came and told it you. But you will think, is it not presumptuous to act in that way, as if God were bound to hear us? It would indeed be presumptuous if you trusted in your own merits, but not when your confidence is grounded on the goodness and fidelity of God. It might be called a holy presumption, by which one abandons himself completely and with full confidence to the divine goodness; a presumption that is most pleasing to God, and which always characterized the intercourse of the saints with Him.

St. Gregory of Nazianzen writes of his sister Gorgonia that she generally poured forth her prayers with a holy presumption. On one occasion she fell grievously ill, and going into the church, she threw herself on her knees before the altar and threatened Our Lord that she would not go away until He restored her to

We must not doubt, then, that God will hear our prayers.

After the example of holy servants of God.

---

[1] Creditis quia hoc possum facere vobis? Utique Domine. Tunc tetigit oculos eorum, di cens : secundum fidem vestram fiat vobis.—Matt. ix. 28, 29.

[2] Omnia quæcunque petieritis in oratione credentes accipietis.—Ibid. xxi. 22.

[3] Amen dico vobis, quia quicunque dixerit huic monti: tollere et mittere in mare; et non hæsitaverit in corde suo, sed crediderit, quia quodcunque dixerit fiat, fiet ei.—Mark xi. 23.

[4] Abiit mulier in viam suam, et comedit, vultusque illius non sunt amplius in diversa mutati.—I. Kings i. 18.

health.[1] Palladius relates that a young man possessed by the
devil was brought to Paul the Hermit. The humble man did
not dare to exorcise the Evil One in his own name, but said to
him: "Go out; the Abbot Anthony commands you."[2] But
the demon paid no attention and went on cursing Paul and Anthony; I will not go out, said he; you may do your worst!
Then Paul betook himself to prayer. What is the meaning of
this, O Lord, said he with a sort of displeasure, as it were; wilt
Thou not, then, command the devil to obey me? I have had to
do with him now for nearly half a day; and now I tell Thee
that "I will not eat nor drink until I die of hunger, unless Thou
grantest my prayer and commandest the demon to depart from
this man."[3]   And at that moment the devil went away and
never came back. Surius relates in the Life of St. Catharine of
Siena, under the date of the 29th of April, that when the Saint's
mother died suddenly without the sacraments, she cried out
with the utmost fervor and confidence in God: How, O Lord, is
that the way in which Thou keepest Thy promises? Hast Thou
not assured me that no one in my family shall die an unhappy
death, and now Thou hast allowed my mother to depart without
the sacraments? Hear me, O Lord; I will not leave this place
until Thou restorest my mother to life again. O wonderful
power that the confident prayer of the just has over the almighty
God! Her mother was restored to life and lived for many years
after. Still more wonderful was the effect of the prayer of St.
Anianus. The king of Babylon had told the Christians that, if
their faith was true, they should be able to move mountains, and
therefore, if within a given time they did not make the mountain
he pointed out to them change its position, they should either
renounce their faith or else be put to death as liars. There was
no use in saying to the king that it is unlawful to tempt God,
and that we should not ask Him to perform miracles without
urgent necessity; that Christ, our Saviour, taught us to pray humbly, but not rashly, and that prayer is designed to help human
weakness, but not to gratify curiosity. The barbarian king
would not have seen the force of such an argument. The
Christians were in a state of the greatest consternation, and earnestly begged of God to help them, since they did not dare to

---

[1] Minitans non prius altare dimissuram, quam esset nacta sanitatem.

[2] Egredera, dixit abbas Antonius.

[3] Non edam neque bibam, donec moriar, nisi me nunc audiens hunc dæmonem ab homine ejeceris.

ask Him to work a miracle. Anianus, then bishop of Alexandria, in Egypt, full of confidence in the divine goodness, went to the king and said to him: If your majesty wishes to be persuaded that the promises of the God whom we adore are not deceitful, look at that high mountain that you wish to be moved, and you will see it not only move, but actually run. And then raising his voice, he cried out: Mountain, in the name of that God who has promised His faithful that even the mountains will obey them, I command you to come towards this town, and to obey me at once. Hardly had he ended his speech, when, to the great astonishment of both king and people, the huge mountain left its place and moved along as rapidly as a ship before a favoring gale. [1] It overturned trees and houses, and hurried on over torrents with such rapidity that the king was afraid it would destroy the whole city, and he begged the bishop to stay its course. The holy man then commanded the mountain again, and it immediately obeyed this new order, and stood still; [2] and being fixed, there it remains unto the present day.

Mark, my dear brethren, how exactly God keeps His promise of not refusing anything to a prayer that is made with faith and confidence. But what am I saying of a prayer that is actually made? For God hears His servants who have confidence in Him even before they say a word of prayer, according to His promise by the Prophet Isaias: "And it shall come to pass, that before they call, I will hear;" [3] as soon as they have the mind to ask, their petition shall be granted. That this is the case is confirmed by many examples in the lives of the saints, and by what the pious Tauler writes of a great servant of God, who by her prayers obtained all she wished from God. Many were in the habit of recommending their wants and necessities to her prayers, and she readily undertook to help them. It often happened that she forgot to say the prayers she had promised; but nevertheless those who had had recourse to her were fully satisfied and returned thanks to her for having helped them. She would then say to them: My good people, you are mistaken; you have no reason to be grateful to me, for, to tell you the truth, I had completely forgotten you. She asked Our Lord how it happened that the petitions of those people were granted before she said a word

Whose prayers God often heard before they were uttered.

---

[1] Mons continuo moveri cœpit, de loco suo recedens. tantaque celeritate versus Babylon veniens, quanta navis per æquora vento pellitur.—Pet. de Natal. in Cat. Sanct., l. ix., c. 19.

[2] Sicque ibidem fixus, usque hodie manet.—Ibid.

[3] Eritque antequam clament, ego exaudiam.—Is. lxv. 24.

of prayer for them, and she received the following answer: " I decreed to do as you wished, because you had the intention of praying for it." [1] The holy Abbot Apollonius once encouraged his monks to ask a special favor from God on Holy Saturday, after they had partaken of dry bread and vegetables. Come, my brethren, said he; let each one of you beg of God to give him on to-morrow, that joyful day, whatever food is the best for him. They made a difficulty of praying for such a favor as that, for they did not think it necessary. Apollonius, then, full of confidence in God, said: " Well, then I will pray for you all." "Let it be so," [2] they replied. Hardly were the words spoken, when there appeared amongst them a number of youths whose exceeding beauty declared them to be angels, and who brought all sorts of grapes and different kinds of fruit and food unknown in that country, in such abundance and of such surprisingly lasting quality that the monks had a sufficient supply, not only for Easter Sunday, as Apollonius had desired, but also for the whole time that elapsed between Easter and Pentecost. Consider now, my dear brethren, if the confident prayer of a just man is so powerful with God, even in things that concern mere temporal welfare, such as health, freedom from want, and even the pleasures of the body, how much more powerful will it not be in things that are necessary or advantageous for the soul's salvation, of which Our Saviour says: " Seek ye therefore first the kingdom of God and His justice, and all these things shall be added unto you." [3]

From this it follows that confidence in prayer is a sign of predestination, and leaving off prayer a sign of reprobation.   From this I conclude that it is a beautiful mark of predestination to place one's confidence in God, and to hold familiar intercourse with Him in constant prayer. On the other hand it is a mark of reprobation to have no confidence in God, and to go so far as to give up prayer. As long as the sheep bleats it can be found by the shepherd; but if the wolf has caught it by the throat and prevented it from crying out, there is no help for it, and it will be devoured. One of the thieves who were crucified with Our Lord was saved; the other was lost. Why? The one raised his voice in confident prayer to the Saviour: " And he said to Jesus: Lord, remember me when Thou shalt come into Thy

---

[1] Ego sic fieri prout optaveras decrevi, quia tu ita petere cogitasti.—Tauler, serm. i. de circumcis.

[2] Ita fiat.

[3] Quærite ergo primum regnum Dei et justitiam ejus, et hæc omnia adjicientur vobis. —Matt. vi. 33.

kingdom." [1] This was enough to ensure his entry into paradise that very day. "And Jesus said to him: Amen I say to thee, this day thou shalt be with Me in paradise." [2] The other gave way to despair, and refused to pray, so that the hellish wolf dragged him away even from the very side of Our Lord. The soul without prayer, says St. John Chrysostom, is like a town without walls, into which the enemy can easily find his way; it is a garden that is not watered, so that everything in it dries up. I know not, says the learned Eusebius, whether I should not look on it as an act of desperation for a Christian to give up prayer; for he who refuses to eat is desperate; he who cannot eat is sick; he who has nothing to eat is poor; but he who refuses to eat when he might is desperate, or else beside himself. Prayer is the food and nourishment of the soul; therefore he who does not pray is poor in grace, which, generally speaking, is not given without prayer; he is sick in his soul, which is not strengthened by prayer; nay, he is in a desperate state, because he refuses to use the means necessary for his recovery. " Blessed be God, who hath not turned away my prayer, nor His mercy from me." [3] But how dost thou know, David, that God has not turned away His mercy from thee? Because, answers St. Augustine in the person of David, God has still left me the spirit of prayer; and as long as I pray willingly and with confidence in God, I can be sure of His mercy. From this I conclude also that no one, and much less one who is of good will and is resolved to serve God truly, has reason to doubt concerning his soul's salvation and future happiness in heaven; for in confident prayer he has a means of obtaining everything from God.

Ask, then, dear Christians, and you shall receive. In all your necessities, temptations, and dangers of soul imagine that you hear the words that were spoken by a heavenly voice to the mother of St. Gregory of Tours. During the great plague of Auvergne, when miraculous signs of approaching death were exhibited on the walls of the houses of the victims, St. Gregory's mother, as the saint himself testifies, saw a similar forewarning in her own house in the sudden changing of wine into blood. Terrified beyond measure, the pious matron felt sure that every

Conclusion and exhortation to pray with confidence.

---

[1] Dicebat ad Jesum : Domine, memento mei dum veneris in regnum tuum.—Luke xxiii. 42.

[2] Et dixit illi Jesus : Amen dico tibi : hodie mecum eris in paradiso.—Ibid. 43.

[3] Benedictus Deus, qui non amovit orationem meam et misericordiam suam a me.—Ps. lxv. 20.

one in the house would be swept off by the plague. As she was giving way to the bitterest lamentations, she heard a voice from heaven saying to her, " Pray, and you will be freed." [1] And so it turned out; she went to the grave of St. Benignus, prayed, and was freed from the plague; so that, while other houses were filled with mourning and lamentation, and dead bodies were being constantly borne through the streets, neither death nor pestilence nor any malady whatsoever troubled her. " While all the neighboring houses were marked, ours alone escaped." [2] In the same way should each one of you take those words to himself, Pray, and you will be freed. Are you cast down and sorrowful? Pray, and you will be freed. Does the devil sometimes suggest doubts to you regarding your salvation? Pray, and you will be freed. Whatever be your wants of body and soul, pray, all of you, with confidence in God; He is your father, who is very willing to have you with Himself in heaven, and therefore will not refuse you any grace that will help to bring you there. He is a faithful God, who has promised to give you everything you ask Him for to that end in the name of His Son, and if you ask with confidence He can refuse you nothing. Say, Hallowed be Thy name by me in all my works, O Lord, and grant that Thy holy will may be always and in all circumstances done in and by me; protect me from all occasions of sin, and do not allow me to forget Thee and myself so far as to consent to grievous sin. O heavenly Father, give me true humility, without which I cannot possess the kingdom of heaven; give me patience in the crosses Thou wilt send me, and meekness and charity towards my neighbor. Raise my heart and mind to heavenly goods; give and preserve in me a child-like confidence in Thee, that I may serve Thee as Thou desirest, with joy, continue in Thy love to the end, and at last enjoy Thee in heaven. Ask, and you shall receive. Amen.

Another Introduction to the same sermon for the third Sunday after Epiphany.

Text.

Sicut credidisti fiat tibi.—Matt. viii. 13.
" As thou hast believed so be it done to thee."

---

[1] Ora, et liberaberis.

[2] Signatisque vicinorum domibus, domus nostra inviolata permansit.—S. Greg. Turon. apud Sur. in Vita S. Benigni.

Introduction.

We find two strange beggars in to-day's gospel, my dear brethren. Both ask a favor from Christ, and neither says what he wants. The leper stands before Him and merely says: " Lord, if Thou wilt, Thou canst make me clean." But what is the meaning of that? Our Lord knew beforehand that He could cure him. The centurion's prayer consisted in the words, " Lord, my servant lieth at home sick of the palsy, and is grievously tormented." But this, too, was known to Our Lord, and He might well have said to them, What do you want of Me? For they should have explained themselves better; the one should have said: Lord, clean me from my leprosy; and the other: Heal my servant. Is not that the case, my dear brethren? But no; never could those two men have prayed better than they did; for they thereby showed the great faith and firm confidence they had in Christ, feeling certain that the mere mention of their being in want would suffice to secure His help. Nor were their hopes disappointed; for Our Lord, seeing their confidence, at once said to the leper: " I will; be thou made clean," and to the centurion: " Go, and as thou hast believed, so be it done to thee." O my dear brethren, what might we not receive from God, if we only prayed with similar confidence and assured hope! For it is certain that, etc.—*Continues as above.*

FORTIETH SERMON.

ON THE GOODNESS OF GOD IN SOMETIMES NOT HEARING OUR PRAYER.

Subject.

1. We know not what we ask for when we pray for a temporal blessing, or to be saved from a temporal evil. 2. Therefore God is very good to us when He refuses to hear our prayers, and it would often be a great misfortune for us if He granted them.—*Preached on the feast of St. James the Apostle.*

Text.

Nescitis quid petatis.—Matt. xx. 22.
" You know not what you ask."

Introduction.

Is it any wonder that the mother's prayer for her two sons was refused when she did not know what she was asking? Truly, when one does not know what he prays for his request is unreasonable. For the two brothers either thought that the kingdom in which they wished to have the first places was an earthly one, and in that case they knew not what they asked, for, as Our Lord said, His kingdom is not of this world, or else they meant the kingdom of heaven, and in that case, too, they displayed the same amount of ignorance, since they put forward their request without any previous merits on their part; they wished to fly before their wings were grown; they wished to reap where they had not sown; they claimed an eternal reward before having earned it, and therefore with justice did Our Lord send them away with the reproof, "You know not what you ask." My dear brethren, we are surprised and sometimes even complain that, although we ask so often and for so many things, we are not heard, in spite of having in our favor that promise of the almighty God, "Ask, and you shall receive." How does that happen? Ah, when I consider the matter, I find the same fault in ourselves that Christ reproved in the two disciples: we know not what we ask; for if we ask for heaven and eternal goods, we wish to obtain them without working for them; we cry out daily, "Thy kingdom come," and by our sinful lives we shut the gate of that kingdom against ourselves. Hence we know not, or better, we do not wish for what we ask, as I have fully explained on a former occasion. But when we pray for temporal goods, to which our desires generally tend, then we seldom know what we ask for, as I now intend to prove.

Plan of Discourse.

We know not what we ask for when we pray for a temporal blessing, or to be saved from a temporal evil; the first part. Therefore God is very good to us when He refuses to hear our prayers, and it would often be a great misfortune for us if He granted them, the second part, or rather the conclusion to be drawn from the first, to the end that we may learn and know how to pray in a more intelligent, salutary, and useful manner.

Do Thou teach us this, O God of goodness, through the intercession of Thy Mother Mary, and of our holy guardian angels.

He who   How can he who knows not what is good and what evil understand what he prays for when he desires to have the former or to be freed from the latter? Perhaps what he looks on as wicked is good, and what he considers good is wicked. Hence, if he ventures to entertain such desires, and they are fulfilled, he will find himself disappointed, and must acknowledge, when too late, that he was wrong. He acts just as imprudently as a man born blind who tries to distinguish between colors. For how can he know what is black or white? He is like a traveller quite unacquainted with the country, who on coming to a cross-road determines which to take solely by the appearance of the roads; for he is as likely as not to select one that is beset with robbers and murderers, so that his choice brings him into imminent danger of death. *knows not what is good or bad for himself knows not what he desires.*

So it is with us mortals in things that concern our temporal welfare, as well as that of our immortal souls; we are blind and know not what is good or bad, useful or injurious for us. " What needeth a man to seek things that are above him," asks the wise Preacher, " whereas he knoweth not what is profitable for him in his life, in all the days of his pilgrimage? " [1] We are inexperienced travellers, who consider only the outside and the beginning of things; but what their result will be in the future we neither know nor see. " For the thoughts of mortal men are fearful, and our counsels uncertain, says the Holy Ghost in the Book of Wisdom; " hardly do we guess aright at things that are upon earth, and with labor do we find the things that are before us." [2] We often look on that as a great piece of good fortune which subsequent experience teaches us to be a great misfortune; we often shun as an evil what is really for our advantage. And where could we get this knowledge from? " There is great affliction for man," says the wise Ecclesiastes, " because he is ignorant of things past, and things to come he cannot know by any messenger." [3] In olden times, indeed, the prophets foretold future events; but they knew them by divine revelation. Does God perhaps speak to us now in the same way, or give us any idea of how we shall fare in various circumstances? No, indeed; for even in present things, that we see with our eyes and touch *We mortals know not what is good or bad for us, even in temporal things.*

---

[1] Quid necesse est homini majora se quærere, cum ignorat quid conducat sibi, in vita sua numero dierum peregrinationis suæ ?—Eccles. vii. 1.

[2] Cogitationes enim mortalium timidæ ; et incertæ providentiæ nostræ : difficile æstimamus quæ in terra sunt, et quæ in prospectu sunt invenimus cum labore.—Wis. ix. 14, 16.

[3] Multa hominis afflictio quia ignorat præterita, et futura nullo scire potest nuntio.—Eccles. viii. 6, 7.

with our hands, we are ignorant and blind, and know not whether they are good or bad for us, especially in what concerns the salvation of our souls; how, then, could we know the future? Oh, no! this knowledge God has reserved for Himself alone. He knows best, and has already foreseen from all eternity what is good and profitable or bad and injurious for each one.

Hence we know not what we pray for when we ask for temporal things.

How, then, can we reasonably offer up prayers to God for some temporal good, or that He may avert some temporal calamity, since we do not know and cannot, humanly speaking, know whether what we ask is good or bad for us? Are we not often like those little children who stretch out their hands to grasp the fire, wondering at the beautiful shining thing, and burning their fingers? Are we not often in our endeavors to avoid and free ourselves from temporal evils like those same children who struggle and try to resist being tied up in swathing clothes, although the temporary inconvenience they suffer will be the means of saving them from having crooked limbs? Do we not often, like a sick man, reject the wholesome medicine that was intended to cure us, and put it away from us altogether because we find it somewhat bitter to the taste, while we long for appetizing food, that will only shorten our lives? " O children," says the Lord, " how long will you love childishness, and fools covet those things which are hurtful to themselves? " [1]

Many have asked for and obtained things that were injurious to them, like the prodigal.

Consider, my dear brethren, the state of the prodigal while still in his father's house. He was in want of nothing; he had sufficient food, clothing, and the means of becoming amusement; he was treated as the son of rich parents. But he was discontented in spite of all, for he knew that his father's eye was always on him, watching his every movement, and that displeased his youthful fancy. He wanted to be away and his own master, and to dispose as he wished of the property that was coming to him. Freedom was the great object of his wishes, and therefore he gave himself neither rest nor peace till he gained it, and kept constantly praying his father: " Father, give me the portion of substance that falleth to me;" and his importunity was so great that the father had to give way at last: " And he divided unto them his substance." [2] And now at last the son is quite satisfied and goes off as pleased as if the whole world belonged to him. But, foolish child, you know not what you have desired, and still

---

[1] Usque quo parvuli diligitis infantiam, et stulti ea quæ sibi sunt noxia cupient.—Prov. i. 22.

[2] Pater, da mihi portionem substantiæ quæ me contingit ; et divisit illis substantiam.—Luke xv. 12.

less what you have received! Much better would it have been for you if your father had refused your request, and paid no attention to your prayers. But go now and enjoy yourself. In a short time you will find out what it is that you were so anxious for, and you will learn by sad experience that your imaginary good fortune was in reality a grievous calamity for you; for you will be reduced to such extremities that you will be glad to appease your hunger with the husks of swine: "And he would fain have filled his belly with the husks the swine did eat; and no man gave unto him." [1]

Consider that renowned hero of old, the mighty Samson. He happened once to cast his eyes on a Philistine woman, whose beauty so captivated him, that he ran off at once to his parents, as we read in the Book of Judges: "He came up and told his father and his mother, saying: I saw a woman in Thamnatha, of the daughters of the Philistines; I beseech you, take her for me to wife." [2] His parents wished him to marry one of their own tribe, and reminded him that the law forbade him to marry a strange woman. "Is there never a woman," said they to him, "among the daughters of thy brethren, or among all my people, that thou wilt take a wife of the Philistines, who are uncircumcised?" [3] But all their remonstrances were unavailing; he had fixed his heart on the woman, and no other would satisfy him. "And Samson said to his father: Take this woman for me, for she hath pleased my eyes." [4] And his father had to go and make arrangements for the marriage: "So his father went down to the woman, and made a feast for his son Samson." [5] At last he was satisfied. Although this happened, as the Scripture says, in accordance with a divine decree, yet Samson knew not what he was asking, or what a dear price he had to pay for that marriage, and how many difficulties it caused him afterwards. Never after that had he a moment's rest; he was constantly engaged in fighting with the Philistines, and in the end he lost his freedom, his honor, his authority, and his life.

In the Book of Genesis I find another example of the same

Samson

Rachel.

[1] Cupiebat implere ventrem suum de siliquis, quas porci manducabant, et nemo illi dabat.—Luke xv. 16.

[2] Ascendit et nunciavit patri suo et matri suæ, dicens: vidi mulierem in Thamnatha de filiabus Philistinorum, quam quæso ut mihi accipiatis uxorem.—Judges xiv. 2.

[3] Numquid non est mulier in filiabus fratrum tuorum, et in omni populo meo, quia vis accipere uxorem de Philistiim, qui incircumcisi sunt?—Ibid. 3.

[4] Dixitque Samson ad patrem suum: hanc mihi accipe, quia placuit oculis meis.—Ibid.

[5] Descendit itaque pater ejus ad mulierem, et fecit filio suo Samson convivium.—Ibid. 10.

kind. Rachel was constantly sighing for a son; it seemed to her an impossibility to endure any longer the shame of her sterility. "Give me children," said she to her husband, "otherwise I shall die." [1] At last God heard her prayers: "The Lord also remembering Rachel, heard her; and she bore a son, saying: God hath taken away my reproach." [2] But she was not yet satisfied: "The Lord give me also another son," [3] was again her prayer. And again God heard her, but this time she died in child-birth: "And when her soul was departing for pain, and death was now at hand, she called the name of her son Benoni, that is, the son of my pain. So Rachel died." [4] What had she received then? She wished to have children, that she might not die of sorrow: "Give me children, otherwise I shall die." They were given to her, and on that very account she died in great agony. See, my dear brethren, how all these people knew not what they were wishing for and asking; they desired to have what they thought good for them, and when they received it, they found themselves completely mistaken.

And many wished to be freed from an evil which was a source of the greatest good to them.

And how many, too, as we read in the Sacred Scriptures, desired to be freed from some imaginary evil, which after all turned out to their best advantage? How troubled Joseph was while in prison in Egypt! How earnestly he implored the butler to put in a good word for him, that he might be released! "Only remember me," he said, "when it shall be well with thee, and do me this kindness, to put Pharao in mind to take me out of this prison." [5] But be satisfied, Joseph! You know not what you ask and desire; it is not good for you to be released now; the prison is still the best place for you. If the butler had remembered his promise to Joseph, and entreated Pharao to release him, truly, Joseph's desire for freedom would have been gratified; but then he would have been compelled either to serve some other Egyptian master, or else to return to his own country; and in that case, who would have interpreted the dream that Pharao subsequently had? The two years' imprisonment that Joseph still had to suffer was the cause of his being raised to the dignity of viceroy of Egypt, and

---

[1] Da mihi liberos, alioquin moriar.—Gen. xxx. 1.

[2] Recordatus quoque Dominus Rachelis, exaudivit eam. Et peperit filium, dicens: abstulit Deus opprobrium meum.—Ibid. 22, 23.

[3] Addat mihi Dominus filium alterum.—Ibid. 24.

[4] Egrediente autem anima præ dolore, et imminente jam morte, vocavit nomen filii sui Benoni, id est, filius doloris mei. Mortua est ergo Rachel.—Ibid. xxxv. 18, 19.

[5] Tantum memento mei cum bene tibi fuerit, et facias mecum misericordiam, ut suggeras Pharaoni, ut educat me de isto carcere.—Ibid. xl. 14.

placed in a position to save so many people from perishing of hunger. Again, in the case of the prodigal, how he longed for the husks that were given to the swine, that he might satiate his hunger with them, and his longing was fruitless! But this very extremity of misery that he suffered was the cause of his at last opening his eyes. "And returning to himself, he said: How many hired servants in my father's house abound with bread, and I here perish with hunger? I will arise and will go to my father. And rising up he came to his father." [1] And his father received him with joy as his well-beloved child. Mark that it was hunger and want that drove this poor son back to his father, and restored to him his former prosperity. "You know not what you ask." Those people did not in truth know what was good or bad for them.

And is it not the same in the world nowadays? I take you yourselves to witness, my dear brethren. Let each of you consider his own experience, and recall to mind those things that he desired most eagerly, prayed for most fervently, and received with the utmost joy and satisfaction, and he will have to acknowledge that those very things were to him frequently a source of uneasiness, chagrin, and difficulty, and that he would have been far better off if he had never received them. That imaginary piece of good luck, that lucrative property, that honorable position, that employment, that profitable business, that you made the object of your earnest desire until you obtained it, like the prodigal in the Gospel,—must you not confess that sometimes it brought you in nothing but envy, jealousy, hatred, persecution, disunion, enmity, trouble and labor, disquiet and anxiety? To what must many a one ascribe his intolerable domestic trials, his secret anguish, his poverty and want, his daily moanings and lamentations, if not to that marriage which, like Samson, he desired as the one thing to complete his happiness, strove for many years, and at last secured, with the result that his life is now poisoned by constant hatred and disunion, reviling and cursing, until it is made a hell on earth for him? How many parents have not, like Rachel, wearied Heaven with their prayers and devotions to obtain children, or to preserve them in health? and yet those very children, because they were undutiful, or stupid, or weakly and delicate, were to their parents the source of noth-

Confirmed by experience.

---

[1] In se autem reversus dixit: quanti mercenarii in domo patris mei abundant panibus, ego autem hic fame pereo! Surgam et ibo ad patrem meum. Et surgens venit ad patrem suum.—Luke xv. 17, 18, 20.

ing but disappointment, trouble, and shame. And such you will find to have been the case in many instances which you know better than I can tell you. So it is; "you know not what you ask;" we cannot say what is good or bad for us, and therefore we know not what we desire or ask for.

Much less do we know what is good for our souls.

Now, if we are so ignorant in things that concern our bodily and temporal welfare, how much less can we know whether the object of our prayers and wishes is good or not for our eternal welfare? Here we must indeed all acknowledge that we are stone-blind. How many would be now in hell for all eternity if they had obtained the health, riches, or honor before men that they longed for, who have actually gained heaven by means of sickness and weakness, poverty and want, contempt and lowliness! How many would now be in heaven, rejoicing with the angels and saints of God, if their prayers had not been heard, and if they had not obtained what they so eagerly desired; who, when their prayers for temporal prosperity were granted, began to lead perverse lives, continued therein, and after an unhappy death were hurled into the abyss of hell!

And we complain without reason when our prayers are not heard.

You pray, then, and sigh, and send forth your petitions to God; you get others to pray and have Masses said to obtain the gift of health, or to free your husband, wife, child, or friend from illness.—Why?—Is that a question to ask? you think. Is it not better to be in good health than to be sick?—It is in your opinion; but do you know whether or not it is better for your soul?—Most certainly it is; for when I am strong I can go to church, and join in public devotions; I am very willing to lead a good life and serve my God alone.—Nonsense; you know not what you ask. If you were in good health, the chances are you would think still less of devotion, of the service of God, and of leading a pious life, and that you would abuse your health and bodily strength, your eyes, ears, and other senses, to offend God in many ways. This sickness or infirmity that now keeps you at home, or even confines you to bed, is a means of preserving you from many dangers and occasions of evil. The pain you have to suffer makes you think of the eternal joys of heaven, and impels you, since you cannot avoid the suffering in any case, to make it a means of gaining those joys, by bearing it patiently. So that sickness is much better for your soul. If your child were strong, healthy, clever, well-made, and amiable, you would in all probability, through over-fondness for it, neglect its precious soul,

and teach it all the vanity and luxury of the world, so that you
and your child would be lost forever. As it is, your child's
stupidity, or sickness, or deformity is the cause that you at least
attend to its spiritual welfare. Therefore you should allow God
to manage for you as He pleases; He knows best what is for
your good and that of your children. You pray and send forth
your sighs to heaven to be freed from some temporal calamity,
to obtain success in that important business or lawsuit, to be
saved from disgrace or dishonor, and that the minds of those
who now persecute you, as you think, for your torment alone,
should be changed. But why do you pray for that? Is it not
because you imagine it is good for you? Yet you know not
what you ask. If your prayer were heard, your soul would in
all probability suffer. If all your wishes were gratified, if you
had nothing to annoy or trouble you, you would fix your heart
on earthly things, and forget death, judgment, heaven, hell,
and eternal torments. The misfortune from which you now
suffer, the loss you have sustained, the ill-success of your business
undertakings, the lawsuit you have lost, the hard-hearted,
merciless husband, the obstinate, peevish, disobedient wife,
whose faults you must bear with the utmost patience, the man
who persecutes you, opens your eyes and makes the vanities of
the world bitter and insipid to you, and compels you often to
fly for refuge to God by prayer; let Him, then, deal with you as
He pleases, for He knows best what is good for your soul. You
pray and complain to God of your poverty and the secret want
that you and your children have to suffer; and you ask for
more money and means for providing for your family. Why?
Oh, you exclaim; if I were not so poor, if I were as well off as
my neighbor, on whom fortune seems to rain down her choicest
blessings, how easily I could then attend to the divine service,
give generous alms to the poor, and perform different works of
Christian charity and mercy! But now there is neither joy nor
pleasure in my life, and I am wearied of it! Ah, you know not
what you ask and desire. If things prospered with you according to your wish, if you had everything in abundance, likely
enough the last thing you would think of would be the service of
God; you would in all probability be like the rest of the world,
for whom temporal prosperity and riches are nothing but so
many chains by which the devil ties them down to a life of sin
and vice; as the Apostle says to Timothy: "But having food

and wherewith to be covered, with these we are content. For they that will become rich fall into temptation, and into the snare of the devil, and into many unprofitable and hurtful desires, which drown men into destruction and perdition."[1]

For the prosperity we desire is generally bad for the soul.

When are true virtue and the fear of God more difficult to be found, when is the soul in greater danger, than in the midst of temporal prosperity and abundance? "Thou hast been favorable to the nation, O Lord, Thou hast been favorable to the nation; art Thou glorified?"[2] exclaims the Prophet Isaias. Thou hast bestowed much wealth and many temporal blessings on those men; have they therefore blessed Thy holy name? Have they served Thee with zeal? Have they not rather gone farther from Thee on that account, and become more proud and haughty, more avaricious, unchaste, intemperate, and slothful in Thy service? When did Saul, who was at first so good that, according to Thy own words, there was no one like him,—when did he turn out so ungrateful and wicked? Was it not after Thou hadst raised him to the throne? When did the wise Solomon bend the knee before idols and offer them incense? Was it not while he was living in abundance? Truly that is the case. "Solomon surpassed all in enjoyments," says St. Jerome, "and that is perhaps the reason why he fell so shamefully."[3] Therefore, O man, cease complaining; the providence of God wishes to lead you to heaven by the surest road, through that poverty and want or hard work by which you have to earn a modest subsistence. He knows what is good for you, but you yourself do not. You know not what you ask. Thus, my dear brethren, we are all blind and ignorant, and cannot say what is good or bad for our temporal well-being, much less for the welfare of our souls. Hence, when we pray for temporal blessings, we know not what we ask from that God whose providence cannot go astray in its arrangements, and who rules us by His infinite wisdom. This fundamental truth will serve as an introduction to the

Second Part.

Hence we have often cause to

I ask you now whether you think we have reason to rejoice always when God hears our prayers and gives us all we desire,

---

[1] Habentes autem alimenta, et quibus tegamur, his contenti sumus. Nam qui volunt divites fieri, incidunt in tentationem, et in laqueum diaboli, et desideria multa inutilia et nociva, quæ mergunt homines in interitum et perditionem.—I. Tim. vi. 8, 9.

[2] Indulsisti genti, Domine, indulsisti genti ; numquid glorificatus es ?—Is. xxvi. 15.

[3] Solus in deliciis Solomon, et forsitan ideo corruit.

and to complain and think He deals hardly with us when He refuses to grant our petitions? Ah, far different should be our opinion on the matter. For we should rather thank Him humbly when He refuses to hear us, and fear incurring His displeasure when He gives us what we ask for. This is the teaching of St. Augustine; " God," he says, " sometimes gives us in His anger, and sometimes refuses us in His goodness." [1] What an outcry the Israelites raised in the desert when they wished for flesh to eat! " For a mixed multitude of people that came up with them burned with desire, sitting and weeping, the children of Israel also being joined with them, and said: Who shall give us flesh to eat?" [2] Did God hear their tears and prayers? Yes, and He sent them such an abundance of quails that the Prophet David compared them to the dust of the earth and the sand of the seashore: " And He rained upon them flesh as dust, and feathered fowls like as the sand of the sea; so they did eat, and were filled exceedingly, and He gave them their desire." [3] O my God, what goodness and mercy to that ungrateful people, who murmur against Thee! They can now eat as much as they wish, and are fully satiated. But, alas, we should rather say: How they are punished! for it would have been far better for them if they had never seen the meat that the Lord bestowed on them in such abundance. " And yet the flesh was between their teeth," says the Scripture, " neither had that kind of meat failed," and they still had enough of it, " when behold the wrath of the Lord, being provoked against the people, struck them with an exceeding great plague." [4] In our own times, too, it is frequently an effect of the divine anger when God hears the prayers of men and grants them all they wish for; He fulfils their desires, but they often find therein their eternal ruin. But, O Lord, why dost Thou hear them, then? Why dost Thou not refuse to grant their petitions? They have not asked Me for advice; they thought they knew better than I what was good for them; they have not submitted their will to Mine; they were not satisfied with the decrees of My providence; they wished to find happiness by ways and means that suited their own whims

fear the anger of God when He hears our prayers.

---

[1] Deus aliquando iratus dat ; aliquando propitius negat.

[2] Vulgus promiscuum, quod ascenderat cum eis, flagravit desiderio, sedens et flens, junctis sibi pariter filiis Israel, et ait: quis dabit nobis ad vescendum carnes ?—Num. xi. 4.

[3] Pluit super eos sicut pulverem carnes; et sicut arenam maris volatilia pennata. Et manducaverunt et saturati sunt nimis, et desiderium eorum attulit eis.—Ps. lxxvii. 27, 29.

[4] Adhuc carnes erant in dentibus eorum, nec defecerat hujusmodi cibus ; et ecce furor Domini concitatus in populum percussit eum plaga magna nimis.—Num. xi. 33.

and inclinations. If, then, they wish to go to ruin, I let them have their way; they can use their freedom; they have made themselves unworthy of My grace, of the blessing I would have conferred on them by refusing to grant their prayers, and now I say to them with displeasure what I formerly said to the Chananean woman through pity: "Be it done to thee as thou wilt." [1] I give you the prosperity you desire; live long with your friends; be merry and healthy, as you wish; be rich as you wish; attain a high position in the world, as you wish; let everything go according to your desires; but you will find out afterwards how it will end with you.

And He often confers a special grace on us when He refuses to hear us. You see, therefore, my dear brethren, that it is often a special gift of God to refuse to hear our prayers, and to withhold from us what we desire. " He sometimes refuses us in His goodness." Through love for us, He denies us what He foresees we should make a bad use of, as the same St. Augustine says: " he who would abuse what he wishes to have, does not receive it, because God takes pity on him." [2] It was by a similar grace, as the holy Doctor continues, that God allowed St. Paul to pray so long and fervently to be freed from a troublesome temptation, and yet did not hear him, because He would otherwise have deprived him of the opportunity of practising humility and self-denial. In the same way, too, God does not always hear the prayers of His well-beloved souls and dear friends in the sense in which they wish to be heard and which they think is good for them; for He knows best what is for their greater advantage. " Oftentimes," says St. Isidore, " God refuses to hear many according to their wishes, that He may hear them for their salvation." [3]

Shown by similes. And in what better manner could He show His love for us as our father, or His skill as our physician? What does the loving father do when his child cries for a knife? He puts it away at once, and showing the child his empty hand, says: See. there is no knife there. But the child cries out again, there is one on the table. No, says the father; you are mistaken; and he makes a sign to have the knife taken away and hidden. The child still continues to cry; but the father takes no notice, and

[1] Fiat tibi sicut vis.—Matt. xv. 28.

[2] Male usurus eo quod vult accipere, Deo potius miserante non accipit.—S. Aug. tract. 74 in Joan.

[3] Sæpe multos Deus non exaudit ad voluntatem, ut exaudiat ad salutem.—S. Isid. de Summo Bono, l. iii., c. 7.

is determined not to give it the knife. Is that harshness? No, it is fatherly love. The knife is not good for the child; it would cut itself with it. The child does not know that, but the father does. How the poor man ill with fever tumbles and tosses about! He cannot bear anything on him; he tries to get out of bed, and cries out for cold water. Oh, he exclaims, will you let me die of thirst? Am I to be smothered with heat in this bed? What does the doctor do? He pretends to take no notice, and tells the nurse to cover the sick man better still, lest he should die before his time. The sick man does not understand the reason of this, but the doctor does. Senseless man! how often have you not complained that God has turned a deaf ear to your prayers, and imagined that He is bound to give you all you ask for, because He is your merciful, heavenly Father? He is your loving Father, that is true; but you are a silly child, and do not know what is good for you. Often you ask Him, as you think, for bread; but in reality it is a stone you desire; must He grant such a useless request? You think you are asking Him for a fish; but what you desire is really a venomous serpent. Do you expect Him to hear your prayer to your own destruction? Such are the similes used by Our Lord Himself when speaking of prayer in the Gospel of St. Matthew. God deprives you of consolation by the death of your husband, wife, child, or dear friend; He takes away some pleasure from you by misfortune or loss, whether you like it or not; He gives you that bitter chalice of suffering or calamity to drink, whether it pleases you or not; and meanwhile He allows you to cry, and moan, and sigh to Him for help, and to act like the sick man, but He, like the wise physician, takes not the least notice, since He knows best what is conducive to your welfare. You, indeed, seek what is good for you, but such, too, is the object of His desires. In what does your greatest good consist? You cannot say, because you are a child, a sick man; but God knows all about it, and arranges everything to that end, because He is your father and physician. Place yourself, then, and all that belongs to you, in His hands; allow Him to do with you what He pleases, and be assured that everything will turn out for the salvation of your soul.

But are we, then, never to pray to God, but to keep always quite still when we desire temporal blessings or to be freed from temporal miseries? And can we never hope to be heard when we address such prayers to Him, although we have been hitherto

How to pray for temporal things.

recommended to pray for those things? No, my dear brethren, that does not at all follow from what I have said. God wishes us to pray to Him for such things. He desires to be acknowledged as our father and the only source of all good, which we must receive from Him alone; but prayers for temporal things must be offered with due preparation of heart and in a proper manner. How, then? With perfect resignation of our will to the will of God, and with an earnest desire not to receive anything but what is for the good of our souls and for the honor and glory of God, so that it is a matter of perfect indifference to us whether we obtain what we ask or not, and we are quite ready to accept from the hand of our heavenly Father one thing as well as the other, whether it is suitable to our inclination or opposed to it, sweet or bitter to us.

If we do not wish to pray foolishly.; If we pray without that preparation and disposition, we know not what we ask. If you pray, O man, without that resignation, and obtain all you ask for, oh, do not rejoice too much, nor exult in the thought that the treasures of heaven have been opened to you; but rather fear and tremble, because your prayers have been heard. Do not say, like those of whom the Prophet Zachary speaks, "Blessed be the Lord, we are become rich." [1] My desires are fulfilled. Blessed be God for having heard my prayer! The happiness or prosperity, that you take as a sign of the divine favor, is perhaps only a proof of the wrath of God; it may be that He has given you in His anger what He would have refused you in His goodness. But if you pray with that intention and preparation of heart, and your prayers are heard, then look on what has been given to you as an additional motive to serve God with the utmost zeal and humility. If, on the other hand, He turns a deaf ear to you, if He refuses to help you in your necessities, be not troubled therefore, but rather rejoice and thank the good God because He has not granted your request; for that refusal on His part is a sign of His tender love and affection for you; He acts towards you as the loving father with his child, or the skilful doctor with his patient. Only bear your trial with Christian patience and the assured confidence that you will hereafter receive all the greater treasures of glory in heaven. It is as easy for God to grant as to refuse your request if it is good for your soul; why does He not grant it? What pleasure can that loving Lord, who shed His blood for

---

[1] Benedictus Dominus, divites facti sumus.—Zach. xi. 5.

us, find in leaving you groaning under the weight of affliction and misfortune? Therefore be always satisfied with the will of God.

Hence, my dear brethren, when we pray for temporal things, let us explain our wants to God with child-like confidence, but without doing violence to His providence by our prayers; let us act like the sisters of Lazarus when their brother lay at the point of death; all they said was: " Lord, behold, he whom Thou lovest is sick." [1] They did not cry out like the father who was praying for his son, " Lord, come down before that my son die." [2] It was enough for them that the Lord knew of their brother's illness; otherwise they left themselves entirely in His hands. So also should each one of us pray: Lord, behold I am sick. Lord, I am in trouble and adversity. Lord, my father, mother, husband, wife, child, or friend is at the point of death. Lord, my business is falling off. I have nothing to eat. I am unjustly persecuted. I am in danger. I have suffered a great loss. Do Thou, O Lord, say, for Thou canst do so without trouble, let it be done; but do not say, be it done as thou wilt. No, my God, not as I will, but as Thou wilt; do not give me what I desire, but what is for the good of my soul. I am a child and know not what is good for me; I am sick and know not what is wholesome for me; do what Thou knowest to be best for me. " Give me," I beg of Thee with Thy servant Augustine, " give me in this life what I ask, if Thou wishest to do so." [3] Give me health, fortune, prosperity; but do not regard my wish and inclination; give, if it is pleasing to Thee and good for me; and if Thou wilt not give, because it is bad for me. then I beg of Thee, leave me in my poverty, trouble, or suffering; " but if Thou wilt not, then be Thou my life, which I always seek." [4] Be Thou my health, my fortune, my riches, my care, my only Good, which I will always seek and love. That is the way to pray, my dear brethren; let us pray like that, and then we shall know what we ask for. Amen.

On the Prayer of Married People, and on Morning Prayer, see the First Part. On False and Useless Prayer, see the Second Part. On Prayer before Confession and during time of Calamity, and on the Necessity of Prayer in order to Persevere in Grace, see the Third Part.

Conclusion and resolution to pray thus in future.

---

[1] Domine, ecce quem amas infirmatur.—John xi. 3.
[2] Domine, descende priusquam moriatur filius meus.—Ibid. iv. 49.
[3] Da, si vis dare in hac vita, quod quæro.
[4] Si autem non vis, tu esto vita mea, quam semper quæro.

ON CONFIDENCE IN GOD.

ON THE HAPPINESS OF HIM WHO PUTS HIS CONFIDENCE IN GOD.

Subject.

Happy is he who in all his necessities places all his hope and confidence in God.—*Preached on the first Sunday of Advent.*

Text.

His autem fieri incipientibus, respicite et levate capita vestra, quoniam appropinquat redemptio vestra.—Luke xxi. 28.

" But when these things begin to come to pass, look up and lift up your heads, because your redemption is at hand.

Introduction.

Terrible will be the coming of Our Lord to judge the living and the dead. There will be signs in the sun, moon, and stars that will fill the world with terror. The powers of heaven will be moved, and the sea will send forth a mighty roaring. All the peoples of the earth will be stricken with dread. " Men withering away for fear and expectation of what shall come upon the whole world." And in those terrible circumstances we are encouraged to rejoice and lift up our heads towards heaven with an assured confidence: "But when these things begin to come to pass, look up and lift up your heads," to show the joy that animates you. Yes, truly, says Christ, Our Lord; even in those terrible circumstances you, my faithful servants, must rejoice. Even when the wicked are pining away for fear, " lift up your heads;" then must your joy and hope be all the greater; then must you look forward to your redemption with still greater confidence. O my dear brethren, if we always kept in the

36

friendship of God, and if we had, moreover, a lively hope and confidence in Him, how much trouble, anxiety, and sorrow we should avoid! We often sigh and groan under the miseries of this wretched life; wherever we turn we find hundreds of dangers and necessities of soul and body. Ah, only serve your God! Have confidence in your God! Fly to your God for refuge!

Plan of Discourse.

Happy he who in all his necessities places all his hope and confidence in God. Such is the whole subject of this sermon, in which I begin to treat of this matter. Therefore, if we wish to be happy, let us live piously and trust in God.

Obtain this grace for us from thy Son, O Mary, through the intercession of our holy guardian angels.

Although Christian hope aims chiefly at the invisible and spiritual goods that we confidently expect from God in the necessities of the soul, such as protection in temptations, deliverance from sin and the dangers of sin, and from an unhappy death and eternal damnation, that we may possess God, our supreme Good, whom we desire above all things, yet this hope can and must also be extended to temporal goods, such as health, food, and other bodily necessities, the welfare of our children, success in business, fair weather, general peace, and so on; blessings which it is not only lawful for a Christian to desire, but which he can hope for also in a meritorious manner, provided his hope and desire are directed to the attainment of his last end, the honor and glory of God, and the good of souls. Hence we can and should hope and trust to be preserved from temporal calamities, or to be freed from them if we are actually suffering them. It is of this latter hope that I now intend to speak. Happy is the man, I repeat, who in all temporal necessities puts his whole hope and confidence in God, and flies to Him for refuge. Why? I need not go to much trouble to prove it, for with a little reflection our reason and faith will show us why clearly enough. *(We can and should put our trust in God alone, even in temporal affairs.)*

For, where can I better place my confidence than in Him who, as I know for certain, will console me in my troubles if I fly to Him for refuge? Now, in such a person as that two things are required: first, He must have the power, and, secondly, the will to help me. If one of these be wanting, my confidence is badly placed; nor shall I be able to find the help I hoped for. Thus, if in poverty I were to put my trust in a poor workingman, who *(Because he from whom I hope for certain help must be able and willing to help me.)*

has hardly enough to keep himself and his family from starving, and to look to his help to become rich, every one would say that my hope is a foolish one. But why? I should ask; the man is a good friend of mine, and wishes well to me. Yes, his will is good, there is no doubt of that; but he wants the power; the poor fellow has not the means of making you rich. On the other hand, if I were to place this firm confidence in a rich man who is a noted miser, and never gives anything to the poor, my hope would again be an ill-founded one. But why? He is able to help me, and can give me a hundred ducats if he wishes. Hundred ducats, indeed! He will not give you a farthing; he is able, of course; but the will is wanting. Hence both are required, the power and the will, to make my hope and confidence assured.

Neither of these do we find in men. Not the power,

Now, my dear brethren, we can find hardly any one on earth in whom we can thus trust, since men are wanting either in the power or in the will to help us, or even in both. For, no matter how great may be the power that some possess, it still remains a limited one, dependent, defective, which weakens itself by rendering assistance to others. What I give to another I take away from myself, and so make myself unable to give as much in future. The powerful ones of this earth are kings, princes, and sovereigns; but they are still only men, that is, if they have power, they are not almighty; and therefore the Prophet David warns us: " Put not your trust in princes, in the children of men, in whom there is no salvation." [1] Great is the blindness of those who perform some crime in obedience to their masters, and then look to them for protection. When Absalom commanded his servants to slay his brother Amnon at table, in the presence of the other princes, he told them to carry out his orders without fear: " Strike him and kill him; fear not; for it is I that command you; take courage and be valiant men." [2] The servants trusted in their master's power, and accomplished the murder: " And the servants of Absalom did to Amnon as Absalom had commanded them." [3] How did they fare afterwards? The Scripture does not say; but it hints pretty broadly at their fate when it tells us that Absalom had to fly for his life on the occasion, so that he could hardly have been able to protect his servants. Is there a prince in the world who can free you from a headache, or a fever, or an

---

[1] Nolite confidere in principibus, in filiis hominum, in quibus non est salus.—Ps. cxlv. 23.

[2] Percutite eum et interficite; nolite timere; ego enim sum, qui præcipio vobis; roboramini et estote viri fortes.—II. Kings xiii. 28.

[3] Fecerunt ergo pueri Absalom adversus Amnon, sicut præceperat eis Absalom.—Ibid. 29.

unprovided death? Where is the king powerful enough to save your land from an inundation, your vineyard from hail, yourself from a mortal injury? The Prophet Jeremias bewails with hot tears the folly of those who place their confidence in men, no matter how powerful they are: " While we were yet standing our eyes failed, expecting help for us in vain, when we looked attentively towards a nation that was not able to save." [1] Right was the answer given by king Joram to the widow who appealed to him for help in the famine. " Save me, my lord, O king," she said; "and he said: If the Lord doth not save thee, how can I save thee?" [2]

And even when the good will to help is found amongst men, it is very inconstant and changeable, and is little to be relied on. A sour look, an incautious word, may deprive you of your seemingly best and most faithful friend. The promises and offers of service that people make are mostly empty compliments, uttered in the spirit of worldly policy. When the hour of need comes, those fine words vanish into thin air. You entrust a matter of importance to some one who is under an obligation to you, and who has offered his services; you rely on his ability, but hardly are you gone a few steps away from him, when he forgets you; out of sight, out of mind. When Joseph was in prison in Egypt, he told Pharao's butler that he would soon be reinstated in his former position, and begged of him to say a good word to the king for him. Joseph's prophecy was fulfilled, and after the lapse of three days the butler was restored. Truly, it would seem that Joseph had now good reason to hope for a speedy release; but days, weeks, months, nay, two whole years passed by, and Joseph was still in prison. Was it perhaps because the butler's prayer had no influence on the king? No; but when he regained his freedom he forgot all about Joseph: " But the chief butler, when things prospered with him, forgot his interpreter." [3] So little reliance is to be placed on the promises of men. And even if they do not forget, they still often refuse to help when they could do so, because it might cost them some trouble, or expose them to danger if they kept their word. When Sedecias was besieged by the Chaldeans in Jerusalem, he expected Pharao,

Nor the will.

---

[1] Cum adhuc subsisteremus, defecerunt oculi nostri ad auxilium nostrum vanum; cum respiceremus attenti ad gentem quæ salvare non poterat.—Lam. iv. 17.

[2] Salva me. domine mi rex. Qui ait: non te salvat Dominus; unde te possum salvare ?—IV. Kings vi. 26, 27.

[3] Et tamen succedentibus prosperis, præpositus pincernarum oblitus est interpretis sui.—Gen. xl. 23.

king of Egypt, to help him, and asked him to send at once as many soldiers as possible to his assistance. Pharao set out rather late, but when he saw the army of Nabuchodonosor, he was afraid to risk his soldiers' lives against it, and went back, while Nabuchodonosor continued the siege. Jerusalem was taken and plundered, and Sedecias, after his eyes were put out, was led captive into Babylon, as we read in the twenty-fifth chapter of the Fourth Book of Kings. Such is the way of the world; every one seeks his own advantage, and even those whom you think your best friends will deceive, betray, and abandon you if they find their own interest at stake. Even if there is one or another who has both the power and the will to help, he can use it only in a very limited way and in certain circumstances; there is no human power able to help in every necessity and danger. Thus, my dear brethren, it is to no purpose that we rely on men, and no one can esteem himself happy merely because he has many rich and powerful patrons. The contrary is rather the case, as we learn from the lips of infallible Truth: "Cursed be the man that trusteth in man, and maketh flesh his arm." [1]

God alone has power to rule everything in the world.

Christians, lift up your hearts! Place all your hope and confidence in heaven! Fly to your God for refuge; on Him alone you can fully rely, for it is on God alone that our happiness or misery, our prosperity or adversity, depends. "The power of the earth is in the hand of God," says the wise Ecclesiasticus; "the prosperity of man is in the hand of God." [2] He is the almighty and sovereign Lord of all created things, who can dispose of them all according to His good will and pleasure. Everything that happens on earth and in heaven, in the water and under the earth, sin alone excepted, happens solely because His all-wise providence has so ordained and not otherwise. Therefore in the holy Scripture He describes His occupations, not indeed according to the majesty of His own nature, but to suit the narrowness of our understanding. For instance: "He walketh about the poles of heaven." [3] He considers the plans and works of men. He hides Himself in the abysses of the earth. He calls to the darkness. He commands the light. He weighs the winds in a balance. He sets bounds to the sea. He touches the mountains, and they smoke. He measures the waters and weighs the heavens in His hand. He holds up the universe on three fingers. He has

---

[1] Maledictus homo qui confidit in homine, et ponit carnem brachium suum.—Jer. xvii. 5.
[2] In manu Dei potestas terræ ; in manu Dei prosperitas hominis.—Ecclus. x. 4, 5.
[3] Circa cardines cœli perambulat.—Job xxii. 14.

weighed the mountains in scales, and the hills in a balance. He
sits upon the globe of the earth, and the inhabitants thereof are
as locusts.   He stretches out the heavens as nothing, and spreads
them out as a tent to dwell in.   So speak the Prophets Isaias,
David, and others.   Why do they say such strange things of the
almighty God?   To give us to understand, says St. Gregory of
Nazianzen, that God rules the world, and arranges everything in
it. [1]

And. as God Himself says elsewhere, to show us that all
created nature is as wax in His hands, He turns it as He pleases:
He gives a sign to the fire, and contrary to its nature, it fans
the three youths in the fiery furnace like a cool breeze, while it
burns even the spirits in hell.   He gives a sign, and the sun
stands still at the command of Josue; it goes back at the prayer
of the sick king Ezechias, and turns day into night; it hides itself at the death of Jesus Christ, and makes night of day.   He
gives a sign, and the mountains at the word of St. Gregory
Thaumaturgus remove from one place to another.   He gives a
sign, and the waters of the sea divide to allow the Israelites to
pass over dry-shod.   He gives a sign, and the raven feeds Elias;
the lions crouch at the feet of Daniel in the den and eat up the
disobedient prophet, that we may know that He is the ruler of
the world, and understand that all the elements must obey Him;
that the great council-chamber is His providence, which arranges and disposes what is to happen to every one on earth.   "Good
things and evil, life and death, poverty and riches, are from
God." [2]

*All creat-
ures must
obey Him.*

We generally attribute events to the working of creatures or
to changes of fortune.   A poor maiden who fears God is sought
for in marriage by a rich lord.   Oh, what a lucky thing for her!
we think.   But we should rather say: What a wonderful disposition of providence in her regard!   A rich man loses all he has.
What a misfortune! we say.   But we should rather think and
say: What a decree of God's providence in that man's regard!
One is raised by some great man's favor to a high position; another is mercilessly oppressed and persecuted by his enemies,
and reduced to the utmost poverty.   What a happiness for the
one, we think, to have had such a powerful patron! what a misfortune for the other to have got into the hands of such ruthless

*Nothing
happens
without His
permission.*

[1] Mundum hunc agit, et gubernat universa.
[2] Bona et mala, vita et mors, paupertas et honestas a Deo sunt.—Ecclus. xi. 14.

men! But we are wrong in both cases. We should rather think: What a wonderful act of divine providence to raise that man by means of his patron, and to humble that other by means of his cruel oppressors! For it is God who gave the beneficent thought to the benefactor; it was God who permitted the others to wreak their cruelty on the object of their resentment as a salutary chastisement for him. It is God who suggests to the physician the medicines he ought to use to restore the sick person to health, or to make him worse. It is God who moves that wealthy man to feelings of mercy and charity, that he may secretly help this or that decent poor person. "The Lord killeth and maketh alive," sings Anna in the joy of her heart; "He bringeth down to hell and bringeth back again. The Lord maketh poor and maketh rich, He humbleth and He exalteth, He raiseth up the needy from the dust, and lifteth up the poor from the dung-hill, that he may sit with princes." [1] The Lord gives and takes away, and does what He pleases in all circumstances.

So that God alone has power to help us in all our necessities.

Therefore, my dear brethren, God has unlimited power and sovereign authority to help in all difficulties and necessities. no matter what they may be. He can give peace in time of war, health in sickness, consolation in trouble, riches in poverty, protection in persecution, food in famine. And in all this His power is absolute and unlimited, so that, no matter what He gives away, He is none the poorer; His utmost liberality cannot lessen His treasures; His generosity cannot be wearied by any number of petitioners. In the Lord God, says St. Fulgentius, "there is no falsehood, because there is no difficulty for His omnipotence to do as it pleases." [2] Now, if all this is true,—and faith assures us of it,—where can we better place our undoubting hope and full confidence, if not in the almighty God, the ruler of all things?

He has also the will to help those who trust in Him.

Yes, you think; we have, of course, no doubt that the almighty God is able and knows how to help us by His providence; but often He does not wish to help us, and allows us to groan under our trials and crosses. And are we therefore to doubt of His good will in our regard, provided we fly to Him with confidence for refuge? Christians, where is our faith? Think of what

[1] Dominus mortificat et vivificat, deducit ad inferos et reducit. Dominus auperem facit et ditat, humiliat et sublevat, suscitat de pulvere egenum, et de stercore elevat pauperem, ut sedeat cum principibus.—I. Kings ii. 6, 7, 8.

[2] Nulla est falsitas, quia in faciendis nulla omnipotentis est difficultas.

we are. We are children of God; He is our Father. Is it possible that such a Father does not wish to help His children, who love Him with all their hearts, trust in Him completely, resign themselves altogether to Him, and call upon Him in their necessities? Can the promises of a faithful and infallible God be broken? promises that He has so often and so clearly renewed, assuring us that He is willing to help those who trust in Him? Are not these words clear enough, "Call upon Me in the day of trouble; I will deliver thee, and thou shalt glorify Me"? [1] Such is the divine promise made by the Prophet David. Are not these words clear enough, "I will deliver thee in that day, saith the Lord, and thou shalt not be given into the hands of the men whom thou fearest; but for a certainty I will deliver thee, because thou hast put thy trust in Me"? [2] Is not this promise plain enough, "Cast thy care upon the Lord, and He shall sustain thee; He shall not suffer the just to waver forever"? [3] Such, again, is His promise by the Psalmist. "Come to Me, all you that labor and are burdened, and I will refresh you," [4] as He tells us by the holy Evangelist St. Matthew. "Casting all your care upon Him, for He hath care of you," [5] such are the words of St. Peter. Does He not say often enough: "Ask, and it shall be given you;" [6] "seek, and you shall find" what you desire; knock, and the door shall be opened to you? "for every one that seeketh, findeth." [7] He who asks anything from Me, is sure to get it. Is not this enough to convince us that God has an earnest will to help in all his necessities him who trusts in His providence?

Ah, if only one of those promises were made by some king or monarch of the earth, how his subjects would hasten to take advantage of it! For who would doubt that such a great lord would faithfully keep his word? Demetrius, king of Athens, wishing to know in what circumstances his subjects were, published throughout the whole kingdom that all who had any petition to present to him should only come forward, and their requests

We all trust in th promises the great.

---

[1] Invoca me in die tribulationis : eruam te, et honorificabis me.—Ps. xlix. 15.

[2] Liberabo te in die illa, ait Dominus ; et non traderis in manus virorum quos tu formidas; sed eruens liberabo te ; quia in me habuisti fiduciam.—Jer. xxxix. 17, 18.

[3] Jacta super Dominum curam tuam ; et ipse te enutriet ; non dabit in æternum fluctuationem justo.—Ps. liv. 23.

[4] Venite ad me omnes qui laboratis et onerati estis, et ego reficiam vos.—Matt. xi. 28.

[5] Omnem sollicitudinem vestram projicientes in eum, quoniam ipsi cura est de vobis.—I. Pet. v. 7.

[6] Petite, et dabitur vobis.—Matt. vii. 7.

[7] Omnis enim qui petit, accipit.—Ibid. 8.

would be at once granted. You can imagine, my dear brethren, what a vast number of petitions were handed in to him, and how joyfully every one awaited the fulfilment of his hopes. Demetrius read all the petitions, and then threw them into a river, nor did he grant a single one of them. See how vain it is to trust to the promises of men. But mark, too, how the mere promise of even a deceitful man can inspire one with hope and confidence.

So that, if we do not trust in God, we are wanting in faith.

Now God cries out, not once, but a hundred times, " Come to Me, all you; ask, and you shall receive." Hope in Me, and I will save you. Whatever you ask, only have confidence, and you will obtain it. These are the words of God, who is almighty and can keep His promise; of God, who is infinitely good and has the will to keep it; of God, who is infinitely faithful and must necessarily keep it; and yet we cannot be persuaded to put our whole confidence and hope in Him! What, in God's name, is the cause of that? Ah, nothing else but the want of a lively faith, on which hope is grounded. We do not believe firmly; we do not bring before our minds undoubtingly and in lively colors the almighty power, goodness, and faithfulness of God, and therefore we are so often despondent. So it is, my dear brethren. How many of us do not deserve the reproof that Our Lord gave to St. Peter when the latter was on the point of sinking into the waves: "O thou of little faith, why didst thou doubt"?[1] If we are suddenly overtaken by some calamity, what sighs and lamentations, what fears and despondency we give way to! And if the first " Our Father " we say has no effect, how slothfully we say the second, thinking that all our prayers will be of no avail, while we hardly dare to go as far as the third, through sheer want of confidence! " O thou of little faith, why dost thou doubt?" You do not believe as you ought, and therefore your hope sinks to the ground.

He who has a lively faith hopes everything from God.

If we always had a lively faith, and a firm confidence in God, nothing would seem too difficult, nothing so impossible as not to be effected by flying to God for refuge, as St. John Chrysostom says. "Let no servant of God doubt," he exclaims; " for, although he desires difficult things, and asks for miracles, he cannot be deserted by the almighty God."[2] He must not give way to the least doubt; he will certainly obtain all he wishes;

---

[1] Modicæ fidei, quare dubitasti?—Matt. xiv. 31.

[2] Nullus ex cultoribus Dei dubitet ; quamvis beneficia difficilia speret, quamvis miracula super se venientia postulet, deseri a summo Deo non potest.

for he who loves God with his whole heart, who trusts in Him alone, who flies to Him for refuge with child-like confidence, must necessarily be heard, provided only that what he asks is for the good of his soul. It is impossible for such a one to be abandoned by the almighty God.

Read the history of the patient Job. It is well-known into what poverty, misery, and desolation that pious man fell; how he was robbed of all his property, and infected with an ulcer that covered his body from head to foot, so that he had to sit on a dunghill and scrape away the matter that was flowing from his sores; yet he not only regained his former wealth, health, and prosperity, but received from the Lord twice as much as he had before. Why? Because in all his troubles and sufferings he never lost for a moment his confidence in God. Hear what he himself says: "Although He should kill me, I will trust in Him." [1] By which he means to say: If God were to afflict me to such an extent that death was already before my eyes, yet would my confidence in Him not be lessened, but I would still continue to hope that He would preserve my life. Yes, that He certainly would do: "And He shall be my saviour." [2] In the thirteenth chapter of the Second Book of Paralipomenon you may read how a small number of the men of Juda put to flight a large army of Israelites: "And there fell wounded of Israel five hundred thousand valiant men." And how did they manage to secure such a victory? They were armed with confidence in God alone. "The children of Juda were exceedingly strengthened, because they had trusted in the Lord, the God of their fathers." [3] David was so confident in his reliance on the protecting arm of God, that he feared no one on earth: "If armies in camp should stand together against me," he said with the utmost confidence, "my heart shall not fear. If a battle should rise up against me, in this will I be confident;" [4] that is, I will put my trust in the Lord. In a gloomy desert of Syria there dwelt a man named Isuardus, who was formerly the rich lord of Castella, and who through a vehement desire of imitating the voluntary poverty of Our Lord had constructed a small cell for himself

As the servants of God have always done.

---

[1] Etiamsi occiderit me, in ipso sperabo.—Job xiii. 15.
[2] Et ipse erit salvator meus.—Ibid. 16.
[3] Corruerunt vulnerati ex Israel quingenta millia virorum fortium. Vehementissime confortati filii Juda, eo quod sperassent in Domino Deo patrum suorum.—II. Paralip. xiii. 17, 18.
[4] Si consistant adversum me castra, non timebit cor meum ; si exurgat adversum me prœlium, in hoc ego sperabo.—Ps. xxvi. 3.

there.   After a time he had consumed all his food, and knew
not where to procure a fresh supply, so that he began to suffer
the pangs of hunger.   In these straits his sole refuge was his hope
in the Lord,[1] as his historian says.   Lord, he exclaimed, Thou
hast said that we must place our confidence in Thee, and Thou
wilt provide for us ("Cast thy care upon the Lord, and He
shall sustain thee"[2]); Lord, I hope in Thee; help me, then.
And God rewarded his confidence with a supply that lasted him
his whole life.   He sent a raven to him, that dug with its claws
in the earth until it found the root of a certain herb that grew
plentifully in that part; the bird then took the root in its beak
and brought it to the servant of God, thus saying to him in its
own way that here he had the food sent him by God.   Isnardus
tried the root, and found it so succulent and good that he never
used any other food during the remainder of his life.   On one
occasion two strangers, who had formerly been his subjects, happened to pass by the place; they recognized their former lord,
and were hospitably received by him; but all he had to set
before them consisted in the roots.   He told them at the same
time how God's fatherly providence had shown them to him by
means of the raven.   The strangers asserted when they returned
home that they had never tasted such good and nourishing
food.

And even the elements obey them; shown by examples.   By means of a similar hope and confidence in God men who
were otherwise weak and powerless miraculously compelled the
elements to obey them.   Moses divided the waters; Josue stayed
the sun in its course; Elias and Eliseus brought down fire from
heaven, and raised the dead to life; Gregory moved mountains;
St. Paul did not hesitate to say that he could do all things: "I
can do all things in Him who strengtheneth me,"[3] in whom I
place my confidence.   St. Sylvester, a monk in Sicily, had once
to bake some bread in a great hurry; but he had nothing at hand
to draw the burning coals out of the oven; trusting in God, he
crept in himself, and removed them with the hem of his garments, and then got out without having sustained the least injury.   St. Placidus, while still a youth, fell into the water and
was being carried down by the current, when St. Benedict commanded Maurus, his disciple, to run and save him.   Maurus
ran on the top of the water, as if it had been dry land, and

[1] Totam spem suam in Dominum erigebat.

[2] Jacta super Dominum curam tuam, et ipse te enutriet.—Ps. liv. 3.

[3] Omnia possum in eo qui me confortat.—Phil. iv. 13.

brought out Placidus by the hair. St. Elizabeth once put out a great fire by filling a sieve with water, as there was nothing else at hand, and emptying it on the burning pile. As the holy Bishop Corbinianus was once travelling along the shore of the Tuscan Sea on a Friday, he was reminded that he could have nothing but meat to eat; but as he refused to eat meat, his major-domo said to him: Sir, how can you procure fish here? The servant of God raised his eyes to heaven, and saw an eagle flying through the air; he pointed to it, and said: That bird is bringing us fish. Nor was he deceived. The eagle darted into the sea like a flash of lightning and caught a large fish, which it placed at the feet of the holy man, so that he and his retinue had quite enough to eat. The holy Abbot Mutius, as we read in the Lives of the Fathers, was once on his way to visit a dying monk, and was surprised by night while still a long distance from the convent. What was he to do? He did not take long to reflect. In the name of Jesus Christ, he called out to the descending sun, I command you to stand still , that I may reach the sick man by daylight. And behold, the sun stayed its course until he had accomplished his journey. His companions were amazed. What do you wonder at? said the holy man to them. Are we not assured by Christ Himself, "If you have faith as a grain of mustard-seed, you shall say to this mountain: Remove from hence thither, and it shall remove, and nothing shall be impossible to you" ? [1]

Well known is the incident related in the life of the holy Bishop Martin. He was once travelling through a forest and fell into the hands of robbers, who were on the point of putting him to death, but he showed not the least sign of fear. One of the band, astonished at this, asked him if he felt no uneasiness. Why should I? was the answer: I never felt easier in my mind than I do now; for I know well that, the greater the danger, the speedier is God's providence in coming to the help of those who trust in Him. Such, too, were the sentiments of Alfonso, king of Naples; he was once hearing Mass, when a fearful earthquake suddenly shook the walls of the church, and so filled the people with dread that they rushed out at once; he, however, remained quietly kneeling where he was, and told the priest, who was also influenced by the general consternation, to continue the holy sacrifice. Being asked afterwards how he preserved his pres-

This confidence alone reassured them in all circumstances.

---

[1] Si habueritis fidem sicut granum sinapis, dicetis monti huic: transi hinc illuc, et trans ibit, et nihil impossibile erit vobis.—Matt. xvii. 19.

ence of mind in such imminent danger, he answered in the words of the Wise Man: "The heart of the king is in the hand of the Lord;"[1] he who trusts in God has nothing to fear.

Happy, therefore, he who trusts in God.

Happy, then, he who places his hope in God with a firm confidence! "Blessed be the man," says God Himself by the prophet Jeremias, "that trusteth in the Lord, and the Lord shall be his confidence. And he shall be as a tree that is planted by the waters, that spreadeth out its roots towards moisture: and it shall not fear when the heat cometh. And the leaf thereof shall be green, and in the time of drought it shall not be solicitous, neither shall it cease at any time to bring forth fruit."[2] See, says St. Jerome, explaining this passage; there you have a lively picture of the Christian who loves God, has confidence in Him, and in the time of necessity calls on Him for help. Blessed will that man be in heaven and on earth; blessed amongst men on earth; blessed by the angels in heaven and the elect of God; blessed by the sovereign God Himself, whose help and grace he is assured of whenever he wishes.

Hence we should fly to Him for refuge in all our necessities with firm hope and confidence.

"Be you humble, therefore," I conclude, my dear brethren, in the words of St. Peter, "under the mighty hand of God, that He may exalt you in the time of visitation; casting all your care upon Him, for He hath care of you."[3] In all necessities and afflictions of body and soul our sole refuge must be His mercy, and with an assured confidence we must cry out to Him, like children to their loving father, Behold, O heavenly Father, how matters stand with me now; Thou knowest my wants; Thou art almighty and canst help me; Thou art infinitely good and hast the will to help me; Thou art infinitely faithful and hast promised to help those who put their trust in Thee. Now I cast myself in the lap of Thy providence; deliver me out of this trouble, if Thou knowest such deliverance to be for the good of my soul; show me that Thy word cannot fail, that no one has ever put his hope in the Lord and been confounded. "In Thee, O Lord, have I hoped, let me never be confounded."[4] Amen.

---

[1] Cor regis in manu Domini.—Prov. xxi. 1.

[2] Benedictus vir qui confidit in Domino, eterit Dominus fiducia ejus. Et erit quasi lignum quod transplantatur super aquas, quod ad humorem mittit radices suas; et non timebit cum venerit æstas. Et erit folium ejus viride, et in tempore siccitatis non erit sollicitum, nec aliquando desinet facere fructum.—Jer. xvii. 7, 8.

[3] Humiliamini igitur sub potenti manu Dei, ut vos exaltet in tempore visitationis: omnem sollicitudinem vestram projicientes in eum, quoniam ipsi est cura de vobis.—I. Pet. v. 6, 7.

[4] In te, Domine, speravi; non confundar in æternum.—Ps. xxx. 2.

Another Introduction for the feast of the Visitation of the B. V. M., when it falls on the third Sunday after Pentecost.

Text.

Beata quæ credidisti.—Luke i. 45.
" Blessed art thou that hast believed."

Introduction.

By faith we mean not only that virtue by which we believe and profess as infallibly certain all that God has revealed, because He is infinite Wisdom and Truth, but also that other virtue of hope and confidence in God which is founded on faith, and by which we confidently hope to obtain all that is advantageous to our salvation from God. It was to this confidence that Our Lord alluded in the Gospel on several occasions when healing the sick. "O woman, great is thy faith,"[1] said He to the Chananean woman; that is, great is thy confidence in Me. "As thou hast believed," said He on another occasion, "so be it done to thee;"[2] and again: "if thou canst believe."[3] And to Peter, reproving his want of confidence, "O thou of little faith, why didst thou doubt?"[4] Mary, Queen of heaven, blessed art thou that hast believed! With good reason did St. Elizabeth utter thy praises in those words; for by thy faith and confidence in God thou art exalted above all creatures, and blessed amongst women; by thy firm trust and confidence in God thou hast brought down thy Creator from His high throne in heaven, and given a saviour to the world. Ah, if we had but a little of this virtue, how much better we should be! My dear brethren, we often sigh and groan, etc.—*Continues as above.*

FORTY-SECOND SERMON.

ON PLACING OUR CONFIDENCE IN GOD ALONE.

Subject.

We often find that God does not help us in our temporal necessities, although we fly to Him for refuge, because we do not place our hope and confidence in Him alone.—*Preached on the second Sunday of Advent.*

---

[1] O mulier, magna est fides tua.—Matt. xv. 28.　[2] Sicut credidisti, fiat tibi.—Ibid. viii. 13.
[3] Si potes credere.—Mark. ix. 22.　　[4] Modicæ fidei, quare dubitasti?—Matt. xiv. 31.

Text.

Tu es qui venturus es, an alium expectamus?—Matt.xi. 3.
"Art Thou He that art to come, or look we for another?"

Introduction.

Such was the question that John caused to be asked, not because he doubted that Christ was the true Saviour of the world —for he had already pointed Him out and announced Him to men,—but that his disciples might know for certain who Our Lord was, and might thus be deterred from expecting another Messias. What answer did Christ make to the question? " Go and relate to John what you have heard and seen. The blind see, the lame walk, the lepers are cleansed, the deaf hear, the dead rise again." This should suffice to show your master that I, and no other, am the Messias; for it is only by the almighty power of God that such miracles can be wrought. My dear brethren. we have an almighty God, whose least sign all creatures must obey; who alone can free us from all our necessities and sorrows, and who has given His promise to help those who put their confidence in Him and call upon Him. Therefore we should place all our hope and trust in Him, and indeed in Him alone; for there is no other who has the same power and good will to help us that He has. Happy, then, is he who trusts in God alone. Such was the subject of my last sermon. But now methinks I hear some exclaim: Yes, but I have now been hoping and trusting for such a long time; I have prayed and sighed so often, but I am none the better for it all; I am just as badly off as I was at the beginning. Now do you know why you have not been helped? You were expecting assistance from some one else; you did not place your hope and confidence in God alone; and that is the reason why your prayers and appeals to God are so often fruitless, as I shall now show.

Plan of Discourse.

We often find that God does not help us in our temporal necessities, although we fly to Him for refuge, because we do not place our hope and confidence in Him alone, but expect help from some one else. Such is the whole subject. Therefore put your confidence in God alone.

Give us Thy grace to this end, O God; we ask it through the intercession of Mary and of our holy guardian angels.

But what is the meaning of that, " because we do not place our
hope and confidence in God alone" ?   Must we, then, in all adverse and disagreeable temporal circumstances keep quite still,
and refrain from seeking the help of other men, and expect God
alone to help us?   In that case the sick man should not have
recourse to the doctor, but wait till God restores him to health.
The man of business, or the tradesman who is brought to poverty by misfortune, should give up his work or his business, and
wait till God sends him something to eat.   The beggar should
not appeal to others to help him, but expect his daily bread from
the hands of God alone.   The man who is in doubt regarding
some important matter, on which great gain or loss depends,
should not take counsel with other men, or seek patrons, or ask
others for assistance, but leave the whole conduct of the matter
to God alone.   He who is attacked, persecuted, injured, and
wounded even to death by his enemy must not take up arms to
defend himself, but trust solely in the protection of the almighty
God; and so on in other dangers and necessities.   But, my dear
brethren, I do not mean to say that; help yourself, and God will
help you, says the old proverb.   To trust in God in the way you
suppose would be nothing else than presumption.

*We must al-
so make use
of natural
means in
our neces-
sities.*

There is no doubt that God wishes us to use our diligence and
the natural means we may have at hand to avert calamities, but
in such a way as not to place our hopes of safety in those human
means, but in God alone; for He alone it is who has given those
means the power of helping us, and without His assistance all
our efforts would be fruitless.   The sick man must not ascribe
his restoration to health to the doctor, the tradesman or man of
business must not attribute to his own industry the success that
has crowned his efforts, the beggar must not thank his entreaties
for the alms received, the man who was in doubt must not think
that the happy turn things took was owing to the advice he got
or to the help and patronage of men, the persecuted man must
not thank his weapons for his safety; no, in all those cases the
success is to be attributed to God alone.   For, as St. Paul says,
there is one who sows, and another who waters; but it is God
who gives the increase.   " Therefore neither he that planteth is
anything, nor he that watereth; but God that giveth the increase." [1]   Men, creatures, our own efforts and other means by

*But so as
not to put
our trust in
them alone,
but in God,
who gives
them power
to help us.*

---

[1] Itaque neque qui plantat est aliquid, neque qui rigat: sed qui incrementum dat, Deus.
—I. Cor. iii. 7.

which we seek to help ourselves, to free ourselves from trouble or danger, must be looked on as mere instruments which God, the supreme Master, has placed in our hands for our deliverance. Hence, just as when I hope to obtain from a painter a beautiful picture, I do not place my hopes in his brush, although he must make use of it, but in his skill alone, so, too, when I expect God to help and assist me in my necessities and dangers by those means, I do not place my hopes of success in them, but in the providence of God alone. And that is the meaning of trusting in God alone.

Herein are wanting they who blame creatures for adverse circumstances that happen.

Now, my dear brethren, most men are grievously wanting in this respect. For, in the first place, we are wont, when anything disagreeable occurs, to put the blame on the wrong cause, like the child that clenches its fist and threatens the rod because it has hurt it. True, the pain the child feels comes from the rod immediately; but if it could reason, it would say: The rod has hurt me, but not of itself, for it is a lifeless thing that hung on the wall until some one took it down. Who was it, then, that caused me the pain? My father or mother, who took the rod and beat me with it. Must I, then, be angry with my parents? God forbid! They love me, and mean well with me. Why did they beat me? I committed a fault; I told a lie, or was disobedient, or sulky. That was the first cause of my pain; so that I must put the whole blame of it, not on the rod, nor on my father or mother, but upon my own fault; and if I wish not to be beaten again, I must not be guilty of it in future. So would the child reason, if it knew how. In the same way should we consider the calamities that befall us. That wicked, cruel husband, that idle, useless wife who causes me such trouble every day, that disagreeable neighbor, that false friend who persecutes me, that bad season that has destroyed my crops, that war that has brought me to poverty, etc., all these are so many rods that have hurt and still hurt me. But who takes them in hand and strikes me with them? My heavenly Father, whose just providence has ordained those trials for me. Why does He act in that way? Because I have done wrong, or that I may avoid wrong doing in future, so that I myself am the sole cause of my sufferings. But we do not think of that; like the child we bite the rod, and pour out our wrath and throw the whole blame on men and other creatures, that are the immediate cause of our trouble; and hence it comes that we have to bear trials and crosses without heavenly consolation or merit for our souls.

Such is the way in which we act in regard to our hope and And ascribe success or failure to human means. confidence, when we ascribe the prosperous or adverse circumstances of our lives more to creatures and human intervention than to God and His providence. If we have still to bear the weight of the misfortune from which we tried to free ourselves, —for instance, the lawsuit on which so much depended is lost; the sickness still remains dangerous; the gain we sought is unattainable; poverty is at the door—oh, then we think, the lawyer is in fault; if he had minded his business better, I should not now be the loser. That wicked man stood in my way, and prevented me from succeeding. The doctor does not know his business; therefore I am not any better. Such is the tenor of the letter that St. Gregory of Tours wrote to queen Austregildis, who, when she was on her death-bed, commanded all the doctors to be put to death, as she blamed them for not curing her; but on God she never cast a thought. And if we are successful, if the suit is won, the sickness cured, the loss made good, the necessity provided for, then we think to ourselves: For this I have to thank the lawyer, the doctor, the patron who took my part, the good friend who helped me. If it were not for him, I should never have done so well. Ah, that is a clear proof that we do not place our confidence and hope in God alone, although we have already appealed to Him for assistance. And on that account God will not hear our prayers the next time we fly to Him for refuge. We should rather say, if things go wrong: May the will of God be done! He has arranged this for me. And if things go well, Thanks be to God, who has suggested the right thing to the lawyer, the doctor, the patron and friend! Blessed be God, who has given those natural means the power of helping me so well!

Another proof that we do not place our confidence in God They, too, are wrong who first have recourse to human means. alone is the fact that in impending calamities our first thoughts are directed to what we can effect by our own industry or by the help of others; and if we see that we can do little or nothing, then, more through despair than through child-like confidence, we appeal to God by prayer as the last resource. Thus you may hear some sick people sighing forth, after they have spent months and years in bed: Alas, I have done everything now, but all is of no avail! I see that I must try something else, and rely on God; He will be my best friend after all. Thus God is made the last resource in an emergency. Ah, unhappy we, exclaims St. Bernard with indignation: "Why do we hesitate to cast away all miserable, vain, useless, and deceitful hopes," [1] so that we may place our confidence in Him who alone can and will help us?

God should be the first to whom we appeal. God is the foundation on whom all natural means rest, and without His coöperation nothing in the world can be of any avail. Therefore He should be the very first we think of in our troubles and difficulties; to Him we should fly for refuge first of all. We should begin by prayer, asking God to help us, and then, trusting in Him alone, make use of natural and human means. The hope that rests on men and on human industry is compared in holy Scripture to a wave of the sea. The hope of the just, which is built on God alone, is compared to a mountain on land. Mark this beautiful simile, my dear brethren. When the wind rages over the sea, it throws up the waves on high like mountains; but how long do they remain in that position? Almost in the same moment they fall down again into the depths. So it is with the hope of the worldling, says the Holy Ghost: "The hope of the wicked is as a thin froth, which is dispersed by the storm." [2] On the other hand, the mountain on land stands firm, no matter how the winds may blow. Such is the hope of those who trust in God alone: "They that trust in the Lord shall be as Mount Sion; he shall not be moved forever." [3]

There are some who lose heart if they are not helped at once. Thirdly, the weakness of our hope in God is shown when we experience no relief nor help after having prayed and made use of natural means. Then we lose heart at once, and if we are encouraged or consoled either publicly in sermons, or by inward spiritual inspirations; if we are told to continue praying, to hope in the Lord, and not lose confidence in Him, we often think with a sort of chagrin: Yes, no doubt prayer is good; hope is good; confidence in God is good; but! And what do you mean by that wretched "but"? Nothing else than that you are wanting in true hope and confidence in God, as if He either could not or would not help you. And can you imagine that such a weak faith as that will move the Lord God to assist you? No, indeed! There could not be a worse way to try to gain His fatherly affection, His grace and favor, or to ensure His help in your need.

---

[1] Utquid cunctamur abjicere spes miseras, vanas, inutiles, seductorias ?—S. Bern. serm. ix. in Ps. xc.

[2] Spes impii tanquam spuma gracilis, quæ a procella dispergitur.—Wisdom v. 15.

[3] Qui confidunt in Domino sicut mons Sion ; non commovebitur in æternum.—Ps. cxxiv. 1.

Finally, there are some who, when public calamity or scarcity is impending, no longer give the usual alms to the poor. Do you know why they do that? One would think the act was suggested by avarice and parsimony. But no; it comes from nothing else than their want of confidence in God, and in God alone. They trust too much for the means of subsistence in the property or money they have left, and are afraid that, when the general pressure comes, they will have to suffer if they continue to be generous to the poor. As if the faithful God, who expressly said: " Give, and it shall be given to you," [1] "he that giveth to the poor, shall not want; he that despiseth his entreaty, shall suffer indigence," [2]—as if, I say, the almighty and most faithful God could not support them with a little as well as with a great deal.

Tell that tradesman or shopman to act honestly in his work or business, and to give up cursing, swearing, lying, and cheating. Oh, he will say to you, it is easy to talk; he who tries to act honestly nowadays will soon come to grief; we must endeavor to make a little profit now and then, or we shall not be able to get on. Tell that man-servant or maid-servant, or that housekeeper, to leave the house which is the proximate occasion of sin for them. Alas, they will say, how am I to live if I go away? All these people are wanting in confidence in God; they look for the means of subsistence to vice and sin; they do not hope that God would help them if they kept His law, as if He had or wished to have no providence for them.

Nay, there are some who trust more in the devil than in God. It would seem almost impossible to find a man who looks for any good from that evil spirit, who is well known as the worst enemy of the human race; and yet there are only too many in the world who depend on him. I will say nothing of sorcerers and those unhappy souls who enter into a formal compact with the demon. But how many are there who make vain observations of numbers and chances, thinking to find some luck therein! How many are there who use certain herbs, minerals, rings, ciphers, writings, words, and similar things to produce effects for which they are utterly inadequate, unless in so far as the demon interferes with them? All these people put their confidence more in the devil than in God. And could a greater folly be

[1] Date, et dabitur vobis.—Luke vi. 38.

[2] Qui dat pauperi non indigebit; qui despicit precantem, sustinebit penuriam.—Prov. xxviii. 27.

imagined! True, the natural powers of the devil are great; but he cannot use them unless as far as God allows him; and God keeps him constantly under restraint. Without the divine permission he cannot produce the slightest breeze in the air, nor move the smallest leaf on a tree; much less can he procure wealth for men. And yet people trust that unhappy deceiver, and refuse to trust God. In a word, there are few men in the world who place their confidence in God alone.

Hence God does not help, because we do not trust in Him alone.

Meanwhile they moan and sigh: Ah, I have prayed so long and so often that God might take this trouble from me, help me in my necessity, or free me from this trial. To that end I have performed many devotions; I have been to confession and Communion, given alms, and had Masses said; but there is no help for me, and I am just as badly off as before. Now, the very reason why there is neither help nor consolation for you, and why God does not hear you, is that you do not fly to Him with a real confidence; you do not trust in God alone; you rely more, or at least in the first place, on creatures, on your own industry, on human means; and therefore, I repeat, God does not and will not help you.

Shown from Scripture; in the Ammonites.

Read the holy Scriptures, and you will see that, as a general rule, He abandons those who put their trust in men. The town of Hesebon was looked on as impregnable, for it was surrounded by water in the midst of a deep valley, and a besieging army could not come near it. The citizens therefore felt very secure. They heard that some neighboring places were attacked and taken, but they did not feel the least alarm, and continued to indulge in all kinds of riotous and luxurious living, laughing at the idea of an enemy attacking them or approaching their walls. But God told them by the Prophet Jeremias how vain was their confidence. "Why gloriest thou in the valleys? thy valley hath flowed away, O delicate daughter, that hast trusted in thy treasures, and hast said: Who shall come to me? Behold I will bring a fear upon thee, saith the Lord God of hosts, from all that are round about thee; and you shall be scattered every one out of one another's sight, neither shall there be any to gather together them that flee;"[1] for you have relied, not on Me, but on your walls.

---

[1] Quid gloriaris in vallibus? defluxit vallis tua, filia delicata, quæ confidebas in thesauris tuis, et dicebas: quis veniet ad me? Ecce ego inducam super te terrorem, ait Dominus Deus exercituum, ab omnibus qui sunt in circuitu tuo; et dispergimini singuli a conspectu vestro, nec erit qui congreget fugientes.—Jerem. xlix. 4, 5.

In the sixteenth chapter of the Second Book of Paralipome- non the Scripture says of king Asa: "And Asa fell sick, in the nine and thirtieth year of his reign, of a most violent pain in his feet." To whom did he appeal for help? To the Lord, his God? Ah, if he had done that it would have been well for him. "And yet in his illness he did not seek the Lord, but rather trusted in the skill of physicians,"[1] whom he called together from all parts of his kingdom. But not one of them could allay the pain he suffered, or save him from death; abandoned by God, he died in fearful torments: "And he slept with his fathers; and he died."[2] Asa, says Cajetan, was punished, not because he had recourse to the physicians, but because he placed all his confidence in their skill, and did not seek the true God. Hear this, all ye who in sickness and misfortunes not only neglect to call on God, like Asa, but, terrible to think, actually seek help and advice from the devil by having recourse to people of suspicious character, or by using different superstitious means of healing diseases, averting temporal losses, finding lost things, and so on. Oh, if he who puts his trust in men is accursed ("Cursed be the man that trusteth in man"[3]), what sort of a curse will fall upon him who hopes and trusts in diabolical arts?

Naaman, one of the richest and most influential princes of Syria, was, as we read in the Fourth Book of Kings, infected with a loathsome leprosy. "He was a valiant man and rich, but a leper."[4] Physicians vied with one another in their efforts to relieve him, but to no purpose; until at last Naaman acted on the advice of a servant maid, dismissed the physicians, and went to see Eliseus, the prophet of God. "So Naaman came with his horses and chariots, and stood at the door of the house of Eliseus."[5] The prophet told him to wash seven times in the Jordan. Hardly had he done so, when "his flesh was restored like the flesh of a little child, and he was made clean."[6] De Lyra, speaking of this, asks: Who made Naaman a leper? It was God, he answers. Why did He not cure him before? Because Naaman trusted too much in the skill of men. He wished

---

[1] Ægrotavit etiam Asa anno trigesimo nono regni sui dolore pedum vehementissimo, et nec in infirmitate sua quæsivit Dominum, sed magis in medicorum arte confisus est.— II. Paral. xvi. 12.

[2] Dormivitque cum patribus suis, et mortuus est.—Ibid. 13.

[3] Maledictus homo qui confidit in homine. Jerem. xvii. 5.

[4] Erat autem vir fortis et dives, sed leprosus.—IV. Kings v. 1.

[5] Venit ergo Naaman cum equis et curribus, et stetit ad ostium domus Elisæi. Ibid. 9.

[6] Restituta est caro ejus sicut caro pueri parvuli, et mundatus est.—Ibid. 14.

to show him that help and counsel can be had only from the Lord, and therefore that we should place our hope in God alone in all our necessities. And Naaman acknowledged this after he was made clean; for he went back to the man of God. " In truth I know," said he, " there is no other God in all the earth, but only in Israel, " [1] from whom alone we must expect help.

In Joseph in Egypt. Even the most faithful servants of God have sometimes been left quite desolate when they placed their confidence anywhere except in the Lord. Well known is the innocence of Joseph; how obedient and respectful he was to his father Jacob; what a sincere love he had for his brothers, wicked as they were, and how angelic he was in his purity, which he kept untarnished in the midst of the most violent temptations and allurements,—all virtues that are most dear to the heart of God. Yet he was falsely accused as an adulterer, thrown into prison, bound with chains, and kept there for some years without hope or help, although no doubt he often called on God during the time, for he loved God with his whole heart. There you have an example of a just and innocent man, abandoned, as it were, by God in the most dreadful misfortune. Ah, that is truly the case, would the wisdom of the world say; unhappy Joseph, of what good to you now is that virtue and piety with which you so earnestly strove to gain the favor of God? He now leaves you in the lurch. If you had obeyed your mistress, you would have been secure of her protection, and would fare much better than you now do in that wretched prison. See now how vain and idle your hope is. Oh, foolish reasoning of the senseless world! Cannot the God of infinite reason restore to the light of day from the gloomy dungeon one who puts his trust in Him? Cannot the Almighty place even a slave on the throne, if He pleases? And such was in reality what He did for Joseph. Yet I cannot help thinking with astonishment, Why did the wise, almighty, and faithful God allow innocence to languish in a dungeon for such a long time? Why did He not liberate His beloved Joseph long before? Do you wish to know the reason? It was because Joseph had not deserved to be freed before, says St. John Chrysostom; because he had not placed all his confidence in God. How was that? Joseph had prophesied to the chief butler of Pharao that he would soon be liberated and be restored to his former position; and then he thought to himself, Now is my chance;

[1] Vere scio quod non sit alius Deus in universa terra, nisi tantum in Israel.—IV. Kings v. 15.

now I shall have some one to intercede for me. "Only remember me," said he to the chief butler, "when it shall be well with thee, and do me the kindness to put Pharao in mind to take me out of this prison; for I was stolen away out of the land of the Hebrews, and here without any fault was cast into the dungeon." [1] Hear, says St. Chrysostom, what Joseph desires; his wish now is to be helped by men; but for that very reason God will justly refuse to help him. Now, Joseph, so does the Lord seem to address him, do you hope and rely on men, as if My providence alone were not enough to save you? You will see, then, what it is to put your trust in men. For the butler, once things prospered with him, forgot all about his promise: "But the chief butler, when things prospered with him, forgot his interpreter," [2] and the unlucky Joseph had to remain some years still in prison, through a decree of divine providence, because he had relied too much on human help. Such is the teaching of SS. John Chrysostom and Augustine. "Justly," says the former, "as it seems, did he suffer thus, that he might learn not to trust in men, but in God alone." [3] And St. Augustine has not the least hesitation in asserting the same thing. "There is not the least doubt," he says, "that for the sake of chastising holy Joseph God did not allow the chief butler to remember what Joseph asked him to do," [4] because he had relied too much on human aid. But when at last Joseph, having found his hopes frustrated, no longer relied on men, but trusted in God alone, how did things go with him then? From being a prisoner and a slave, he became viceroy of Egypt.

Thus God has promised His help and assistance only to those who trust in Him alone. "Because he hath hoped in Me," He says by the Psalmist. "I will deliver him; I will protect him because he hath known My name." [5] To encourage us to this undivided confidence, Our Lord gives us a beautiful exhortation in the Gospel of St. Matthew, when speaking to those timid and

Therefore we should rely on God alone.

---

[1] Tantum memento mei, cum bene tibi fuerit, et facias mecum misericordiam ut suggeras Pharaoni ut educat me de isto carcere: quia furto sublatus sum de terra Hebræorum, et hic innocens in lacum missus sum.—Gen. xl. 14, 15.

[2] Succedentibus prosperis præpositus pincernarum oblitus est interpretis sui.—Ibid. 23.

[3] Merito et ipse hoc passus existimatur, ut disceret, in hominibus non esse fidendum, sed spem omnem in Deo dirigendam.—S. Chrys. hom. viii. in Ep. ad Tim.

[4] Sine ulla dubitatione credendum est quod pro castigatione sancti Joseph non permisit Deus magistrum pincernarum, ut in mente haberet quod ei sanctus Joseph, cum de carcere dimissus est, supplicaverat.—S. Aug. serm. lxxxii. de temp.

[5] Quoniam in me speravit, liberabo eum : protegam eum, quoniam cognovit nomen meum.—Ps. xc. 14.

pusillanimous people who are always in dread lest the necessary food and clothing should be wanting to them. " Consider the lilies of the field, how they grow: they labor not, neither do they spin; " and yet the Lord clothes them with a snow-white and beautiful garment, that no art can imitate, so that not Solomon in all his glory was clothed as one of them. " How much more you, O ye of little faith! " [1] How much more readily will not your heavenly Father provide for those who trust in Him? Mark how Our Lord speaks of the lilies of the field, not of those that grow in gardens. Why? The lilies and flowers that grow in gardens owe their flourishing condition to the diligence and labor of the gardener, who plants them in carefully prepared ground, waters, and looks after them. But no one takes any care of the lilies of the field; they do not receive any aid from human hands, but expect all their growth from heaven alone; and therefore the Lord looks after them and cares for them. Such, then, should be the nature of our confidence; we can, indeed, and must make use of human means, but at the same time we should rely on God as if we had them not, and from Him alone expect the help we are in need of.

After the example and teaching of holy servants of God.

The holy king David understood this well, when he said to the Lord: " Give us help from trouble, for vain is the salvation of man." [2] The forces of the Syrians, the Ammonites, and the Idumeans had united against David, and were prepared to attack him. He had an army powerful enough to resist all those foes, and generals who had been always victorious, and so could have easily hoped for a complete victory; yet he did not think himself justified in trusting this army. My soldiers, he thought. are indeed not used to flee before the enemy; they have been always victorious hitherto; but still they are only mortals, and can easily fall into disorder and be vanquished. If I, then, put my trust in them, I shall run the risk of finding myself disappointed; but if I trust in Thee, O my God, I can be certain that I shall not be overcome by my enemies; therefore I beg of Thee, " Give us help from trouble, for vain is the salvation of men." He, of course, made use of his army; but all his confidence he placed in the almighty protection of God. Such, too, were the dispositions of St. Ignatius Loyola. the founder of our Society. Whatever seemed to him to be advantageous for the glory of God and the

[1] Considerate lilia agri, quomodo crescunt: non laborant, neque nent. Quanto magis vos. modicæ fidei !– Matt. vi. 28. 30.

[2] Da nobis auxilium de tribulatione, quia vana salus hominis.—Ps. lix. 13.

good of souls he at once undertook with the greatest courage. He built and founded many houses in Rome for the poor and for those unfortunate women who are driven by want to lead a bad life; and that he did sometimes without as much as even a penny in his possession, to the great astonishment of others, who often reproved him for his presumption in thus undertaking a great work without any means of carrying it out. But, said he to them, shall I not trust in my God? You know not what a source of income is a firm faith and an assured confidence in God alone. To hope in what you really have is not hope; to have confidence that you will succeed in carrying out that for which you are abundantly supplied with human means is not confidence. The poor man, who has nothing, calls upon God, and God hears him. A rich and noble gentleman, who had offered to help Ignatius whenever the latter was in need, complained that he was so sparing of asking from him, and that he had not more confidence in his promises. Sir, said Ignatius, it is now more than thirty years since I, being enlightened by God, have learned that, although one must make use of all lawful means in furthering things that are to the divine honor and glory, yet we must not rely on those means, but place our confidence in God alone, for whose honor the work is undertaken. If, therefore, you wish to offer me your help thus generously, I accept it with thanks; but you must know that I do not rely on you and your money, nor on any other creature, but solely on God. Such, too, is the teaching of St. Basil in the following words: "As we owe adoration to no one but God alone, so also we should not place our confidence in any one but God, the Lord of all things."[1]

Hear this, ye afflicted souls, who complain that you are abandoned by all men, and that you can see no means of deliverance from your misery; ah, all the more favorable is the opportunity you have to place all your hope in God. Believe that you do not say too much when you exclaim: I have no one but God to look to. But in having Him you have all; and even if it seems to you that you are abandoned by Him, you must still continue to hope that He will not leave you, or that He has left you only for a time, provided you keep your confidence in Him and remain in His grace; for that is an infallible sign that He has not forgotten you, since He never forgets those who put their trust in Him.

Conclusion and exhortation to the suffering.

---

[1] Sicut nulli alii nos praeterquam soli Deo cultum tribuere par est, sic etiam neque in ulla alia re spem nostram constituere debemus, quam in Deo, omnium rerum Domino.—S. Basil. in orat. ii. de Principat.

"Blessed is the man," says St. Basil, "who lays aside all hope in this world, and places his whole confidence in God."[1]   Only fear God, love Him with your whole hearts, and cast yourselves and all your miseries into His fatherly hands.   Say with king David: "But it is good for me to stick close to my God, to put my hope in the Lord God."[2]   Yes, O my God; why should I trust in men, who have so often deceived me?   "To Thee is the poor man left; Thou wilt be a helper to the orphan."[3]   There is no one but Thou, O my God, who can protect and help me.   In Thee alone have I help enough, certain and confident that my hopes will not be in vain.   Amen.

Another Introduction to the same sermon for the fourth Sunday after Pentecost.

Text.

Per totam noctem laborantes nihil cepimus; in verbo autem tuo laxabo rete.—Luke v. 5.

"We have labored all the night and have taken nothing; but at Thy word I will let down the net."

Introduction.

Beautiful is the lesson that St. Peter here teaches us.   The night being calm and still, he thought he was sure to catch a great many fish; but with all his labor he caught nothing, as he himself acknowledges: "Master, we have labored all the night, and have taken nothing."   Christ enters into the boat.   "Launch out into the deep," said He, "and let down your nets for a draught."   Here Peter might certainly have been doubtful with regard to the success of the experiment; for he had already failed to catch anything during the night, when the time is more favorable for fishing, since the fish do not then see the meshes of the net, and are thus more easily captured than in the day-time.   He might then very well have said: There is no use in trying any further.   If I have been unsuccessful during the night, I cannot reasonably hope for anything in the day-time.   Nevertheless, said Peter, "at Thy word I will let down the net;" and behold, at the the first draught he caught so many that the net was torn, and two boats were filled with the haul almost to sinking.   See how different the result of his labor was.   Was not the water the same

[1] Beatus qui omni spe rerum hujus mundi se orbavit, ac in solo Deo omnem spem fixit.—S. Basil. orat. de virt. et vit.

[2] Mihi autem adhærere Deo bonum est, ponere in Domino Deo spem meam.—Ps. lxxii. 28.

[3] Tibi derelictus est pauper; orphano tu eris adjutor.—Ibid. ix. 14.

by day as by night? By all means. And did they not work as
hard during the night as they did in the day-time? Without
doubt, and harder too, for they must have cast the net a hundred times in the night, whereas in the day they let it down only
once. Why, then, did they catch such a quantity of fish, while
their labor in the night remained fruitless? Our Lord wished to
show them thereby what can be done by human industry alone,
and what can be done by the help of the almighty God. In the
night Peter hoped to be successful, relying on his own efforts;
but during the day he had no hope except in the words of
Christ. "At Thy word I will let down the net." My dear
brethren, one word was enough to inspire Peter and his companions with a firm confidence in Christ, while the good God,
who is infinitely faithful, has given us a hundred promises.
"Come to Me," He says, "all you that labor and are burdened;"
come to Me in all your trials and troubles, "and I will refresh
you." [1] Have confidence in Me, and I will help you; ask, and you
shall receive. But all these promises cannot induce us to have
confidence and to put our trust in God. Nay, methinks I hear
some saying with Peter: "We have labored all the night, and
have taken nothing." I have hoped and confided so long; I have
prayed and sighed so much; but hitherto I have not received any
assistance; I have still the same troubles to bear. But do you
know why you have not been helped? Like Peter, you have relied
too much on your own industry and on human means; you have
not placed your confidence in God alone. etc.—*Continues as above.*

FORTY-THIRD SERMON.

ON CONFIDENCE IN GOD IN SEEMINGLY DESPERATE CIR-CUMSTANCES.

Subject.

When we are in such evil plight that there seems to be, humanly speaking, no hope for us, then should our hope and confidence in God be all the firmer.—*Preached on the third Sunday
of Advent.*

Text.

*Nihil solliciti sitis; sed in omni oratione, et obsecratione, cum
gratiarum actione, petitiones vestræ innotescant apud Deum.*—
Phil. iv. 6.

[1] Venite ad me omnes qui laboratis et onerati estis, et ego reficiam vos.—Matt. xi. 28.

" Be nothing solicitous; but in everything by prayer and supplication with thanksgiving let your petitions be made known to God."

Introduction.

Rejoice in the Lord, just Christian, who serve your God: " Rejoice in the Lord always: again I say, rejoice." [1] Such is the exhortation that St. Paul gives you in to-day's epistle. And why should the children of God be sorrowful? What can be wanting to you, who have an infinitely good and faithful Lord as your father? " Be nothing solicitous," but in all your troubles and necessities fly to Him with confidence. Hope and trust in the Lord, and as we have seen in the last sermon, in the Lord alone, for He alone can and will help you. Ah, think some; there is no more hope or confidence for me; my circumstances are desperate! What? Desperate? Then so much the better; for on that very account you can and must place your confidence all the more firmly in God and await His help, as I told you in a few words towards the end of the last sermon, and now proceed to explain more in detail.

Plan of Discourse.

When we are in such evil plight that there seems to be, humanly speaking, no hope for us, then should our hope and confidence in God be all the firmer. Such is the whole subject of this sermon.

O almighty, good, and faithful God, keep us always in Thy friendship, and give us a sure hope and a firm confidence in Thee alone! This we beg of Thee through the intercession of our Mother Mary and of our holy guardian angels.

When one sees no chance of success there is no more reason for natural hope.

But how can one hope when affairs are in a desperate condition? And how can one hope all the more that things will turn out well? Is that credible, or possible? Hope, generally speaking, is the expectation of some future good that is difficult of attainment; such is the definition given of it by the Angelic Doctor, St. Thomas. [2] But when the desired good seems unattainable, is it not more the object of despair than of reasonable hope? The husbandman willingly works in the field and spares no labor or trouble as long as there is a prospect of a harvest. The soldier in battle fights bravely at the risk of his life as long

[1] Gaudete in Domino semper; iterum dico, gaudete.—Phil. iv. 4.
[2] Objectum spei est bonum futurum, arduum, possibile haberi.

as there is a chance of gaining the victory. The merchant travels over land and sea, to his great discomfort and disquiet, as long as there is hope of making profit. The student bears all the tedium of his years of study, because he thinks he will be able to excel in some science and thus attain a good position. The sick man does violence to himself, and against his will takes the most bitter medicines and pills, as long as there is any reasonable hope of recovering his health. But if all these people see that their trouble and labor will not help them to the desired end; if such great difficulties and impediments present themselves, that no means will enable them to gain the object of their wishes; oh, then their reasonable hope falls to the ground. The husbandman gives up his labor, the merchant his long journeys, the soldier fights no longer, the student ceases to study, the sick man refuses to take the prescribed medicines; for they all have good reason to despair of success. This is true, my dear brethren, when we speak of natural hope, which is founded merely on human and natural means.

But it is quite different with supernatural hope and confidence in God. This should never fail, nor be wanting in the least degree, but rather increase, the more difficulties and impediments stand in the way. Nay, when we see that the natural means we have hitherto used are of no avail, and know that they will be of no avail in the future; when we have exhausted all our ingenuity to no purpose; then must that hope be all the greater, more certain, and more fervent, that in spite of former failures we shall yet attain the desired end. Why so? Because supernatural hope is not founded on natural means, nor on our own industry and labor, so that it is not interfered with by their want of success; but it rests on the almighty God, to whom nothing is impossible, whose infinite power is not limited by any difficulty or hindrance, who with a single sign of His will can restore what is already despaired of; and all that He can do just as easily as He can refuse His help when things seem, humanly speaking, to be progressing favorably. Therefore I can never have reasonable grounds to waver in a hope of this kind, no matter how slight may seem the chances of success, as I explained on another occasion, when speaking of prayer in public calamities.

Not so with supernatural hope, that is founded on God.

And I added then, that my hope should rather increase and become more assured and fervent, because it is founded on the God of infinite goodness and infinite wisdom, who is more than

For He often allows things to get into a

desperate
state, that
we may as-
cribe our
success to
Him alone.

ever willing to help those who trust in Him when they are deprived of all human assistance, and who often defers coming to
their aid until affairs are in a desperate condition, partly to prove
our hope and see if it rests constantly on Him alone, and partly that
we may look on our success as a pure benefit from God. If He
heard our prayers at once when we appeal to Him, besides using other means in our impending or actual necessities, then we
should often ascribe our success, not to God's goodness, but to
our own efforts and industry, or to other creatures and human
means, and so we should neglect to thank God as we ought.
And this we know by experience. When some important matter
has been brought to a fortunate termination; when the husband,
or wife, or child, or friend about whom we were in a great state
of trouble recovers from a dangerous illness; when we escape
an evil that threatened us; how do we act? We are filled with
joy and exultation; we offer and receive a thousand congratula-
tions; but what thanks or service do we render the good God for
the benefit bestowed on us? Do we become more fervent in the
love of God and of our neighbor, more humble and modest in
our outward demeanor, more generous to the poor, more devout in prayer, more diligent in frequenting the holy sacraments,
more careful in training up our children in a Christian manner,
more studious in avoiding the occasions of sin, more vigilant in
shunning even deliberate venial sins? No, indeed! We go the
old gait, as we did before; hardly do we once offer a word of
thanks to God. That is an evident sign of gross ingratitude or
of crass ignorance, since we do not look on our success as a pure
benefit from God. Therefore, I repeat, God defers helping us;
He allows us to plague ourselves and to try all possible means;
He waits till things have reached such a point that we have no
more hope of bringing them to a successful termination by natural means. Then, if our trust and confidence in Him is not
gone, He brings matters to a better state, either at once or gradually, that we may be compelled to acknowledge and confess
that nothing but the all-powerful hand of God could help us,
and thus fulfil our obligation of gratitude to Him.

Proven from
Scripture.
Susanna.

Read the holy Scriptures, and you will find that God often
acted in that manner towards His servants. Thus, for instance,
in the thirteenth chapter of the Book of Daniel, you will find
the history of the chaste Susanna. Pure and stainless as was
the life of that holy matron, yet she had to suffer from the tongue

of calumny, and that, too, an the part of the judges of the people, who accused her publicly of the heinous crime of adultery and, having suborned false witnesses, caused her to be sentenced to be stoned to death. Alas, a hard and bitter fate for one so rich, noble, and innocent, who had hitherto been held in the highest esteem throughout Judea on account of her piety and holiness! And now she had to stand her trial publicly before the people, in presence of her husband, her parents, and relations, as a shameless adulteress. What was she to do? Her friends were filled with pity for her, but could not help her. "Therefore her friends and all her acquaintances wept."[1] So strong was the testimony of the elders against her, that she had no one to say a word in her favor: "And she, weeping, looked up to heaven; for her heart had confidence in the Lord."[2] Oh, since that is the case, thou hast no evil to dread, Susanna! No one who has ever trusted in the Lord has been deceived or disappointed. Meanwhile there was no prospect of help far or near; the people believed the elders: "The multitude believed them as being the elders and the judges of the people."[3] The punishment prescribed for adultery in the divine law was that the guilty one should be publicly stoned to death; the sentence was pronounced, and all cried out unanimously that it was a just one: "They condemned her to death."[4] Susanna, what thinkest thou now? "Her heart had confidence in the Lord." "O eternal God," she exclaimed, "who knowest hidden things, who knowest all things before they come to pass. Thou knowest that they have borne false witness against me."[5] But still she was led away to be put to death; "and when she was led to be put to death,"[6] when they had already taken up the stones to cast at her, then Susanna, with a dying voice as it were, cried out to God: "Behold, I must die, whereas I have done none of these things which these men have maliciously forged against me."[7] And now, when there seemed to be not the slightest gleam of hope for her, what occurred?

---

[1] Flebant igitur sui, et omnes qui noverant eam.—Dan. xiii. 33.

[2] Flens suspexit ad cœlum ; erat enim cor ejus fiduciam habens in Domino.—Ibid. 35.

[3] Credidit eis multitudo quasi senibus et judicibus populi.—Ibid. 41.

[4] Condemnaverunt eam ad mortem.—Ibid. 41.

[5] Deus æterne, qui absconditorum es cognitor, qui nosti omnia antequam fiant, tu scis quoniam falsum testimonium tulerunt contra me.—Ibid. 42, 43.

[6] Cumque duceretur ad mortem.—Ibid. 45.

[7] Ecce morior, cum nihil horum fecerim, quæ isti malitiose composuerunt adversum me.—Ibid. 43.

Whom God
did not de-
liver until
all hope
seemed lost.
" The Lord raised up the holy spirit of a young boy, whose name was Daniel; and he cried out with a loud voice: I am clear from the blood of this woman." [1] He protected the innocent, and convicted the elders of falsehood. They were stoned, and Su-. sanna set free, while from that time forward she was held in still greater honor and love by the people and by all posterity. " With that all the assembly cried out with a loud voice, and they blessed God, who saveth them that trust in Him." [2] See there, my dear brethren, how wonderfully God knows how to help when things seem desperate. What think you of this, you pu- sillanimous Christians, who become cast down at once if you do not experience present help in your necessities, and lose all hope and courage? Is hope in God of no avail when human means cannot help us? Is it a vain hope, when, naturally speaking, everything seems to be lost?   No, says Eusebius; not alone does God not abandon the just who trust in Him, but He renders them help and assistance beyond their hopes. Mark that in this example. God might have sent Daniel earlier to detect the fraud of the elders, before Susanna was brought before the tri- bunal; the almighty God could easily have done that; but then the wonderful manner in which He rendered assistance would not have been so evident, nor would such praise have been given to Him. As it was, however, " all the assembly cried with a loud voice, and they blessed God, who saveth them that trust in Him." And with regard to Susanna's immediate friends, " Helcias and his wife praised God, for their daughter Susanna, with Joakim her husband, and all her kindred." [3] They, too, offered the trib- ute of their praises. To whom? Not to Daniel, who had dis- covered the fraud of the elders, and freed Susanna from death, but to God, from whom alone, as they all well knew, help could be expected in such desperate circumstances.

The history
of Daniel.
The name of Daniel here reminds me of another proof of my subject and an example of the wonderful manner in which the providence of God acts towards His servants who put their trust in Him. Daniel was specially dear to king Darius, on account of his extraordinary knowledge and prudence, and the king had

---

[1] Suscitavit Dominus spiritum sanctum pueri junioris, cujus nomen Daniel; et exclamavit voce magna: mundus ego sum a sanguine hujus.—Dan. xiii. 45, 46.

[2] Exclamavit itaque omnis cœtus voce magna, et benedixerunt Deum, qui salvat sperantes in se.—Ibid. 60.

[3] Helcias autem et uxor ejus laudaverunt Deum pro filia sua Susanna, cum Joakim, marito ejus, et cognatis omnibus.—Ibid. 63.

even determined to place him over the whole kingdom. "Daniel excelled all the princes and governors, because a greater spirit of God was in him."[1] "And the king thought to set him over all the kingdom."[2] His enemies even had to acknowledge his innocence and holiness. "They could find no cause, nor suspicion, because he was faithful; and no fault nor suspicion was found in him."[3] Yet by divine permission Daniel was brought, through the envy and jealousy of the chief men of the kingdom, to the greatest straits, so that his condition was as desperate as that of any man could well be. The king was forced against his will by the importunate representations of the satraps to condemn Daniel, whom he loved so well, to be thrown to the lions, because he had transgressed the royal command by praying three times a day to the true God, as you may see in detail in the sixth chapter of the Book of Daniel. So that he was thrown into the den, where the hungry lions eagerly awaited him as their prey: "Then the king commanded; and they brought Daniel, and cast him into the den of the lions."[4] And lest any one should try to liberate him, "a stone was brought, and laid upon the mouth of the den; which the king sealed with his own ring, and with the ring of his nobles."[5]

But we might think, is it thus the infinite justice of God allows hatred and envy to gain the upper hand, and publicly to triumph over innocence and righteousness? Does the God of infinite fidelity, then, abandon His faithful servant, and give him up as a prey to wild beasts, to be devoured alive by them, and that, too, under such circumstances, that there seemed not the slightest hope for him—so that Daniel is lost, and the hope he placed in God is doomed to disappointment? No, my dear brethren, God does not abandon him; it is one of the wonderful ways of His providence to allow men to fall into the utmost straits, that they may know that God alone is their helper in need, and that they may thus have cause to glorify His almighty power. The lions, hungry as they were, did not dare to touch Daniel. "My

With whom God acted in the same manner.

---

[1] Daniel superabat omnes principes et satrapas; quia spiritus Dei amplior erat in illo.—Dan. vi. 3.

[2] Porro rex cogitabat constituere eum super omne regnum.—Ibid. 4.

[3] Nullamque causam et suspicionem reperire poterunt, eoquod fidelis esset; et omnis culpa et suspicio non inveniretur in eo.—Ibid.

[4] Tunc rex præcepit, et adduxerunt Danielem, et miserunt eum in lacum leonum.—Ibid. 16.

[5] Allatusque est lapis unus, et positus est super os laci; quem obsignavit rex annulo suo et annulo optimatum suorum.—Ibid. 17.

God hath sent His angel," as the Prophet himself acknowledges, " and hath shut up the mouths of the lions, and they have not hurt me."[1] And what was the result? Even what God sought; namely, the confession that God is our helper in extreme need, and the public glorification of His holy name. When Darius saw on the next day, to his great joy, that Daniel was in the midst of the lions unhurt, he freed him at once, and published an edict throughout his whole kingdom commanding his subjects to adore the God of Daniel, who had done such wonderful things for His servant. "Then king Darius wrote to all peoples, tribes, and languages, dwelling in the whole earth: It is decreed by me, that in all my empire and my kingdom all men dread and fear the God of Daniel; for He is the living and eternal God forever; and His kingdom shall not be destroyed, and His power shall be forever. He is the deliverer and saviour, doing signs and wonders in heaven and in earth; who hath delivered Daniel out of the lions' den."[2] See how the glory of God was thus exalted and published.

Therefore we must never waver in our trust in God.

From this we learn, first, that we cannot place our hopes in any man on earth, no matter who he is. Daniel had as his patron and protector the king himself, and yet that very king, to please his courtiers, condemned him to be thrown to the lions. Has not David warned us: " Put not your trust in princes; in the children of men, in whom there is no salvation"?[3] Secondly, Daniel was saved from the lions by a miracle, and came forth unhurt out of the den: "And Daniel was taken out of the den, and no hurt was found in him."[4] Why? The Scripture gives the reason: " Because he believed in his God;"[5] that is, because he placed all his confidence in the almighty God alone. So should we, too, when things seem to have reached their worst, never allow our confidence in God to waver. Nay, since God is wont to let our circumstances get into a seemingly desperate condition, that we may look on the help He will send us as a benefit from

---

[1] Deus meus misit angelum suum, et occlusit ora leonum, et non nocuerunt mihi.—Dan. vi. 22.

[2] Tunc Darius rex scripsit universis populis, tribubus, et linguis habitantibus in universa terra : A me constitutum est decretum, ut in universo imperio et regno meo tremiscant et paveant Deum Danielis. Ipse enim est Deus vivens, et æternus in secula ; et regnum ejus non dissipabitur, et potestas ejus usque in æternum. Ipse liberator atque salvator, faciens signa et mirabilia in cœlo et in terra ; qui liberavit Danielem de lacu leonum.—Ibid. 25, 26, 27.

[3] Nolite confidere in principibus ; in filiis hominum, in quibus non est salus.—Ps. cxlv. 2,3.

[4] Eductusque est Daniel de lacu, et nulla læsio inventa est in eo.—Dan. vi. 23.

[5] Quia credidit Deo suo.—Ibid.

Him, our hope and confidence in such circumstances should rather be all the greater and more fervent.

Come now, poor desolate orphans; you have no father or mother to care for you; you have no friend to take your part; no one to put in a good word for you; not a soul in the world to take the least interest in you; humanly speaking, there is nothing for you but wretchedness and misery. Still, do not lose courage on that account; the almighty God is your father; only present your petitions to Him; cast yourselves into His lap with full and perfect confidence; He will care for you; He will feed and provide for you. Say to Him: "To Thee is the poor man left; Thou wilt be a helper to the orphan." [1] Sorrowing widow, your husband is taken from you by a premature death, and has left you with a houseful of little children; the business or occupation by which you managed to provide for yourself is in the grave with him. What can you do now? Humanly speaking, there is no hope for you. Poor citizen, you sit at home with your wife and children, sighing in the words of Christ when the hungry crowd was following Him in the desert: "Whence shall we buy bread, that these may eat?" [2] You work as hard as you can the whole day to try to earn enough to keep body and soul together, but it is only with great difficulty you succeed. What are you to do? Humanly speaking, your only hope is the beggar's staff. Poor peasant; you have exhausted nearly all your resources; your little farm has been plundered; your hay, oats, straw, cows, and oxen have been taken from you; next harvest your creditors will expect you to pay them something of what you owe them; but your debts are so great that you could not pay them in many years. What are you to do? Humanly speaking, there is no hope left for you, and you will die of hunger and sorrow. But for that very reason none of you should lose heart; only love your God and hope in Him; He is the almighty Lord, who can make everything right in a moment; those trials He sends you are simply intended to prove your hope and to see if it is firm and well grounded. Only see that you do not disturb the order of Providence by want of confidence or faith; do not yourselves force God to withdraw from you the help He is prepared to give you if you fly to His fatherly lap with child-like confidence. The Lord knows the best time for coming to your assistance and consoling you; He says to you

Exhortation to all in trouble to confide in the Lord.

[1] Tibi derelictus est pauper: orphano tu eris adjutor.—Ps. ix. 14.
[2] Unde ememus panes, ut manducent hi ?—John vi. 5.

what Christ said to His Mother at the marriage-feast of Cana, when the wine failed, and she through compassion begged of Him to help: " My hour is not yet come." [1] It is not yet time for Me to help you; but it will come, if you only continue to trust in Me. " Have confidence in God always," says St. Augustine, " and leave yourself in His hands as far as you can. For then He will not cease to take care of you, and will not allow anything to happen to you unless what is for your good, although you may not understand what He does to you." [2]

With that confidence we can do anything, after the example of the servants of God in the Old Law. Oh, if we only had that firm faith and trust in God, we should be almighty, as St. Bernard does not hesitate to say: " God makes those who hope in Him almighty." [3] Strengthened by a similar confidence, the young David, when the army of Israel was filled with dread, and the soldiers were hiding like mice in the holes in the earth, with nothing but his sling in his hand, attacked and overcame the huge and well-armed Goliath, and put the enemy to flight. " Thou comest to me," he said undismayed to the giant, " with a sword, and with a spear, and with a shield; but I come to thee in the name of the Lord of hosts, the God of the armies of Israel; and the Lord will deliver thee into my hand, and I will slay thee, and take away thy head from thee; and I will give the carcasses of the army of the Philistines this day to the birds of the air, and to the beasts of the earth; that all the earth may know that there is a God in Israel " who is able to protect us; " and all this assembly shall know that the Lord saveth not with sword and spear." [4] Ezechias, king of Juda, had no army to oppose the great force that Sennacherib had sent against him; nor was there any help to be expected from any other king or country. Confidence in God was his only resource; he went to the Temple and with his people prostrated himself before the Divine Majesty, and prayed: " And now, O Lord our God, save us out of his hand, and let all the kingdoms of the earth know that Thou only art the Lord." [5]

[1] Nondum venit hora mea.—John ii. 4.

[2] Constanter Deo crede, eique te totum committe, quantum potes. Ita enim ipse te sublevare non desinet, nihilque tibi evenire permittet, nisi quod tibi prosit, etiamsi nescias.—S. Aug. in Solil. c. 15.

[3] Omnipotentes facit omnes, qui sperant in eo.

[4] Tu venis ad me cum gladio, et hasta, et clypeo; ego autem venio ad te in nomine Domini exercituum, Dei agminum Israel; et dabit te Dominus in manu mea, et percutiam te, et auferam caput tuum a te; et dabo cadavera castrorum Philistiim hodie volatilibus cœli et bestiis terræ; ut sciat omnis terra, quia est Deus in Israel; et noverit universa ecclesia hæc, quia non in gladio nec in hasta salvat Dominus.—I. Kings xvii. 45, 46, 47.

[5] Et nunc, Domine Deus noster, salva nos de manu ejus, et cognoscant omnia regna terræ, quia tu es Dominus solus.—Is. xxxvii. 20.

What was the effect of this prayer? God sent Ezechias, not any human aid, but an angel, who in one night slew a hundred and eighty-five thousand men, the whole army of the Assyrians, so that Sennacherib alone with difficulty escaped. [1] Abias, king of Juda, and Jeroboam, king of Israel, were arrayed against each other; the latter had eight hundred thousand of the bravest and most experienced warriors, "who were also chosen and most valiant for war," as the Scripture says. [2] The former, too, had good soldiers, but they were only half as numerous. Yet Abias conquered, in spite of the great disparity of the forces, and slew five hundred thousand men of Israel, and put the remainder to flight. What had enabled that weak army to gain such a signal victory? "God is the leader of our army," [3] said Abias with full confidence in God before setting out to fight. Zara, the Ethiopian king, went against Asa, king of Juda, with ten hundred thousand men. Asa had only five hundred and eighty thousand to oppose to him, and yet he gained a complete victory: "And the Ethiopians fell even to utter destruction." [4] How did Asa manage that? His army was indeed strong, but he did not trust in it; "he called upon the Lord God and said: Lord there is no difference with Thee, whether Thou help with few or with many; help us, O Lord our God; for with confidence in Thee and Thy name we are come against this multitude." [5] Armed with this confidence, he attacked the enemy and conquered. For the Lord slew them, and his army fought against them." [6] Strengthened with a similar confidence, Judith, a weak woman, slew Holofernes and put his army to flight, when all the citizens of Bethulia were down-cast and despairing.

The same firm reliance enabled St. Dominic, as well as many other Christians, to provide for himself and his brethren miraculously when they were in the utmost need. In his convent in Rome, in which there were at the time a great many monks, there was on one occasion not even a bit of bread for them to eat. He sent two of them out into the city to beg; but God de- *In the New Law.*

---

[1] Egressus est autem angelus Domini, et percussit in castris Assyriorum centum octoginta quinque millia.—Is. xxxvii. 36.

[2] Qui et ipsi electi erant, et ad bella fortissimi.—II. Paral. xiii. 3.

[3] In exercitu nostro dux Deus est.—Ibid. 12.

[4] Et ruebant Æthiopes usque ad internecionem.—Ibid. xiv. 13.

[5] Invocavit Dominum Deum, et ait: Domine, non est apud te ulla distantia, utrum in paucis auxilieris, an in pluribus; adjuva nos, Domine Deus noster; in te enim et in tuo nomine habentes fiduciam venimus contra hanc multitudinem.—Ibid. 11.

[6] Quia Domino credente contriti sunt, et exercitu illius prœliante.—Ibid. 13.

creed that in such a large and wealthy city they could not get anything by way of alms except one small loaf, which they gave out of charity to some other poor persons; thus they had nothing. Dominic praised their charity and went into the choir to pray, after which he ordered the bell to ring as usual to assemble all the brethren for meals. Some of them shook their heads; why should we go to an empty table? said they; we have not a bit of bread, nor anything else to eat. Have courage, said Dominic; the Lord will provide; He knows that we have nothing; but hope in Him. Having said grace, they sat down. Still nothing came. After they had given up all hope, two young men entered the refectory, laid down before each a snow-white loaf, and vanished. Dominic sent to the cellar for something to drink, although he knew that there was nothing there. But behold, they found a cask full of the choicest wine. The bread lasted them for three days, and the wine for many weeks. Animated with a similar hope, the Roman emperor Ferdinand II., when in extreme danger, gained a complete victory over his rebellious subjects. Almost all the princes of the empire had conspired against him; they had already taken most of the towns and provinces of Germany, and were on their march to Vienna to make the Emperor prisoner. In Vienna the heretics raised a revolt against him. Could any more desperate circumstances be imagined? And yet, how mighty is he who trusts in God alone! Ferdinand threw himself on his knees before a crucifix. Lord, he exclaimed, Thou seest that I have nothing to hope from man; wilt Thou make me a laughing-stock to Thy enemies? Here I am; let Thy holy will be done! But if Thou hast decreed otherwise for me, Thou alone canst still help me. "Hardly had I said that prayer," he acknowledged afterwards to his confessor, "when I was filled with hope and consolation, assured that God would frustrate all the designs of my enemies." And so it turned out in reality; for Ferdinand overthrew the rebels and took their ringleader prisoner. Only recall to your minds, my dear brethren, different things that have occurred in our own times, and you will have to confess that God helps in an equally wonderful manner all His servants who trust in Him. I am sure you all know to what I am alluding.

Trustful abandonment of ourselves to the   Is it not true, then, that "God makes those who trust in Him omnipotent"? Let us therefore constantly rely on God, resign ourselves to His providence even in the greatest extremities, and say to Him with child-like confidence, as David did when he was persecuted: "Let not the humble be turned away with confusion; the poor and needy shall praise Thy name." [1] Lord, Thou knowest how things are with me; I cannot help myself in this extremity by any human aid; all natural means are of no avail. Behold me prostrate at Thy feet; do with me as Thou wilt; but remember that I place my whole confidence in Thee and do not forget what Thou hast promised to those who trust in Thee alone; do not ever allow it to happen that one who humbly hopes in Thee should be deceived. No, that cannot, that will not be. With this confidence alone I am sufficiently assured of Thy help. Amen.

For other sermons on the same subject, see the foregoing Third Part.

Another Introduction to the same sermon for the Fifth Sunday after Pentecost.

Text.

Oculi Domini super justos, et aures ejus in preces eorum. —I. Pet. iii. 12.

"The eyes of the Lord are upon the just, and His ears unto their prayers."

Introduction.

Happy the man who is in the state of grace, that is, in the friendship of God! The eyes of the Lord are upon him in all places, at all times, looking after him and seeing that no harm comes to his soul. The ears of the Lord are continually open to hear his cries in all his necessities. Just souls, rejoice! be of good courage! "Who is he that can hurt you?" [2] asks St. Peter in to-day's epistle; you, who have such a powerful protector to defend you? What can be wanting to you, since you have such a generous Lord always ready to grant your petitions? Only fly to Him with confidence in all your necessities, etc.—*Continues as above.*

[1] Ne avertatur humilis factus confusus: pauper et inops laudabunt nomen tuum.—Ps. lxxiii. 21.

[2] Quis est qui vobis noceat ?—I. Pet. iii. 13.

FORTY-FOURTH SERMON.

ON BEING ALWAYS CONFIDENT IN GOD.

Subject.

God often uses means that run directly counter to the end in view, that He may bring those who trust in Him to that end. Therefore we should never allow our confidence in Him to fail under any circumstances.—*Preached on the fourth Sunday of Advent.*

Text.

Erunt prava in directa, et aspera in vias planas.—Luke iii. 5.

" The crooked shall be made straight, and the rough ways plain."

Introduction.

Vain would it be for weak mortals to attempt to fill all the valleys of the world, to throw down all the hills and mountains, to make straight all the crooked ways, and plain all the rough ones. But the task is possible, nay, even easy for God; He who made all things out of nothing can just as easily, if He pleases, level the mountains, fill up the valleys, and make the crooked ways straight. My dear brethren, we have hitherto treated of Christian hope, and have learned first, that in all our necessities we must first fly to God for refuge, with an assured confidence that we shall find consolation, help, and safety with Him, because He alone has the power and at the same time the will to help us. Secondly, that we must not put this confidence in any creature, nor in human means, although we can and should make use of them, but in God alone; because He is the one from whom natural means must, as mere instruments, receive the power of helping us, and without His will all such means are utterly worthless. Thirdly, when we see that no means that we have used hitherto have been of any avail, and we foresee, moreover, that they will not help us in the future; nay, when, humanly speaking, affairs are in a desperate state, then we must not allow our trust and confidence in God alone to waver, but rather be all the more hopeful of help from Him; because this supernatural confidence is not founded on natural means, but on the God of infinite power, goodness, and fidelity, who is able to help us even then, and who for the most part allows our affairs to get into a desperate condition, that He may then help us, and that we may ascribe the help received to Him alone. There you have a short *résumé* of the subjects treated of in the three last sermons; it may be of some good to those who have not heard them. There is still another point, my dear brethren. When we see not only that we cannot do anything with human means, but that there are obstacles in the way which run directly counter to the end we have in view, must we then still continue to hope for success, if it is for our good? Certainly; we must not waver the least in our confidence in God; because nothing can resist His almighty power, and He often allows things to take that course with us mortals, as I shall now show.

Plan of Discourse.

God often uses means that run directly counter to the end in view, that He may bring those who trust in Him alone to that end. Therefore we should never allow our confidence in Him to fail under any circumstances. Such is the subject of to-day's sermon.

Grant us all the grace to observe the conclusion of it, we beg of Thee, O God of goodness, by the intercession of Mary and of our holy guardian angels.

Yet that seems incomprehensible. To use means that run directly counter to the end proposed, with a view of gaining that end! That is as if I set a blind man, who wishes to go to France, on the road to Austria, telling him that he will get to France in that way. Or as if, when I wish to light a fire to warm myself, I put cold water on the hearth instead of burning coals. Or as if I were to take poison for the purpose of preserving my life. Who, then, can reasonably imagine that God, in order to keep me in good health, would send me a grievous and dangerous illness? or allow my property to be plundered or stolen, in order to provide me with the means of subsistence? or suffer me to be put to public shame and ridicule and persecution, in order to preserve my good name and honor? or place nothing but obstacles in my way, in order to secure my success in some weighty matter? or deprive me by death of the husband whose labor was the sole support of the family, that He might enable me and mine to obtain a becoming livelihood? How can

It seems impossible to us to attain an end by contrary means.

that be? Who can understand such things? True it is, my dear brethren; such things seem to our weak understanding absurd, incomprehensible, nay, impossible.

But the Lord tells us by the Prophet Isaias that we must not judge rashly of what we cannot understand: ." For My thoughts are not your thoughts, nor your ways My ways, saith the Lord. For as the heavens are exalted above the earth, so are My ways exalted above your ways, and My thoughts above your thoughts."[1] All that I have said we shall be able easily to understand, if we only remember that He is God. We believe and acknowledge that He is infinite wisdom; we must, then, also confess that He is able to bring about the desired result by means that tend in quite a contrary direction. We believe and acknowledge that He is almighty, to whom nothing is impossible; hence we must also confess that He can cause temporal prosperity by misfortune; that He can exalt by humbling, protect by persecution, enrich by poverty, give true peace to the soul by first depriving it of consolation, and turn the instruments that were prepared for our destruction into the means of bringing us happiness and prosperity.

But, not to lose so much time in speculating on what God can do by His almighty power, I say that most frequently God uses such contradictory means to bring men to the end they wish for. Let us examine the holy Scriptures here and there, and we shall find that to be the case (for the best way of finding out how God is likely to act is to see how He has acted on other occasions). After the general deluge, in which God drowned the whole world in order to punish its inhabitants for their sins and vices, He said to the Patriarch Noe: "This is the sign of the covenant which I give between Me and you, and to every living soul that is with you, for perpetual generations."[2] What was the sign? "I will set My bow in the clouds, and it shall be the sign of a covenant between Me and the earth. And when I shall cover the sky with clouds, My bow shall appear in the clouds; and there shall no more be waters of a flood, to destroy all flesh."

Marginal notes:
But God can easily do that.

And He often uses such means, as He did after the deluge.

[1] Non enim cogitationes meæ, cogitationes vestræ ; neque viæ meæ, viæ vestræ, dicit Dominus. Quia sicut exaltantur cœli a terra, sic exaltatæ sunt viæ meæ a viis vestris, et cogitationes meæ a cogitationibus vestris.—Is. lv. 8, 9.

[2] Hoc est signum fœderis, quod do inter me et vos, et ad omnem animam viventem, quæ est vobiscum in generationes sempiternas.—Gen. ix. 12.

[3] Arcum meum ponam in nubibus, et erit signum fœderis inter me et inter terram, cumque obduxero nubibus cœlum, apparebit arcus meus in nubibus ; et non erunt ultra aquæ diluvii ad delendum universam carnem.—Ibid. 13, 14, 15.

St. Augustine asks here, Why did God choose the rainbow, and that too in the clouds, as a sign of a clear sky? Before, the clouds had discharged torrents of water, which had inundated the earth; and now the same clouds were to be the sign of fair weather; that which might reasonably give the world cause to fear another deluge was now to be the proof that they were safe from that danger. How can such things be explained? God, answers St. Augustine, wishes thereby to show that He can attain His end by the most contradictory means, and that, where His providence works, all obstacles and impediments lose their efficacy; [1] and thus by a divine decree an impending misfortune is often the sign of coming prosperity.

When the Hebrew people were dying of thirst in the desert, and there was no water to be found anywhere, God said to Moses: "Behold, I will stand before thee, on the rock Horeb, and thou shalt strike the rock, and water shall come out of it, that the people may drink." [2] What was he to strike the rock with? "Take in thy hand the rod wherewith thou didst strike the river, and go." [3] But, O Lord, Moses might have answered, how can that be? The rock is very hard, and when struck, is more likely to give forth sparks of fire; how can I, then, hope to bring water out of it? With the same rod I struck the river of the Egyptians, and the water was turned into blood; I struck the Red See with it, and the waters dried up; how can I expect it to bring water out of the rock? But Moses knew better the way in which God is wont to act, and that He shows His almighty power in the means He uses; therefore without the least hesitation Moses struck the rock, and the clear water burst forth in an abundant stream. Who would have thought that possible? And yet God caused it to come to pass. *And with the Israelites in the desert.*

You know what happened to Jonas. God sent him to the city of Ninive to announce its speedy destruction to the inhabitants on account of their wicked lives. "Arise and go to Ninive, the great city, and preach in it; for the wickedness thereof is come up before Me." [4] Jonas was unwilling to go: "And Jonas rose up to flee into Tharsis from the face of the Lord." [5] *With the Prophet Jonas.*

[1] Ubicunque fuerit providentia, frustrantur universa contraria.

[2] En ego stabo ibi coram te, supra petram Horeb ; percutiesque petram, et exibit ex ea aqua, ut bibat populus.—Exod. xvii. 6.

[3] Virgam, qua percussisti fluvium, tolle in manu tua, et vade.—Ibid. 5.

[4] Surge et vade in Ninivem, civitatem grandem, et prædica in ea, quia ascendit malitia ejus coram me.—Jonas i. 2.

[5] Et resurrexit Jonas, ut fugeret in Tharsis a facie Domini.—Ibid. 3.

He took ship and sailed away. Truly, that was not the way to
Ninive, quite the contrary. Yet the Lord brought him to Ninive by that very way. "But the Lord sent a great wind into
the sea; and a great tempest was raised in the sea, and the ship
was in danger to be broken."[1] What happened after that?
By divine decree Jonas was thrown into the sea, and a huge
whale swallowed him. But God wished him to go to Ninive;
why, then, did He allow him to be cast into the sea, and to become
the prey of the monster? Surely, there was no chance of escape
for Him; the whale must certainly devour him. And how, then,
can he go to Ninive and announce the impending destruction of
that city? But God knows what He is doing, and can attain
His end by the most unlikely means. The whale bore Jonas
about for three days and nights as if he were in a ship, and at
last cast him out on the shore, not far from Ninive, as many
authors think. Mark, my dear brethren; Jonas flies from
Ninive; he is thrown into the sea, and swallowed down by the
fish, and in that seemingly impossible manner God brings him
where He wishes to have him. "For where divine providence
works, all obstacles lose their efficacy."

With Moses and Joseph in Egypt.

How many have not been helped by God, preserved in life, and
raised to most honorable positions by the very means that seemed
best adapted to bring about their utter destruction! Moses was
to be as a God for king Pharao in Egypt; what were the
means used to effect that? The very means that were employed
to destroy him and all the Hebrew people. Pharao decreed that
all Hebrew children should be drowned as soon as they were born:
"Pharao therefore charged all his people, saying: Whatsoever
shall be born of the male sex, ye shall cast into the river."[2] Such
was the fate in store for Moses; he was put into a basket and laid
by the bank of the river. Was that a way to raise him to the
dignity for which he was intended? Truly, it was the means
that the all-wise providence of God selected, by whose decree
the daughter of Pharao happened just then to come down to the
river. "And behold, the daughter of Pharao came down to wash
herself in the river."[3] She saw the beautiful child on the bank,
and through a natural feeling of pity had it taken up and given

---

[1] Dominus autem misit ventum magnum in mare, et facta est tempestas magna in mari, et
navis periclitabatur conteri.—Jonas i. 4.

[2] Præcepit ergo Pharao omni populo suo, dicens : quidquid masculini sexus natum fuerit,
in flumen projicite.—Exod. i. 22.

[3] Ecce autem descendebat filia Pharaonis, ut lavaretur in flumine.—Ibid. ii. 5.

over to a Hebrew woman, who was Moses' own mother, to be nursed: "And Pharao's daughter said to her: take this child and nurse him for me, and I will give thee thy wages."[1] The mother took the child with joy, "and when he was grown up she delivered him to Pharao's daughter. And she adopted him for a son."[2] Thus Moses was brought up in the court, until by God's command he became a ruler over Pharao, and the saviour of his own people. Before Moses' time, God had resolved to make Joseph viceroy of Egypt; what means did He use to that end? Even those which seemed best adapted to ruin Joseph utterly. His brothers could not bear him, because he had prophesied that they should one day prostrate themselves before him; and animated by hatred and envy, they determined to put him out of the way. They "cast him into an old pit,"[3] and finally sold him as a slave to the Ishmaelites. Now, said they with sardonic laughter, "it shall appear what his dreams avail him."[4] This very act on the part of his brothers helped Joseph to come to Egypt, where after many wonderful adventures he was at last placed on the throne, and his brothers, driven by hunger, were obliged to come and bend the knee before him. "They sold him," says St. Gregory, "that they might not have to do him homage: they did him homage, because they had sold him."[5] "Wherever God's providence works, all obstacles lose their efficacy."

The three holy kings were, as we read in the Gospel, led from the East by a star to find and adore the new-born Saviour of the world; when they came near to Jerusalem, they lost sight of the star, so that they knew not where to go. Why, I ask, did God deprive them of the guiding star at that time? Who was to show them the place in which they would find Christ? Herod was to do that. Herod? He who would not tolerate any other king in Juda except himself? whose only object was to slay Christ and all those who adored Him? who at the very first question the three kings asked him, "Where is He that is born king of the Jews?"[6] was filled with rage and confusion? ("And king Herod,

With the three kings on the journey to Bethlehem.

---

[1] Ad quam locuta filia Pharaonis, accipe, ait, puerum istum, et nutri mihi; ego dabo tibi mercedem tuam.—Exod. ii. 9.

[2] Adultumque tradidit filiæ Pharaonis, quem illa adoptavit in locum filii.—Ibid. 10.

[3] Miserunt eum in cisternam veterem.—Gen. xxxvii. 24.

[4] Tunc apparebit quid illi prosint somnia sua.—Ibid. 20.

[5] Quem ideo vendiderunt, ne adorarent; adoraverunt, quia vendiderant.—S. Greg. hom. x. in Ezech.

[6] Ubi est qui natus est rex Judæorum?—Matt. ii. 2.

hearing this, was troubled, and all Jerusalem with him."[1]) Was he the man to point out the place where Christ was born? Ah, unhappy travellers, you will surely fare badly with him; it would have been better if you had not seen him at all. And yet it was Herod who against his will helped the kings to find the place and to adore Our Lord. " And assembling together all the chief priests and the scribes of the people, he inquired of them where Christ should be born. But they said to him: In Bethlehem of Juda."[2] Whereupon Herod called the Wise Men, "and sending them into Bethlehem, said: Go, and diligently inquire after the child."[3] Thus does God bring the ship into the desired haven even with a contrary wind; " for where God's providence works, all obstacles lose their efficacy."

With the Apostles in the preaching of the Gospel.

Jesus Christ wished to have His holy Law and Gospel preached and spread throughout the world. Whom did He choose as instruments to perform this great work? Twelve poor, ignorant, and unskilled men, such as the Apostles then were; and when He was sending them forth, He said to them: " Behold, I send you as sheep in the midst of wolves;"[4] and He adds: " Therefore fear them not."[5] But, O Lord, what a strange thing that is to say, " I send you as sheep in the midst of wolves; therefore fear them not"! Shouldst Thou not rather have said the opposite: I send you as sheep in the midst of wolves; therefore you have good reason to fear them, and to dread lest, with all your labor, you may accomplish nothing; for we know how wolves act towards sheep. They tear them to pieces and devour them. Truly, adds Our Lord in most impressive words, so they will treat you also, my dear apostles; they will fall on you like cruel wolves, drag you from one town to another, and publicly scourge you: " For they will deliver you up in councils, and they will scourge you in their synagogues;"[6] and after a long continued persecution they will cruelly put you to death. But for that very reason be of good heart: " Therefore fear them not." Behold, I send you; it is I who lay this heavy charge on your shoulders; the very means that will be chosen to destroy you and My Gospel will help you to spread it throughout the

---

[1] Audiens autem Herodes rex, turbatus est, et omnis Jerosolyma cum illo.—Matt. ii. 3.

[2] Et congregans omnes principes sacerdotum et scribas populi sciscitabatur ab eis, ubi Christus nasceretur. At illi dixerunt ei: in Bethlehem Juda.—Ibid. 4, 5.

[3] Et mittens illos in Bethlehem, dixit: ite, et interrogate diligenter de puero.—Ibid. 8.

[4] Ecce ego mitto vos, sicut oves in medio luporum.—Ibid. x. 16.

[5] Ne ergo timueritis eos.—Ibid. 26.

[6] Tradent enim vos in conciliis, et in synagogis suis flagellabunt vos.—Ibid. 17.

world. And such was really the case. How did the Christians after the preaching of the Gospel increase so rapidly in every part of the world? By the very means that were used to prevent that increase; namely, by persecution, by the slaughtering and murdering of Christians in almost every country of the world. The more they were persecuted, the more numerous did they become. The blood of the martyrs was the seed from which Christians sprang. [1] Wherever divine providence works, there all obstacles lose their efficacy.

We see from the Lives of the Saints and other histories that God is wont to act in the same way with others. Thus, for instance, we are surprised at the means by which God raised Athenais, who was born of honest but lowly parents, to the highest dignity and fortune on earth. For after the death of her parents the innocent girl was thrust out of her home by her merciless and avaricious brothers, and thus, abandoned by all, she was forced to seek help and support from the pious Empress Pulcheria. The Emperor Theodosius, the brother of Pulcheria, happening to see Athenais, was struck with her appearance, and chose her as his bride, and placed on her head the crown of the East. We are surprised to see how God raised Adrian VI. to the pontifical throne; namely, by means of the plots and machinations of his enemies, who tried to have him turned out of the imperial court, and successfully, too; but thus they brought it about against their will that he was raised by the king of Spain first to the episcopal dignity, then to the cardinalate, and finally to the papacy. We are surprised to read how St. Ignatius Loyola founded the Society of Jesus; by means, namely, which seemed to render such an undertaking absolutely impossible. The whole world almost was against him; Catholics, non-Catholics, clergy, laity, gentlemen, ladies, spiritual and temporal superiors; and yet the power and wisdom of the almighty God enabled Ignatius to see the Society spread over the world in his own life-time. Consider again, my dear brethren, what has occurred this very year, and still continues. These are the wonderful dispensations of the almighty providence of God, who chooses not the high-ways, but the paths and by-ways, to bring to the wished-for end His servants who trust in Him.

But why? First to show His unlimited power, which nothing can successfully oppose, nor frustrate; as Mardochai said

[1] *Sanguis martyrum semen est Christianorum.*

trust in His omnipotence. to Him: " O Lord, Lord, almighty King, for all things are in Thy power, and there is none that can resist Thy will, if Thou determine to save Israel. Thou art Lord of all, and there is none that can resist Thy majesty." [1] Secondly, to purge our confidence in Him of all natural and human hope, so that we may ascribe our success in all cases to Him alone, when we consider that natural means have been rather a hindrance than otherwise. Thirdly, to strengthen all the more our confidence in Him alone, so that even in the most desperate circumstances we may never lose the hope of success, provided it is good for our souls. That want of courage is very common amongst us when we fail in our attempts, or when the contrary to what we have desired happens. For instance, the children fly to God for help during the dangerous sickness of the father or mother, that they may not be deprived of their chief means of support; meanwhile the father or mother grows worse, and dies. There is no hope for us any more, think the children. Good parents have a wicked, disobedient son, with whom they have fruitlessly tried exhortations, threats, and punishment to bring him to his senses; they appeal to God, and confidently leave their son to Him. Meanwhile the latter becomes more wicked and dissolute day by day. Ah, think the parents, all our trouble is in vain! That man has a just lawsuit; if he does not win it, he is ruined. He has long ago recommended the matter to God with confidence; but although his claim is just, his antagonist, being richer, gains the day. Alas, he thinks, I am a ruined man! I will now have to beg my bread. A pious, zealous servant of God has undertaken to convert a soul, to extirpate some common vice, to further the honor and glory of God; he places his whole confidence in God and relies on His assistance. But he finds nothing but opposition everywhere; it seems almost impossible for him to attain the proposed end. Vain are all my efforts, he thinks; I must let the stone lie, since I cannot lift it. There are some even who exclaim in despair, what is the use of praying, of being devout to the saints? I will give it all up.

Therefore our confidence in God should never waver. No, that is not the way to have confidence in God. Put your unshaken trust in that almighty Lord, who uses the most contrary means to attain the wished-for end, and is wont thus to act that our hope in Him may be all the firmer. He can and

---

[1] Domine, Domine, Rex omnipotens, in ditione enim tua cuncta sunt posita, et non est qui tuæ possit resistere voluntati, si decreveris salvare Israel. Dominus omnium es, nec est qui resistat majestati tuæ.—Esth. xiii. 9, 11.

will provide for the children, if they but trust in Him, even by the death of their father or mother, and provide for them better than if their parents were alive and in good health. He can and will convert that wicked son, even after he has grown worse, and when the parents least expect it. He can and will make up to that man what he lost, as he thought, in that law-suit, and that even by means of the unjust antagonist; or, if the case is really lost, He can restore to him twofold by some unforeseen stroke of good fortune. He can and will bring that zealous soul to the accomplishment of its wishes, in spite of all opposition, provided there is no wavering in confidence in that Lord whose providence in its working causes all obstacles to lose their efficacy. "All things are possible to him that believeth," [1] said Our Lord to the father whose son was possessed by the unclean spirit, and who asked Christ to free him. He who trusts in his God, and with child-like confidence appeals to Him, can and will receive everything from Him.

Who had more reason to give up all hope and confidence, nay, to despair of having any posterity, than Abraham? God had promised to increase his descendants by his son Isaac beyond all peoples. "And God said to Abraham: Sara, thy wife, shall bear thee a son, and thou shalt call his name Isaac, and I will establish My covenant with him, and with his seed after him. . . and he shall become nations, and kings of peoples shall spring from him." [2] And yet soon after Abraham was commanded by God to slay his son Isaac as a sacrifice. "He said to him: Take thy only son Isaac, whom thou lovest, and go into the land of vision; and there thou shalt offer him for an holocaust upon one of the mountains which I will show thee." [3] What is the meaning of this? Abraham might easily have thought; Isaac is to continue my family, and now I must sacrifice him? That is the very way to destroy my hopes of posterity and to put an end to my family. Yet Abraham set out with his dear son: "So Abraham, rising up in the night, saddled his ass, and took with him two young men, and Isaac, his son." [4] When they came to the place pointed out

After the example of the Patriarchs Abraham and Job.

[1] Omnia possibilia sunt credenti.—Mark ix. 22.

[2] Ait Deus ad Abraham: Sara, uxor tua, pariet tibi filium, vocabisque nomen ejus Isaac, et constituam pactum meum illi in foedus sempiternum, et semini ejus post eum. . . eritque in nationes, et reges populorum orientur ex eo.—Gen. xvii. 19, 16.

[3] Ait illi: tolle filium tuum unigenitum, quem diligis, Isaac, et vade in terram visionis, atque ibi offeres eum in holocaustum super unum montium, quem monstravero tibi.—Ibid. xxii. 2.

[4] Igitur Abraham de nocte consurgens, stravit asinum suum, ducens secum duos juvenes, et Isaac, filium suum.—Ibid. 3.

by God, he laid his son on the altar; "and he put forth his hand, and took the sword to sacrifice his son."[1]   Did Abraham then despair of having posterity by Isaac?   No, he still remained firm in his hope.   What God promises, he thought, must be fulfilled.   God has assured me that Isaac shall continue my family; therefore it will be so, even after I have slain him, although I cannot imagine how it will be brought about.   "In the promise also of God, says St. Paul of him, he staggered not by distrust, but was strengthened by faith, giving glory to God: most fully knowing that whatsoever He hath promised, He is able also to perform.   Who against hope believed in hope."[2]   Why against hope?   Because, humanly speaking, he could not hope under the circumstances to have descendants by Isaac; and yet he hoped, relying on the divine promises.   Hear what St. Zeno says: "That is against hope which seems impossible, but becomes possible by the hope which firmly trusts in God."[3]   That is the meaning of the words of the patient Job: "Although He should kill me, I will trust in Him."[4]   That is, although God acts towards me in such a way as to seem to leave me without any hope, yet will I hope and trust that things shall go well with me.

Exhortation to rely steadfastly on God in all our necessities.

I conclude, my dear brethren, in the words of Ecclesiasticus: "Ye that fear the Lord, hope in Him; and mercy shall come to you for your delight; and know ye that no one hath hoped in the Lord and hath been confounded.   Ye that fear the Lord, believe Him."[5]   Therefore never waver in your confidence in Him, no matter what happens.   He Himself encourages us to this firm confidence; for, if we consider the various names of God that signify His relations with us, they all urge us to put our undoubted trust in Him.   He calls Himself the Lord: "I am the Lord;" not a harsh, exacting Lord, but a good and loving one.   "How good is God to Israel!"[6]   David could not contain himself when reflecting on this unspeakable goodness, but invites all men to ac-

---

[1] Extenditque manum, et arripuit gladium, ut immolaret filium suum.—Gen. xxii. 10.

[2] In repromissione etiam Dei non hæsitavit diffidentia, sed confortatus est fide, dans gloriam Deo, plenissime sciens, quia quæcunque promisit, potens est et facere.   Qui contra spem in spem credidit —Rom. iv. 20, 21, 18.

[5] Contra spem autem est, quod non videtur esse possibile ; sed possibile hac spe fit, cum Dei dicto indubitanter ac firmiter creditur.—S. Zeno, serm. de spe.

[4] Etiamsi occiderit me, in ipso sperabo.—Job xiii. 15.

[5] Qui timetis Dominum, sperate in illum, et in oblectationem veniet vobis misericordia, et scitote quia nullus speravit in Domino et confusus est.   Qui timetis Dominum, credite illi.—Ecclus. ii. 9, 11, 8.

[6] Quam bonus Israel Deus!—Ps. lxxii. 1.

knowledge and praise it: "Give praise to the Lord, for He is good; for His mercy endureth forever."[1] Whom can the servant trust in more than in his master, when he knows that the latter is not only powerful, but also good and loving? He is called a shepherd, and a good shepherd: "I am the good shepherd,"[2] a shepherd that does not leave his sheep, but protects them against the wolves. To whom should the timid sheep fly for protection, if not to its loving shepherd? He is called a father, and He acts in such a fatherly manner to us, that He not only feeds us on earth, but has reserved for us in heaven an immortal inheritance; and He wishes us to address Him by the name "father." Do we need any further inducement to put our trust in such a good Lord, such a loving Father, such a faithful Shepherd? Ah, my God, he who recognizes Thee under those loving titles has never cause to waver in his confidence in Thee: "Let them trust in Thee who know Thy name."[3] The Lord Himself commands us to have confidence in Him: "Be of good heart,"[4] He says. He wishes us to trust in Him with our whole hearts: "Have confidence in the Lord with all thy heart."[5] He wishes us to rely on Him always: "Hope in thy God always."[6] Always, in want and in plenty, in prosperity and adversity, in temptations, dangers, accidents, when there seems to be no hope, "hope in thy God always." Now let each one say to himself, my dear brethren: If God wishes us all to trust in Him, and to trust in Him always and with our whole hearts, then He will help me, and will provide for me in my necessities, and will not disappoint me in the hope I found on Him. "Why does God," asks St. Augustine, "so often tell us to lean on Him, if He is not willing to support us? God is not deceitful; He does not offer His help for the purpose of afterwards withdrawing and giving us a more severe fall."[7] Besides, what magnificent and oft-repeated promises we have from God! One of them alone should suffice: "Ask and you shall receive." "Trust in the Lord, and do good." What shall be the consequence? "And

---

[1] Confitemini Domino quoniam bonus; quoniam in sæculum misericordia ejus.—Ps. cxvii. 1.

[2] Ego sum pastor bonus.—John x. 11.

[3] Sperent in te qui noverunt nomen tuum.—Ps. ix. 11.

[4] Habete fiduciam.—Matt. xiv. 27.

[5] Habe fiduciam in Domino ex toto corde tuo.—Prov. iii. 5.

[6] Spera in Deo tuo semper.—Osee xii. 6.

[7] Quare Deus toties nos ad innitendum sibi moneret, si supportare nos nollet? Non est illusor Deus, ut se ad supportandum nos offerat, et nobis innitentibus ei in ruinam nostram se subtrahat.

thou shalt be fed with its riches."[1]   "Delight in the Lord;" that is, treat so confidently with Him, that you actually enjoy yourself with Him.   And what then?   "And He will give thee the requests of thy heart."[2]

As long as we do not hope for anything superfluous.

But there is one thing you must not forget, as St. Augustine says, "You must distinguish between the petition of your heart and the petition of your sensuality.   Many," he continues, "hope for money from God; many hope for fleeting and perishable honors."[3]   Such people despair and think their hopes in God put to shame if misfortune brings them from a high to a lowly position, in which they cannot live as before in abundance; and now the object of their desires is to be restored to their former affluence.   They hope for and desire wealth and honorable position, that they may enjoy the esteem of the world and live in idleness, comfort, and extravagance, indulge in gluttony, conform to the vanity of the world, and gratify their sensuality. Such desires come not from the reasoning heart, but from the unreasoning flesh.   No; God has promised to give what is necessary to the support of the body, but not superfluities that are injurious to the soul.

For other things we must hope confidently.

Place your hope, then, in God, and ask Him for what is necessary, and for other things too, whatever they may be, but with this condition, if they be advantageous for your salvation; and be constant in this hope, not wavering, but certain and assured that your wish will be granted.   Say to yourselves, like Abraham: What God has promised must infallibly be done; He has promised to give me all that is good and useful for me if I trust in Him alone; so that I may be certain of it, even if all the men on earth, all the angels in heaven, and all the demons in hell stood in the way.   Therefore I will continue to hope, and with that hope in all present and future necessities of soul and body I will first fly to God; with that hope I will be consoled in all trials and crosses, being assured, as St. Cyprian says, that, "since all things are God's, he who has God is in want of nothing."[4]

Especially for what concerns our salvation.

But more especially must my hope be directed to the eternal goods of the future life in heaven, which are the object of Christian, supernatural hope.   All that I can desire and hope for in

---

[1] Spera in Domino et fac bonitatem ; et pasceris in divitiis ejus.—Ps. xxxvi. 3.

[2] Delectare in Domino, et dabit tibi petitiones cordis tui.—Ibid. 4.

[3] Discerne petitionem cordis tui a petitione carnis tuæ.   Multi de Deo sperant pecuniam; multi de Deo sperant honores caducos et perituros.—S. Aug. in Ps. xxxix.

[4] Cum Dei sint omnia, habenti Deum nihil deerit.

this life passes away with time, and I should only use it in so far as it can help me to attain possession of the good that will last forever. Therefore, O my God, with regard to my temporal wants, I place my prayers and hopes altogether in Thy hands; and I beg of Thee never to grant any wish of mine in that respect, unless in so far as Thou knowest it to be good for my soul. But strengthen more and more my hope of eternal joys; let me say, with Thy servant David: " What have I in heaven? and besides Thee, what do I desire upon earth? Thou art the God of my heart, and the God that is my portion forever." [1] Ah, what a consolation for me to think and say: I am weeping in sorrow; I am suffering trouble; I am persecuted by men; I have to bear hunger, thirst, and poverty; yet I am certain that Thou, my God, hast care of me, that it may be well with my soul! And I am assured, too, by Thy Apostle, " that the sufferings of this time are not worthy to be compared with the glory to come, that shall be revealed in us." [2] I hope in all this, and await with a child-like and firm confidence, like the blind Tobias, an eternal reward: " We look for that life which God will give to them that never change their faith from Him." [3] That life Thou hast promised, in the Gospel of St. Matthew, to me and to all those who love Thee and trust in Thee alone: " Be glad and rejoice, for your reward is very great in heaven." [4] In and with this hope will I live and die. Amen.

Another Introduction to the same sermon for the seventh Sunday after Pentecost.

Text.

Numquid colligunt de spinis uvas, aut de tribulis ficus ?—Matt. vii. 16.

" Do men gather grapes of thorns, or figs of thistles? "

Introduction.

It would be a vain and foolish hope to expect grapes from thorns, or figs from thistles; that will not and cannot be. True,

---

[1] Quid mihi est in cœlo, et a te quid volui super terram? Deus cordis mei, et pars mea Deus in æternum.—Ps. lxxii. 25, 26.

[2] Quod non sunt condignæ passiones hujus temporis ad futuram gloriam, quæ revelabitur in nobis.—Rom. viii. 18.

[3] Vitam illam expectamus, quam Deus daturus est his qui fidem suam nunquam mutant ab eo.—Tob. ii. 18.

[4] Gaudete et exultate, quoniam merces vestra copiosa est in cœlo.—Matt. v. 12.

such a thing could not proceed from natural causes alone: but with the almighty God even that is possible and easy. He who can make bread out of a stone, and wine out of water, can also, if He pleases, bring forth grapes from thorns and figs from thistles. My dear brethren, we have hitherto treated, etc.—*Continues as before.*

ON THE CONFORMITY OF OUR WILL WITH THE WILL OF GOD.

ON THE HONOR SHOWN TO GOD BY CONFORMITY WITH HIS WILL.

Subject.

To be always resigned to the will of God in all circumstances is a virtue by which we give God the greatest honor and glory. —*Preached on the feast of the Nativity of Our Lord.*

Text.

Gloria in altissimis Deo, et in terra pax hominibus bonæ voluntatis.—Luke ii. 14.

" Glory to God in the highest, and on earth peace to men of good will."

Introduction.

Never was there more done to promote the exterior honor and glory of God than on this day of grace, on which Jesus Christ, the Incarnate Son of God, in obedience to the will of His heavenly Father, was born in the stable at Bethlehem. Then was fulfilled what David foretold in his person. " Burnt-offering and sin-offering Thou didst not require. Then said I: behold, I come. In the head of the book it is written of me, that I should do Thy will. O my God, I have desired it." [1] With reason, then, did the angels exult on this night, and sing: " Glory to God in the highest." But are men to have no part in this great joy? Certainly; " and on earth peace to men of good will." To what kind of men? To men of good will; that is, to those who, after

---

[1] Holocaustum et pro peccato non postulasti ; tunc dixi, ecce venio. In capite libri scriptum est de me, ut facerem voluntatem tuam. Deus meus, volui.—Ps. xxxix. 7-9.

the example of the new-born Saviour, are always in conformity with the most holy will of God. Not only do they find true peace and rest on earth, but they give to their God in the highest the greatest honor and glory. This conformity with the will of God, my dear brethren, consists of two things. First, that men do what God wills, and how, when, and because God wills, as I have already explained. Secondly, that they do with complete satisfaction whatever the will of God has decreed for themselves and ordered in the world. This is that most beautiful and perfect virtue which gives the greatest honor and glory to the Lord God; and that resignation and conformity God demands of us by countless titles as our sovereign Lord; it makes us confident that things go well with us; it alleviates and sweetens trials; it gives us a heaven of consolation even in this life; it consummates our happiness with God. How are we to practise this beautiful virtue? That we shall see to our consolation in the following sermons. To-day I confine myself to the first proposition, and I say:

Plan of Discourse.

To be always resigned to the will of God in all circumstances is a virtue by which we give God the greatest honor and glory. Such is the subject of this sermon.

Christ Jesus, who on this day didst come into the world, and wert born in a stable, to do, not Thy will, but the will of Him who sent Thee, inflame our hearts, that after Thy example we may be always resigned to the will of Thy heavenly Father! This we beg of Thee through the merits of Thy virginal Mother, of whom Thou wert born, and of Thy holy angels, who sang exulting at Thy birth, "Glory to God in the highest, and on earth peace to men of good will."

The honor of God is, properly speaking, the greatest good of God.

Strictly speaking, praise, honor, and glory belong to no one but God alone. "To the king of ages, immortal, invisible the only God," says St. Paul, "be honor and glory forever and ever." [1] And in this honor consists the only good that God can receive from His creatures; therefore the honor of God is, as it were, of infinite value. For the greatness and excellence of every good must be measured by the greatness and dignity of the person to whom it belongs. Thus the honor of the general is of much more importance than that of the drummer-boy; the

[1] Regi sæculorum, immortali, invisibili, soli Deo, honor et gloria in sæcula sæculorum.— I. Tim. i. 17.

honor of a noble is more important than that of a poor peasant; the honor of a mighty emperor is more important than that of a lackey. Who, then, can estimate the value of the honor and glory of the sovereign God? What are all kings, emperors, and earthly sovereigns, what are all creatures, past, present, and to come,—nay, all the creatures that could possibly be made, in comparison with God? The prophet Isaias answers: "Behold, the nations are as a drop of a bucket, and are counted as the smallest grain of a balance; behold, the islands are as a little dust. All nations are before Him as if they had no being at all, and are counted to Him as nothing and vanity."[1] Therefore the honor of all creatures taken together is as nothing when compared to the least portion of the honor of God.

From this it follows, my dear brethren, firstly, that man can do nothing more noble or excellent than to further the honor and glory of God; and the smallest work, for instance, a momentary thought offered to God in the state of grace, is much greater and more valuable than the whole world and all it contains. What wonderful things men have invented since the beginning of the world! What beautiful works of art, miracles of skill, as they might be called, have come forth from the hands of artists! What almost impossible feats of heroism have been performed on land and water by celebrated generals! And yet the poor peasant girl who sweeps out the stable with a good intention, and thereby gives honor to God, performs a far greater action, and one far more excellent and worthy of praise, than all the exploits of Alexander, who conquered the earth and the sea. Why so? Because those great deeds are an honor only to a mortal man, while the poor maid with her abject toil gives honor to God. O Christians, if we only thought of this always, what great things we might do every day! Secondly, it follows that the destruction of a whole kingdom, nay, that of heaven and earth, and all creatures, is of far less significance than the least loss or injury affecting the honor of God; so that the lives and property of all men should be sacrificed to save the divine honor from injury; and if it were necessary to increase it, that all men should give up all they have, their comfort, honor, and good name, their health, and life itself; not one should hesitate a moment, or think whether he should make the sacrifice or not;

Side note: Hence man can do nothing more excellent than to further the glory of God.

---

[1] Ecce gentes quasi stilla situlæ, et quasi momentum stateræ reputatæ sunt ; ecce insulæ quasi pulvis exiguus. Omnes gentes quasi non sint, sic sunt coram eo, et quasi nihilum et inane reputatæ sunt ei.—Is. xl. 15, 17.

but each one should think himself happy in being able thus to further the honor and glory of God. And we may look on it as beyond a doubt, that any sacrifice we could possibly make under such circumstances would be far less worthy of consideration than if some vile slave were to give a few drops of blood in honor of the greatest monarch on earth; for all the goods of creatures put together are nothing in comparison, have no proportion whatever, to the good of the Creator. Again, the honor and glory of God is the only end of all that the Lord has done outside Himself. "The Lord hath made all things for Himself." [1] He creates the world, He sends His only-begotten Son down on earth to become a poor little child; He allows Him to be nailed to the cross; He promises us an eternal heaven as a reward for our good works; He threatens the wicked with eternal torments; all this He does for His own sake, for His own honor and glory. Hence it follows that there is no better means of becoming like to God than to further His honor and glory in all things, as He does Himself.

Now there is no one who honors God more than he who practises conformity to the divine will. Now to my subject. The Lord God is never more honored and praised by creatures than when they not only do His holy will in all things, but also unite their will with His in all circumstances, and approve of and are fully satisfied with whatever God wills. For is it not an honor for God that a creature so submits to His wish and desire that He can use that creature as He pleases, without the least opposition? That He can dispose of him according to His pleasure; do with him what He wills; place him here or there; treat him with friendliness or apparent severity; give him sweet or sour, honor or shame, riches or poverty, joy or sorrow, consolation or trouble, health or sickness, life or death, as it may seem good to Him, without ever hearing the least word of complaint? Thus the creature is always, as far as his will is concerned, well-disposed towards God, always satisfied and contented with His decrees; he has always in his thoughts and on his lips the words that Our Lord addressed to His heavenly Father in the Gospel of St. Matthew: "Yea, Father, for so hath it seemed good in Thy sight." [2] What more dost Thou desire from me, O my God? My property? my honor and good name? my friends and relatives? my father and mother? my sisters and brothers? my sons and daughters? my rest and

---

[1] Universa propter semetipsum operatus est Dominus.—Prov. xvi. 4.
[2] Ita, Pater, quoniam sic fuit placitum ante te.—Matt. xi. 26.

comfort? the change of my mode of life and occupation? my health and prosperity? my life itself? Behold, I am ready; all that I have, all that I am, all that I possess in and outside myself is in Thy hands. Take what Thou pleasest, when and where Thou pleasest. Pay no attention to the opposition of my sensuality, to the resistance of my inclinations. My wish and desire is, that Thou shouldst dispose of everything according to Thy most holy will and pleasure, without at all taking into account my inclinations, my temporal well-being, or the blind desires of my heart. If Thou wilt, place me in the lowliest position; however hard it may be to my vanity, Thou shalt find no opposition in my mind and my will. There is nothing that I am not ready to accept—misery, losses, trouble, and difficulties,—in order to fulfil the secret, but, at the same time, most just decrees of Thy holy will. What honor and glory, I repeat, is given to God by a soul thus earnestly disposed! Hear how He boasts of it by the prophet Isaias: Thou shalt not be called by thy name any longer; "thou shalt be called by a new name, which the mouth of the Lord shall name. Thou shalt be called, My pleasure in her. . . because the Lord hath been well pleased with thee. And thou shalt be a crown of glory in the hand of the Lord, and a royal diadem in the hand of thy God." [1]

And in truth, if the honor and glory that is shown outwardly is nothing else but inward esteem and the praise and love that spring from it, what more sure sign of the esteem and love of God could be found than the disposition of him who is always *By this conformity he honors all the divine perfections.* and in all circumstances satisfied with the will of God? For he honestly believes and acknowledges what God is; by this conformity alone of his will with that of God he acknowledges, honors, and praises almost all the divine perfections at once. He acknowledges and highly appreciates the wonderful providence of God, for he is perfectly certain that whatever happens in the world, sin alone excepted, is ordered and arranged by it. He acknowledges and honors the infinite prudence and wisdom of God; for, without inquiring into the reason of this or that, and without the least doubt, he is convinced that God does everything rightly and justly. He acknowledges and praises the fatherly goodness of God, for he is persuaded that God arranges everything for his greater good. He acknowledges and praises

[1] Vocabitur tibi nomen novum, quod os Domini nominabit. Vocaberis, Voluntas mea in ea. . . quia complacuit Domino in te. Et eris corona gloriæ in manu Domini, et diadema regni in manu Dei tui.—Is. lxii. 2, 4, 3.

the infinite fidelity and good will of God, for he has no fear of any evil or harm from Him. He acknowledges and praises the unlimited sovereignty of God over all creatures, for he looks on it as most right and just that all should submit to Him in every circumstance with the utmost humility and most ready obedience. He acknowledges and praises the omnipresence of God; for he believes that He, present in all His creatures, secretly carries out His inscrutable decrees by their means. He acknowledges and praises the infinite knowledge of God; for he is certain that God is well aware of all his troubles and necessities. He acknowledges and praises the almighty power of God, who is able to help him, and to direct all things for his greater good. He acknowledges and praises the infinite mercy of God, in whose lap he casts himself, to whose protection he flies in all dangers of soul and body, with child-like confidence. He acknowledges and praises the infinite justice of God, to which he completely gives himself up to be punished for his sins as God may please. And, finally, he gives proof of a most perfect love of God, which cannot ascend any higher, as it were; for he is a dear friend of God in adverse as well as prosperous circumstances, and even in the hardest trials and calamities does not utter a word of complaint nor even admit a thought against the divine decrees. He is, as it were, one will and heart with God; he is pleased with everything that God wills, and as God wills; whatever is done to him by God is sweet and agreeable to him.

Without it, no virtue is pleasing to God.

In a word, this conformity and satisfaction with the will of God is an epitome of all virtues and of Christian piety and holiness; and all other virtues, if they are to be pleasing to God, must be directed to it. Father Nuremberg, in his book on this virtue, calls it "A Divine Life." [1] Humility is not pleasing to God; meekness, chastity, generosity, mercy, temperance, patience, even devotion and zeal for the divine honor, are not pleasing to God, if they are not in conformity with His will and practised according to His pleasure. Prayer, fasting, alms-giving, visiting the poor and those in prison, hearing Mass, chastising the body, going to confession and holy Communion—all that gives no honor to God if in certain circumstances He does not approve of it or will it. King Saul thought he had done wonders when he kept the best of the flocks of the Amalekites to offer in sacrifice to God, although Samuel had told him on

[1] Vita Divina.

the part of God to destroy and slay without sparing. "Blessed be thou of the Lord," he cried out exultingly to Samuel; "I have fulfilled the word of the Lord."[1] But what thanks did he get? "The Lord hath also rejected thee from being king." Why "hast thou done evil in the eyes of the Lord?"[2] What? Evil? asked Saul in amazement. I have devoted as a sacrifice of thanksgiving to the Lord for the victory whatever has remained alive. And the people, too, have determined to offer the best of the flocks and herds in sacrifice: "For the people spared the best of the sheep and of the herds, that they might be sacrificed to the Lord thy God."[3] What sacrifice? exclaimed the Prophet. "Doth the Lord desire holocausts and victims, and not rather that the voice of the Lord should be obeyed?"[4] Do you think God is pleased with the homage of a sacrifice that you offer Him against His will, and simply through some fancy of your own? You should have done what He commanded, and not what appeared good to yourself. Away with you; "the Lord hath rejected thee." The only honor and glory that God expects from His creatures is that they should be ready to obey His least sign as His servants, and their obedience must be free, unconstrained, so that they willingly do whatever, however, and whenever He pleases, and allow Him to rule them as may seem best to Him. Two brethren once came to St. Macarius and asked him to teach them how to pray. That requires but few words, was his answer; you must often raise up your hands or your minds to God, and say: Lord, be it done according to Thy good will and pleasure; to say this, and say it sincerely, is the most perfect and pleasing offering that we poor mortals can make to God.

And truly if ever there was a man in the world who knew how to honor and glorify God, it was Our Lord and Saviour Jesus Christ, who was brought down from heaven to earth by the honor and glory of His Father, and who says of Himself: "I seek not My own glory; but I honor My Father."[5] How did He do that? Hear what He Himself says: "For I always do the things that please Him."[6] The fulfilment of His Father's will He elsewhere calls His food and drink: "My meat is to do

Christ honored His Father by that conformity.

---

[1] Benedictus tu Domino, implevi verbum Domini.—I. Kings xv. 13.

[2] Abjecit te Dominus, ne sis rex. Quare fecisti malum in oculis Domini?—Ibid. 23, 19.

[3] Pepercit enim populus melioribus ovibus et armentis, ut immolarentur Domino Deo tuo.—Ibid. 15.

[4] Numquid vult Dominus holocausta et victimas, et non potius ut obediatur voci Domini?—Ibid. 22.

[5] Ego non quæro gloriam meam; sed honorifico Patrem meum.—John viii. 50, 44.

[6] Quia ego, quæ placita sunt ei, facio semper.—Ibid. 29.

the will of Him that sent Me." [1] This is what David testifies to,
speaking in the person of Our Lord, as I told you in the introduction: "In the head of the book it is written of Me, that I
should do Thy will. O my God, I have desired it, and Thy law
in the midst of my heart." According to the unanimous teaching of theologians, God could not have laid on the sacred humanity of Our Lord a single command binding under pain of
sin, since otherwise He would not have been free to violate that
command. When therefore Christ says that He is obedient to
the Father, we must understand Him to mean that He resigns
Himself joyfully to everything that He knows in various circumstances to be pleasing to His heavenly Father: "O my God, I
have desired it." The Eternal Father was pleased that His Son
should be born poor: "My God, I have desired it." Behold,
I have neither house nor home; I am lying in a miserable stable,
exposed to wind and weather, with no better bed than a little
straw; I am poorer than the poorest beggar's child! The Eternal Father was pleased that His Son should submit to the hard
law of circumcision, like those born of sinful men, and bear the
mark of a sinner: "My God, I have desired it;" even for this
I am ready, O God, because such is Thy will. The Eternal
Father was pleased that His Son in the very beginning of His
life should be persecuted by men, and have to fly into the idolatrous land of Egypt, in the middle of the night, and there live
amongst heathens: "My God, I have desired it;" I am ready,
since it is Thy will. The Father was pleased that His Son
should spend thirty years hidden and unknown in the mean
house at Nazareth, working as a carpenter's apprentice, and subject to His mother and foster-father, earning His bread by the
sweat of His brow: "My God, I have desired it;" let it be so,
My God, since such is Thy will. The Father was pleased that
His Son should spend the three last years of His life going about
with ignorant, uncouth fishermen, and with wicked Pharisees
and Scribes, who sneered at Him and watched every word He
said in the hope of being able to find fault with Him: "My
God, I have desired it;" in this, too, I resign Myself completely
to Thy will. And finally the Father was pleased that His innocent Son should suffer the most cruel torments in His soul
and body and good name, and that He should be condemned to
die on the cross as the worst of criminals: "My God I have

---

[1] Meus cibus est ut faciam voluntatem ejus qui misit me. –John iv. 34.

desired it;" be it so, O God; I am indeed willing, although I could more than satisfy for the sins of the world with far less trouble; although the torments that are before Me are so hard for My human nature, that the bare thought of them forces Me to sweat blood, and fills My soul with sorrow unto death. "Nevertheless, not as I will, but as Thou wilt." [1] See, my dear brethren, how Christ, the Son of God, honored His Father, and gave Him the greatest glory, by being always contented and satisfied with His holy will and pleasure. Therefore He has taught us to say daily: "Our Father. . . . Thy will be done on earth as it is in heaven."

Mark these words; we must wish and desire, if we are willing to give due honor to God, that in all circumstances and occurrences the will of God should be done by us as it is done in heaven. The heavenly spirits are called by David attendants and servants of God, whose only duty is to do His will: "Bless the Lord, all ye His hosts; you ministers of His, that do His will." You who are always ready to obey His least sign: "you that execute His word, hearkening to the voice of His orders." [2] Even the greatest princes of heaven are so determined to do the will of God that, if He gave them the least sign of His pleasure that they should come down on earth and become gardeners and pull up weeds, or till the ground with great labor like husbandmen, or undertake any other lowly occupation, they would do so with the utmost joy, and make a heaven for themselves out of the work they perform in obedience to the will of God. For they know well that the honor and glory of God, which they prize and value above everything, consists in nothing else but conformity with His will. Consider for a moment, my dear brethren, the office which the holy guardian angels have undertaken to fill. Bright and noble creatures as they are, they are not ashamed to spend years and years at the side of some vile mortal, from the first moment of his life to the last, even though he be a most wicked sinner, a Jew, or Turk, or unbelieving heathen, or a most godless idolater, who blasphemes the true God, or a wicked sorcerer, who gives himself up to the devil and enters into a compact with that evil spirit to commit the worst kind of sins. In spite of this, those most pure spirits of heaven are most patient in their attendance on such men; they protect and defend them

In this way God is honored by the angels.

---

[1] Verumtamen non sicut ego volo, sed sicut tu.—Matt. xxvi. 39.

[2] Benedicite Domino omnes virtutes ejus, ministri ejus, qui facitis voluntatem ejus. . . facientes verbum illius, ad audiendam vocem sermonum ejus.—Ps. cii. 21, 20.

as children given over to their care by God; nay, as St. Bernard says, they serve them; and the angel who has to guard a poor beggar is just as satisfied with his position as if he had charge of the greatest monarch of earth, because such is the will of God, who has appointed to each angel the soul he has to look after.

By the four elements.

But why do I speak of the angels? Consider all things under heaven, the sun, the moon, the planets, the stars, the elements, fire and water, air and wind, the earth and the animals on it; these, too, honor and glorify their Creator by complete conformity with His will; for each of them in its place constantly does what He has decreed. The sun gives light and constantly runs its appointed course, flying round in the orbit fixed for it with the velocity of an arrow shot from a bow. Fire heats and consumes with the utmost rapidity whatever is given to it as fuel. Water flows, the wind blows, the earth stands still, the wild beasts attack those who come too near them; and all that is according to the qualities that God has given to each one, and in obedience to His command. Nay, those same creatures allow God to do with them as He wills, even if it be against their nature and inclination. If God wishes the sun to stay its course, it is ready to obey Him, as it did at the prayer of Josue: "Move not, O sun, toward Gabaon, nor thou, O moon, toward the valley of Ajalon. And the sun and the moon stood still, till the people revenged themselves of their enemies." And that lasted for a whole day: "So the sun stood still in the midst of heaven, and hasted not to go down the space of one day."[1] If God wishes the fire to lose its natural heat, and to become even cold, against its nature, it is ready to obey Him, as it did in the Babylonian furnace, in which, although it shot forth flames nine and forty cubits high, the three youths felt it as a cooling breeze. "He made the midst of the furnace like the blowing of a wind bringing dew," says the Scripture of the angel who stood by them; "and the fire touched them not at all, nor troubled them, nor did them any harm."[2] If God wishes water to become solid, and to stand still, or earth to move from place to place, they are both ready to obey. Thus the sea stood like a wall on both sides, until the Israelites passed over dry-shod; on the other

---

[1] Sol contra Gabaon ne movearis, et luna contra vallem Ajalon. Steteruntque sol et luna, donec ulcisceretur se gens de inimicis suis. Stetit itaque sol in medio cœli, et non festinavit occumbere spatio unius diei.—Jos. x. 12, 13.

[2] Fecit medium fornacis quasi ventum roris flantem, et non tetigit eos ommino ignis, neque contristavit, nec quidquam molestiæ intulit.—Dan. iii. 50.

hand, the mountains often changed their places at the command of the servants of God. If God wishes the wind to cease blowing, it is ready to obey, as it was when it hearkened to the voice of Christ, when the ship in which He was with the disciples was in danger of being lost: "Then rising up, He commanded the winds and the sea, and there came a great calm." [1]

Does God wish lions to become meek lambs, or fishes attentive scholars, or birds servants, or ravens feeders of men, they are willing to obey Him even against their nature and instinct. Thus the fierce lions watched over the Prophet Daniel in the den, and licked his feet. The fishes, at the command of St. Antony of Padua, lifted up their heads out of the water and listened to his sermon. A raven brought half a loaf every day to St. Paul the hermit, and when St. Antony visited him it brought a whole one. Father Joseph Anchieta of our Society, being unable once to bear the fierce rays of the sun, called out to a bird that was flying past, and told it to bring a number of its companions: it obeyed, and there came a whole swarm of them together, and they spread out their wings to shade him from the sun, accompanying him thus on his journey, until the sun went down, when he dismissed them with his blessing. With reason did the three youths in the furnace sing: "All ye works of the Lord, bless the Lord; praise and exalt Him above all forever." Sun and moon, fire and water, heat and cold, birds and beasts, ice and snow, day and night, light and darkness, lightnings and clouds, mountains and hills, seas and rivers, and all creatures, praise ye the Lord and exalt Him above all forever! For they do so in reality when they obey His least sign and fulfil the will of their Creator.

O my God. how Thy unreasoning creatures put to shame me and many other men on account of our uneasiness, discontent, vain fears and anxieties, disobedience and obstinacy, when Thou commandest anything opposed to our sensuality or comfort! Thou willest now and then that this or that person should say or do something against me; but I am not at all satisfied therewith; I cannot bear it; I give way to impatience and anger and desires of revenge. Thou wilt that this man should live in poverty and want; but he is not resigned to Thy holy will; he curses and swears at his fate, although he cannot thereby change it. Thou wilt that this other should lie sick in bed, and suffer pain; but

By all other creatures.

How much more should not men thus honor God!

---

[1] Tunc surgens imperavit ventis et mari, et facta est tranquillitas magna.—Matt. viii. 26.

he is not at all satisfied with that; he grows impatient and wishes for nothing so much as health. Thy will is that another should bear his daily annoyances and domestic crosses for Thy sake; but he is unwilling to do so, and tries to vent his displeasure in cursing, swearing, and invective. Thou wilt that each one should serve Thee truly according to his state; but almost every one desires a position different to that in which Thou hast placed him. Thus Thy holy will and our miserable will run directly counter to each other; what wonder is it, then, that most men lead wretched, unhappy, discontented lives? For how can there be true peace and contentment when Thy will is opposed? "Who hath resisted Him, and hath had peace?"[1] asks the patient Job. Oh, how much less honor, O Lord, Thou receivest from reasoning men than from Thy unreasoning and lifeless creatures! And yet we should look on it as an honor and happiness to allow Thee, our heavenly Father, who meanest so well with us, to dispose of us according to Thy will, and we should receive everything, sweet and sour, from Thy hand with the utmost satisfaction. What honor and happiness it is for a poor mortal to increase and further Thy glory, O God, by that uniformity and resignation!

Exhortation and resolution always to practise conformity to the will of God.
Therefore, my dear brethren, let us all earnestly endeavor to will at all times what God wills. But He wills everything that happens, and ordains it, sin alone excepted; therefore let us be completely resigned to the will of God, and be satisfied with all that He is pleased to do, no matter what it is. Always to do what God wills, always to be satisfied with the will and decree of God, herein consists the greatest virtue, holiness, and perfection of man. Ah, would that we were disposed as the Cistercian monk was of whom Cæsarius tells us! He wrought daily wonderful miracles, so that the mere touch of His clothing healed the sick, although no greater signs of holiness were to be seen in him than in his brethren. The abbot thought this looked suspicious, and, calling the monk to him, asked him what sort of a life he was leading that God worked such miracles by him. I do not know, answered the monk; I watch, fast, pray, and work like my brethren; I never do more or less than they; I live in no other manner than that prescribed by the rules of the Order. Yet there is one thing, I know, for which I give God most sincere thanks: I am never disturbed nor annoyed, no matter what happens; things may go well or ill with me and every one

---

[1] Quis restitit ei, et pacem habuit ?—Job ix. 4.

else in the world, I am always contented and satisfied, for I think to myself: The good God wishes to have it so; may His holy will be done! " And what were your feelings," asked the abbot, " when that fine property of our convent, that brought in so much every year, was attacked by wicked men and burnt? Were you not sorry, as the others were?" "To tell you the truth," answered the monk, " I was not in the least put out by it, but ascribed it all to the will of God, and I said to myself at once: The good God wills it so, therefore it must be for our good. If He gives us something, we owe Him our humble thanks; if He takes from us by misfortune what He has given, we must be equally satisfied with His holy will." Then the abbot knew the reason why God worked such miracles by means of that monk, namely, his perfect conformity with the divine will. So it is, Christians. He who has advanced so far that he is always content with the will of God, he, I repeat, is an epitome of all virtue and has reached the highest point of perfection. Let us, then, with thankful hearts say in all circumstances with Christ our Saviour: "Yea, Father, for so hath it seemed good in Thy sight." I will live in this state, because such is Thy holy will; in this state I will suffer this or that, because it is pleasing to Thee; so I will be, and so I will remain, for such is Thy will; nor do I desire to be otherwise than as Thou wilt have me. Thus shall I give honor to Thee, O God in the highest, and I shall experience that peace which the angels announced to-day to men of good will. Amen.

Another Introduction to the same sermon for the thirteenth Sunday after Pentecost.

Text.

Non est inventus qui rediret, et daret gloriam Deo.—Luke xvii. 18.

"There is no one found to return and give glory to God."

Introduction.

Mark the great advantage gained by those ten lepers on account of their ready obedience to the words of Christ. "Go, show yourselves to the priests," said Our Saviour to them. But they might have thought, Art Thou not the Son of God, who hast power over all diseases? The mere touch of Thy garment is enough to restore health. Why, then, dost Thou send us to the priests to be healed by them? Why dost Thou not say, as Thou

didst to another leper, "I will. Be thou made clean"?[1] Then
we should be cleansed at once from leprosy, and should not have
to go any farther. But they said nothing of the sort, and simply
went as they were commanded; "and it came to pass, as they
went, they were made clean." So far they were quite right; but
nine of them did wrong in not returning to thank their Benefactor, as Our Lord Himself complained: "Were not ten made
clean? And where are the nine? There is no one found to return and give glory to God but this stranger." Hitherto, my
dear brethren, we have treated of the first part of the virtue of
conformity and resignation of our will to the will of God, which
consists in this, that we do what, when, how, and because God
wills us to do. But how few there are of us who thus give God
the glory of fulfilling His will in all things! To be, then, in perfect conformity with the divine will, it is not enough for us to
do what God wills, but we must also be satisfied with all that
God chooses to do with us. This is that most beautiful virtue
of which I am beginning to speak to-day; but I fear there are
not many who glorify God by it. A most beautiful virtue, I repeat, by which the greatest honor is given to God, etc.—*Continues as above.*

FORTY-SIXTH SERMON.

ON THE JUSTICE OF CONFORMING OUR WILL TO THE WILL OF GOD.

Subject.

With infinite right does God require of us men that we should
in all things do His holy will, and in all things be perfectly
satisfied with His holy will—*Preached on the feast of St. Stephen,
the first Martyr.*

Text.

*Stephanus autem, plenus gratia et fortitudine, faciebat prodigia
et signa magna in populo.*—Acts vi. 8.

"And Stephen, full of grace and fortitude, did great wonders
and signs among the people."

Introduction.

History does not tell us what miracles St. Stephen wrought
among the people. Yet we need not examine into them, for

[1] Volo: mundare.—Matt. viii. 3.

we find in Stephen himself a most surprising miracle of fortitude and the love of God, which he showed in his zeal in pro-
moting the glory of God, and also in freely offering himself to
undergo all sorts of pains and torments according to the divine
will. How undismayed he preached Jesus Christ as the true
God in the synagogue, in presence of his bitterest enemies!
How heroically he upbraided them with their wickedness!
" You stiff-necked and uncircumcised in heart and ears," he
said to them, " you always resist the Holy Ghost. Which of
the prophets have not your fathers persecuted? And they have
slain them who foretold of the coming of the Just One, of whom
you have been now betrayers and murderers." [1] They were filled
with rage at these words: " Now, hearing these things, they were
cut to the heart, and they gnashed with their teeth at him.
They stopped their ears, and with one accord they ran violently
upon him. And casting him forth without the city, they stoned
him." [2] But this did not deter the intrepid servant of God from
publicly professing his faith in Jesus Christ, while he left to
the disposition of divine providence his martyrdom and death.
He suffered as if it did not concern him in the least, so that,
while the stones were raining down on him, he prayed with his
last breath for his persecutors: " And falling on his knees, he
cried with a loud voice, saying: Lord, lay not this sin on their
charge. And when he had said this, he fell asleep in the
Lord." [3] O my dear brethren, if we had only a spark of this
fortitude and conformity with the will of God, what great things
we might do for the divine honor! And what good reason we
have to endeavor to acquire this virtue! I have already shown
that we can give God the greatest honor by conformity to His
will. I now go on to speak of the justice of this virtue.

Plan of Discourse.

*With infinite right and by countless titles does God require of
us men that we should in all things do His holy will, and in all
things be perfectly satisfied with His holy will. Therefore we are*

[1] Dura cervice et incircumcisis cordibus et auribus, vos semper Spiritui Sancto resistitis.
Quem prophetarum non sunt persecuti patres vestri ? Et occiderunt eos qui prænuntiabant
de adventu Justi, cujus vos nunc proditores et homicidæ fuistis.—Acts vii. 51, 52.

[2] Audientes autem hæc dissecabantur cordibus suis, et stridebant dentibus in eum. Con-
tinuerunt aures suas, et impetum fecerunt unanimiter in eum, et ejicientes eum extra civitatem, lapibabant.—Ibid. 54, 56, 57, 58.

[3] Positus autem genibus, clamavit voce magna, dicens : Domine, ne statuas illis hoc peccatum. Et cum hoc dixisset, obdormivit in Domino.—Ibid. 59.

guilty of the greatest injustice towards Him when we oppose His will and decree even in the smallest things. Such is the subject of this sermon.

That we may always abandon ourselves with joyful hearts to Thy holy will, grant us, O Lord worthy of all love, Thy powerful grace, which we humbly beg of Thee through the merits of Mary, of our holy guardian angels, and of Thy faithful servant Stephen.

By various titles we can acquire a right to a thing.

A right to a thing means, according to theologians, the lawful power to dispose of it as one wills, so that no one else has any title to interfere in this complete dominion over it. There are different titles by which one can hold or acquire such a right; for instance, there is the title of purchase. I have bought a house with my own money, and taken possession of it; therefore it belongs to me; I can live in it, if I wish, or let it to another; I can allow it to remain empty; I can change it inside or outside; I can give it away or sell it, or let it fall down, just as I please; no one can prevent me doing any of these things with it, and if any one tried to interfere with me I could say to him: What is it to you? I am the owner of my own house; I can make what use I please of it, because I have bought it with my own money. Men have had a similar right in former times, and have it still, too, in different countries, especially amongst heathens and infidels, over other men, who are bought and sold in the market like oxen. These slaves must serve their master with the most perfect obedience and readiness, and do whatever he commands them, except that he has not the right to order them to do anything against the law of God, or to take away their lives, which latter power is not granted by God to any private individual. Again, there is the title of trade and profit, which gives a right to a thing; what I gain in a lawful manner belongs to me, and I am the owner of it. The same is to be understood of a lost thing that I find, if the owner of it cannot be discovered, and there is no hope of discovering him. There is also the title of gift; what is given to me by another is my own when I accept it, and even my benefactor himself cannot take it back from me without doing me an injustice, nor can he in the least interfere with any use I may wish to make of it. A title to a thing can also be acquired by long and peaceable possession of it, although one may not know how the thing first came into his possession. And there are several other titles. But of all the titles that give man the dominion and property of a thing, there is none better than that which gives one the dominion of what he himself has invented or made with his own hands or his own ingenuity. Who has a greater right to the picture than the painter who has painted it to show his skill and for his own pleasure? To whom does the tree belong, if not to the gardener who has planted it on his own ground? To whom does the chair belong, if not to the carpenter who has made it for himself? It is in his power to sell the chair or to keep it, to throw it away, to break it in pieces, to fling it into the fire, to place it in this room or that, just as he likes. And if the picture, the tree, the chair had reason, they would not have the least right to find fault with the use their master makes of them, but must, so to speak, obey him as creatures do their creator, from whom they have received their being, and in all circumstances they must be ready to do his will and to allow him to use them as he wills.

Now to our subject, my dear brethren. Oh, how infinitely great and perfect is the Master that we have! A Master whose sovereign and almighty power has neither end nor limit. Who else is that Master but He of whom David speaks when he says: "For the Lord is a great God, and a great King above all gods. For in His hands are all the ends of the earth; and the heights of the mountains are His."[1] He is the true God of heaven and earth, before whom all the crowned heads of the world must bend the knee, whose slightest sign they must obey as humble slaves; to Him we all belong without exception, with everything in and outside of us. His sovereignty and almighty power extend not merely to the exterior works which we perform to please Him, not merely to the outward goods and possessions which we can use for our enjoyment, but also (and that can be said of no master with regard to his slave, of no monarch with regard to his subjects) to our souls and all their faculties, our memory, understanding, and will, nay, even our most secret thoughts and desires; and He has an infinite right, by countless titles, to require that we should use all those faculties according to His pleasure. *God has an infinite right to our will, so that we should always submit it to His.*

And, firstly, He has that right from the title of creation, which is in itself more than enough. "Know ye that the Lord He is God," says the Psalmist;[2] "He made us, and not we our- *From the title of creation.*

---

[1] Quoniam Deus magnus Dominus, et rex magnus super omnes deos. Quia in manu ejus sunt omnes fines terræ, et altitudines montium ipsius sunt.— Ps. xciv. 3, 4.

[2] Scitote quoniam Dominus ipse est Deus; ipse fecit nos, et non ipsi nos.—Ibid. xcix. 3.

selves." From all eternity He had in His divine mind the idea of how He would make and form us in time; He is the only Master whose hands could fashion us from nothing, therefore all that we are and have and can do comes from Him and belongs to Him by right. If the carpenter has such an undisputed right to the chair which he has made for himself that he can use it when, how, and where he pleases, although he has not made the wood of the chair, nor given it its nature and being, but simply cut the wood into the accidental form and shape of a chair, what an unlimited right, then, must not the Lord God have over us and all that belongs to us! What an all-perfect service and complete submission we owe His most just decrees, since we are the works, the master-pieces of His hands; since He has given us, not merely the outward form and stature that we have, but also our whole being and essence, and has made us altogether for Himself! So that we are not our own masters. Nor have we the lawful right to dispose of anything that is ours, unless according to God's will and pleasure. Nor have we the smallest reason to complain that He has given us too little, or because He chooses to take away what He has given us. If He has bestowed on me a weak intellect, little ability of mind or strength of body, and little or nothing of the goods of this world, He is the Master; He was not bound to give me even what He has given; He might have given me far less, nay, He might have left me in the abyss of my nothingness forever. What would I say to the ragged beggar who is dissatisfied with the penny I give him, and murmurs against me, saying: Is that all you have for me? can you not give me something more? Away with you, I should answer; I am not bound to give you anything. Take what you have got, and be thankful. Just as little reason have we to complain of God, no matter how He deals with us.

From the title of preservation. And that all the more (herein consists God's second title to perfect dominion over us and all we have) because we have not merely received our whole being from Him, as our First Cause and Creator, but also every moment we must still receive the same being from Him by preservation. In this respect no other work is in need of its maker. If the picture or the chair is finished, it is and remains a picture or a chair, although the painter with his brush or the carpenter with his tools goes away, or is carried off by death. It is not so with us. If you hold in your hand a glass that you wish to break into a thousand pieces, what have you to do? Must you take a hammer, and strike hard at it? By no means; all you need do is to open the fingers of the hand in which you hold the glass, and it will of itself fall to the ground and break in pieces. In the same way, if God were to withdraw His preserving hand from us for a moment, what would become of us? We should sink into our original nothingness. Without the coöperation and help of God, all my faculties of soul and body are utterly useless. If I wish just to give a passing thought to something, I cannot do it by myself; God must help me to think. I am looking at you now, my dear brethren, but I could not do so, although my eyes are healthy and I keep them open, if God did not help me to form the image. I am speaking now; but I could not do so if God did not help me to form the words and to move my tongue. I cannot even wish or desire a thing, unless God helps me to form the act of the will, the wish, the desire. In a word, according to the teaching of St. Paul, I can do nothing without the present help and influence of the divine omnipotence. "For it is God who worketh in you both to will and to accomplish." [1] Thus God is always occupied with our preservation, and consequently whatever we have and are is completely under His dominion, in His power.

From this it follows that there should not be in us the least thing that is not perfectly in accordance with His will and pleasure; and, if it is an injustice to take away from a man what belongs to him, or to interfere with him in the lawful use of his own property, how unjustly then do we not act towards God by opposing even once His holy will, or by withdrawing from Him even one single thought by employing it contrary to His will and pleasure? Some one enters by night into another man's garden and takes away the apples from his tree; what a noise the owner makes when he discovers the theft! He does not hesitate to accuse the culprit before the authorities, and to demand restitution for the theft. And in what does the injury consist? In the fact that the apples were stolen from a tree planted in the man's ground. Yet he did not make the ground, nor fix the roots on the tree, nor cause the latter to grow. He did not water it with the rain that fell from the clouds, nor fructify it by the heat of the sun; not even the stalk of an apple could he make by his own skill, much less the fruit itself. And now he complains that the fruit was taken from him unjustly, simply because it

By which we are specially bound to do all things according to His will.

---

[1] Deus est enim qui operatur in vobis et velle et perficere.—Phil. ii. 13.

grew in his garden! What are we then to think of the right that the sovereign God has to complain of us if we even once withdraw and steal away our wills from His ordination and disposition? for He is not merely lord and master of the land on which we walk and stand, not merely owner of the tree, that is, of our bodies and souls, but He is also the lord and master and preserver of everything that our will can do or bring forth.

The title of redemption and purchase. But supposing even that we were not created by God; that we had received nothing from Him; that we were not constantly in need of being preserved by Him: yet we should still belong to Him by different titles, and be strictly bound to do, not our own, but His holy will, and to allow ourselves to be ruled, not according to our own fancy, but according to His good will and pleasure. One of these titles is that of purchase. Hear what St. Paul says to all men: "Know you not that your members are the temple of the Holy Ghost, who is in you, whom you have from God, and you are not your own. For you are bought with a great price." [1] As if he wished to say: Poor mortals, what do you complain of? Why do you sigh and moan when things do not go according to your fancies? What do you wish for? What is the object of your desires? It is not for you to long for what you like, or what seems good to you; for " you are not your own," you are bought; God has bought you, to Him you belong. And what price did He pay for you? A great price; the infinite price of His precious blood. For, as we well know, we were all given over to the devil as fuel for hell by the sin of our first parents, and the Incarnate Son of God paid the price for us to His heavenly Father by suffering the shameful death of the cross, and thus He freed us from the slavery of the devil and bought us for Himself. If, then, the trifling sum that the master pays for his slave gives him such a right that the latter is bound to order his life according to his master's pleasure, and to allow his master to deal with him as he pleases; nay, if the trifling wages paid amongst us to a servant gives the master such a right that the servant must act, not according to his own will, but according to the will of his master (St. Paul binds servants expressly to obey their masters in all things pertaining to their service, as they would obey God Himself: " Servants be obedient to them that are your lords according to the flesh, with fear and trembling,

---

1 An nescitis quoniam membra vestra templum sunt Spiritus Sancti, qui in vobis est, quem habetis a Deo, et non estis vestri. Empti enim estis pretio magno.—I. Cor. vi. 19, 20.

in the simplicity of your heart, as to Christ: with a good will serving, as to the Lord, and not to men."[1] The Prophet David says: "As the eyes of servants are on the hands of their masters, as the eyes of the hand-maid are on the hands of her mistress;"[2] that is, servants should be so ready to obey their masters that the latter must be as confident of the fulfilment of their commands as if the service was already performed),—if that is the case, I say, then God has an infinite right to our will and to all we have, because He has bought us, not with a trifling salary or a few ducats, such as we give our servants, but with His own life's blood for His service. And we on our side are bound by an infinite obligation to be ready at all times to obey the least sign of our Master, and to do His will perfectly as soon as we know it, whatever He may command us to do, and to submit our will to His, approving and accepting everything that is pleasing to Him, rejecting and disapproving what is contrary to His will.

There is, moreover, a fourth title on our side, obligatory indeed on us, but coming nevertheless from our free will, and accepted by God; and that is the title of gift. For in holy baptism, after having renounced the world, and publicly declared war against the devil and the flesh, we gave ourselves, our souls and bodies, our memory, understanding, and will, and everything we have in and outside of us, to the Lord God, to be disposed of as He chooses, forever, thus devoting ourselves to Him as His servants; and that offering we have frequently repeated afterwards. In fact, we have acted towards God in this matter almost as St. Paulinus of Nola did when he offered himself as a slave to the barbarians in order to ransom the son of a widow who was held captive by them. That present we still daily ratify when we say: "Thy will be done on earth as it is in heaven." So that, if we had any right to live according to our own will and pleasure, we have once for all given it up to God. Therefore, as he who has of his own free will given me something would do me an injury if he tried to take it back or to interfere with me in the use of it, so we cannot take from God without injustice the will that we have given Him that He may use it according to His pleasure, and do with us what He chooses.

In former times there was amongst some people the follow-

The title of gift.

---

[1] Servi, obedite dominis carnalibus cum timore et tremore, in simplicitate cordis vestri, sicut Christo.—Ephes. vi. 5, 7.

[2] Sicut oculi servorum in manibus dominorum suorum, sicut oculi ancillæ in manibus dominæ suæ.—Ps. cxxii. 2.

ing law: If a debtor was unable to pay, he was given over as a slave to his creditor, the latter thus acquiring more or less right over his person, according to the greatness of the debt. There, my dear brethren, you have a new title for the right that God has over our wills, and for that obligation by which we are bound to do everything according to His pleasure and to allow Him to dispose of us as He chooses. Ah, what an immense debt we owe the almighty God! Nor do I now speak of the debt we incur by the manifold sins we have committed since we came to the use of reason. Can any of us say with truth that he is free from sin, that he never offended God in his whole life? Well indeed is it for him who can say that. But, as St. Augustine remarks, the very fact of his being free from sin is a still greater benefit that he owes the Almighty. Besides the debt contracted by sin, count, if you can, the numerous benefits, the natural and supernatural graces and talents, that God has so freely bestowed on you since your birth; what else are they but debts that you are bound to make some return for? Consider now, O man, what you have in and outside yourself to pay them off. Not the least thing will you find that you do not owe Him already on other titles; and therefore, if you still had any right left over yourself, you would be bound to give it all up to God; and as He has left you free will to such an extent that you may abuse it to do evil against His will, or use it to do good according to His will, He demands of you with the greatest right, and will be content if you satisfy that demand, that you should submit your free will to Him in all things, and be always ready to do what He wills, to omit and avoid what He does not will, and to accept with resignation whatever He has decreed for you, so that He may dispose of you in all circumstances according to His pleasure.

The title of God's endless perfections.   Finally, if we could blot out all those titles that God has over our wills; if God had not created us nor given us all we have, so that we did not belong to Him on that account; if He did not preserve us every moment of our lives, so that we should not be obliged to devote all our actions to Him; if He had not shed His precious blood and suffered the shameful death of the cross to save us from eternal damnation, so that we should not be bound therefore to give Him our wills; if we had not sacrificed and offered ourselves to Him, so that we did not thus belong to Him, and He had not the slightest right to make any demand of us: what then? He would still have an infinite right to the perfect conformity of our will with His, and to rule and dispose of us as He pleases, by the sole title of His infinite, divine perfections, majesty, and dignity, by which He infinitely surpasses all creatures. For, as the philosopher Aristotle says, natural sovereignty is founded on the excellence of nature; and hence it is that reasoning man is superior to the unreasoning beast, that the husband commands the wife, and that the ignorant must allow themselves to be instructed by the learned. A man who is of lowly origin, says St. Jerome, is generally looked down upon and badly served.[1] But servants do not dare to act in that way with persons of noble birth.[2] The greater and more important the master, the more obedient the servants.[3] It is looked on as an honor to obey the command of a great man, although it may be a difficult one. " There is no doubt that all are eager to fulfil the wishes of a king; they are even desirous to receive his commands; and they look on it as meritorious on their part not only to obey the command, but even to receive it; so that, the higher a person is, the greater the favor of being allowed to serve him."[4] Daily experience teaches us that such is the case with earthly sovereigns. Now, since God infinitely surpasses in excellence and perfection all the kings, emperors, and monarchs of earth, and all created things in heaven and on earth, because He is the only supreme, immense, most wise, powerful, beautiful Good, worthy of all love, honor, and service, He has an infinite right to all sovereignty and dominion over all created things; and as He has the right to be loved by us with our whole hearts for His own sake, so He has also the right to expect that we should do His holy will and pleasure in all things without the least opposition and with the utmost satisfaction; and therefore that we should be always in perfect conformity with His most blessed will.

Now, my dear brethren, since the unlimited right that God has over our will is founded on so many titles, can we be so unjust, so shameless, as to do the least act, say the smallest word, nay, form even a thought in any way opposed to His divine will? How could we move a hand or foot, unless according

Thus we are strictly bound in all things to conform to the will of God.

---

[1] Viles et ignobiles dominos palam contemni videmus, eisque ad minima quæque præcepta in faciem resisti solere.—S. Hieron. ad Demet., c. 1.

[2] At hoc in personas nobiles jam non admittitur.—Ibid.

[3] Quantoque potentiores domini, tanto servi ad obedientiam promptiores.—Ibid.

[4] Certe ad regis imperium ita omnes parati sunt, ut etiam optent juberi; et non solum bene merituros esse credunt si jussa fecerint, sed tanquam jam meruissent, quod jussi sunt; ita pro dignitate præcipientis servitium beneficii loco ducitur.—Ibid.

to the will of God? How could we bear to have a hair on our heads, a hem on our garments, that is not arranged perfectly according to God's will, to say nothing of its being contrary to that will? How could we give way to displeasure, or make the least complaint, when God decrees something for us that is contrary to our sensuality, inclination, or fastidious nature? If God were to act with us as the carpenter does with the chair he has made, which he throws about here and there as he wishes, or even breaks into pieces; or as the gardener does with the tree he has planted, which he cuts down if he chooses and casts into the fire; as the infidel does with the slave, whom he overburdens with hard labor, or chastises with hunger, thirst, and blows, should we have the right to make the least objection? Must we not humbly say like the high-priest Heli, when Samuel announced to him the destruction of his children and his children's children: "It is the Lord; let Him do what is good in His sight"?[1] He is our sovereign Lord, and we are His servants; He has to command, and we have to obey; let Him do and accomplish in us and all belonging to us whatever is pleasing to Him.

Especially as He uses His right over us for our good. But we are not ruled and governed by God as those unhappy slaves are by their barbarous and cruel masters. The unlimited, infinite right that He has over us by countless titles to dispose of us according to His good will and pleasure He does not, so to speak, use for His own advantage (for what can God expect from our poor service? With the utmost obedience we cannot increase His happiness one iota), but for our good, that it may be well with us here and hereafter; that, free from all unnecessary cares and anxieties, we may repose under His protection and in His fatherly arms, abandoning ourselves with confidence to His providence, in the full assurance that all will be for our welfare. If He sometimes decrees for us things that go against our sensuality and inclinations, we are nevertheless sure that He does not act with the intention of torturing us and showing in us His almighty power, but that He has in view the good of our souls; because He alone knows best what is advantageous for our spiritual welfare, and He has pledged His divine word that in all circumstances, and in all the decrees and visitations of His providence, He will, as far as He is concerned, seek only our advantage.

And prom- Moreover, He does not ask us to submit to Him for nothing,

---

[1] Dominus est ; quod bonum est in oculis suis, faciat.—I. Kings iii. 18.

although, as we have seen, He has right enough to demand that ises us a temporal and eternal reward for conformity to His will. of us; but He promises, as the reward of our conformity with His will, the indescribable joys of His heaven, which we are to possess with Himself. Nay, He does not wait till death to reward us; for even during the present life He bestows on us a portion of the reward, by giving to those who abandon themselves with full resignation to His will (as we shall see in other sermons on the same subject) a sort of heavenly happiness upon earth; nay, He arranges and disposes His divine will according to their will and desire. And with regard to the soul, God gives them everything they wish for in order to work out their salvation. With regard to the body, God has often accommodated His will to that of His servants whose wills were in conformity with His. Witness St. Thomas of Aquin, who, being sick on one occasion, wished to have fresh herrings, a dish that was very rare in the place where he was; but God sent them to him by a miracle. A similar incident happened to our Father Peter Canisius, a truly apostolic man, who once longed for a certain sort of bird, which was not to be found in the country in which he was; he signified his wish to God, and it was immediately satisfied, for a bird of the desired kind flew into the room and allowed itself to be caught and killed. There are many similar examples in the Lives of the Saints. So generous is God to His just servants who are fully resigned to His will, that He always keeps His eyes on them to see what they want, and His ears open to hear what they desire, as the Prophet David says: "The eyes of the Lord are upon the just, and His ears unto their prayers. The just cried, and the Lord heard them." [1]

Ah, my God, is it then necessary to bring forward so many Conclusion and act of resignation to the will of God. motives to induce me to submit my most wretched will to Thy most holy, just, and righteous will? If Thou hadst left me altogether to my own will, if I could always do and omit what suits my own fancy and choose what is pleasing to me, even then I should humbly and fervently beg of Thee to take charge of me, and to deign to look after me and those belonging to me. For I know, and have unfortunately only too often experienced, how things went with me and into what a miserable state I fell, whenever I used my freedom against Thy holy will. What would then become of me if Thou wert to allow me to act in

---

[1] Oculi Domini super justos, et aures ejus in preces eorum. Clamaverunt justi, et Dominus exaudivit eos.—Ps. xxxiii. 16, 18.

everything according to my own will? Oh, no, great God! Behold, I give myself to Thee body and soul, with everything I have in and outside myself! "Receive, O Lord, all my liberty,"[1] I beg of Thee in the words of my holy father Ignatius. It belongs already to Thee by countless titles. Make what use of me Thou wilt; place me where Thou wilt; rule and govern me and mine in the manner most pleasing to Thee. Do not consider whether Thy decree is agreeable to my sensuality and corrupt nature, or not; take not those things into account, but dispose of me as Thou wilt; my reasoning will shall always say what Thy beloved Son, my Saviour Jesus Christ, has taught me by word and example: "Not as I will, but as Thou wilt."[2] Not my will, but Thine be done; for Thou art my Creator, and I am Thy creature; Thou art my preserver, and I am in need of Thee at every moment; Thou art my Redeemer, and I am. so to speak, the slave Thou hast purchased; Thou art my sovereign Benefactor, and I am Thy debtor; Thou art the best, most perfect, most beautiful and infinite Good, whom I must honor and love with all my heart, whom, with Thy grace, I will honor and love with all my heart here on earth, and hereafter in heaven. Amen.

Another Introduction to the same sermon for the seventeenth Sunday after Pentecost.

Text.

Diliges Dominus Deum tuum ex toto corde tuo.—Matt. xxii. 37.
"Thou shalt love the Lord thy God with thy whole heart."

Introduction.

As I have often told you, to love God is to do what God wills and when, how, and because God wills, and to be satisfied with all the arrangements of God's providence. To love God with our whole hearts is to do and omit everything, without the least exception, that God wishes us to do and omit, and at the same time in all circumstances, whatever they may be, to be satisfied and content with the will of God. This is that most beautiful virtue which gives most honor to God, as I have already explained. Now, continuing the same subject, my dear brethren, even if God receives no honor thereby, it is nevertheless most just for us to conform our wills to His in all things; for He has

---

[1] Suscipe, Domine, universam meam libertatem.
[2] Non sicut ego volo, sed sicut tu.—Matt. xxvi. 39.

an infinite right to that conformity. And this is the subject of my sermon to-day, etc.—*Continues as above.*

FORTY-SEVENTH SERMON.

ON THE ADVANTAGE OF CONFORMITY WITH THE WILL OF GOD.

Subject.

To be always resigned to the will and decree of God is most prudent with regard to ourselves. 1st. Because we are thereby assured of our own advantage and consolation. 2d. Because thereby our sorrows and pains even in the greatest trials are lessened and sweetened.—*Preached on the feast of the Epiphany.*

Text.

Vidimus enim stellam ejus in oriente, et venimus adorare eum.—Matt. ii. 2.

"For we have seen His star in the East, and are come to adore Him."

Introduction.

In the three holy kings we have a perfect model of conformity with the will of God. And in the first place, how ready and eager they were to do the will of God! The mere sign of the new-born Saviour, which they had seen in the sky, was enough to make them set out at once to seek Him. The Patriarch Abraham showed indeed a similar obedience to God when he left his home and country to go into a strange land; but He did so at the express command of God: "And the Lord said to Abraham: Go forth out of thy country, and from thy kindred, and out of thy father's house, and come into the land which I shall show thee."[1] And God promised him a great blessing if he were obedient: "And I will make of thee a great nation, and I will bless thee, and magnify thy name, and thou shalt be blessed."[2] But these kings came at a mere sign from their Creator; the bare sight of the star was enough for them, without any promise. They required nothing more to induce them to leave their kingdoms, their homes, their repose and comfort, and to set

---

[1] Dixit autem Dominus ad Abraham: egredere de terra tua, et de cognatione tua, et de domo patris tui, et veni in terram quam monstrabo tibi.—Gen. xii. 1.

[2] Faciamque te in gentem magnam, et benedicam tibi, et magnificabo nomen tuum, erisque benedictus.—Ibid. 2.

out: "We have seen His star, and are come." Again, how cheerfully they submitted to the arrangement of divine Providence! They set out, and knew not whither. Their intention was to seek and adore the Saviour, but they had no idea of where they should find Him. They travelled on dangerous roads through unknown countries, and knew not what might happen to them. They were indeed comforted and consoled by the presence of the star that showed them the way; but after a time even that vanished from their sight by divine decree; so they were left in ignorance of where they had to go. Yet, as they were content with the will of God in all circumstances, they did not lose courage or grow faint-hearted. Their arrival was a source of great trouble to Herod and to the whole city of Jerusalem: "And king Herod, hearing this, was troubled, and all Jerusalem with him." But they were free from care and anxiety, firmly resolved not to give up the object of their journey, in spite of troubles, difficulties, and dangers, until they had found the new-born King of glory. With that resignation and determination of will they set out again: "And behold, the star which they had seen in the East went before them, until it came and stood over where the Child was;" and they entered full of joy, and in preference to many others had the happiness of seeing and adoring their incarnate God and Saviour. My dear brethren, are we thus ready and willing to do and omit at the least sign what God wishes us to do and omit? Are we just as contented and satisfied with the will of God in all circumstances, in spite of troubles, difficulties, and discomforts, as these holy kings were? Indeed, it would be only just and right that we should be always thus disposed towards our God, who, as we have seen in the last sermon, has by countless titles the right to expect that from us. Now, supposing that God did not require that of us, and that we were at liberty to upset His decrees and His providence, and to act according to our own fancies, even then it would be prudent and reasonable for us, if we seek our own consolation and advantage, to be always in conformity with the will of God; as I shall now show.

Plan of Discourse.

To be always and in all circumstances resigned to the will of God is most prudent with regard to ourselves; because we are thereby assured of our own advantage and consolation. This I

shall show in the first and longer part. Because thereby our sor-
rows and pains even in the greatest trials are lessened and sweet-
ened; as I shall show in the second part.

O merciful Saviour, who hast so wonderfully led, comforted,
and drawn to Thyself by a star the three holy kings, because
they were always resigned to Thy will, draw our hearts also to
Thee by the star of Thy grace, that we may be always in conformity with Thy holy will, and experience the great advantage
and consolation Thou givest to those who resign themselves
cheerfully to Thy decrees. This we ask of Thee through the intercession of Thy Mother Mary, and of our holy guardian angels.

When of two things I know not which is good or bad for me, *He who knows not which of two things is good for him acts well by leaving the choice to one who understands and wishes well to him.* then prudence requires me to leave the selection to some one
who knows more of the matter than I do, and who certainly has
the good will to direct me properly. With the choice of such a
friend I can be quite satisfied. Is not that the case, my dear
brethren? For instance, you go into a room in which there are
three packets lying on the table, one full of gold, the other of
lead, and the third of sand. They are indeed of different
colors, but still it is impossible for you to know what each packet contains. You are allowed to choose which you will; how are
you to make your choice? The first seems the most beautiful
and brilliant in color; but perhaps that is the one that is filled
with sand; and what better would you be for selecting it? There
you stand looking at them, but all your looking is of no avail.
Now, would you not be glad to have some one to tell you all
about it? I can do that; I know the contents of each packet,
and besides, I am a good friend of yours; I think that you would
willingly rely on a sign that I should give you, or a word that I
should speak to direct your choice, rather than run the risk of
making an irrevocable blunder by choosing for yourself. Or, to
speak more to the purpose, there are on the table many dishes
with various kinds of food; but the half of them are poisoned,
and you have no means of distinguishing them from the others.
Would you dare to stretch forth your hand and take one, and eat
of it? I imagine that you would not act so rashly, no matter
how savory the food, and you would prefer to wait till your host,
who is your good friend, comes in and tells you which dish you
can eat with safety. There is many a blind man who allows himself to be led about even by a dog. Why? Because he cannot
see, while the dog has good eyes, and is faithful to him. If he

happens to get into a marshy place, and cannot find his way out, would he not be glad if some one were to come and stretch forth his hand to help him? I think so.

We mortals do not know what is good or bad for us.

Since that is the case, then, my dear brethren, it is a prudent and sensible thing for us mortals to allow God to lead us on the road by which He wishes us to travel, to leave to Him all the care regarding ourselves and those belonging to us, and to be satisfied with, nay, to accept with cheerfulness, whatever He has decreed for us from eternity in all circumstances and occurrences. For what else are we but blind, ignorant mortals, who do not understand, especially in things that concern our souls, what is good or bad for us? " What needeth a man," asks the wise Preacher, " to seek things that are above him, whereas he knoweth not what is profitable for him in his life?" [1] We often stretch out both arms to grasp something we think to be gold, and in reality it is but a sack full of dust and ashes. We long for food that we imagine to be good for us, and when we swallow it, we find that we have brought death on our souls, because it is poisoned. We generally judge of things by their outward appearance only; but we have no idea of what may be hidden under that, nor of how they will turn out for us. What we have hitherto called good luck and prosperity is in truth misfortune and adversity; what we consider misfortune is often the very best thing that could happen to us, as far as our salvation is concerned.

We think that what pleases our senses is good ; but herein we are often deceived.

We are like one who is in a ship with no other idea than to enjoy the fresh air; he thinks every wind a fair one as long as it is mild and gentle, no matter in what direction it blows him; but if it blows him with violence into port, he is annoyed at it. But the sailor, whose whole idea is to get into port, understands the matter better; he calls that a foul and contrary wind which the other approves of, and wishes for the wind which the other so much objects to. So do we act, generally speaking. We give that the name and character of a good thing which seems pleasant and agreeable to our corrupt nature and sensuality; we shun and avoid as an evil what is opposed to it; but meanwhile we are ignorant of the end that the all-wise and all-ruling providence of God wishes to attain by His decrees in our regard. " This is the will of God," says St. Paul, " your sanctification." [2] The end

---

[1] Quid necesse est homini majora se quærere, cum ignorat quid conducat sibi in vita sua ?—Eccles. vii. 1.

[2] Hæc est voluntas Dei, sanctificatio vestra.—I. Thess. iv. 3.

that He has in view is to bring us all to the haven of salvation. But what is our will? Oh, we must not hesitate to acknowledge it! Our will is temporal wealth and riches; our will is the esteem and good opinion of the world: our will is our comfort, repose, health, pleasure, the delights of the body; to this are directed most of our thoughts, wishes, and desires; what is contrary to this will we look on as a misfortune, a calamity.

No, that alone is good and to be desired which helps us to our last end, the salvation of our soul, and not what flatters our senses; that alone is evil and bad for us which keeps us from that end and hurts the soul, not that which causes us pain and against which we have a natural repugnance. But how are we to know what that is? Ah, here we must acknowledge the weakness of our understanding, and humbly confess that we know nothing about it, that we are stone-blind in this respect. How many men have found the riches they so ardently desired to be deadly poison, which brought them eternal death, while the poverty they hated and shunned would have helped them to eternal life! How many are helped to preserve the health of their immortal souls and to avoid the dangers of sin by the bodily illness and weakness in which they sigh and moan, while the health they wish for would be the cause of their eternal ruin! How many have been brought to a knowledge of themselves, so that they now serve God with true humility, by a humiliation, disgrace, or persecution that seemed very hard for them to bear; who, if they had enjoyed the esteem of men, which they desired, and which seemed good to them, would have forgotten their God and been brought to eternal shame! How many have had their eyes opened, so that they now lead pious lives, by crosses and trials the very name of which filled them with dread and aversion, who, if they had the comfort and wealth they longed for, would have indulged in all kinds of vice, and would have lost their souls! In a word, he who now finds in the circumstances of his state of life a ladder by which he can ascend to heaven, provided he works earnestly with the grace of God, would in other circumstances, which he perhaps imagines to be better for him, fare badly, and be miserable for eternity.

Many have been helped to their greatest happiness by misfortune; many to their greatest misery by prosperity.

Was Naaman any worse for the hideous leprosy with which God had afflicted him? Yet he was full of impatience and disgust on account of it. But if he could have foreseen what a great advantage that very disease would bring him, not all his

Shown by examples from Scripture.

money, nor that of his Syrian king, would have seemed enough
to pay for it according to its value; for he not only regained his
bodily health, but also came to the knowledge of the true God
by means of his sickness. " In truth I know," said he with exultation to the Prophet Eliseus, after he had washed seven times
in the Jordan and come out clean, "there is no other God in all
the earth, but only in Israel." [1] What a desirable good was the
sickness of the palsied man in the Gospel of St. Matthew, who
on account of it heard from the lips of Our Lord Himself the
joyful words: " Be of good heart, son, thy sins are forgiven
thee "! [2] A hundred years of health would not have brought him
such happiness as that. On the other hand, would it not have
been a thousand times better for king Antiochus to have spent
his whole life sick in bed? for when he recovered the health he
prayed for so earnestly he fell into all sorts of vices and sins.
Hard, no doubt, and bitter must his public disgrace have been to
king Manasses, when his enemies brought him as a prisoner to
Babylon and cast him into a dungeon. But be satisfied, Manasses! Rejoice rather, instead of giving way to sadness; for that
prison, that disgrace, will bring you more glory than if you were
on the greatest throne on earth. Such indeed was the case with
him, for while in confinement he learned to know himself and
his God, and from being a monster of wickedness became a holy
man. " And after that he was in distress," says the Scripture,
"he prayed to the Lord his God; and did penance exceedingly
before the God of his fathers. And he repaired the altar of the
Lord, and sacrificed upon it victims, and peace offerings, and
praise; and he commanded Juda to serve the Lord, the God of
Israel." [3] And on the other hand the proud and haughty Aman
had never such cause for weeping as when he boasted of having
attained the very summit of his ambition, for not long after his
pride brought him to the gallows: " So Aman was hanged on
the gibbet; " [4] and lost his life and his soul together. Finally,
how many are there not who owe their good fortune and eternal
happiness to the loss of temporal goods, which we mortals make

---

[1] Vere scio quod non sit alius Deus in universa terrra, nisi tantum in Israel.—IV. Kings v. 15.

[2] Confide, fili, remittuntur tibi peccata tua ?—Matt. ix. 2.

[3] Qui postquam coangustatus est, oravit Dominum Deum suum, et egit poenitentiam val-de coram Deo patrum suorum. Porro instauravit altare Domini, et immolavit super illud victimas, et pacifica et laudem ; præcepitque Judæ ut serviret Domino Deo Israel—II. Paral. xxxiii. 12, 16.

[4] Suspensus est itaque Aman in patibulo.—Esth. vii. 10.

so much of! If the apostles had been rich, and not as poor as they were, they would never have been raised to such a high dignity by Our Lord, who always selects the lowliest and most abject. What happened to king Solomon? Into what an abyss of vice he fell through his abundance! "Solomon was unrivalled in prosperity," says St. Jerome, " and perhaps on that account he fell so lamentably."

Remarkable is the history of Eulogius, as related by Causinus. *Shown by an example.* He was a poor, lowly man, who lived among the rocks and caves of the mountains, and earned his bread by quarrying stones; but he was always resigned to the will of God and led a good and holy life. When he returned home to his poor hut after a hard day's work, he used to assemble all the beggars of the neighborhood and share with them the scanty wages he had earned during the day; and while at work he kept himself in constant union with God by prayer. In a word, Eulogius in his poverty and lowliness was a great saint and servant of God. Now it happened that a pious hermit named Daniel once shared his hospitality during the night; he was amazed at the great virtue and generosity of his host to the poor, and begged of God for three weeks to give the poor man something more of the goods of the world, that he might do more for the honor of God and for the poor. At last God heard his prayer. Eulogius, while engaged in his usual labor, found a great quantity of gold. He was thus made rich at once, but (alas, who would have thought it?) he was also changed in another way; he thought no more of prayer; he no longer knew the poor and needy, and did not give them a penny of the treasure he had found; all his thoughts were centred in his wealth, and he who was before so satisfied and happy in his poverty, was now filled with anxiety as to how he could keep his treasure from being stolen or demanded from him by his sovereign. For safety's sake, then, he went to Constantinople, to the court of the emperor, where by means of his gold he in a short time secured an honorable position; and forgetting his God, whom he had before served so well, nay, forgetful even of himself, he gave himself up to a life of vice. Daniel, hearing of this, and quite confused at the result of his imprudent prayer, went at once to Constantinople to see Eulogius, and exhorted him to give up his evil ways. How, said he, can you be so ungrateful to the good God who has gratuitously bestowed such good fortune on you? But all his preaching was of no avail, and he was driven away by blows. His only resource now was prayer. He threw himself on his knees, repented of the fault he had committed, and begged of God day and night with burning tears to bring back Eulogius to his former state, that his soul might not be lost forever. Oh, how wonderful the efficacy of the confident prayer of the just! Daniel was heard again. Eulogius fell into disgrace with the emperor, was deprived of his office, and being detected in a conspiracy against the emperor, had to fly for his life. And well for him, too, because he can now come to his senses. His money was gone; he had not a penny to buy a piece of bread. What was he to do? He had to go back to his hut, and take up his hammer and crowbar and earn his bread as before. And now, being poor again, he became as holy as he had been formerly. Such are the fruits of desiring another state instead of that to which God has called us. And so, too, the loss of temporal goods is often for our greater advantage, much as we may deplore that loss; and the disgrace we so dread, the humiliation before the world, the lowly, poverty-stricken state in which we weep and moan, are all for the good of our souls, while temporal prosperity is often nothing else but deadly poison for our souls. In a word, we know not what is good or bad for our salvation.

Hence it is for our advantage to allow God to do with us as He pleases; for He knows what is best for us, and wishes well to us.

Since that is the case, how comes it that we blind mortals have such a disgust for the one thing, and such a longing for the other; that we dolefully complain of the one, while we rejoice at the other, although we do not understand which of the two is conducive to our eternal welfare? Does not prudence, then, require us to submit completely to the divine will, and to allow God's providence to dispose of us as He wishes? Nay, should we not earnestly beg of God to call us to that state, with all its circumstances, which He knows to be good for us, and accept everything from His hand, with full resignation to all His decrees? It is God, and God alone, who knows for certain, and has known from all eternity, what is useful or injurious at all times, in all circumstances; He is at the same time our best friend, on whom we can safely rely; all that He seeks is our salvation, and He is more anxious about it than we are; He will arange everything for our good, provided we are satisfied with Him and resign ourselves into His hands with child-like confidence. Nor does this require much proof. God is our Father, our Saviour, our Spouse, our Brother, our supreme Good, as He says Himself, and

He has frequently promised that all shall turn out for the good of the just. " And we know that to them that love God," says St. Paul, "all things work together unto good." [1] This alone should suffice to keep us in constant quiet and contentment, caring for nothing unless the perfect fulfilment of His holy will in all things.

How unwise, then, for us to complain when we think that things are not going well with us, or that we are unfortunate? We act like the peasant of whom Elianus tells us; he was cutting wood with some others, and had gone with his pitcher to fetch water from a spring, when, looking down, he saw in the water an eagle entangled in the coils of a serpent. Taking his axe, he cut the serpent in pieces, and the eagle, being thus freed, flew away. He returned to his companions with the water, and they all quenched their thirst; but when he himself was about to do the same, the eagle, by divine permission, flew at him, and striking the pitcher, broke it, so that the water was spilled. The peasant, in a rage, began to abuse the eagle; you ungrateful bird, he exclaimed; is that the treatment I have deserved from you? I have saved your life, and now you will not allow me to take a drink of water? But his anger did not last long, and his abuse was soon changed into thanksgiving, for all his comrades, who had drunk of the water, fell dead on the spot; thus he learned that what he looked on as an injury was in reality a benefit for him. My dear brethren, if we only knew, when we are visited by poverty, sickness, humiliations, crosses, and trials, how well God means with us in depriving us of the goods we desire, which are in reality a deadly poison for our souls, as many have found to their cost, instead of complaining and giving way to impatience, we should rather thank divine Providence for being so good to us, and be always satisfied with what God ordains, rejoicing even in our hearts that things do not go as we wish and according to the cravings of our sensuality and corrupt nature, but rather according to the good will and pleasure of the God of infinite goodness and wisdom, who loves us so much.

We complain without reason when we think things go wrong. Shown by an example after the manner of a simile.

Nay, since we do not know what is good or bad for our spiritual welfare, and since God alone knows it with certainty, we should be afraid to ask anything of Him absolutely that concerns our temporal welfare or bodily comfort, as I have shown on another occasion; and if the Lord gives us our will in any such matter, we

Hence in all things we should be resigned to the will of God, like pious Christians.

[1] Scimus autem quoniam diligentibus Deum omnia cooperantur in bonum. ·Rom. viii. 28.

should fear lest our choice be not the right one. Far safer for us would it be to confine ourselves to the humble prayer of Our Lord, "Not as I will, but as Thou wilt."[1] Such was the way in which St. Pardulph acted; he was stone-blind, and all the blind people in the country used to come to him to be cured; but he never uttered a syllable of a prayer to God that he himself might recover his sight; all he said was: As far as I am concerned, O Lord, may Thy will be done. Equally resigned and contented with the will of God was St. Francis Borgia of our Society; while still in the world as Duke of Gandia, his wife became dangerously ill, and God allowed him to choose whether she should be restored to health or not. My Lord and my God, sighed Francis with a sorrowful heart, why dost Thou act so with me? What fault have I committed, that Thou shouldst now leave to my choice that which depends altogether on Thy will? No, dear Lord, I have nothing to say; my desire is to do Thy holy will in all things; for who knows better what is good for me than Thou, my God? Let it be, then, as Thou pleasest; ordain and decree, not only with regard to my wife, but for me and my children, whatever is most pleasing to Thee. The only thing I ask of Thee is that Thy holy will be done. Simple apparently, but in reality well-meant and sensible, was the prayer that another pious servant of God used to say daily; every day he said the A B C, letter by letter. What was his object in doing so? Behold, he said, my Lord and my God, with these letters every word is made; all I have to ask of Thee is Thy grace and friendship, for I know not what is good or bad for me. Do Thou now put the letters together; spell with them poverty, riches, sickness, health, annoyance, comfort, shame, the esteem of others, persecution, repose, death, life; and give me then a sign that I may know which of them Thou wishest me to take; with that I will be satisfied. O Christians, what a beautiful prayer! Let us at all events have those dispositions in our hearts, and in all circumstances and occurrences say or think what Our Lord said to His heavenly Father, "Yea, Father, for so hath it seemed good in Thy sight."[2] With that prayer, that thought, that resignation to the will of God, we can be certain that things will always go well with us, and, moreover, that our pains and sorrows in adversity and trials will be much lessened and sweetened, as we shall see briefly in the second part.

[1] Non sicut ego volo, sed sicut tu.—Matt. xxvi. 39.

[2] Ita Pater, quoniam sic fuit placitum ante te.— Ibid. xi. 26.

Second Part.

Let no one imagine that the thought, It is the will of God, and complete resignation to that holy will, can make our weak nature utterly insensible to all crosses and annoyances, so that our flesh and senses feel no pain or sorrow. No, we are not angels, nor stocks or stones; we are and remain weak mortals. Even Our Lord Jesus Christ, although He was in perfect conformity with the will of His heavenly Father, and was fully satisfied with all His decrees, yet felt the thorns and scourges, the nails and other torments of His Passion, as He showed clearly enough by the anguish caused Him in the garden at the mere thought of them. We feel, then, the pressure of adversity, although we are resigned to the will of God, that is true; but what I mean is that by resigning ourselves to the will of God we mitigate and lessen in great part the pain we feel; for, as the poet says, "the burden that is willingly borne becomes light,"[1] although in itself it may be heavy enough. The reason of this is that, when we feel pain, there are two parts of our nature affected by it. There is the outward agony felt by the flesh and the body; and still worse than that, there is the inward opposition of the will, which objects to that pain, and is uneasy under the infliction, which it tries to get rid of. Thus the flesh is made to suffer, and at the same time the will and the mind. Now, if the will ceases to oppose, and submits to the suffering, it is freed from pain, and there is less to suffer than when one is tormented in both parts. Is not that the case, my dear brethren? Truly, there cannot be a doubt of it.

He who suffers willingly feels less pain than he who suffers unwillingly and impatiently.

For instance, there is a pious man, who imposes on himself a week's fast as a penance; there is also a criminal, who, being in prison, has nothing but bread and water to eat for a week. The latter does nothing all day but sigh and moan, and swear and curse, and long and wish: Ah, if I had only made my escape sooner, the officers of justice would not have caught me, and I could at least have a bit of meat with my bread, etc. The other is quite satisfied with his fasting. Which of the two suffers the most? The criminal, of course, because he is forced to fast against his will. But the penance and mortification is the same in both cases. Both have to be satisfied with bread and water. No matter; the first performs his penance willingly, while the other is tormented by his will, which is opposed to it. In the same

Confirmed by experience.

---

[1] Leve fit, quod bene fertur onus.

way, a single blow given by a stranger out of anger or treachery, against one's will, hurts far more than ten blows that a servant of God gives himself through zeal for the divine honor, or to gain the souls of others, or to atone for his sins, no matter how severely he may scourge himself. The bitter or insipid medicine that one takes at the doctor's orders sometimes occasions less disgust than burnt or ill-cooked vegetables that are sent to table by a careless cook. All that is natural enough; "the burden that is willingly borne becomes light."

Hence he who is not resigned to God's will has a two-fold torment to suffer. There you have, my dear brethren, in a few words the effect of the resignation and conformity of the human will with the will of God in crosses and trials; it takes away that which causes the most pain, namely, the opposition and uneasiness of the will; for the latter peacefully submits to the divine decrees, and always thinks and says: "Yea, Father, for so hath it seemed good in Thy sight;" may Thy will be done; while another man, who does not think of this, but gives way to anger and impatience in adversity, has a twofold torment to suffer: one from the trial itself, and the other from his obstinate, dissatisfied will. And what good does he derive in the end from his anger and impatience? Is he freed from the cross that annoys him sooner than he who bears his trial with patience and resignation? No, indeed; his sufferings are rather protracted thereby. The sick man tosses and tumbles about in bed, and moans and sighs; is he any better for that? Will he get well the quicker? Not by any means; his sickness will rather be increased by his discontent and restlessness. The poor laborer or tradesman, in a fit of desperation, throws his hammer or axe behind the door; does that enable him to support his family better? No, for his earnings will become less, and he will end by being a beggar. One who has suffered a great loss by misfortune sits down and tears his hair, and gives way to the most passionate grief; will he thus be able to recover what he has lost? Not by any means; his conduct will not bring good luck into the house, and his murmuring and obstinacy will only unfit him for business, while he has, moreover, to bewail the loss of the hair he has pulled out in his bad temper. A wife has much to suffer from her husband; when he comes home drunk, he often beats her and treats her most cruelly; but she never bestows a thought on the divine will; she cries and screams, and curses and swears, and scratches and bites her husband. What does she gain by it all? Nothing but sore bones. And

I could have told her as much beforehand, for if she had been patient the blows would not have been half so severe. A man has been injured and insulted by his neighbor; he curses and swears and abuses him in all the moods and tenses. Has he thereby got back his good name? No, indeed; he has rather injured himself still more in the opinion of all decent people, who cannot look on one who behaves in that manner as a good Christian. Some people give way to excessive grief at the premature death of a dear friend, and weep day and night (there is nothing to be said against that, and such tears can well consist with patience and interior resignation to the will of God, as I have shown on another occasion); but they do not think of God, and become quite melancholy and misanthropic through grief, refusing to hear a word of consolation. Will they thus be able to restore the dead to life? Ah, they might cry and moan a long time before doing that; their friend is dead, and they are shortening their lives by their immoderate grief, so that they may expect to die before their time. Thus these people have acted in such a manner as to give the almighty God good reason for punishing them by fresh calamities, because they are not obedient children, but rebellious slaves.

If all these and many more like them had only made use of their right reason, and summoned their faith to help them; had they bestowed more attention on the truths of their religion, and considered that the death, the injury, the trouble, the loss, comes from the hands of God, that it is according to His will they now suffer and are tormented, and with that thought resigned themselves to the divine will, saying; "Yea, Father, for so hath it seemed good in Thy sight," what would they have gained then? First, they would have been freed from the suffering caused them by their own obstinate wills, their uneasiness and discontent, which made their crosses all the heavier. Secondly, in the midst of their sorrows they could at least have had the consolation from heaven that arises from the thought: I am now an instrument that the providence of God uses to fulfil His will; I am now suffering what God wills and because God wills. I am now furthering the honor and glory of my sovereign God, since I resigned myself to His will. I am now earning eternal joy and glory for myself in heaven. I am now showing that I am a dear friend and child of God, who as my loving father chastises me for my own good. Now I am taking on myself a share of

While he who is resigned receives great consolation and alleviation in his sufferings.

the sufferings of my crucified Saviour; and so on. O Christians, think of this, and see for yourselves whether such heavenly comfort cannot alleviate and sweeten and lessen even the greatest torments! Now prudence requires us to choose the lesser of two evils, and there is no doubt that the grief in which one has some consolation is far less than one in which consolation is altogether wanting, not to speak at all of suffering in such a way as to bring upon one's self perhaps eternal torments in the next life.

Conclusion and resolution to be always resigned to God's will.

Let us, then, my dear brethren, bear with patience, willingness, and readiness the daily cross that God lays on us, which we must bear in any case, whether we will or not; for God is not to be put out of His way by our opposition. Let us be contented in all circumstances, to our own great advantage, to God's honor and glory, to the great alleviation of our sufferings, to the comfort of our souls; for if we are not contented, we must still suffer the same trials, to our great harm and loss of merit, to the lessening of the divine honor, to the useless trouble of our own minds, to the increasing of our torments, without finding any consolation either from God or in ourselves; therefore let us always say with resignation: " Yea, Father, for so hath it seemed good in Thy sight." Thou knowest what is good for me; let Thy holy will be done in me! " Give me what Thou wilt, and as much as Thou wilt, and when Thou wilt," as Thomas à Kempis says; " place me where Thou wilt, and act freely with me in all things; for behold, I am Thy servant, prepared for everything," according to Thy holy will. Amen.

Another Introduction to the same sermon for the sixteenth Sunday after Pentecost.

Text.

Ipse vero apprehensum sanavit eum.—Luke xiv. 4.
" But He taking him, healed him."

Introduction.

Why did Our Lord heal this dropsical man by the mere touch of His hand? The man had asked nothing of Him, for the Gospel merely says: " Behold, there was a certain man before Him, that had the dropsy;" he simply placed himself before Christ as if to show himself and to say: Here I am, O Lord! Thou knowest what is the matter with me; a word from Thee will be enough to heal me. In my opinion, my dear brethren, it was the silence of the man that moved Our Lord to restore him to health before being asked. Mary and Martha acted in the same way when their brother Lazarus lay dangerously ill. They sent to Christ this message; "Behold, he whom Thou lovest is sick."[1] We know well that Thou art the Lord from whose hands must come sickness and health, life and death. It is enough for us that Thou knowest how it is with our brother; if Thou wilt restore him to health, we shall rejoice; if Thou wilt allow him to continue in his illness, we shall be satisfied. Ah, my dear brethren, if we were all thus resigned to the will of God, so that in all the accidents and changes of life we merely show ourselves to the Lord God, who is present in all places, and say to Him: Thou knowest, O Lord, how it is with me; I am poor; I am sick; I am desolate; I am in trouble; I am heavily burdened by this or that cross; Thou canst help me if Thou wilt; but if Thou wilt not, may Thy holy will be done! what honor and glory we should give to God thereby, an honor He expects from us with the greatest right founded on countless titles, as I have already explained.—*Continues as above.*

FORTY-EIGHTH SERMON.

ON CONFORMITY WITH THE WILL OF GOD IN ADVERSITY.

Subject.

This thought, It is the will of God, should suffice to enable us to bear every stroke of adversity 1. with patience; nay, 2. with joy.—*Preached on the feast of St. Joseph, Spouse of the Blessed Virgin.*

Text.

Joseph autem, vir ejus, cum esset justus.—Matt. i. 19.
"Joseph, her husband, being a just man."

Introduction.

The Wise Man says of the just servants of God: "Whatsoever shall befall the just man, it shall not make him sad."[2] Such a just man was Joseph, the foster-father of Our Lord Jesus Christ, the chaste spouse of the ever blessed Virgin Mary, and the chosen

---

[1] Ecce, quem amas infirmatur.—John xi. 3.
[2] Non contristabit justum quidquid ei acciderit.—Prov. xii. 21.

patron of our land of Treves: "Joseph, her husband, being a just man." The Lord God, who generally mingles sorrow with joy even for His just servants on earth, did not spare the foster-father of His Son. I will say nothing now of the lowly state, contemptible in the eyes of the world, in which Joseph lived; for he had to earn his bread as a poor tradesman, although he was of royal descent. And yet he was contented in his poverty, even before he had the consolation of seeing his Saviour. Was it not a hard and bitter trial for him, tossed about as he was by fear and hope, by love and sorrow, to have to think of putting away from him his beloved spouse Mary? And yet, as St. Jerome says, even under those circumstances Joseph formed no evil suspicions of the Blessed Virgin, but resigned himself at once without further investigation to the providence of God. Was it not a hard and bitter thing for him, when the Blessed Virgin was on the point of bringing forth Our Lord, to be turned away from all the inns at Bethlehem in the cold winter time, so that he was compelled to find shelter in a stable open to the four winds of heaven, where there was neither chair, nor bed, nor fire? But such was the will of God, and Joseph was satisfied therewith. Was it not a hard thing for him, a wonderful act of resignation, to rise in the middle of the night at the command of the angel, and fly with Mary and the Child into the strange and unknown land of Egypt? Nevertheless he set out at once without a murmur, because such was the will of God. Was it not a hard thing for him to lose his beloved Son in Jerusalem for three days? Was it not hard for him to die, and to be separated from the society of Jesus and Mary, and to descend into Limbo? But the fact that all these things were ordained by God was enough to make Joseph submit to them with the utmost resignation, nay, even joy. Sorrowful and oppressed Christians, who sigh and groan under the pleasure of adversity, how well would it be for you if like St. Joseph you always thought to yourselves: This is the will of God; this sickness, this poverty, this death, this misfortune, this trouble comes from God! Then you would find relief in the greatest troubles, and would be resigned to God's will with patience, nay, even with joy, in all circumstances, as I shall now show to the consolation of all who are in trouble.

Plan of Discourse.

This thought, It is the will of God, should in itself suffice to enable us to bear every stroke of adversity with patience, as I shall show in the first part. This thought, It is the will of God, should in itself suffice to enable us to bear every stroke of adversity with joy, as I shall show in the second part.

Heavenly Father, it is pleasing to Thee that we should do Thy will in all things; let it then be pleasing to Thee now (we beg this of Thee through the intercession of the Mother of Thy Son, of His foster-father, and of our holy guardian angels) to give us Thy powerful grace, that in all circumstances and misfortunes we may think and say with patient, joyful hearts, " Thy will be done."

There is a certain well-known game amongst children that I *God plays with us when He visits us with trials; shown by a simile.* am sure we all played when we were young, and it consists in this: one who is counted off for the purpose lays his head in the lap of another, having his eyes blindfolded, so that he can see nothing of what is going on around him; he then puts his hand on his back, palm upwards, and another child strikes it, when the first has to guess who it was that struck him; he gets up and looks around; ha, he exclaims, it was you! No, says the other; you are wrong; down with you again. And again a blow is given on the hand. Again the child starts up; now I have you, he cries; I know your hand! Wrong again; down with you once more! And so the game goes on until the child guesses the one who struck him, when he is released. It seems to me, my dear brethren, that the almighty God plays a game of that sort with us when He visits us with trials and crosses in this life. And He Himself says, speaking of His wisdom and providence: " I was delighted every day playing before him at all times, playing in the world; and My delight is to be with the children of men. Now, therefore, ye children, hear Me: hear instruction, and be wise, and refuse it not." [1] This game is carried on in order, as we daily experience. To-day one gets the blow; to-morrow, another; one is hit a little harder; but there are few who have not something to bear, because there is hardly one in the world who has not some cross, or trouble, or trial to put up with. Many, who find the blow too hard, as they think, have tearful eyes and sad hearts; but God finds pleasure therein, not indeed because they are afflicted, but because, as He foresees, the blow will do good for their souls, and will make them zealous in His service,

---

[1] Delectabar per singulos dies, ludens coram eo omni tempore, et deliciæ meæ esse cum filiis hominum ; nunc ergo, filii, audite me ; audite disciplinam, et estote sapientes, et nolite abjicere eam.—Prov. viii. 30-33.

so that they will go to heaven and rejoice with Him for all eternity.

We are dissatisfied with them because we forget they come from God. Many act like the children in the game I have mentioned, who think they have been hit too hard, or that they have had to remain blind-folded for too long a time; they begin to murmur and complain, to abuse, and quarrel, and strike back, and that they do because they are not able to guess the hand that struck them. And truly, all our uneasiness and discontent, our impatience and unwillingness, our murmurs and complaints, our want of courage and our despair in our daily crosses, come almost entirely from the fact that we do not acknowledge, or at least do not recollect with a lively faith, whose hand it is that strikes us and sends us misfortunes. We are ignorant and inexperienced in what concerns the principal truths of our religion, or our evil inclinations blind the eyes of our understanding, so that we do not recognize the Author of our sorrows; thus we generally lay the blame on the wrong person, on creatures and on chance, although such things are mere instruments that an invisible hand makes use of to strike and chastise us. Therefore we are impatient and discontented; and we make our troubles worse, instead of finding relief or consolation.

And lay the blame on creatures. For instance, one is stricken in his worldly goods; he loses money or money's worth, and almost goes out of his mind with grief. Now, who has done that? Guess. Thieves and robbers have done it, by taking away my money. No, my good friend, you are wrong! Down with you again; you must remain in trouble without any consolation! Business gets bad; the income grows less every day, and poverty is at the door. Guess now, who did that? My debtor, who has become bankrupt, did it. No, you are wrong, try again. Then the lawsuit that I have lost through injustice, because the judge was bribed by my opponent, is to blame for my misfortune. No; wrong again. Then it was the bad season, the cold winter, the dry summer, that ruined my fields and vineyards, so that for some years nothing has grown in them. O nonsense! if you cannot make a better attempt than that you will never find out, and you will get no relief in your trouble and sorrow. If you had said: The blow comes from my extravagance in dress, from my prodigality, from my idleness, then you would have been somewhat nearer the mark, although you would not have quite hit it; for there is another cause at work, which has sent those trials to you on account of your prodigality, extravagance in dress, or idleness. Another is smitten in his honor and good name. He feels the blow and gives way to anger and discontent. But wait a moment; think first who it is that has struck you. That enemy of mine is to blame; he cannot bear the sight of me; I know the fellow well; he is capable of anything, and has run me down and blackened my character, that I may lose my position. Those talkative scandal-mongers have been at work behind my back; they have put the worst construction on my actions, and thus taken away my good name; but they will suffer for it one day or other. But what are you saying? You are quite wrong. It is another hand that has struck you, and until you guess who it is you will have to bear the full brunt of your trouble; there will be no help for you; you will go on cursing and swearing and make yourself worse instead of better. A third is smitten in his bodily health; a toothache, or headache, or fever attacks him. Guess now where the blow comes from. From heat; from cold; from unhealthy fasting fare; from rain and wind; from trouble and anxiety. If I had kept in out of the cold air; if I had been allowed to eat meat; if that person had not provoked me to anger, so that I got into a violent passion, I should be all right now. No, no; that is a very bad guess of yours; if you cannot make a better one than that, you will find no consolation in your troubles. A fourth is smitten in the affections; he is deprived of some dear friend; father or mother or pet child is taken from him by death. Alas, what an overwhelming sorrow! he thinks. But after all, who has struck the blow? Merciless death has done it; that illness that was not looked to in time, that doctor, who did not understand his patient's constitution, is to blame. No, you must guess better than that, or you will find no comfort in your sorrow, and your weeping and wailing will not help you. Another is stricken daily in his soul with bitterness, sorrow, trouble, despair almost, on account of his daily crosses; there is no end to his moanings and lamentations. Look around you now, and see who is the cause. That ill-tempered, cross-grained husband; that peevish, quarrelsome wife; that unruly child; those unfaithful servants; that troublesome neighbor; that perjured, false friend. Oh, no, you are quite wrong; that is not the hand that has struck you; you must rise higher in your thoughts, or else you will have a hell on earth, without comfort, merit, or alleviation. Well, then, since nothing else is to blame, it must be the devil who sends these misfortunes to me; they are the result of magic, of the black art, etc. Oh, poor wretches that we are, how great is our blindness! We go wrong at the very start, and that is the reason why we are still impatient and discontented.

It is God alone who sends us crosses, as Job well knew.

I admit that those creatures are the immediate instruments from which our crosses come; but, I repeat, it is a far different hand that uses them to strike us with. Let us try to learn a lesson from Job; he knew at the first blow he got whose hand it came from. "The hand of the Lord hath touched me," he says. [1] Mark those words, my dear brethren; it is the hand of the Lord that has struck me, I know and feel it well. And how hard it struck him! He was, as the Scripture says, one of the richest and greatest men of the East: "This man was great among all the people of the East." [2] Besides landed and other property, he owned "seven thousand sheep, and three thousand camels, and five hundred yoke of oxen, and five hundred she-asses, and a family exceeding great." [3] One day there came to him messenger after messenger to tell him with tearful eyes that all his cattle were taken away, his house burnt to the ground, his servants slain, so that in a moment he was reduced to the utmost poverty, and had nothing left him out of all his wealth but a noisome dunghill. Truly, that was a severe blow! Unhappy Job, who was it that struck thee? Was it not the Sabeans, the Chaldeans, who plundered thy property and slew thy dependents? Such was the report brought by the messengers. But no, Job made a better guess: "The Lord hath taken away." [4] Another came to announce to him a still severer blow: all his dear children, seven sons and three daughters, were carried off in one day by death, not after a long illness, nor through old age, nor in the presence of their father, but they were buried in the ruins of their house that fell in on them. Afflicted father, what was the cause of that terrible calamity? Was it not the hurricane that threw down the house in which thy children were? No, "The Lord hath taken away" my children from me. Nor were his misfortunes yet at an end, for, as the Scripture says, he was smitten with a most grievous ulcer, so that there was not a sound place in him from the crown of his head to the sole of his foot, and

[1] Manus Domini tetigit me.—Job xix. 21.
[2] Eratque vir ille magnus inter omnes orientales.—Ibid. i. 3.
[3] Et fuit possessio ejus septem millia ovium, et tria millia camelorum, quingenta quoque juga boum, et quingentæ asinæ, ac familia multa nimis.—Ibid.
[4] Dominus abstulit.—Ibid. 21.

forced by the intolerable pain and stench, he had to take refuge on a dung-hill, where he scraped the corrupt matter off his body with potsherd. [1] Miserable man, who afflicted thee thus grievously? Was it not the evil one? No; I know well who did it. "The hand of the Lord hath touched me." His misery was increased by the mockery and abuse and contumely of wicked tongues. Truly, a heart-breaking affliction! Unhappy Job, who is the cause of it? Is it not thy own relations, thy wife even? No; no matter where the blow comes from, there is one thing I am certain of; it is the Lord who has ordained it for me: "The hand of the Lord hath touched me;" it is He who thus chastises me. Excellent guess!

O my dear brethren, if we turned our thoughts in the same direction in adversity, what great consolation we should find for our souls! It is an undoubted truth, which I shall not now delay to prove, that all trials, whatever may be their name, have their origin in the hands and all-wise arrangements of the almighty God. If we only remembered this with a lively faith, we should soon find relief. But, you exclaim, what good will it do me to remember it? Will that free me from the trial, just as the child who guesses the name of the person who struck him in the game is allowed to get up? Yes, it will; for at all events that thought will encourage you to overcome impatience, and will alleviate your pain in great part by making you suffer contentedly. Mark the effect that thought had on Job: "The Lord hath taken away;" "the hand of the Lord hath touched me." Then I am satisfied; I have nothing to say against it: "In all of these things Job sinned not by his lips, nor spoke he any foolish thing against God." [2] All he did during his severe trials was to praise and bless God: "The Lord gave and the Lord hath taken away; as it hath pleased the Lord, so is it done; blessed be the name of the Lord." [3] Nay, he even said to his wife, when she was mocking him: "If we have received good things at the hand of God, why should we not receive evil?" [4] If I have been so richly endowed to my great joy and satisfaction by the generous hand of God, why should I not with equal satisfaction receive evil from the same hand? This thought, my dear

If we thought of that, we should be patient and contented under trials.

---

[1] Qui testa saniem radebat sedens in sterquilinio.—Job ii. 8.

[2] In omnibus his non peccavit Job labiis suis, neque stultum quid contra Deum locutus est.—Ibid. i. 22.

[3] Dominus dedit; Dominus abstulit; sicut Domino placuit, ita factum est; sit nomen Domini benedictum.—Ibid. 21.

[4] Si bona suscepimus de manu Dei, mala quare non suscipiamus?—Ibid. ii. 10.

brethren, should cause the same feeling of satisfaction to us in all adverse circumstances; for if I remember with a lively faith that it is God who sends me this cross; that it is the hand of the Lord that now torments and afflicts me; that it is the will of God for me now to suffer this trial; oh, then I must acknowledge that it is a good, holy, and just thing for me to suffer, and that nothing can be holier, better, or more just than what God does to me or ordains for me, although I may not know the reason why He acts thus in my regard. "If we do not understand why the thing happens," says St. Augustine, "let us leave it in the hands of His providence, because it is not done without reason." [1] Does not faith teach you, O man, exclaims St. John Chrysostom, that the Lord God has a care of even the least of His creatures; that nothing happens without His will and permission; that He has a most weighty reason for everything He does; that He loves you, especially if you are in the state of grace, with a love far surpassing that of the father and mother for their only child? What more do you want then, to content you, no matter how things go with you? "You need not go further than this; this one thought should suffice to console you." [2]

And should I not receive at all events with patience and contentment a blow from the hand that was pierced with a nail for my sake, and fastened to the cross? Should I give way to discontent and murmuring against a God who, as I know for certain, means well with me, and ordains not even the least thing for me that He knows not to be for my good? Do we not often see with our own eyes how readily and willingly the sick man, who is anxious to regain his health, gives himself up to the hands of the doctor, whom he allows to torture and plague him in every conceivable way? Food and drink, for which he has the greatest desire, are forbidden him, and the sick man overcomes himself and abstains; the bitterest and most insipid pills are prescribed for him; he shuts his eyes and swallows them, although the taste of them provokes the utmost disgust in him, and he knows not of what they are made. If he has to be bled, he stretches out his arm, and allows himself to be cut and burnt; and although the intolerable pain causes him to cry out, so that he can be heard in the next house, he bears it without a word of

And should receive them willingly from such a loving God.

---

[1] Si non intelligamus quare quid fit, demus hoc providentiae ipsius, quia non est sine causa.

[2] Nihil igitur ultra pervestiges ; etenim ad consolationem hæc tibi sufficiunt.

complaint against him who is the cause of it; nay, he gives him money for torturing him. Why? Because such are the commands of the doctor, and the sick man thinks they must be good for him, so he is satisfied, although the doctor is a man who can err in his ideas of curing illnesses, and as a matter of fact has often erred in them. And we hesitate to repose that much confidence in the God of infinite wisdom, who cannot err in His decrees, and who is most desirous of our salvation; who gave His sweat and blood to provide us with a wholesome remedy for our souls? Shall we resist Him, and refuse to be satisfied with His will in all things, although He may sometimes hit us rather hard? No! I repeat with St. Chrysostom, " you need not go further than this; this one thought should suffice to console you," it is the will of God; this blow comes from the hands of God; that one thought should be more than enough to make you patient and satisfied in your sufferings. Say, then, whenever the cross weighs heavily on you, as the Prophet David said, " I was dumb and I opened not my mouth, because Thou hast done it." [1] I will be silent and not say a word of complaint, much less will I murmur, because Thou hast done it, because Thou hast so ordained it. This trouble, pain, misfortune, poverty, disgrace, annoyance that I have to suffer from this or that person are hard blows; they hurt me; but I know the hand they come from; it is Thine, O Lord. " Yea, Father, for so hath it seemed good in Thy sight." [2] I am contented; everything Thou dost to me is right, holy, and just. That is the way, my dear brethren, to bear one's cross with patience, and that patience comes from the thought, Such is the will of God. The same thought is, moreover, reason enough for us to bear all our crosses and trials even with joy and pleasure, as we shall see in the

Second Part.

What? you exclaim; to bear adversity with joy and pleasure? Can I, then, feel pain and joy at the same time? Can I be troubled and at the same time pleased? Can I weep for sorrow, and laugh with joy? No, that cannot be, or else it must be the result of a trick, like that of those comedians, who laugh on one side of their face while they cry on the other; and in that case one of the two feelings is not real. No, my dear brethren, I do not

Joy in suffering consists in peace and contentment of mind.

[1] Obmutui et non aperui os meum, quoniam tu fecisti.—Ps. xxxviii. 10.
[2] Ita, Pater, quoniam sic fuit placitum ante te.—Matt. xi. 26.

mean that we can laugh and enjoy ourselves in adversity, pain, and suffering, although some of the martyrs of Christ did so, even in the midst of their torments; but that grace is not given to all. Still I say that we can bear trials with joy. "Do you think," says the philosopher Seneca, "that laughter and enjoyment are one and the same thing?"[1] Or that he alone is joyful who opens his mouth to laugh, and that all who weep are sad? Oh, no, if such are your ideas, they are very often completely wrong. Many a one puts on a cheerful countenance, while his heart is oppressed with sorrow and anxiety. Many a one weeps at a funeral for outward appearance' sake, and yet he is rejoiced at heart to be freed from a burden, or to come in for a good legacy. The joy of which I speak, and that St. Paul experienced when he wrote to the Corinthians ("I am filled with comfort, I exceedingly abound with joy in all our tribulation."[2]),—that joy, I say, is a joy without laughter, which can exist with the bitterest tears; a joy that is not felt by the body, but that consists in the imperturbable repose and contentment of the mind. Let the body and the imagination suffer as much as they will; let the heart be filled with sorrow; still the mind can remain undisturbed and quiet in the midst of it all. And that is the right way to rejoice; that is the joy promised by Our Lord to His faithful servants, when He says: "Take up My yoke upon you, and learn of Me, because I am meek and humble of heart; and you shall find rest to your souls."[3] Mark those words; He says: you will find rest, not for your bodies, but to your souls.

Although our natural inclinations are thwarted and disturbed.

No, suffering Christians, I cannot take away your sorrow from you, nor forbid you to weep, when the hard blow is given you at which nature is forced to cry out. Suppose your beloved husband or dear child dies; or you suffer great loss in your temporal affairs; or your husband is a drunkard, and ill-treats you (and there are wretches wicked enough to do that, and to maltreat the wives whom they should love next to God and heavenly things, and to act towards them as if they were servants or even worthless rags); in such circumstances I cannot be so hard as to find fault with you for shedding tears or feeling pain; much less would I advise you to laugh or give outward signs of pleasure.

---

[1] Nisi forte judicas illum gaudere, qui ridet?

[2] Repletus sum consolatione, superabundo gaudio in omni tribulatione nostra.—II. Cor. vii. 4.

[3] Tollite jugum meum super vos, et discite a me, quia mitis sum et humilis corde; et invenietis requiem animabus vestris.—Matt. xi. 29.

By no means; weep and be sorrowful, and sigh without fear; your heart can and does feel the weight of affliction, the trouble you are in forces you to weep and sigh; but impatience does not consist in that, as some imagine; otherwise Christ, the Son of God, would have given way to impatience in the garden of Gethsemani and on the cross on Calvary (and we could not think that without blasphemy); for in His trouble and grief He sweated blood and complained to His heavenly Father. You can, I say, feel the anguish and sorrow; but let your mind, that is, the reasonable judgment of your will, be undisturbed and composed, and in that way rejoice that you are suffering pain, that you are sorrowful, that you weep and moan.

That spiritual repose and joy you may have if you remind yourself earnestly that the blow comes from God, that it is the will of God, and with that certainty say resignedly, "Yea, Father, for so hath it seemed good in Thy sight." Thou wilt that I should now be afflicted; yea, Father, be it so, since it is pleasing to Thee. Thou hast appointed this cross for me in this hour, and wilt that I should now sigh and moan; therefore I will sigh and moan, since such is Thy will. I desire nothing else but what Thou wilt, and therefore I rejoice that Thy adorable will is now being accomplished in me in this sorrowful manner. That is the way to rejoice, my dear brethren, even when we are sad; to rejoice even because we are sad, and weep, and lament. Ah, you think, but there's the rub! Truly, there's the rub; but it is altogether in our will. How so? If you love your God truly with all your heart above all things, as you are bound to love Him, it must be an easy matter for you to rejoice in that way in the midst of crosses and trials, when you think: this is the will of God; it is God who gives me this hard blow.

That joy we can have if we remember that the trial is from God.

I will explain myself by a simile. A young man clad in splendid raiment goes through the streets of the town in winter time; he is suddenly hit with a snow-ball so severely that he winces with pain. He looks around full of anger, and grasps his sword; who is the rascal, he cries out, who thus dares to insult me publicly? And if he could catch the guilty one, he would certainly run him through. Meanwhile he hears a voice from a window saying in a laughing tone: I did it. Still more annoyed at this, he looks up, and there he sees his intended bride smiling and greeting him. At once his expression changes; he takes his hat off and makes her a deep bow, and if he has time, he runs up

The love of a creature often sweetens suffering for us; shown by an example.

to her in all haste, kisses her hand, and thanks her for the favor conferred on him, which he thinks of the whole day with satisfaction, and evens dreams of at night. And what is the cause of the sudden change? Does he feel the pain no longer since he looked up to the window? Certainly he does, just the same as before. Why, then, was he in such a rage at first, while he is now so gay and happy? That is the work of the dear hand that threw the snow-ball; he knows now that it was not ill-meant, and takes it as a sign of favor and love; he willingly submits to such things from the object of his affections. In the same way the courtier would look on it as a great favor to receive such a blow from his sovereign, although it might cause him some pain.

How much more should not the love of God do that! O my Lord and my God, I am ashamed to have to use such similes in explaining Thy holy truths! Fie, for shame! a wretched piece of flesh, that in a short time will rot in the grave and be the food of worms, can make what would otherwise be the greatest insult, to be revenged with blood, so sweet and agreeable that one forgets the pain through joy! Nay, many a one is ready to shed his blood and to encounter sword and spear and death itself, for the sake of pleasing a worthless creature. But that loving hand of our heavenly Father, who calls Himself the Spouse of our souls, who has been hankering for our hearts from all eternity up to the present moment, who loved us even to the shameful death of the cross, whom we hope to see and to love forever in heaven; that hand, I say, is not worth so much in our sight that it can sweeten a trifling sorrow, or induce us to receive with contentment the loving blow it inflicts! A hard snow-ball strikes you, O man, when you are weighed down by crosses and trials, when poverty oppresses you, or grief at the death of a friend, or persecution, or disgrace, or some other affliction; your fastidious nature, when it feels the smart, breaks out into expressions of discontent, murmurs and complains, swears and curses its ill-fortune. But think a little; see first who it is that has thrown the ball at you. Do not, however, look to earth; raise your eyes and thoughts to heaven; it is from there that the ball has been thrown by that Lord of whom Job says: "He commandeth the snow to go down upon the earth." [1] Imagine, and indeed it is the truth, that you hear your loving Lord and God crying out to you with a friendly laugh: I have done it.

---

[1] Qui præcipit nivi, ut descendat in terram.—Job xxxvii. 6.

If you still continue to murmur and complain after such a thought as that, if you still refuse to be resigned, oh, then you can come to the conclusion that you do not love God truly with your whole heart.

If the Lord had no good intention with regard to us when He sends us sorrows and trials, if His only object were to enjoy Himself by plaguing us mortals with all sorts of afflictions, should we not look on it as the greatest honor and happiness to be thus able to please and satisfy such a great Lord? Now our faith teaches us quite the contrary; namely, that God has no pleasure in our sufferings. "Thou art not delighted in our being lost," said Sara to the Lord; "because after a storm Thou makest a calm, and after tears and weeping Thou pourest in joyfulness." [1] "He who made man in His goodness," says St. Gregory, "will not permit him to be tormented unjustly." [2] Much more will He have pity on our misery. "I have compassion on the multitude," [3] sighed Our Lord, when the people were without food for three days. He seems to be angry when He punishes us and sends us trials; but in reality the blows He gives are loving ones, intended for our good. *Ecce fingo contra vos malum,* "Behold, I frame evil against you," He says by the Prophet Jeremias, or, according to the meaning of the word *fingo,* I act as if I were doing you harm. Thus He behaves like the lady in the simile I brought forward, who pretended to try to hurt the young man, although in reality she was only showing her affection for him. In the same sense are we to understand the words of St. Paul: "Whom the Lord loveth, He chastiseth." [4] "All that have pleased God," says Judith, "passed through many tribulations remaining faithful." [5] All without exception, in whom God is pleased, have to pass through tribulation; that is, in going through it, they are caught by the hand of God.

Therefore the thought: This is the will of God; what I now suffer, the cross I have to bear, is sent me by God, because He loves me, should be enough for me, if I love the Lord with all my heart, to resign myself joyfully to His will. Hear, my

Marginal notes: Especially since it is through love that He sends us crosses. Therefore, after the example of pious Christians,

---

[1] Non enim delectaris in perditionibus nostris; quia post tempestatem tranquillum facis, et post lachrymationem et fletum exultationem infundis.—Tob. iii. 22.

[2] Qui benigne hominem condidit, nequamquam injuste cruciari permittit.—S. Greg. in moral.

[3] Misereor super turbam.—Mark viii. 2.

[4] Quem enim diligit Dominus castigat.—Heb. xii. 6.

[5] Omnes qui placuerunt Deo, per multas tribulationes transierunt fideles.—Judith viii. 23.

we must always remember that trials are according to the will of God. dear brethren, the beautiful reflection that St. Francis Borgia, the third General of our Society, made on this point. He came home late one winter's night, covered with snow, and found the gate of the college locked, as all had gone to bed. He rang the bell as hard as he could, but to no purpose. Thus he was kept ringing and waiting for some hours. At last some one awoke, opened the gate, and seeing that it was the Father General, began to make all sorts of excuses, and to beg pardon for having kept him out so long in the cold. Francis laughingly made answer: "My dear Father, I am very grateful to you for a special consolation that I owe to your keeping me waiting so long. Do you know what I was thinking of, as I stood there covered with snow? I imagined that I saw my dear Lord in heaven, amusing Himself throwing the snow-flakes at me, just as a man sometimes does with his servant; and therefore, since everything happens by His decree, He kept your eyes closed in sleep, that He might continue the game with me longer. I was indeed tired, cold, and wet, but I was well contented at heart, and so much did that thought console me, that I should have willingly stayed there the whole night, if you had not come."

And joyfully accept everything from His hand. Let us think the same, my dear brethren, in all occurrences which are disagreeable, painful, and contrary to our nature and sensuality. Wherever the suffering comes from, whether from inward or outward things, from reasoning or lifeless creatures, from men or the demon, from our own domestics or strangers, from father or mother, from brothers or sisters, from enemies or friends, it should make no difference. Let us always raise up our eyes to heaven, and look on it as certain, and say to ourselves: This is all arranged above; God wills it so; it is the Lord who has given me this blow; this hard knock comes from heaven, from that loving and amiable hand. Well therefore is it for me that I can be the means of giving pleasure to such a great Lord, who loves me so much. "As it hath pleased the Lord, so is it done: blessed be the name of the Lord." This cross, this poverty, this desolation, this disgrace, this persecution and oppression, this illness and pain, is a love-token given me by God: "Yea, Father, for so hath it seemed good in Thy sight." I accept it willingly; I thank Thee for it; I humbly kiss the gracious hand that strikes me and means so well with me; behold, I am ready for all Thou wilt do to me; "may Thy most holy, righteous, and adorable will be done in me, by me, and about me and all belonging to me, O Lord." Pardon me, O Lord, for having been so often impatient, discontented, and almost desperate in my former crosses and trials. I am sorry for it from my heart! I acknowledge that all I gained thereby was merely to make my cross heavier and more troublesome; but it was because I did not know or think that it was Thy loving hand that gave me the blow; otherwise I should not have acted so unbecomingly. Yea, Father, since such is Thy will, I am fully satisfied with it. Yea, Father, since such is Thy will, I take up the cross with joy. Yea, Father, whatever Thy will may be in future, so let it be done; blessed be the name of the Lord under all circumstances, in all crosses and trials. Amen.

Another Introduction to the same sermon for the eighteenth Sunday after Pentecost.

Text.

Confide, fili.—Matt. ix. 2.
" Be of good heart, son."

Introduction.

Oh, what a great blessing that poor palsied man owed to his sickness! If he had not been ill, they would not have brought him to Our Saviour, and so he would not have been enlightened by Him, nor repented of his sins, nor been forgiven them. But now he hears the consoling words: " Be of good heart, son, thy sins are forgiven thee;" and he was restored, besides, to bodily health. Thus what we look on as an evil and a misfortune serves by divine ordination, even when we know nothing about it and are not thinking of it, as a means to further the salvation of our souls, which should be our sole concern on this earth. Therefore, as I have said before, if we seek and love our own advantage we can do nothing better than to resign ourselves cheerfully to the providence of God, allowing Him to do with us what He pleases. Ah, if we only thought of this with a lively faith when we are afflicted; if we only thought, I say, This sickness, this poverty, this death, this misfortune, etc., comes from God, the worst part of our sorrow would be taken away, and we should always hear in spirit the words, Be of good heart, my soul. So it is, my dear brethren, as I shall now show to the comfort of all who are in sorrow, etc.—*Continues as above.*

FORTY-NINTH SERMON.

ON THE HAPPINESS OF HIM WHO IS CONTENT WITH THE WILL OF GOD.

Subject.

He who completely resigns his will to the will of God, and is always satisfied with His decrees, is the happiest man on earth: 1. In his own imagination; 2. In reality.—*Preached on the feast of the Purification of the Blessed Virgin.*

Text.

Postquam impleti sunt dies purgationis ejus, secundum legem Moysi.—Luke ii. 22.

" And after the days of her purification according to the law of Moses were accomplished."

Introduction.

The law of purification, as far as it concerned women after childbirth, as laid down in the Book of Leviticus, consisted of two parts: First, "If a woman shall bear a man-child, she shall be unclean seven days."[1] Besides these seven days she had to remain thirty-three days longer in her purification, during which time she could not touch anything holy, nor enter the house of God, but was looked on as unclean: " She shall touch no holy thing, neither shall she enter into the sanctuary, until the days of her purification be fulfilled."[2] Secondly, after the lapse of those forty days, she had to stand at the door of the temple, and if she were too poor to offer a lamb, she had to bring two turtle doves, " one for a holocaust, and another for sin; and the priest shall pray for her, and so she shall be cleansed."[3] Such, my dear brethren, was the law in those days.   Now think of this; that law was observed by the most holy Virgin, who was never stained by the least sin, and who was purer than the angels; she covered her innocence and holiness with that garment of sin; like an ordinary woman she appears to-day before the door of

---

[1] Mulier si pepererit masculum, immunda erit septem diebus.—Levit. xii. 2.

[2] Omne sanctum non tanget, nec ingredietur in sanctuarium, donec impleantur dies purificationis suæ.—Ibid. 4.

[3] Unum in holocaustum, et alterum pro peccato; orabitque pro ea sacerdos, et sic mundabitur.—Ibid. 8.

the temple; like a sinner, she brings her offering! But why? For there is no doubt that she was not bound by the law, and her observance of it seemed to injure her maidenly fame before the world. That is true, but she acted according to the will of our heavenly Father, whose most holy Son had to submit to the law of circumcision. And Mary, the immaculate Mother of His Son, had also to submit like a sinner to the law of purification. Such was the will of God. And that one thought was enough to induce the holy Virgin to resign herself to God's will with the utmost joy and satisfaction. My dear brethren, if we wish to be true children of the Mother of God, we must try to imitate her as well as we can in this virtue, which is most pleasing to God, and like her to be always resigned to His holy will. By doing so we shall suffer no loss or injury; nay, we shall rather attain the greatest happiness that can be enjoyed on earth, as I shall now show.

Plan of Discourse.

He who completely resigns his will to the will of God, and is always satisfied with His decrees, is the happiest man on earth. Such is the whole subject. He is the happiest in his own imagination; the first part. He is the happiest in reality; the second part.

Mary, Queen of all faithful servants of God, and you, O holy angels, ministers of God, obtain for us by your intercession the grace to practise this virtue, and thus to have on earth a foretaste of the happiness that you enjoy in heaven.

All our happiness or misery, as we mortals judge by our senses of such things, consists, so far as this life is concerned, mostly in our own imagination and fancy, that is, in the judgment we form regarding the thing as to whether it is bad or good for us. The wise Epictetus remarks this. "Men are influenced," he says, "not by things, but by the opinions they form of them;"[1] and that is evident enough. A simple-minded man finds, for instance, a piece of copper overlaid with gold; he hides it away, imagining that it is pure gold and worth a great deal of money; he is as happy with his copper as another would be with real gold and silver. But if he finds a precious stone, and thinks it to be glass, he lets it lie there, or throws it away; he has neither pleasure nor profit from it, because he is ignorant of its value. A child

Marginal note: Happiness and misery on earth consist mostly in the imagination.

---

[1] Homines turbantur, non rebus, sed quas de rebus habent opinionibus.

is happier and more contented with the few pence it saves up
than many a one who possesses thousands. I remember that once
when I was a child my father put into my hand a kreutzer and
a piece of gold, telling me I could take which I preferred; and
I chose the kreutzer. Why? Because I thought to myself, With
this I can buy apples and nuts, but I do not know what to do
with the piece of gold. On the other hand, there was another occasion, on which our house caught fire and was burned
to the ground, along with half the houses of the town, so that
we were forced to take shelter in a little garden-house outside
the town; but I well remember that I and other children were
dancing with joy at the sight of the flames, while my parents
and grown-up friends were bewailing their loss. But what did
I know about loss? I was glad to be in the garden, and to see the
fire; that was the greatest delight for me, although I was a suffer-
er like the others. Thus the whole matter depends on the imagination.

Shown by
an example.

Since I have begun to speak of children, my dear brethren, I
will bring forward an occurrence related by Famianus Strada in
his famous History of the Wars of the Netherlands; it happened
in the year 1570. The sea had inundated a great portion of
Holland and Friesland, so that in the latter country alone twenty
thousand people and a large number of cattle lost their lives.
When the waters subsided a little, they found on the shore a
cradle in which there was a child with a living cat; the cradle
had been cast on the shore by the waves, and the child was tran-
quilly sleeping beside the cat. Now I ask, had not the child, as
well as the other inhabitants of the place, lost its friends and
relations, its brothers and sisters, nay, perhaps its parents? Was
not the house in which it was born carried off by the waves?
Was it not exposed to the fury of the elements? Was it not in
imminent danger of losing its life? for it would not have been a
difficult matter to upset the cradle and drown the child and the
cat? There is no doubt of it. How was it then possible for the
child not to be frightened, and to lie there so quietly? Perhaps,
you say, because it was asleep. Good; but now I ask, how could
it sleep in such a dreadful storm, amid the roaring of the waters,
while its life was hourly exposed to the utmost danger, and after
having experienced such a grievous loss? Would any of you
have slept in such circumstances? Oh, you exclaim, what is
there to be surprised at? The child was too young to have any

idea of the loss it suffered, or of the danger it was in. Quite right; but from this I make the same conclusion as before, and you must acknowledge that it is true, as Epictetus says, that "men are influenced, not by things, but by the opinions they form of them." The child had ears like other people, and could hear the turmoil of the winds and waves; it had feeling, and doubtless was aware that its cradle was shaken about; it had eyes, and could see that it was alone with the cat on the waters, for it is not likely that it slept the whole time, since the storm lasted for some days. It was awake, then, sometimes, and went to sleep again under such terrible circumstances. If you or I were in that cradle, we should hardly be able to draw a breath for fear. But what is the reason of the difference between us and the child? Why should it be calm and quiet in the danger, while we, if we were similarly situated, would be filled with anxiety? It is all to be traced to the influence of the imagination and fancy. The child was accustomed to be rocked in its cradle, and probably thought that its mother or some one else was rocking it; at all events, the storm that was the cause of rest and sleep to it would have made us tremble with fear, because our imaginations would have represented to us the imminent danger that threatened our lives.

Again, if the child, on awakening and not finding its mother or any one near it, and seeing that its only companion was the cat, commenced to cry and scream, would that have helped it in any way? Would its danger have been lessened thereby? Or would it have been brought sooner to land? Not by any means; it would only have disturbed its peaceful sleep, made itself unhappy, and perhaps by its struggles upset the cradle. And if it had been drowned like so many others, would it not have been far better to have met death calmly and quietly than to have added to the terrors of drowning by useless clamor, tears, and struggles, as the other victims of the inundation did? Without doubt. And yet the same wind and water, the same circumstances and causes, nay, the same death, as far as the mere loss of temporal life is concerned, had to be met by all. So it is; but all did not form the same estimate or opinion of the danger and the death. It is clear, then, that it is not the outward circumstances, nor misfortunes, nor trials, nay, not even death itself, that is the cause of our trouble and distress, but simply the imagination and opinion that we form of the evil. Consequently,

Hence he who wishes to be happy must amend his imagination.

in order to live calmly, contentedly, and happily, all we have to do is to lay aside or amend our judgment about those adverse circumstances. If we succeed in convincing ourselves that there is nothing bad or injurious in the world save and except sin alone, and that everything that happens is for our eternal welfare, then we should be rid at once of all disquiet and uneasiness, and should live contentedly and happily.

That is best done by conformity with the will of God. But, you ask, how can we lay aside or amend that judgment? We are driven about in this world as on a stormy sea of trials, difficulties, miseries, and wretchedness; how can we convince ourselves against our own judgment that those things are good and desirable? Ah, Christians, truly we can do so, if we only acknowledge with a lively faith who it is that sets this sea of adversity in motion; if we only earnestly persuade ourselves,—and indeed it is the truth,—that all calamities and troubles come from the hand of God, and are ordained specially by Him for each one of us; that thus it is our God who rocks us in these crosses, as the child is rocked by its mother in the cradle; then, indeed, we should be peaceful and contented like the child in the midst of the bitterest trials and misfortunes. So it is; the conformity and perfect resignation of our will to the will of God takes away and corrects all wrong fancies and opinions about things, and places the mind in a state of imperturbable repose and contentment. For, as I have often said before, when one really believes and is firmly convinced that everything that happens in the world, sin alone excepted, is according to the decree and will of God, he must also be firmly convinced that everything that happens is good, right, holy, and cannot be better, because it is ordained by the God of infinite wisdom, justice, and holiness. He who thinks and believes, This state of mine is appointed for me by the inscrutable decrees of God; this care and trouble, this annoyance, this poverty and want, this loss and injury, this weakness and sickness, this death or misfortune, comes from the loving hand of God,—he must also say, Therefore there is no evil in it; it is ordained for my greater good; I am not to be disturbed at it, or to complain of it, but should rather rejoice and return thanks to God. And in consequence of that firm persuasion, since he loves God with his whole heart, and wills all that God wills, he is completely resigned to the divine decrees, and says with the high-priest Heli: "It is the Lord; let Him do what is good in His sight;"[1] and with the patient Job: "The Lord

[1] Dominus est; quod bonum est in oculis suis, faciat.— I. Kings iii. 18.

gave, and the Lord hath taken away; as it hath pleased the Lord so is it done: blessed be the name of the Lord:"[1] and with our dear Saviour: "Yea, Father, for so hath it seemed good in Thy sight:"[2] "not what I will, but what Thou wilt."[3] "Therefore, since nothing in the world can happen to him but according to God's will and decree, there is nothing in the world except sin that can appear to him to be an evil, or disturb his repose, or sadden his mind. In all accidents and occurrences he is contented, happy, and joyful in the Lord. What else is that but being happy, at least as far as the imagination is concerned? But he is also happy in reality, as I shall now show in the

Second Part.

In what consists the true happiness of a man on this earth? Describe to me a happy man.. Is he not one who has all he wishes and desires, and in the manner in which he wishes and desires? whose every undertaking goes according to his wish? whose will is always done without the least opposition? who is not aware of anything further to wish for, and who has not the least fear of anything ever happening to thwart him? Truly, you must acknowledge that, as Salvianus says, such a man as that is the favorite of fortune: "There are none happier than those who are what they wish to be."[4] For all our trouble, disturbance of mind, displeasure, discontent, besides being the effect of our imagination, must also be attributed to the fact that we are forced to be or to do something that we do not wish to be or to do; or that others do not act as we wish them to; or that something crosses our will or our plans; or that we cannot have what we desire to have. From this opposition and thwarting of our will come all our difficulties and troubles, and the mental disturbance that daily tortures us and drives us about hither and thither, as if we were at the mercy of a furious storm. Hence the miser, although he has more money than he can use during his whole life, is never happy, but always discontented. Why? Because he is always longing for more, and never has as much as he desires to have. Show me the man who has lands and riches, and the honors and pleasures of the world in abundance, but who is discontented be-

He is truly happy who has all he wishes for.

---

[1] Dominus dedit, Dominus abstulit; sicut Domino placuit, ita factum est; sit nomen Domini benedictum.—Job 1. 21.

[2] Ita, Pater, quoniam sic fuit placitum ante te.—Matt. xi. 26.

[3] Non quod ego volo, sed quod tu.—Mark xiv. 36.

[4] Nulli lætiores sunt, quam qui hoc sunt, quod volunt.

cause things do not go according to his will, and I will show you a man who is apparently happy, but really miserable and worse off than the poor peasant who sits in his wretched thatched hut, eating a piece of dry bread with a contented mind.

Such is he who is always content with the will of God.

But where can we find a man who has everything that he wishes and desires? Methinks we should seek him in heaven. True, the blessed in heaven, who see God face to face, are the only ones who are happy in the most perfect degree; yet we can find a foretaste of that happiness here on earth in the man who has completely abandoned his will to the will of God; who in all circumstances and occurrences first of all fixes the eyes of his mind on the providence of God, and is completely satisfied with His decrees. For since everything in this world, sin excepted, happens according to the will and decree of God, and all that God wills must be fully accomplished, and that man desires and wishes for nothing but what is pleasing to God, it follows that in all the accidents and events of life his will is fulfilled and is never thwarted in the least.

For everything happens to him according to his wish.

Therefore he has at all times, in all circumstances, whatever he wishes and in the manner he wishes to have it, as Salvianus says. Is he humbled and shamed before the world, despised and persecuted by men? Others may pity him, but he himself is contented and satisfied. He wishes to have things so, because such is the will of God, who has ordained it for him. Is he poor and needy? does he suffer loss in his temporal goods? If so, his desire is fulfilled, since such is the will of the God whom he loves so much. He has sometimes hardly bread enough to keep himself from dying of hunger; he can hardly find a drink of water to quench his thirst, or a rag of clothing to cover himself with, or a bit of fuel to warm himself with; he has not a bed to sleep in at night, in spite of the earnest efforts and conscientious use he makes of natural means; truly that man is in a most miserable state, thinks the world. But the world is wrong; he is the happiest man on earth. Why? Because he has what he wants; it is his will to be as he is, since such is the will of God. He is always weak and delicate; for months at a time he has to keep the bed; he cannot come to church or to public devotions, and is tortured by pain night and day; is he not unhappy? Not at all, for he is satisfied with the will of God; God wills him to suffer, consequently he wills it himself, so that his desire is fulfilled. He gives way to natural sorrow; he sighs, moans, and

weeps; is he not unhappy now at all events? No, for even under those circumstances his mind is at peace and undisturbed,
his faith, his judgment, remain the same; this is the will of God,
he thinks, and he is just as resigned as ever; it is his wish to
moan, sigh, and weep, because that is pleasing to God, because
God wills him to sigh, moan, and weep with sorrow. If he is
even hindered or thwarted in some good purpose by the efforts
of the most wicked men, he remains undisturbed and contented,
for the customary thought occurs to him, such is the will of
God.

He is in just the same dispositions with regard to things that
happen outside himself. Is the sun shining? He is satisfied.
It is raining, or snowing, or hailing; the wind howls, the thun-
der roars: he is quite contented; the will of God is done, and
that is all he wants. People speak on all sides of wars and blood-
shed, of dangerous and contagious illnesses, of scarcity and
famine; the bad weather, the cold winter, the dry summer, they
say, will do a great deal of harm to the fields and vineyards; they
are all filled with dread and consternation; alas, they exclaim,
what will become of us poor people? Yet what do they gain by
their lamentations except to make their sufferings worse? All
he has to do is simply to collect his thoughts; such is the will
of God, he says to himself; come what may, then, it will be all
for the best; without God's will I shall not die of hunger, or
cold, or sickness; without His permission not the least harm can
befall me; but if He wishes me to suffer hunger, cold, sickness,
or death, I am ready; whatever pleases the Lord will be done;
may His name be blessed, whatever He does to me. In a word,
let the whole world be destroyed, *impavidum ferient ruinæ;*
he will go with it, but calmly and contentedly, because such is
the will of God, and he desires nothing but the accomplishment
of that will. Wish him happiness, and he will answer, with that
beggar of whom Tauler writes, that he has never spent an unhappy day or hour, nor has he ever had to complain that things did
not go according to his wishes. Nay,—and those who are over-
anxious and fearful should mark this,—if he feels but little devotion in his usual prayers and pious exercises, or even feels no
devotion at all, and is filled with desolation; if he has no more
relish or pleasure in God than if he were a dry stick; if even the
desire to accept everything according to the will of God seems
to have left him; he still remains contented and satisfied as far

And every-
thing in the
world goes
according to
his wish.

as his reasoning will and inward consciousness are concerned; for he thinks to himself: This desolation and dryness of spirit, this apparent unwillingness to do good, this weariness of God and heavenly things, I now desire to have and willingly accept, because such is the will of God, who now wishes me to suffer in this way. That, my dear brethren, is what the Wise Man says of the just servant of God: "Whatsoever shall befall the just man, it shall not make him sad." [1] Nothing that happens to him can disturb him, or deprive him of his peace of mind.

Herein consists true happiness on earth.

This is the peace that the angels joyfully announced to the world at the birth of Our Lord, in the words, "Glory to God in the highest, and on earth peace to men of good will;" [2] that is, whose will is always in conformity with the all-perfect and holy will of God. And in this consists the greatest joy and happiness that we can have on earth. Picture to yourself, as far as you can, all other pleasures, joys, and delights, heavenly joys alone excepted, and you will find none that can be compared to this. It is a foretaste of eternal bliss, an earthly paradise, an astonishing glory in this vale of tears, which has some resemblance to that of the elect in heaven, where the greatest joy of the blessed is to have, as it were, one heart, soul, and will with God, and to be ready to obey His least sign, and to fulfil His holy will, looking towards Him not otherwise than a hungry child does towards the dish on the table from which it expects something to eat. Nay, I may venture to say that this complete and constant conformity and contentment with the will of God is an unchangeable and lasting happiness, which begins here on earth, but instead of being ended by death, is simply transferred from this life to eternity.

The servants of God knew that well: shown by examples.

Wise was the answer given by Alfonso, king of Arragon, when he was asked whom he considered the happiest man on earth. Was he a great artist, a renowned hero and general, a mighty king or emperor? "I have spent some considerable time," said Alfonso, "thinking of what the happiness of this life consists in; for I have a great desire for it, and the result of all my speculations about the matter is, and I hold it for certain and undoubted, that he alone is truly happy who is completely resigned to the providence of God, allowing Him to act as He pleases, and always satisfied with His will." Cassian tells us of a pious old

---

[1] Non contristabit justum quidquid ei acciderit.—Prov. xii. 21.

[2] Gloria in altissimis Deo, et in terra pax hominibus bonæ voluntatis.—Luke ii. 14.

Christian who lived in Alexandria in the midst of idolaters, like a lamb among wolves; they surrounded him on one occasion and tossed him about from one to the other like a ball, abusing, cursing, and beating him most cruelly; but the old man never uttered a word of complaint, or showed the least sign of annoyance. One of his tormentors at last asked him what miracles his Christ had worked. "This," answered the old man quietly, "that I am able to bear all your insults and ill-treatment with meekness, and without losing my peace of mind; for I keep on reminding myself that it is His holy will that I should now be tormented." St. Mary Magdalene of Pazzi found such superabundant consolation and inward joy of heart in the conformity of her will with the will of God that she once forgot herself and burst forth into sighs of love. "Lord," she exclaimed, "Thou knowest that from my youth I have never desired anything but what is pleasing to Thee, and if I knew now that it was Thy will for me to be tortured forever in hell, I should at once cast myself into those everlasting flames." Then she said to those who were standing by, and who were amazed at her words, "You do not know how sweet is that one word, the will of God." Gerson tells us of another servant of God, who was equally resigned to the divine will; the devil appeared to him in the likeness of an angel, and told him that all his works of penance were of no use, as he was to be lost forever. "Very well," was the answer; "I serve my God not merely for the sake of going to heaven, but because He wishes me to serve Him; if He chooses to reject me and condemn me to hell for eternity, He is the Lord, and may His holy will be done; meanwhile I will continue to serve Him, because such is His will." I do not mean to say, my dear brethren, that this most perfect conformity and satisfaction with the will of God is necessarily required from all, otherwise I should make many despair of practising this beautiful virtue; I merely wish to show what complete repose and happiness it brings to the human heart, so that the fear of the greatest evil, which in our estimation is the fire of hell, cannot disturb our tranquillity.

Ah, my dear brethren, what else do we seek or desire on this earth but to be happy? And see how easy it is for us to have our wish if we only earnestly consider with a lively faith the chief truths of our religion (one of which is that, with the sole exception of sin, nothing happens in the world without being arranged by divine Providence), bring them before our minds,

Hence he who wishes to be happy must always be satisfied with the will of God.

and then judge and form our opinion according to them. "Submit thyself, then, to Him," I conclude in the words of Eliphaz to Job, "and be at peace; and thereby thou shalt have the best fruits."[1]   Do you wish things to go well with you, to enjoy peace and contentment under all circumstances, to have all your desires granted, to be happy on earth?   Then submit to Him; be satisfied with your God and His will, whatever He does to you; think always, in all the accidents of life: Such is the will of God, and say, Yea, Father, Thy will be done!   That is all you need do, and you will have peace; you will be and will remain happy.   It was by this exhortation that Father Nicholas Zucchi of our Society, who died in the odor of sanctity, brought many souls not only to holiness of life, but also to great peace and joy of heart.   To those who had a special desire of saving their souls he used to say the words of the Psalmist: "Delight in the Lord, and He will give thee the request of thy heart."[2]   He happened once to be called to a young man who was dying, and was asked by him if he recognized him.   I do not remember ever to have seen you before, was the Father's answer.   Eight months ago, said the sick man, when I was in the Roman College, I asked you to teach me the right way of serving my God truly and zealously, and all you said to me was, "Delight in the Lord, and He will give thee the requests of thy heart;" that is, my only joy should be to try to do the will of God in all things, and to be always satisfied with that will.   What good that exhortation, which I have taken well to heart, has done me, you can see after my death in the sealed writing which you will find under my pillow.   He then asked the Father's blessing, and shortly afterwards peacefully expired.   Father Zucchi found the writing and read it three times over with great consolation; for the young man described in it the sweet repose and exceeding heavenly joy of heart that he experienced, in addition to other graces given him by God, from the time when, in obedience to the exhortation, he began to practise perfect conformity with the will of God. The same statement was made to Father Zucchi on her death-bed by a nun at Rome, who had learned from him to be always contented, and rejoice with the will of God.

Conclusion and resolution.   O my Lord and my God!   Poor mortal that I am, in not having sooner known or thought of this truth!   What uneasiness,

[1] Acquiesce igitur ei, et habeto pacem ; et per hæc habebis fructus optimos.—Job xxii. 21.
[2] Delectare in Domino, et dabit tibi petitiones cordis tui.—Ps. xxxvi. 4.

disquiet, anxiety, despair, nay, how many sins I might have avoided, which I brought upon myself by my anger and impatience, by abusive words, by cursing and swearing in crosses and trials! This alone I now complain of and repent of with my whole heart, that I did not sooner submit to Thy holy will, and to Thy all-wise decrees. If I had done so, I should have been much more contented and satisfied in those circumstances, in which for the future I am determined to submit to Thee with all the powers of my soul. Yea, Father! Be it as Thou wilt, and in what manner Thou wilt, in heat and cold, in rain and snow, in wind and weather, in war and peace, in fertility and scarcity, in all the natural events that occur outside of me, be it as Thou wilt, when, how, and as long as Thou wilt; such, too, is my will. Yea, Father! Be it when and how Thou wilt, in hunger and thirst, in poverty and want, in shame and disgrace, in persecution and contempt, in difficulties and annoyances, in sorrow and trouble, in sickness and health, in death and abandonment, in anguish and depression, in life and death, in everything that concerns me and mine, I give myself up to Thee with my whole heart, and throw myself into Thy fatherly arms; do with me in these and all other things whatever is most pleasing to Thy holy will. If I am not really in earnest, then I will beg of Thee daily, O my God, to give me a will that is always satisfied with Thine; so that I may always sincerely say: "Yea, Father, for so hath it seemed good in Thy sight," and thus begin to enjoy on earth the happiness that I hope to enjoy in heaven with Thy angels and saints. Amen.

Another Introduction to the same sermon for the feast of All Saints.

Text.

Gaudete et exultate, quoniam merces vestra copiosa est in cœlis.—Matt. v. 12.

"Be glad and rejoice, for your reward is very great in heaven."

Introduction.

Wonderful are those words of the holy Gospel, "Blessed are the poor; blessed are they that mourn; blessed are they that hunger and thirst; blessed are they that suffer persecution; blessed are ye when they shall revile you and persecute you, and speak all that is evil against you." Who could believe those words to be true? For the whole world cries *no* to them. Poverty, humiliation, sadness, hunger, thirst, contempt, persecution, the loss of the esteem of men, are all hateful in the eyes of the world, and are feared and avoided by it as the greatest evils. And yet Jesus Christ, the infallible truth, calls happy those who suffer such things for His sake. Therefore the world must be wrong when it pities such men as if they were unhappy. Yes, you say, they will be happy in heaven, for by patiently bearing the miseries of earth they lead holy lives. To be holy here, and happy hereafter, that is only what we have to expect according to the divine promises. And so it is, my dear brethren. And should not that be a sufficient inducement to us to bear the miseries of this life for a short time for God's sake? Meanwhile I will tell you something that will probably surprise you. I wish to make you holy and at the same time happy, not only in heaven, but here on earth as well, so that, if you do as I tell you, I shall be able to say to you, "Be glad and rejoice;" for your reward is exceedingly great, not only in heaven, but on earth, too. What do you think of that? Ah, you say, that cannot be; for I cannot be happy here unless I gratify all my inclinations, and satisfy them completely. But I cannot be holy unless I mortify myself and fight against those inclinations with violence. How is it possible for me to gratify my desires and to mortify them at the same time? And, consequently, how is it possible to be holy and happy at the same time? Nevertheless it is all possible enough, and all we have to do is, as we have seen already, to conform our will to the will of God in all circumstances, and to be satisfied with His decrees. And I have already explained how perfect holiness consists therein. But now I shall show that therein, too, consists perfect happiness on earth, etc.—*Continues as above.*

FIFTIETH SERMON.

ON THE GREAT FAVOR HE ENJOYS WITH GOD WHO IS CONTENT WITH HIS WILL.

Subject.

1. He who completely resigns his will to the will of God, and is always satisfied with the divine decrees, is in the greatest favor with God. 2. Answer to a question.—*Preached on the feast of the Annunciation of the Blessed Virgin.*

Text.

Ecce ancilla Domini; fiat mihi secundum verbum tuum.—
Luke i. 38.

" Behold . the hand-maid of the Lord; be it done to me according to thy word."

Introduction.

That was the wished-for word, for which the souls in Limbo had been sighing so long, which men on earth were anxiously awaiting, and the angels in heaven were looking forward to: " Be it done to me according to thy word." For as the holy Fathers say, the Son of God did not wish to become man until the Virgin Mary, whom He had chosen as His mother, had given her consent. Hence St. Bernard thus addresses her: " Say the word, and conceive the Word;" ' give your consent, that the Word may become flesh for the good of the world. And Mary is ready at once: " Behold the hand-maid of the Lord; be it done to me according to thy word." Thus the Son of God is conceived, to the great happiness and salvation of the world, and the Virgin is raised to the dignity of Mother of God. O my dear brethren, if we only thought and said with the same willingness and contentment in all accidents and events, behold, I am a servant, a hand-maid of the Lord, " be it done to me according to thy word, " how peacefully and happily we might live! For, as I have already shown, true happiness on earth is found in the full conformity of our will with the will of God; since he who is thus resigned, desiring nothing but what is pleasing to God, has all he wishes. But that is not all his happiness; for full conformity with the will of God brings him much higher, since thereby he becomes not only the happiest amongst men on earth, but he also enjoys the special favor of God in heaven, as I shall now show.

Plan of Discourse.

He who completely resigns his will to the will of God, and is always satisfied with the divine decrees, is in the greatest favor with God in heaven. This I shall prove in the first part. In the second part I shall answer a question which the subject has perhaps already suggested. Both parts I shall make as brief as possible.

¹ Loquere verbum, et suscipe Verbum.

Mary, Virgin Mother of God! thou hast surpassed all creatures in the other virtues, and more especially in the perfect conformity of thy will with the will of God. Obtain for us from thy dear Son even a part of this virtue, through the intercession of the holy angels; so that, after thy example, we may at all times, in all circumstances, think and say with contented wills: Behold, I am the servant or hand-maid of the Lord; "be it done to me according to thy word."

It is looked on as a great happiness to enjoy a king's favor. The world looks on him as the happiest of courtiers who is highest in the favor of his sovereign. And what a great to-do they make about that favor! What a commotion there is when the favorite is pointed out; see, that is the man; nothing is done without him; he is the king's favorite, and never leaves his side. Oh, what trouble, care, and anxiety people undergo, what money they spend, what bitter pills they swallow, before they can attain to such an honor! And how much hatred, envy, and calumny one who has attained it is exposed to! And yet the sovereign is but a man, who, when he closes his eyes in death, takes all his favorite's happiness with him to the grave. Nay, even during the life-time of the sovereign, since he is disposed one way to-day, and another to-morrow, all that is necessary sometimes to disgrace the favorite is a mere suspicion of infidelity, a false charge, a word uttered without any evil intention, that is taken up in a bad sense. Nor is that anything new in the world. Aman, who yesterday was the favorite of king Assuerus, to-day hangs on a gibbet: "So Aman was hanged on the gibbet." [1] In spite of all that, however, it is still considered a great matter to secure the favor of a king or prince.

What a happiness it must, then, be to enjoy the favor of God! What great happiness it must, then, be for a poor mortal to stand high in the friendship of the Prince of princes, the King of kings, the Monarch of heaven and earth, the great, infinite God, in comparison with whom all the princes and rulers of earth are infinitely less than the poorest beggar or the lowliest slave; whose favor I can keep as long as I wish, once I have secured it; whose friendship cannot be taken from me by all the efforts of my enemies, nor by all the machinations of the hellish spirits, and who will never be removed by death or abandon me first! Oh, what a happiness it is to be and to be called even a servant of God! What a great dignity that is! Holy people would not give it up for all the riches and honors of the world.

---

[1] Suspensus est itaque Aman in patibulo.—Esther vii. 10.

The disciples of Christ have always made a boast of that title; thus St. Paul calls himself: "Paul, a servant of Jesus Christ;"[1] and St. James: "James, the servant of God and of Our Lord Jesus Christ."[2] The same title is used by the Pope, the Vicar of Jesus Christ; "the servant of the servants of God."[3] Why do they not call themselves apostles, and not servants of Christ? Didymus of Alexandria answers by saying: Just as, when men are signing their names, they add whatever honorable titles they enjoy, in order to give authority to their signatures, so also these holy men add their title of servant of God. "That they look on as more honorable than all the royalty of earth,"[4] since God is such a great Lord. David was a rich and mighty king, yet he could not find any higher title to boast of: "O Lord, for I am Thy servant," he says twice in succession; "I am Thy servant, and the son of Thy hand-maid."[5] And why should we be surprised at that? For even the Queen of heaven and earth, the blessed Virgin Mary, when she was made Mother of God and was raised above all the angels, contents herself with the name of servant and hand-maid of the Lord. "Behold the hand-maid of the Lord," she exclaims. Now, if it is such a great honor and happiness to be a servant, a hand-maid of God, what must it then be to be and to be called His beloved friend?

Oh, truly, all other gifts and graces of God must yield in dignity to this friendship! Imagine you possess infused knowledge like Solomon, or even still more than he had; that you have greater wisdom than Daniel, so that you can see distant and future things, and have power to work miracles and to heal the sick; that, like St. Peter, your shadow is able to cure diseases, and that, like St. Gregory Thaumaturgus, a word of yours is enough to move mountains from one place to another; truly, you would think that something great, and would look on yourself as the most fortunate man on earth. But what good do all these gifts do you? By instruction the ignorant man is benefited, and not the teacher; by healing the sick the physician does not become more healthy; he who frees another from the devil is not any better himself therefore, since he was not possessed by the evil spirit. If you have not the friendship of God,

This favor is more to be prized than all the other gifts of God.

---

[1] Paulus, servus Jesu Christi.—Rom. i. 1.
[2] Jacobus, Dei et Domini nostri Jesu Christi servus.—James i. 1.
[3] Servus servorum Dei.
[4] Æstimantes hanc appellationem supra regna totius orbis consistere.
[5] O Domine, quia ego servus tuus ; ego servus tuus et filius ancillæ tuæ.—Ps. cxv. 16.

all these gifts would not contribute an iota to your happiness, and you would be of far less account than the lowly peasant who is in the friendship of God. "If I speak with the tongues of men and of angels," says St. Paul, "and if I should have prophecy, and should know all mysteries, and have not charity, I am nothing;"[1] that is to say, if I am without the grace that makes me the friend of God. Although, generally speaking, God gives the grace of miracles rather to His friends than to His enemies, yet He has sometimes conferred it on the latter also. Thus He endowed Saul with the gift of prophecy, so that he took his place amongst the prophets, even after his perversion. The wicked high-priest Caiphas was enabled by Him to prophesy; the idolatrous Balaam had grace to predict the most remote future events; the traitor Judas could drive out devils and work miracles. Nor should we be surprised at this; for these gratuitous graces are more for the benefit of others than for that of the recipient; so that he who is an enemy of God is not any better for them, except that they enable him to do good to another. God makes use of sinners who are endowed with those graces merely as instruments to further His glory, just as He sometimes uses unreasoning animals for the same purpose. Since, then, the Lord God bestows those gifts even on His enemies, it follows that the grace which makes man a friend of God is much more to be prized, and raises him to a far greater happiness. What are we, then, to think of him who is not merely a friend, but who is and is called the intimate friend and favorite of God?

He who is always in conformity with the will of God is a special friend of God. Such is the dignity and happiness to which they are raised, in preference to others, who are always resigned to the will of God, and fulfil it with readiness and satisfaction. Hear what Christ, Our Lord, says of them in the Gospel of St. John: "I will not now call you servants."[2] "You are My friends, if you do the things that I command you,"[3] and act according to My will. And to show how intimate that friendship is, He says in the preceding chapter: "If any one love Me, he will keep My word, and My Father will love him, and We will come to him, and will make Our abode with him."[4] Where are you now, Aristotle and

---

[1] Si linguis hominum loquar et angelorum, et si habuero prophetiam, et noverim mysteria omnia, charitatem autem non habuero, nihil sum.—I. Cor. xiii. 1, 2.

[2] Jam non dicam vos servos.—John xv. 15.

[3] Vos amici mei estis, si feceritis quæ ego præcipio vobis.—Ibid. 14.

[4] Si quis diligit me, sermonem meum servabit, et Pater meus diliget eum, et ad eum veniemus, et mansionem apud eum faciemus.—Ibid. xiv. 23.

you other philosophers, who maintained that there can be no true friendship between those who are very different from each other either in nature or position, as, for instance, between a master and his servant, between a learned and an ignorant man? That is not the case at all. There is not so much difference between heaven and earth, between the tower of Babel and an ant-heap, as there is between God and me, a mere mortal. God is the Lord of hosts, and I am a miserable worm of the earth; God is infinite wisdom, and I am of myself a blind and ignorant man; God is omnipotence itself, and I am weakness itself; God is infinitely rich, and I am a poor, wretched creature; God is infinitely holy, and I am born in sin, subject to the eternal curse; God is an eternal, immortal, infinite, immense, incomprehensible Good; I am a mortal, transitory, miserable creature, who in a short time will become the food of worms in the grave. And yet that great God is my friend, and I am His friend, provided my will is fully conformed to His, and I endeavor to do His will in all things, and to be always satisfied with it. I am, then, a friend of God, not merely like other just men who are in the state of grace, but I am a specially beloved friend of God, an intimate friend, a favorite of God, in whom the monarch of heaven has a special pleasure, whom He delights to converse with. My name is " His will is in me," because He is pleased with me; such is the promise He makes by the Prophet Isaias to all His faithful servants, who are always in conformity with His will. " Thou shalt be called, My pleasure in her; because the Lord hath been well pleased with thee. And thou shalt be a crown of glory in the hand of the Lord, and a royal diadem in the hand of thy God."[1]

But it is not enough that I am called an intimate friend of God; I am something more than that; I stand much higher in the divine favor; I approach much nearer to God when I am constantly resigned to His will. Hear this: " For whosoever shall do the will of My Father, that is in heaven," no matter who he may be, what of him? " He is my brother, and sister, and mother."[2] Let us, my dear brethren, briefly consider those words, who it was that spoke them, and in what circumstances they were uttered, and take them deeply to heart; then we shall see that man cannot have or imagine a greater, higher happiness

Christ looks on such a one as His brother, sister, and mother.

---

[1] Vocaberis : Voluntas mea in ea ; quia complacuit Domino in te. Et eris corona gloriæ in manu Domini, et diadema regni in manu Dei tui.—Is. lxii. 4, 3.

[2] Quicunque enim fecerit voluntatem Patris mei, qui in cœlis est, ipse meus frater, et soror, et mater est.—Matt. xii. 50.

as a reward for conforming his will to that of God. He who
says those words is the Son of God, Eternal Wisdom and Truth,
who cannot be deceived or speak falsely; He assures us that He
looks on the man who always tries to do the will of His Father,
as a brother, a sister, and a mother at the same time; that He
loves him with the tender love of one brother for another, of one
sister for another, of the child for its mother. How highly should
we not value the honor of being a brother of Jesus Christ according to the flesh, a sister of Jesus Christ, the Son of God?
How do we not honor and praise and hold in high esteem Mary,
the Virgin Mother of God, who conceived and brought Him forth
into the world? And that is truly right and just, ever blessed
Virgin! Thou canst not be sufficiently praised, honored, and esteemed by us according to Thy merits. " Blessed is the womb
that bore Thee," [1] we may well cry out, as the woman in the
Gospel did to thy Son. And yet Christ says that between Himself and him who does the will of His Father there will be as
close a relationship, as friendly a love, as there is between Himself and His Mother. Mark, too, that those are the words of that
Son who loved His Mother with greater tenderness than ever
son did father or mother. And in what circumstances did He
say them? Even whilst His Mother was standing at the door,
wishing to speak to Him. " And one said unto Him: Behold,
Thy Mother and Thy brethren stand without, seeking Thee." [2]
What answer did Christ make? " Stretching forth His hand
towards His disciples, He said: behold My mother and My brethren. For whosoever shall do the will of My Father that is in
heaven, he is My brother, and sister, and mother." [3] But, O
dear Lord, how is that possible? Canst Thou love any one as
much and esteem him as highly as Thy own Mother? Is she
not the dearest and best of all to Thee? Truly Thou hast loved
her, and dost still love her in heaven, more than all creatures
that are, have been, or can be. But why? Not so much because Thou hast taken flesh in her immaculate and blessed womb,
but rather because she, Thy virginal Mother, is among all creatures, angels, and men the one who most perfectly fulfils the will
of Thy heavenly Father in all circumstances. This is what Our

[1] Beatus venter qui te portavit.—Luke xi. 27.

[2] Dixit autem ei quidam : ecce mater tua et fratres tui foris stant quærentes te.—Matt. xii. 47.

[3] Et extendens manum in discipulos suos, dixit : Ecce mater mea et fratres mei. Quicumque enim fecerit voluntatem Patris mei, qui in cœlis e t, ipse meus frater, et soror, et
mater est.—Ibid. 46-50.

Lord Himself says. When the woman cried out: "Blessed is the womb that bore Thee," He answered: "Yea, rather blessed are they who hear the word of God, and keep it;"[1] that is, they who, having known and understood the will of God, fulfil it perfectly, as My Mother does. If there had been any creature in the world more resigned to God's will than Mary, Christ would have loved and prized that creature more than His own Mother.

O great God, I must cry out with astonishment, in the words of holy Job: "What is a man that Thou shouldst magnify him? or why dost Thou set Thy heart upon him?"[2] Behold, what we are bound to do as Thy slaves and most obedient servants, even if Thou wert not willing to reward us for it, what we are bound to do by countless titles of creation, preservation, redemption, Thy own sovereign dominion, namely, to filful Thy will in all circumstances with resigned, contented, and joyful hearts, that Thou thinkest so much of as to look on Thyself as under an obligation to us on account of it, and to reckon it as equal to the benefit Thou didst receive from Thy dearest Mother! True indeed are the words that Thy servant David utters in his astonishment: "But to me Thy friends, O God, are made exceedingly honorable."[3] Too great is the honor in which Thou holdest Thy intimate friends! Could a mortal man hope for any greater dignity or happiness on earth, my dear brethren, than to be in such high esteem, favor, and grace with the almighty God? *(What happiness for a poor mortal to be thus esteemed by God!)*

Nay, there is, I may say, a still higher dignity to which God will raise those who fulfil His will readily and with satisfaction. He, the great God, will submit Himself and His will to them, and will be their attendant and servant in eternal happiness. Are you surprised at this? Yet it is the truth; He says so Himself in the Gospel of St. Luke: "Blessed are those servants whom the Lord, when He cometh, shall find watching," that are ready and willing to do His will and pleasure. What reward shall they have? "Amen I say to you, that He will gird Himself, and make them sit down to meat, and passing, will minister unto them."[4] These words seemed incomprehensible to St. Thomas Aquinas; filled with astonishment on account of them, he cries out: What is this? "The almighty God submits Himself so far *(Nay, Christ will minister to such a one in heaven.)*

[1] Quinimo beati qui audiunt verbum Dei, et custodiunt illud.—Luke xi. 28.

[2] Quid est homo quia magnificas eum? aut quid apponis erga eum cor tuum?—Job vii. 17.

[3] Mihi autem nimis honorificati sunt amici tui, Deus.—Ps. cxxxviii. 17.

[4] Beati servi illi quos cum venerit Dominus, invenerit vigilantes: Amen dico vobis quod præcinget se, et faciet illos discumbere, et transiens ministrabit illis.—Luke xii. 37.

to holy souls, that He becomes their hired servant, as it were, while each one of them becomes His god."[1] Passing, He will minister to them; He will go around and wait on them, because during their life-time they waited on Him by joyfully resigning their wills to His. My dear brethren, who should not strain every nerve to practise this contentment and conformity with the will of God? If we had no other motive for it but the great favor, grace, and happiness that we thus gain with God, would not that in itself suffice? Now, what are the means by which we can attain to the practice of this beautiful virtue, which is so pleasing to God? That I shall explain to you on another occasion. I have now to answer an objection that has perhaps occurred to many of you since I began to speak on this subject. I shall do so briefly in the

Second Part.

Must we, then, keep still in all occurrences?

But, one might say, if what we have heard up to this is true; if all that happens in the world, save sin alone, happens according to the will and all-wise decree of God; if God wishes me to be circumstanced as I now am; if I must be satisfied with the will of God in everything that occurs to me; nay, if I should even rejoice that the Lord thus ordains things for me—then I can and must give up all care and trouble regarding myself and those belonging to me. Then should I and mine keep still and calmly wait with the utmost contentment what it may please God to decree for us. Nor dare I use any means to oppose that decree; for I must not offer opposition to the will of God. Nay, I must not even desire any change in myself or my state, but must leave things as they are fixed by God. Therefore, if I am now sick, I must be satisfied, because it is God's will, and I need not send for the doctor, nor take any medicine, in order to regain my health; otherwise I should oppose the will of God by desiring health while He wishes me to be sick. If I am now poor, and have great difficulty in supporting myself and my family, I must be satisfied, because such is the will of God; nor should I trouble myself about work or business in order to bring my affairs to a better condition, as by doing so I should oppose the will and all-wise decree of God, striving for riches and earthly goods while God wishes me to be poor and in want. If I have been unjustly deprived of what belongs to me, or if

---

[1] Deus omnipotens sanctis animabus in tantum se subjicit, quasi sit servus emptitius singularum, quilibet vero ipsarum sit deus suus.—D. Thom. 63, de Beat. c. 2.

my good name has been taken from me by calumny, I must be satisfied, and say with the patient Job: "The Lord hath taken away;" it is His will that I should suffer this loss of my worldly goods or good name. Nor can I denounce the unjust man to the authorities, nor seek to have my good name or property restored to me; otherwise I should oppose the divine decree by wishing to have things different to what God wills them to be. My child is disobedient, my servants obstinate or unfaithful, my husband or wife is the cause of much annoyance to me; what am I to do? I must be satisfied; it is the will of God that I should suffer this annoyance. Therefore I must not reprove the child, servant, or wife, nor punish them, lest I should act contrary to the will of God. My house is on fire, what am I to do? I must be satisfied and look on with folded hands, and not try to put the fire out; for it is the will of God that my house should be burnt, and I must submit to His will. And so on in other accidents and calamities. For instance, enemies, thieves, robbers, or murderers come into our town or country, and plunder and lay waste all before them; we must let them do as they please, and not try to prevent them, nor use violence against them; for it is the will of God that we should be harassed in that way. The times are dangerous through bad and unfruitful seasons, contagious sickness, impending war, plague, or famine; we cannot even have public prayers to avert those calamities, lest we should oppose the will and decree of God; but we must be satisfied and contented with whatever comes. How could people live in the world under those circumstances?

I must acknowledge that the difficulty is apparently a reasonable one and hard to answer. Yet such is not really the case, for I can solve it in one word. Since you are now poor, sick, persecuted, afflicted, it is God's will and decree for you to be so; that is true; yet God wishes you to use natural means to cure your sickness, for every one is bound to preserve his life and health for the divine service as long as he can conveniently. God wills you to labor and work hard in your poverty, in order to support yourself and your family as well as you can according to your state. God wishes you to try to save your house, since it is now on fire. God allows you to seek to regain in the ordinary lawful way what you have been unjustly deprived of. God wishes you to correct paternally and punish the faults of your wife, your children, your servants. God wishes that in public

Answer: No; we can and should use natural means to avert misfortunes.

as well as private calamities and afflictions we should fly to Him by prayer.

But, you insist, that is acting directly against the first will of God, by which He decreed that I should be sick, poor, persecuted, afflicted. No, it is not against the will of God; for, according to the unanimous teaching of the holy Fathers and of the theologians, God has a twofold will; one by which He absolutely decrees a certain thing, because it is pleasing to Him; the other by which He decrees a thing under certain conditions, that is to say, according as men act in this or that manner. Thus God will condemn me to hell forever if I die in the state of mortal sin. In the same way He often wishes men to continue in their illness and to die of it if they do not use medicines to regain their health. He wills your house to be burnt to the ground if you do not try to save it by putting the fire out, and He absolutely wills you to do this latter if you conveniently can. Are you, then, sick, poor, persecuted, afflicted to-day? If so, be satisfied and resigned to the will of God; for such is His will with regard to you to-day; but it may be also His will that you get well to-morrow if you use the proper medicines; that you be better off to-morrow if you work hard to that end; and so on in all the other accidents and circumstances of life which may be changed by human industry.

But if you have to-day used all the human means in your power to free yourself from your trials, and still remain in the same sickness, poverty, and affliction, then you have done your part, and you can safely say: It is the will of God for me to suffer this sickness or poverty; yet it is not forbidden, but is according to the divine will, that you should make another effort to better your condition to-morrow; and so on. The holy Bishop Remigius gives us a beautiful example of this. He had foreseen that in the coming year there would be a great scarcity of food, and therefore he collected a large quantity of corn, in order to be able to help the poor people; but some drunken, good-for-nothing young fellows began to jeer and laugh at his foresight. What is our Jubilarius up to now? they asked sneeringly. (Remigius had been fifty years a priest, and such was the name they gave him.) I think he wants to raise the price of corn. So saying, they ran to the barn in which the corn was stored. and set it on fire. When Remigius heard of this, he rode to the place at once, hoping to put out the fire; but he was too late; the corn was all consumed. What was the poor Bishop to do now? His pious and holy intention had thus been completely frustrated. When he saw that there was no more hope, he dismounted from his horse, went up close to the fire, and said without the least sign of anger, and with a smiling countenance: " The heat is a good thing, at all events." For he thought to himself: I have done my best, and have failed; the Lord gave, and the Lord hath taken away; blessed be the name of the Lord.

From this we see, first, how in all circumstances, whatever they may be, one can always be peaceful and contented, and think, Such is the will of God for the present; and yet, without acting against conformity with the will of God, try to make things better. Secondly, that we must not be at all anxious for the future; but, after we have done our best to bring things to a successful issue, leave the result in the hands of God with full contentment and satisfaction, being ready and willing at the same time to accept whatever He may please to decree for us. For instance, we might think: All my labor and trouble is of no avail; I am just as poor as ever I was; well, then, be it so! God wills it, and I also, O Lord; may Thy holy will be done! I have tried to get a better position, and have not succeeded; such is the will of God, and such, too, is my will, O Lord. May Thy holy will be done! I have tried to regain my rights, to have my property or honor restored to me; but to no purpose; I have lost my lawsuit. Let it be so, then; it is the will of God. Yes, my heavenly Father, I am satisfied; Thy holy will be done. I have for a long time tried to get rid of my domestic crosses; but things are just as bad as ever. Let it be so, then, since such is the will of God. Yea, my heavenly Father, may Thy holy will be done! All the medicines I take are not of the least good to me; I am still as sick as ever; therefore I wish to be sick, since God wishes it. Yea, my heavenly Father, may Thy will be done! Finally, all hope is lost, death is at hand, I cannot avoid it. I will, then, go into eternity, since such is the will of God. Yea, heavenly Father, may Thy holy will be done! I resign myself to Thy mercy; into Thy hands I commend my spirit. That is the way, my dear brethren, to be fully resigned to the will of God in all circumstances; that is the virtue which contains all other virtues, and to which I have been trying to encourage you and myself as well.

How to resign ourselves daily to the will of God.

Let us, then, make once for all the firm resolution to practise it with all possible diligence. Let us often think with a lively faith, God is a Lord of infinite wisdom, justice, and holiness, so that whatever He decrees for us must be good, right, and holy. To God alone belongs all honor, praise, and glory, and He places His greatest exterior honor in this, that creatures are in full conformity with His will; therefore, we ought to look on it as our greatest happiness and joy thus to honor and glorify Him. God is our most loving Father, who knows what is good for us, and who ordains all for our greater eternal good; therefore, we ought to be contented and rejoiced that everything happens to us according to His holy will and pleasure. In any case, God does what He wills, no matter whether we oppose Him in our impatience or not. Therefore, prudence and common sense require us to accept from His hand with a contented spirit that which He will send to us even against our will if we are obstinate, and in the latter case we shall have no merit. In this conformity with the will of God consists the greatest peace of heart and happiness which we can enjoy on earth; and in it, too, consists the highest happiness that we can have with God in heaven. What else are all these motives, O God,—and one of them should suffice,—but so many fetters and chains which draw and force me with violence, as it were, to submit to Thy holy will in all circumstances with full satisfaction? Yea, heavenly Father, so shall it be; my greatest efforts shall tend to have my will in perfect conformity with Thine. Above all I will avoid the least thing that is contrary to Thy will, and never omit what I know to be pleasing to it. Whenever I am in adversity, no matter where it comes from, I will at once collect my thoughts, and say to myself: Such is the will of my heavenly Father: "Yea, Father, for so hath it seemed good in Thy sight." Thus, since I shall do and omit what Thou wishest me to do and omit, Thou wilt be satisfied with me; and at the same time, since I shall accept with satisfaction all Thou ordainest for me, I shall be satisfied with Thee. Thus we shall both be one. O my God, do this in me by Thy powerful grace, that I may remain always united with Thy holy will, until I shall see Thee in Thy kingdom, where I shall be perfectly united with Thy will forever. Amen.

Another Introduction to the same sermon for the fifth Sunday after Epiphany.

Text.

Triticum autem congregate in horreum meum.—Matt. xiii. 30.
" But the wheat gather ye into My barn."

Introduction.

So it will be in the end; the weed goes into the fire, the wheat into the barn. When the two are growing in the field, if we were to judge of them by outward appearances, we should say that the weeds are better than the wheat; for the former seem more beautiful on account of the red, white, and yellow flowers they produce. But in the end, when the harvest time comes, and one has to be separated from the other, the good man of the house forms a far different judgment, for he knows the difference. "Gather up first the cockle, " he says; "and bind it in bundles to burn, but the wheat gather ye into my barn." By this parable, my dear brethren, according to the explanation given by St. Augustine, Our Saviour wishes to represent this world as a vast field. By the weeds He means the wicked; by the wheat, the good, who order their lives according to the law and will of God, as the holy martyr St. Ignatius said: " I am the corn of Christ, and must be ground by the teeth of the wild beasts." The wicked, as long as they are mixed up with the good, seem to be the happier of the two, since they are generally better provided with the things of this world, and spend their time in pleasures and vanities, while by divine decree the good are tried by many afflictions and calamities. If we were to judge in this case, too, by mere appearances, we should grudge the happiness of the wicked, and have a heart-felt pity for the good; and really, in the opinion of the world, the poor, sick, persecuted, humbled servant of God passes for a very miserable mortal indeed. But the world may think what it will; it is not its opinion that makes us unhappy, but our own imagination, as Salvianus says: " No one is unhappy on account of the opinion of others, but on account of his own." [1] Even if good men are sorely tried in this life, what a great change there will be at the end, when the heavenly Husbandman shall give the word for death to separate the two sorts of men, and the angels will take

---

[1] Nemo aliorum sensu miser est, sed suo.

the wheat away from the weeds! Into the fire with the cockle!
Such shall be the sentence; "but the wheat gather ye into My
barn," that it may enjoy eternal happiness. Yet we need not
wait till then; if the poor, oppressed man, who is so unhappy in
the eyes of the world, is only satisfied with God and His holy
will, he is the happiest of men even here, because he wills all
that God wills, etc.—*Continues as above.*

FIFTY-FIRST SERMON.

ON THE MEANS OF ATTAINING CONFORMITY WITH THE WILL OF GOD.

Subject.

To attain perfect conformity of our will with the will of God,
1. The first means is constant prayer to God. 2. The second
means is the constant practice of this virtue.—*Preached on the
feast of SS. Philip and James, Apostles.*

Text.

Non turbetur cor vestrum.—John xiv. 27.
"Let not your heart be troubled."

Introduction.

Why should you be troubled or disturbed, My dear disciples,
whom I have chosen to tread in My footsteps and to do the will
of My heavenly Father as you have seen Me do it? You, for
whom eternal dwellings have been prepared in My Father's
house: "In My Father's house there are many mansions; I go
to prepare a place for you; and I will take you to Myself, that
where I am you also may be"?[1] Therefore "let not your
heart be troubled." You will indeed have to suffer persecution
from men for My name's sake; you will be hated by all; they
will scourge, crucify, and kill you; but no matter what happens
to you, "let not your heart be troubled." For such is the ordination of My heavenly Father for you, that you may have greater
glory in His heavenly dwelling. Such is the meaning of the
words that Christ addressed at the time to His disciples, and
which He now speaks to all Christians who mean well towards
Him, "Let not your heart be troubled." You, too, My faith-

---

[1] In domo Patris mei mansiones multæ sunt; vado parare vobis locum; et accipiam vos ad
meipsum, ut ibi sum ego, et vos sitis.—John xiv. 2, 3.

ful servants, have no cause for uneasiness as long as you continue to submit your will to the will of My heavenly Father in all things; nay, by that very means you will obtain repose and contentment of heart, and will give My Father the greatest glory, and gain for yourselves the greatest happiness in heaven and on earth. This, my dear brethren, I have already explained in detail when speaking of the conformity of our will with the will of God. It still remains to be seen how we can attain to the practice of this virtue, on which so much depends. The means of doing so I will now suggest to you.

Plan of Discourse.

To attain perfect conformity of our will with the will of God, the first means is constant prayer to God, as I shall show in the first part. The second means is, the constant practice of this virtue, as I shall show in the second part.

That we may faithfully use both means, give us Thy grace, O God, which we ask of Thee through the intercession of Mary and of our holy guardian angels.

The most necessary means of preserving the life of the body is to take food and nourishment; and it is so necessary that nothing can supply for it if it is wanting. A man can live without clothing, bedding, house, or money; but it is, humanly speaking, impossible to live for any length of time without food, unless, indeed, the Almighty works a miracle, as He has sometimes done, in favor of His servants. Therefore hunger is reckoned as the worst of torments, under the influence of which men have been known to eat cats, dogs, mice, and rats; nay, we read in the History of the Jews that during the siege of Jerusalem under Titus there were some mothers who ate their own children. The same thing happened in Treves; when the people were suffering from famine and pestilence, history tells us, that a woman cooked and ate her own child.

Food is necessary to preserve the life of the body.

My dear brethren, what food is to the preservation of the bodily life that is prayer to the soul and the preservation of the spiritual life, as the holy Fathers say. This is the meaning of what the Prophet David says: "I am smitten as grass, and my heart is withered, because I forgot to eat my bread;" [1] that is, because I have left off praying to God. Mark those words; he does not call prayer simply nourishing food, but bread; to show

Prayer is the food of the soul.

[1] Percussus sum ut fœnum, et aruit cor meum; quia oblitus sum comedere panem meum. —Ps. ci. 5.

that, as bread is generally used with all other kinds of food, and no food is relished without it, so prayer must be used with all the other means that are ordained to preserve the spiritual life of the soul.

And as necessary for the attainment of virtue as the soul is to the body. St. John Chrysostom is not satisfied with comparing prayer to bread or any other kind of food; he makes the necessity of it far greater when he says: "What the soul is to the body, that is prayer to the soul."[1] At a pinch a man might live for one, two, three, or four days without bread or other food; but he could not live a moment without his soul. And this is the reason why Jesus Christ, our Saviour, has left to the world that exhortation that St. Paul afterwards so deeply impresses on all men: "We ought always to pray, and not to faint."[2] For, as the human body is always enlivened and kept up by the indwelling soul, no matter whether we sit, or walk, or wake, or sleep, or work, or eat, or drink, so also the soul and its supernatural life must be strengthened and supported in all its actions by prayer to God.

This necessity is founded on our wants, which God alone can supply. The truth of this is evident from the nature of prayer. For it is either a petition that we present to God, begging something from Him and hoping to obtain it, and that is the case generally with vocal prayer and the aspirations that we make use of frequently during the day; or else it is a union of the mind with God and divine things, by means of the frequent recollection of God and divine things, by keeping in the presence of God, or by the inward intention by which all our works and even outward actions are directed to God; and this latter is the sense in which we must understand the words of Our Lord, "We ought always to pray, and not to faint." Both these qualities of prayer show how necessary it is for all men at all times to obtain the spiritual goods they are in need of. With regard to the first, the prayer of petition and asking from God, it is as necessary to a man as it is for a poor cripple, who has neither money nor friends to help him, to beg for his food and to entreat the charitably disposed to assist him. How else could the poor man live, since he has no money to buy food, and cannot use his hands to earn it? If he does not find people to help him, he must die of hunger; and if he refused to beg under those circumstances it would be an evident sign that he wishes to put an end to his own existence. Now, are not the wants of our souls much greater than the temporal wants of such a man? Can we form

[1] Quod corpori est anima, hoc animæ est oratio.
[2] Oportet semper orare, et non deficere.—Luke xviii. 1.

even a good thought without the assistance of the almighty God? And, therefore, have we not good reason to beg of God unceasingly to come to our assistance, and to look on him who gives up prayer as in a most desperate state, and far worse off than the cripple who says to himself: What is the use of my begging and crying for help? I know very well that it will not do me the least good. Of twenty whom I ask for alms there is hardly one who gives me anything; I will beg no longer. But could such a thought as that enter our minds, my dear brethren, about the almighty God, since we have His infallible promises that our prayers shall never be fruitless, and whatever we ask for the good of our souls and in a proper manner shall always be granted? With regard to the other species of prayer, namely, union with God by constant recollection of His presence, it is also necessary for one who wishes to keep from sin for any length of time. Unhappy is the soul that separates itself from God and does not cultivate a familiarity with Him. What will become of it? What becomes of the little infant that is abandoned by its mother? of the limb that is cut off from the body? How can either preserve its life?

Since that is the case, my dear brethren, since prayer is so absolutely necessary for our spiritual welfare, how much more necessary must it not be to attain to the practice of that important virtue which contains all the other virtues, in which our greatest piety and holiness consists, and on which therefore our salvation depends,—the virtue of perfect conformity and resignation of our will to the will of God? To do and omit in all circumstances what God wills, how, and because God wills, is the first requisite; and it is often a very hard and difficult thing, since we have to do many things that we do not like, and omit many that we are inclined to do, while we must also overcome our desires, and trample on human respect and the usages of the world. How could we expect to be able to do that exactly, in the midst of doubts and distracting occupations, when we do not know what God wills us to do or avoid, unless we first humbly beg light from Him, and seek to know His will by fervent prayer? To be in all circumstances satisfied and contented with the will and decree of God, even in the most trying and disagreeable occurrences, against which all the inclinations of our nature rise up in arms, this is the second requisite for the virtue of which we are speaking. But how could we think of attaining such perfection without the divine aid, and therefore without prayer?

Much more necessary is prayer to attain conformity with the will of God.

Therefore
we must
earnestly
beg of God
to give us
this virtue.

Hence, if we are desirous of this beautiful virtue, ah, let us pray humbly, fervently, constantly with the Catholic Church: "give us, O Lord, a true conformity with Thy will."[1]　Be assured that the frequent repetition of this one little prayer, even in thought, with a sincere heart, brings more profit to the soul than spending two or three hours in the church reading a prayer-book, without rightly understanding what we are saying, or really meaning our prayers to be heard.　Before all the duties and occupations in which we are engaged during the day, let us ask the divine assistance in these or similar words: Grant, O Lord, that I may do this work according to Thy will and pleasure.　In all doubts as to whether we should do or omit this or that, let us, with St. Paul, ask advice from God: "Lord, what wilt Thou have me to do?"[2]　Tell me by my holy guardian angel what is pleasing to Thee, and in what manner I am to do it.　That we should do more especially, and some time beforehand, in important matters on which a great deal depends; as, for instance, when we wish to know whether we should choose this office, this employment, this trade or business, this state of life.　I have explained this matter fully when speaking of the choice of a state of life.　Our holy Father St. Ignatius has prescribed for his children a rule commanding them never to ask a superior for anything without first having taken counsel with God by prayer, to see if it is His holy will that the request should be granted. How much more, then, ought not Christians to take a similar precaution in things on which their eternal happiness or misery depends?　Let us pray, and pray humbly, earnestly, constantly: Grant, O Lord, that we may be fully satisfied with Thy decrees, so as to be able to say with truth and sincerity in all circumstances and occurrences, in all trials and calamities: Thy will be done on earth, as it is in heaven!　O heavenly Father, may Thy will be done in me and mine!　Whenever we say the Our Father we should repeat those words with special fervor and attention in this sense: Grant, O Lord, that I may always know Thy holy will and do it; that I may be fully satisfied with it in all circumstances.　More especially should we repeat this prayer when suffering annoyances or afflictions that are hard for our nature: Heavenly Father, Thou hast decreed this for me; may Thy holy will be done!　Only give me patience, and bend my

---

[1] Da nobis, Domine, veram cum tua voluntate concordiam.

[2] Domine, quid me vis facere?—Acts. ix. 6.

obstinate will, that it may be fully conformed to Thine, etc.

Yet, my dear brethren, prayer alone will not suffice, unless we *But, besides* set to work in earnest. God wishes us to be virtuous, but He *prayer, we* will not interfere with our virtuous works; He will help us to *use other* do them, if we ask His help in a becoming manner; but we, *means.* on our side, must work with His grace and help. The mother does her best to encourage and teach her child how to walk; but the child must move its feet or it will never learn. Therefore, the second necessary means of attaining to conformity with the will of God is the constant practice of this virtue, as we shall see in the

Second Part.

I do not think we need wait long for an opportunity of practis- *First; we* ing this beautiful virtue; every hour of the day we have oppor- *tise this vir-* tunities enough. But how are we to set about it? From small *tue in small* things we must go on to great ones, and he who wishes to reach *things.* the summit of perfection must commence at the bottom of the ladder. If you wish to get to the top of a ladder, do you begin by setting your foot on the highest rung? No, that would not do; you must begin at the first, and from that go on to the second, and from the second to the third, from the third to the fourth, and so on, until you gradually reach the highest. A child never learns to walk all at once: it must first know how to set down its feet properly, and, then take one step after another, holding on by a bench; in a little while it will be able to walk slowly with-out any support; and at last it can go as fast as it wishes without danger. Such is the manner in which we have to learn to prac-tise the virtue of conformity with the will of God. Perfect sat-isfaction and resignation in all circumstances is a far too high and glorious virtue to be attained at a jump; the whole secret of its practice consists in profiting by the ordinary opportunities that are daily offered us; then, after a time, we shall be able to bear the greatest misfortunes and adversities without any in-ordinate disturbance of mind, remembering that those things come to us from the good God.

There is no one in the world who has not daily to contend with *For which* things that are contrary to his will and inclination. They may *we have* come from our own imprudence or inexperience, from the weak- *opportuni-* ness and fastidiousness of nature, from carelessness and forget- *ties.* fulness, or from the wickedness and malice of others with whom we have to do; or from chance as we imagine; or from unavoidable causes that we could not foresee or prevent. Whatever be their origin, our whole lives are thickly strewn with those sharp thorns, as we may call them, which excite in our hearts many a movement of hatred, envy, anger and displeasure, of fear and anxiety, of impatience and annoyance, of disquiet and uneasiness, that, for a few moments at least, unsettles our peace of mind. For instance, an expression escapes us that we would gladly recall a moment after; another person says something that annoys us; a servant is careless or slow at work; a child annoys us by its crying; our food is not properly cooked or is too salt; while eating I bite my tongue; some awkward person treads on your toe; you knock your hand against something that hurts it; while working, a splinter gets under your nail; you cut yourself with a knife or other sharp instrument; your work does not go to your satisfaction; a glass, a pitcher, or a basin gets broken; your clothes are torn; as you are going about the house in the dark, the light gets blown out; you cannot sleep at night, or somebody disturbs you when you want to rest; the weather is disagreeable; you are kept too long at the door before it is opened to you; your business, contrary to your expectations, brings you in little or nothing during the day; and there are countless similar occasions, on which our fastidious nature is apt to feel disturbed and put out.

This practice will gradually teach us how to conform to the will of God in greater misfortunes.

It is in little things like those in which an impatient man, who does not try to restrain his passions, is wont to break out into cursing, swearing, and blasphemy: it is in such little things, I say, that we have an excellent opportunity of practising the virtue of conformity with the will of God, provided we recover ourselves at once, remember divine Providence from which these things come, and think to ourselves, Such is the will of God; Lord, may Thy will be done! I acknowledge that one cannot hope to practise great and heroic virtues by means of such things; yet, there is not the least doubt that in the long run we can attain to a high degree of virtue, perfect peace of mind and undisturbed satisfaction by means of them. It is certain that he who is diligent in finding out how he can offer and present such trifling things to God, and who receives them from the hand of his heavenly Father with a contented will, not only adds enormously to his merits by that constancy in practising virtue, but also becomes capable of conforming his will to that of God, even in the most disagreeable accidents and circumstances of this life.

Only try it for a time, my dear brethren, and you will find that what I say is the truth.

But if we have no opportunity of practising conformity with the will of God, besides what is offered us in those ordinary occurrences of life, then we can have recourse to another practice that is most pleasing to God and useful to ourselves; namely, that of fully offering ourselves and all that we have daily to the most holy will of God. For, although great misfortunes do not happen to us every day, yet we can every day offer ourselves to God, and protest that we are ready to accept such visitations, and to bear them if it is His holy will. This was what our holy Father St. Ignatius did; his daily prayer was: Receive, O Lord, all my liberty, take my memory, understanding, and will, etc.; my body and soul, and all that Thou hast given me; my honor and good name, my health, my life, and the end of my life; I give it all to Thee, and submit and deliver it wholly to Thy adorable will. Only one thing I ask of Thee: give me Thy love, and I am rich enough, nor do I desire anything else. Oh, truly, that is a beautiful prayer, my dear brethren! Happy he who says it with a sincere heart! *(margin: We can also daily offer ourselves to God to suffer great trials if He wishes.)*

For the same purpose it would be well to put one's self frequently to the proof, in order to see if we can accept with contentment and satisfaction any great calamity that God might be pleased to send us. An architect keeps on hand all kinds of plans of buildings, great and small, although no one has asked for them, so that in case a plan is required, he may have it ready at once. So each one can make in his own imagination a plan of some misfortune or calamity that might happen to him, foresee it and represent it to his mind, as if it were already present, and he felt the pressure of it; and then think: what if this misfortune really happened to me? Would I then be resigned to the divine will? For instance, if I were to lose this important law-suit, or this employment which brings me in such a good income; if the business in which I have embarked all my fortune goes to the bad; if my house should be burnt down; if my husband or wife should be confined to bed for years with a painful illness, so that we could earn nothing; if I should lose the favor of my master; if my dear friend were to be taken away from me by death; if the child that is the joy of my life, should be led astray and become the cause of the greatest trouble to me; if my husband, with whom I have lived so peacefully hitherto, should *(margin: And we can imagine that God sends us great trials, and then see how we are disposed with regard to them.)*

change, and turn his love into hatred, and fill the house with quarrelling and contention; if I should be put to public shame or disgrace; if my only son were to die; if the great God were to summon my husband or wife from the world, and to leave me helpless and alone with my poor children; how would I be disposed in such a case? Truly, it would be a hard blow for me, a bitter nut to crack! Yet it might happen, perhaps it will happen; supposing it did, what should I do? To try to resist it would be vain; to give way to murmurs and complaints, to cursing and swearing, to moaning and lamentations would be to no purpose. The cross would come to me from the God who means so well with me; would it not be right, then, for me to accept it from Him willingly, readily, and submissively? Truly, it would be so! Then I will anticipate the will of God, which I do not yet know, and from this moment fully abandon myself to what the good God may please to decree for me and mine. Yes, O my Lord and my God, behold here I am, ready for every thing; may Thy holy will be done. Only if Thou sendest me this cross, give me the grace of patience, that I may bear it with contentment. In that way, my dear brethren, by that heroic resolution and determination to surrender our will to God, we not only gain great merit, but if the misfortune really comes, we have already half conquered it: for the evils that we foresee do us less harm. After the Society of Jesus was spread throughout the world, and was already doing much for the glory of God and the salvation of souls, St. Ignatius used to say: if news were now brought to me, that the whole Society would be certainly disbanded and abolished, truly it would be sad news indeed! Yet I believe that even in that case I should regain my peace of mind and contentment, if I only spent a quarter of an hour in fervent prayer to God, and remembered that it happened according to His will.

Finally, when troubles come, we must at once submit to the will of God. Finally, if one of those calamities I have mentioned, or a similar great misfortune, really happens to you, what then? Oh, do not lose much time in giving way to useless sorrow, or in complaining of the conduct of men, or blind chance, to which you attribute your sufferings; but cast yourself at once at the feet of your heavenly Father, and beg Him humbly to give you grace and strength to bear the trial with constancy. How does one act who is mortally wounded? Does he run after the person who inflicted the wound? No, for that would not heal it. If he is prudent, he will go at once to the nearest doctor, who can cure him. Such, too, should be our conduct in all trials and misfortunes. I am daily mortally wounded, we should say to ourselves; my heart is sorrowful even to death; I must run, then, at once to the only Doctor who can cure and comfort me; that is to God, my heavenly Father. Would you prefer to run after him who has inflicted the wound? Then go, but to the same God; for it is He who has afflicted you; cast yourself into His fatherly lap; kiss the well-meaning hand that has struck you, and say: "Yea, Father, for so hath it seemed good in Thy sight." May Thy holy will be done; I accept the wound Thou hast inflicted on me. Thou alone canst and must now heal and comfort me.

If, in such circumstances, the devil suggests blasphemous thoughts, or your natural inclinations rise up in rebellion against the divine decrees, or men, as is generally the case when other people are the cause of our misfortunes, try to arouse your anger, or to make you curse or swear or complain; then think and say to those false advisers what Jesus Christ said to Peter, when He commanded him to sheathe the sword that he had drawn to defend his Master in the garden: "The chalice which My Father hath given Me, shall I not drink it?"[1] Will you prevent me from drinking the chalice of suffering that my heavenly Father has poured out for me? Will you try to persuade me not to take it from His hand? From that hand which has created me, when I was not; which has preserved me every moment till now; which leads and guides, protects and defends me; which has always been so generous to me? "Go behind me, Satan, thou art a scandal unto me; because thou savorest not the things that are of God, but the things that are of men."[2] Be still, ye rebellious and unruly thoughts! Ye false friends, carnal men, depart from me! You are a scandal to me! You do not understand the things of God; you are my enemies, because you try to turn me away from the only true Friend I have in the world, and to make me look with suspicion on my beloved Father! Away with you! I am satisfied with my God; He has sent me this sorrow; shall I not then bear it without a murmur? If my sworn enemy had afflicted me in this manner, out of mere hatred, and with a desire of tormenting and injuring me, then you would have some apparent grounds for advising me to resist

And overcome all opposition by the thought: it is the will of God.

---

[1] Calicem quem dedit mihi Pater, non bibam illum?—John xviii. 11.

[2] Vade post me, satana, scandalum es mihi : quia non sapis ea quæ Dei sunt : sed ea quæ hominum.—Matt. xvi. 23.

him. But "the chalice which my Father hath given me, shall I not drink it?" He is the best, most loving and merciful of all fathers, from whom I have received and hope every good thing; I am certain and assured that He loves me, that in all His decrees, besides His own honor and glory, He seeks the welfare and advantage of my soul, and that, as far as He is concerned, He desires me to be happy in heaven; can I then doubt that this suffering which He now sends me is for my good? And how do I know what is good for me? If this misfortune had not happened, if I had not lost my property or that law-suit, if my money had not been taken away, if I were still in good health, if I were not thus disgraced and put to shame, perhaps I should be lost forever! If my dear child, or husband, or friend had lived for some years longer, perhaps he would have died in the state of mortal sin and have been hurled into hell. I do not know that, but my God knows it; and He orders all things with the greatest wisdom and justice. And be it as it may, Thou hast done it, O God! It is Thy will, O my heavenly Father, and this one thought should suffice to make me resign myself to Thee with my whole heart. Thou art the Lord, who canst dispose of me and mine as Thou wilt, and hast that right by countless titles; truly, Thou deservest that I should give Thee this honor and glory, and contentedly accept this trial from Thy fatherly hand! Nor will I oppose Thee in any way: "Not my will, but Thine be done." I thank Thee, and rejoice that Thou now fulfillest Thy holy will in me; and if it were in my power to resist Thee, and turn away this trial from myself, even then I should willingly accept it, for the sole reason that I know that it is Thy will, O God, that I should have it. Therefore, with my whole heart I will say: "Blessed be the name of the Lord; as it hath pleased the Lord, so is it done." So let us pray, my dear brethren; so let us daily accept the ordinary crosses of our lives, and so offer ourselves to God, that, when greater trials are sent us by Him, we may take them from His hand with resignation. Then we shall have attained that beautiful virtue in which all our holiness consists, by which God is most honored, which brings us the greatest repose and happiness on earth, and which will surely make us happy with God and His saints in the kingdom of heaven. Amen.

Another Introduction to the same sermon for the sixth Sunday after Epiphany.

Text.

Simile est regnum cœlorum grano sinapis.—Matt. xiii. 31.
" The kingdom of heaven is like to a grain of mustard-seed."

Introduction.

From the mustard-seed, which is the smallest of all seeds, grows a shrub like a tree, in the branches of which the birds of the air rest and build their nests. So says Our Lord in to-day's Gospel. What is the meaning, my dear brethren, of saying that heaven is like the grain of mustard-seed? In my opinion, it is nothing else than that our eternal happiness or misery generally has its origin and commencement in some small thing which we either regard properly for the love of God or despise through contempt. For from small things we go on to great. So it is. And, to speak to the point, a slight act against the known will of God, that is, when I refuse to do what God wishes me to do, or to avoid what is displeasing to Him, or resist His decree in some small matter; a trifle of that kind is often so deeply felt by God, that He will deprive me of the graces He had prepared for me, and allow me to fall into sin and to lose my soul. On the other hand, a trifling service that I offer to God with well-meaning heart, after having known His will, a ready act of resignation to His decrees in some slight trial, is often so highly esteemed by God that He will therefore bestow on me special favors and extraordinary graces, by which I am enabled to grow in virtue and to gain heaven. This I have already explained, if you remember, in another sermon. I then drew the conclusion, and draw it now, too, that in order to make sure, we should do and omit all that God wishes us to do and omit, without even the least exception; and that, in all circumstances, without the least exception, we should be satisfied with God's will and decree. In that properly consists the full conformity of our will with the will of God, which gives God the greatest honor and glory, and ourselves the greatest happiness in heaven and on earth, as we have heard already. It now remains, etc.—*Continues as above.*

On Conformity with the will of God in our Respective States of Life; On Confident Resignation of Ourselves to the Will of God, see the foregoing first part. On the Confident Resignation of the

Care of our Salvation to the will of God, see the following fifth part. On the Example of the Blessed Virgin, of the holy Angels and of St. Joseph, with respect to this conformity, see the sixth part.

ON THE LOVE OF OUR NEIGHBOR.

ON THE MOTIVES FOR LOVING OUR NEIGHBOR.

Subject.

We must love all our fellow-men, no matter who they are: 1. Because they are worthy of our love; 2. Because Jesus Christ is worthy that we should love them for His sake.—*Preached on the Seventeenth Sunday after Pentecost.*

Text.

Diliges proximum tuum sicut teipsum.—Matt. xxii. 39.
" Thou shalt love thy neighbor as thyself."

Introduction.

There we have the foundation of the whole law, " Thou shalt love the Lord thy God with thy whole heart; Thou shalt love thy neighbor as thyself." This love of our neighbor is as rare among men in the world as the love of God, even amongst those who imagine they love their neighbor. For in what narrow limits they confine that love! Friends, relations, benefactors, and those who agree with our opinions and suit our fancies, generally share all our love among them. All others we look on as strangers; and if a work of Christian charity is required in their behalf, Oh, we think and say, what is the man to me? I do not know him; I owe him nothing; he has not deserved anything from me; I cannot bear him, nor suffer to be in his company, etc. Christians! That is not according to the words of the law, "Thou shalt love thy neighbor as thyself," that is, all men, no matter who they are. Why so?

Plan of Discourse.

Thou shalt love thy neighbor as thyself, no matter who he is; because in himself he is worthy of your love. This I shall show in the first part.   Thou shalt love thy neighbor as thyself, no matter who he is; because Christ deserves that, for His sake, you should love your neighbor.   This I shall show in the second part.

Mary, Mother of fair love, and you holy guardian angels, obtain for us all a true love of our neighbor, because Jesus Christ our Saviour expects it from us.

The portraits of great men are held in honor.   When you enter the houses and rooms of rich people, you see all kinds of paintings on the walls, some of which are enclosed in silver or gilt frames.   Many a simple-minded person might think: What is the use of wasting so much gold and silver and rich stuff on those bits of painted canvas?   Why go to that expense for such useless things?   If the value of the gold or silver were given to the poor, or spent otherwise, there would be some sense in it.   But, my good friend, some one who knows the difference might answer, you do not understand those things; the costly frames are not for the sake of the picture, nor of the colors in which it is painted; but rather for the sake of the person whom it represents.   There is the portrait of the emperor, there that of our elector; on the other side, that of the grandfather of the master of the house, and that of his father; this picture, although it is rather soiled looking, is an original of one of the most celebrated painters of his time.   Therefore, it is well worth while to adorn such pictures as those with costly frames.

Brothers, comrades, and companions love each other.   Again, when we see two brothers or sisters, or comrades, or travelling companions, acting towards each other with special affection and confidence, we are not surprised thereat.   Every one looks on it as a matter of course; they have been brought up in the one house by the same parents; they have been lodging together for many years; they are fellow-countrymen and have been on a journey together in a foreign land.   If such people were not on friendly terms with each other, where could friendship be found?

Our neighbor is the image of God.   Thou shalt love thy neighbor, O man! O Christian! that is, each and every one in the world without exception.   Do you wish to know the reason why you should love him?   Open the eyes of your faith: oh, what a precious image and picture you will see in him!   No matter what his outward appearance may be, or his inward disposition; no matter how ragged, poor, lowly, abject, miserable, unknown he may seem, he is a living image of the mighty Monarch of heaven and earth; he has in his body a soul as beautiful as an angel, in which is reflected the likeness of the Most Blessed Trinity. That soul is an original of the God of infinite wisdom, knowledge, and power, nor has any one laid a hand on it but God Himself, nor does it owe its origin to any one but God; it is made for nothing else but God; it has no other end and aim but God, no other resting-place but God, and expects no other reward but God. That soul is an original which may not be bought or sold for any price less than the life blood of God. Oh, human soul, in what great honor and esteem Thou must be held! O parents, be careful of the precious souls of your children, that they may not be lost forever! Christians, labor every day with the utmost diligence for the salvation of your immortal souls: for that is the only necessary business you have to attend to, as long as you are on this earth! Christians, I add, as a conclusion to be drawn from this, honor and love your neighbor, who is such a beautiful image of God! For, if a lifeless picture, that is made of worthless colors, is esteemed and honored merely because it represents some great man or good friend, or because it is a celebrated work of art, what honor and love are not due to the master-piece of God's hand, which is a living image of the Ever Blessed Trinity? When the young Tobias presented himself before Raguel, the latter, although he had never before seen him, at once received him with the utmost love and friendship, because he saw that his features resembled those of the elder Tobias, whom he loved dearly, not merely on account of relationship, but also on account of his excellent character: "And Raguel received them with joy. And Raguel looking upon Tobias, said to Anna his wife: How like is this young man to my cousin?" And at once he began to speak of his dear friend, but when he found that the young man was his son, he embraced him with tears of joy: "And Raguel went to him, and kissed him with tears, and weeping upon his neck, said: A blessing be upon thee, my son, because thou art the son of a good and most virtuous man." [1] O Christians, when we consider our neighbor in the light of faith, we, too, must acknowledge and say: How like this man is to our God of infinite beauty! And when we have thus considered him, provided we love God, must we not confess that, on that account alone, there is not one in the world who is not worthy of esteem and love?

---

[1] Suscepit eos Raguel cum gaudio. Intuensque Tobiam Raguel dixit Annæ uxori suæ: quam similis est juvenis iste consobrino meo? Et misitse Raguel et cum lacrymis osculatus est eum, et plorans super collum ejus dixit: Benedictio sit tibe fili mi; quia boni et optimi viri filius es.—Tob. vii. 1, 2, 6, 7.

He is our brother.

But there is a much closer connection and relationship between us, by which we are bound to love each other mutually. For all human beings are brothers and sisters; we are all children of a common father, not only because we are descended from the same father Adam, according to the flesh, but also because, by the far more excellent birth of the soul, we are children of our eternal Father, who is in heaven. "Have we not all one father?" said God by the Prophet Malachy to the priests of the Old Law, who in their hearts despised the common people; "Hath not one God created us? Why, then, doth every one of us despise his brother?"[1] If men were bound to love each other with fraternal affection in the Old Law, what love and union are not required amongst us Christians by the New Law, that most perfect and all-holy law of love published by Jesus Christ? For we are born again in the blood of Christ, adopted as children of God, and thus related, we cry out unanimously to heaven, as Our Saviour Himself has taught us, as our elder Brother: "Our Father, who art in heaven." Nor does each one who prays say "my Father," but "our Father," "so that," as St. Chrysostom says "whenever we pray, we must remember that we are all brothers and sisters, who have the one heavenly Father." "We do not say," says St. Cyprian, "give me this day my daily bread; forgive me my trespasses; lead me not into temptation; deliver me from evil; but, give us our daily bread; forgive us our trespasses, etc." Why? "We pray for all the people, because all the people are one,"[2] to show that we must foster a mutual love as if we were but one individual, and had but one heart, mind, and will; therefore, the good I wish myself I must also wish all others; and what I do not wish to happen to myself I must desire to avert from others, according to the practice of the early Christians, as we read in the Acts of the Apostles: "And the multitude of believers had but one heart and one soul; neither did any one say that aught of the things which he possessed was his own, but all things were common unto them."[3] Oh, truly happy times!

Our comrades and table companions.

That love and union of hearts should exist amongst us Christians, because we are all brothers and sisters, children of a common Father, and also because we have a common mother, the

---

[1] Numquid non pater unus omnium nostrum? numquid non Deus unus creavit nos? Quare ergo despicit unusquisque nostrum fratrem suum.—Malach. ii. 10.

[2] Pro toto populo oramus, quia totus populus unum sumus.—S. Cyprian. de Orat. Dom.

[3] Multitudinis autem credentium erat cor unum et anima una; nec quisquam eorum quæ possidebat, aliquid suum esse dicebat, sed erant illis omnia communia.—Acts iv. 32.

holy Catholic Church, in and from which we receive spiritual
life from God. For by baptism we are born again in Christ, we
are brought up from our youth in the holy doctrine and teaching
of the Church, we are fed like comrades at the same table, and
our food and drink is the precious, adorable flesh and blood of
Jesus Christ. "Ah," says St. Chrysostom, considering this, and
addressing those Christians who live in hatred and disunion;
"will you not love and act towards one another as children of the
same heavenly Father? Then, at all events, have some respect
for the Table in which you all participate."[1] That Table on
which Jesus daily offers Himself as a Victim to His Father, and
gives Himself to us as the food of our souls. Even murderers,
when they have once eaten bread and salt together, cease to plot
against each other, and become comrades; but we Christians cannot live in peace and harmony, although we so often receive together the Sacrament of Love of the most meek Lamb, and are
united in Christ!

Finally, we are all travelling companions, who are going on the
same road to the same fatherland, namely, to heaven, where our
Almighty Father and many of our brothers and sisters, who have
gone before, await us, that, being united with them in the most
perfect love, we may enjoy the same inheritance with them, and
possess the same eternal joys. The inheritance that children expect after the death of their parents in this life is often a cause
of strife, disunion, and contention between brothers and sisters.
Nor is that to be wondered at; for since the amount to be left them
is limited, the greater the number of children, the less the share
that comes to each one, while, on the other hand, each wishes to
have the best and largest share; thus arise envy and jealousy,
quarrelling and contention, hatred and enmity, if there is only a
suspicion that the inheritance is not fairly divided. But it is
quite different with what we have to expect from our Father in
heaven; for it is infinite and inexhaustible, and cannot be lessened or diminished by any number of claimants. Each one shall
have as his portion the infinite God Himself, whom we shall all
possess together; so that our inheritance shall be a bond to unite
the hearts of the elect in intimate and joyful love. From this I
conclude, that my neighbor, no matter who he may be, is worthy
of my love, since he is a human being created for the same end
as myself, to love me and be loved by me for all eternity. Should

He is with us on the journey to our heavenly fatherland and inheritance.

---

[1] Vereamini igitur mensam illam, cujus omnes participes sumus.

I, then, hate or injure him who is really on the journey with me to the same place, in which, as I hope, we shall all live forever in perfect love? Should we not even now commence to do that which we wish and desire to continue throughout eternity?

The mutual love of men is the cause of the greatest happiness on earth. Nay, should we not do that which is the cause of the utmost happiness to us here on earth? For if each one loved his neighbor as himself, what a wonderful change there would be in the world! Almost all vice would be abolished; almost everything that troubles our hearts and minds would be removed. Pride and vanity, which now make us seek and extol ourselves above others; avarice and the concupiscence of the eyes, which are the cause of so many injustices on account of that wretched " mine and thine," and that occasion so much quarrelling and contention, the fruitful source of revengeful feelings, envy, jealousy, irreconcilable hatred, persecution, oppression, calumny, detraction, cursing, swearing, wars, and murders; these capital sins, which are the sources and causes of all the troubles and trials of life, would all be removed, if Christian, brotherly love reigned in our hearts: each one would honor and esteem his neighbor as himself, would wish and do good to him as to himself, would rejoice at his prosperity as at his own, and help him in danger and necessity as he would wish to be helped himself. All would have the same wish without the least fear or suspicion of being envied, cheated, betrayed, or injured by another; in a word, the world would become a picture of the future heavenly Jerusalem, which will be a dwelling of the most perfect repose, union, and peace; because there the most perfect love will unite all hearts together.

Therefore our neighbor is worthy of our love. O my God! should not all these considerations induce us mortals to love one another sincerely? Was it necessary for Thee to command us under pain of eternal damnation to love one another? And Thou, Jesus Christ, our Saviour, hadst Thou to work so hard to impress on the hearts of Thy Christians this law of love, which is in itself so attractive? Mark, my dear brethren, this new title and motive which should impel us to love our neighbor. Let us blot out all the other titles, that of our being children of God, brothers and sisters of the same Father and Mother, comrades at table and travelling companions, co-heirs to the kingdom of heaven, and let us suppose, moreover, that there is absolutely nothing in our neighbor to make him worthy of our love; yet does Jesus Christ well deserve that, for His sake we should love our neighbor. This we shall see in the second part.

Second Part.

Amongst all the commandments of God and the Gospel-laws, there is none that Jesus Christ took more interest in, or inculcated on all men more earnestly by word and example, than the law which commands us to love our neighbor. For, in the first place, He puts it in the same rank as the law that commands us to love our sovereign God. " Master," said the lawyer in to-day's Gospel, " which is the great commandment in the law?" And the answer was: " Thou shalt love the Lord thy God with thy whole heart, and with thy whole soul, and with thy whole mind. This is the greatest and the first commandment. And the second is like to this: Thou shalt love thy neighbor as thyself." Mark, says St. Chrysostom, how Christ makes, as it were, no distinction between the love of God and the love of our neighbor, although there is an infinite difference between God and man; so that He holds one love in as high esteem as the other, as if to say: to love God and to love your neighbor is the same thing in My eyes. Nay, it would seem as if the Apostle St. Paul preferred to some extent the law of the love of our neighbor to that of the love of God, for he says that the whole law is fulfilled by him who loves his neighbor: " Owe no man anything, but to love one another: for he that loveth his neighbor hath fulfilled the law:"[1] thus he writes to the Romans. " For all the law is fulfilled in one word: ' Thou shalt love thy neighbor as thyself:'"[2] thus to the Galatians. The meaning of the Apostle is, not that a man who blasphemes God, swears falsely, does not observe the fast-days, still keeps the whole law if he only loves his neighbor, but that a man who, for God's sake, has a sincere love for his neighbor, will not offend the Lord by any kind of sin, so that he will keep all the other commandments as well. It is necessary for us to love our neighbor, as well as to love God; yet, as St. Augustine says, the holy Scripture looks on one as enough, since these two loves are inseparable. God wills us to love our neighbor for His sake; from which it follows that it is impossible for me to obey this command unless I love God. " By the love of God the love of our neighbor is generated, and by the love of our neighbor the love of God is nourished;" such are the words of St. Gregory; "for he who neglects

The law that commands us to love our neighbor Christ has taken specially to Himself.

[1] Nemini quidquam debeatis, nisi ut invicem diligatis: qui enim diligit proximum, legem implevit.—Rom. xiii. 8.

[2] Omnis enim lex in uno sermone impletur; diliges proximum tuum sicut teipsum.—Gal. v. 14.

to love God is certainly unable to love his neighbor." [1] And St. John says straight out that he who does not love his neighbor cannot love God: "If any man say, I love God, and hateth his brother, he is a liar. And this commandment we have from God, that he who loveth God love also his brother." [2] Even the holiest actions that I perform to please God are only false and lying signs of a love for Him, unless I love my neighbor as myself. It is to no purpose that I leave the world and all I have for God's sake; to no purpose that I renounce all sensual and carnal pleasures; to no purpose all my prayers and devotions: all my watching, fasting, penance, mortification and chastising of the flesh, all my crosses and trials, if I still have a wilful anger and hatred in my heart against a single person in the whole world. I may say with the lips and with tears of devotion, all this I do for Thee, O my God; but as long as I have that secret hatred against my neighbor, I am a liar and do not speak the truth. For "this commandment we have from God, that he who loveth God love also his brother."

He calls it His own law.

Again, Christ calls this commandment His commandment: "This is My commandment, that you love one another, as I have loved you." [3] Not, says Maldonatus, that the fulfilment of the other points of the law is of no importance in His sight, or that He does not care if we keep the other commandments; but He wishes to recommend this one commandment of love to us in a special manner, as the foundation of His holy Gospel, and an object most pleasing to His Sacred Heart; not otherwise than as a father who has several children, says of one of them: this is his mother's son, but this is my son. He does not wish thereby to intimate that the other children are not his too; his meaning is, that of all his children the one whom he thus singles out is his favorite, and the object of his special care. In the same sense, Christ says, "this is My commandment," the one which is dearest to Me, "that you love one another." Therefore, when the disciples of St. John complained that they had always to hear the same exhortation from their master, "My little children, love one another," and they consequently desired something new, St. John said to them that he knew nothing better; "for it is the

---

[1] Per amorem Dei amor proximi gignitur, et per amorem proximi, amor Dei nutritur: nam qui amare Deum negligit, profecto amare proximum nescit.—S. Greg. l. 7. Moral c. 10.

[2] Si quis dixerit quoniam diligo Deum, et fratrem suum oderit, mendax est. Hoc mandatum habemus a Deo, ut qui diligit Deum, diligat et fratrem suum.—I. John iv. 20, 21.

[3] Hoc est præceptum meum, ut diligatis invicem, sicut dilexi vos.—John xv. 12.

precept of the Lord, and if it is observed, it will be enough." [1]

In the third place, Christ calls it a new law: " A new com- *He calls it a new law.* mandment I give unto you: that you love one another." [2] But why does He say that? This commandment is as old as the world; for the law of nature bound the first men to brotherly love and friendly intercourse with one another; while the law of Moses contains the express words: " Thou shalt love thy friend as thyself:" [3] and at all times the law was: " Do unto others as you wish they should do unto you." Hatred, anger, vindictiveness, injustice, detraction, contumely, cursing and swearing, deceit and treachery, are vices that were always forbidden. Meekness and charity, compassion for the miserable, generosity towards the poor, readiness to help others in their necessities, etc., are virtues to which men were always bound. Why, then, does Christ say, as if He was bringing forward something novel, " A new commandment I give unto you: that you love one another?" St. John Chrysostom and St. Cyril answer this question by saying: that it is a new commandment, because it is to be kept in a new manner, on account of a new title, and a new motive. [4] Our Lord's meaning was: hitherto you have received this commandment from God as your Creator and sovereign Lord, whom you are bound to obey, either through fear of eternal punishment, or through hope of an eternal reward; but now I command you anew to love one another as your Redeemer, who will give My life's blood for you; as your Brother, who will make you children of My Father, who has thus adopted you as My brethren with the prayer and the command that you love one another on My account and for My sake. And if hitherto neither the hope of reward, nor the fear of punishment, nor the authority of your Legislator could inspire you with that love, you should, at all events, practise it for the sake of the love that you owe your Redeemer and Saviour; for I command you anew to love one another, and I enforce that commandment with all My authority: for My sake you must love one another.

Fourthly, we would do well to note the time and the circum- *Which He published just before His Passion and death.* stances in which He so specially inculcated this command on His disciples. When was it? On the very night of the Last Supper, when He gave them His last will and testament. Before He went

[1] Quia præceptum Domini est, et si fiat, sufficit.
[2] Mandatum novum do vobis; ut diligatis invicem.—John xiii. 34.
[3] Diliges amicum tuum sicut teipsum.—Lev. xix. 18.
[4] Mandatum novum, quia novo modo servandum.

to His death He said to them: "These things I command you, that you love one another."[1] When a father is at the point of death, he calls his children to his bed-side to give them his last exhortations; what he then says to them is generally what they are most inclined to observe; and it remains, too, most deeply impressed on the memories of the children. Oh, they say, after ten or twenty years, or more, this or that was enjoined on me by my father on his death-bed; I must never forget it during my whole life; I must faithfully observe it, and never act contrary to it. And if any one tries to hinder them from fulfilling their father's last words, they exclaim at once, as St. Augustine says: "What? Must I not do that which my dear father commanded me with his last breath? Must I not observe the last injunction that he laid on me, when about to depart from this life?" "Ah," continues the holy Doctor, "my brethren, consider this with Christian hearts: if the words of the dying parent are so sweet, so pleasing, so authoritative to his heirs, what should be the power of the last words of Christ with His heirs?"[2] Love one another, He says, My children, do not forget it; this is the commandment that I, your dying Father, give you; this is the expression of My will before I am nailed to the cross for you: "These things I command you, that you love one another;" inculcate it on all Christians that they must love one another. And, accordingly, the Epistles that the Apostles wrote afterwards to the different churches are filled with exhortations to the love of our neighbor, especially the Epistles of St. Paul and St. John. St. Paul says that he does not think it even necessary to say anything more of that love; for he writes thus to the Thessalonians: "But as touching the charity of brotherhood, we have no need to write to you; for yourselves have learned of God to love one another."[3]

He wishes His disciples to be known by this love. Fifthly, the surest sign by which the disciple and follower of Christ is to be known is brotherly love: "By this shall all men know that you are My disciples, if you have love one for another."[4] "As a sign of being His disciple," says St. Basil, "He does not require miracles or prodigies; but He says: 'By this

[1] Hæc mando vobis, ut diligatis invicem.—John xv. 17.

[2] Fratres, cogitate visceribus Christianis; si hæredibus sunt tam dulcia, tam grata, tam magni ponderis verba patris ituri in sepulchrum; hæredibus Christi qualia debent esse verba novissima?—S. Aug. in I. Joan. 10.

[3] De charitate autem fraternitatis non necesse habemus scribere vobis: ipsi enim vos a Deo didicistis ut diligatis invicem.—I. Thess. iv. 9.

[4] In hoc cognoscent omnes, quia discipuli mei estis, si dilectionem habueritis ad invicem.—Johu xiii. 35.

shall all men know that you are My disciples, if you have love one for another.'"[1] All other things are only deceitful signs of a disciple; but this love is a true one and cannot deceive. Neither the cross, with which all My faithful shall sign themselves, nor the announcing of My name, which they acknowledge everywhere, nor the prayers and outward works of devotion, with which they honor Me, nor the miracles, exorcisms, healing of the sick, and raising of the dead which they perform in My name, shall be undoubted signs of true Christianity; for all these things can proceed from deceit and hypocrisy, and many will come at the last day to Me with such works; but I will say to them: I know you not. By this alone can all the world know for certain who are My disciples, when, by mutual, fraternal charity, the words will be verified: "The multitude of believers had but one heart and one soul."

Finally, in return for the countless benefits that we have received and continue to receive from Him, the only return of gratitude that Our Lord requires of us is, that we should love our neighbor; for He puts our neighbor in His own place, and says that whatever we do to him He shall accept it as if it were done to Himself: "So long as you did it to one of these My least brethren, you did it to Me."[2] That service that you rendered your neighbor, you rendered to Me; that alms you gave to that beggar and those decent poor, you gave to Me; that visiting the sick, comforting the afflicted, that meekness in bearing the faults of others, that pardoning of injuries, all these I have accepted as if you had done them to My own Person. Do you acknowledge that you are deeply indebted to Me? Then love your neighbor, and you will pay off all, and I shall be satisfied. He protests that he who injures his neighbor injures the apple of His eye, that is the tenderest and dearest member of His sacred body: "He that toucheth you toucheth the apple of My eye."[3] On the last day Christ will, so to speak, forget everything that was done either to please or displease Him, and will bring forward the works of charity that have been performed or omitted with regard to one's neighbor, as the sole reason for reward or punishment. "Come, ye blessed," He will say to the just, "possess the kingdom prepared for you." Why? "For I was hungry

He commands us to love our neighbor in His place.

---

[1] Ad declarationem suorum discipulorum, non signa et mirabiles potentias exigit; sed ait: in hoc, etc.

[2] Quamdiu fecistis uni ex his fratribus meis minimis, mihi fecistis.—Matt. xxv. 40.

[3] Qui enim tetigerit vos, tangit pupillam oculi mei.—Zach. ii. 8.

and you gave Me to eat." "Depart from Me, you cursed." Why?
For I was hungry and you gave Me not to eat." [1] "So long as
you did it to one of these, My least brethren, you did it to Me."
O Christians, what do we owe Our Saviour? Just souls, what
do you owe Him for the many graces and benefits He has bestowed
on you? Sinners, what do you owe Him for the amazing patience
with which He has borne with your sins, for the many times He
has forgiven you and freed you from the pains of hell? What
return can or shall we make Him? Behold, the return is a sweet
and easy one to make: only love your neighbor as yourselves:
He requires nothing more of you; with that He is satisfied; all
His right to a return He has, so to speak, renounced in favor of
our neighbor: as we act towards him, so do we act to Jesus
Christ, our Saviour.

Therefore, every one deserves that we should love him, after the example of pious Christians.

Where are you now who so often say, when a work of charity
is expected of you: What is the man to me? I do not know him;
I owe him nothing: he has deserved nothing from me; I cannot
bear him, etc? What? Is, then, Jesus Christ nothing to you?
Do you not know your Saviour? Do you owe Him nothing?
Has the Son of God deserved nothing from you? Can you not
bear Jesus? You must know, then, that what you have given
or refused to that man you have given or refused to Christ.
Even if the man is not worthy of your love, certainly Jesus
Christ deserves that you should love him for His sake. Ask St.
Elizabeth, queen of Hungary, what she found to love in the lepers that she attended day and night; what beauty or amiability
she discovered in the sick and wounded, whom she fed with her
own hands in the hospitals, and whose beds she made for them.
What! she will exclaim, what are you asking! Is not my Saviour Jesus Christ beautiful and amiable, and worthy enough of
my love for me to render Him this slight service and trifling
attendance in the persons of whom He has said: "As long as
you did it to one of these, My least brethren, you did it to Me "?
Ask all those charitable servants of God who have given up all
they had, and spent their whole lives in caring for unknown
poor and sick people, some of whom have even voluntarily sold
themselves into slavery, that they might redeem other slaves who
were utterly unknown to them; ask what they found so attractive in those miserable men that, for their sake, they sacrificed

---

[1] Venite benedicti ; esurivi enim et dedistis mihi manducare. Discedite a me maledicte;
esurivi enim et non dedistis mihi manducare.—Matt. xxv. 34, 35, 41, 42.

their own lives. Ask that mother who received the murderer of her own son into her house, and hid him until he had an opportunity of escaping the officers of justice who were in pursuit of him; ask all those who have done good to their worst enemies what amiable qualities they found in those wicked men, from whom they received nothing but insults and injuries? What! they will exclaim, where is your faith? Are not these men worthy of the same love that we owe Our Lord Jesus Christ? And so it is in reality. Depict your neighbor in the blackest colors; say that he is a worthless, good-for-nothing, wicked man, whom no one can bear; say that he does all the mischief that lies in his power; no matter how you described him, it still remains true that Christ has said of him, that what you do to such a man you have done to Himself; and, therefore, it is true, that Christ is well deserving that you should love even such a man for His sake.

"But before all things," I conclude in the words of St. Peter, "have a constant mutual charity among yourselves." [1] Before all things, before all other works of devotion, before all that you do, be sure that you foster this mutual love. Your neighbor, as the image of God, as your brother, as your comrade and travelling companion, as your co-heir to the kingdom of heaven, is well deserving of that love. Love one another; it is the command of the Lord, the special and dearest law of Jesus Christ, our Saviour, who has commanded us to love our neighbor in His place, and who will give us a clear receipt for all we owe Him, if we only love our neighbor. O my Saviour, how have I hitherto with truth been able to say that I love Thee with my whole heart, since I must now, to my great confusion, acknowledge that I have so little loved him whom Thou hast put in Thy place? Alas, how unbecomingly I have acted towards Thee, if Thou hast taken to Thyself all that I have done to my fellow-man! How many services I have refused Thee! How often I have despised Thee in my own mind! How often I have hated Thee, spoken evil of Thee, wished harm to Thee, ill-treated Thee! If it is true, and I have Thy own word for it, that Thou feelest as done to Thyself what I do to my neighbor, ah, what will become of me? How can I hope or expect to regain Thy favor, if Thou measurest out to me in the measure in which I have loved my

Conclusion and resolution to love our neighbor.

---

[1] Ante omnia autem, mutuam in vobismetipsis charitatem continuam habentes.—I. Pet. iv. 8.

neighbor? Pardon me, O God, for I have not known the truth so clearly before! Above all, I will now detest and repent of the sins I have committed against fraternal affection, because such sins displease Thee more than all others. Above all, I will practise the law of charity, because that law is the dearest to Thee. Whenever I experience a feeling of dislike towards my neighbor, and am inclined to hate him, I will at once remember that it is Jesus Christ Himself who is the object of those feelings. Do Thou, O God of love, give to us all and preserve in us a loving heart, that we may love one another truly in this life according to Thy will, until we shall all love one another in heaven, and rejoice with Thee forever. Amen.

FIFTY-THIRD SERMON.

ON THE WAY AND MANNER IN WHICH WE SHOULD LOVE OUR NEIGHBOR.

Subject.

We must love our neighbor as Christ has loved us: that is, 1. with a patient, meek love; 2. with a beneficent love; 3. with a general love.—*Preached on the Eighteenth Sunday after Pentecost.*

Text.

Videns Jesus fidem illorum, dixit paralytico: Confide, fili.
—Matt. ix. 2.

"And Jesus seeing their faith, said to the man sick of the palsy: Be of good heart, son."

Introduction.

A brilliant example of the sincere love of our neighbor is given us in to-day's Gospel in Jesus Christ, our Saviour, for He comforted and healed the paralytic as soon as ever He saw the thoughts that were in the minds of those who brought the poor man to Him, and before they had spoken a single word to Him: "And Jesus, seeing their faith, said to the man sick of the palsy: Be of good heart, son," I will help you and cure you. Mark, my dear brethren, how beneficent the love of Our Saviour! And in the second place, how meekly He answers the envious Scribes and Pharisees, who were watching all His actions out of hatred, and were decrying Him as a blasphemer, when He could easily have punished them! "And Jesus, seeing their thoughts, said: Why do you think evil in your hearts?" I will show by healing this sick man that I have the power to forgive sins. There you have the example of a meek and patient love. Thirdly, there was no one present who did not experience His love and beneficence: He healed the paralytic man; He filled with consolation the man's friends who had brought him; He proved His divinity to the scribes and Pharisees by working a miracle, and He moved all who were present to acknowledge God, to adore and praise Him: "And the multitude, seeing it, feared, and glorified God that gave such power to men." See how general was the love of Jesus Christ; and from this, too, we may learn how we should love our neighbor according to the express command of Our Lord: "This is My commandment, that you love one another, as I have loved you." [1] We have seen how Christ loved us mortals; from that we must learn how to love our neighbor. There you have the subject of this instruction, or rather meditation.

Plan of Discourse.

Christ has loved us mortals with a patient, meek love; such should be also the nature of our love for our neighbor. The first point. Christ has loved us mortals with a beneficent love; such should be our love for our neighbor. The second point. Christ has loved us mortals with a general love; such should be our love for our neighbor. The third point.

Christ Jesus, who hast commanded us to love one another as Thou hast loved us, give us all Thy powerful grace, that we may do what Thou hast commanded; this we ask of Thee, through Thy dearest Mother Mary and our holy guardian angels.

So that Christ has loved us men with a meek and patient love. These virtues are, according to the Prophet Isaias, a sign by which the future Messias and Redeemer of the world was to be known. "Behold my servant," says the Prophet; "I will uphold him; my elect, my soul delighteth in him: I have given my spirit upon him. He shall not cry, nor have respect to person, neither shall his voice be heard abroad. He shall not be sad, nor troublesome." [2] "But I, as a deaf man," says king David, in the person of Our Lord, "heard not, and was as a dumb man

(margin note: How patient and meek the love of Christ for us mortals!)

---

[1] Hoc est præceptum meum, ut diligatis invicem, sicut dilexi vos.—John xv. 12.

[2] Ecce servus meus, suscipiam eum : electus meus, complacuit sibi in illo anima mea : dedi spiritum meum super eum. Non clamabit, neque accipiet personam, nec audietur vox ejus foris. Non erit tristis, neque turbulentus.—Is. xlii. 1, 2, 4.

not opening his mouth. And I became as a man that heareth not: and that hath no reproofs in his mouth: "[1] like a lamb that is led to the slaughter not opening its mouth. And, indeed, what is the whole life of Our Lord but a constant practice of patience and meekness? To speak only of the three last years of it, which He spent going about doing good to all men, in towns and villages, in forests and deserts; what had He not to bear with from the ungrateful, stiff-necked, wicked people, to whom He made known His divine truths? With what meekness, modesty, and willingness He suited Himself to the different temperaments He had to deal with, so as to win the hearts of the people! How many a refusal He met with in all places! How many acts of opposition and proofs of obstinacy He had to put up with! How many blasphemous and contumelious expressions were uttered against Him by the envious scribes and Pharisees, both publicly, in His presence, and privately, behind His back, all of which He was well aware of; but He bore them in silence, as if He knew nothing about them. What sort of men did He choose for disciples, to be with Him constantly? Poor, unknown, uncultivated, ignorant, coarse, and faulty fishermen. What patience and meekness He had to employ in order to instruct them and train them in His own spirit! Often they did not even understand, as the Gospel says, what He was explaining to them; so that He had to repeat the same truths over and over again, until they at last managed to have some idea of them. They often quarrelled with each other, and then He had to come between them and make peace; but in spite of the great trouble they occasioned Him daily, He still lived with them in love and friendship, and wished to be always in their company.

Especially during His Passion. But never did His meekness show itself more clearly than in His Passion and death. Consider, my dear brethren, the unheard-of injuries heaped on Him by His enemies in their diabolical rage. He was injured in His property; for Judas, His own disciple, stole His money, and the soldiers took away all His clothes, and cast lots for them before His face. He was injured in His body; from head to foot He was a mass of wounds: His head was pierced with thorns, His face defiled with spittle and bruised with blows, His hands and feet were pierced with nails, all the members of His body were torn with the scourges. He was in-

---

[1] Ego autem tanquam surdus non audiebam : et sicut mutus non aperiens os suum. Et factus sum sicut homo non audiens, et non habens in ore suo redargutiones.—Ps. xxxvii. 14, 15.

jured in His honor and good name; many ascribed His miracles to sorcery and magic and dealings with the devil; His doctrine was decried as sedition; His beneficence was looked on as a means employed by Him to get the people on His side, so as to spur them on to revolt. He was treated as an ambitious man, who wished to set himself up as a king, and, therefore, called Himself the Son of God. He had to bear all the insults that could possibly be offered to a mock king: instead of a sceptre, a reed was put into His hand; instead of the royal purple, a red rag was thrown over His shoulders; instead of a crown, the sharp thorns were placed on His head, and in this guise He was greeted as a king. Besides that He was treated as a false Prophet: His eyes were bandaged, He was struck on the face, and asked in mocking tones to prophesy who had struck Him. As the vilest of criminals, He was buffeted on the face before the tribunal. He was laughed at as a good-for-nothing, and, when He was hanging on the cross between two thieves, He had to hear the insults of those who derided Him, because, as they thought, He could not save Himself from their hands. All these injuries and insults He had to put up with, although He had never given the least cause for them, and had rather deserved to be treated with the utmost veneration. Had He not good reason to forget His patience on this occasion, especially as He was the Almighty Lord, who could so easily have defended Himself? Yet He bore it all in silence, with as much meekness and patience as if He felt not the least pain; nay, in the midst of His torments, He continued to do good to His persecutors. Judas was determined to betray Him, and after many loving exhortations and remonstrances, Jesus cast Himself at the traitor's feet and washed them, with a view of thus bringing him to repent. Peter thrice denied Him through fear of a wretched servant-maid, and, in spite of that, Jesus made him head of His Church and His Vicar on earth. Although He complained that His heavenly Father had abandoned Him, yet He never ceased to pray for grace and pardon for His tormentors.

All this, Christians, reminds us of what Christ said of Himself on another occasion: "Learn of Me, because I am meek and humble of heart." [1] It teaches us, too, what should be the nature of our love for our neighbor; namely, that it must be a meek love, by which we bear with one another's faults and failings, and

So should we love our neighbor.

[1] Discite a me, quia mitis sum et humilis corde.—Matt. xi. 29.

suffer in a patient and friendly spirit what might otherwise cause us to feel hurt and annoyed. If we had to live only with angels, who are not subject to bad temper, to sin, nor to any other fault, then there would be no room for meek and patient love on earth, nor would it be of any use to us; or, if we were obliged to have that love only for those who are gentle in their disposition, who know how to treat us well, and do not contradict us in the least, or whom we have a special affection for, then there would be no great art in being meek and patient; or, to speak better, patience and meekness would be without merit, and no virtue. But as it is, we are bound to love all men, and, according to the law of Jesus Christ, in the manner in which He has loved us; and at the same time we must live and deal with people who have peculiar imaginations and dispositions, and are full of rash judgments, of faults and imperfections, just as we ourselves have our faults. The one is proud, the other clownish; one is too sharp, the other too stupid and simple; one is of a passionate and hasty disposition, the other, melancholy and peevish; one is too sensitive and quarrelsome, the other, too obstinate and headstrong; every one has his faults. To try to amend them all would be vain labor: it is not in our power to make people faultless. So that to preserve peace and brotherly love, according to the express command and the example of Jesus Christ, all we can do is to be patient and meek in bearing with our neighbor's disagreeable qualities, as St. Paul says to the Galatians: "Bear ye one another's burdens, and so you shall fulfil the law of Christ." [1] Oh, if all only had that love, what a change there would be! What a happy place the world would then become! What peace there would be everywhere on earth, according to the promise made by Our Lord to the meek: "Blessed are the meek, for they shall possess the land." [2]

Many fail in this point. How is it with me in this respect? So should each one ask himself. Has my love for my neighbor hitherto been a meek, patient love? Have I learned to bear patiently and meekly the faults and failings of others? They have to bear with mine; so that it would be an injustice for me to expect them to bear a hundred faults in me, while I am unwilling to overlook the least short-coming in them. And yet, have I not often been guilty of this injustice? How often, instead of acting in a friendly manner towards my neighbor, have I not shunned and avoided him? When he came in by one door, I went out by the other, because I

[1] Alter alterius onera portate, et sic adimplebitis legem Christi.—Gal. vi. 2.

[2] Beati mites, quoniam ipsi possidebunt terram.—Matt. v. 4.

could not bear his manner or behavior, because he had some natural defect that seemed intolerable to me, although he was not to blame for it. How often, when I could not avoid his company, have I not given expression to my dissatisfaction by an unfriendly countenance, by sour looks, and other signs of secret contempt? I have acted towards him as Joseph's brethren did towards their innocent brother; I could not speak a friendly word to him, nor look at him in any but a hostile manner. How often have I not addressed him in a harsh, overbearing way? How often have I not complained to others of his bad temper and natural faults, and said that it was an intolerable thing for me to have to do with such a man? If I succeeded in overcoming myself for a time for God's sake, and concealed my dislike for him so far as to meet him in a friendly manner, I still felt a secret joy when others noticed or found fault with his defects. And all this came from a want of meekness and patience in bearing with his faults.

Alas, I am thus driven to the conclusion that the love I have had for my neighbor has been altogether unlike that which Jesus Christ had for us; that the true love which He requires has as yet found no place in my heart, and that the many protestations I made to God in prayer, offering to bear with my neighbor's faults, were only empty forms without meaning. For I have not had patience or meekness enough to overlook even one of his faults, or to bear a single word of contradiction from him. Yet, even if I had not been wanting in patience and meekness, I should still have had but one quality of sincere love, which must not merely exist in the heart, but also show itself in work. Just as Thy love was for us, O merciful Saviour! for it was not merely meek and patient, but also most beneficent. So, too, should be our love for our neighbor, my dear brethren, as we shall see in the

Hence they do not love their neighbor as Christ commands.

Second Part.

The same love that made Jesus Christ bear so meekly and patiently the imperfections of those with whom He had to do, and the terrible torments and insults heaped upon Him by the Jews and wicked soldiers, the same love, I say, moved Him to use all His divine power to do good to men: "Who went about doing good," [1] as the Scripture says of Him. He wandered through towns and villages, forests and deserts, seeking whom

How beneficent the love of Christ to us mortals!

[1] Pertransiit benefaciendo.—Acts x. 38.

He might benefit. He drove the evil spirits from the possessed, comforted the afflicted, fed the hungry, healed the sick, cleansed lepers, raised the dead to life, sought out and converted sinners. He entered into the houses of sinners, sat down to table with them, and made no account of the wicked things that were said of Him, as long as He had an opportunity of showing His generous love to man. In a word, all His thoughts, words, actions, and every step and movement He made, from the first moment of His Incarnation to His last breath on the cross, was intended for nothing else but our eternal welfare: "For us men and for our salvation." Nay, He seemed to forget Himself that He might do good to others. How many miracles did He not work to help them in their necessities, and free them from their miseries! But what did He do when He Himself was in the greatest straits? When He was fasting forty days and nights in the desert, and was hungry, He could easily have turned stones into bread, or water into wine, to refresh Himself. But He did not work such miracles for Himself: they were for the good of others. When the wine failed at the marriage-feast of Cana, He could work a miracle. "I have compassion on the multitude," He said in the desert; "for behold, they have now been with Me three days, and have nothing to eat." [1] And to help them, He miraculously multiplied a few loaves, so that they all had enough. The same pity induced Him to change water into wine at Cana. When He was seized by the soldiers and taken prisoner in the garden of Gethsemani, it would have been easy for Him to tear asunder His bonds, and free Himself from their hands. But no; His only care was that His disciples should be suffered to go unharmed; if you seek Me, He said, here I am; drag Me forth if you will; but one thing I command you, let these go in peace: "Jesus answered: I have told you that I am He; if, therefore, you seek Me, let these go their way." [2] With reason does St. Peter Chrysologus say, considering these words: "Christ is a man for Himself, a God for me." [3] That is, for the love of others He was an all-powerful God to help them in their necessities and work miracles for them; but when there was question of Himself, He was, as it were, a weak man.

So should   O Christians! hear again those words: "This is My com-

[1] Misereor super turbam, quia ecce jam triduo sustinent me, nec habent quod manducent. —Mark viii. 2.

[2] Respondit Jesus: dixi vobis quia ego sum; si ergo me quæritis, sinite hos abire.— John xviii. 8.

[3] Christus sibi homo, mihi Deus.

mandment: that you love one another, as I have loved you." My love for you, as you know by experience, was always a benefi- cent love. "This is My commandment: that you love one an- other;" such, too, should be the nature of your love. That is what St. John, the beloved disciple, seeks to inculcate on us in the words of his first epistle: "My dearest, if God hath so loved us, we also ought to love one another." [1] "Be ye, therefore, fol- lowers of God," says St. Paul, "as most dear children, and walk in love, as Christ also hath loved us." [2] But, dear Saviour, we are not able to work miracles for our neighbor, as Thou hast done. We have not, like Thee, the power of multiplying bread for the poor, of changing water into wine for the thirsty, of giving sight to the blind, hearing to the deaf, speech to the dumb, of freeing those possessed by the devil, of restoring the sick and dying to health, of raising the dead to life. How, then, can we love our neighbor as Thou didst? Ah, methinks I hear Our Lord answering: Can you not, then, do good to one another without working miracles? Have you not every day a thousand opportunities of showing kindness to one another? Are there not beggars enough crying for alms either in the public streets or at your doors? Are there not decent poor enough, who have to work hard and yet can hardly manage to support themselves and their children, who are ashamed to beg, although they are far more deserving of alms than public beggars? If you cannot multiply bread for them, you can, at least, help them now and then with your bread and money. Are there not desolate sick people in your neighborhood? If you cannot restore them to health, you can, at all events, visit them, and do what your means will allow for them. Are there not afflicted people enough who groan and sigh under the pressure of misfortune without help or consolation? If you are not able to free them from their troubles, you can, at least, frequently address a word of comfort to them, and say a word in their favor when you get the chance. Daily there are people, known and unknown, neighbors, friends, domestics, whom you can serve in different ways by acts of love and kindness. In these, then, and countless similar circum- stances, you can and should, according to the example I have given you, prove your beneficent love for your neighbor. "This

be our love for our neighbor, for which we have op portunities enough.

---

[1] Charissimi, si sic Deus dilexit nos, et nos debemu salterutrum diligere.—I. John iv. 11.

[2] Estote ergo imitatores Dei sicut filii charissimi; et ambulate in dilectione, sicut et Christus dilexit nos.—Ephes. v. 1, 2.

is My commandment: that you love one another, as I have loved you."

There are not many who use those opportunities.

Truly, O Lord, I have opportunities for so doing; but how have I behaved in them hitherto? Am I not one of those selfish people of whom Thou complainest by Thy apostle St. Paul: "For all seek the things that are their own, not the things that Jesus Christ's"?[1] That is, they are concerned for themselves alone; but take no trouble to help the other members of Christ. Christ is, as far as His own advantage is concerned, a weak mortal; but for others, He is the generous, almighty God. Can I not say exactly the opposite of myself with truth; I am a god for myself; a man for others? As long as things go well with me, they may go with others as they wish; as long as I am rich, others may look out for themselves; as long as I can eat, drink, and sleep well, amuse myself and indulge my senses, others may suffer hunger and thirst, and weep and wail as they please; as long as I can gratify my expensive tastes in dress, others may go ragged and naked; it does not matter to me. Nay, have I not, perhaps, by my excessive extravagance, by my sensual, luxurious mode of life, contracted debts that I cannot pay, and made myself unable to help the poor as I ought? When the duties of my state or employment oblige me to help my neighbor and come to his assistance, do I always do so with becoming zeal and diligence? Do I fulfil that duty with pleasure, as if I were helping my Lord and Saviour Himself? Have I not, perhaps, neglected certain matters that were placed in my hands, or deferred them because they were entrusted to me, by poor people, from whom I could not expect much in the way of payment? Have I at least so much love for my neighbor, that I wish him from my heart that good that I am unable to procure for him? Do I rejoice at his good fortune, as if it were my own? Do I compassionate him in trials and adversity, and condole with him if he is unfortunate? True Christian love requires all this of me.

But do quite the contrary.

But, alas! have I not always done quite the contrary? Instead of wishing and doing good to my neighbor, through fraternal affection, as to myself, how often have I not done him harm, and caused him sorrow and affliction? How often have I not wished evil to him, and rejoiced when he suffered misfortune or loss? How often have I not been disturbed and dis-

---

[1] Omnes enim quæ sua sunt quærunt, non quæ sunt Jesu Christi.—Philipp. ii. 21.

pleased, through envy and jealousy, at his good fortune or success?   How often have I not tried through hatred to hinder
those who were about to render him a service?   How often have
I not tried to run him down before others, by speaking evil of
him?   How often have I not turned away the poor from my door
in a rude and harsh manner, instead of giving them alms?
How often have I not added to the troubles of poor widows and
orphans, instead of taking an active interest in their welfare?
How often have I not been harsh and cruel to my servants, nay,
even to my wife and children, to whom I owe the greatest love
and kindness?   Ah, again do I see that I have nothing of the
true spirit of the love of Jesus Christ!   And what judgment must
I form of myself, when I consider the third quality of this love;
namely, that it must be general, like the love that Jesus Christ
had for us?   This, my dear brethren, is briefly the

Third Part.

General love consists in this, that it extends itself to all men, Christ extended His
without exception.   Such was the love of Jesus Christ.   He came love to all
down from heaven on earth and took human nature on Himself, men.
in order to save, as far as in Him lay, all men from hell, and to
make them eternally happy.   Therefore He gave Himself to all,
without exception; Jews and heathens, great and small, rich
and poor, young and old, received from Him the same instruction
and doctrine, the same remedies for body and soul.   He was
never deterred by the want and poverty of the one nor unduly
influenced by the wealth and authority of the other.   No one
was too mean in His sight, no one too unknown or strange, nay,
no sinner too wicked to be offered His favor and plentiful grace.
Even to those who openly declared themselves as His sworn enemies He was willing to do good and to give grace; He invited
them to come to Him for that purpose, and called out to them
in the most friendly terms.   He sought them diligently, and
often wept bitterly with heartfelt pity for those who, through
wickedness and obstinacy, refused to receive His grace.

"This is My commandment: that you love one another, as I He who
have loved you."   If my love for my fellow-men is not great does not
love all
enough to impel me to love all without exception, then I have men has
not a true Christian love, but a mere hypocritical one; for the not true,
supernatu-
motive that, as we have seen already, should induce me to love ral Chris-
my neighbor is the fact that he is the image of God, my brother, tian charity.

my comrade, my travelling companion, my co-heir to heaven, and because Christ wishes me to love him. But this motive is not limited to a few; it holds good for all men; and, therefore, I cannot have a true love for one man without loving all. And just as it is a false repentance to say, I am sorry for having stolen, because I have offended my God thereby, but I am not sorry for having committed a sin of impurity, since the offence against God is the general motive of repentance for all sin; in the same way, it is a false love to say: I love that man, because he is an image of God, my brother, my comrade, my travelling campanion, my co-heir, and because Christ wishes me to love him; but I do not love that other, and cannot bear the sight of him nor wish him well. When Our Lord published the law commanding us to love our enemies, just as our heavenly Father causes His sun to shine on the good and the wicked, and pours down His rain on the just and unjust, He adds: "For if you love them that love you, what reward shall you have? Do not even the publicans this? And if you salute your brethren only, what do you more? Do not also the heathens this?"[1] If you love only certain persons to whom you are drawn by a natural inclination; if you do good, and are inclined to do good, only to those who are agreeable to you, or who are closely connected with or related to you, or from whom you expect something in return; "do not also the heathens this?" And how, then, could you be distinguished from the heathen and the Turk? Even amongst the wildest barbarians, there are friends who love each other. Now, my Gospel must have a mark of holiness to distinguish and raise it above mere natural love such as is found amongst heathens and barbarians. Therefore I say to you: "Love your enemies; do good to them that hate you; and pray for them that persecute and calumniate you; that you may be the children of your Father who is in heaven."[2]

But very few love in that manner.

O my God! how sublime and perfect is this love! But, at the same time, how rare it is in the world! Do we not now live in those unhappy days of which Thou hast prophesied, O Lord, that when they come the charity of many shall grow cold? "And then shall many be scandalized, and shall betray one an-

---

[1] Si enim diligitis eos qui vos diligunt, quam mercedem habebitis? Nonne et publicani hoc faciunt? Et si salutaveritis fratres vestros tantum ; quid amplius facitis. Nonne et ethnici hoc faciunt.—Matt. v. 46, 47.

[2] Diligite inimicos vestros ; benefacite his qui oderunt vos ; et orate pro persequentibus et calumniantibus vos ; ut sitis filii Patris vestri qui in coelis est.—Ibid. xliv. 45.

other, and shall hate one another. And because iniquity hath
abounded, the charity of many shall grow cold. "[1] Alas, it is
already growing only too cold amongst us, so narrow are the limits in which it is circumscribed! We have certain likes and dis-
likes, and according to them we act towards our fellow-man. We
have special friends for whom we spare neither money, nor services, nor trouble, nor labor; but for others we have nothing,
know nothing, do nothing. From some we can bear anything;
from others, not even a jocose word. In that office, in which we
should serve all with the same readiness and diligence, we have our
particular objects in view, our special attractions; for while we
are unwearied in our efforts for some, we are utterly indifferent
to the interests of others. Amongst those who live according
to worldly policy there is hardly a spark of true, supernatural,
Christian charity. The greetings, compliments, and expressions
of good will that are mutually exchanged are matters of form,
mere flatteries and deceits; there is hardly a man in the world
whom those people love for God's sake, and because Christ wishes
them to love him. "One loves," says St. Chrysostom, "because he is loved in return; another, because he is honored; a
third, because he has received a benefit; a fourth, because he
hopes for some good thing; nearly all love on account of their
own advantage. But you will with difficulty find any one to
love his neighbor for Christ's sake."[2] The rich despise and
contemn the poor; those who are of noble birth hardly conde-
scend to look at the lowly born, and speak of them as the common herd; although we are all made by our Creator of the same
clay; although we are all made to the image of God, and are
brothers and sisters of Jesus Christ and co-heirs to the same
heaven; and therefore our love for one another should be general,
according to the express command of Our Lord. With regard
to the beneficent love of one's enemies and of those who have
injured us, we must not dare to say a word about it to most
people. They would look on it as an utter impossibility, although that commandment is laid upon us by the Son of God,
who does not order us to do impossible things; and that, too, under pain of eternal damnation. O charity of Jesus Christ!
where art thou? It is only to be found in some pious souls,

---

[1] Tunc scandalizabuntur multi, et invicem tradent, et odio habebunt invicem. Et quoniam abundavit iniquitas, refrigescet charitas multorum.—Matt. xxiv. 10, 12.

[2] Christi vero causa difficile quemquam invenies, qui amicum ut oportet, diligat.—S. Chrys.
Hom. 61. in Matt.

whose example God allows us to see for our edification, although there are few who follow it.

Prayer for a true love of our neighbor, such as Christ had. O my God and Saviour, who commandest me to love my neighbor as Thou hast loved us men, give me what Thou commandest! Give me that patient love, that takes everything in the best sense, and meekly bears with the faults and failings and disagreeable qualities of all men! Give me Thy beneficent love, which knows not how to refuse, and is nourished by a willingness to serve others! Give me that general love which excludes no one, but extends itself to all for Thy sake! Ah, my Lord, patient and meek as my love for my neighbor may be, it will never be as patient and meek as Thine for me, and never shall I have so much to suffer from others as Thou hast had to suffer from me, wicked and ungrateful sinner that I am! Beneficent as my love may be, much as I may try to please my neighbor, or desire to do him good for Thy sake, I shall never go so far as to confer as many benefits on him as I owe to Thy generosity, and still daily and hourly receive from Thee. And if I were to extend my love and active beneficence to all men with whom I have any intercourse, would that be a great thing for me to do, since Thou hast filled the whole earth with Thy goodness and mercy, and hast extended Thy love even to Thy tormentors and to those who crucified Thee? O Lord, imprint Thy example deeply in my heart, that I may always keep it fresh in my memory, and as often as I have to deal with people remember Thy law: "This is My commandment, that you love one another, as I have loved you," and may thus endeavor, if only at a distance, to imitate Thy patient, beneficent, and general love. Amen.

On the Small Number of those who Love their Neighbor as Themselves, see the foregoing second part. On the Love of Our Enemies, and the Forgiveness of Injuries, see the sixth part.

ON FRATERNAL CORRECTION.

ON THE REASONS FOR FRATERNAL CORRECTION.

Subject.

Each one should be impelled to practise the duty of fraternal correction: 1. by the love of God; 2. by the love of his neighbor.—*Preached on the ninth Sunday after Pentecost.*

Text.

Amice, quomodo huc intrasti, non habens vestem nuptialem?—
Matt. xxii. 12.

" Friend, how camest thou in hither not having on a wedding garment? "

Introduction.

Did none of the many guests who were invited notice that this poor man was not clad in a seemly fashion? Truly, some of them must have remarked it. Why, then, did no one take the trouble of reminding him in a friendly manner, and warning him to change before the king should come in? If that had been done, the wretched man would have had time to go home and put on something better, if he had it; and thus he would have avoided the great misfortune of being cast into the exterior darkness. But this is only a parable, my dear brethren, and not history; if the thing had happened in reality, who knows how the guests would have behaved? Oh, how many there are who daily lose by their sins and vices the precious wedding-garment of sanctifying grace! How many are cast into the exterior darkness of hell who would have amended their evil ways, and escaped those eternal flames, if only they had had some zealous lovers of souls to give them a friendly warning and admonish them fraternally to amend their lives!—a thing we might often do in different circumstances, if we only had the good will. But most people do not think of this. And yet it is a duty imposed on all Christians. This is a subject, my dear brethren, that I have long been seeking an opportunity of speaking about, because I have not yet directly treated of it: I mean, the duty of fraternal correction. And what of it? It is required of us all by the love of God and the love of our neighbor; and we are bound to it by God's express command. But in what manner should fraternal correction be given, and in what manner taken? There you have the subject of the four following sermons and instructions. To-day I begin with the first, and I say:

Plan of Discourse.

The reasons for fraternal correction are, the love of God and the love of our neighbor. Such is the whole subject. The love of God requires it; the first part. The love of our neighbor requires it; the second part.

Christ Jesus, give all of us here present the true love of Thee and of our neighbor, so that we may prevent sin and be most diligent in helping souls to amend. This we ask of Thee, through the intercession of Mary the Refuge of sinners and of our holy guardian angels.

The object of fraternal correction is to induce others to repent, when they have sinned. Fraternal correction, in a general sense, means admonishing our neighbor with the intention of inducing him to avoid evil or to do good, in whatever manner that admonition is given. For instance: we may mildly remonstrate with, or more sternly reprove, a person, according to circumstances, when he is actually doing or saying anything against the law of God, by representing the deformity of the vice to which we know he is addicted; by wholesome advice, when he is about to put himself in danger of sin; by cutting off the occasion in which he is, or which he seeks and loves; by paternal chastisement, if he refuses to amend, and our duty requires that of us; by secretly reporting his conduct to those who are better able to correct him than we are, if our correction fails to do good; by bringing him to sermons and devotions, where we hope that some good thoughts may be suggested to him; and, finally, if there is no other way, by trying to give him good and edifying example, and by fervent prayer that God may prevent him from committing sin, or may enable him to amend his life.

It is re- To this correction we are all bound, my dear brethren, due proportion being observed, according to our different states and quired of us by the love of God, who is offended by sin. opportunities. If there were no special command given us to this effect; if there were no evangelical counsel to exhort us to it; if it were left altogether to our own choice, still a sincere love of God would certainly impel us to practise fraternal correction. For if I love my friend truly, I rejoice in his welfare, and sympathize with his sorrows and misfortunes, while I spare no efforts to save him from evil, although there is otherwise no bond between us, nor am I bound to him in any way by contract or agreement. The fact of his being my friend is enough to make me abhor the idea of his incurring misfortune, or suffering harm. Now, the greatest evil, the worst harm, the greatest injury and insult, the worst misfortune, so to speak, that can be inflicted by His creatures on our Lord and God, who is infinitely happy in Himself, is sin alone, by which He is dishonored, despised, contemned, and grievously offended. Sin is an act of rebellion on the part of the creature against the Creator; an odious ingratitude towards the God of infinite goodness; an act of hatred and wrath against the God of infinite beauty; a defiance and mockery to the very face, so to speak, of the God who is present everywhere; a shameful abuse of the divine coöperation, for God is forced, as it were, against His will to take part in the offence offered Himself, inasmuch as He must help to perform the sinful act; it is a shameful rejection of God, of that sovereign Good worthy of all love, and a selling of ourselves to the devil forever for some wretched thing. Sin, as far as it can, attempts the life of the eternal God, and, as St. Paul says, crucifies anew the Son of God, our Saviour, who is now reigning in glory .And if an insult of that kind is offered the Almighty in my presence, can I look on with dry eyes, with speechless mouth, with an unchanged countenance, with an undisturbed heart? Should I tolerate that injustice, and not hinder it, if I can, by admonition, exhortation, correction, or complaining of it to others? If so, I should not be worthy of being called a child, a friend, a servant, a creature of God, or, at all events, it would not be true for me to say that I love my God, as I am bound to love Him, with my whole heart, my whole mind, and all my strength.

O princes and kings of earth! you have, as is right, your Dutiful subjects try to punish at once all who are officers to watch with careful eyes that no one does anything against your written laws and commandments, and to administer due punishment to the transgressor. Princes and kings of earth!

guilty of disrespect to their sovereign. who would dare, even behind your backs, to utter a word against you, not to speak of offending you in your very presence, and before your faithful servants? Oh, what a commotion there would be if any such thing occurred! If there was any one present who had a drop of honorable blood in his veins, he should be ready to shed it and to give his life to boot, dearly as he might love it, to defend your honor, and to punish the wretch who has dared to insult you! "I will go and cut off his head," he would cry out, full of wrath, like that faithful servant of David, when his royal master was insulted by Semei; "why should this dead dog curse my Lord the king?" [1] Where is my sword? I will go at once and strike off his head. The least insult or act of disrespect to a sovereign, says Tertullian, is like the sound of drum or trumpet, which calls all the subjects to arms: "Every man becomes a soldier against those who are guilty of treason, in order to punish such a crime." [2]

Much more should we do so when God is dishonored. And the King of kings, the Lord of hosts, the great God worthy of all love, before whom all the potentates of earth must bend the knee, cannot find servants zealous enough for His honor, or jealous enough of the respect due to Him, to correct those who wound His honor and infinite majesty in their presence, and to recall them by a few words to a sense of duty! God is offended; God is dishonored; God is murdered, as it were, by sin; can any true servant of God, who loves his Master, sit still and look on calmly? Could he be such a coward as not to admonish the delinquent, if possible, to prevent his crime and to make him amend his ways?

Especially if we wish to act as dutiful children of our heavenly Father. What should we think of a son who looks on while his father is being maltreated by some wicked fellow, and stands there quietly while he is being kicked and buffeted, and does not make the least effort to help him, although he could easily do so? We should say that that son is undutiful, and unworthy of having an honorable man as his father. It is an indelible disgrace to the memory of the Emperor Gallienus that, when he heard that his father was taken prisoner by the Parthians, he showed neither anger against the barbarians nor sympathy for his father; but without deigning to say a word by way of answer to the messenger who brought him the news, as if it were of no concern to him, turned to a friend and asked him what he was to have for

---

[1] Vadam et amputabo caput ejus. Quare maledicit canis hic mortuus domino meo regi? —II. Kings xvi. 9.

[2] Contra reos læsæ majestatis omnis homo miles.

dinner on that day. To know that his father was in prison, and yet not testify grief thereat, nor declare war on those who had captured him, although it might easily have been done, is a most cruel and unworthy act on the part of a son. In such circumstances, a dutiful son would find in his respect and love for his father a superhuman strength, so that he would be ready to dare wounds, and even death itself, in his efforts to free his beloved parent. Atus, the son of Crœsus, was born dumb and remained so, until excitement at a sudden danger in which his father was loosened the string of his tongue: Crœsus was attacked by a man with a drawn sword, who was about to pierce his heart, when Atus cried out: "O man, slay not my father!" O Christians, is not the Lord God our Father, our most faithful and loving Father, who has not His like upon earth; to whom we pray daily, "Our Father who art in heaven;" who shows us His fatherly love by heaping benefits on us every moment? And we, who say we are His children, see and hear daily the sins and vices with which men treat Him so unbecomingly; we see and hear their unchastity and impurity, their uncharitable talk, their swearing and cursing, by which they publicly insult the Almighty, nay, as St. Paul says, again crucify and slay Him; and shall we tolerate that? Shall we look on coldly, and not rather do our best to put a stop to it? Should we not cry out to the malefactors, "O man, slay not my father"? What are you doing? Why do you speak and act in such a manner? Do not slay our heavenly Father! But if we neglect to do this, especially when there is a hope of our doing some good thereby, is it possible that we have still a child-like love of God in our hearts?

There is no one who has not some friend to whom he is attached; now, I ask, if that friend were insulted, despised, and ill-treated, would not any honorable man be hurt and afflicted, if he were looking on? Would he not feel angry with the person who thus misuses his friend, and try to prevent him by every means in his power? We ourselves are so sensitive that a word is sometimes enough to put us in a passion, so that we can hardly restrain ourselves from taking revenge if we have the opportunity. Should we not have the same feelings at the sight of the injuries that are offered to God, from whom we have received all the good things we possess, who is our best Friend, and whom we must love more than ourselves? The great God (consider this, my dear brethren), who is not at all in need of our ser-

We are jealous of our own honor and that of our friends: should we not be so, too, of the honor of God?

vices, is so jealous of our honor and welfare, if we only love Him, that He takes to Himself all the injuries that others do us. "Amen, I say to you," He exclaims, "as long as you did it to one of these, My least brethren, you did it to Me."[1] Nay, He says even: "He that toucheth you toucheth the apple of My eye,"[2] and threatens the eternal flames of hell to those who dare to nourish hatred and anger against one of His servants and to call him a fool. And we, who are in need of our God at all moments, in all circumstances, should we not also take to ourselves the injuries offered to Him, and at all events correct with a gentle admonition him who dares to insult the Almighty by sin? Where is our charity? where is our sense of decency? nay, where is our faith?

If we love God, then we should try to prevent the sins of others, as pious Christians do.

Ah, if we had only a spark of the true love of God, we should look on it as the greatest happiness and honor to be thus able, in some degree, to further the honor and glory of God! Our holy Founder Ignatius, who had always in his thoughts and on his lips the words, "all for the greater glory of God,"[3] after having succeeded in building in Rome several houses of refuge for persons who had fallen into vicious ways, he himself having begged the money to build those houses, when he was laughed at for spending money so foolishly, as there was little hope of reclaiming such persons, used to answer: if, with all my trouble and labor, I succeeded in preventing one of those persons from committing sin even during one night, and thus saved my God from being insulted by that sin, my labor would be more than rewarded, and all the money I have spent would be well laid out. On another occasion he went into an ice-cold river during the winter-time, and remained there with the water up to his neck, because he knew that a young man was to pass by on his way to a house of ill-fame; and his intention was to keep that young man even once from committing mortal sin. That holy man understood well and teaches us all by his example what it is to offend God, and what a sincere love God requires of His servants; he knew, too, what it is to save one's fellow-mortal from sin. And this is another motive that should urge us not to neglect the duty of fraternal correction; namely, the love that we owe our neighbor, as we shall see in the second part.

[1] Amen dico vobis, quamdiu fecistis uni ex his fratribus meis minimis, mihi fecistis.—Matt. xxv. 40.

[2] Qui enim tetigerit vos, tangit pupillam oculi mei.—Zach. ii. 8.

[3] Omnia ad majorem Dei gloriam.

Second Part.

If, as we have seen already, I can save my neighbor from some great danger, misfortune, or calamity, without any great loss to myself, there is no doubt that the law of charity binds me to do so under pain of sin, even if the man were nothing to me otherwise. Thus, if I were to refuse a piece of bread, that I can easily spare, to a man who is on the point of dying of hunger, or not to help out of a pit one who has fallen into it, and whom I can save by merely stretching out my hand to him, or not to give due warning to a blind man whom I see to be in imminent danger of falling over a precipice, who would say that, in such circumstances, I am free from a sin of cruelty and want of charity? I should evidently act against the fundamental law: " Thou shalt love thy neighbor as thyself;" for if I were in similar circumstances I should reasonably wish some one to help or warn, or pull me out of the pit, or save me from dying of hunger. Esirlanda tells us of a nobleman, a native of Jerusalem, who, by incautiously eating some food that had been bewitched, lost the outward appearance of a human being, and seemed to all who beheld him to be an ass. By this transformation he lost the power of speech, but not reason; he heard all that was said in his presence, but could not make himself known. The first to drive him away were his own companions, who were seeking him everywhere, although unknown to them he was in their very presence; as he was trying to enter into a boat with them they drove him off with blows. Many were the attempts he made to go into the houses, and to stretch forth his hands for help; but there was nothing but blows for him wherever he went. Three whole years this transformation lasted, and during that time he had to bend his back beneath heavy burdens. Once he happened to pass by a church in which the priest was saying Mass and was just raising the sacred Host on high to be adored by the people; the poor wretch at once threw himself down on his knees, load and all, and behaved with such devotion that all who saw him came to the conclusion that it could not be an ass, but a human being who showed such a sense of reverence for the holy Mass. At once people began to suspect that witchcraft had something to do with the matter; and their suspicions were correct. The animal and the woman who owned him were taken into custody and strictly observed, until at last the whole thing was brought to light. The witch was burned alive and the young man recovered his former

The law of charity binds me to help my neighbor as well as I can in his bodily necessities.

stature. Suppose now, my dear brethren, that some one knew that the young man was bewitched, and yet took no trouble to free him; would you not look on him as guilty of the greatest cruelty? To see a man changed into the likeness of a beast of burden, to be able easily to help him, and yet not to stir a finger in his behalf, could any greater heartlessness be imagined? I am sure that if you had been present on the occasion, you would not have allowed a reasoning being to be so ill-treated.

Much more should I help him when his soul is in danger.

Oh, necessities of the body and necessities of the soul! Deformity of body and deformity of soul! Danger of body and danger of soul! Sickness of body and sickness of soul! Death of body and death of soul! can you, indeed, be weighed in the same balance? Even as little as the mortal can be weighed with the immortal, the temporal with the eternal. Mark now, O Christian, your neighbor has sinned, as you know, and is still in the same danger and occasion to sin; your neighbor will sin, as you are well aware; your neighbor sins actually in your presence. Alas, what is he doing? what has he done? whither is he going? His soul is deformed and changed into a most horrible figure of a brute beast, for in the Holy Scriptures sinners are generally spoken of as beasts: "I am become as a beast before Thee;"[1] "many dogs have encompassed me;"[2] "fat bulls have besieged me."[3] What will he do now? His soul is hurrying blindly into the abyss of hell. How will he save himself? His soul has actually fallen into the imminent danger of eternal death. Could his deformity, his danger, his misfortune, his necessity, be greater or more deplorable? Now, if the law of Christian charity requires of each one to help his neighbor if he can when the latter is suffering from danger, want, or bodily deformity,—although that is of little importance,—how much more does not the same law require us to help our neighbor in that utmost danger, necessity, and deformity of the soul, on which all depends, and to try to save him, if possible, from the wretched state in which he is?

That I can do, to my own great gain, by fraternal correction.

And that can be done, and without any harm to us, nay, to the great merit of our souls, by fraternal correction, admonition, and reproof, as Jesus Christ, our Saviour, tells us in the Gospel of St. Matthew: "If thy brother shall offend against thee, go and rebuke him;" act the apostle towards him; admonish and

[1] Ut jumentum factus sum apud te.—Ps. lxxii. 23.
[2] Canes multi circumdederunt me.—Ibid. xxi. 17.
[3] Tauri pingues obsederunt me.—Ibid. 13.

reprove him. What will be the consequence? " If he shall hear thee, thou shalt gain thy brother."[1] Oh, what an act of charity! what a precious gain, to have saved the soul of one's brother! to have saved a soul, that is more precious in the sight of God than all the treasures of earth, which have been created by God for the sole purpose of saving souls! to have saved a soul, a precious pearl, for the sake of which the Eternal Son of God left all that is in heaven, came down upon earth, and labored hard for thirty-three years! A soul that can be bought with nothing less than the blood of Jesus Christ, which He shed for it, even to the last drop! What an immense gain, I say, to save such a soul from the jaws of hell! What a gain to prevent that soul from being condemned to curse and blaspheme its God forever; to help it to love, praise, and bless Him for eternity in heaven! Oh, what a great gain! what a great, meritorious, holy, divine work, to which all others must yield! " No sacrifice," says St. Gregory, " is so grateful to God as zeal for souls."[2] To pray, fast, distribute our goods to the poor, build churches and temples to the great God, and found hospitals for the sick and refuges for the poor, are indeed meritorious and holy works in the sight of God; but to save even one soul is a work of charity which far surpasses all the others in greatness and merit. Hear what St. John Chrysostom says: " Although you may give immense sums of money to the poor, you will do a great deal more by converting one soul."[3] For he who gives money to a poor man appeases his hunger; but he who corrects a sinner hinders him from committing sin."[4] In the one case, the body is saved from the pangs of hunger; in the other, the soul is saved from the flames of hell. " My brethren," cries out St. James, " if any of you err from the truth, and one convert him, he must know that he who causeth a sinner to be converted from the error of his way shall save his soul from death, and shall cover a multitude of sins."[5]

It was this consideration that made the apostles and their successors travel through the whole world, preaching the Gospel, and filled them with indescribable consolation and joy, in the _This gain inspired th saints to undertake._

[1] Si autem peccaverit in te frater tuus, vade et corripe eum ; si te audierit lucratus eris fratrem tuum.—Matt. xviii. 15.

[2] Nullum quippe tam gratum Deo sacrificium est, quam zelus animarum.

[3] Etsi immensas pecunias pauperibus eroges ; plus tamen effeceris, si unicam converteris animam.

[4] Qui peccantem correxit, impietatem extinxit.

[5] Fratres mei, si quis ex vobis erraverit a veritate, et converterit quis eum, scire debet, quoniam qui converti fecerit peccatorem ab errore viæ suæ, salvabit animam ejus a morte, et operiet multitudinem peccatorum.—James v. 19, 20.

the greatest labors to save a soul.

midst of their many trials and sufferings. If they had been asked what was the reason of the incessant labors they undertook, of their unwearied activity, they would have answered that it was to gain the precious souls of their brethren that were redeemed by the blood of Jesus Christ, for the sake of which they would be quite ready to sacrifice their comfort and convenience, their honor and good name, their health and their lives, and, moreover, to undergo public disgrace and all the torments of martyrdom. This was the gain that St. Paul longed for, when he offered himself to God to become an anathema for his brethren, that he might win over their souls to Christ. This was the gain that drove St. Francis Xavier to the distant Indies and Japan, in order to convert the heathens there. "Lord," was his usual prayer, "Lord, give me souls!" This was the gain that the seraphic St. Catharine of Siena desired, when, like St. Paul, she offered to undergo the pains of hell for all eternity, under the condition that the gates should be closed after her, never to be opened again; the gain, namely, of the precious souls of her brethren. This was the gain that Jesus Christ Himself sought as the reward of all His labor, and of the bitter death He suffered on the cross, as He Himself says: "The Son of man is come to seek and to save that which was lost." [1]

That zeal is wanting to most people who have opportunities enough of exercising it.

O love of God and of our neighbor, where art thou nowadays? If, my dear brethren, we cannot with the apostles and apostolic men go about the world to convert the souls of our brethren and win them over to God, yet we have many an opportunity of showing zeal for souls by hindering, lessening, and decreasing the number of our neighbor's sins, by fraternal correction and admonition. But, alas, I must say again: O love of God and of our neighbor, how cold thou art grown in this particular! There are adulterers enough in the world (of Treves I know nothing) who sin just as David did, but perhaps not so secretly; but where shall we find a Nathan to warn them, or at least urge others who have more influence over them to admonish them of the evil of their ways? There are unjust people and usurers enough in the world who, like Achab, use every means in their power to become possessed of their neighbor's property; but where can we find an Elias hardy enough to reprove them? There are still unchaste Herods enough in the world; but were shall we find a John the Baptist to say to them: it is not lawful? There are proud Eudoxias

[1] Venit enim Filius hominis quærere et salvum facere quod perierat.—Luke, xix. 10.

enough in the world who give others a bad example of luxury and extravagance; but were is the John Chrysostom to tell them the truth about themselves? There is still many a revengeful Theodosius to be found in the world; but where is the Ambrose who tries to restrain them from sin?   We see and hear daily in company how the good name of our neighbor is injured by calumnious and uncharitable conversation; how piety and God and His saints are made subjects of ridicule; how whole neighborhoods are scandalized by cursing and swearing; where is the zealous Tobias who shows either by sharp reproof, or by other signs, that such talk is displeasing to him and says: "Speak not so, for we are the children of saints " ? [1]   We see here and there how that young man and young woman, how that servant man and servant girl spend hours in each other's company at home in the evenings, in the dark night; we know very well that they are not saying their prayers (oh, that wretched sitting at the door in the evening!); we know that that young man or woman has managed to slip out of the house at night, or has gone to meet some one, God knows where!   Where is the zealous neighbor or inmate of the house who reports their conduct to their parents, as he is in duty bound to do, or to their master or mistress, that it may be put a stop to?   In a word, we see and hear daily that the great God is offended by many sins; that the precious souls of our fellow-mortals are hurried on in swarms to eternal ruin; and although we might sometimes hinder that to a great extent, we do not take trouble to do so; it gives us as little concern as if a cat or a dog were falling into a pit.   Yet, in the latter case, we often take pity on the poor animals, and bring a ladder to help them out: but we are unconcerned when we see the immortal souls of our fellow-creatures falling into the abyss of hell!   O love of God and of our neighbor, what small room thou hast in our hearts, although we daily make the most beautiful professions of love in our prayers: My God and my all, we exclaim; I love Thee with my whole heart! I love Thee above everything in heaven and on earth!

Ah, would to God that there were not to be found in such great numbers those murderers of souls who, instead of endeavoring to further the honor of God and their neighbor's salvation, seem to devote all their efforts to extending the kingdom of the demon, and bringing other souls along with their own to hell! By their impure talk, and the indecent pictures they expose publicly,

Many on the contr help to r souls.

---

[1] Noli ita loqui ; quoniam filii sanctorum sumus.-- Tob. ii. 17, 18.

or by reading bad books, or dressing in a scandalous manner, they are to many an innocent soul the occasion of sinful thoughts and desires.   They act as go-betweens to encourage an impure passion; they are teachers of the devil's school, who endeavor by ridicule, and even threats, to turn away from their devotions the pious who otherwise have no sympathy with their evil ways; nay, even parents are sometimes guilty in this respect, by not tolerating innocence and piety in their children, and by acting as devil's agents to corrupt the innocent by word and example.   O scandal-givers!   O betrayers of souls! see how terribly you sin against the love of God and your neighbor!   Woe to you when the angry God will demand of you the souls that you have ruined! when that curse shall fall upon you which Jesus Christ has uttered against all who give scandal: " Woe to that man by whom the scandal cometh!" [1]

Conclusion and resolution to help our brother by fraternal correction.   Far be this woe from us, my dear brethren!   Far different shall be the conclusion we now make, namely, never in future to allow an opportunity of hindering evil or doing good to pass by, when we have any hope that our warnings or admonitions will be effectual.   Thereby we shall prove that we love our God, not merely with the lips, but in reality, with our whole hearts, since we thus take an active interest in furthering His honor and preventing sin.   We shall show thereby that we love our neighbor, not merely with the lips, but with the heart and sincerely, since we thus try to save the souls of our brothers and sisters from hell, and to bring them with us to heaven, where our joy and glory will be all the greater, the more companions we have with us to show us eternal gratitude for the love we had for their souls, and to join with us in praising God forever.   Amen.

Another Introduction to the same sermon for the Ninth Sunday after Pentecost.

Text.

Videns civitatem, flevit super illam, dicens: quia si cognovisses et tu.—Luke xix. 41, 42.

" Seeing the city, He wept over it saying: If thou also hadst known."

Introduction.

Wood and stone, walls, houses, and palaces of Jerusalem, that were soon to be reduced to ashes, it was not on your account

[1] Væ homini illi per quem scandalum venit !—Matt. xviii. 7.

that Jesus wept so bitterly. It was the thought of the precious souls of the inhabitants of Jerusalem, that were going to their eternal destruction in their obstinacy and blindness, and to be given over as a prey to the demons; it was the thought of those precious souls, for the sake of which He came down on earth, that forced such bitter tears from the eyes of the Saviour: "Seeing the city, He wept over it." And indeed tears were all He had now to give for it; for what had He not done to bring those souls again on the right path? How He warned, exhorted, threatened, reproved, in all the streets and by-ways in His sermons! "If thou also hadst known!" If thou hadst taken those well-meant exhortations to heart! But all is in vain; there is no means of saving thee now: thou wilt die in thy sins and be lost forever! "He wept over it;" thus Jesus bewails the irreparable loss of souls. My dear brethren, how many souls there are nowadays in all the towns and villages of the world who live in sin and die in sin! But which of us takes that loss to heart so much as to shed even one tear at it? Yet our tears would be of little avail. Which of us, let me ask, would, after the example of Our Lord, take the trouble of keeping his neighbor from sin by brotherly correction and admonition, and thus save him from eternal ruin? Yet we have many opportunities of so doing, etc.—*Continues as above.*

FIFTY-FIFTH SERMON.

ON THE DUTY OF FRATERNAL CORRECTION.

Subject.

Many are bound by justice under pain of sin to fraternal correction. 2. All are bound to it occasionally by a special law of God.—*Preached on the Twentieth Sunday after Pentecost.*

Text.

Abiit ad eum et rogabat eum, ut descenderet et sanaret filium ejus.—John iv. 47.

"He went to Him, and prayed Him to come down and heal his son."

Introduction.

It is no wonder that this man was so anxious for the recovery of the sick person, for the latter was his son; but why did he come himself? for he was a great man, a ruler, and could have sent one of his servants to Our Lord to ask Him to heal his son? But no, he was not satisfied unless he came himself, for his fatherly love would not let him rest otherwise: "He went to Him, and prayed Him to come down and heal his son." And according to his wish and desire he heard from Our Lord the consoling words: "Go thy way, thy son liveth." My dear brethren, we have already begun to speak of fraternal correction, by which the souls of our fellow-men, sick and dying through sin, can be saved from death and restored to health. I have shown how that correction is required of us by the love of God and the love of our neighbor. But unfortunately in this matter we are as if we were dumb, or as if our neighbor's welfare did not concern us. Yet it does concern us, and we are bound to further it under pain of sin, as I shall now show.

Plan of Discourse.

Many are bound by justice under pain of sin to fraternal correction. This I shall show in the first and longer part. All are bound to it occasionally by a special law of God. This I shall show in the second part.

O God of goodness, grant by Thy powerful grace that we may all unite our efforts to further Thy honor, and glory, to prevent sin and vice in ourselves and others, and to induce the wicked to amend their lives. Help us to this by thy intercession, O Virgin Mother Mary, and you, holy guardian angels.

Everyone is bound in justice to keep to the terms of the contract he has made. He who has made a contract or an agreement with another is bound in justice to fulfil his part of it. Thus, if I were surety for your debtor, I should be bound to do my best to enable you to have the money that is due to you. A steward or servant who has agreed with you for a yearly wage is bound to look after your property and your house, and justice requires him to take all possible care to make your property as profitable as possible and prevent it from being injured by theft or otherwise. He who has undertaken to keep your money, or money's worth, safe for you, is bound to do all he can to prevent it from being lost; and so on. Of this there is not the least doubt.

Many, by virtue of their state or office. Now, my dear brethren, there are many men in the world who, by virtue of their office or position, have entered on a tacit agreement with God by which they bind themselves to look after the

welfare of certain souls as best they can, in order to prevent
them from being lost forever. Who are they? All superiors,
whether lay or ecclesiastical, who have to protect the interests
of their subjects in towns or villages: such as parish priests and
those who have a care of souls with regard to their parishioners;
preachers with regard to their hearers; teachers with regard to
their scholars; parents with regard to their sons and daughters;
masters and mistresses with regard to their servants and other
domestics; husbands with regard to their wives; in a word, all
those who have any position of superiority or authority over
others. When entering on their state or occupation they made
a tacit contract with God by which they took upon themselves
the care of their subjects, as sureties, stewards, and depositaries
of God, binding themselves thereby to use all possible diligence
to lead on their subjects to good, to keep them from evil, and
to induce them to amend their lives if they are in sin.

have made a contract with God to look after the souls of others.

Therefore they are bound in justice not only to admonish,
warn, and exhort in a fatherly manner those subjects of theirs
whom they see to be in sin or in the danger of sin, but also to
reprove and punish them if warnings or threats have proved unavailing; so that they who are careless or forgetful of this duty
are guilty of all the sins and vices that they failed to correct and
prevent in their subjects. "If," says St. Augustine, "we permit those who are under our authority to commit sin before our
eyes, we make ourselves partakers in their guilt." [1] We are
just as guilty as if we ourselves committed the sinful act; for
"he who does not correct what should be corrected is guilty of
the sin." [2] And God will one day require the souls of those
subjects at our hands, as He Himself says: "At the hand of
man, at the hand of every man, and of his brother will I require
the life of man." [3] At the hand of the husband, the father,
the master, the mistress, the superior, I will require the soul
that was allowed to be lost to Me, through want of correction
and admonition; he who is responsible for that loss must make
it good at his own cost; his own soul will have to answer for all
the sins that have been committed through his carelessness.

Hence they are bound to do so by fraternal correction and admonition.

And this is perfectly just; for it is a recognized practice even
in worldly concerns. If your debtor has run through his prop-

And if they neglect to do so, God

---

[1] Si eos in quos nobis potestas est, ante oculos nostros perpetrare scelera permittimus, rei coram ipsis erimus.—S. Aug. lib. v. contra Jul.

[2] Qui non corrigit resecanda, commisit.

[3] De manu hominis, de manu viri, et fratris ejus requiram animam hominis.—Gen. ix. 5.

erty, and has become unable to pay what he owes you, you look to the person who went surety for him, to see that you get what you have a right to; nor can the latter shirk the obligation, for he should have looked better after the man for whom he went surety, and not suffered him to live so extravagantly. If the money you have deposited with another is stolen, or the property you have left in his care injured, then, according to all theologians and jurists, he who undertook the care of it is bound to make restitution to you out of his own goods, if the theft can be traced to any wilful and gross carelessness on his part. Why so? He has not stolen your property, nor received a single penny of your money. No matter; he was not diligent in keeping it, as he was bound to be by the contract he entered into; and on account of this carelessness he is bound in conscience to indemnify you out of his own goods. In your absence you have entrusted your house and shop to your servant; the servant finds a comfortable seat, and goes to sleep with the door open, so that thieves get into your shop and run off with what they can lay hands on. What will you say to that when you come back? What will you think of your servant when you find out how he has looked after your property? It does not take you long to consider about that! You worthless fellow! you say to him; make good what was lost through your laziness, or else you will soon become acquainted with the inside of a prison, to teach you, and all like you, how to mind your business. But why are you so strict with the poor man? Is that right on your part? What harm has he done? He only fell asleep, and there is surely no great harm in that? Yes, you answer; but he should have looked after my house and property better; I hired him for that purpose; and therefore he should either have shut the door or else kept his eyes open; his going to sleep was the cause of the robbery; therefore he must either pay me or go to prison. And you are perfectly right, nor can any one find fault with your mode of acting under the circumstances.

O superiors, pastors of souls, teachers, husbands, masters and mistresses, and you especially, Christian parents, mark this well: you are sureties for the souls of those under your care. A precious treasure has been entrusted to you by God; souls, the houses and dwellings of God, have been placed in your charge that they may not be stolen away from Him by the devil. Woe to you if through your want of care, or neglect of due admonition, or reproof, those souls are squandered, that trea'sure lost, those houses broken into! What will you have to do in that case? You must make good the loss with your own property; God will demand your souls instead, and that, too, with the utmost strictness. Hear what the Holy Ghost says by the Wise Man: "My son, if thou be surety for thy friend, thou hast engaged fast thy hand to a stranger, thou art ensnared with the words of thy mouth, and caught with thy own words. Do therefore, my son, what I say and deliver thyself; because thou art fallen into the hand of thy neighbor. Run about, make haste, stir up thy friend; give not sleep to the eyes, neither let thy eyelids slumber." [1] These words are applied by SS. Gregory, Bernard, Thomas of Aquin, and the Venerable Bede to all those who are in any way bound to look after the souls of others, and to take an interest in their salvation. And who is it to whom you have given your hand and word? Is it not to Jesus Christ, your Saviour and the Redeemer of souls? Yes, beyond a doubt. Why, then, does the Holy Ghost speak of Him as a stranger? Mark the reason:

Suppose that you are well off, and that you undertake to be surety with a man for his debtor. While you are signing the agreement, oh, how friendly the man is to you! He is as polite and cordial as if you were his dearest friend. But wait a little; when the time has elapsed, and the debtor is unable to meet his obligation; what then? Oh, then the creditor acts quite differently; he sends word to you at once, and lets you know that you have to pay. The time is up, he says; you went bail for that man; give me now what he owes me. And if you do not pay immediately he sends the officers of justice to your house to take possession of your property, and tries by every means to compel you to pay the debt. Why has he changed so suddenly in your regard? At first he was quite friendly to you; he spoke kindly and was most cordial. Yes, but then is not now; things are seen in a different light now that the time for payment has come. He is quite a stranger to you; he knows you no longer, unless in so far as he is determined to exact his own from you to the last farthing. So will Christ act with those who by their state or office have charge of the souls of others. "Christ is called a

Explained by other similes.

---

[1] Fili mi, si spoponderis pro amico tuo, defixisti apud extraneum manum tuam, illaqueatus es verbis oris tui, et captus propiis sermonibus. Fac ergo quod dico fili mi, et temetipsum libera; quia incidisti in manum proximi tui; discurre, festina, suscita amicum tuum; ne dederis somnum oculis tuis, nec dormitent palpebræ tuæ.—Prov. vi. 1-4.

stranger," says St. Thomas speaking of the words of the text I have quoted, "because although He is a friend at the time of the agreement," when one undertakes the charge of the souls of others, "He is a stranger when the day of reckoning comes,"[1] if the duty has not been properly performed. Therefore, "my son, if thou be surety" waken up the souls entrusted to you; admonish, reprove them if they have done evil or are in danger. Do not go asleep over your weighty charge, be not negligent; save them from the danger, that you may not have to pay for them one day with your own soul.

Most people are careless of this duty.

But alas, how few there are who care about this! How carelessly most people perform their duty in this respect! How many there are who go to sleep, and let thieves enter into the house of God, and have neither eyes to watch over the souls entrusted to them, nor tongues to warn them, nor hands to punish them when necessary? Public abuses, scandals, sins, and vices, are sometimes allowed loose rein in a community, and thereby many souls are betrayed and ruined; while those who could and ought to speak in order to prevent the mischief have not courage to open their mouths; they act as if they were asleep, and allow the temples of God, precious souls, to be robbed and plundered. Sometimes the servants in a house lead wicked lives either with each other, or with people of the neighborhood; but the master and mistress who could prevent that, and are bound in duty to prevent it, keep silent as if they were asleep in broad daylight. That servant, they think, does his or her duty in the house, and is diligent at work: that is enough for us; as far as other matters are concerned, they may look out for themselves. If the servants spend the Sundays and holy-days in drinking, or frequent bad company, or encourage dangerous intimacies; whether they pray or curse, go to sermons, or elsewhere; whether they frequent the sacraments or not; that is their own affair. It is enough for us that they are faithful. If we were to warn or admonish them, they might perhaps leave us, and where would we get others to suit us so well? That is all such people care about. How are the children of the family often brought up? In what vanity, idleness, and dangerous customs they squander away the best years of their youth! What evident occasions of sin and dangers of losing their innocence they are allowed to frequent,

---

[1] Dicitur autem Christus extraneus; quia amicus est in sponsione, sed erit extraneus in exigenda ratione.

while no restraint is placed on their intercourse with the opposite sex, and the parents meanwhile look on as if they were asleep! We must let young people have their fling, they say; they must act, and dress, and amuse themselves like others; we did so ourselves in our young days; it would not do to be too hard on the poor children. But whether the poor children have a good or a bad soul,—and that soul God has entrusted to the parents' charge,—that they do not think of; whether they are pious or wicked, whether they will rejoice or suffer in eternity, whether they will go to heaven or to hell, that is the last thing that troubles the parents, as if it were not the least concern to them. Married women do not always live in a Christian manner; instead of looking after their children and domestics they sometimes spend the day sleeping, dressing, paying useless visits, talking and chatting, gambling, and otherwise amusing themselves, thus wasting their time doing nothing, and would to God that they did not often do worse! Meanwhile the husband, who could and ought to change that state of things, says nothing, and acts as if he were asleep. Even if his wife's misconduct afflicts him, he has not courage to do his duty, and obey the law of fraternal correction and admonition. What can I do? he says. Patience! I must let things take their course, or else I shall have a peevish, discontented wife to contend with. Thus, precious souls are betrayed and stolen away from God, their Creator, because they who should have guarded the house and undertook to do so are careless and indifferent.

Alas, how will they fare when Christ will appear to them as a stranger, and demand an account of the souls that they thus allowed to slip through their hands? To no purpose will they try to excuse themselves by saying: but I have done no harm; I did not lead those under my care into the vices to which they abandoned themselves; I did not tell my servants to swear, or curse, or not to go to church, or to frequent bad company, or to cultivate dangerous intimacies; I did not advise my children to lead idle, useless lives; nor was I pleased to see my wife neglecting her household duties, and squandering our income so foolishly. I neither taught them those evil habits nor did I give them bad example; how, then, can I be accountable for their sins? Ah, that you will soon see! Neither did that surety tell the debtor to squander away his property; he would far rather have seen him able to pay what he owed. The servant who went

In vain do they try to excuse themselves by saying they do no evil.

asleep in the shop did not invite the thief to come in, nor did he show him the goods or ask him to steal them; he would have been far better pleased if the thief had remained away altogether. But he slept when he should have remained awake; and that alone is enough reason for having him punished.

For they can lose their souls by neglecting to correct their subjects. All those who have charge of the souls of others, especially masters and parents, need of a certainty commit no other sin to lose their own souls than that neglect of paternal vigilance and correction. Woe to me, they will one day cry out; woe to me, not because I myself have led a bad life, or have enticed those under my care to evil, by giving them scandal or bad example; but woe to me, they will exclaim, with the Prophet Isaias: "because I have held my peace." [1] Woe, and eternal woe, to me, because I have kept silent when I should have admonished! Woe to me because I have not done what the duties of my state required of me and restrained those under my care from committing sin! Woe to me for having slept when I should have been awake and watched their actions! Woe to me for not having reproved and chastised them when they did wrong! Woe to me for having permitted them to follow the customs of the vain world, and to mix so freely with the opposite sex! Woe to me "because I have held my peace!"

All others, too, are bound to fraternal correction. A good thing for me, perhaps some will now say, that I am not a superior, or pastor of souls, or preacher, or master, or father, or mother; I have only myself to look after and be responsible for; so that I am free from that duty and need not trouble about rendering any account for not having admonished or corrected others. True, you are not so strictly bound in justice as those others are; yet do not be in too great a hurry to conclude that you are free from every obligation in that respect. Whoever you may be, you are bound under sin according to your ability and opportunity, to fraternal correction, by a special law of God, which He has imposed on all men, as I shall briefly show in the

Second Part.

By the law of God in the Old Testament. It is certain and undoubted that it is the will of God that all sins and vices should be corrected and reproved, in whatever manner it may be done. Now, superiors, parents, and pastors of souls have authority in this way over their own subjects alone,

---

[1] Quia tacui.—Is. vi. 5.

and not over others; neither can they know everything nor find out always where sin is committed. There are millions of sins committed behind their backs that they can know nothing about, and therefore cannot prevent by correction. Hence it is clearly the will of God that all men should perform this duty with regard to each other, and try to help one another to the best of their ability to avoid sin and to amend their lives. Such is the meaning of the words of the wise Ecclesiasticus: " He gave to every one of them commandment concerning his neighbor." [1] The law of God both in the Old and New Testament speaks expressly of this. In the Book of Leviticus the Lord says to Moses: " Speak to all the congregation of the children of Israel, and thou shalt say to them; thou shalt not hate thy brother in thy heart; but reprove him openly, lest thou incur sin through him." [2] In the Book of Ecclesiasticus the Lord says, over and over again: " Reprove a friend, lest he may not have understood, and say, I did it not; or if he did it, that he may do it no more. Admonish thy friend, for there is often a fault committed. Admonish thy neighbor before thou threaten him, and give place to the fear of the Most High." [3]

In the New Law Christ expressly commands us in the Gospel of St. Luke: " If thy brother sin against thee, reprove him." [4] Or, as those words are interpreted, if he sins to thy knowledge, or in thy presence, reprove him. And in the Gospel of St. Matthew: " If thy brother shall offend against thee, go and rebuke him between thee and him alone; if he shall hear thee, thou shalt gain thy brother; and if he will not hear thee, take with thee one or two more. And if he will not hear them, tell the Church." [5] If he will not hear you, tell those who have more authority over him. St. Paul, too, writes in the same sense, in his Epistles to the Ephesians, the Thessalonians, the Galatians, to Timothy, and to Titus. Hence the holy Fathers and theologians conclude that we are bound to practise fraternal correction, not

The law of Christ in the New Testament.

---

[1] Mandavit illis unicuique de proximo suo.—Ecclus. xvii. 12.

[2] Loquere ad omnem coetum filiorum Israel, et dices ad eos: non oderis fratrem tuum in corde tuo; sed publice argue eum, ne habeas super illo peccatum.—Levit. xxix. 2, 17.

[3] Corripe amicum, ne forte non intellexerit, et dicat : non feci ; aut si fecerit, ne iterum addat facere. Corripe amicum ; saepe enim fit commissio. Corripe proximum, antequam commineris, et da locum timori Altissimi.—Ecclus. xix. 13, 15, 17, 18.

[4] Si peccaverit in te frater tuus, increpa illum.—Luke xvii. 3.

[5] Si autem peccaverit in te frater tuus, vade et corripe eum inter te et ipsum solum ; si te audierit, lucratus eris fratrem tuum ; si autem te non audierit, adhibe tecum unum vel duos. Quod si non audierit eos, dic ecclesiae.—Matt. xviii. 15, 16, 17.

by a mere counsel, but by a law which obliges us under sin; and he who does not try to correct his neighbor whom he sees doing wrong becomes a participator in his guilt. "He who can correct and neglects doing so," says St. Gregory, "certainly participates in the sin."[1] With all those who sin I sin too," says St. Prosper, "when I do not reprove them;"[2] provided I have the means and opportunity of doing so. Nearly the same words are used by SS. Ambrose, Bernard, Augustine, Leo, and others.

Therefore, no one is excused from this.

Now come forward all you who, when there is question of fraternal correction, have in your hearts or on your lips the words of Cain: "Am I my brother's keeper?"[3] What have I to do with others? I have to look out for myself; it is my own soul that I must try to bring to heaven; let others try to do the same for themselves; let each one bear his own burthen and account for his own actions; I have enough to do to mind myself, and I find so many faults and failings in myself that I have neither time nor inclination to trouble myself about those of others. What is it to me? Ah, fine talk that! What a pity you do not speak and think in that way when you indulge your curiosity about the actions of others, and by rash judgments and unfounded suspicions put the worst construction on them! What is it to me? I have to look out for my own soul. So should you think and say when you backbite your neighbor, or listen eagerly to uncharitable conversation; when you talk about faults that you merely suspect in him, or make his secret faults the subject of ridicule and laughter, causing them to appear much worse than they are in reality. What is it to me? What have I to do with others? So should you think and say when you speak of the known sins of your neighbor to those who cannot correct him, and do that through hatred, dislike, vindictiveness, because he has done you some injury, or out of mere talkativeness. That would be the time for you to say: what is it to me? I have nothing to do with others, I must look after myself and my own soul. As we shall see next Sunday, fraternal correction does not require such spying, detraction, talking, and fault-finding. I will then explain how fraternal correction is to be given. No; such prying and idle talk does

---

[1] Qui potest emendare et negligit, participem procul dubio se constituit.—S. Greg. l. 10 Moral.

[2] In omnibus peccantibus, pecco, quando non increpo.

[3] Numquid custos fratris mei sum ego?—Gen. iv. 9.

not prevent sin, but rather increases it; it does not gain the souls of our brethren, but rather takes away their good name and reputation. But when opportunity offers to give your neighbor a wholesome admonition, when you see or know of him doing wrong to warn him charitably, to keep him away from evil, and give him a mild reproof if you reasonably hope that it will do him good; or if you are aware that sin is committed in your neighborhood, to tell the pastor of the parish about it, who has ways and means of preventing it; that I say, concerns you and all men, that is what the love of God and of our neighbor, the express law of God, and the good of souls require.

Therefore if your brother sins, go and rebuke him. Each one will find opportunities enough of doing this, as I have already explained, provided he wishes to help his neighbor to amend. Remember how often you have given others scandal and been the occasion of sin to them, thus helping in the ruin of souls. That consideration alone should be sufficient to induce you to be all the more zealous in atoning for the harm you have done and in gaining new souls to God. Consider the example of St. Paul. After his conversion he hardly took time to refresh his body, emaciated as it was by a three days' fast, but at once set about the work of converting sinners to Christ; he who before was a persecutor, as soon as he became a Christian himself, began without delay to induce others to follow his example: "And immediately he preached Jesus in the synagogues, that He is the Son of God." [1] We have another example in David. When he had repented of his sins his first resolution was to become a teacher and an apostle, to warn others from following the broad road of vice, and to lead them to God: "I will teach the unjust Thy ways; and the wicked shall be converted to Thee." [2] This was what Our Lord said to St. Peter, after having foretold his lamentable fall: "And thou being once converted, confirm thy brethren." [3] His meaning was: thou wilt indeed rise after thy fall; but remember, at the same time, that thou art bound to help thy brethren, and to sustain them by word and example. Follow these examples, and you will atone to God for your former faults. If you have formerly hindered others in their devotions, try now to encourage them therein: "Confirm thy brethren." Have you given scandal by dissolute conduct or extravagance in

Exhortation to practise fraternal correction after the example of pious Christians.

[1] Et continuo in synagogis prædicabat Jesum, quoniam hic est Filius Dei.—Acts ix. 20.

[2] Docebo iniquos vias tuas, et impii ad te convertentur.—Ps. l. 15.

[3] Et tu aliquando conversus, confirma fratres tuos.—Luke xxii. 32.

dress? try now by your modesty and piety to atone for those sins. Have you been to others a stumbling-block; have you led them into sin? try now to keep others from sin, as an atonement for those whom you have betrayed: "Confirm thy brethren." Oh, what a weight of punishment deserved by your sins you can thus get rid of ! "He shall cover a multitude of sins." [1]

Conclusion and resolution.
Oh, yes, my God, when I think of the number of souls I have turned away from good and led into evil I shudder with fear! Alas, how many have I not led astray by bad example and advice, by approving of their sinful actions, by flattery and caresses, by allurements and unbecoming conversation, by sinful gestures and behavior, by extravagance in dress, by a dissolute mode of life! Ah, my God, there is hardly an end to the sins I have caused others to commit! Woe to me if Thou shouldst require all those souls at my hands; how should I be able to pay Thee, since I have but one soul at my disposal? Therefore, I will in future carefully seek out every occasion of working for the good of souls, and will observe the precept of fraternal correction, so that I may make some restitution at least for Thy injured honor, and gain other souls to unite with me in praising Thee for all eternity. Amen.

Another introduction to the same sermon for the tenth Sunday after Pentecost.

Text.

Qui in se confidebant tanquam justi, et aspernabantur cæteros.—Luke xviii. 9.

"Who trusted in themselves as just, and despised others."

Introduction.

That is what we generally do; we notice the least mote in the eyes of another and can hardly see the great beam in our own. We can find fault with, condemn and reprove the faults, failings, and sins of others, like the hypocritical Pharisee in to-day's Gospel: "O God, I give Thee thanks that I am not as the rest of men, extortioners, unjust, adulterers," public sinners. But we try to hide our own faults from ourselves, to cloak and excuse them. In a word, we can overlook anything in ourselves, nothing in others. If, instead of talking about our neighbor and looking down on him when we see faults in him, we were to

---

[1] Operiet multitudinem peccatorum.—James v. 20.

correct him in the way in which he is most likely to take correction and profit by it, that is, in a brotherly manner, and thus help him to amend, we should act as the love of God and of our neighbor require, as I explained already. But in this respect we are generally dumb, and have no courage to undertake to help him to amend, as if his welfare did not concern us in the least, etc.—*Continues as above.*

FIFTY-SIXTH SERMON.

ON THE MANNER IN WHICH FRATERNAL CORRECTION SHOULD BE ADMINISTERED.

Subject.

How we should fraternally admonish and correct others.— *Preached on the Twenty-first Sunday after Pentecost.*

Text.

Et iratus dominus ejus, tradidit eum tortoribus.—Matt. xviii. 34.

"And his lord being angry, delivered him to the torturers."

Introduction.

Three different states of mind are to be observed in this lord. First, he acts towards the servant who could not pay his debt, with the strictest justice: "As he had not wherewith to pay, his lord commanded that he should be sold, and his wife and children, and all that he had, and payment to be made." Secondly, he behaves with the utmost compassion and generosity towards the same servant. For when the latter cast himself at his feet, and begged for mercy, he not only set him at liberty, but even remitted the whole debt: "And the lord of that servant, being moved with pity, let him go and forgave him the debt." Thirdly, when the ungrateful servant acted so pitilessly to his fellow-servant, the lord changed his compassion, goodness, and generosity into just wrath and anger: "And his lord being angry, delivered him to the torturers." To come to the point at once, my dear brethren; we have hitherto treated of fraternal correction, by which we can help our neighbor to avoid sin and amend his life; and I have shown, in the first place, that it is required of each one by the love of God and the love of our neighbor; while, in the second place, I have proved that we are bound to it under pain of sin; many in justice, all by virtue of a special law of God. Now, the question is, how should one, who is concerned for the divine honor and his neighbor's welfare, act when he has to administer fraternal correction or admonition, so that he may attain his end, and not make matters worse instead of better. We can learn that from the Lord in the Gospel; namely, we must not be too harsh and severe to our neighbor at first, but warn him in a friendly manner, and, if he promises to amend, show a brotherly sympathy for him; but if we see that it is necessary, and that the promised amendment does not follow, we should reprove him with a holy anger. This is what I intend to explain in to-day's instruction.

Plan of Discourse.

How we should fraternally admonish and correct others; such is the whole subject.

O Holy Ghost, enlighten our hearts, that we may learn how to help others to avoid sin and to amend their lives; this we ask of Thee, through Thy Virginal Spouse Mary and our holy guardian angels.

A doctor must use great skill and prudence in prescribing for his patients.

If a doctor were to treat all his patients in the same way, and to give them all the same medicine, it would be an evident sign that he knows little of his profession, and we should expect him to kill more of his patients than he would cure. There is an old story of a doctor who used to fill his pockets in the morning with all kinds of prescriptions, and when called to visit a sick person he would, after having felt his patient's pulse, dive down into his pocket, take out the first prescription he put his hand on, and give it to the sick man, saying: Here, send this to the apothecary's, and may God have you in His keeping! And so he did with all his patients. Would you like to trust such a doctor as that? I should think not; for what is good for one kind of illness is bad for another; what will cure one man who has a fever might bring to the grave another who has the very same fever. No, a good doctor must have a clear understanding, prudence, and foresight; he has to take into consideration the symptoms of the disease, the age, constitution, strength, and other circumstances of the sick person; so that he may know what sort of medicine he has to administer in different cases, whether it should be strong or weak, sweet or bitter, cooling or heating,

how often and in what quantity it has to be given. He gives
pills to one and a sudorific to another; he bleeds one, but not
the other; the one he takes very gently and quietly, the other
violently, according to the circumstances of the patient; and thus
he can hope for the best results from his treatment.

My dear brethren, what the medicine prescribed by the doctor
is to the diseases of the body that is the.fraternal correction
given by a well-meaning Christian to the spiritual maladies of
his neighbor. The one intends to save the body; the other, the
soul from death, and to keep it alive. Therefore, the latter, as
well as the former, if he hopes to do any good, must use great
prudence and caution, and take every circumstance into consideration, lest, by administering the correction in an unskilful manner, he do more harm to his neighbor than good. These circumstances are generally comprised in the words so well known
to theologians: who, what, where, by what means, why, how,
when. That is, I must first consider who the person is whom I
have to correct; what is the sin I wish to warn him against; what
is the place in which I intend doing so; what are the means I intend using to carry out my purpose; what is the motive for which
I wish to correct him; how and in what manner I am to undertake the task; and, finally, at what time should I do it so as to
have the best results. We shall consider those circumstances
more in detail, taking them in order. Nor am I speaking of
those who are bound in justice to correct others, but only of those
whom charity obliges to perform that duty.

So, too, must he who undertakes to correct others; and he must consider every circumstance.

First, then, I must see who the person is whom I think to be
in need of correction from me; whether he is a stranger or an
acquaintance of mine. Private individuals are rarely obliged
to administer correction to a stranger whom they are not acquainted with, although they may be well aware that he is not
leading a Christian life, unless, indeed, the case is one in which I
can be of assistance to others in inducing him to amend, or if he
indulges in sinful actions or words in my presence, so that the
opportunity is offered me of giving him a friendly warning, or
of showing my displeasure at his conduct. Thus zeal for souls
often drove St. Francis Xavier into taverns, where he used to sit
down with those who were drinking there, and drink and play
with them, so that he might have an opportunity of warning
them and keeping them from the sins of cursing, swearing,
quarreling, and so forth, that are generally committed in such

Namely, who the person is whom he has to correct.

places.   If the person is well known to me, and is a neighbor
or friend of mine, then I must consider whether he is of a higher
or lower position than I, or whether he is equal to me in worldly
standing.   In the first case, as for instance, if a son has to admonish his father, or a daughter her mother, or a subject his superior, or a young man one who is advanced in life, a poor man
one who is wealthy, an ignorant man one who is learned and well
educated; then common sense tells us that we must be very courteous, careful, and modest in what we say; we must give the admonition with all respect, humility and reverence, if we hope to
produce any good effect by it.   Such is the advice given us by
St. Paul in his Epistle to Timothy: " An ancient man rebuke
not, but entreat him as a father. " [1]   You must not reprove him
in harsh terms, but rather implore of him, as your father, to take
in good part what you have to say.   Other acquaintances of ours,
who are of lower or equal position, we can, after due examination
of the matter, take to task with greater freedom and severity, reminding them of their duty, but always in such a way as to observe all the circumstances of fraternal correction given in a
proper manner.

What is to
be correct-
ed.   The next circumstance is, what have we to warn him of; in
what am I bound to admonish my neighbor?   St. Augustine tells
us this: " You must not seek out for something reprehensible;
but rather reprove what you have seen; otherwise, we should seem
to be spies on the actions of others." [2]   To go about here and
there prying into the affairs of our neighbors through curiosity,
to watch or ask how this or that one lives, what he does, what
happens in this or that company, and that with the sole object
of finding something to criticise and condemn, that is not at all
required.   Such is, indeed, the duty of superiors, parents, and
masters with regard to their subjects; but in a private individual it
would be mere curiosity, and the mark of an idle man, who is more
inclined to meddle with his neighbor than to attend to his own
business; it would be acting like the envious Pharisees of whom
the Gospel says: " They watched Him, " [3] meaning Our Lord.
No; what you see yourself, that you must correct.   You satisfy
your obligation if, when you happen to see your neighbor going
wrong, or find out without actually making inquiries, that he is

[1] Seniorem ne increpaveris, sed obsecra ut patrem.—I. Tim. v. 1.

[2] Non quærendo quid reprehendas; sed videndo quid corrigas ; alioquin videremur explor-
atores vitæ aliorum.

[3] Observabant eum.—Luke xiv. 1.

leading a bad life, or if there is a general belief in the neighborhood that such is the case; you satisfy your obligation then, by
admonishing him at a fitting time.

The third circumstance is, where, in what place, the correction should be given. This question is answered by our divine
Master, Christ Himself: "If thy brother shall offend against thee,
go and rebuke him between thee and him alone." Fraternal correction, if it is to be profitable, must be administered in secret,
and not in the presence of others, for we must not put our erring
brother to useless shame, or unjustly lessen his good reputation;
since that would rather excite his anger than induce him to amend
his evil ways. Unless, indeed, he gives public scandal by improper,
impure, or blasphemous discourse, or by indecent actions; then
charity and zeal for the divine honor require us to show our displeasure at such language or actions, either by some outward sign,
if the person is of a higher position than we are, or by interrupt-
ing the conversation. Christ our Saviour has taught us this,
not only by word, but also by example. Peter had sinned, and
that, too, grievously, when he denied his Master three times in the
court of the high-priest. Our Lord heard all he said; did He reprove him? Certainly He did. But how? Was it by harsh and
severe words? No; for that was not the place for such a reproof; the court was full of servants, and Our Lord did not wish
to put Peter to shame before them. How did He, then, act? He
looked at Peter, but with such compassion and deep meaning
that His look pierced the heart of the apostle more profoundly than
any words, and brought him to see and repent of his sin with bitter
tears. But on another occasion, when Peter wished to deter his
Master from undergoing the torments of His death and Passion,
and when they were only accompanied by a few well-known disciples, who probably heard nothing of what was going on, Our Lord
reproved him sharply: "Go behind me, satan," He exclaimed,
"thou art a scandal unto Me; because thou savorest not the
things that are of God."[1] Even with the hard-hearted and obdurate Judas He employed a wonderful mildness in this respect,
for at the Last Supper He did not reprove his treachery openly,
lest He should put him to shame before the other disciples; but
spoke of it in such a way that Judas alone could understand
what He alluded to, while the others could not know anything
about it.

Where the correction is to be given.

---

[1] Vade post me sathana; scandalum es mihi; quia non sapis ea quæ Dei sunt.—Matt. xvi. 23.

Many are the faults committed in this respect by husbands and wives, who, when they have to administer what they think to be a wholesome reproof, wait till the whole family is assembled at table, and then commence upbraiding in sharp and cutting words before servants and children; so that the only likely result of their reproof is mutual recrimination, or cursing and swearing, or even blows. That is not the place for a wholesome Christian admonition. Young wives are sometimes more guilty in this way, when they go after their husbands to the taverns, and reprove their drunkenness before the assembled guests. There can be no possibility of doing good in such a place as that by admonition. Others, again, have not courage enough to administer the reproof to the erring one alone, but wait till there are three or four friends together, when they seem to have more courage, and speak hardily of faults they wish to correct. But the place is ill chosen, and, instead of doing good, the correction is far more likely to do harm, by putting the person to shame. "Rebuke him between thee and him alone."

With what means should the correction be given? With regard to this circumstance I must consider whether, for instance, I have reasonable grounds for hoping that my admonition will do good if administered privately; otherwise, according to the nature of the case, I should ask others to help me. Who should they be, and how must I manage the matter? Can I make known my neighbor's fault to the first I meet? Not by any means! That would be detraction, a fault, as I have already explained, that I should be guilty of by complaining, under pretext of being displeased at their sins, of the failings of others to their friends and acquaintances. Servants sin in this way by speaking of the faults of their masters and mistresses in the neighborhood, for the purpose of seeking consolation in the confidence and sympathy of others. No, I repeat, that is not the way to administer wholesome correction. How can I do it, then? If I have to ask others to help me, I must tell them what I want them for. Certainly, but you must tell only those who are in a position to help you. We read in the Book of Genesis that Joseph accused his brothers of a grievous crime; but to whom? It is not written that he accused them to his neighbors, but to his father.[1] "To his father," says Abulensis, "who was able to prevent a repetition of the crime.[2]" Now, we know whom we have to

---

[1] Accusavitque fratres suos apud patrem.—Gen. xxxvii. 2.

[2] Apud patrem qui poterat remedium adhibere.

appeal to in such a case. If a child commits a fault, I should tell its parents. If servants keep dangerous company, I should tell their employers. The faults of parishioners I should make known to the parish-priest; of penitents to their confessor, or to other superiors, if the case requires it, and there is no other means available. This is the meaning of the words of Our Lord: "If he will not hear them, tell the Church." If your brother will not listen to you or to others, and refuses to amend after you have privately admonished him, tell the Church; and if that does not help, commend the matter to God and say no more about it.

Why; what should be the motive and intention in administering fraternal correction? This is the fifth circumstance. The only motive should be the pure love of God and of our neighbor, and our intention should be to prevent sin, which is the greatest dishonor to God, and the greatest evil to our neighbor. If I have any other motive, the correction is not Christian nor honestly meant, but, as the wise Ecclesiasticus says, "a lying rebuke,"[1] a hypocritical and false admonition. Ah, how lamentably most people fail in this respect! They appear to have some zeal for the divine honor and their neighbor's salvation, and sometimes persuade themselves that they have it; but when the day comes on which God will examine justice itself with a lantern, as He Himself says, then it shall be made evident that it is not always a zeal for God and for souls, but rather self-love and hatred that is the motive of the reproof; nay, it may even be a sort of jealousy excited with regard to the very vices that are reproved, "There is a lying rebuke in the anger of an injurious man; and there is a judgment that is not allowed to be good."[2] Do you wish to know where those wrong intentions come from? *(margin: What should be the motive.)*

For instance, those with whom I associate, either through choice or necessity, are quite opposed to my natural inclinations and disposition, so that they are a source of annoyance to me; oh, in a case of that kind I am ready at once to administer reproof and correction, and I am not at a loss for either words or courage to say what I think! But, on the other hand, there may be even greater faults in the same persons, that are not the occasion of any trouble or discomfort to me; and I say nothing about them, make no effort to correct them. An evident proof that my re- *(margin: Many reprove without a good intention.)*

---

[1] Correptio mendax.

[2] Est correptio mendax in ira contumeliosi ; et est judicium, quod non probatur esse bonum.—Ecclus. xix. 28.

buke is not a sincere, but a lying one, and that it proceeds, not from zeal against sin, nor from the love of my neighbor, nor from a desire of doing good to his soul, but from self-love, which does not allow me to bear his faults with patience. Again; from those whose humor and disposition happen to chime in with mine, and for whom I have an affection, I can bear anything, and I do not like to say a single word of contradiction to them, although they now and then deserve a word of Christian reproof on account of their faults; but they who have somehow or other incurred my anger, or against whom I have a natural dislike, are not at all likely to be spared by me if they commit even the least fault. Nay, if I am disputing with some good friend, and in the course of argument he contradicts me, so that I get angry, I am then very apt to rebuke him with all the faults I know him to be guilty of, which I should otherwise never dare allude to. Again a sure sign that my rebuke is a lying one, which does not come from hatred of sin and zeal for souls, but from passion, anger, and hatred towards my neighbor. In the Sacred Scriptures the Holy Ghost compares the wicked man to a stormy sea: "The wicked are like the raging sea, which cannot rest."[1] Hector Pintus says that when the sea storms and rages, it throws up on the shore all the filth that was before buried in its depths: "the sea pollutes the shore to cleanse itself."[2] As long as we are left in peace, we have hardly a word to say about our neighbor's faults; but when we are contradicted or reproached with our own faults, we begin to rage and storm; then everything comes out; under the pretence of protecting our honor, we attack our neighbor's fair fame with all sorts of uncharitable remarks. To clear ourselves we throw mud at others, and accuse them of the faults with which we are reproved, so as to divert suspicion from ourselves. Truly, that is not a well-meant correction, but a lying rebuke, given in anger and proceeding from passion. Even envy and jealousy regarding the same vice can sometimes be our motive in correcting our neighbor. Thus a wife who loves her freedom too well, and is not as faithful as she should be, often accuses her husband of being too familiar with others, and lets him feel the full brunt of her anger. Why? Because she wishes to turn away suspicion from herself, that she may be still more at liberty to indulge her unlawful passion. Oftentimes,

[1] Impii quasi mare fervens, quod quiescere non potest.—Isa. lvii. 20.
[2] Mare ut se purget littus coinquinat.

also, one will reprove her companion with being too familiar with some admirer or other, and say that her conduct is apt to give scandal; that people are beginning to talk, etc.   What is her object in giving that advice?   Simply the wish to secure the attentions of the same admirer for herself.

Father Cataneus writes that in a certain town in Italy an unjust miser used to beg of a preacher to condemn the vice of usury, as he knew it to be very common in the town.   The preacher praised his zeal, as he thought it, and his desire to promote the glory of God and the salvation of souls; and in several sermons animadverted very strongly on the vice complained of.   But do you know why the miser was so anxious about the matter?   He cared nothing whatever for the good of souls, but he hoped that others like himself might be converted by the sermons, and renounce all unjust practices, thus leaving him more room to enrich himself by usury.   Oh, what a lying rebuke that was!   No; the honor of God, the salvation and amendment of our neighbor, should be the only motive to induce us to correct our brother, if we wish to do so in a Christian manner. *Shown by an exampl*

When should the correction be given?   As soon as ever we hope to do some good thereby; nor should we wait till the vice has become so inveterate that there is little hope of inducing our neighbor to amend.   When the unhappy prince Amnon was murdered in broad daylight by the servants of his brother Absalom, Jonadab, one of David's courtiers, knew of the matter long beforehand.   But it was not till the foul deed was accomplished and the whole court thrown into the utmost confusion thereby, as if a similar fate was in store for all the princes, that Jonadab stood up and declared that Amnon was the only victim, and that Absalom had been already plotting his destruction for two years.   If he had disclosed the plot to the king in time, what great evils would he not have prevented!   As it was, Amnon lost his life; Absalom had to fly into exile, and David was forced to shed many a bitter tear.   Such is the fault of many who for a long time observe the bad conduct of their neighbors' children, but do not venture to speak to the parents until there is hardly any hope of inducing the children to amend.   More especially do parents err in this respect when they spare the rod while their children are young, thinking some allowance must be made for their youth, and that afterwards there will be time enough to bring them back on the right path.   But there is little chance of cor- *When the correctio should be given.*

recting them then; you might as well try to tame a wolf when it is grown old. Punishment, when it is required, should be administered while the children are young; afterwards it will be too late, and the parents will, like David, find in their children a source of bitter sorrow and trouble, nay, of shame and disgrace. Therefore, fraternal correction should be given when there is still reason for hoping that it will do some good. Again, just as every place will not do for this correction, so also should the proper time be chosen, no matter how pure the intention may otherwise be. "All things have their season,"[1] says the wise Ecclesiastes: and it is especially necessary that I should wait till my neighbor is in the proper mood to listen to me, before I proceed to correct him. It is a general rule with doctors never to give medicine to a sick man, and much less to bleed him, while he is in the height and delirium of a fever; otherwise he would only be made worse, and would be placed in imminent danger of death; therefore they wait until the fever has somewhat subsided. "Stir not the fire with a sword,"[2] says Pythagoras; or else you will cause the flames to burst forth with still greater violence. In the same way when a man is in the heat of a violent passion, it is not the right time to administer fraternal correction; in such circumstances a word of rebuke would be like stirring the fire with a sword, or bleeding a man in the height of fever; it would only inflame his passion still more. Jonathan gives us a beautiful example of how we should act in similar circumstances. He was obliged to witness daily the blind fury with which his father persecuted David, hunting him from place to place and seeking his life. He was very willing to protect his innocent friend; but as his father was always in a violent rage, he restrained himself until he found the latter in a good humor at table. Then he profited by the opportunity, and represented to Saul the innocence and fidelity of David, and the injustice of persecuting such a man; and on one occasion his remonstrance made such an impression that Saul swore that he would never again do the least thing to harm David, but rather make him his friend. "And when Saul heard this, he was appeased with the words of Jonathan, and swore: As the Lord liveth he shall not be slain."[3] So much depends on selecting the proper time

---

[1] Omnia tempus habent.—Eccles. iii. 1.

[2] Ignem gladio ne fodito.

[3] Quod cum audisset Saul, placatus voce Jonathæ, juravit: vivit Dominus quia non occidetur.—I. Kings xix. 6.

for administering fraternal correction. Great is the mistake, therefore, of those women who, when their husbands come home drunk at night, abuse them and the vice of drunkenness in all the moods and tenses. Oh, my good women, that is not the time for you to correct your husbands! The only result you could hope for under such circumstances is a severe beating. You should keep quite still, or if you say anything, let your words be only those of praise and encouragement, and wait with your correction until the drunken fit is over; then you will have reason for hoping that a few modest words of reproof will not fail to do good.

In what manner should the correction be given? This I put in the last place, because it depends on the other circumstances and follows from them. For if the love of our neighbor and the desire of his good should be the only motives for correcting him, if the most suitable time and place should be selected for administering the correction, it follows that it should be given in the manner most likely to move our neighbor's heart and mind to amend his ways. Amongst private individuals (it is otherwise with regard to parents and other superiors) the best means of doing that is to observe the utmost friendliness and mildness of manner and language, so that the person corrected may see that we act out of pure desire for his spiritual welfare. A harsh, domineering manner, or a sarcastic reproof, or words that would cause him to feel shame, would make matters worse, and fill the person with a desire of revenge for the insult we offer him. No, that is not the way in which the almighty God has told us to correct our neighbor. "The just man shall correct me in mercy,"[1] says David. "The servant of the Lord must not wrangle," says St. Paul, "but be mild towards all men, apt to teach, patient, with modesty admonishing them that resist the truth;"[2] and, again, writing to the Galatians on fraternal correction, he says: "Brethren, and if a man be overtaken in any fault, instruct such a one in the spirit of meekness, considering thyself lest thou also be tempted."[3] Each one should remember that he, too, is a sinful mortal, subject to many faults and imperfections; and therefore, when he has to correct his brother, he should do so in the spirit of Jesus Christ, who never harshly re-

How it should b given.

---

[1] Corripiet me justus in misericordia.—Ps. cxl. 5.

[2] Servum Domini autem non oportet litigare ; sed mansuetum esse ad omnes, docibilem, patientem, cum modestia corripientem eos qui resistunt veritati.—II. Tim. ii. 24, 25.

[3] Fratres, si præoccupatus fuerit homo in aliquo delicto, hujusmodi instruite in spiritu lenitatis, considerans teipsum, ne et tu tenteris.—Gal. vi. 1.

proved any sinner (except the hypocritical Pharisees, who, after repeated exhortations, refused to be converted), but always encouraged them by gentle words to amend; such as, "Be not unfaithful; go and sin no more," etc. Such were the words He used to Thomas, to the paralytic man, to the adulteress, to Magdalene, and to other public sinners. Even before the written law, when Lot wished to deter his fellow-citizens from the commission of an abominable crime, he did not address them in violent terms, or curse them, or swear at them; but with the greatest mildness begged of them not to be guilty of such a sin: "Do not so, I beseech you, my brethren, do not commit this evil." [1]

Explained with regard to particular cases.

So, too, my dear brethren, should we correct each other. And that our neighbor may have still less reason to feel ashamed, it would often be advisable for us not to speak too bluntly of his fault, but rather to hint at it in a general way, and at the same time to excuse his intention. For instance; this is a matter in which you are wont to act so and so, and you seem to attach no importance to it; I can, of course, easily believe that you have no bad intention therein; but I wish you would ask your confessor about it and see what he has to say; at all events, I should feel myself troubled in conscience if I were to act as you do, etc. Often we might speak of the matter as if it concerned others in general: Alas, how common such and such a vice is in the world! People act as if they were allowed to do as they please; what a pity that men should be so blind, and expose their souls to the risk of eternal damnation! etc. Such was the manner in which Nathan reproved David for the crimes of murder and adultery; he began with a parable and laid the blame on an imaginary person. There was a rich man, he said, who took away a poor man's sheep and ate it; and when David grew angry, and said that the man should die, Nathan spoke more clearly, and said to him. "Thou art the man." [1] Sometimes, also, we might acknowledge our own weaknesses: Alas, what miserable mortals we are! I have often made the resolution not to meddle in other people's affairs; but we see and hear so much of this or that vice, that I can hardly keep it, etc. Sometimes we might lead the conversation to the virtuous example of others. and praise especially in them what we know the person we wish to correct is deficient in. And so on.

---

[1] Nolite, quæso, fratres mei, nolite malum hoc facere.—Gen. xix. 7.

[2] Tu es ille vir.—II. Kings xii. 7.

Ah, my dear brethren, if we only had a zealous love of God and of our neighbor, that alone, since love is acute, would teach us how to act so as to help each other to amend. Do Thou, O God of pure love, inflame us all with true charity, that we may not only try to do Thy holy will in all things, but also endeavor, when opportunity offers, to keep our brethren from violating Thy law, to encourage them in Thy service, and thus to increase the number of Thy elect, with whom may we praise and bless Thee for all eternity. Amen.

Another Introduction to the same sermon for the eleventh Sunday after Pentecost.

Text.

Et loquebatur recte.—Mark vii. 35.
" And he spoke right."

Introduction.

To speak when one should hold his tongue is to speak wrong; to speak when duty requires us to do so is to speak with reason; yet it does not always mean that we speak even then as we should, for we may err grievously in our manner of speaking. To speak when and what and as we should speak is to speak right, and in this consists the beautiful art of Christian wisdom and eloquence. To come to our subject, my dear brethren; we have hitherto treated of fraternal correction, by which we can help our neighbor to avoid sin and to amend his life; and I have shown that it is required by the love of God and of our neighbor, and that we are bound to practise it, many of us in justice, all of us by a special law of God. Now, the question is, how should one who is concerned for the honor of God and the welfare of his neighbor administer fraternal correction so as to be of real help to his neighbor, instead of making him worse, and that it may be said of him, " he spoke right "? This question I will answer in this instruction.

Plan of Discourse.

How and in what manner fraternal correction should be administered; such is the whole subject.

Christ Jesus, who alone hast the art of making the dumb speak aright, teach me now and those who are here present how to speak right, so as to prevent sin and help others to amend their lives. This we beg of Thee, through the intercession of Mary and of our holy guardian angels.

FIFTY-SEVENTH SERMON.

ON READINESS TO ACCEPT FRATERNAL CORRECTION.

Subject.

He who is corrected should accept brotherly admonition with gratitude.—*Preached on the twelfth Sunday after Pentecost.*

Text.

Reddite ergo quæ sunt Cæsaris, Cæsari, et quæ sunt Dei, Deo. —Matt. xxii. 21.

" Render therefore to Cæsar the things that are Cæsar's and to God the things that are God's."

Introduction.

How gently, and at the same time how prudently, Our Lord dealt with those Pharisees! They wished to ensnare Him in His speech, as the Gospel says: " Then the Pharisees going, consulted among themselves how to ensnare Him in His speech." For if He had answered their question, "Is it lawful to give tribute to Cæsar, or not," by saying no, it is not lawful, they would have had cause enough to accuse Him before the judges and have Him condemned to death. But if, on the other hand, He had said that they were bound to pay the tribute, then they could have accused Him of being an enemy of the Jewish people. But Our Lord evaded all their snares by the simple answer: " Render therefore to Cæsar the things that are Cæsar's and to God the things that are God's." By those words, too, He gave them a well-meant and fatherly instruction as to what they owed their Lord and God, and what they owed their lawful superiors. Would to God that they had only taken that lesson to heart and profited by it; had they done so, their lot would not have been such a wretched one. We have already heard, my dear brethren, that fraternal correction is necessary, and also how it should be given in order to do good to our neighbor. I now go on to speak of the person who has to be corrected, and to show in what manner he should take the correction; and this will be the last point we shall have to consider concerning this subject.

Plan of Discourse.

He who is corrected, should accept brotherly admonition with gratitude; such is the whole subject of this sermon and exhortation.

That we may acknowledge and fulfil it, grant us all Thy light and grace, O Lord of hearts, through the intercession of Mary and of our holy guardian angels.

Reason itself tells every one of us that we should be grateful to a well-meaning friend for the benefit he bestows on us. If there were no looking-glass in the whole world, the human eye would be unfortunate, for although it could contemplate all the riches and beauty of the earth, it could not see itself, nor know what it looks like, or whether it was beautiful or ugly, white or black, blue or grey. That service is rendered us by the looking-glass, which is always ready to show us our own countenances, and to let us see whether we are handsome or ugly; and if it had reason and free will, so that it could grant its services or refuse them, we should be thankful to it for showing us any spots that might be on our faces, since once we have seen them we can wipe them off. If there were no doctor in the world, sick people would be badly off, and would not know what to do; therefore the patient, like the wounded man in the Gospel who was cared for by the Samaritan, owes gratitude to the doctor, who, after having felt his pulse and considered the symptoms of his disease, prescribes the medicines that are required to restore him to health. A poor man owes the greatest gratitude to him who gives him a rich alms, even without being asked for anything, and thus helps him in extreme necessity and saves his life. The traveller who has lost his way is bound to be most grateful to him who puts him on the right road again. Is not that the case? But what does it all mean? That the showing the spots on the face, the curing the disease, the alms-giving, the putting the traveller on the right road, are all benefits without which the first would be dirty, the second sick, the third starving, the fourth still wandering off the road. *Every benefit deserves gratitude; shown by similes.*

From these similes, my dear brethren, you may see what a great benefit is fraternal correction and admonition. It is a fatal consequence of original sin that our nature is so blinded that we not only seek with all possible diligence to hide our faults from the eyes of others, but, as far as we can, even from ourselves. Self-love makes us most unwilling to acknowledge our *We are often ignorant of our own faults, and thus go on insensibly to our ruin.*

own short-comings; we carry, so to speak, our own faults on our backs, where we cannot see them; nay, we often imagine that what is really scandalous is becoming in us, and we count as virtues those sins and vices that are condemned by God. Thus the vain worldling looks on as good and lawful whatever is according to the usages of the perverse world in outward behavior, dress and conversation; although such usages may be altogether wrong according to the Christian law and in the sight of God, and may be the means of leading those that follow them on the broad road to hell. One who is accustomed to sinful and scandalous language justifies himself by the plea that he only wishes to amuse others and create a laugh. The vindictive man, who for years nourishes hatred and anger against his neighbor; the passionate man, who lives in constant strife and discord with his wife, thinks he has a right to do as he pleases in that respect, without committing any grievous sin. The impure man, who keeps up an unlawful intimacy, thinks that his sin is known to no one but himself and God, although it may be the talk and scandal of the whole neighborhood. The unjust man tries to persuade himself that everything is lawful for him, as long as he can add to his store. How many sins does not the drunkard commit of which he has not the least recollection when the drunken fit is over? How many are there not, who, through want of thought, talk of everything that comes into their mind, thus often wounding Christian charity, and inflicting grievous harm on their neighbor's good name, and giving scandal besides to those who listen to them; and yet they do not advert to the fact that they are addicted to such a pernicious habit; for if they did advert to it, they would certainly take steps to amend. How many parents look on their children as good and holy, although in reality they are addicted to many vices and sins, on account of the want of care and watchfulness on the parent's own part? yet the latter are not a whit troubled at the state of things and make no effort to amend it. Thus we often bear about with us a soul defiled with abominable vices, although we flatter ourselves that we are quite pure and innocent; we are sick unto death, and are not aware of it; we are poor, naked, and hungry in our souls, and we think ourselves rich and not in need of alms; we are running straight along the broad path that leads to hell, and we imagine that we are on the road to heaven. In a word, we lead unchristian, sinful, wicked lives, and through culpable carelessness and ignorance we refuse to acknowledge that to be the case; or through want of reflection we think nothing of it. The malice of sin, the danger in which we are, seldom occurs to our minds, unless our attention is called to it by some one else.

Now in those circumstances a good Christian, who is really zealous for the honor of God and the good of souls, comes to you and exhorts you, or administers fraternal correction, by which he enables you to see the deformity and malice of this or that vice; and that he does with the best intentions in your regard, out of pity for your soul, and a sincere desire for your welfare; he does it also with all possible meekness and modesty, as we have seen in the last sermon. That man is the looking-glass that shows you the spots and stains. What spots and stains? Not those which merely disfigure your face in the eyes of men, and which are not worth thinking of; but the abominations that defile your soul, and make it an object of disgust in the sight of God, beautiful as it is by nature. He is the physician who shows you your disease and the means of curing it. What disease? Not one that threatens the life of the body; but one that imperils the life of your immortal soul. He is the merciful and generous friend, who gives you a rich alms, although you have not asked him; as St. Thomas Aquinas says, " to correct the erring is a kind of spiritual alms." [1] What sort of an alms is it? Not a piece of bread which is able to still the pangs of hunger for a day; but the bread of life which can rescue the soul from extreme danger forever. He is the faithful guide, who shows you where you are going astray, and leads you back to the right path. How were you going astray? It is not merely a matter of lengthening your journey from one place to another by a few hours, and of being no worse off for having lost your way; but of bringing you back from the road that was taking you every moment farther and farther away from heaven, and would at last have brought you to the depths of hell.

He who corrects us fraternally shows us our faults with a well-meaning heart, that we may correct them.

Now if the service rendered by the looking-glass, the doctor, the generous friend, the faithful guide, deserves gratitude from every honest mind, because it is a benefit, although a small one, with what thankfulness should you not take the well-meant exhortation and admonition of your neighbor, which you have every reason to consider as a far greater benefit? Ah, dear

Hence we should be most grateful to him, as to our benefactor.

---

[1] Corrigere delinquentem, est quædam eleemosyna spiritualis.

Christian, you prize as friends those flatterers and time-servers who know how to win your favor by saying what will please you and approving of everything you do; who never tell you the truth, but always seek to tickle your ears with flattery; who, when you are most defiled with sin, are capable of saying to you: Oh, how beautiful you are! who, when death is already in your face, can exclaim: I have never seen you looking so well! who, when you have lost your way in a gloomy forest, cry out to you: go on, you are on the right road!   These are the people whom you consider your best friends; these you lend a willing ear to; in them you trust, although their false praise and flattery are only leading you on to destruction.   Believe me, and be assured that you have no better friend in the world than he who is charitable enough to tell you the truth when you have done wrong, and to admonish and exhort you in a brotherly manner. And therefore it is but right that you should take what he says as a great benefit which deserves your gratitude, and humbly acknowledge your fault and firmly resolve to amend it.

And should take the correction with gratitude, after the example of prudent and pious men.   The Scripture tells us that Joseph accused his brethren, and adds immediately after, that he was his father's favorite: "Now Israel loved Joseph above all his sons, because he had him in his old age." [1]   I should have thought that his brothers would have complained of him, and murmured against him because he had accused them to his father; but there is not a word of their having done so.   They were indeed filled with anger against him, but it was on account of something else; and when they were on the point even of putting him to death, they said not a word of the accusation, but only of his dreams: "Behold, the dreamer cometh," [2] they exclaimed; not, behold, our accuser cometh. Still better did David, although he was an annointed king, receive the reproof addressed to him by the Prophet Nathan, on account of the adultery and murder that he had committed, and the public scandal he had given thereby.   Ah, it is true, he sighed; I acknowledge my sin; most grievously have I erred; "I have sinned against the Lord." [3]   O Nathan, thou man of God, be thou blessed a thousand times for having opened my eyes, and caused me to see my wickedness! Help me now to appease the wrath of God and to atone for the scandal I have given!

[1] Israel autem diligebat Joseph super omnes filios suos, eo quod in senectute genuisset eum. —Gen. xxxvii. 3.

[2] Ecce somniator venit.—Ibid. 19.

[3] Peccavi Domino.—II. Kings xii. 13.

Such too was the manner in which St. Francis Regis took a reproof that was once given him. According to his usual custom
when giving missions, he preached most zealously to the people,
and on one occasion his companion, who was still very young
and not yet a priest, found fault with some things he had said,
and especially with the manner in which he treated his subject,
which he condemned as being too simple. The holy man listened
humbly, and then said in a friendly tone: " I thank you for having been so good as to warn me of my fault." What would he
not have said, how great would not his gratitude have been, if
his companion had warned him of some real fault against the commandments? Menochius tells us of a nobleman who found hospitality for some days with the Bishop of Verona, who honored and
esteemed him very much on account of his great natural gifts. One
fault the Bishop had noticed in him at table, and therefore when
the nobleman had left the house, he sent a letter after him saying
that he thanked him for the honor done his house, and that he
took the liberty of sending him a present which he hoped he would
accept. The nobleman looked for the present, but all he found
was an admonition calling his attention to the fault committed
at table. And how do you think he took it, my dear brethren?
Oh, said he to the messenger, would to God that such presents
were more in vogue; if they were, men would be much richer and
better than they now are. Greet the Bishop from me, and offer
him my most heartfelt thanks; I shall never during my whole
life forget the valuable present he has made me. Of all the
benefits he conferred on me while I was in his house, there is
none I value so highly as this warning; and I will try at once to
profit by it. And as long as he lived he kept up a constant cor-
respondence with the Bishop in order to show his gratitude and
his desire for his friendship. These and many others like them
knew what a great benefit it is to be corrected in a fraternal manner. And therefore in respectable families the custom is still
kept up of making the children kiss the rod with which they have
been punished, in order to show that they look on the punishment as a benefit, and that they respect even the instrument
with which it is administered. True indeed, my dear brethren,
are the words of that nobleman! If fraternal correction and admonition were usual presents amongst men, and I add, if they
were always received with a thankful heart, oh, what a great matter that would be, and how much it would improve the lives and

morals of the Christians of our days! How many sins and vices would be avoided, how many sinners converted, how many scandals removed! Then would there be a far greater number of devout servants of God, who would have courage to warn their neighbor of his faults; whereas now they must keep silence, as they have good reason for fearing that their correction, instead of earning gratitude, will only excite hatred, and instead of doing good, will only make matters worse.

Alas, how small the number of those who take fraternal correction with humility and thankfulness, and look on it as a real benefit! Instead of thanking the glass that shows them their deformity, they act like the notorious Thais. Happening once in her old age to look in the glass, and seeing the many wrinkles on her forehead and her sunken cheeks, she got into such a rage that she flung it out of the window and swore that she would never look at one again. Why so? In her youth she spent much time before the glass; why did she get in such a rage against it? Because she could not bear the sight of her wrinkled and now ugly face; and therefore the glass which showed her her deformity became hateful in her eyes. Instead of being grateful to the well-meaning doctor who prescribes for their diseases, they act like those sick people who, when they are forbidden certain kinds of food and drink, turn away from the doctor with aversion and will have no more of him. Instead of being grateful to the good friend who is willing to aid their poor souls with spiritual alms, they act like those who, although they are poor in reality, try through pride to pass for rich people. If you give them an alms, what? they exclaim; what do you take me for? Do you think I am a beggar? Keep your alms for yourself; I am not in want of it. Instead of being grateful to the guide who has shown them where they have gone astray, they act like a foolish traveller, who, being told by a peasant whom he meets that he has lost his way, begins to abuse and curse. What brings that fellow here? he says. Can he not mind his own affairs? He has quite upset me with his uncalled-for remarks. I will go on my own way and not take any notice of him.

They are very glad to see others punished for their faults; but their own they do not wish to be interfered with. As a Cistercian Abbot was once returning home from a chapter with his companion, he lost his way in a gloomy desert. There he saw some people clad in the same kind of habit he wore himself, and was by them most courteously invited into their monastery with his companion. The Abbot readily accepted the invitation, and was brought into a magnificent monastery, in which there was a well-furnished guest-room as well as several other rooms fitted up with every convenience. He could not sufficiently admire the modest deportment, down-cast eyes, and general amiability of the monks. In the evening he and his companion were treated to a splendid supper, and were then shown to their rooms with every mark of the most scrupulous courtesy. In the morning the Superior came to the Abbot and humbly begged him to address a few words of spiritual advice to the monks before leaving. The Abbot consented, the bell was rung, and a great number of monks flocked into the hall. The beginning of the sermon was listened to in silence; the middle of it too was received with approbation; but when the Abbot began to speak of pride, and said to them: do you not know, my dear brethren, that pride drove the angels out of heaven, there was at once such a commotion among the audience that several of them rose up and went out. The Abbot, not in the least disconcerted, continued his discourse; oh, how many angels and archangels were turned into devils through pride! At these words the confusion became still greater; many began to cough, and others noisily left the hall. Still the preacher continued: oh, how many possessed glorious thrones in heaven, and are now lying like horrible ghosts deep in the abyss of hell! Hereupon all the monks, with the exception of one, went out, looking daggers at the Abbot, and giving loud expression to their displeasure. The latter, scandalized at this conduct, and seeing himself deserted by all except one, turned to him and asked him what was the cause of the displeasure the monks showed when he was speaking of the pride of the angels. You must know, most Reverend Father, was the answer; that we are all devils, and like yourselves, Reverend Fathers and Abbots, we listen with pleasure when the faults of others are spoken of; but we cannot bear to have the truth told us about ourselves. He then vanished at once and the hall and monastery and all the rest of the monks with him. The terrified and astonished Abbot found himself in the midst of a morass, which it cost him a great deal of trouble to get out of.

There is a strong resemblance between those demons and people who cannot listen to a word of admonition. For they do not wish their faults to be seen or known; they do not desire to

And that because they do not wish to know or

know anything of the diseases they are suffering from; their pride is hurt at the idea of their being looked on as poor; they refuse to acknowledge that they have strayed from the right path, or else they do not wish to amend their evil ways. Thus the looking-glass, the doctor, the friend, the guide, who comes to them with fraternal correction, is an object of hatred in their eyes. They abuse and turn him away. Mind your own business, they say to him; I do not want your warnings; wait till I send for you before you preach to me. Thus it is that truth causes hatred, according to the old saying, and as St. John the Baptist experienced, when he admonished the unchaste Herod. "It is not lawful for thee to have thy brother's wife,"[1] said he. But the saint had to suffer for telling the truth. Away with him at once, exclaimed Herod; out of my sight with that troublesome preacher. "Herod himself had sent and apprehended John, and bound him in prison for the sake of Herodias."[2] Sad, too, is the return made for their charity to preachers and confessors, instead of the gratitude due to their well-meant admonitions, when, according to the obligations of their office, they warn their hearers and penitents and exhort them to renounce certain vices. It is not lawful, they say; that injustice, that company, that scandalous abuse, that drunkenness, that gambling and idleness, is not lawful; it is not according to the law of Christ; it will surely lead to hell. But what do they get for their warnings? Abuse, invective, curses, and ridicule; such are the thanks given them. Nay, they who are warned sometimes become through spite more hardened in evil; because their pride will not allow them to acknowledge that they are wrong.

But woe to those who refuse to profit by admonition! Hear what the Holy Ghost says by the wise Ecclesiasticus: "He that hateth to be reproved walketh in the trace of a sinner;"[3] or, as others read it: in the trace of the devil; he is a follower and imitator of the devil. Why? Because the devil is so proud that, as we have seen already, he does not like to hear his faults spoken of, and at the same time he is so hardened and obstinate in guilt that, even if he could, he would not lay aside his wickedness or free himself from it. How can we distinguish a wise man from a fool? By the way in which he takes correction, as

---

[1] Non licet tibi habere uxorem fratris tui.—Mark vi. 18.

[2] Ipse enim Herodes misit ac tenuit Joannem, et vinxit eum in carcere, propter Herodiadem.—Ibid. 17.

[3] Qui odit correptionem, vestigium est peccatoris.—Ecclus. xxi. 7.

the Holy Ghost again says, by the wise Solomon: "Rebuke a wise man, and he will love thee. Teach a just man and he shall make haste to receive it."[1] On the other hand, "he that hateth reproof is foolish."[2] and he shows clearly enough that he hates his own soul. The punishment of this folly even in this life will be that he who refuses to listen to reproof will be blinded by flatterers and wicked men, and by divine permission become more hardened in his evil ways.

The holy Scripture gives us a striking example of this in the person of the wicked king Achab. The Prophet Micheas had already given him a most salutary warning; but for that very reason he had become hateful to Achab. "Did I not tell thee," said the latter to Josaphat, king of Juda, "that he prophesieth no good to me, but always evil? Therefore I hate the man and cannot bear the sight of him. Hear then, said Micheas, what the Lord intends to do with thee: "I saw the Lord sitting on His throne, and all the army of heaven standing by Him on the right hand and on the left. And the Lord said: Who shall deceive Achab king of Israel, that he may go up and fall at Ramoth-Galaad?" Then Satan stood up: "And there came forth a spirit and stood before the Lord, and said: I will deceive him." "By what means?" asked God; how wilt thou deceive him? "And he said: I will go forth and be a lying spirit in the mouth of all his prophets," that they may conceal the truth from him, say what they know will please him, and thus lead him on to his ruin. "And the Lord said: Thou shalt deceive him, and shalt prevail: go forth, and do so." Whereupon the unhappy Achab, following the flattering talk of his false prophets contrary to the well-meant advice of Micheas, went out against his enemies and was slain, so that the dogs licked up his blood on that day. "And the battle was fought that day, and the king of Israel stood in his chariot against the Syrians, and he died in the evening: and the blood ran out of the wound into the midst of the chariot, and the dogs licked up his blood, according to the word of the Lord which He had spoken."[3] May you not expect the same fate,

Shown in the case of Achab.

---

[1] Argue sapientem et diliget te. Doce justum, et festinabit accipere.—Prov. ix. 8, 9.

[2] Qui odit increpationem insipiens est.—Ibid. xii. 1.

[3] Num quid non dixit tibi, quia non prophetat mihi bonum, sed semper malum? Vidi Dominum sedentem super solium suum, et omnem exercitum coeli assistentem ei a dextris et a sinistris. Et ait Dominus: quis decipiet Achab regem Israel, ut ascendat et cadat in Ramoth Galaad? Egressus est autem spiritus, et stetit coram Domino, et ait: ego decipiam illum. In quo? Et ille ait; egrediar et ero spiritus mendax in ore omniun prophetarum ejus. Et dixit Dominus: decipies et praevalebis; egredere et fac ita. Commissum est ergo praelium

O wicked Christian? You avoid and hate the prophets of the Lord, preachers, confessors, and other pious servants of Christ, who tell you the truth. You cannot listen patiently to them when they condemn your usury, the dangerous company you keep, your vanity and luxury, and other vices; you treat them with contumely and insult; but what will the Lord do at last? He will permit the spirit of lies to influence you. He will allow others like yourself, who are of the same mind as you, to confirm you still more in your evil ways; wicked friends will flatter you, and approve of all you do. Even your confessor, whom you select for that express purpose, will hide the truth from you, and solve all your doubts in the way most pleasing to you. Yes, Sir, or Madam; you can do that; there is no great harm in it; you need not be scrupulous with regard to it, etc. But what will be the end of it all? Hear the sentence of the Almighty: "The man that with a stiff neck despiseth him that reproveth him shall suddenly be destroyed, and health shall not follow him." [1] That is what you gain by despising correction.

Yet pious Christians should not fail to obey the law of fraternal correction.

Meanwhile, pious Christians, this should not interfere with your zeal for the divine honor. It is true that a private individual is never bound under pain of sin to administer fraternal correction when he has reason for believing that he can do no good to his neighbor thereby (a private individual, I say; for it is otherwise with regard to preachers, who are in duty bound to speak the plain truth and to condemn prevailing vices, although they foresee that their words will have little or no effect. Nay, even if they had reason to think that many would become worse on account of their sermons, still they should not allow themselves to be deterred from following the example of Christ, who condemned the vices of the Pharisees, although He foresaw that they would only be made worse thereby). There is no such obligation for private individuals; yet one should not be too desponding in this matter, nor too easily give way to doubts with regard to the good effects of his reproof. If now and then you do no good, yet your words have not been uttered altogether in vain; you have done your duty, and your reward will be just as great in heaven as if you had succeeded. Mark, says St. Bernard, that Christ

In die illa, et rex Israel stabat in curru suo contra Syros, et mortuus est vespere; fluebat autem sanguis plagæ in sinum currus. Et linxerunt canes sanguinem ejus, juxta verbum Domini quod locutus fuerat.—III. Kings xxii. 18-22, 35, 38.

[1] Virgo qui corripientem dura cervice contemnit, repentinus ei superveniet interitus; et eum sanitas non sequetur.—Prov. xxix. 1.

has not told you to gain your brother; but to rebuke him; He does not say; go and gain him; but go and rebuke him; if he shall hear thee, thou shalt gain thy brother." If he obstinately refuses to hear you, you cannot help that and are not responsible for it. Even if, contrary to your expectations, your neighbor were only to become worse in consequence of your reproof, you did not foresee that; you meant well towards him, and whatever harm has been done him, he may thank himself for it. "When vices are reproved," says St. Bernard, "and scandal is caused thereby, it is to be imputed to him who has committed the reprehensible act, and not to him who has reproved it." [1] And generally speaking, even when the person who is admonished blushes with shame, or becomes angry, it does not follow that the rebuke is totally lost on him; for afterwards when he thinks calmly of the matter, he must come to the conclusion that the correction was well meant, that it was founded on fact, etc. Thus if he does not amend at once, he will do so gradually, although shame does not allow him to acknowledge that at first.

O dear Christians! I conclude in the words of St. Bernard: "may that zeal and love of justice, that hatred of iniquity flourish in us, and may none of us ever flatter vice," [2] but when and wherever it is possible let us never be wanting in doing our part to help our neighbor to amend his life. Let us admonish each other in the spirit of charity; especially should parents with regard to their children, and superiors with regard to their subjects, be most particular in the performance of this duty. Let those who are admonished take the correction with gratitude, and thus let us mutually help each other to put an end to sin, and to extend the kingdom of God daily, until by means of this mutual help we shall eternally rejoice with God in heaven, in the most perfect love and union. Give us all, O God, Thy powerful grace to this end. Amen.

Conclusion to be most zealous in helping ou neighbor t amend, as far as we can.

Another Introduction to the same sermon for the twelfth Sunday after Pentecost.

Text.

At ille dixit: qui fecit misericordiam in illum.—Luke x. 37.

"But he said: he that showed mercy to him."

[1] Cum arguuntur vitia, et inde scandalum oritur, ispe sibi scandali causa est, qui facit quod argui debeat, non ille qui arguit.—S. Bern. super cantice.

[2] Ferveat in nobis zelus ille, ferveat amor justitiæ, odium iniquitatis, nemo vitia palpet. —S. Bern. Serm. de Joan Bapt.

Introduction.

Even the envious Scribes had to confess that the Samaritan, who was so good to the wounded man, really acted as a neighbor should; truly, " he that showed mercy to him " must be looked upon as that man's neighbor. My dear brethren, what the Samaritan did to the body to the wounded man, that, as we have heard already, is done to the sick and wounded souls of his brethren by the good Christian, who gives them well-meant, fraternal correction. But what do you think of the wounded man? How must he have been disposed towards the Samaritan? How did he take the care that was so lovingly bestowed upon him? Did he perhaps reject it, and say in an angry tone of voice: why do you interfere with me? Go your own way, and leave me alone? I am comfortable enough, and do not want your bandages and oil. If he had acted thus, would not all who heard of it say without hesitation that pain had caused him to lose his mind? No, there is not the least doubt that he accepted with gratitude the services rendered him, and was grateful for them to his dying day. There you have an example of how he who is corrected should take the correction; and this is the last point we have to consider with regard to this subject, etc.—*Continues as above.*

ON CHARITY TOWARDS THE POOR SOULS IN PURGATORY.

FIFTY-EIGHTH SERMON.

ON THE REASONS THAT SHOULD URGE US TO HELP THE SOULS IN PURGATORY.

Subject.

We should be generous to the poor souls in purgatory: 1. On account of the great need in which they are; 2. On account of the great advantage we ourselves shall derive therefrom.— *Preached on the feast of St. Lawrence, Martyr.*

Text.

Dispersit, dedit pauperibus; justitia ejus manet in sæculum sæculi.—II. Cor. ix. 9.

"He hath dispersed abroad, he hath given to the poor: his justice remaineth forever."

Introduction.

Not without reason are those words used in the Epistle of to-day, for as we know from the history of his life, St. Lawrence was a very generous friend to the poor. A short time before his martyrdom he had distributed amongst them all the remaining treasures of the Church, so that not a farthing was left to apply to any other purpose. If we imitate him in this respect, my dear brethren, according to our ability, he will be sufficiently honored by us to-day, and we shall have received sufficient fruit from his life. I have often exhorted you to be merciful and generous to the poor and needy in this world; but there are other beggars who are much worse off and far more deserving of compassion, for whom I long have been seeking an opportunity of putting in a good word. The text of to-day and the fiery torments endured by St. Lawrence supply me with this opportunity; for I allude to the poor souls in purgatory. God of goodness, place powerful words on my tongue; most holy Virgin, Mother of mercy, and you, holy guardian angels, help me also; and you, too, holy souls still burning in the fire of purgatory, obtain for me by your prayers the grace to fill all who are here present with a heartfelt and generous compassion towards you! Relying on your help, I shall now try to move myself and my hearers to that compassion and generosity by the twofold consideration of your need and of our advantage.

Plan of Discourse.

We should be generous to the poor souls in purgatory, on account of the great need in which they are, as we shall see in the first and longer part; on account of the advantage we ourselves shall derive therefrom, as we shall see in the second part.

If the little trouble I am now about to take, and my good will can be of any help to you, poor souls, you are heartily welcome to it.

He who, without much trouble or loss to himself, can help his neighbor in necessity is bound to do so.

If I see another in extreme necessity, and can help him without any loss to myself and without much trouble, I am certainly bound to do so. This is the command of God, the law of charity in the Gospel, the teaching of theologians, and even of the light of reason itself. So that he who omits a charitable work of that kind is looked on by all as guilty of the greatest cruelty. Who does not wonder, when reading the Sacred Scriptures, at the cruelty of the Samaritan woman, who so long denied a drink of water to Our Lord when He was thirsty and asked of her a drink, although she had a full pitcher of water by her and the whole well to draw from? Who is not indignant at the boorishness of Nabal, who so churlishly refused the humble request of David for a little food for himself and his followers? Who does not condemn the hard-heartedness of the rich glutton who allowed the poor Lazarus to sit at his door amongst the dogs and refused him even the crumbs that fell from his table? We cannot bear to see even a dumb beast in the agonies of death. If I were to cry out to you; your calf lies in a morass and cannot get out; your dog or your cat is howling in the fire; would you not run at once and save the poor animal?

The souls in purgatory are in great straits

Poor souls! brethren of Jesus Christ! co-heirs of His glory, from which you are excluded on account of what you still owe His justice; you who have to suffer in the midst of flames until you pay your debt; in what pitiable and extreme necessity you are! If, my dear brethren, purgatory were nothing but a prison in which *because they are in prison.* those souls are confined, and kept away from the sight of their Creator, could any bodily suffering be compared with theirs, when we consider the qualities of those souls and all their circumstances? There is an old saying that no prison can be beautiful, even if it is your own room, or the hall of an imperial palace inlaid with gold; the mere fact of your being a prisoner takes away all the beauty of it. Chain up a dog that is accustomed to run loose, and see what he will do; how he howls and barks and runs to the length of his chain, and gnaws at the wood to which it is fastened, in the hope of getting free! Put a bird in a cage, and see how it flutters about, trying one wire after another with its beak, to see if there is any hole big enough to let it escape! Shut up a cat in a room, and it will clamber up the walls and run its head out of the window until it gets free. Wolves and other wild beasts have been known to gnaw off their foot when it was caught in a trap, in order to escape. If imprisonment is then such an intolerable thing even for unreasoning animals, that are after all slaves by nature, and given over to us to use them as we please, what a torment must it not be for a rational being who is by nature free?

And the greater the dignity and excellence of the person imprisoned, the more he feels his confinement. A servant feels *Although as friends of God they have a right to the greatest happiness and the possession of God.* the loss of liberty, but much more is it felt by a rich and noble lord, a prince, or a king; because these latter had greater liberty, and were accustomed to rule, so that they are more sensitive to anything that limits their freedom. Judge for yourselves now, my dear brethren, how grievous imprisonment must be for a soul that of its nature must have the greatest freedom, so that in a moment it should be able to penetrate iron and stone, and to raise itself from earth to heaven as it wishes; a soul that now possesses the great dignity of being a child of God, a prince of the heavenly kingdom, which belongs to it by right, because it left this life in the state of grace: a soul that now clearly knows that God is its only and supreme Good, that loves nothing more than its God, that sighs only for its God, and yet is kept violently apart from Him in a gloomy prison, under the earth, in the neighborhood of hell, according to the general opinion, and is thus prevented from the enjoyment of its last end! Oh, truly a fearful torment! nay, we might almost say, a hell itself!

To be able to form some idea of that torment, imagine, my *Their straits*

and tor-
ments;
shown by a
simile.
dear brethren, the great desire, and, at the same time, the inex-
pressible grief of a father, who, returning after a long voyage, full
of the hope of seeing again his dear wife and children and friends,
from whom he has been absent for years, finds that on his arrival
in harbor he is kept in quarantine for six months, because he has
come from a country that is infected with the plague; and there
he has to remain shut up all that time, without being allowed to
see any one from outside. What do you think would be the poor
man's feelings under those circumstances? To be in his own
country, in his own town, so near his loved ones, and yet unable to see them; how long must not the hours of his imprisonment seem to him? How he counts the months, the weeks, the
days that have to elapse before he is set at liberty!

Confirmed
by exam-
ples from
Scripture.
Consider what Absalom must have felt when on his return
from banishment, although he was allowed to go to Jerusalem,
he heard the command of his father: "Let him return into
his house, and let him not see my face."[1]   This command, says
the Scripture, caused him such sorrow that he preferred to die
rather than bear it. Why, he sighed to himself, why should I
go back to my own house? Am I to have my father's palace,
tower, and gardens constantly before my eyes, and yet not be permitted to see him? Would it not be better for me to go far
away into banishment again? "Wherefore am I come from Gessur? It had been better for me to be there; if he be mindful of
my iniquity, let him kill me."[2] If he has forgiven me, why
does he subject me to such a punishment? But otherwise let
him kill me; for I would prefer that to living so near him and
not being allowed to see his face. Imagine what Jacob must
have felt when, after seven long years of toil and labor, he expected to get possession of his beloved Rachel, and found that
Laban had deceived him, and that he had to work seven years
more before obtaining the object of his desires.

On account
of their de-
sire to see
God, the
torments of
the poor
souls are
greater
than those
of the bride
Again, imagine one who has been chosen as the bride of a
great king, and who is on her way to join her beloved spouse,
but is taken prisoner by her enemies and kept in close confinement. What desires and wishes she must form for freedom; what
longings that do violence to the human mind and cause the
utmost torment she must constantly feel! Yet almost infinitely greater is the torment of a soul in purgatory, that sighs with

---

[1] Revertatur in domum suam, et faciem meam non videat.—II. Kings xiv. 24.

[2] Quare veni de Gessur? melius erat mihi ibi esse ; quod si memor est iniquitatis meæ,
interficiat me.—Ibid. 3?.

the most ardent longings for the sight of its God, and yet has to who is separated from her bridegroom. sigh in vain. Sceptres, crowns, and all that is glorious or great on earth; created beauty and everything in the world that can attract our love; ah, what are ye all in comparison with the supreme and most beautiful of all goods, God Himself? Painful desires and longings of one creature for another, ah, what are ye in comparison with the yearnings of a soul that is already close to God by its full knowledge, and yet is kept in prison, unable to see its beloved God, its promised Bridegroom? It seems to me that I hear such a soul crying out from purgatory in the words of the Psalmist: "My tears have been my bread day and night: whilst it is said to me daily: where is thy God?"[1] This sad thought is always before my mind: where is thy God? thy last end? the centre and fulfilment of all thy happiness? Where is He? Did not all my efforts on earth tend solely to possessing Him for all eternity? "When shall I come and appear before the face of God?"[2] When will that longed-for moment arrive when I shall be freed from this prison? How many years have I spent here already? How many days, months, years will have to elapse during which I shall still be deprived of the possession of my God? "Woe is me that my sojourning is prolonged!"[3] Fearful is the duration of my imprisonment! Is there no one to stretch out a helping hand to me? No one to open a door of escape for me?

Ah, my dear brethren, we pity poor prisoners on earth, al- Hence pity should urge us to try to help them. though they are generally criminals, murderers, and thieves. Our hearts, if they are not of stone or iron, would melt to see them confined in gloomy dungeons, behind iron bars, pallid, half-naked, lying on straw, covered with filth and vermin; and to console them a little in their sad state, we send them food and clothing. Should not the same pity influence us with regard to the poor souls, who are servants and dear friends of God, and are confined in a far more painful prison? The former are indeed deserving of compassion, although their only punishment, so far, is that they have to remain in prison until their sentence is pronounced; but the latter are kept away from the God whom they so long and desire to possess, and have to suffer in the fire of purgatory.

[1] Fuerunt mihi lacrymæ meæ panes die ac nocte, dum dicitur mihi quotidie: ubi est Deus tuus?—Ps. xli. 4.

[2] Quando veniam et apparebo ante faciem Dei?—Ibid. 3.

[3] Heu mihi quia incolatus meus prolongatus est!—Ibid. cxix. 5.

All the
more so,
because
they are
imprisoned
in fire.

Ah, that one word, fire, is sufficient to give us an idea of their torments. If no soul were confined in it longer than one day or a few hours, it would still be a place of terrible torments. What can be more terrible, more horrifying, than the idea of burning for such a long time? Go and look at a furnace in which iron is melted; imagine that you are about to be cast into it alive; your flesh creeps at the bare thought! Think of the gridiron, on which, as historians tell us, St. Lawrence was roasted over a slow fire for some hours; could you bear that torment for even half an hour? Your blood runs cold at the mere thought of it! Oh, no, you could not bear it! And meanwhile, what have you been considering? That which is nothing more than a painted fire, compared to that in which the poor souls are burning. What? A painted fire? Yes, says St. Polycarp; and do you wish to know why?

And in such
a fire that
all natural
fire is as
nothing
compared
to it.

In the first place, the more fire is confined, the less air it has, the greater also is its force and violence; it works far more powerfully in a confined space than in the open air. When a handful of powder is ignited in a mortar, the small flame that comes from it drives the heavy iron shell high into the air as if it were a child's ball, and shatters with it everything it comes across, as with a thunder-bolt. The strongest walls, towers, mountains, and rocks are blown up by subterranean mines. Imagine now the force of that fire which is confined in the middle of the earth, where not the least breath of air can reach it, and how it rages and roars against the poor souls! In the second place, an instrument does more or less work according as the hand that wields it is stronger or weaker. Give a child a rod and let him beat you with it; you can bear twenty blows from him without feeling pain; but if a strong man beats you with the same rod, he will cause the blood to spurt out from your hand in a few moments. The celebrated hero Scanderbeg could cut a Turk in two with one blow of his sword. The Sultan desired to see the sword that could do such wonders, and Scanderbeg sent it to him; but when he had tried a long time and found that he could do nothing remarkable with it, he complained that the wrong sword had been sent him. No, said Scanderbeg; I have sent you the right sword, but I could not send you my arm. My dear brethren, what is the fire that men can enkindle for their uses on earth? It is a rod or a sword, but it is, so to speak, placed in the hand of a weak child; that is, it is an element which cannot produce any effect beyond its own natural powers. But the fire of purgatory is an instrument raised above its nature by the mighty arm of God's justice, which, as it is all-powerful, gives it, as it were, an infinite increase of intensity. Therefore, according to the opinions of the holy Fathers, it comprises all imaginable torments that men can suffer. "This fire," says St. Augustine, "although it is not eternal, excels all the pains that any one ever suffered on this earth."[1] "The least pain of purgatory," says St. Thomas of Aquin, "exceeds the greatest of this life."[2] "Nay," exclaims St. Gregory, "take away the blasphemies, the despair, and the eternity from hell, and you will not be able to distinguish between the condition of a lost soul in hell and a soul in purgatory; because the fire in which the elect are purified is one and the same with that in which the damned are tormented."[3] The Church, too, prays for the departed in the following terms: "Deliver the souls of the faithful departed from the pains of hell."

In this terrible fiery prison the poor souls are confined for weeks, months, years, for twenty, fifty, a hundred years, or even longer, and since they cannot help themselves, they keep crying out to us: have pity on me! have pity on me! Give me even one Communion, one Mass, one rosary, one act of mortification, even one good work of the many that you perform every day! What you thus bestow on me will be of the greatest help in lessening my torments and shortening the time of my imprisonment. Ah, have pity on me! "But," continues St. Augustine, "there are few who make any response to the appeal!" O my brethren, how cruel that is! The sick man calls from his bed, and there is some one to bring him medicines and to comfort him; a dog howls at the door and there is some one to open it for him; an animal falls into a pit and it is helped out, "but the faithful soul cries out in its torments, and no one heeds it."[4] What cruelty on the part of reasoning beings! The Emperor Henry after having taken a city that had obstinately resisted him, fulfilled a threat he had before uttered, and commanded his soldiers to put all the inhabitants to the sword, not sparing even the child in its mother's womb. The citizens seeing no hope of

From the midst of this fire the poor souls daily cry to us for help.

---

[1] Hic ignis, etsi æternus non sit, excellit omnem pœnam, quam unquam passus est aliquis in hac vita.—S. Aug. in Ps. 37.

[2] Pœna purgatorii minima excedit maximam hujus vitæ.—S. Thom. Dist. 1. q. 1.

[3] Eodem igne et crematur damnatus, et purgatur electus.—S. Greg. in Ps. 37.

[4] Clamat autem in tormentis fidelis, et non est qui respondeat illi.

mercy, as a last resource assembled all the children from six to ten years of age, and sent them to the emperor's tent, with orders to fall down prostrate before him and implore his mercy in the words: "Lord, be merciful." The sight of those innocent children so moved the heart of the emperor that he wept, and spared the city.

It would, then, be very cruel not to help them since we can do it without any loss, nay, to our great profit.

Ah, Christians, if I could now cause the floor of the church to open and show you that terrible prison, what a mournful procession would meet your gaze, crying out: father, mother, have pity on me! Son, daughter, have pity on me! Husband, wife, have pity on me! Brothers, sisters, friends, relatives, have pity on me! Should not the sight of such sorrow and suffering move us to shed tears of compassion? Yet such are in reality the cries sent forth by those poor souls, although we cannot hear them with our bodily ears. O my dear brethren, how cruel it is to pay no attention to them, to make no effort to help them, especially since we can do so easily by applying to their advantage a share of our daily actions, to their great relief and without the least loss or additional trouble to ourselves! But why do I say without loss? It is rather of the greatest advantage to us to help the poor souls, and therefore we are still less to be excused if we refuse to show them mercy, as I shall briefly prove in the

Second Part.

We may expect them to help us even while they are in purgatory if we help them.

Although the blind heathens thought that the souls of men die with their bodies as if they were dumb beasts, so that they could not hope for any return or advantage from them; yet they were wont to show the greatest honor to the memory of the departed. According to historians, many millions were spent in building splendid monuments and mausoleums to keep fresh the memory of the dead. What would they have done if they had believed that their souls were immortal and destined to live in a far happier country, where they could make a rich return for all the honor and generosity shown them, as our faith teaches us? Oh, what a great interest is brought in to us by the small capital we expend for them! What graces and favors we owe to the few works of devotion that we perform during our lives for the relief of the poor souls! As time does not permit it, I will say nothing now of the benefits we have to expect from the souls themselves whom we help; for it is certain that since they are friends of God and in full conformity with His will, although they are in torments and cannot help themselves, yet they can pray to God for others. Let those speak of it who know it by experience, and who found the poor souls helping them in doubts, dangers, difficulties by land and sea, at home and on a journey; they will be able to tell you that hardly had they finished their prayer when they experienced immediate relief, as we shall hear more in detail in a future sermon. Thou knowest, O Lord, how many benefits I for my part owe those souls! I do not say this, my dear brethren, to praise myself, but to honor and extol the divine goodness, which is so desirous that we should help the souls it keeps prisoners that I am never wont to commence any important work without first praying for the poor souls, and I must acknowledge that I always found evident assistance and success in the work undertaken. If these souls are so powerful while still in prison, how much more will they not be able to do for us when by our good works they shall be freed from their sufferings and be enabled to enter heaven?

All I have to ask you now is this; will the God of infinite fidelity and generosity allow our charity and mercy to go unrewarded? Was it then merely to deceive us that He said: "Blessed are the merciful, for they shall obtain mercy"?[1] Is there no meaning in that magnificent promise of His: "Give, and it shall be given to you: good measure and pressed down and shaken together and running over shall they give into your bosom. For with the same measure that you shall mete withal, it shall be measured to you again,"[2] especially as Our Lord says that what we do to the least of His brethren He will take as having been done to Himself? What help and grace may we not expect from that mercy in the hour when we are most in need, the hour of death? Are we not expressly assured of this by the Prophet David: "Blessed is he that understandeth concerning the needy and the poor: the Lord will deliver him in the evil day"?[3] that is, in the dangerous hour of death the Lord will take care of him and free him from the hands of his enemies. Then he will be helped by those souls, far more faithful to him than his friends and relatives, and his deathbed will be surrounded by those whom he

God will not allow our charity to go unrewarded, especially on our deathbed.

---

[1] Beati misericordes, quoniam ipsi misericordiam consequentur.—Matt. v. 7.

[2] Date et habitur vobis: mensuram bonam et confertam et coagitatam et supereffluentem dabunt in sinum vestrum. Eadem quippe mensura qua mensi fueritis, remetietur vobis.—Luke vi. 38.

[3] Beatus qui intelligit super egenum et pauperem: in die mala liberabit eum Dominus—Ps. xl. 2.

either freed from purgatory or relieved therein, and who will now bring him heavenly help and consolation in return.

According to the interpretation of Bellarmine, this seems to be the meaning of those words of Our Lord in the Gospel of St. Luke: "Make unto you friends of the mammon of iniquity; that when you shall fail, they may receive you into everlasting dwellings." [1] And there have been some who, when at the point of death, saw souls standing round them like an army defending them from the attacks of the devil and ready to accompany them into heaven. What help and grace may not be expected as the reward of this mercy after death, if one has to spend some time in purgatory to pay off his own debts! Oh, if I had the happiness to free even one soul from that prison, and that I had to go there myself after death, would that now happy soul look on with indifference, while I, its benefactor and the promoter of its happiness, languish in torments with the severity of which it is well acquainted? Would it not intercede with God for my speedy liberation? And with what confidence could I not look to that soul and say as Joseph did when the butler was released from the Egyptian prison: "Only remember me when it shall be well with thee, and do me this kindness: to put Pharao in mind to take me out of this prison." [2] Remember me, I might say; think of me, blessed soul! A year or two ago I brought you liberty; do not now forget me who have to suffer as you had then! Remember me now when it is well with you; intercede for me with God, with whom you can do all things, and beg of Him to free me from this prison. Remember how it was with you when you were here; how you longed for the moment of your liberation to come: it was I who helped you thereto; show now the same mercy to me, so that by your assistance I may soon come to heaven and rejoice with you. The butler forgot Joseph for a long time, my dear brethren, but we may be certain that such a soul, which clearly sees in the beatific vision all the prayers that are addressed to it, will not long remain insensible to them. Of that I cannot have the least doubt.

And again, I often ask myself if it is possible for one to be lost forever who tries to bring others to heaven? Is it possible for a Christian to be damned who makes every effort to free souls

---

[1] Facite vobis amicos de mammona iniquitatis; ut cum defeceritis, recipiant vos in æterna tabernacula.—Luke xvi. 9.

[2] Memento mei cum bene tibi fuerit, et facias mecum misericordiam: ut suggerat Pharaoni, ut educat me de isto carcere.—Gen. xl. 14.

from purgatory? No, answers St. Chrysostom; God is too good and faithful not to show mercy to him who has been merciful. Otherwise why should He at once invite into His kingdom those who fed Him, gave Him to drink, freed Him from prison, visited and consoled Him in sickness, if He should condemn to hell the Christian who renders Him all those services in the persons of the poor souls? No, I say again; the poor souls themselves would not allow that. If their benefactor was at the last gasp in the state of sin, and in danger of being sent to hell for all eternity, they would unanimously cry out to God for a powerful grace of repentance for him, saying like the Jewish people when Jonathan's life was in danger after he had routed the Philistines, on account of his having eaten a little honey against his father's command: "Shall Jonathan then die, who hath wrought this great salvation in Israel?"[1] Shall he perish who saved us from the hands of our enemies? No, we cannot allow that; not a hair of his head shall fall to the ground. What? those souls would cry out; shall he, O good God, be condemned to hell forever who has shown us such great charity? It is to him we owe it that we are freed so soon from our torments and have come to enjoy eternal rest with Thee; and must he now be among the reprobate? Ah, be merciful to him according to Thy promise, for he has been merciful to us.

Let us make trial of this, my dear brethren, and by frequent works of mercy make friends of the departed; and we shall find that we have not lost, but gained, by our trouble. There have been many, I know there are some still, who keep nothing for themselves, but give all their satisfactory works to the poor souls, and in my opinion they themselves are the gainers thereby. If we do not wish to be so generous, then let us at least give a part of our satisfactory works to the poor souls every day; this is an alms that the most needy beggar can bestow as well as the richest lord; and then we shall see that the words of my text are true: "He hath dispersed abroad; He hath given to the poor: His justice remaineth forever."

---

[1] Ergone Jonathas morietur, qui fecit salutem hanc magnam in Israel?—I. Kings xiv. 45.

FIFTY-NINTH SERMON.

ON THE MOTIVES AND MEANS FOR HELPING THE SOULS IN PURGATORY.

Subject.

1. To help the souls in purgatory is a most excellent act of the love of God. 2. By what means we can and should especially help those souls.—*Preached on the sixth Sunday after Pentecost.*

Text.

Misereor super turbam.—Mark viii. 2.

" I have compassion on the multitude."

Introduction.

The privations of these poor people who were almost dying of hunger bring before my mind the sufferings of the poor souls in purgatory, who have to remain in that prison, not merely for three days, but in many cases for years and years, unceasingly sighing and crying out to heaven: have mercy, Lord, have mercy! Free us from this prison, that we may see Thee whom we so long for! And meanwhile that omnipotent and most merciful Lord, who was moved to compassion at the sight of the hungry multitude, so that He wrought a miracle to supply their wants, hears the sighs and complaints of the suffering souls, and, as far as He Himself is concerned, has the greatest desire to free them at once, and bring them to heaven; but His divine justice demands full satisfaction for the debt they owe Him on account of their sins, and to that end He recommends them to those who are still living on earth, and who can help them by satisfying for them. Hence they cry out to us in the words of the Prophet Job: " Have pity on me, have pity on me, at least you my friends," [1] our brothers and sisters! My dear brethren, if our hearts are human they should be easily moved to compassion, and we should try in every possible way to help those poor souls in their extreme necessity. For this is an act of the most excellent charity towards our neighbor, as I have proved on a former occasion, and I hope that I have inspired many to promise rich alms to

---

[1] Miseremini mei, miseremini mei, saltem vos amici mei.—Job xix 21.

the poor souls. That we may be faithful to this promise and keep it exactly, I now continue and say:

Plan of Discourse.

To help the poor souls is also a most excellent act of the love of God; the first part. By what means especially, we can and should help those souls, I will show in the second part.

Merciful God, we again beg of Thee through the Mother of mercy and our holy guardian angels, to fill the hearts of all here present with that mercy that is so desirable in Thy sight, so that we may exclaim: "I have compassion on the multitude."

He who loves another seeks to give his friend pleasure and joy on every possible occasion, and to further his honor whenever he can. Therefore, if I truly love God, I cannot better prove the sincerity of my love than by endeavoring to do that in which I know He takes a special delight, and by which the divine honor is especially increased. Such is the way in which Jesus Christ proved His love for His Father, when He said: "I do always the things that please Him;"[1] and again: "I seek not My own will, but the will of Him that sent Me."[2]

He who loves God seizes every opportunity of pleasing Him.

Now, my dear brethren, although he who is in the state of grace gives honor to God by every good work, yet he does so especially when he helps the poor souls, because he thus gives the Almighty special pleasure, and extraordinary honor and glory. How is that? Imagine that there is a rich and noble lord, whose dear son has gone into foreign lands, and having ventured too far, has been captured by Turks, or other barbarous people, and been kept a close prisoner. What must, not only the unfortunate son, but also the loving father, feel at this misfortune? Alas, sighs the former day and night, like the Prodigal in the Gospel: "How many hired servants in my father's house abound with bread, and I here perish with hunger?"[3] His servants are well provided for; but I must lie here in a dungeon, laden with chains! Alas, who will free me, and bring me back to my father's house? And meanwhile the unhappy father sighs and laments: unfortunate child, why didst thou go so far away from me? Ah, who will bring thee back to me? When shall I have the happiness and joy of receiving thee

That is done especially by him who helps the poor souls. Shown by similes.

---

[1] Ego quæ placita sunt ei facio semper.—John viii. 29.

[2] Non quæro voluntatem meam, sed voluntatem ejus qui misit me.—Ibid. v. 30.

[3] Quanti mercenarii in domo patris mei abundant panibus; ego autem hic fame pereo?—Luke xv. 17.

into my house? Suppose now, my dear brethren, that I happened to be in Turkey with a foreign embassy, and that I was able to redeem that son either by money or by influence, and to bring him back unhurt to his father; what indescribable joy I should cause, not only to the ransomed slave, but also to his father, who had bewailed his loss so bitterly! He would always look on me as his greatest benefactor, on account of that ransom, and would feel obliged to show me the liveliest gratitude in return for the service I have rendered him. Is not that the case? Again, imagine the state of the bridegroom, who expects to bring home his beloved spouse after the marriage festivities, and finds that she falls suddenly ill of some dangerous malady, so that the doctors either give up all hope of her recovery, or fear that she will remain ill for many years. Could a greater favor be done the bridegroom under those circumstances than to restore his bride to health? Judge of the joy he would feel if some one were to come forward with a powerful remedy that at once restores her to perfect health.

For the poor souls are dear children and spouses of God.

Now to our subject, my dear brethren. Every soul in purgatory is a dear child of God; and they are more assured of that relationship than the most pious and holy souls in this life, whose conscience gives testimony, as St. Paul says, "that we are the sons of God, and if sons, heirs also; heirs indeed of God. and joint-heirs with Christ,"[1] but who are not certain, at all events infallibly, that they will always remain children of God, for they are constantly in danger of losing the grace of God by sin, and becoming children of eternal damnation. But the soul in purgatory is beyond all danger, doubt, and fear, and is quite assured and certain that it is and will always remain a chosen child of God, and can infallibly expect to share in the eternal inheritance. Now if, according to the testimony of the holy Scriptures, no father or mother on earth has such a tender love for his or her only son as the Lord God has for His children, even for those who being still in this life can become children of the devil, how exceedingly great and tender must not be the love of God for a just soul in the next life? And, therefore, how great must not be the desire of the Almighty God to receive His beloved child into His own house, that is, into the kingdom of heaven, and to see him there? Every soul in purgatory is a

---

[1] Quod sumus filii Dei, si autem filii, et hæredes, hæredes quidem Dei, cohæredes autem Christi.—Rom.viii. 16, 17.

beloved spouse of Christ, whom He has won by shedding His blood on the cross. " I will betroth thee to Me forever,"[1] He says to each just soul by the Prophet Osee; but on condition that thou remainest faithful to Me till the end of thy life. There is no need for this condition with the souls in purgatory; the espousals are fixed for all eternity; they are already on their way to the city of God; everything is ready for the marriage-feast, and no spouse on earth is so eager to get possession of his bride as Jesus Christ is to receive the soul that He has bought with His blood. " My delight is to be with the children of men,"[2] He says Himself; as if their society were a source of new joy to Him, and He could not be completely happy until they share in His bliss.

Meanwhile these dear children of God, as during their pilgrim- They are kept in pris on away from God. age on earth they wandered from the right path, either by grievous sins of which they repented or by small daily faults and transgressions, have fallen into the hands of the enemy, and are kept imprisoned in a gloomy dungeon far from their Father's house. These spouses of Christ are suffering more than mortal pains, and cannot yet go to the feast prepared for them; for the infinite justice and holiness of God require that they should pay the necessary amount of satisfaction. Our heavenly Father hears those dear children of His, Christ hears His beloved spouses sighing and moaning in their prison, and longing to be released; He has the greatest desire to help them and bring them to Himself in heaven; but His justice does not permit it, and insists on full atonement for all, even to the last farthing.

Now, I leave you to judge, my dear brethren, what a So that he who frees them does an act that is very pleasing to God. great act of charity it is, and how it must be specially pleasing to God, to satisfy the claims of His justice by prayers and other good works, and so to free those souls out of prison, and enable them to enter heaven even an hour sooner, and to share in the glory of their heavenly Father and Spouse. Let it suffice to re-member what He Himself says in the Gospel, namely, that He will accept that act of charity with as much joy and pleasure as if it were done to Himself: " Amen I say to you, as long as you did it to one of these My least brethren, you did it to Me."[3] That these words are to be especially understood of the souls in

---

[1] Sponsabo te mihi in sempiternum.—Osee ii. 19.

[2] Deliciæ meæ esse cum filiis hominum.—Prov. viii. 31.

[3] Amen dico vobis, quamdiu fecistis uni ex his fratribus meis minimis, mihi fecistis.—Matt. xxv. 40.

purgatory is evident from the following remarkable words of St. Gertrude, as we read in Denis the Carthusian: "As often as you free a soul you give the Lord as much pleasure as if you had released Himself from captivity; a benefit that He will reward you for at the proper time." [1]

And also promotes the honor and glory of God. I will say nothing of the great honor and glory that, besides the pleasure, we can thus give to the Almighty. For by that act of charity we send to God souls that will praise His infinite majesty sooner than they otherwise would have done, and will most perfectly know, love, and honor Him in heaven. We poor mortals, as long as we are wandering about in the darkness of this vale of tears, can neither know nor praise God properly; but when the soul, separated from the body, first sees the face of its God it receives a most perfect knowledge of that most supreme Good worthy of all love, and from that knowledge must necessarily spring seraphic flames of love that will burn incessantly for all eternity. I imagine that I am now looking at a soul flying upwards from purgatory into heaven; with what joy and exultation it offers its first meed of thanks to God's mercy; how submissively it adores the Infinite Good and His infinite perfections! Methinks I hear it intoning the canticle of praise of the heavenly citizens: "Holy, holy, holy! Alleluia! Praised be God! Glory and honor to Him for all eternity!" Oh, I cannot help thinking what a great act has been performed by that man who assisted that soul out of purgatory, and hastened its entrance into heaven; for he is the cause of all that love, gratitude, praise, honor, and glory that are offered the Divine Majesty sooner than they otherwise would have been! And from this, too, we may conclude, without the least fear of doubt, that the help rendered the suffering souls must be inexpressibly dear to God.

Therefore we should help the poor souls. Ah, my dear brethren, should not this one motive be enough, if we truly love God, to animate us to help the poor souls in every possible way? Think of the countless benefits we owe the Divine Goodness every moment of our lives; there we have a means of making a return for them, and of paying our own debts to some extent. Let us, then, make use of the means that are best adapted to free from purgatory those souls that are so dear to God. What are those means? That we shall see in the

---

[1] Quoties animam aliquam liberatis, hoc adeo Domino acceptum est, quasi ipsum ex captivitate redemissetis ; quod beneficium reddet vobis tempore opportuno.

Second Part.

Immediately after the death of one of our loved ones we are wont to spend the time in giving way to grief and lamentation, in preparing a mourning dress and a respectable funeral, and in receiving visits of condolence, mostly from people who are little concerned about the death of our friend; they wish to show their sympathy out of courtesy alone, because such is the custom, and their visits are often wearisome enough to us under the circumstances. Amongst all those troublesome preparations, that are not of the least use to the deceased, we hardly bestow a thought on his soul, which is then most in need of help. That is, indeed, a selfish system of mourning, which is directed more to our own honor than to freeing the soul of the departed from purgatory, for which latter object little or nothing is done. The souls in purgatory attach no value to magnificent funeral obsequies, and are not in the least benefited by them. St. Jerome, after having described how St. Antony buried the body of St. Paul, the first hermit, in the sand, reproaches the vain world with the pride of those who prepare splendid funerals for their departed friends, cover the dead bodies with costly stuffs, surround their coffins with countless lights, and bury them in magnificent tombs. " How is it," he says, " that pride can still find a place in the midst of mourning and lamentation?"[1] With all this useless extravagance, nothing is done for the help or consolation of the soul. Those people are not aware that they can show their love for the departed soul far better with a short prayer than with all that vain pomp. " Do you wish to honor the dead?" asks St. Chrysostom. " Then give alms; for what is the use of vain weeping?"[2] What advantage is to be derived from useless funeral pomp? " You should rather put forth every effort to help the departed by alms, prayers, and Masses."[3] " Men must weep and show their sorrow; we cannot refuse them the consolation they find in shedding tears at the death of a dear friend," says St. Augustine; " but with far greater earnestness, zeal, and care should they endeavor to help the departed soul by sacrifice, prayer, and

---

[1] Cur ambitio inter luctus lachrymasque non cessat?

[2] Vis mortuum honorare? Fac eleemosynas; quæ tibi ex multis fletibus utilitas?— S. Chrys.

[3] Nitere quantum potes, ut juvetur non lachrymis, sed prece, supplicationibus, eleemosynis, oblationibus.—Idem.

almsgiving." [1] In the Book of his Confessions, he praises his mother, St. Monica, because on the approach of her death she gave no instructions concerning the embalming of her body or her burial. [2] "She left us no injunctions concerning matters of that kind; her only request was that she should not be forgotten at the altar." [3] The same truth was clearly demonstrated by means of a miracle to a Venetian nobleman by Father Paul Montorfano. While he was Superior of a convent of Theatines, the noble sent him a large sum of money that he might celebrate the anniversary of his ancestors in the convent church. The servant of God was, however, more intent on having the ceremonies carried out with piety than with much outward pomp; whereat the proud noble was mightily dissatisfied. He remonstrated with Father Paul, saying that such a large sum of money ought to have secured more magnificence in the office; when the Father led him into a room, and putting all the money he had received into one scale of a balance, wrote the De Profundis on a piece of paper and put it into the other, and, wonderful to relate, the little piece of paper weighed down the heavy gold. The proud noble then saw and was convinced that a short prayer is of far more use to a soul than splendid obsequies.

But fervent prayer is. And so it is in truth, my dear brethren. The prayer of the just is one of the most excellent and powerful means of relieving the souls in purgatory. It is called by St. Augustine the "key of heaven," [4] by which the closed gate of heaven is opened especially to the poor souls; and therefore the devil leaves no stone unturned to frustrate or prevent the prayers of the just for the departed. Such is the testimony given by St. Teresa, who freed and brought to heaven by her prayers a vast number of suffering souls. "Once," she says, "as I was going to my oratory to say the office for the dead, a most fearful apparition came and sat down on my book, so that I could not read. Three times I drove away the evil spirit by the sign of the cross, but as soon as I commenced to read the psalms he came back and prevented me, until at last, by constantly using holy water,

[1] Impleant homines erga suos officia postremi funeris, et sui humani lenimenta moeroris; verum illa quæ adjuvant spiritus defunctorum, oblationes, orationes, erogationes, multo pro eis observantius, instantius, abundantius impendant.

[2] Imminente die resolutionis suæ non cogitavit corpus suum sumptuose contegi, aut condiri aromatibus, aut monumentum concupivit, aut curavit sepulchrum patrium.

[3] Non ista mandavit nobis; sed tantummodo memoriam sui ad altare tuum fieri desideravit.

[4] Clavis cœli.

I banished him and was able to finish my prayer. I then saw
some souls going up to heaven, who only wanted the few prayers
that the hellish foe tried to hinder." So far St. Teresa. We
read in the life of St. Dominic of the wonderful power of the
rosary to help the poor souls. A noble lady, named Alexandra,
was miraculously raised to life by the Saint, that she might receive the last sacraments; she acknowledged that she had died
in the state of grace, but was condemned to purgatory for two
hundred years on account of the sins she had given others occasion to commit, and besides that, she had to suffer five hundred
years longer because she had indulged in such extravagance of
dress that she had been to many the occasion of impure thoughts
and desires; she hoped, however, to be freed soon by the rosar-
ies that were to be said for her by her fellow-sodalists of the
confraternity to which she belonged. After having said this,
she again departed this life. St. Dominic and the members of
the confraternity of the rosary prayed so fervently for her soul
that fifteen days after Alexandra appeared to him surrounded by
glory to thank him.

Another still more powerful means of helping the poor souls And gen-
is almsgiving and other works of mercy. Such is the teaching erous alms.
of St. Thomas: "Almsgiving has a greater power of satisfying
than prayer." [1] By this means Cæsar Costa, Archbishop of
Capua, lessened his own sufferings in purgatory. During his life-
time he had given a poor priest money to buy a cloak; after his
death he appeared to the priest surrounded by flames, and humbly
begged of him the loan of that mantle for a short time. When
it was given to him he covered himself with it from head to foot,
and thereby considerably lessened the heat of the flames. By
the same means Guda freed her royal spouse Sanctius from purgatory. Amongst other acts of charity she had given a cloak to
a poor priest, and behold, a fortnight after, the deceased king
appeared surrounded with heavenly glory and covered with the
cloak that Guda had given to the priest. In the same way, too,
Father Hilarion, a discalced Carmelite, freed his father's soul, by
giving to an unknown young man, who had asked him for something to eat, the best part of his own food. When the supposed
young man, who was in reality an angel, had eaten all the food
given him, he sent word to the Father that he need not pray

---

[1] Eleemosyna completius habet vim satisfactionis, quam oratio.—S. Thom. in 4. Dist. 15
q. 2. a. 2.

any more for the soul of his deceased parent, for the latter was now in heaven; having said these words, he disappeared. This event is related in detail by Charles Rosignoli of our Society.

The forgiveness of injuries. The third means is readiness to forgive injuries and to love our enemies; for since this love is more heroic and makes man more like to God, so also it brings the departed relief more speedily and efficaciously. A proof of this is the example recorded in detail by Father Paul Segneri. There was in Bologna a rich and noble widow to whose house an assassin, utterly unknown to her, had fled to escape the pursuit of the officers of justice. Through pity she concealed him, and even after she had learned that it was her only son, the sole hope of her declining years, who had been slain by him in the public street (I leave you to imagine, my dear brethren, with what grief she heard the news), she still continued to practise the duties of Christian charity toward the murderer; for she gave him her murdered son's best horse and a bag of gold that he might more easily escape. After this heroic act, she went to pray for her son, when he appeared to her in glory, and said: Cease praying for me, mother; the heroic act of virtue that you performed in pardoning my murderer and doing good to him has freed me from purgatory, in which I should otherwise have had to spend many years. O my dear brethren, love your enemies! Do good to those that hate you, pray for those who persecute and do evil to you; and you will most certainly and efficaciously help the poor souls.

Indulgences. Perhaps you would wish to know how you might help them with still less trouble? We have the means of doing that almost daily in the indulgences that the Church of Christ so frequently grants; that is, by the satisfaction for the punishment due to sin, which flows from the merits of Christ and His saints as from an inexhaustible spring, whereby countless souls have been already freed from purgatory, and been enabled to enter into the joys of heaven, according to the testimony of St. Mary Magdalene of Pazzi, to whom God revealed this truth when she was in ecstasy. Almost every time you receive holy Communion, or say the rosary or litany, or do some work of charity, or attend morning devotions, you can gain an immense treasure, with which, if you wish to offer it for the poor souls, you can pay off what they still owe the Divine Justice. Think of this, and keep it constantly before your minds.

Fasting, mortification, penitential works, patience in adversity, nay, all good works that are performed in the state of grace, are also available to help and relieve the souls of the departed, but, according to the Council of Trent, there is nothing better for that purpose, nothing which the poor souls long for more eagerly, than the holy Mass, in which the flesh and blood of Jesus Christ, that is, an infinite treasure of satisfaction, is offered to our heavenly Father for the living and the dead. [1] That the poor souls themselves have frequently acknowledged, and amongst others a monk, who appeared to one of his brethren at Clarvaux, during the lifetime of St. Bernard, and thanked him for having freed him from a long purgatory, and enabled him to enjoy the beatific vision. Being asked what gave him most relief in his sufferings and helped most to his release, he took the Brother by the hand, and leading him into the church where several Masses were being read, " there, " he said, " there are the arms of the grace of our God, by which I have been freed. " [2] This is the might of the divine mercy; this is the saving sacrifice that takes away the sins of the world! A similar example is recorded in the History of St. Dominic. The Blessed Henry Suzo had agreed with another Brother of the Order that whichever of the two should survive was to say two Masses a week, for a whole year, for the other's soul. Some years after, Suzo's companion died. Many were the prayers and works of penance that the survivor offered for his soul, but he completely forgot the promised Masses, until the deceased appeared to him with a sorrowful countenance, and sharply reproved his neglect. Suzo tried to excuse himself by reminding him of the prayers and mortifications he had offered for him; but the other cried out: " it is blood, blood, O my brother, that I want to cool me in those flames; your penances and fervent prayers are of little help to me in the sore strait in which I am, if the blood of Jesus Christ, which is offered in the holy Mass, does not descend into those flames. The Masses you have promised are what I want. " The holy Irish Archbishop St. Malachy, had, as St. Bernard testifies, said many Masses for the soul of his deceased sister; and at last he gave up saying them. After thirty days had elapsed, he heard his sister's voice during the night complaining bitterly, that she had to wait for thirty days in the vestibule

But chie the holy Mass.

[1] Animas in purgatorio detentas potissimum acceptabili altaris sacrificio juvari.—Sess. 25, Decr. de Purgat.

[2] Ecce, hæc sunt arma gratiæ Dei nostri, quibus ereptus sum.

of the church expecting help from her brother, and she had received none; whereupon Malachy began to say Masses for her again, and then she showed herself to him at the church door clad in mourning. As he continued the Masses, he saw her again, in the church this time, but still clothed in a dark brown mourning dress. Still continuing the daily Mass for her, he saw her at last ascending to heaven clad in the garment of glory, in company with other blessed souls.

Hence they are very cruel who do not at once execute the pious legacies of the departed. From this we can see how cruel it is to neglect or defer fulfilling the last wishes of our deceased friends, with regard to pious legacies. The learned Laymann, Sylvester, and other theologians and jurists, quoted by Father Reiffenstuel, are unanimous in affirming that he is guilty of mortal sin who, without just reason, through avarice or carelessness, defers for a notable period the execution of such testaments. The delay of six months, that is granted in Canon Law to executors, is only intended to save them from the punishment inflicted by external tribunals on those who are guilty of such negligence. But neither the divine nor the natural law, nor equity, nor justice, could tolerate such a delay in conscience, and they who are guilty of it commit a mortal sin. You defer for such a long time the saying of the Masses or the giving the alms willed by your former friend, and meanwhile he has to languish in the midst of frightful torments!

Exhortation to be charitable to the poor souls. I conclude, my dear brethren, in the words of St. Bernard: " Arise then, Christians, and help the suffering souls; let your sighs and prayers intercede for them, and the sacrifices you offer satisfy for them. " [1] Help them by fervent prayer, by alms-deeds and works of Christian charity, by forgiving injuries, by indulgences, by patience in trials, but especially by the blood of Jesus Christ by hearing holy Mass, a means that we can employ daily. Imagine, when you are entering the church to hear Mass, that you see the poor souls standing at the door like beggars, and with folded hands imploring an alms from you; remember, too, that they are all dear children of God, who are kept away from their heavenly Father, and are sighing to be released from their prison. If you are often moved to help those who appeal to your charity at the church-door, truly you should remember that the poor souls are far more deserving of compassion, and that you

[1] Surgite ergo in adjutorium animabus, interpellate gemitibus, orationibus intercedite, satisfacite sacrificiis.

can help them without spending a penny, and give them a rich alms by hearing holy Mass. Renew your former resolutions and promises, trusting in the words of God Himself, " Do good to the just, and thou shalt find great recompense: " [1] not only from God, but from the released souls as well. Amen.

This last sentence contains the subject of a sermon that I intend to preach when the opportunity offers.

SIXTIETH SERMON.

ON THE GRATITUDE OF THE SOULS IN PURGATORY TOWARDS THEIR BENEFACTORS.

Subject.

Wonderful is the gratitude of the souls in purgatory towards their living benefactors ; therefore, if we love ourselves and our own advantage, we should be merciful and generous to the departed.—*Preached on the thirteenth Sunday after Pentecost.*

Text.

Filia mea modo defuncta est.—Matt. ix. 18.

" My daughter is even now dead."

Introduction.

Such is the way of the world; the one goes first, and the other follows, into a long eternity. My daughter died yesterday; my son is buried to-day; my father, mother, brother, sister, husband, wife, friend, is dead! And what then? Weeping, moaning, and lamentation are to be heard in the house of death on the part of children, parents, and other friends and relatives; that lasts for one, two, or three weeks, and then the departed is forgotten as if he had never lived. If he is sometimes remembered with a secret sigh, it is generally a useless sigh, a vain remembrance. Few there are who trouble themselves as to the lot of souls in the next world; and yet that should be the first thing to occupy our thoughts, that we may help them, if they are in purgatory, with prayers, Masses, almsgiving, and other good works. I have already shown that to help the poor souls is a most excellent act of charity not only towards the departed, but also towards God Himself. And now I add: that help is a

---

[1] Benefac justo, et invenies retributionem magnam.—Ecclus. xii. 2.

work of charity even towards ourselves, because we can expect a hundredfold reward from the poor souls for the assistance we render them, as I now proceed to show.

Plan of Discourse.

The wonderful gratitude of the poor souls towards their living benefactors; such is the whole subject. Therefore, if we love ourselves and desire our own advantage, we should be generous and merciful to the departed, such shall be the conclusion.

Do Thou, O God, help us by Thy grace to observe it; we beg this of Thee through the intercession of Mary and of our holy guardian angels.

The poor souls show their gratitude to their benefactors in every possible way. They recognize the benefit.

True gratitude is shown by three things: the heart, the mouth, the hands. The heart, inasmuch as I acknowledge the benefit with thankfulness and do not forget it; the mouth, inasmuch as I give my benefactor outward signs by words or otherwise of my gratitude; the hands, inasmuch as I make him what return I can for his kindness. In all these three ways the souls in purgatory prove their gratitude to those on earth who have helped them. First, who will doubt that they acknowledge the benefit received? For they experience that their torments are lessened or shortened; they think to themselves, who can the kind-hearted mortal be who has procured us this relief from God? And I say, too, that they are most grateful; for, the greater the pains, the fiercer the fire that tortures them, the higher also must be their esteem of the charity and kindness that procured them alleviation. Moreover, it is evident that the departed know either by divine revelation, or by their guardian angels, who they are who help them on earth.

They thank their benefactors.

For often they have in person thanked their benefactors in a most heartfelt manner even for slight favors, as we read in the Lives of the Saints. To pass by countless other examples of souls that have appeared to express their gratitude, that zealous servant of God, Father Conrad of the Seraphic Order of the Minorites, as he was praying one night in a church for a lately deceased Brother, (and his prayer was indeed a short one, consisting merely of an Our Father with the versicle, "Lord give him eternal rest,") the Brother at once appeared to him, and after having respectfully thanked him: "O Father," he exclaimed, "if you only knew what great relief that one short prayer has given me, you would certainly say it again! I beg of you then for

God's sake to repeat it." Thereupon the Father said it over again, and kept on saying it, until the soul was released and with joyful thanksgiving ascended up to heaven. When the holy Bishop Bristanus, who was accustomed to pray at night in the church-yards, came to the concluding words of his prayer, "may they rest in peace," he often heard voices from the grave saying: "Amen, amen, we thank you!" Father Julius Mancinellus of our Society was most familiar with the souls in purgatory, who used to visit him in a friendly manner, and tell him how grateful they were to him for the relief that God gave them on account of his prayers. Many times they were seen to come into the church and with bended knees and folded hands to hear his Mass. Still more intimate was their intercourse with St. Frances of the Order of Discalced Carmelites; wherever she went she was accompanied by souls who thanked her or recommended themselves to her prayers; during the night they surrounded her bed, as if to protect her, and as soon as she awoke: God greet thee, servant of God, they would exclaim; may Jesus be always with thee! During her illness she was waited on by them; when temptations were impending from the devil they warned and exhorted her to be on her guard; when she said the rosary they would take her hand and reverently kiss it as the instrument that had brought them such comfort in the midst of their torments. See, my dear brethren, how grateful the poor souls are to their benefactors.

But their gratitude does not consist in words alone; they show it also with their generous hands, for they make a hundredfold return for the benefits conferred on them. In the first place, they show it by their fervent prayers, by which they receive from God copious graces for those who have helped them, and that, too, not merely after their release, but while they are still in purgatory. How can that be? Are they able to do good and to obtain favors by their prayers, while still in that prison? Certainly, only not for themselves; the souls in purgatory are always practising the principal virtues, and making acts of the most lively faith, the firmest hope, the most ardent charity, the most perfect repentance, the most complete resignation to the will of God; but all these and other virtues, perfect though they may be, do not aid them in the least in their progress to eternal glory, nor can they thereby obtain the least diminution of their pains. They are in a state in which they must suffer, because they can-

They make a return to their benefactors by praying for them.

not satisfy any longer, and therefore they are obliged to appeal
to the charity of the living for help. " They expect us to help
them," writes St. Augustine, " because the time of working has
gone by for them."[1] Nevertheless, although they cannot do anything for themselves, yet they can assist us who are still on earth,
performing our pilgrimage. Such is the express teaching of
two eminent theologians, Cardinal Bellarmine and Suarez, the
latter of whom says: " those souls are holy and dear to God,
they love us and know, at least in a general way, the dangers that
threaten us, and the need in which we are of the divine assistance. Why, then, should they not pray for us, although they are
suffering what they owe the Divine Justice, since we, who are
debtors in this life, pray for others, and the Fathers who were
in Abraham's bosom prayed for the living, as we read of Onias
and Jeremias?"[2] So far Suarez. The blessing that king David
wished the citizens of Jabes on account of their charity towards
the deceased king Saul: " Blessed be you to the Lord, who have
showed this mercy to your master Saul, and have buried him,"[3]
that blessing, I say, the suffering souls wish with far more earnestness than David to their benefactors. St. Brigid once heard
them praying in purgatory in a loud voice: "O merciful God,
reward a hundredfold the charity of those who by their good
works help us out of this darkness to Thy eternal light, and to
the sight of Thy divinity!" Now, my dear brethren, when those
souls pray in that manner, how readily will not God hear them,
since they are His dear children? St. Catharine of Bologna
says that whenever she wished for some grace from the Most
High, she always had recourse to the intercession of the holy
souls, and she was rarely disappointed; nay, she adds, that she
obtained by their means many favors that she failed to obtain
through the intercession of the saints in heaven. This is even
in our own days the experience of pious Christians who in all their
undertakings and necessities first offer their prayers to God for
the souls departed, and are nearly always blessed with success, as
I know well to be the case in one instance. If they are so pow-

---

[1] Expectant nos ut juventur per nos : tempus enim operandi jam profugit ab eis.

[2] Illæ animæ sunt sanctæ, et charæ Deo ; nosque ex charitate diligunt, noruntque saltem generaliter pericula nostra, et quantum indigeamus divino auxilio. Cur ergo non orabunt, etiamsi suis pœnis solvant, quod debent ; nam nos etiam in hac vita qui debitores sumus, pro aliis oramus ; et Patres qui erant in sinu Abrahæ pro viventibus orabant, ut de Onia et Jeremia refertur.—Suarez, t. iv. Disp, 47. Sect. 2, n. 4.

[3] Benedicti vos Domino, qui fecistis misericordiam hanc cum domino vestro Saul, et sepelistis eum.—II. Kings ii. 5.

erful while actually in the midst of their torments, we can easily conclude how much more they will be able to do when they are freed from purgatory and admitted into the joys of heaven. With reason may we believe that the first request they will make at the throne of grace will be for those who have opened the gate of heaven for them, and procured their entrance into eternal happiness. And it is equally certain that they will never cease to pray for their benefactors when the latter are in danger, either of soul or body.

Again, we find countless instances in which they have come to the assistance of their benefactors in necessity, sickness, and in the dangers of war and death. I will relate one or two for you. Christopher Landoval, Archbishop of Seville, was commanded by Clement VIII. to make known to the world what happened to him when he was a student in the University of Louvain. From his childhood he was accustomed to give all his pocket-money in alms to help the poor souls; and on one occasion the money sent him from Spain did not reach him in due time, so that he was put to the greatest straits even to find enough to eat; but what pained him most of all was that he could give no more alms. Hungry as he was, he went to the church to pray at least for the departed souls, since he could not help them otherwise; but hardly had he knelt down, when a beautiful young man, richly clad in the garb of a traveller, presented himself before him, and courteously invited him to an inn to take some refreshment and hear the latest news from Spain. Christopher went with him, although not quite at his ease, for he thought the stranger was something more than natural. When the meal was over, the young man gave him a well-filled purse of gold, telling him to use it to supply his wants, as he, the stranger, would be sure to receive it back again from Christopher's father in Spain; whereupon he left him. Christopher at once made inquiries to find out where he came from; but no one in Louvain knew anything of him, nor could he get the least information regarding him when he afterwards returned to Spain; neither had any one appeared to claim the money from his father. He therefore came to the conclusion that the stranger was a soul out of purgatory, who had come to help him through gratitude. He was confirmed in this belief by the fact that the purse of money lasted him exactly to the day on which the usual remittance, which had been delayed, arrived from Spain.

Helping them in necessity.

In sickness and danger of death.

Still more certain was the help experienced in the danger of sickness and death, in the year 1649, by a certain William Friessem, a well-known publisher at Cologne. The following are the contents of a letter that he wrote to Father James Monsfort, of our Society: " I have to tell your Reverence of the wonderful manner in which my little son and my wife were restored to health. I have read the book that your Reverence sent me to print, which treats of charity towards the departed souls; while engaged in reading it, I was told that my little son, four years old, was dangerously ill, that the doctors had no hope of his recovery, and that preparations had been already made for his funeral. At once I put my confidence in and fled for refuge to the souls in purgatory; I went to the church and vowed to give away to the clergy a hundred copies of the work treating of charity towards the poor souls, that many might be inflamed with the desire of helping them. After having made that vow, I returned home and found my son much better, and the next day he was as well as if nothing had been the matter with him. Hardly three weeks had elapsed, when my wife was suddenly attacked by a trembling in her limbs, so that she fell in a faint to the ground; her illness increased to such a degree that no medicines were of any good, and she seemed at the point of death. Still I did not lose courage; for experience had taught me to have great confidence in the souls in purgatory. I ran to the same church, repeated my prayer to the merciful God, redoubled my vow, and promised to give two hundred copies of the work to devout persons. I also appealed to the souls in purgatory, and conjured them for the love of God to take pity on me. Hardly had I finished my prayer and returned home, when my servants came out congratulating me and assuring me that my wife had recovered from her faint, that she was able to eat and drink, and was nearly as strong as before. I found that what they said was quite true, and in a short time she was completely restored, and was able to accompany me to church to return thanks to God. Your Reverence can firmly believe every word I have written; I call God to witness that what I say is the truth." So far the publisher.

In dangers of war.

The day would not be long enough for my sermon, my dear brethren, if I were to bring forward the many instances in which people have been saved from imminent danger of death either through sickness, or in war, or from their enemies, or from murderers, on account of their charity to the poor souls. Eusebius, Duke of Sardinia, who used to give the tenth part of his income for the relief of the suffering souls, was beaten in battle by Ostorgius, a powerful king of Sicily, and was already driven out of one town. His army, which was much smaller than that of the enemy, began to grow disheartened; but his courage revived when he saw one morning a mighty force of about forty thousand brave soldiers horse and foot, all clad in white, approaching and offering him their services. Whereupon Ostorgius, terrified, left the town he had taken, and desired to make peace with Eusebius. The latter thanked God and the strange army, when the general of those soldiers said to him: Know, Eusebius, that almost all those soldiers are souls that have been freed by you from purgatory, and have been sent to help you by the Lord of hosts. Continue in your devotion to the suffering souls, for as many of them as you will free will be your protectors in heaven, to intercede with God for your welfare.

Nearly similar was the experience of Father Louis Monaci, a religious. He was alone on a journey, and according to his usual custom was saying the rosary for the souls departed. Two robbers were lying in wait to take his life, but the grateful souls would not abandon their benefactor; they surrounded him in the guise of soldiers deputed to guard him, and the robbers had to take to flight. In the same way a brave, noble, and pious warrior, who trusted more in the protection of heaven than in his weapons, was singularly helped by the souls in purgatory. Besides other pious practices, he was wont, whenever he passed by a church-yard, to stop a moment and offer up a prayer for the souls of those who were buried there. One day, as he went out unarmed to take a walk, his enemies, who under the pretence of revenging an insult, were plotting against his life, followed him, and were already very close to him. The brave soldier was well aware of what they wanted, and therefore quickened his pace, until he came to the charnel-house of an old church-yard; he sprang over the wall and hid himself there, although the place offered but little protection. When he found himself in the church-yard, he remembered his usual pious custom; but he was in doubt as to whether he should first try to make his escape and then say his usual prayer, or not. On the one hand there was the imminent danger that threatened

And in danger from assassins.

him, which urged him to save his life, and escape from his enemies as quickly as possible; on the other hand he was kept back by his firm resolution to pray for the souls of the departed, which urged him to adhere to his pious practice, and leave his safety to God. Having thought the matter over for a time, he at last determined to remain where he was, saying to himself: I would rather die than give up my habit of praying for the dead; the Almighty God can save me from my enemies, no matter how embittered they may be against me. So he remained where he was, and said his customary prayer to the great astonishment of his enemies themselves, who by this time had entered the church-yard, and were rushing at him with drawn swords. As they were on the point of attacking him and running him through, they suddenly saw that a number of soldiers, who had appeared unexpectedly on the scene, surrounded him to defend him from their attacks. There is no doubt that these soldiers were the souls of those for whom the devout knight had prayed, and that his charity to them merited for him from God the signal protection that was afforded him. His enemies, astounded at what had happened, and fearing for their own lives, took to flight at once. The knight did not yet know of the help that had been sent him; and when his short prayer was at an end, he rose up and looked around, but could see no one, for they had disappeared as quickly as they had come. He was amazed at this, and could not explain it until some time after, when overtures for peace having been made through the intervention of a good friend, and the hostile parties being on the point of giving each other the hand in token of friendship, the knight's former antagonist asked him who were the soldiers that stood around him in the church-yard, and what he was doing there waiting so calmly. Then followed a mutual explanation, and all saw at once that the soldiers were souls out of purgatory, who had come to defend their benefactor, and since he had dared the danger of death to help them, they appeared armed to defend him. When this wonderful event was made public, "it excited in many," as the historian says, "a most pious wish to help the poor souls, who also render assistance in their turn when it is needed."[1] Still more remarkable is what occurred to another devout lover of the holy souls, who used to say the

---

[1] Excitavit in pluribus piisimum affectum opitulandi animabus defunctorum, quæ vicissim subveniunt suffragantibus iu tempore opportuno.

Litany of the Blessed Virgin for them every night before retiring to rest. He had two sworn enemies, who once stole into his room with the intention of putting an end to him; but when they approached the bed of the sleeping man, they could not see him nor find him anywhere, so blinded were they by the poor souls. On another evening, the good man, overpowered by sleep, said only half of his usual Litany, and went to bed; during the night the same assassins came into his room, and found only half a man lying in the bed as if he had been sawn in two; thinking that some one else had killed him, they went away. But when they saw him on the following day make his appearance in the streets as fresh as ever, they could not conceal their astonishment, and told him what had happened to them when they wished to murder him. The good man, till then ignorant of what had occurred, said to them: doubtless I was saved by my devotion to the souls in purgatory, for I pray for them every night; but yesterday evening I said only half my usual Litany, so on that account you saw the half of me lying in bed. They then made friends, and were inflamed with a great desire to help those poor souls who make such a good return for the benefits done them.

Now, my dear brethren, if they are so ready to help miraculously in bodily dangers and necessities those who do them good, how much more care will they not take of the souls and eternal salvation of their benefactors? What will they not do to save from eternal flames those who have saved them from temporal fire? Truly we can have no doubt of this! Witness that wicked young man who, in the year 1620, scandalized the whole city of Rome by his godless life; yet, in the midst of his wickedness, he still kept up a devotion to the poor souls, and used to pray, give alms, and have Masses said for them. This devotion saved the life of his body and of his soul. Hear how wonderfully that happened. One evening, as he was riding alone, he saw the quarters of a murderer who had been executed a short time before hanging on a tree. He stood still and prayed for the departed; and while he was praying, he noticed that the dismembered limbs began to move, came down from the tree, and again formed themselves into an entire body. We can easily imagine the consternation of the young man. The apparition came up to him, caught the horse's bridle, and said to the young man: Dismount quickly; lend me your horse for awhile, and wait

But chie in spirit dangers

here till I come back. So the dead rider went forth, and before he had gone far, the young man heard four shots, and saw the rider fall from his horse as if he were killed; but he got up again, mounted, and brought the animal back to its owner. Did you hear, he said, the report of the shots? They were intended for you. Your enemies were lying in wait for you there, and you would have been lost body and soul. You have to thank your devotion to the souls in purgatory, unworthy as it was, for your escape. Now, go and lead a better life. The young man, filled with amazement and repentance, returned, entered a strict Order, and there lived till his death in the practice of the greatest austerities. O happy soul! what would have become of you if you had not shown that slight charity to the departed?

At the hour of death. My dear brethren, the greatest extremity and danger in which the human soul can be on earth is the last death-struggle, in which hell strains every nerve to prevert the agonizing soul, and to bring it to destruction; but it is in this very extremity that the souls in purgatory are most on the alert to protect and defend their benefactors. Amongst many others whom these souls have helped in their last moments is one mentioned by Cardinal Baronius. He writes that a certain dying man who had a hard struggle at the last hour with the hellish foe, saw the heavens open, and some thousands of soldiers clad in white descend, who comforted him, and assured him that they would stand by him in this dangerous combat. The dying man, full of consolation, asked them who they were. We are souls freed from purgatory by you, they answered; and we have come to repay the benefit we owe you, and to bring you with us to heaven. The dying man then breathed his last with joyous heart and countenance.

After death they pray that their benefactors may be freed from purgatory. Nor are those grateful souls content with this. Even after the death of their benefactors they show their gratitude to them by freeing them sooner from purgatory; according to the wish expressed by that prudent woman, Noemi, in favor of those who are charitable to the dead: "The Lord deal mercifully with you, as you have dealt with the dead."[1] It has often happened that the dead rose out of their graves in the churches and cemeteries, and with many prayers held a sort of funeral procession for some one recently deceased, who had helped them during life. Paula of St. Teresa, a holy Dominican Nun at Naples,

---

[1] Faciat vobiscum Dominus misericordiam, sicut fecistis cum mortuis.—Ruth i. 8.

once saw in ecstasy Our Lord descending into purgatory, and taking out a soul here and there. She asked Him why He selected those souls out of so many, and He said it was because they had been especially charitable to the dead during their lives. Now, He continued, I return like for like, and bring them sooner out of their torments, according to My promise, that the merciful shall find mercy. All that I have just told you, my dear brethren, in a few words, is related in detail by Father Charles Rosignoli in his book: The Wonders of God in the Souls in Purgatory.

From this we can conclude how meritorious are the works of charity that we perform for the departed, and that instead of doing ourselves harm thereby we may rather expect a hundred-fold return from those grateful souls. If there are still some hard hearts that cannot be moved to compassion for them, I certainly cannot promise such people much good fortune in the next life, if, indeed, they will be lucky enough to get to purgatory to satisfy there for their sins; for God Himself says by the Apostle St. James: ''Judgment without mercy to him that hath not done mercy.'' [1] And I might say to them that they will be left in that painful prison till they have paid the last farthing, without help or alleviation, as I have already explained on another occasion. Let us, then, my dear brethren, be more prudent in this matter to our present and future advantage. We shall remain steadfast, then, shall we not? in our former resolution to help the poor souls every day in every possible manner; and if we know not of any soul in particular whom we should pray for, let us, according to a pious custom, appoint certain souls for each day in the week, and offer our good works for them on that day. For instance, to-day for the souls in purgatory who are most dear to the Mother of God; to-morrow for those who have most honored their guardian angels; the day after for those who were devout to St. Joseph; another day for those who reverenced the Blessed Sacrament, or Jesus crucified, and so on. Some keep note-books in which they write down different names of the dead, and whatever name they happen on, they pray for that person, and offer up their devotions for him. Charity is acute, as the saying goes, and if we have a true love for the poor souls, it will suggest to us different ways in which we can help them, and save them from their torments.

Therefore if we seek our own advantage we must be generous to the departed.

---

[1] Judicium sine misericordia illi qui non fecit misericordiam.—Luke ii. 13.

If we show this love to the departed, the words of Noemi shall be verified in us: "The Lord deal mercifully with you, as you have dealt with the dead." Yes, we shall experience that mercy in life in all the dangers and necessities of soul and body; we shall experience it at the end of our lives in our last agony; we shall experience it after this life in purgatory, and, finally, we shall experience it with the blessed souls in heaven. Amen.

The Love of our Neighbor Requires us to Help the Souls in Purgatory: see the first part. Each one of us has Reason to dread Purgatory: see the fifth part. On Generosity to the Living Poor and Needy: see several sermons in the first and second parts.

ON CHARITY TOWARDS ONE'S SELF.

ON HUMILITY.

Subject.

The humble man is great: 1st. before the Lord God in heaven; 2nd. before men on earth.—*Preached on the feast of St. John the Baptist.*

Text.

Erit enim magnus coram Domino.—Luke i. 15.
" For he shall be great before the Lord."

Introduction.

A wonderful thing! God Himself gives testimony of St. John even before he was born into the world, that he would be great before the Lord; and John as soon as he came to the age of reason hid himself in the desert, that no man might know him or esteem him. He did all that lay in his power to make himself small and insignificant, while Christ, on the other hand, spread his name everywhere. The Pharisees asked him once, as they took him to be the Messias, on account of the holiness of his life: " Who art thou?"[1] " Art thou Elias?"[2] And he said: " I am not."[3] Yet the angel Gabriel says of him that " He shall go before Him in the spirit and power of Elias."[4] " Art thou the prophet?"[5] again asked the Pharisees. " And he answered: no."[6] Yet Our Lord says of him: " Yea, I tell you, and more than a prophet."[7] " Art thou the Christ?" asked the Pharisees. What a question, exclaimed John. " And he confessed, and did not deny; and he confessed: " I am not the

---

[1] Tu quis es?—John i. 19.   [2] Elias es tu?—Ibid. 21.   [3] Et dixit; non sum. Ibid. 21.
[4] Ipse præcedet ante illum in spiritu et virtute Eliæ.—Luke i. 17.
[5] Propheta es tu?—John i. 21.   [6] Et respondit: non.—Ibid.
[7] Dico vobis, plus quam prophetam.—Matt. xi. 9.

Christ."[1] Nay, he added that he was not worthy to loose His shoe-latchet: "The latchet of whose shoe I am not worthy to loose;"[2] and Christ calls him the man of whom it is written: "Behold, I send My angel before Thy face, who shall prepare the way before Thee."[3] At last they said to him: "Who art thou? what sayest thou of thyself? He said: I am the voice of one crying in the wilderness."[4] And Christ extols him above all men born of women: "Amen, I say to you: there hath not risen among them that are born of women a greater than John the Baptist."[5] Thus he who humbles himself shall be exalted, and he who lowers himself shall be raised by God. On another occasion, my dear brethren, when speaking of pride, I showed that the proud man who seeks for honor finds none either with God or men, but loses all honor with both; now I say that, on the other hand, the humble man, who flies and contemns worldly honor and praise, receives both, and becomes great before God and men, as I shall now show.

Plan of Discourse.

The humble man is great before the Lord God in heaven; the first and longer part. The humble man is great before men on earth; the second part.

O greatest of mothers and most humble of virgins, since I am now beginning to speak of that virtue that was always most dear to thee, obtain for us from thy beloved Son the grace that our hearts may be inflamed with a love of humility! And do you, holy angels, who could not bear the pride of Lucifer, help us by your intercession!

Virtue alone makes men great in the sight of the Lord God.

It is virtue alone and the state of grace that make a man great and honorable before God. For that sovereign Lord does not regard the person of man. Whether one is great or small, a prince or a peasant, noble or lowly born, beautiful or ugly, learned or ignorant, makes little matter to the Almighty God. These are not the qualities that He looks to, or considers of importance. It is virtue alone that earns His protection, esteem, and good-will, and deserves to be held in honor by Him.

---

[1] Et confessus est, et non negavit; et confessus est, quia non sum ego Christus.—John i. 20.
[2] Cujus ego non sum dignus, ut solvam ejus corrigiam calceamenti.—Ibid. 27.
[3] Ecce ego mittam angelum meum ante faciem tuam, qui præparabit viam tuam ante te.—Mark i. 2.
[4] Quis es? quid dicis de te ipso? Ego vox clamantis in deserto.—John i. 22, 23.
[5] Amen dico vobis, non surrexit inter natos mulierum major Joanne Baptista.—Matt. xi. 11.

Now, it is humility alone that increases and preserves virtue in the soul of man, just as pride is the root of all vice, according to the words of the wise Ecclesiasticus: "Pride is the beginning of all sin."[1] From it come avarice and injustice, since the proud man wishes to be more magnificent than others; anger and hatred if one says a word of contradiction to him; revenge, for he cannot allow the least stain to rest on his honor; obstinacy, since he will not allow himself to be moved to change his opinion, although it may be contrary to truth, lest he should have to confess himself in the wrong; envy, inasmuch as he imagines that his honor is lessened by the exaltation of another; laziness and sloth in the divine service, for he is ashamed of having the name of being pious; nay, even impurity springs from pride, although it is a dishonorable vice, because God, who cannot bear pride, often allows those who think too much of themselves to sink into the depths of shameful sins and thus to dishonor themselves. "Pride is the beginning of all sin."

Just as pride is the root of all vice,

On the other hand, according to the testimony of Holy Writ and of all the Fathers, the beginning, foundation, and root of all virtue is Christian humility. "Humility is the root of all virtue," says St. Bernard.[2] St. Augustine calls it a tower, a bulwark, a castle which protects and defends all the virtues.[3] Nay, he continues, "the whole religion of the Christian consists in humility."[4] Whatever virtue a man has, whatever good he does, is but another aspect of humility. What is faith? Humility of the understanding, which submits and surrenders itself in things that it cannot understand. What is Christian hope? Humility of spirit, by which man, knowing his own weakness and frailty, keeps himself constantly between fear and confidence, relying on the divine mercy. What is the love of our enemies? Humility of the heart, by which we love, and patiently and meekly bear with those whom every inclination of our nature urges us with violence to hate. What is patience in trials? A humbling of one's self, by which man acknowledges that it is right and just for him to submit to the Almighty God, and to bear with resignation the punishments He inflicts, knowing that they are well deserved. Temperance, mortification, penitential works and austerities, what else are they but a humbling of the outward senses, which are thus kept in check that

So humility is the root o all virtue.

[1] Initium omnis peccati est superbia.—Ecclus. x. 13.
[2] Radix omnis virtutis humilitas.
[3] Turris et firmamentum virtutum.
[4] Tota religio Christiani humilitas est.

they may not rise in revolt against the law of God. Even the love of God itself, the queen of all virtues, must have some share of humility, as St. Paul says: "Charity is not puffed-up, is not ambitious." [1]

Not only is humility the foundation of all virtue, but no virtue can subsist when humility is wanting, according to St. Gregory: "he who collects virtues without humility is like one who carries dust in the wind," which is at once blown away. [2] If I see a servant lifting a large chest without any trouble, oh, I think, there is no great treasure in that chest; it is empty and contains nothing but wind; but if it requires the united strength of many to lift it, then I see at once that there must be something in it. If you walk through the fields when the corn is ripe for the harvest, you will see many ears standing straight up, while others are bowed down towards the earth; what is the reason of the difference? They all grow in the same field. Ask the husbandman, and he will tell you; those ears, he will say, that stand up straight we do not like to see, because they contain but little corn, and are only worthless straw; but those that are bent down we like to look at, because they are full of corn and are valuable. The same may be said of a man. If he is bent to earth in inward and outward humility, although we do not see much good in him, yet we can pronounce, without fear of error, that he is rich in virtue, that a great treasure is hidden in his soul. But if he lifts himself on high in his thoughts and behavior, then he is proud and vain; no matter how pious he may seem to be, I still think of him that he is only a man of straw, an empty vessel containing nothing but air, in which there is nothing of value.

All works of devotion and virtue lose the name of devotion and virtue, and become vices, when humility is wanting to them and they proceed from pride. The holy Gospel of Christ preaches fasting and bodily austerites; but if humility does not accompany them, and vainglory has a share in them, then they are mere hypocrisy, which the same Gospel condemns in the Pharisee. The Gospel of Christ preaches almsgiving and the works of mercy; but if they are performed without humility, through vanity, and to gain the esteem of men, then they are condemned in the Scribes. The Gospel of Christ preaches constant prayer

---

[1] Charitas non inflatur, non est ambitiosa.—I. Cor. xiii. 4, 5.

[2] Qui sine humilitate virtutes colligit, in ventum pulverem portat.

but humility must go with it; otherwise it will not justify us, and will be of little or no good to us. Examine all the degrees of holiness: the hermits in the deserts, the confessors of the faith in their penances and austere lives, the martyrs in their torments, the virgins in their angelic chastity, apostolic men in their labors for the honor and glory of God; if one of them is wanting in humility, you can say with certainty that what you admire in him is nothing else but mere vanity, a shadow, a lie, and a deceit.

In a certain place (it is not so long since this occurred) there was Shown by
an example. a person who had gained a great reputation for sanctity on account of her seemingly great austerities and the wonderful miracles she wrought. So great, however, was the number of the latter that it aroused suspicion, and a prudent Father of our Society undertook to examine into the matter, and see whether all was genuine or not. He went to the person, and after a few preliminary remarks said to her: I have heard a great deal of the holy life you lead, and that you even work miracles. Alas, was the answer, how should a poor sinner like me work miracles! So I thought, said the Father; I knew there could be no truth in it; the people are so easily deceived. What? exclaimed the other indignantly; you think the people are deceived in me? what harm do you see in me? and so on. That will do, said the Father; I want no more than that; and he went away. There is no humility there, thought he, and therefore there can be no sanctity; and his judgment was confirmed shortly after, for it was found that the person was a witch, who worked apparent miracles by the help of the devil in order to deceive the people. Where there is no humility there can be no virtue. " Without it," says St. Chrysostom, "we are abominable, wicked, unclean."[1] Therefore he used to say that if he were obliged to choose one of the two, either to take all the vices with humility alone, or all the virtues with pride alone, he would select the former, because with pride he would lose all virtue, but with humility he would soon extirpate all vice.

Consider the Pharisee in the temple; what does he say? He The just become
wicked by
pride, and
the wicked
just by humility. stands before the altar and thanks God that he does not live like the wicked; " he goes through a long list of the good works he is wont to perform; " I fast twice a week, I give tithes to the priests, I share my goods with the poor and give alms." Judg-

---

[1] Sine illa abominabiles, et scelesti, et immundi sumus.

ing by outward appearances, you would say that the man has all the virtues. Now look at the poor wretch, the public sinner, standing behind the door. He has committed all kinds of sins, and made himself notorious by the public scandal he has given. The Son of God looks on both, and when He has considered them attentively, He rejects the Pharisee with all his good works, and receives the public sinner in spite of his vices: "This man went down into his house justified rather than the other."[1] What is the reason of that? "Because," answers St. Chrysostom, "the virtues of the Pharisee were accompanied by pride, and the vices of the publican by humility."[2] If ever there was a wicked man on the face of the earth it was king Achab, of whom we read: "There was not such another as Achab, who was sold to do evil in the sight of the Lord; and he became abominable."[3] Therefore the Lord, being embittered against him, ordered the Prophet Elias to foretell his fate: "In this place shall the dogs lick thy blood: I will bring evil upon thee,"[4] and upon thy children. A severe sentence from the immutable God! And yet what evil happened to Achab? None at all. How was that? "When Achab heard these words, he rent his garments and put hair-cloth upon his flesh, and fasted and slept in sack-cloth, and walked with his head cast down."[5] Just God! where is the execution of the sentence Thou hast pronounced? Ah, Prophet, exclaims the Lord: "Hast thou not seen Achab humbled before Me?" His humility has covered all his crimes. "Therefore, because he hath humbled himself for My sake, I will not bring the evil in his days."[6]

Thus humility makes men great before God.
My dear brethren, the conclusion I draw from this is the following: If virtue alone makes men great and honorable in the sight of God; if humility alone is the foundation and support of all virtues and no virtue can subsist without humility; then it follows necessarily that only he who is humble and despises worldly honors deserves true praise, honor, and esteem from the Almighty God.

It makes us
Besides, what greater honor can there be for a servant than

---

[1] Descendit hic justificatus in domum suam ab illo.—Luke xviii. 14.

[2] Quia omnium virtutum comes fuit superbia ; omnium vitiorum comes fuit humilitas.

[3] Non fuit alter talis, sicut Achab, qui venundatus est ut faceret malum in conspectu Domini, et abominabilis factus est.—III. Kings xxi. 25, 26.

[4] In loco hoc canes lambent sanguinem tuum : inducam super te malum.—Ibid. xix. 21.

[5] Cum audisset Achab sermones istos scidit vestimenta sua, et operuit cilicio carnem suam, jejunavitque et dormivit in sacco, et ambulavit demisso capite.—Ibid. 27.

[6] Quia igitur humiliatus est mei causa, non inducam malum in diebus ejus.—Ibid. 29.

to be in all things like his master? "It is enough for the dis- like to the Son of God
ciple," says Christ, "that he be as his master, and the servant
as his lord."[1] Can a poor mortal be seated on a higher throne
than when he is next to the King of glory, Jesus Christ? But
how can he attain that dignity, if not by humility? This requires no proof; for there never was a man on earth who was so
humble inwardly and outwardly as Jesus Christ, the Son of God.
The Prophet Isaias calls Him: "Despised, and the most abject
of men,"[2] because He behaved as if He were the lowliest of men.
He "emptied Himself," says St. Paul, "taking the form of the
servant."[3]

It is in His humility alone that He invites us to imitate Him: For it is in this virtue alone that He asks us to imitate Him.
"Learn of Me," He says to us all, "because I am meek and
humble of heart."[4] I have created heaven and earth by a word,
and all nature is obedient to My voice; you have seen how I
gave speech to the dumb, sight to the blind, hearing to the deaf,
health to the sick, life to the dead; but it is not miracles that
you must learn of Me. "Learn of Me, because I am meek and
humble of heart;" learn of Me to be humble. You have seen
how temperate I was in eating and drinking, how strict in fasting and watching, how merciful to the poor and needy, how
constant in prayer and meditation, how poor with regard to all
the necessaries of life, how zealous in preaching and converting
sinners, how patient under the bitterest sufferings. These are
indeed virtues to which I have often exhorted you, and of which
I have given you an example; but it is not in those that I
especially wish you to imitate Me; humility is the chief thing
that I recommend you to learn from Me, because I practised it
unceasingly under all circumstances during My whole life. I
have watched, but not always; fasted, but not always; preached,
but not always; I have been humble at all times, in all things, in
all My actions. Examine My whole life, all the words I have
spoken, all the steps I have taken, the signs I have made, My
manner and behavior, My clothing and bedding; all will cry out
to you: "Learn of Me, because I am meek and humble of heart."
This humility of Mine is preached to you by the crib in the stable, the swaddling-clothes that My Mother wrapped Me in, the
workshop in the cottage at Nazareth, the circumcision in the

---

[1] Sufficit discipulo ut sit sicut magister ejus, et servo sicut dominus ejus.—Matt. x. 25.
[2] Despectum et novissimum virorum.—Is. liii. 3.
[3] Semetipsum exinanivit, formam servi accipiens.—Philipp. ii. 7.
[4] Discite a me quia mitis sum et humilis corde.—Matt. xi. 29.

temple, My baptism in the Jordan, the cross on Calvary, the tomb in the garden; all these are preachers that cry out: "Learn of Me, because I am meek and humble of heart." I do not send you to school to the patriarchs and prophets, nor to My apostles and saintly disciples, for you must learn of Me. I Myself, your Master, your Redeemer, your Sovereign God, will be for you the Model of the most complete humility; from Me you must learn how humble you should be. If you have learned that from Me, I require nothing more from you; if you have rightly understood this one lesson, you have grasped all the other virtues with it. It was by this humility that I wished to earn My honor and glory, although it belongs to Me by right. So it is, my dear brethren. "He humbled Himself," says St. Paul, "becoming obedient unto death; even to the death of the cross. For which cause God also hath exalted Him, and hath given Him a name which is above all names: that in the name of Jesus every knee should bow of those that are in heaven, on earth, and under the earth." [1] "So that," exclaims St. Augustine in astonishment, "to this are reduced all the treasures of knowledge and wisdom hidden in Thee: that we should learn it of Thee as a great thing that Thou art meek and humble of heart? O divine Saviour! is it, then, such a great thing to be lowly and humble before the world, that it cannot be learned, unless from Thee, who art so great? Truly such is the case!" [2] It is only from the example of such a great Master that we can learn voluntary humility of the heart. Therefore He says: "Learn of Me, because I am meek and humble of heart." "How great, then," exclaims St. Gregory, "must not the virtue of humility be, since He who is great beyond comparison became little even to His passion, for the sake of teaching that alone!" [3] O humility, cries out St. Bernard, how precious thou seemest in my sight, after such a glorious example! Since Jesus has sanctified thee in His own person, should I be ashamed of thee? Could there be any higher degree of honor for me than to be humble, as my God was?

God has an   Finally, can I gain the favor and esteem of any mightier lord

---

[1] Humiliavit semetipsum, factus obediens usque ad mortem : mortem autem crucis. Propter quod et Deus exaltavit illum, et donavit illi nomen quod est super omne nomen: ut in nomine Jesu omne genu flectatur cœlestium, terrestrium et infernorum.—Philipp. ii. 8–10.

[2] Huccine redacti sunt omnes thesauri sapientiæ et scientiæ absconditi in te, ut hoc pro magno discamus a te, quoniam mitis es et humilis corde? Ita magnum est esse parvulum, ut nisi a te, qui tam magnus es, disci omnino non posset? Ita plane.

[3] Quanta ergo humilitatis virtus est, propter quam solam edocendam, is, qui sine æstimatione magnus est, usque ad passionem factus est parvus ?—S. Greg. Moral. l. 34, c. 18.

than the God of heaven and earth? But I am infallibly assured
of it, if I am humble. He " looketh on the low, " says the holy
Prophet David of Him, "and the high He knoweth afar off. " [1]
His eyes are on the humble; the deep valleys are filled with His
treasures, but the lofty mountains He looks at only from a distance. " God resisteth the proud, " says St. James, " and giveth grace to the humble; " [2] it is for the latter alone that He
keeps all His favors. " Every one that exalteth himself," says
Our Lord, " shall be humbled, and He that humbleth himself
shall be exalted." [3] " Whosoever therefore shall humble himself
as this little child, he is the greater in the kingdom of heaven." [4]
He tells us by the Prophet Isaias that He dwells in the humble:
" Thus saith the High and the Eminent that inhabiteth eternity;
and His name is Holy, who dwelleth in the high and holy place,
and with a contrite and humble spirit, and to revive the heart
of the contrite." [5] In the Book of Ecclesiasticus He says that
He will stamp His divine mark on the heart of the humble.
Amongst the many virtues by which David won the heart of God
humility is specially mentioned: " See my humiliation. " [6]
Mary herself, the most holy and at the same time most humble
Mother of God, gives testimony to the great pleasure God had in
her humility: " Because He hath regarded the humility of His
handmaid." [7] The praise given Him by the humble is most dear
to Him; therefore they are specially invited to praise Him: " O ye
holy and humble of heart, bless the Lord: praise and exalt Him
above all forever." [8] He comforts the humble: " Who comforteth
the humble." [9] He wishes us to do good to the humble: " Do good
to the humble." [10] He threatens those who are violent and unjust
to the humble: " Woe to them that do violence to the cause of the
lowly of My people!" [11] " Lord, I am not worthy," [12] said the hum-

especial pleasure in and esteem for the humble man.

---

[1] Humilia respicit, et alta a longe cognoscit.—Ps. cxxxvii. 6.

[2] Deus superbis resistit, humilibus autem dat gratiam.—James iv. 6.

[3] Omnis qui se exaltat, humiliabitur, et qui se humiliat, exaltabitur.—Luke xviii. 14.

[4] Quicumque ergo humiliaverit se sicut parvulus iste, hic est major in regno cœlorum.
—Matt. xviii. 4.

[5] Haec dicit Excelsus et Sublimis, habitans æternitatem, et sanctum nomen ejus in ex-
celso et in sancto habitans, et cum contrito et humili spiritu, ut vivificet cor contritorum.
—Is. lvii. 15.

[6] Vide humilitatem meam.—Ps. ix. 14.

[7] Quia respexit humilitatem ancillæ suæ.—Luke i. 48.

[8] Benedicite sancti et humiles corde Domino : laudate et super-exaltate eum in sæcula.
—Dan. iii. 87.

[9] Qui consolatur humiles.—II. Cor. vii. 6.

[10] Benefac humili.—Ecclus. xii. 6.

[11] Væ. .. et vim facerent causæ humilium populi mei.—Is. x. 1, 2.

[12] Domine, non sum dignus.—Matt. viii. 8.

ble centurion, and on account of those very words he was held in higher esteem than all the high-priests and princes of the Jews. "The latchet of whose shoe I am not worthy to loose," said St. John the Baptist; on account of that humility Christ bent down before him, that he might baptize Him. "Depart from me, for I am a sinful man, O Lord," [1] said St. Peter; and on account of that humility he was made the foundation of the Church. "I am not worthy to be called an apostle," [2] says St. Paul; and that very humility made him one of the greatest of the apostles. "He that humbleth himself shall be exalted." Hear this, ye proud ones! how long will you run after empty air, without gaining anything? Why do you work so hard for empty honor and esteem of men on earth? Do you wish to mount up high? Then be humble, and you will gain true honor and esteem with God. "Be small in your own eyes, that you may be great in the sight of God," [3] says St. Augustine. Yet you still hanker after honor and glory before men; despise all honor then, and be humble; for humility brings true praise and honor, and makes us great before men on earth, as I shall briefly show in the

Second Part.

Humility also makes us great before men.

You might think that I am contradicting myself when I say that humility is the road to honor and praise before the world; for how can I ascend to the top of a high tower, if I do nothing but always sink down deeper and deeper? Can I ever hope to become rich, if I throw away all my money, and trample it under foot? Will I ever reach the town, if I run away from it as fast as my feet can carry me? Shall I be able to walk in the bright light of day, if I always seek the darkness, and blow every light out? Now, what else does the truly humble Christian do but fly the praise and esteem of men; conceal from them his virtues and every praiseworthy quality he has; nourish a vile opinion of himself, and behave outwardly with a lowly Christian modesty; despise all that is great in the opinion of the world and readily bear all evil talk, abuse, shame, and everything that can make him contemptible in the eyes of the world; be friendly with simple, common, and lowly people, as well as with those of a higher station; and submit himself and serve others whenever he can? But that is to fly honors, to crawl down from the tower,

[1] Exi a me, quia homo peccator sum Domine.—Luke v. 8.
[2] Non sum dignus vocari apostolus.—I. Cor. xv. 9.
[3] Esto parvulus in oculis tuis, ut sis magnus in oculis Dei.

to reject praise, and, as it were, to hide one's self in a dark hole after having blown out the light? And can that be a means of gaining honor and glory before men? There is not a doubt of it, my dear brethren. It seems incomprehensible to the children of the world, but it is true nevertheless; there is no more certain way to honor and glory, even before men, than Christian humility.

For as there is nothing more intolerable than to see a man having a high opinion of and extolling himself, so there is nothing more pleasing and agreeable than to see one who is truly humble. According to the old saying, we must praise virtue, at least in our hearts, even in our enemies. The humble man may seem vile and lowly outwardly; yet every one must secretly admire and esteem him, and therein consists true honor. "If you wish to be glorious," says St. Chrysostom, "do not desire glory. All honor him who does not seek honors; but they despise the ambitious man." [1] "By flying glory she merited it," says St. Jerome of Paula; "for it follows humility like a shadow." [2] Run towards the sun as fast as you can, says this holy doctor, the shadow of your body will follow just as quickly, and the farther you go the longer will your shadow become. The humble man flies honors; he does not wish for them; but whether he likes or not, glory comes after him like a shadow, and the more he tries to humble himself, the more does the shadow increase in the esteem and admiration of men.

For the humble man is as agreeable to others as the proud man is intolerable.

This is what the all-wise decrees of the Almighty effect in the minds of men, to the praise and glory of humility and self-abasement, as the Blessed Virgin sang in the Canticle: "He hath scattered the proud in the conceit of their heart. He hath put down the mighty from their seat, and hath exalted the humble. Because He hath regarded the humility of His handmaid: for behold from henceforth all generations shall call me blessed." [3] Because, on the one side, the man who humbles himself, and for God's sake renounces all praise and glory, gives praise, honor and glory to God alone; and, on the other, God has promised to honor those who honor Him; so that even against their will He exalts His servants, as almost all the saints found by experience, and the more they try to hide their virtues, the more does He bring

The more the humble man flies honor, the more does God exalt him. Shown from Scripture.

---

[1] Si vis esse gloriosus, noli gloriam concupiscere. Honores non quærentem, omnes honorant; ambientem vero aspernantur.

[2] Fugiendo gloriam merebatur, quæ humilitatem quasi umbra sequitur.—S. Hieron. Ep. xxvii. ad Eustod.

[3] Dispersit superbos mente cordis sui; deposuit potentes de sede, et exaltavit humiles. Quia respexit humilitatem ancillæ suæ; ecce enim ex hoc beatam me dicent omnes generationes.—Luke i. 51. 52, 48.

them forward before the world.   Abraham was humble, so that when God spoke to him in a friendly manner he hardly dared to keep up the conversation, and at last acknowledging his nothingness, he said: " I will speak to my Lord, whereas I am dust and ashes." [1]   And what did he merit thereby?   That glorious promise: " In thy seed shall all the nations of the earth be blessed." [2] Thou lookest on thyself as but dust and ashes; but I will give thee an undying name throughout the whole world.   " I will bless thee, and I will multiply thy seed as the stars of heaven, and as the sand that is by the sea-shore: thy seed shall possess the gates of their enemies." [3]   Moses was humble; the daughter of Pharao had adopted him and caused him to be brought up in the royal court; but he put aside all the trappings of grandeur, trampled them under foot, ran away from the palace and hid himself amongst the sheep, which he guarded forty years, as a lowly shepherd, according to the learned Philo.   And how he afterwards resisted the honor offered him by God, and besought the Lord not to make him the leader of His people!   " Who am I that I should bring forth the children of Israel out of Egypt?" [4]   " I beseech Thee, Lord, I am not eloquent from yesterday and the day before: and since Thou hast spoken to Thy servant, I have more impediment and slowness of tongue." [5]   But the more he shunned honors and tried to avoid the dignity offered him, the more did God exalt him: " Behold, I have appointed thee the God of Pharao." [6]   You wish, said the Lord, to avoid earthly honors, and now I will make you greater than a king; I now appoint you as a God over Pharao.

Confirmed by an example.   But why should I delay to seek for proofs of this from the Old Law, since the humility of Christians has always shone brightly enough?   Which of the hermits despised honors more than Antony, who did not think himself worthy of being in the company of the lowliest peasant of Egypt?   And yet this humility so gained the heart of the great emperor Constantine that he thought it a privilege to be able to correspond with Antony. Which of the founders of Orders was more humble than St.

---

[1] Loquar ad Dominum meum, cum sim pulvis et cinis.—Gen. xviii. 27.

[2] Benedicentur in semine tuo omnes gentes terræ.—Ibid. xxii. 18.

[3] Benedicam tibi, et multiplicabo semen tuum sicut stellas cœli, et velut arenam quæ est in littore maris : possidebit semen tuum portas inimicorum suorum.—Ibid. 17.

[4] Quis sum ego ut educam filios Israel de Egypto ?—Exod. iii. 11.

[5] Obsecro, Domine, non sum eloquens ab heri et nudiustertius ; et ex quo locutus es ad servum tuum, impeditioris et tardioris, linguæ sum.—Ibid. iv. 10.

[6] Ecce, constitui te Deum Pharaonis.—Ibid. vii. 1.

Francis of Assisi, who did not hesitate to ask the beggars in the streets to give him the crusts that they did not care to eat? And yet, besides the esteem in which he was held by the rest of the world, even the Sultan of Turkey admired his humility and held him in high honor. Which of the holy matrons abased herself more than Melania, one of the richest and noblest ladies of Rome, who, after she had distributed two millions amongst the poor, made a pilgrimage to Jerusalem, and came back to Rome clad in torn garments, and sitting on an ass, without saddle or bridle, that she might make herself ridiculous? But the more she sought shame and contempt, the more honor was shown her against her will; for, surprised at her exceedingly humble appearance, the whole Roman senate was moved to go out and meet her with great pomp, and welcome her back; an honor that would never have fallen to her lot had she retained her former wealth and dignity. Hear what St. Jerome says of Pammachius, a Roman senator, who, wishing to be unknown to the world, and to serve God with his whole heart, laid aside his dignity and splendor, and put on a poor habit in a convent. When Pammachius was a senator, says the Saint, his name was known in Rome, but not much outside of it; he then surpassed many in dignity, but there were also many who surpassed him; " but now all the Churches of Christ speak of Pammachius," although he wishes to be unknown; " and the world wonders at the poor man, whom it did not know when he was rich." [1] So true is it that glory follows the humble man like his shadow.

Yes, truly, it is to no purpose, holy servants of God, that you try to hide your virtues and holy lives! Go, if you wish, and conceal yourselves in the gloomiest deserts, in the caves of the earth, where no human eye can see you; yet the honor that you shun will follow you over mountain and valley; that God who exalts the humble will, as He often has done, betray you; He will send princes and kings and whole nations in procession to you, to seek you out in your solitudes and bend the knee before you. God will make your name great and honored in the world, either by angels, or by miracles, or by the demons themselves. We see and have experience of this daily. The poor monk, who has left the world and its vanities, whenever he leaves his cell to appear in humble guise in the streets, does he not receive more

And by daily experience.

---

[1] At nunc omnes Christi Ecclesiæ Pammachium loquuntur; miratur orbis pauperem quem hucusque divitem nesciebat.

tokens of respect and honor, from great and small, than if he had continued in his former position? Thus does the Almighty wish to honor humility. Nay, even pride must put on the garb of humility to save itself from being shamed, and to receive some honor. How many a one speaks slightingly of himself and his actions, only that he may get more praise and glory from others? How many a one undertakes the meanest offices, only that he may be exalted? "Oh, what a glorious thing is humility!" exclaims St. Bernard; "for even pride has to use it as a cloak, lest itself should be put to shame," [1] and to gain a little honor. But since such humility is only false and merely apparent, so the honor that it gains does not last long, is false, and vanishes like smoke before the wind. Evidently, then, true Christian humility is the only sure way to gain honor before God and man.

Conclusion and resolution to practise true humility.

Rejoice, then, ye lowly and poor, who can say with David: "It is good for me that Thou hast humbled me." [2] Happy and thrice happy those who can say of themselves with the same Prophet: "Lord, my heart is not puffed up, nor are my eyes haughty." [3] Thou, O God, knowest all things; Thou provest the reins and the heart; Thou knowest that I do not wish to exalt myself: that I do not arrogate to myself any of those things that Thy mercy has deigned to bestow on me, Thy unworthy servant; that I do not seek the praise or esteem of men, and that my only desire is to please Thee. "I will make myself meaner than I have done, and I will be little in my own eyes," [4] which, knowing my own weakness, I will keep a check on. I will be humble before Thee, whom I will always honor and adore in all places. I will be humble in the eyes of men, to whose judgment I will readily submit for Thy sake. I will be humble in my own thoughts, acknowledging that I am in truth nothing of myself, that I have nothing and can do nothing, and that on account of my sins I deserve shame and contempt. I will be humble in my words, which shall never boast of anything but the humility of my Lord Jesus Christ. I will be humble in my works, of which I desire to leave all the honor and glory to Thee; humble in my dress and behavior, which shall be of such a kind as to show that I make profession of the Gospel of the most humble Jesus; humble in my heart, with which I shall constantly sigh and pray to

[1] Gloriosa res humilitas, qua ipsa quoque superbia palliare se appetit, ne vilescat.
[2] Bonum mihi quia humiliasti me.—Ps. cxviii. 71.
[3] Domine, non est exaltatum cor meum, neque elati sunt oculi mei.—Ibid. cxxx. 1.
[4] Vilior fiam plus quam factus sum ; et ero humilis in oculis meis.—II. Kings vi. 22.

Thee: Lord, give to me, increase and preserve in me, true humility, that I may attain the honor Thou hast promised the humble; not honor before the world, which I do not desire, but honor with Thee in heaven. Amen.

Another Introduction to the same Sermon for the feast of the Visitation of the Blessed Virgin.

Text.

Intravit in domum Zachariæ et salutavit Elizabeth.—Luke i. 40.

"She entered into the house of Zachary and saluted Elizabeth."

Introduction.

Two things I find most admirable in the Visitation of the Blessed Virgin; one is her wonderful humility, the other, the exaltation that immediately followed it. Humility, inasmuch as she deigned to go on foot to visit her cousin St. Elizabeth, and to act as the servant of a creature while she was actually carrying the Most High in her bosom. Exaltation, inasmuch as this very humility was made the occasion of her greatest praise and glory before God and men. She was so anxious to keep secret the mystery of the Incarnation that was accomplished in her womb, that she did not reveal it even to her spouse St. Joseph; and now all is openly declared. "Blessed art thou amongst women," cried out Elizabeth, enlightened by the Holy Ghost, "and blessed is the fruit of thy womb. And whence is this to me, that the mother of my Lord should come to me?" Thus the Blessed Virgin herself, seeing that her dignity was made known, was obliged to declare it with her own lips: "He hath regarded the humility of His handmaid," said she; "He that is mighty hath done great things to me." So it is, my dear brethren; he that humbles himself shall be exalted. On another occasion, when speaking of pride, I showed that, etc.—*Continues as above.*

On the Humility of Mary, see the sixth part.

ON PATIENCE IN ADVERSITY.

ON THE FIRST ADVANTAGE OF ADVERSITY.

Subject.

The trials of this life draw away our hearts from the love of the world and of creatures; therefore they are good and very useful to us.—*Preached on the feast of St. Andrew, Apostle.*

Text.

O bona crux!—St. Andrew, Apostle.

"O good cross!"

Introduction.

Never have I heard a poor criminal crying out on his way to execution: Oh, thou goodly gallows, for which I have longed so eagerly! Oh, thou desirable wheel, that I have so wished for! Oh, thou sword, that I have desired for such a long time, that thou mightest cut off my head! But often have I heard them say quite the contrary. Accursed theft! Unlucky murder! Had I never thought of you, I should not now be in this miserable state! But to-day I hear one who is being led to execution crying out with joy and exultation: "O good cross, long desired, earnestly loved, constantly sought for, and now at last granted to my earnest desires, receive me!" But holy St. Andrew, what art thou saying? How is it possible to love and esteem an instrument of punishment, that is wont to inspire only horror and dread? Wilt thou not lose thy life on the cross, as well as the criminals who are condemned to that mode of death? Truly, my dear brethren, St. Andrew had nothing but death to expect; but he himself explains the reason of his joy and gladness. "Receive me from men, and restore me to my Master;" for by the cross he was to be taken away from amongst men, and to be enabled to rejoin his beloved Master,

Jesus Christ. Therefore he exclaimed: "O good cross! desired, loved, and sought for!" This teaches us, my dear brethren, the advantage of the cross of adversity and temporal suffering in this life. We often complain of it, and look on it as a sign that God is angry with us; but how well the Lord means with us when He visits us with the cross! His desire is to draw our hearts with violence to Himself, to impel us to seek Him, to love Him, and one day to possess Him forever; and He can find no better means of accomplishing that than the cross and adversity. Why so? Because our heart must be drawn away from the love of the world and of creatures before it can be drawn to the love of God; since, according to the testimony of holy Writ, it is impossible for the love of God and the love of the world to exist together. "If any man love the world, the charity of the Father is not in him."[1] Now, the effect of crosses and trials is to draw our hearts from the love of the world and of creatures, and to fill them with the love of God and of heavenly things. To-day I consider the first point.

Plan of Discourse.

The trials of this life draw away our hearts from the love of the world and of creatures; therefore, they are good and very useful for us. The fruit of the consideration of this truth should be patient resignation of our will to the will of God in all crosses and trials.

Do Thou, O Almighty God, help us thereto by Thy grace, which we beg of Thee through the merits of Mary and of our holy guardian angels, and then we shall think and say in adversity with Thy holy apostle: "O good cross!"

The greatest and heaviest stumbling-block that we find on the way to heaven, the strongest wind that blows us off the path of justice and Christian holiness, is the inordinate love of the world and an inclination towards creatures. Nay, according to the assurance of the Infallible Truth, it is impossible for the love of God and the love of the world to be united in the same heart, as we have seen already in the introduction: "If any man love the world, the charity of the Father is not in him." No one can be at the same time a lover of the world and a lover of his heavenly Father. Why? Because God and the world are two masters that constantly strive against each

Nothing distracts the heart from heavenly things more than the love of creatures and of the world.

---

[1] Si quis diligit mundum, non est charitas Patris in eo.—I. John ii. 15.

other, so that one cannot serve them both together; for if he loves the one he must hate the other; if he obeys the one he must despise the law of the other. The human heart is far too small and narrow to harbor two such masters at once; God wishes to have it altogether for Himself, nor can He brook a rival. And what else is the origin of all sins and vices, if not a love of created things, that is contrary to God? What is pride? An inordinate love and desire of honors and the esteem of men. What is avarice? An inordinate love of temporal goods and riches. What is impurity? An inordinate love of carnal pleasures. What is gluttony? An inordinate love of the delights of the palate. What is anger and jealousy? Sorrow at an offence, or at another's prosperity, springing from self-love. What is laziness and sloth? A love of one's own comfort. In a word, if you get rid of this love, you shut the door against all vices at once.

Adversity makes us disgusted with the world and creatures.

Now, just as this love, which is so disastrous to justice, is supported and increased by prosperity, so it is lessened, extinguished, and even turned into hatred and dislike, by adversity. Here is the proof of that. To make a thing disgusting and hateful to a man all you need do is to show that it is contrary to his interests, that it will disappoint him, that he will fare badly with it. What forced from the Israelites those bitter sighs and prayers which they sent forth to heaven, desiring to leave Egypt? They had already been for long years in that country without expressing any such desire. What was the cause of the sudden dislike they felt to dwell any longer among the Egyptians? Whence came that wish to leave the country in which they were born and bred? Ah, times had changed for them. Under the government of Joseph, the best and most fruitful parts of the land were theirs, and they possessed their goods in peace; no one then thought of the land that God had promised them; Egypt was good enough for them, and they were quite satisfied to remain there. But when they were oppressed, deprived of their goods, and treated as vile slaves; when they had to work hard, and be content with little food and drink; when they felt the blows of the lash on their shoulders, and had to drag stones and bricks like beasts of burden; then there was an end of their satisfaction; they grew tired of Egypt; the bare name of it was enough for them, and day and

night they sent forth sighs and lamentations. " The children
of Israel groaning, cried out because of the works." [1]

My dear brethren, we must acknowledge that this world is not
the land in which we have to dwell forever; that the goods it
can offer us are but transitory, uncertain, deceitful, and vain;
that there is another far happier land reserved for us in heaven,
towards which, as towards our last end, all our sighs, desires,
thoughts, words, works, and chief, nay, only care, should be
directed. We all believe this and acknowledge it; no one doubts
it. But no matter how firmly we are convinced of this truth,
it seldom makes such a deep impression, or has such great effect
on our minds, as to wean our hearts altogether from earthly
things, as long as we are prosperous and can enjoy creature comforts in abundance. For earthly things are able, by their presence and seeming goodness and sweetness, to flatter our senses,
befool our reason, and attract our inordinate inclinations; so
that we often spend the whole day thinking of present
things, while we hardly bestow a thought on eternal and heavenly
things. In prosperity we are like the young man in the Gospel
of St. Matthew, who, with a great desire of saving his soul,
came to Our Lord and said to Him: " Good Master, what good
shall I do that I may have life everlasting?" Are you in earnest
about it? asked Our Lord. Then if so: " If thou wilt be perfect, go sell what thou hast, and give to the poor, . . . and come
follow Me." [2] How did the young man receive this advice?
" And when the young man had heard this word, he went away
sad." [3] He turned away from Our Lord, and went away sorrowful. What was the cause of his sorrow? He should have joyfully
received the advice given him, for his wish was to hear what he
had to do to gain eternal life. Our Lord Himself had told him;
why, then, did he go away sad? Ah, " he had great possessions." [4] Such is the reason assigned by the Gospel. If, like
the apostles, he had nothing to leave but a boat and a few torn
nets, he would easily have made up his mind to abandon all, and
follow Christ; but alas! his heart was taken up with the great
possessions, and he thought it would be too difficult for him to
renounce them; he valued his riches more than perfection, more

*In prosperi-
ty it is very
difficult to
keep the
heart free
from creat-
ures. Shown
from Script-
ure.*

[1] Ingemiscentes filii Israel propter opera vociferati sunt.—Exod. ii. 23.
[2] Magister bone, quid boni faciam ut habeam vitam æternam? Si vis perfectus esse,
vade, vende quæ habes, et da pauperibus, et veni, sequere me.—Matt. xix. 16, 21.
[3] Cum audisset autem adolescens verbum, abiit tristis.—Ibid. 22.
[4] Erat enim habens multas possessiones.—Ibid.

than Christ, more than the kingdom of heaven. "He went away sad;" he returned to the world. Alas! said Our Lord thereupon: "Amen, I say to you: That a rich man shall hardly enter into the kingdom of heaven. And again I say to you: It is easier for a camel to pass through the eye of a needle than for a rich man to enter into the kingdom of heaven."[1] The rich man who lives in prosperity and fixes his heart on worldly goods shall with difficulty save his soul. In a word, my dear brethren, we love what pleases us, become attached to it, and can hardly do without it.

Sickness teaches us the misery of this life. The cross, adversity, want of temporal goods and all worldly consolation, is the teacher best able to impress this lesson deeply on our minds. The cross shows us by actual experience how little we can depend on the world, how despicable and wearisome a thing is this vale of tears. The cross teaches and forces us to wean our hearts from what is transitory, and to seek elsewhere our consolation and the object of our love. What could not be done in many years by the faith, clear though it is; nor by the divine lights and inspirations, striking though they may be; nor by sermons and exhortations, impressive though they be; that is effected by the cross in a few hours. For instance, we are told frequently that health is an inconstant and uncertain good, that we must never depend on it; that the strongest giant can be completely disabled by the slightest accident; that our lives are confined to the space of a few uncertain years; that we are always hurrying on to death, which can seize hold of us at the Creator's least sign; that after death we shall have no time to work out our salvation, and therefore that we should not defer for a moment true repentance and amendment of life, and the zealous practice of virtue, or else we should be guilty of the greatest presumption; but what effect have all those truths on us? Not much; as long as we are young and strong, and feel no pain or ache, those thoughts are put aside as troublesome; we pay no attention to them; we live as carelessly (and often, too, in sin and vice), as if we were never to die. But if a fever or a bad cold attacks us, or a violent fit of pain keeps us in bed, our thoughts soon begin to get more serious; there is an end of our laughter; there are no more amusements, dances, or entertainments; the taste gets bad, the other senses lose their power of

[1] Amen dico vobis: Quia dives difficile intrabit in regnum cœlorum. Et iterum dico vobis: Facilius est camelum per foramen acus transire, quam divitem intrare in regnum cœlorum.—Matt. xxiii. 24.

perception. These painful lessons teach us much that we were unwilling to understand before; they show us that the world, fair as it seems, is bitter and insipid; and we learn at last that the words of St. Paul hold good for us too: "It is appointed unto men once to die;"[1] we humbly acknowledge with the formerly proud Antiochus: "It is just to be subject to God."[2] See what the cross of sickness is able to do!

We are all taught not to put our trust in men, for whose sake, alas that I should have to say it! virtue and justice are so often neglected nowadays. This lesson is utterly disregarded by many, as long as they are prosperous. But if by a decree of God's providence the wheel of fortune is turned the other way; if instead of the favor and esteem we formerly enjoyed we are looked at askance; if we are unjustly deprived of our office or employment; if our friends prove false to us and do not keep their word; that cross at once opens our eyes, and we begin to see clearly what we before had only a dim perception of: namely, that we were building on sand when we placed the favor of men as the foundation of our happiness. Adversity teaches us the truth preached by the Prophet Jeremias: "Cursed be the man that trusteth in man, and maketh flesh his arm."[3]

By humiliations we learn not to trust in men.

Long ago, O holy Apostle St. Paul, thou didst warn preachers in the person of Thy disciple Timothy: "Charge the rich of this world not to be high-minded, nor to trust in the uncertainty of riches;" advise and admonish them not to extol themselves on account of their wealth, not to fix their heart on it, and to use it moderately, as if they had it not, "to do good, to be rich in good works, to give easily," thus using their wealth to their own advantage; "to lay up in store for themselves a good foundation against the time to come, that they may lay hold on the true life."[4] But alas, holy Apostle, all our preaching is of no avail in many instances, as long as those people are at peace in the midst of their riches, as long as their business prospers and their income increases daily! But let some cross come upon them, a heavy loss, an unsuccessful lawsuit or bankruptcy, or unforeseen misfortune caused by war or unfruitful seasons; that

Misfortun teaches us the vanity of worldly goods.

---

[1] Statutum est hominibus semel mori.—Heb. ix. 27.

[2] Justum est subditum esse Deo.—II. Mach. ix. 12.

[3] Maledictus homo qui confidit in homine, et ponit carnem brachium suum.—Jer. xvii. 5.

[4] Divitibus hujus sæculi præcipe, non sublime sapere, neque sperare in incerto divitiarum ; bene agere, divites fieri in bonis operibus, facile tribuere ; thesaurizare sibi fundamentum bonum in futurum, ut apprehendant veram vitam.—I. Tim. vi. 17-19.

will teach them better and quicker, and will soon bring them to see and humbly to acknowledge that everything in the world is vanity and folly, and that they should fix their hopes on God alone.

Death teaches us the inconstancy of human love and friendship.

To no purpose frequently is one exhorted to renounce his love and attachment, which is inordinate and often dangerous, nay, unlawful, for this or that person, whom he calls his joy, his comfort, as long as she is in his sight, and he can see her whenever he wishes. Heaven with its delights, God with all His perfections, must give way to this love; hell with its torments, terrible as they are, is often not able to influence him to put a check on his inordinate desires; nothing can help him, but some cross, which will break asunder the bonds of this attachment. If power is given to death to act, and he comes and tears away the beloved person, and with her all the comfort of the survivor, the sorrow and anguish thus caused will soon teach him the uncertainty of human friendship; the worms that gnaw away the object of his inordinate love will remind him that there is another beauty, another infinite good, on which we can and should fix our hearts firmly.

Deformity teaches us how perishable is earthly beauty.

What foolish vanity, what a number of sins in one's self and others, what evident danger of eternal damnation, comes from so-called beauty, especially in the female sex! Those who have it will spend hours before the glass, tricking themselves out, making idols of themselves to attract admiration, and thus adorned with the utmost extravagance, they appear in public, often, too, in the churches, not to adore God, but to please the eyes of men and win their hearts; such is the chief object of their thoughts, desires, cares, and labors. How can God enlighten such infatuated people, and enable them to see their vanity and misery? The eyes that admire them, the bows that are made to them, the compliments paid them in company, only make them more proud and foolish. What can be done for them, then? I know, O my God! "Fill their faces with shame;" as the Prophet David desires of Thee; "and they shall seek Thy name, O Lord." [1] That will bring them to a knowledge of their folly; when they see that their beauty is transitory, they will be converted and seek Thy name, they will honor and adore Thee. An ulcer or a sore that disfigures their faces (and no more disagreeable cross can be inflicted on them) will be more than enough to

---

[1] Imple facies eorum ignominia, et quærent nomen tuum Domine.—Ps. lxxxii. 17.

humble those dissolute children of the world, and teach them that their beauty is only a flower that blooms in the morning and in the evening fades away. A cross of that kind will remove forever the stumbling block that was the occasion of so many sins.

Finally, not to go more into detail, we hear often enough and believe and experience that there is no true joy to be found in created things; that no man ever had perfect satisfaction in this world, nor real, unadulterated pleasure; and still the saying is true: "the world is bitter, but it is loved." [1] More, sometimes, even than God and heaven, especially by those who are in prosperous circumstances, and who thus do not perceive so keenly the bitterness of the world. How can those people be undeceived? All that is necessary is the cross, adversity: that alone is able to embitter the sweets of life and to make them disagreeable and insipid. A profligate, drunken, avaricious, jealous, or hard-hearted husband; a peevish, ill-tempered, quarrelsome, idle wife, or one who is addicted to gambling; an undutiful, deformed, or sickly child; a troublesome neighbor; a false friend; obstinate servants; stern masters; any one of these and similar domestic crosses is enough to poison the whole day, and to turn into bitterness all the delights that such people seek. I ask your own experience if such is not the case. Thus it is adversity that teaches us to know the world and to hate it. With reason does St. Augustine say: "Adversity forces on the unwilling, enlightens the ignorant, protects the weak, excites the sluggish, humbles the proud, cleanses the penitent, crowns the innocent." [2]

Every tribulation disgusts us with the world.

And this, my dear brethren, is the reason why the good God visits even His chosen, pious, just, and beloved children with all kinds of crosses and trials in this life. He wishes thereby to make them disgusted with the world, that they may know that it is not a place for them to enjoy themselves in, and that by withdrawing their hearts and affections from it they may not be dragged down to eternal ruin with it. In this way He acts not unlike the peacock. Naturalists tell us that when that bird sees its mate always hatching its eggs, and so wearing itself away almost to death, he throws the eggs out of the nest, and breaks them in pieces to put a stop to the hatching. In the same way God sees how parents in their inordinate attachment to their

This is what God has in view when He visits His faithful servants with trials. Shown by a simile.

[1] Amarus est mundus et diligitur.

[2] Compellit nolentem erudit, ignorantem, protegit infirmantem, excitat torpentem, humiliat superbientem, purgat pœnitentem, coronat innocentem.—S. Aug. in Ps. 60.

children neglect their own soul, strain every nerve to enrich their children, allow them all liberty in dress, conversation, idleness, and company; neglect the sacraments on account of the pressure of business, and thus expose themselves and their children to the danger of eternal damnation. He sees how married people, in their inordinate fondness for each other, grow cold in their desires for heavenly things; He sees a man brooding over his gold like a hen on her nest, or else using his wealth for the purposes of vain show and ostentation. He sees how this man will turn the favor of his master, or the esteem he enjoys among men, to a bad use, by making it serve his pride and vanity, or by using it to oppress others. He sees how that girl, infatuated with her own good looks, does all she can to attract attention. Now, in what way does the all-wise God act, if He loves those people and desires to have them with Himself in heaven? I must lose no time! He thinks; the eggs must be broken at once! Go, He says to death; take away that son, that daughter, that husband, that wife, although in the bloom of youth; poverty, misfortune, disgrace, illness, do you go to those others; take from them the wealth they enjoy, their dangerous consolations, their vain beauty, their honor and good name, so that they may learn to despise earthly things, and may not run the risk of losing heaven by a too great attachment to them.

Proved by examples. To say nothing of countless other examples, thus did God act to that English nobleman named Thomas, as Bartholi writes. He was dancing once at the court of Queen Elizabeth, and exhibited such skill and agility that the queen publicly congratulated him, and invited him to come again and dance with herself. Thomas, as we can easily imagine, was nearly beside himself with joy, and put forth his best efforts, so as to surpass his first performance and please the queen still more. But in the middle of the dance, through a dispensation of divine Providence, he became giddy and fell to the ground at full length, to the great amusement of the by-standers. The queen kicked him with her foot: " Get up, you ox," she exclaimed. The apparently unfortunate, but really on account of his accident most fortunate Thomas, thus publicly disgraced, knew not where to turn, or what to do. " Thus passes the glory of the world," [1] thought he to himself. Good, then! Since the

---

[1] Sic transit gloria mundi.

world despises me, I will have nothing more to do with it. He
became a convert to the Catholic faith, and entered our Society,
in which he became a brave champion of the true religion and
of the honor of God, until his death. The annals of the
Dominican Order relate a similar occurence that happened to
the Blessed Peter Gonzalvo, who at first was a secular priest, but
led a very worldly, free, and easy life, not at all suitable to his
state. On one occasion, as he was riding on a magnificent horse
in the streets of Piacenza, dressed far too splendidly for a priest,
the horse stumbled and threw its rider into a dung-heap, so that
he was covered with filth from head to foot. Angry with himself, he cried out, " Serves you right, Peter, you have got what you
deserved!"[1] Such is the reward the world gives its servants. You
have deceived me, O world, but it is for the first and last time!
And thereupon he left everything, entered religion, and became
one of the shining lights of the Dominican Order.

In the same way did God act with that court lady in France, Other ex-
who, through a desire of appearing beautiful, was not content amples.
with what nature had given her, but had recourse to art to em-
bellish herself. As she was of a dark complexion, she used to
paint her face daily with rouge, in order the better to attract
admiration. But her trick was discovered to her great shame,
and also to her eternal salvation. Being in company on one occasion, she engaged in a game of forfeits. She lost, and as a
punishment was obliged at once to wash her face. What could
she do? She was compelled to pay the forfeit; and as the
washing went on, the fresh colors gradually disappeared from
her face and left her own dark complexion exposed to view. She
could not stand being thus put to shame; holding her hands before her face, she ran out of the house to the first convent that
came in her way, where she did penance for her vanity, and
having learned to despise the world, spent the remainder of her
life in the service of God. St. Gregory of Tours writes of St.
Monagundis, that she would never have become a saint if God
had not broken the eggs with which she had become infatuated.
She had two daughters of great beauty, in whom she placed all
her love and all her hope; she lived with them in a very vain
style, quite according to the perverse world, and hardly bestowed
a thought on God during the day. What did the Lord do? He
took away the two daughters one after the other by death, in the

---

[1] Habes Petre, quæ digne commeruisti.

bloom of their youth. The mother, almost in despair, did nothing but weep and lament, and had a mind to starve herself to death, so as to put an end to her sorrow. But after she had calmed down a little, what am I thinking about? she said to herself. Will all my weeping restore my children to life? And what is the good of resisting the Almighty God? Why do I not rather strike out some better plan? God has taken from me all my consolation and joy on this earth; He may as well, then, have myself too into the bargain! No sooner said than done. She entered religion, shut herself up in a poor cell, and became a great saint. None of these people, my dear brethren, would have been so fortunate had it not been for the crosses that God sent them.

Hence God means well with us in chastising us, and we should accept the cross gratefully.

Truly the inventions of the providence and goodness of God, with regard to His elect, are most advantageous to us, although they are often hidden from our understanding, and are disagreeable to our sensuality! If crosses and trials, my dear brethren, were good for no other purpose but that which we have now been considering, should not that alone be enough to induce us to bear our daily contradictions with patience, to receive them from the hands of God with full submission to His will, and to accept them readily, nay, with thanksgiving? For, what greater favor can God bestow on man, who is created not for this world, but for heaven as his last end, than to draw away his heart from the love of the world and its dangerous goods, which constitute the greatest obstacle to his salvation? Why, then, do we sometimes complain that God deals harshly with us, as if He were an unmerciful step-father who is careless of our interests, or who rejoices in our misfortunes through hatred of us? Oh, no, the crosses He sends are all proofs of His love! If He were really angry with us, if He were minded to punish us in His wrath, and reject us from His favor, He would deal quite differently with us; He would not deign to inflict fatherly chastisement on us, but would allow us to run on after our own desires, like so many sinners and worldlings, whom He gives over to their evil inclinations, whose false repose He does not disturb, and whom He permits to go asleep in their vices without awakening them by tribulations.

Conclusion, and resignation to the

Truly, O Lord, I now know how well Thou didst mean with me in sending me the cross! "O thou good cross!" I exclaim with Thy apostle St. Andrew, who loved it so much; what a good thing it is for me that Thou now and then visitest me with trials God
sends us. tribulation! Even the disgust that the miserable world has inspired me with; the experience that I am here in a vale of tears, and that I cannot enjoy true happiness in this life; the sighs with which I have often complained of my lot; even those things are the fruit of the crosses that Thou hast sent me, and if I had been free from them, who knows what a foolish, worldly life I should have led? Now I praise and bless Thee and the merciful decrees by which Thou hast saved me from the world and its vanities, from sin and its dangers. And in future I will leave myself and all that I have completely to Thy providence; I will accept every cross from Thee with patience and thanksgiving. If my inordinate inclinations should attach themselves to any creature to the danger of my soul, oh, then I beg of Thee now to make that creature disgusting to me, even against my obstinate will, so that my whole heart, separated from all that is outside of Thee, may find in Thee, my only sovereign Good, true rest and peace here and in eternity. Amen.

Another Introduction to the same sermon, for the twentieth Sunday after Pentecost.

Text.

Dicit ad eum regulus: Domine, descende, priusquam moriatur filius meus.—John iv. 49.

"The ruler saith to Him: Lord, come down before that my son die."

Introduction.

Thus necessity can drive even great men to God! When did the ruler learn to ask after Christ, to go to Him, and to beseech Him so humbly? Was it not when his son grew sick and was at the point of death? There can be no doubt that he had heard long before of Our Lord's miracles, and yet the thought never occurred to him of going to see Christ, much less of speaking to Him. Nay, perhaps like Herod and the princes and priests, he would have looked on Our Lord as a seditious man, a deceiver of the people, and would have laughed at and persecuted Him, if he had not been in need of His help. The illness and imminent death of his son opened the man's eyes, and at length brought him to the true faith. There we see, my dear brethren, the use of crosses and trials, etc.—*Continues as above.*

SIXTY-THIRD SERMON.

ON THE SECOND ADVANTAGE OF ADVERSITY.

Subject.

The trials of this life draw our hearts to the love of God and heaven; therefore they must be very good for us.—*Preached on the feast of All Saints.*

Text.

Gaudete et exultate, quoniam merces vestra copiosa est in cœlis.—Matt. v. 12.

" Be glad and rejoice, for your reward is very great in heaven."

Introduction.

There are six wonderful statements in to-day's Gospel: " Blessed are the poor" and humble, " Blessed are they that mourn" and weep, " Blessed are they that hunger and thirst; " " Blessed are they that suffer persecution;" " Blessed are they who are reviled by men," and spoken ill of. Who could believe that? The whole world cries *No* to it! Poverty, humiliation, hunger, thirst, persecution, contempt, the loss of reputation; these things are all hateful, and signify calamities that are to be shunned as the greatest evils. And yet it is Jesus Christ, the Infallible Truth, who pronounces happy those who suffer such things for His sake. The world must be wrong, then, in its judgment, when it pities those who suffer. Yes, you exclaim; such men will be happy in heaven, because by patiently bearing their crosses they lead holy and pious lives here on earth. To be holy here and happy hereafter is only a natural consequence that no one can find fault with, and it is consistent with the divine promises. And so it is in reality, my dear brethren. But should not that consideration suffice to induce us to bear with patience and readiness the crosses that God sends us? Meanwhile they are also a source of great happiness to us even in this life. How so? Because although we cannot enjoy the happiness of the elect in heaven here on earth, yet trials incline our hearts and minds to God and heavenly things, so that we can thus have a foretaste of heaven, and can with good reason say to the afflicted:

"Be glad and rejoice," and accept your cross with resignation from the hands of God. I have already shown that adversity withdraws the heart from the world and the love of creatures. Now, when that much is done, what must follow, since the human heart is obliged to fix itself on something, if not that it gives its love to God and heaven? And this is the subject of this sermon.

Plan of Discourse.

The trials of this life draw our hearts to the love of God and heaven; therefore they must be very good for us.

May this consideration be a source of comfort to all sorrowing Christians, O Comforter of the afflicted; a grace that we expect from Thee through the intercession of Mary, of the holy angels, and of all the elect of God in heaven.

If I could see into your minds now, I should in all probability find many of them filled with wonder. What? you ask; can crosses, trials, and adversity win our hearts, and induce us to love Him who thus tries us? That is a fine means of gaining our affections! Strange indeed that any one should try to make us his friends by treating us to kicks and blows, to sorrow and suffering! Show a stick to a dog, a rod to a child, and you need not attempt to strike; the mere sight is enough to make both run away and hide, and be very careful not to show themselves for a long time. Show the child a cake or a lump of sugar, and it will come to you at once and stretch out its hand for it with an eager laugh. Throw to the dog a piece of meat, and you will see how he will fawn on you. If God is in earnest about gaining our love, and keeping us in His service, He should do it with caresses, and not with sour looks; He should please us with gifts and favors, and not chastise us so unmercifully with stripes, misery, and trials. *(Prosperity rarely turns men's hearts to God.)*

Ah, is that your idea, my dear brethren? You are quite wrong then! Far different is the judgment of the Almighty in the matter. Hear what He says by the Prophet Jeremias: "I will give My fear in their heart, that they may not revolt from Me." [1] As if the Lord wished to say: what do you think I should do with this people to make them faithful to Me, so that they will never abandon Me? Shall I always show them a smiling countenance? Shall I fill them with consolation, joy, and pleasure? But if I did that, they would soon turn their backs on Me, they would *(But rather averts them from Him.)*

[1] Timorem meum dabo in corde eorum, ut non recedant a me.—Jerem. xxxii. 40.

never think of Me, for they would imagine that they had enough and were not in need of Me. I have already had experience of that in My chosen people the Jews. I miraculously surrounded them with blessings and benefits; but what thanks did they give Me for them? "He grew fat, and thick, and gross." And having been thus satiated with prosperity, what did he do? " He kicked; he forsook God who made him, and departed from God his Saviour. They provoked Him by strange gods, and stirred Him up to anger with their abominations. They sacrificed to devils and not to God."[1]

Trials force us to seek and love God. Shown by examples from the Old Testament.

What shall I do, then, to make men come to Me, to keep them always in My love and friendship? I know what to do; "I will give My fear in their heart;" I will trouble them; I will fill their lives with crosses, and embitter them with trials; then they will run to Me for help; and to whom else should they run, since I alone can help them? "In their affliction they will rise early to Me;"[2] they will hasten to Me and speak Me fairly; but if I allow things to go well with them, they will remain in their beds till late in the day. Consider what happened to Manasses, king of Juda. A party of Assyrians hid themselves in ambush, at a time when there was no war or hostility between him and the Assyrians and Chaldeans; he was captured and led off prisoner. Nothing was farther from his thoughts than to be thus taken, surrounded, and led off to Babylon. Nor did his captors show him the respect usually exhibited to persons of his condition, when they are in the hands of their enemies. His prison was not a palace, nor a decent house, nor even a habitable room; he was kept like one of the lowest herd, bound hand and foot with iron chains, so that he complained to God of his miserable state. I am bound with iron fetters, he said; and cannot raise my head, nor lift my eyes to heaven; hardly am I able to draw my breath. Nay, he found it difficult to bend his knee to earth, and therefore he begged of God to accept the humiliation of his heart. What a great misfortune, you will think, for such a mighty king, reared in luxury, feared by so many people, honored by so many courtiers, waited on by so many servants, to fall suddenly into such depths of misery! And yet Manasses himself looked on this misfortune as a special mark of the divine favor in his regard.

[1] Incrassatus, impinguatus, dilatatus ; recalcitravit ; dereliquit Deum factorem suum, et recessit a Deo salutari suo. Provocaverunt eum in diis alienis, et in abominationibus ad iracundiam concitaverunt. Immolaverunt dæmoniis, et non Deo.—Deut. xxxii. 15-17.

[2] In tribulatione sua mane consurgent ad me.—Osee vi. 1.

While he was prosperous, he was the most wicked and impious of kings; he had filled the whole kingdom with scandals and idolatry, profaned the temple, and shed the blood of the innocent inhabitants of Jerusalem in torrents; in a word, he was hastening to eternal ruin as fast as he could go. But in the midst of his wicked career God threw those fetters round him, and held him fast. His painful prison became an oratory for him; he entered it an abandoned sinner, but came out a contrite penitent. After his imprisonment, which did not last very long, he governed his kingdom in a holy manner, and is now living forever in heaven; while if that misfortune had not happened to him, he would probably be in hell. Such, too, was the effect of adversity on king Nabuchodonosor. He had conquered many countries and kingdoms; he was lord of almost countless peoples, and ruler of half the world; but in a moment he was hurled from the pinnacle of prosperity into the depths of wretchedness. A sudden rebellion on the part of his subjects filled him with fear to such an extent that he voluntarily went into banishment, hid himself in the depths of a gloomy forest, and there spent seven years without house, or home, or bed, exposed to wind and rain and snow, without a friend or a servant, or any one to help and console him. No other food had he during that time but herbs and bitter roots; he had not even the heart to emerge out of his solitude and show himself again amongst men. He became so emaciated and savage-looking that he lost even the semblance of a human being. At last after the lapse of seven years his eyes were opened, and he was reconciled to God and to his subjects at the same time. " Now at the end of the days, I Nabuchodonosor lifted up my eyes to heaven, and my sense was restored to me: and I blessed the Most High, and I praised and glorified Him that liveth forever." [1] Nor does he grow tired praising God, but protests that he will ever glorify the King of heaven; for He is just in His judgments and can humble those that extol themselves: " Therefore I Nabuchodonosor do now praise, and magnify, and glorify the King of heaven: because all His works are true, and His ways judgments, and them that walk in pride He is able to abase." [2] Thus openly and candidly did he write and speak, because he

---

[1] Igitur post finem dierum ego Nabuchodonosor oculos meos ad cœlum levavi, et sensus meus redditus est mihi, et Altissimo benedixi, et viventem in sempiternum laudavi et glorificavi.—Dan. iv. 31.

[2] Nunc igitur ego Nabuchodonosor laudo et magnifico, et glorifico Regem cœli : quia omnia opera e us vera et viæ ejus judicia, et gradientes in super biapotest humiliare.—Ibid. 34.

acknowledged that his seven years' humiliation had cured him of his pride and brought him true happiness; for many Fathers of the Church hold that he remained steadfast after his conversion, and died a happy death.

From the New Testament.
Our Lord and Saviour Jesus Christ during the three last years of His life on earth always had a crowd of people following Him to listen to His instructions. What sort of people were they? We do not read that there were amongst them any of the rich, the high-priests or the chief men, who lived in abundance and luxury. Who were they then? The poor, whom He fed by miraculously multiplying bread, the blind, the lame, the paralytic, lepers, those possessed by the devil, who came to Him, " to be healed of their diseases," [1] as St. Luke says. Truly the centurion came, believed, and was converted with his whole house; the ruler also spoke to and adored Him, as we saw in the Gospel of last Sunday; but under what circumstances? The servant of the former was sick, and the son of the latter; if necessity had not driven them to Our Lord, the chances are they would never have thought of Him. The disciples themselves, while the sea was calm, made no appeal to their Divine Master, though He was in the boat with them; but when the storm arose and the sea grew angry; when " a great tempest arose in the sea, so that the boat was covered with waves," [2] and they were in danger of drowning, oh, then they knew how to cry out to Him for help! " His disciples came to Him, and awaked Him, saying: Lord, save us, we perish." [3] Thus, says St. Gregory, " the evils that assail us compel us to fly to God." [4] For it is under the pressure of calamity that we find out how much we are in need of the divine assistance.

Explained by a simile.
Horace describes a man named Opimius, who was very rich, but, as is often the case with such people, very avaricious and miserly. He fell into such a deep lethargy that he could not be awakened; his friends and acquaintances did their best for him; they pulled his hair, his beard, his ears; they shook him from side to side; but all to no purpose; the sick man could not be aroused. A doctor was called in who was an experienced man and knew well the character of his patient; what did he do? He had a table brought to the bedside, and emptied on it some bags of money,

---

[1] Ut sanarentur a languoribus suis.—Luke vi. 18.
[2] Motus magnus factus est in mari, ita ut navicula operiretur fluctibus.—Matt. viii. 24.
[3] Accesserunt ad eum discipuli ejus, et suscitaverunt eum dicentes: Domine, salva nos, perimus.—Ibid. 25.
[4] Mala quae nos premunt, ad Deum ire compellunt.

which he shook about, making a great noise. Opimius! he then cried out, what are you about? Do you not hear what they are doing with your money? Your heirs are dividing it already among themselves; if you do not awake quickly, you will not have anything left. At once Opimius opened his eyes; what! he exclaimed; what are you doing with my money, rascals that you are! Away with you! I am not dead yet! Right, said the doctor; keep awake if you wish to live, and look after your money. Thus was the sick man roused out of his lethargy, and freed from the danger of death, solely by the anxiety he felt about his money.

Alas! my dear brethren, how many Christians there are who resemble this Opimius; who are sunk deep in the lethargy of sin, and hardly ever raise their eyes to God and heaven; who live careless of their salvation, and almost dead to all feeling of devotion, and the love of God and heavenly things! The good God, like an experienced physician, uses every means to arouse them, but, generally speaking, to no purpose as long as they are in prosperity. He is compelled then to take from them whatever has attracted their heart and their love, and has caused them to sink into that spiritual lethargy; He deprives them of the creature, the friend, the money or property that they love, and by causing them to feel the pressure of sorrow and calamity. He awakens them with violence, forces them to open their eyes, and to pay more attention to their soul's welfare. "The evils that assail us compel us to fly to God." *[margin: Many would not seek God, if He left them without trials.]*

Absalom made use of the same means on one occasion. He had already sent messenger after messenger to Joab inviting him to come; but the latter did not deign even to notice the invitations. Absalom was indignant at being thus insulted; wait, he exclaimed, I will teach you that I am your master! Go, said he to his servants; "you know the field of Joab near my field, that hath a crop of barley: go now and set it on fire." The servants at once did as they had been ordered: "So the servants of Absalom set the corn on fire." When Joab heard that, says the Scripture; "he arose and came to Absalom to his house." [1] Why, asks St. Eucherius, did he not come before, when he was invited in such a friendly manner? Now he is forced to come against his will, after losing his crops. "Because the pressure of the loss he had sustained was more power- *[margin: Shown by an example, after the manner of a simile.]*

[1] Scitis agrum Joab juxta agrum meum, habentem messem hordei; ite igitur, et succendite eum igni. Succenderunt ergo servi Absalom segetem igni. Surrexit et venit ad Absalom in domum.—II. Kings xiv. 30, 31.

ful over him than the courteous invitation he had received before."[1] And it is characteristic of men that they are more easily drawn to the service and love of God by chastisements than by gifts and blessings. How often does not the Lord invite us by inspirations, and by sending us His servants, preachers and priests, to warn us? But what does He gain thereby? We act as if we heard Him not; where our treasure is, there is our heart, our love. So that the fire of tribulation must do what good works failed to effect.

Confirmed by experience.

And to speak the truth about the matter, my dear brethren, when do we think least of God? When do we feel least inclination for devotion and the love of heavenly things? Is it not when all our earthly desires are satisfied? When the good God sends fruitful seasons, and blesses our labors, is it not then often, nay, generally, the case that the tavern is visited more frequently than the church; that more time is spent in gambling than in hearing sermons and attending devotions? When are idleness, pride, extravagance in dress, prodigality, dangerous meetings, convivial excesses, drunkenness, and impurity, most in vogue? Is it not when we seem to be too well endowed with the goods of this world? And during that time preaching, exhortations, prayers, and threats are of no avail. Take, O Lord, the fire, the rod in Thy hand; "fill their faces with shame," as the Prophet says, and there will soon be an end to their wantonness; suffering will compel them to turn to Thee: "And they shall seek Thy name, O Lord! Let them know that the Lord is Thy name; Thou alone art the Most High over all the earth,"[2] whom we must always love, honor, and fear. So it is. If there is a dearth of provisions; if excessive drought or rain ruins the crops; if there is danger of pestilence; if we or those belonging to us are in danger of death; in a word, when calamity, sufferings, and trials are at our doors; then it is, O Lord, that we seek Thy name; then they who have never learned to read know how to pray; then candles are offered, vows made and alms given; then there is no end of processions, fasting, confessions and Communions; then, at least in outward appearance, men are humble, chaste, meek, and pious; then, O Lord, they seek Thee, they love, honor, and fear Thee! Never yet have I heard of a sick man, who,

---

[1] Nisi quia efficacior fuit ad trahendum damni pressura, quam urbana Absalonis supplicatio.

[2] Imple facies eorum ignominia; et quærent nomen tuum, Domine. Et cognoscant quia nomen tibi Dominus: tu solus altissimus in omni terra.—Ps. lxxxii. 17, 19.

having been pious before his illness, was drawn away from the love and service of God by ill health; but many have I seen who promised mountains in the way of repentance and good resolutions; who sent forth to God the most beautiful sighs of contrition; who were firmly determined to amend their lives if they were restored to health; only let me get well, they exclaimed, and see if I do not make a better use of the precious time given me, and pay more attention to my soul, be more zealous in prayer and exercises of devotion.—things that they never dreamt of while they were in good health and that they will never perhaps think of again, in spite of their fine resolutions, if they recover. " The evils that assail us compel us to fly to God." It is the cross, adversity, that forces us to go to Him, thus verifying the words of the Prophet Baruch: " The soul that is sorrowful for the greatness of evil she hath done, and goeth bowed down, and feeble, and the eyes that fail, and the hungry soul giveth glory and justice to Thee the Lord." [1]

This causes me all the less astonishment, because man is forced *Heaven is gained in many way* by a natural impulse to seek for happiness, and he cannot live without consolation; therefore, since he cannot find happiness or consolation in tribulations and adversity on earth, he must look for it in heaven, and, whether he wishes or not, he is compelled to appeal to God, to serve Him in the hope of finding comfort somewhere, if not in this life, at least in the next. Thus, as St. Bernard says, God draws us to Himself violently by means of trials, and brings us, as it were, against our will, at least at first, to heaven. For, as that holy doctor writes, there are many kinds of people chosen for heaven; " some carry it away by violence, others buy it, others steal it, others are forced to enter it." [2] The first, like soldiers, lay siege to heaven, and they are the voluntarily poor, who freely give up everything and live austere lives in the constant practice of mortification, self-denial and penance. Others, like merchants, purchase heaven, so to say; and they are the merciful, of whom the Gospel speaks, who, by giving alms, make friends and intercessors for themselves, who will obtain for them from God the grace to live piously and to be received into eternal tabernacles. The third, like thieves in the night, steal heaven away, so that no one notices them. Who are they? They are the humble of heart, who live quietly

---

[1] Anima quæ tristis est summagnitudine mali, et incedit curva et infirma, et oculi deficientes, et anima esuriens, dat tibi gloriam et justitiam Domino.—Bar. ii. 18.

[2] Alii violenter rapiunt, alii mercantur, alii furantur, alii ad illud compelluntur.

at home, and conceal their virtues and good works from the eyes of the world. We see nothing remarkable in them outwardly, but in the sight of God they are very holy.

Most people are forced to enter it by crosses and trials. Lastly, the fourth class, which is the most numerous, consists of those who enter the kingdom of God simply because they are forced to do so. Of these the Gospel speaks in the parable of the master of the house, who said to his servant: "Go out quickly into the streets and lanes of the city, and bring in hither the poor and the feeble and the blind and the lame, and compel them to come in, that my house may be filled."[1] They are, says St. Gregory, those whom God visits here below with all sorts of trials, with poverty, humiliation, sorrow, trouble, abandonment, sickness, and persecutions, by which sinners who have left Him are forced to return to Him, and just souls are urged to continue to serve Him faithfully. "They who, broken down by the trials of life, return to the love of God," says the saint, "and who are thus drawn away from the desires of this world, are they not compelled to enter?"[2] Thus, since they can find nothing in the world to love or enjoy, and as they bear their crosses with Christian patience and a good intention for God's sake, although at first they were dissatisfied with them, they are, as it were, forced by violence to enter heaven. When David was hiding in the cave at Odollam many joined him; but who were they? They were all people who were in difficulties, as the Scripture says: "And all that were in distress, and oppressed with debt, and under affliction of mind, gathered themselves unto him."[3] We can see with our own eyes that the greater number of those who often go to church, to confession and Communion, and who pray longer and more zealously, are people who are in trouble and humbled either through poverty or persecution, or illness, or some other misfortune, as it is called in the world, although in reality such crosses are rather to be looked on as benefits from God. And they who are thus driven by their miseries and sufferings to the church, to the holy sacraments and to prayer, what great merit do they not gain for eternal glory by their devotions? And how much do they not increase those merits every day? "By affliction,"

---

[1] Exi cito in plateas et vicos civitatis, et pauperes ac debiles, et coecos et claudos introduc huc; et compelle intrare, ut impleatur domus mea.—Luke xiv. 21, 23.

[2] Qui hujusmodi aversi tatibus fracti ad Dei amorem redeunt, atque a prasentis vitæ desideriis corriguntur; quid isti nisi ut intrent, compelluntur?

[3] Et convenerunt ad eum omnes qui erant in angustia constituti et oppressi ære alieno, et amaro animo.—I. Kings xxii. 2.

says St. Gregory, "we lose earthly things; but by bearing our affliction humbly we multiply our heavenly gifts."[1] Such, too, is the opinion of St. Jerome: "The more we are afflicted in this life by persecutions, poverty, the power of our enemies, or the sufferings of sickness, the greater will be our reward in the next life after the resurrection."[2]

These people seem to me, to express my thoughts clearly on the matter, like a bird imprisoned in a cage, that has to sing to please its owner. If you have caught a beautiful bird that you wish to keep, what do you do? You shut all the doors and windows, that it may not escape; but you are not content with that, for it may still fly away if the door is incautiously opened. Therefore you cut its wings, and to teach it to obey you, you give it no food for a time until hunger forces it to sing, and to fly on your hand, begging food from you. In the same way does God act with many in this life. "My delight," He says, "is to be with the children of men."[3] My joy is to speak to them often, and cultivate their friendship on earth; My still greater joy and most ardent desire is to have them with Me in heaven. Now, when He has caught souls by His grace and brought them to His friendship, to protect them from the many dangers to which He sees them exposed, to keep them faithful in His service, and to prevent them from flying away from Him and falling into the talons of the hellish vulture, He closes all the doors on them; some He shuts up in a room by illness, weakness, or pain; He cuts the wings of others, that is, He allows them to be put to shame, to be disgraced, to be persecuted, so that they may have no wish to be proud or haughty; He cuts off the abundance of earthly goods by losses and misfortune, that they may not set their heart on such things; He puts an end to their dangerous love of a creature, by death and the sorrow it causes, so that they may learn to raise their hearts to heavenly goods. Others He deprives of their nourishment by poverty and secret want, and the withdrawal of all earthly consolation, that they may be compelled to fly to His fatherly arms as the only resource left them, and by prayers and sighs to make known to Him their wants and implore His help, keeping their eyes con-

(margin note) Hence God sends trials to those whom He wishes to bring to heaven. Shown by a simile.

[1] Afflicti terrena perdimus, sed afflictionem humiliter sustinentes, cœlestia multiplicamus. —S. Greg. in Moral.

[2] Quanto in hoc sæculo persecutionibus, paupertate, inimicorum potentia, vel morborum crudelitate fuerimus afflicti; tanto post resurrectionem in futuro majora præmia consequemur.—S. Hieron. Ep. ad. Cypr.

[3] Deliciæ meæ esse cum filiis hominum.—Prov. viii. 31.

stantly fixed on Him, until at length, being comforted by His heavenly consolations, they may be fully resigned to His will, with the assured hope of rejoicing with Him forever in heaven, where He has eternal joys in reserve for His dear children.

Confirmed by examples.   St. Paul was a bird of that kind, caught and imprisoned by God. Wearied by countless persecutions and calamities, tired of earthly things, he used constantly to raise his thoughts to God, and sing in joyful tones: "Our conversation is in heaven." [1] Ignatius, our holy Founder, was a bird of that kind. Never perhaps would he have thought of uniting himself to God so fervently, if the Lord had not clipped his wings, when he was filled with ideas of worldly glory as an officer at Pampeluna, by causing him to be confined to bed by a wound. Then by reading the Lives of the Saints he made a beginning of that life which was destined to become so perfect, and a source of so much honor and glory to God. His favorite exclamation was: "Ah, how vile the earth seems to me when I look up to heaven!" [2] Another bird of the kind, that was caught and kept in close confinement, was that celebrated Spanish hero, Gonzalvo by name, of whom Nieremberg writes. He had reached the summit of earthly ambition, and was held in the utmost esteem by his sovereign, but through excessive ambition and too much confidence in the support of his soldiers, he rose up in rebellion against his lawful king. His soul would have been lost forever if God had not clipped his wings; his army was completely routed in battle, and he himself was forced to fly, disguised as a peasant. He wandered about for a long time in this lamentable condition, in hourly fear of being captured, and at last found refuge in a cave in a remote desert. Here, deprived of all human consolation, he devoted himself altogether to God, whom he served faithfully for many years, leading a most austere life, until his zeal for the divine honor drove him out into the surrounding country, where he preached and worked many miracles; and at last he ended a holy life by a happy death while waiting on the sick in a hospital. A bird of that kind was the holy hermit Leopardus, as St. Gregory of Tours writes. He was married, and lived in the greatest abundance, but being suddenly reduced to the utmost poverty, he stole one night into his brother's house to seek consolation from him; but by divine permission his brother, instead of helping, turned him away with harsh and abusive words. Leopardus, thus

[1] Nostra conversatio in cœlis est.—Philipp. iii. 20.
[2] Quam sordet mihi terra, dum cœlum aspicio.

humbled and abandoned, and quite worn out and hungry,
crawled into a peasant's barn for shelter. Here, in the height
of his temporal affliction, he found the beginning of his eternal happiness. "O my soul," he said to himself, "what art
thou doing? How long wilt thou still hesitate? Dost thou
not see what the world is, and how transitory and deceitful its
goods and pleasures are? Wait no longer, then; embrace with
all thy mind the most sweet yoke of Christ!" Full of this resolution, he went at day-break into solitude, where, unknown to
the world, he led a holy and penitential life. From all this we
may see how true are the words of St. Augustine: "Man knows
that God is a physican, and that tribulation is a medicine to
save our souls, not a punishment to destroy them."[1]

O sorely tried, and yet just Christian! You who have
hitherto been kept within the limits of the commandments of
God like the bird in its cage; you think and say to yourself
sometimes, with a sort of indignant astonishment: I abstain as
well as I can from grievous sins; I am humble, chaste, temperate
enough; I am not particularly addicted to pride and vanity; I
pray earnestly and frequently; why, then, have I to bear such
severe trials in spite of my innocence? Should not the God of
mercy at last put an end to my trouble, and free me from the
miseries I have been so long suffering? Ah, my good friend, be
not astonished, and much less should you lose heart; for your
goodness is the reason why God does not free you from your
cross, and why He has sent it to you. It is on account of the
cross that you keep from grievous sin, that you are humble,
chaste, and temperate, that you are fervent in prayer. If you
had nothing to bear, you would not long be in the grace of God:
if He had not clipped your wings, and shut you up in a cage,
but left the door open to you for all sorts of sensual comforts
and enjoyments, oh, then you would have escaped from His
hand long ago! And how far you would have wandered from
God and heaven! In how many occasions and dangers of
grievous sin you would have fallen! You would have taken
flight where, alas, most people congregate, that is to the broad
road of pleasure, to the gates of death, to eternal ruin! You
do not think of that now; but what you now fail to see you
will understand clearly enough at the end of the world, on that

Marginal note: Therefore we should accept the cross with gratitude.

[1] Intelligit homo medicum esse Deum, et tribulationem medicamentum esse ad salutem,
non pœnam ad damnationem.—S. Aug. in Ps. 29.

great day when all shall be disclosed. That is the day for which the Lord is waiting, to explain to you and me and all men the hidden designs of His providence, and how He brings His elect so wonderfully and surely to heaven by the way of the cross, when it would be impossible to bring them there by any other way. Then you will thank and bless your God a thousand times for that which now seems to give you reason for complaint. Then you will acknowledge that to be a sign of predestination, nay the greatest of all benefits, which the world looks on as a token of harshness, forgetfulness, rejection on the part of God. Therefore be satisfied with God as long as He is satisfied with you, and do now what you will wish to have done when you know better. Be contented with the cross which your heavenly Father has laid on your shoulders; take it willingly from His hand, and thank Him for it in the assured hope that it will be the means of making your salvation all the more certain. Let the children of the world plume themselves on their prosperity, despise you and reproach you, as his friends did the patient Job. Let them say to you: O poor fool, "where is thy God?"[1] Where is your consolation? Where is He whom you have so long served? What else have you from Him but suffering and misery? Say to them by way of answer: therefore do I know that God is with me, and that I am in His grace; therefore I am assured that He will bring me to heaven; my crosses and trials are a sure sign of His good will towards me, and of my predestination.

Conclusion and resolution to bear any trial.

Yes, O Lord, so it is; I acknowledge the truth of this, and therefore in future I will submit with more patience and readiness to all trials and adversities which Thou wilt be pleased to send me! The world is not worth loving; endless thanks be again to Thee for having made it bitter to me! Thou, my God, art the only true, constant, infinitely perfect Good; to Thee, then, shall belong all my love, my heart, and my will; to be and remain always with Thee is my only and most earnest desire and firm resolution. If I cannot be with Thee unless I have to bear crosses and trials, according to Thy good will, O Lord! then I beg of Thee, do not free me from this abandonment, persecution, trouble, or sickness until the hour of my death! Only grant me patience to carry this heavy cross manfully, and to be with Thee here by Thy grace and friendship, and hereafter in Thy glory. Amen.

[1] Ubi est Deus tuus?—Ps. xli. 4.

Another Introduction to the same sermon for the twenty-first Sunday after Pentecost.

Text.

Procidens autem servus ille, orabat eum.—Matt. xviii. 26.
" But that servant falling down, besought him."

Introduction.

Alas! that unhappy servant must have thought, what shall I do? All that I possess is to be taken from me; my house, my wife and children are to be sold, and I myself must go with them into slavery! What am I to do? I must lose no time; I must humble myself, and falling down at my master's feet, beg of him to forgive me. " But that servant falling down, besought him, saying: Have patience with me, and I will pay thee all." Mark there again, my dear brethren, what necessity is able to effect, and how powerful is the influence that trials have over us even . nowadays. I have already shown that they draw away our hearts from the love of the world and creatures, etc.—*Continues as above.*

SIXTY-FOURTH SERMON.

ON CONSOLATION IN ADVERSITY.

Subject.

Patience in adversity, penance and mortification of the senses, bring to the servant of God in this life a supernatural joy, and also a natural joy.—*Preached on the third Sunday after Easter.*

Text.

Tristitia vestra vertetur in gaudium.—John xvi. 20.
" Your sorrow shall be turned into joy."

Introduction.

Hard words those: " You shall lament and weep," My dear disciples, My faithful servants! But at the same time how great the consolation! " Your sorrow shall be turned into joy," therefore be not disturbed, nor frightened at the thought of the sorrow. Hear this, pious Christians, who now live in trials and adversity, resigned to the will of God! Be comforted! your sorrow shall be turned into joy! Hear this, pious Christians, who now mortify your senses by voluntary penances and austerities! Only continue as you have begun; your severity towards yourselves, your present sufferings, shall be turned into joy! Yes, you say to yourselves; such we hope will be the case in the next life, in the glorious resurrection, as we have heard already; but that is still a long way off, and we must have a good deal of patience till it comes. What? How can you speak like that? Do you not know that it is only a little while compared with eternity? Yet if that little while seems too long to you, then I say to you: not only shall your sorrow be turned into the eternal joys of the next life, but also in this life you shall have joy in return for your sorrow, as I now proceed to prove.

Plan of Discourse.

Patience in adversity, penance, and mortification of the senses, bring joy to the servant of God in this life; such is the whole subject. They bring a supernatural joy, as we shall see in the first part; a natural joy, as we shall see in the second part. Let us, then, joyfully bear the cross, either through necessity or by our own free will.

Help us all to do this, O dear Saviour, by Thy grace, which we beg of Thee, through the intercession of Mary and of the holy angels.

The apostles of Christ show that we can have joy and consolation in trials and mortification.

What? shall we look for delights in trials, penance, and mortification? for comfort in austerities? for pleasure in the midst of sharp thorns? for joy in the cross and suffering? for mirth in sadness? How can such things harmonize? Wet and dry, warm and cold, white and black, are not more opposed to each other than joy and sorrow, depriving one's self violently of joy and yet finding pleasure therein. That is true, my dear brethren, as far as the words go and in outward appearance. Yet these latter things can exist together; they must in fact exist together, or else the apostles of Christ would exhort us in vain, and urge us to do an impossible thing, as often as they impress on us the necessity of rejoicing in the midst of suffering. St. James writes in his Epistle: "My brethren, count it all joy," yes, nothing else but joy; what? When everything goes according to your natural wishes and inclinations? No; but "when you shall fall into divers temptations." [1] When you are sunk in a

---

[1] Omne gaudium existimate, fratres, cum in tentationes varias incideritis.—James i. 2.

sea of troubles, and have all sorts of trials to sustain, then your joy should be at its height.   St. Peter, the chief of the apostles, gives us a similar lesson: " If you partake of the suffering of Christ, rejoice." [1]   O glorious St. Paul, if those things could not harmonize, you would have been guilty of mere hypocrisy in saying out so frequently before the world: " I please myself in my infirmities, in reproaches, in necessities, in persecutions, in distresses." [2]   " Who now rejoice in my sufferings." [3]   Nay, he even ventures to say: " I am filled with comfort, I exceedingly abound with joy in all our tribulation. " [4]   Paul, says St. Chrysostom, was as joyful in his sufferings as if he were in a paradise of delights; and although he had the great happiness of being rapt up to the third heaven, and of seeing the bliss of the elect, yet he never rejoiced at that, but only at the trials he had to bear, on which he congratulated himself; and that, too, to such an extent that in the midst of his labors and difficulties he chastised his body with all sorts of penitential exercises in order to increase his joy.

If these things cannot harmonize, then I do not understand how the martyrs of Christ were able to laugh and sing so joyfully in the midst of the most cruel torments; nor how so many other saints, and even tender women, longed so earnestly for the cross, and were not satisfied till it was given them; nay, if the cross laid upon them seemed insufficient, they tortured themselves with iron chains, hair-shirts, rods, and scourges, nor would they have changed those penances for any worldly delights.   Ask a St. Teresa, a St. Catharine of Siena, a St. Mary Magdalene of Pazzi, if she is tired of her cross, and you will hear how Teresa preferred to die rather than to be without suffering.   Let me, O Lord, she used to pray, either suffer or die.   You will see Catharine holding the crown of thorns with both hands. and refusing to change it for any earthly crown.   You will hear Magdalene expressing the wish to live longer, solely for the purpose of being able to bear the cross longer.   Ask St. Ignatius, and he will tell you that there are not chains and fetters enough in all Spain to satisfy his longing for suffering.   Ask St. Francis Xavier, and you will hear him crying out in the midst of his troubles: " still

The martyrs and other holy servants of God.

[1] Communicantes Christi passionibus, gaudete.—I. Pet. iv. 13.

[2] Placeo mihi in infirmitatibus meis, in contumeliis, in necessitatibus, in angustiis.—II. Cor. xii. 10.

[3] Gaudeo in passionibus.—I. Coloss. i. 24.

[4] Repletus sum consolatione, superabundo gaudio in omni tribulatione nostra.—II. Cor. vii. 4.

more, O Lord, still more!" as if he could not be satiated with trials. Those holy servants of God would surely not have been in such dispositions, if they had not found pleasure and joy in the cross. True indeed are the words of St. Paul paraphrased by St. Bernard: "The sufferings of this time are not worthy to be compared with the present grace of consolation that is given on account of them."[1] Even if there were no hope of a future reward, still we should choose suffering in order to taste true joy and consolation in the present life.

Worldlings do not understand this joy.
And in what does this wonderful joy consist, which is hidden in sharp and bitter sufferings? Vain children and lovers of the world, I must not address this question to you; you would not understand it! "Let them alone; they are blind,"[2] I might well say in the words of our dear Lord. They measure joys by the outward senses, and when you speak of pleasure to them, their thoughts at once revert to carnal delights which are common to men with the brute creation. Oh, woe to us poor mortals, if we had nothing more than that to expect for bearing crosses and trials! Far greater and more excellent are the true joys that inwardly delight the mind and the soul, a single drop of which gives us more sweetness than all the vain joys of the world, and of which no one knows anything but he who has tasted them, as St. John says in the Apocalypse: "To him that overcometh," to him that conquers himself, "I will give the hidden manna. . . which no man knoweth but he that receiveth it."[3] That is to say, the God of infinite generosity will give to His faithful servants, who mortify themselves for His sake, or are otherwise tormented by trials, a reward in this life; He will not defer it altogether to the next world, but in the midst of their labors He will bestow on them the hundred-fold that He has promised, and while they are actually suffering, He allows them to taste beforehand the joys of heaven by the inward consolation of the heart and sweetness that He sends them.

Pious Christians have it, because they wish to suffer, since it is pleasing to God.
What, then, is that consolation, that joy? I ask you, holy servants of God, who voluntarily renounce all the pleasures of the world, even those that you might lawfully enjoy, and who bear your crosses and trials with such sweetness. Ah, why do you ask us? they exclaim. How can suffering be anything but a pleas-

---

[1] Non sunt condignæ passiones hujus temporis ad præsentem consolationis gratiam quæ immittitur.—Rom. viii. 18.

[2] Sinite illos ; cæci sunt.—Matt. xv. 14.

[3] Vincenti dabo manna absconditum. . . quod nemo scit, nisi qui accipit.—Apoc. ii. 17.

ure to the soul that loves God, when it is His will for it to suffer? How can it be anything else but a consolation to be able thus to pay off the debts contracted with the Divine Justice by former sins? Must it not be a comfort to withdraw one's heart from the transitory, short, deceitful, and disquieting joys of the world, and to fix it on the true joys of heaven? Must it not give pleasure to have a sure pledge of salvation and of eternal glory? Is it not consoling to be able to defy the devil and put him to shame by patience and mortification? to enter into the society of the martyrs and dear friends of God, who by their sufferings furthered His glory? to attract the attention of all the angels and elect in heaven? to have God in one's heart, and to find Him there, since He has promised to be with those who are in affliction? to have a share in the sufferings of Jesus Christ, and to become like to Him by patiently bearing the cross? to prove one's love for Christ not merely with words, but by deeds, since we carry the cross after Him, and are determined to carry it until death?

Is not a mother often rejoiced to deprive herself of food or drink, to remain awake all night and to submit to many other *Shown by simile.* inconveniences for the sake of her child? And if the child dies, how she weeps and laments, and complains that her only joy is taken from her! although in reality she is thus relieved from many worries and troubles. And would she not willingly undergo any labor, if she could only thereby preserve her dear child's life? Does not a lover think it the greatest happiness to be able to please the object of his affections, no matter at what cost to himself? And must pious souls find less consolation and sweetness in the love of Jesus Christ, our eternal God, whom we not only please in the highest degree, but also accompany in suffering, when we bear the cross and mortify ourselves? It is sweet and honorable to die for one's country, sang the poet of old; how much sweeter and more pleasant must it not be to suffer wounds for Christ? This was the thought that animated St. Procopius to suffer bravely for Christ. After having borne with the utmost fortitude all that the most savage cruelty could inflict on him, he thus addressed the judge: You think you will be able to conquer me by the torments you inflict on me, and make me prove unfaithful to Jesus; but you do not reflect that you are in reality conferring on me the greatest benefit that any man in the world could bestow on me; nay, the tortures you cause me to suffer place me under an obligation of the highest gratitude to you. For what can be more pleasing to one who loves Christ than to suffer?[1] My only concern is that you should find out what joy my martyrdom causes me, and that you should wish to deprive me of it by ceasing to torture me. St. Bernard, I believe you! repeat what you said before: "The sufferings of this time are not worthy to be compared with the present grace of consolation that is given on account of them."

The true joy of the human heart consists in the love and possession of God.

And to speak with truth of the matter, can there be a greater consolation for a reasoning being than that which he finds in God, his Creator? Everything seeks and finds its rest and pleasure in that to which it has a natural inclination. This we see even in senseless and lifeless things. Throw a ball into the air, says St. Augustine, and as soon as the force that has impelled it is exhausted, it sinks back again, and does not find rest until it is on its appropriate element, the earth; and if you were to dig away the ground from under it, it would follow you until it reached the centre. The magnet has received from the Author of nature such an attraction towards the north, that if you rub a needle on it, the latter will constantly turn to the north also. Turn it round and round as you will, now in this way, now in that, it will not rest and will continue to agitate itself as if it had life, until it again looks towards the north, its centre and point of rest; then and then only it remains quite still and immovable. Now, continues St. Augustine, there is not amongst all created things a more powerful impulse and inclination than that which urges the heart of man to God, in order to be united with Him and to rejoice in Him: "Thou hast made us, O Lord, for Thyself, and our heart is uneasy until it rests in Thee!"[2]

Without God there is no true joy.

Seek out, O sensual, luxurious man, whatever there is on earth to delight your eyes, to charm your ears, to tickle your palate, to gratify your senses, to delight your flesh; find out all that can be a source of pleasure to you, and having found it, pile it all up in a heap, and then tell me honestly whether you are truly contented and satisfied? You must acknowledge that you have grasped at nothing but empty air and deceitful vanity, as the Prophet says: "O ye sons of men, why do you love vanity, and seek after lying?"[3] You will be just as uneasy as before, and will have to seek after some new pleasure. Nor is that any wonder, for amongst all things that the world can offer you

[1] Quid enim ei qui Christus amat, jucundius esse potest, quam pati?
[2] Fecisti nos, Domine ad te, et inquietum est cor nostrum, donec requiescat in te.
[3] Filii hominum, utquid diligitis vanitatem, et quæritis mendacium?—Ps. iv. 3.

there is nothing for which you are created. One thing is still wanting to you. All that is outside of God is far too mean and worthless to fill and satisfy the human heart, which is capable of possessing an immense, infinite Good. Nay, continues St. Augustine, God Himself, great and mighty as He is, cannot completely satisfy and content me by created joys, unless He gives me Himself with them. [1] Let Him make me lord and master over heaven and earth, to do with them as I please; let Him place under my dominion all the hosts of heaven, and give me all the sensual joys of the whole world: all this cannot bring me perfect consolation. joy, rest, or happiness. "I know that there is a Creator of all these things; after Him do I hunger and thirst; to Him do I cry out: What have I in heaven? and besides Thee, what do I desire upon earth?" [2] What can I wish for, but Thee alone, O my God, who art my last end, and who alone art that most perfect good that can satisfy me? So far St. Augustine. From this it is clear that man can find no greater joy, no more perfect consolation, than in and with his God. "Truly," says St. Bernard, "that only is solid joy which comes from the Creator and not from the creature. Compared with that all other joy is sorrow, all sweetness pain, all delight is bitter, and all that can give pleasure is burdensome." [3]

And this is the consolation, this the joy, into which the sorrow of the just shall be turned even in the present life. This is what the good God, whose yoke is sweet and whose burden is light, so abundantly bestows on those souls who for His sake either bear the crosses He sends them with patience, or else chastise themselves with voluntary penances. And this gift will be all the greater the less consolation they have and seek from creatures and from the senses, as He Himself has promised so often. If they have a share in My cross, He says by the Prophet Jeremias: "I will turn their mourning into joy, and will comfort them, and make them joyful after their sorrow; and My people shall be filled with My good things, saith the Lord," [4] just as a mother when she finds her child submitting willingly to punish-

This is the joy God so richly bestows on the patient and penitent in this life.

---

[1] Omnino me non satiaret Deus, nisi promitteret mihi seipsum Deus.

[2] Omnium istorum Creatorem scio; ipsum esurio, ipsum sitio; ipsi dico: quid mihi est in cœlo, et a te quid volui super terram?—Ps. lxxii. 25.

[3] Revera illud solum et verum est gaudium, quod non de creatura, sed de Creatore percipitur. Cui comparata omnis aliunde jucunditas mœror est, omnis suavitas dolor est, omne dulce amarum est omne quodcunque delectare possit, molestum est.—S. Bern. Ep. 114.

[4] Et convertam luctum eorum in gaudium, et consolabor eos, et lætificabo a dolore suo; et populus meus bonis meis adimplebitur, ait Dominus.—Jerem. xxxi. 13, 14.

ment gives it milk and sugar to assuage the pain, and wipes away its tears with loving caresses. In the Book of Deuteronomy He says: They "shall suck as milk the abundance of the sea."[1] But is not the sea-water bitter and salt? And on the other hand, what can be sweeter than milk? True, the water in itself is bitter: the cross that My just servants bear with patience, their voluntary mortifications and self-denial, are in themselves painful; but I will mix this water with sweetness, so that they will drink it down like milk, and will find it just as pleasing to the taste: they "shall suck as milk the abundance of the sea." That seems miraculous to those who know nothing of divine consolations; but it is a miracle that God can easily work in pious, faithful souls; He will work it; He does actually work it, as we have seen in the examples of the saints.

As they know by experience.

And such is still the experience of those who for God's sake mortify themselves, and say with determined will: Lord, Thy will be done! I accept this from Thy divine hand; I will bear it and be satisfied with it, because so it is pleasing to Thee. If I could seek for proofs in this town of Treves, I am sure that I should find many who are a thousand times more cheerful in their poverty than the rich are in possession of their wealth and treasures; many who are a thousand times more satisfied in their mean and lowly condition than great lords are in their high dignities; many who have imcomparably more pleasure in the observance of chastity, and in bodily austerities, than others find in sensual enjoyments; many who thank God for having deprived them of earthly joys, and even envy others who have more to suffer than they have. I have known many an instance of this, and have been acquainted with numbers who found that consolation in suffering. Nor can it be otherwise. The words of God cannot deceive; and He has expressly promised that they who for His sake renounce temporal consolations shall receive a hundred-fold more than they have given up. It must be so, for "that only is solid joy which comes from the Creator, and not from the creature;" which is not begged of the outward senses, but sought in the centre and resting-place of our hearts. What I have said up to this has been addressed only to those who know by experience what it is to rejoice in God, and to have heavenly consolation. To the sensual children of the world such things are but castles in the air, and they are as little capable of form-

---

[1] Innundationem maris quasi lac sugent.—Deut. xxxiii. 19.

ing an opinion of supernatural joy as a blind man is of pronouncing on the merits of a fine picture of which he cannot make the least image in his mind. Now to explain my subject still better, I will speak of it in a natural way, and will show that in reality patience under the cross and mortification voluntarily practised for the love of God are the cause of joy to us in this life, even as far as natural joy is concerned. This is briefly the

Second Part.

In what does a joyful, happy life consist? Is it not in the inward peace, joy, and contentment of mind, as I proved more in detail when speaking of conformity with the will of God? Such is the description that even heathen philosophers give of it, and we all know by experience that it is a true one. I may give my outward senses all the delights they are capable of enjoying; but how will that help me to a happy life, if I am at war with myself inwardly, if my mind is disturbed and disquieted? If, on the other hand, my body is filled with pains and aches, or has to contend with hard work and discomfort, what harm will that do me, or how can it trouble me, if I suffer willingly, and am contented and peaceful in the midst of my trials? *Natural joy consists in peace and content of mind.*

Now let us take two individuals and compare them with each other. The one is a sensual, luxurious, unmortified man, who abhors all crosses and flies trials and discomfort, in all things he seeks to gratify himself, and allows all freedom to eyes, ears, taste, touch, and the other senses; he permits his desires and inclinations to rule him and govern him as they will, and has not the least idea of denying himself in anything. The other is one who is patient in adversity, accustomed to trials, and given to mortification and self-denial; he keeps a check on his outward senses and the desires of the flesh, and often does violence to them. Which of these two enjoys the greater peace, pleasure, and contentment of mind? "They are at peace with themselves," says St. Augustine, "who subject their inordinate appetites to reason, and overcome and hold in check their carnal desires. This is the peace which is given on earth to men of good will." On the other hand, where do all the mental troubles and disturbances, that disquiet us so much, come from? Is it not from the inordinate desires that we allow to rule over us, and do not try to master? Hence it is evident that the latter of the two lives in greater peace and quiet than the former. *It is possessed by the mortified men, and not by the voluptuary.*

Let us see whether this is so in practice. The voluptuary is attacked, for instance, by a fever, a catarrh, a tooth-ache, or a head-ache. Oh, what a state he gets into! How he murmurs and complains, and weeps and sighs, and what a commotion he causes in the house, as if the last day were at hand! The other takes no notice of such a little thing; he bears it with patience, and remains calm and satisfied. Lord, he says, may Thy holy will be done! Since no man can avoid the inconvenience caused by the change of weather, the first is disturbed and quite put out by a cold wind, the damp air, cold, heat, walking or standing for a quarter of an hour, the prick of a needle, a spark falling on his hand; it seems as if he ought to be carried about in a litter between two woollen matresses. The other, although he feels the inconvenience, is not disturbed by it; he is anxious to mortify himself, and here he has the desired opportunity; so that, having found what he sought, he is satisfied. Since we have to deal with people, we are often exposed to a word of contradiction now and then, or to some disagreeable act on the part of another. Occasionally people indulge in vituperation and contumelious language; the servants, the children, the husband or wife do not always act as they ought. The one who is not master of his passions, and knows not how to mortify himself, gives way to anger and ill-temper under such circumstances; he actually trembles with passion and his heart is full of bitterness. Thus his inward peace is disturbed; his mind is troubled. The other is master of himself at once; he keeps quiet as if nothing had happened; he rejoices at having an opportunity of overcoming himself; he preserves his peace. The first indulges his curiosity and allows all freedom to his eyes; he sees some perishable beauty that pleases him; he contemplates it, and has a certain joy therein; but how long does it last? No longer than the object which gave rise to it remains in view. And what follows? Nothing but the loss of his inward peace. For a whole day, nay, for weeks and years, he keeps that perishable beauty before his mind; he dreams of it at night, and longs to see it again. But these desires of his are frequently doomed to disappointment; yet he still continues to cherish them, fruitless as he knows they must be; and thus he has nothing from the gratification of his curiosity but discontent, worry, and melancholy. If, like the other, he had mortified his eyes and at once cast them down, or turned them elsewhere, he would have avoided all that trouble, and have kept his peace of mind. His curiosity impels him to hear, know, and inquire into everything; he is apt to talk of whatever comes into his head, and many a time he says things he is sorry for afterwards, while he often hears what fills him with fear and uneasiness. He is like that married man who out of blasphemous curiosity disguised himself as a priest, and went in the dark to hear his wife's confession; his only idea was to tease her afterwards, for he loved her sincerely; but he had to listen while she told him that she had frequently committed adultery. I leave you to imagine how he was tortured by a secret sadness and grief, which he dared tell to no man, and for which there was no remedy. If he had not gratified his godless curiosity, he would have still enjoyed his peace of mind and happiness. The other who is concerned only about his own affairs, and attends only to what he has to do himself, remains ignorant of many things that would indeed please him to hear, but he also is saved from the knowledge of much that would disturb and disquiet him. The first is addicted to the pleasures of the table, and is intemperate; hence he has to suffer head-aches, sickness, evil humors in the blood; he shortens his life, and must expect to die before his time. The other, through mortification, keeps within the bounds of moderation, and the little food and drink he takes, tastes all the sweeter to him; he has a good appetite, after as well as before meals; he is always healthy, cheerful, and in good humor. The first, since a luxurious life necessarily gives rise to a carnal one, seeks for occasions to gratify his impure passions; he thinks he has found joy therein; but what bitter pills he has to swallow before, during, and after those criminal actions! His sleep is often disturbed; he has no appetite for his food; his sense of shame, his good name, his conscience, all must be sacrificed for the sake of his unruly passions. But he cares little for that; the unclean spirit has blinded his eyes, closed his ears, bewitched his heart, dulled his senses, driven away shame, darkened his understanding. Thus an uneasy conscience and the fire of hell itself are all that he has gained by his sensual indulgence, and yet he is not satiated with the sinful pleasure he enjoys. How can such a man have peace of mind? Does not the other feel far happier in the practise of chastity and mortification? And the same may be said of all other inordinate gratifications. See now from what uneasiness, annoyance, and discomfort he is free who seems to torment himself by voluntary mortification. He leads a pleasant, peaceful life on earth, even while he deprives himself of earthly pleasures; he is at peace with himself, with his fellow-man, and with his conscience, and lastly with the God whom he loves above all things.

Therefore, my dear brethren, they deceive themselves who think that preachers are too severe when they exhort people from the pulpit to practise mortification and to shun worldly pleasures and entertainments, and look on them as enemies to all enjoyment. No, Christians, such is far from being the case! Never do we seek and desire to procure for you true enjoyment and pleasure more than when we exhort you to mortify your senses and evil desires, which, according to the law of faith, of reason, and of experience itself, are the only cause of all our unhappiness when we give them loose rein. "God hath called us in peace," [1] says St. Paul; and that is the right way to gain true peace. Wofully deceived, then, are they who consider that the vain children of the world, who indulge their sensuality, are the only happy ones. No, Christians; that cannot be! We see the roses outwardly, but the sharp thorns are hidden from us. "They spend their days in wealth," [2] says holy Job of such people; and it is true! They spend their time in eating, drinking, sleeping, amusing themselves and indulging in sensual pleasures; they have worldly goods in abundance, they gratify their senses, they deny themselves no worldly pleasures; but it is not true that their days are days of happiness. They call out peace! peace! but all their calling cannot give them real peace or enjoyment. Worst of all, then, is the error of those who imagine that the way of the cross and penance, the service of God, is so hard and bitter that it is intolerable. No, Christians, wrong again! "The burden is light, the yoke is sweet, the cross is anointed," [3] as St. Bernard says; it is a sweet suffering, a joyful sadness.

Only make trial of it, if you do not believe what I say; renounce the deceitful joys of the world; deny yourselves, as Christ wishes us to do. "Mortify therefore your members," [4] as the Apostle warns you; mortify your outward senses, your inward desires, "And you shall see," says the Lord by the Prophet Malachy, "the difference between the just and the wicked: and

---

[1] In pace vocavit nos Deus.—I. Cor. vii. 15.
[2] Ducunt in bonis dies suos.—Job xxi. 13.
[3] Onus leve, jugum suave, crux inuncta.
[4] Mortificate ergo membra vestra.—Coloss. iii. 5.

between him that serveth God, and him that serveth Him not."[1]
You will see what a great difference there is between the zealous, true, pious Christian and the tepid man who leads a careless life, and has only the name of a Christian. You will experience the great difference there is between the vain, transitory
and merely apparent pleasure that is to be gained by sensual
gratification and the true, real peace and enjoyment that comes
from mortification. You will agree with St. Augustine, who at
first thought it almost an impossibility to give up worldly joys
and sensual pleasures; but once he had firmly resolved to serve
God faithfully, and had actually commenced to practise mortification, he soon changed his opinion, and cried out in joyful
tones: "Oh, how delightful it has become to me all at once to be
without vain pleasures! Now I am rejoiced at losing what I
formerly feared to lose!"[2] I shall imitate him, then, in future.
The crosses, troubles, and difficulties that God sends me, or
will send me, I shall accept with satisfaction, and keep in
check my outward senses and evil inclinations, mortifying and
chastising my flesh. I have sinned; what an immense debt I
have thereby incurred with the Divine Justice! I can still sin;
what powerful means should I not use to avert such a calamity!
Christ my Lord was never without the cross; how can I call
myself a member of Christ under a thorn-crowned Head if I
live in pleasures and delights, and still expect eternal joys hereafter? Mortification can give me a quiet, peaceful life here below; why, then, should I avoid it, or hesitate to make use of it?
And even if I had not all these reasons to urge me to this step,
or if they should not be verified in my case; I have at all events the
express promise of Our Lord: "Your sorrow shall be turned
into joy." It should, then, suffice for me to know that my short
sorrow and suffering shall be turned into an eternal joy in the
glorious resurrection. Help me to keep this resolution, O God.
Amen.

[1] Et videbitis quid sit inter justum et impium, et inter servientem Deo et non servientem
ei.—Mal. iii. 18.

[2] O quam suave mihi subito factum est, carere suvitatibus nugarum! et quas amittere
metus fuerat, jam amittere gaudium erat!

SIXTY-FIFTH SERMON.

ON THE HONOR GIVEN TO GOD BY PATIENCE IN ADVERSITY.

Subject.

By patiently bearing the cross of trials we give great honor and glory to God; therefore we should consider it an honor and glory for ourselves when we are visited with many trials in this life.—*Preached on Easter Sunday.*

Text.

Jesum quæritis Nazarenum crucifixum.—Mark xvi. 6.
" You seek Jesus of Nazareth, who was crucified."

Introduction.

Why did the angel mention that hateful word, "crucified?" " He is accursed that hangeth on a tree," [1] says the Scripture. Would it not have been enough to have said, you seek Jesus of Nazareth? Those words would have enabled the holy women to understand who was risen from the dead. Why, then, was Our Lord called the crucified one? Oh, says St. Ambrose, the world hates the cross as an instrument of shame; but Christ placed His greatest honor and glory in it. [2] Such were the terms in which He spoke of it to His disciples when announcing to them His approaching Passion and death: " The hour is come that the Son of man should be glorified." [3] For the same reason when St. Peter was led forth to be crucified, he wished to be placed on the cross with his head downwards, lest, as St. Ambrose remarks, " he might seem to arrogate to himself the glory of the Lord." [4] It was by the cross that Jesus Christ gave most honor and glory to His heavenly Father; it was by the cross that He wished to make the glory of His resurrection still more evident to the world. " Ought not Christ to have suffered these things," He said to the disciples on the way to Emmaus, " and so to enter into His glory?" [5] How hateful, my dear brethren, is not the name of the cross of trials and adversity in this life to our natural inclinations. But when we consider it in the light of faith,

---

[1] Maledictus qui pendet in ligno.—Deut. xxi. 23.
[2] Gloria et honor Christi crux est.
[3] Venit hora ut clarificetur Filius hominis.—John xii. 23.
[4] Ne affectasse Domini gloriam videretur.
[5] Nonne hæc oportuit pati Christum, et ita intrare in gloriam suam.—Luke xxiv. 26.

we shall find that we, too, can give no greater honor and glory to
God our heavenly Father, to Jesus Christ our Redeemer, and
therefore to ourselves also, than by patiently bearing the cross
of adversity, as I shall now show to the consolation of all who
are afflicted.

Plan of Discourse.

*By patiently bearing the cross of trials we give great honor and
glory to God: therefore we should consider it an honor and glory
for ourselves to be visited with many trials in this life; such is
the whole subject.*

Christ Jesus, by Thy cross and glorious resurrection from the
dead grant us all the grace, which we beg of Thee through the
prayers of Thy Mother and of our holy angels, to honor Thee
here by bearing our cross, and thus to earn, like Thee, the glory
of the resurrection.

To come to the point at once; in what consists the honor and
glory that God expects from men? In this chiefly, that man
submits completely to God as to his Creator and sovereign Lord,
obeys Him willingly in all possible circumstances, is always resigned to His holy will and decree, and thus publicly acknowledges before the world God's supreme sovereignty. For, as I
have often told you before, God is not in the least need of His
creatures, and He has placed His exterior glory in this, that His
creatures are always ready to do, to omit, and to suffer whatever and as long as He wills them to do, to omit, and to suffer.

*The exter-
nal honor
of God con-
sists in the
perfect
submission
of creatures
to His will.*

Never does man show this full submission and obedience clearer or better than in the trials that he accepts from the hand of
God, and bears patiently for His sake. Why? Mark the reason.
All, even lifeless and unreasoning creatures, honor and praise their
Creator, inasmuch as they always do what He has appointed for
them according to their nature; and there is not a worm that
crawls the earth so mean, or a blade of grass so worthless, that
the mature consideration of it cannot bring man to the knowledge of God and of His wonderful power. But when these
creatures occasionally allow violence to be done to their nature,
so that they either do what is contrary to their inclinations, or
cease to produce their wonted effects, then they give testimony
that should compel the most obstinate and incredulous to acknowledge, praise, and adore the divine omnipotence; and such
effects are called miracles or prodigies. The sun, moon, and

*Even sense-
less and
lifeless
things show
Him that
submission.*

stars honor and praise their Creator, according to the Prophet David: "The heavens show forth the glory of God,"[1] by the regularity with which they keep the course assigned to them, without ever standing still, or going wrong. The mountains and hills praise and honor their Creator, silently indeed, but still in a manner that is easily understood, since they remain motionless in the places assigned to them, and faithfully guard the treasures of metals committed to their care. The torrents and rivers praise and honor their Creator by the rapidity with which they hurry on in their course, until at last they are lost in the sea.

But never do they honor their Creator more than when they obey Him against their nature. All these things, my dear brethren, we have constantly before our eyes; they have been from the beginning of the world up to the present moment; but who wonders at them? Who is there who even once in the day thinks of the sun, the mountains, the rivers? They are nothing new to us; we are accustomed to them; they are simply natural things. But if we were to see the sun standing still, as it formerly did at the command of Josue, who ordered it not to continue its course until he had conquered his enemies; or if we were to see the same sun going back ten degrees at the wish of king Ezechias; or to behold it hiding itself, so that the day is turned into dark night, as happened at the death of Our Lord; if we saw the Moselle suddenly divide itself and stand up like a wall on both sides, so that we could cross over dryshod, without either bridge or boat, as was the case when the Israelites crossed the Red Sea in their flight from Pharao; or if the mountain that we call Paulsberg began to move and change its position before our eyes, as mountains have done more than once at the prayer of holy servants of God, according to the promise of Our Lord: "Amen, I say to you, if you have faith you shall say to this mountain, remove from hence thither, and it shall remove."[2] If, I say, we beheld such wonders with our own eyes, what surprise and astonishment would take possession of us! Would we not exclaim like those who were with Our Lord in the boat when He calmed down the raging sea: "What manner of man is this, for the winds and the sea obey him?"[3] How powerful and mighty God must be, since the sun, the rivers, and the mountains obey His voice! There is no doubt that the sun by its standing still and retiring, the sea by divid-

---

[1] Coeli enarrant gloriam Dei.—Ps. xviii. 2.

[2] Amen dico vobis, si habueritis fidem, dicetis monte huic: transi hinc illuc, et transibit. Matt. xvii. 19.

[3] Qualis est hic, quia venti et mare obediunt ei?—Ibid. viii. 27.

ing itself, the mountains by changing their position in such a short time, gave more honor and glory to God thereby than they had given Him for thousands of years before. Why? Because contrary to their nature and inclination they suffered violence in order to do the will of their Creator.

My dear brethren, to be always in good health and prosperity; to have an abundance of worldly goods; to enjoy a good name and the esteem of men; to be looked up to by everyone; to live in constant peace, pleasure, and quiet; that is a state that is most in conformity with our nature and all its inclinations. It is a state that is the object of the sighs and desires of many men, when they think of the happiness that we must seek in all our actions. See, I say to you; see that man, who has everything he can wish for; how satisfied and resigned to the will of God he is; how completely he accepts all the divine decrees; how respectful and obedient he is to the law of God; how thankfully he receives the benefits bestowed on him; how zealous and diligent he is in attending church and practising devotion, hearing the word of God, and frequenting the holy sacraments; how carefully he brings up his children in the service of God; and so on. What do you think of him? Is he not a good Christian? Truly he is, and a real example of piety; for in our days, alas! they who receive most temporal benefits from God are generally the most ungrateful to Him, and make use of His gifts for purposes of pride, vanity, dissipation, and vice. But that man is good and pious, and always united with the will of God; and I ask you again, What do you think of him? Does he not honor and glorify his Creator by the Christian life he leads, and by his resignation to the divine will? Without a doubt he does; but at the same time you cannot help thinking: if I were as well off as that man, I, too, should be satisfied with the will of God, and should willingly thank and serve Him. For it is natural to accept readily that which we like, and to be satisfied with one who gives us everything we wish for. And you have reason for thinking in that way.

Man, too, honors God by serving Him in prosperity.

But, now I ask you to look at that other man, and see what misery he has to suffer for such a long time. Consider that poor tradesman; how he has to work hard the whole day long to get dry bread enough for himself and his family; that unfortunate citizen, who never has luck in anything he puts his hand to, so that wherever he turns he finds the cross; that wretched peas-

But much more when he does so in adversity.

ant, who has been reduced to the direst poverty by wars and plunderings, so that he has hardly a bit of bread to eat. Consider that poor widow with her family of little children, who has no friends to console her, and is moreover exposed to the attacks of her bitter enemies; that wife, who in addition to the poverty she has to bear daily is also tormented by a drunken, good-for-nothing husband, who curses and beats her; that person who has now been for many years in bed suffering great pain. Oh, truly theirs is a state that has nothing conformable to our senses and desires, but everything in direct opposition to our natural inclinations; but those people are nevertheless just as satisfied as the other in their state, just as resigned and submissive to the will of God; they willingly follow Our Lord on the rugged way of the cross, through thistles and thorns, as well as the other who has a road strewn with roses and flowers. While he thanks God for riches, health, and other blessings bestowed on him, they praise, bless, and honor God by their humble submission for the trials and sufferings He sends them, which they look on as still greater blessings. Never do they give the least sign of impatience; and although nature cannot help groaning under the weight of the cross, which presses out sighs from their hearts and tears from their eyes, yet amidst all their weeping and lamentation, they never utter a word but to signify their complete obedience to the will of God. Lord, Thy will be done! is their prayer; I am satisfied with what Thou hast decreed for me! Now what do you think, my dear brethren? Oh, you think to yourselves with the greatest wonder, that is a different matter altogether! What great pleasure the Lord must have in such souls! What an edifying example they give to the whole community! How they put to shame those vain, luxurious worldlings, who cannot bear a harsh word! What a glory for our holy faith to be able to point to such Catholics as these! What honor and glory for God to have such servants! One of them gives more praise and honor to God and to His holy Gospel than a hundred of those who serve him in prosperity. Even a heathen philosopher cries out at the sight: "Behold a spectacle worthy of being looked at by God! Behold a pair worthy of God: a patient man laden with misfortune."[1]

Shown by   And so it is, my dear brethren. When I represent to myself a

---

[1] Ecce spectaculum dignum ad quod respiciat intentus operi suo Deus! ecce par Deo dignum: vir fortis mala fortuna compositus.

Job, who was so richly endowed with wealth and honors that his like was not to be found in the whole East, and who led such a holy, innocent life, offering every morning a sacrifice of thanksgiving to God; when I represent to myself a Tobias, who as the chief man of his tribe was held in high honor, how grateful he was to God, how diligent in going daily to the temple to adore the one true God, how zealous he was in practising the works of mercy, in feeding the hungry, burying the dead, etc.; when I represent to myself a king David, prostrate before the altar, returning thanks to God for the victory gained over his enemies, and with joyful hymns and canticles offering a hundred victims to the Lord of hosts, I am indeed rejoiced at the honor and glory thus given to God; but I do not wonder much at it, for I cannot help thinking that it is an easy thing when you are endowed with wealth and honor and crowned with victory to appear before the altar to show your gratitude, and kiss the bounteous hand that has been so generous to you. But when I remember that the same Job after losing all his children, his cattle, his houses, his lands, his wealth, after being covered with wounds and sores from head to foot, and being abandoned by all, and left to sit on a dung-hill, still praised and blessed God: "The Lord gave, and the Lord hath taken away; as it hath pleased the Lord so is it done: blessed be the name of the Lord;"[1] when I remember how Tobias was deprived of his sight, and thus blind and helpless was exposed to the mockery of his friends and even of his own wife, and yet how he praised and blessed God, rejoicing in the hope of eternal goods, and saying to his son: "We lead indeed a poor life, but we shall have many good things if we fear God, and depart from all sin, and do that which is good;"[2] when I hear him in his blindness, not merely abstaining from all complaint, but even thanking God for it: "He repined not against God because the evil of blindness had befallen him, but continued immovable in the fear of God, giving thanks to God all the days of his life;"[3] when I remember that David in his humiliations and troubles, persecuted by his own son and driven out of his kingdom bareheaded and barefooted, instead of murmuring or complaining, gives utterance to those

[1] Dominus dedit, Dominus abstulit; sicut Domino placuit, ita factum est: sit nomen Domini benedictum.—Job i. 21.

[2] Pauperem vitam gerimus, sed multa bona habebimus, si timuerimus Deum, et recesserimus ab omni peccato, et fecerimus bene.—Tob. iv. 23.

[3] Non est contristatus contra Deum quod plaga cœcitatis evenerit ei; sed immobilis in Dei timore permansit, agens gratias Deo omnibus diebus vitae suae.—Ibid. ii. 13, 14.

beautiful words: " Let Him do that which is good before Him," [1] let Him decree for me whatever He pleases; He is Lord and Master; if He wishes to take from me my crown, my kingdom, my life, He can do so without paying any attention to my natural wishes and desires; I am satisfied with whatever He arranges for me; " if he shall say to me: Thou pleasest me not: I am ready;" [2] let Him only give a sign as to what He wishes to do with me and mine; I am ready, O Lord, to abandon the throne on which Thou hast placed me, and to sink into the very depths of disgrace; when, I say, I consider how those great men thought and acted under such circumstances, then I am compelled to cry out, " God is wonderful in His saints." [3] How great is the power of divine grace, which can make a weak and sensitive nature so steadfast in enduring trials that are quite opposed to all its inclinations! How the glory of God is published to the world by the fact that He has such servants, who continue to love Him with all their hearts, even in the direst sufferings! These are miracles, as it were, that the world has not yet ceased to wonder at.

Simile showing the difference between serving God in prosperity and in adversity.

They who serve God in prosperity are to my mind like the attendants and courtiers of a king, who are always at the side of their royal master, accompany him wherever he goes, whether it is to the chase, to the theatre, or to the table; dressed in magnificent array, they pay him their respects early and late, and await his commands. But they who serve God in adversity are like those brave soldiers and heroes who fight for their king far away from his presence, and risk their lives and shed their blood for him in the open air, in heat and cold, amidst constant dangers from sword and bullet, daring death daily from fire and sword. Which of these two classes of men give more honor to their king? There is no doubt that one heroic act performed by a soldier at the risk of his life during a siege or a battle makes the king more glorious than all the attendance and waiting of the courtiers. For the latter only make a vain show and parade about their sovereign's person; while the former by their valor make him illustrious as a conqueror, increase his kingdom, extend his power, and make him respected and feared by his enemies and by other monarchs.

To be faith- To pray long and frequently, to hear Mass daily, to give alms

[1] Faciat quod bonum est coram se.—II. Kings xv. 26.

[2] Si dixerit mihi: non places; praesto sum.—Ibid.

[3] Mirabilis Deus in sanctis suis.—Ps. lxvii. 36.

to the poor, and perform other good works of the kind, that, according to most people, is the proper way to be pious and to honor God. It is true those works are laudable, by them we acknowledge our duty to God, and make parade before Him, as it were; but I can say without hesitation that one " Deo Gratias," one " May Thy will be done," spoken from the heart in sorrow and trial, brings, as a general rule, more honor to God than a whole bookful of prayers, or all the outward works of devotion that one performs when things are prospering with him. Not to be impatient when we have all we wish for; not to be angry when no one contradicts us; not to hate, when no one injures us; these are virtues found even in heathens who know nothing of the Christian doctrine: " Do not also the heathens this?" [1] Even the devil pays no regard to such virtue. As long as holy Job was prosperous, the wicked spirit had no great respect for him. The Lord asked him, by an angel who presided over an assembly of the angels, whether he had seen the pious Job in his wanderings through the world: " Hast thou considered my servant Job, that there is none like him in the earth, a simple and upright man, one that feareth God and avoideth evil?" But, replied the demon, is any credit due to him for that? " Doth Job fear God in vain?" He serves Thee in a house filled with everything, with riches, pleasures, servants, and good friends: " Hast thou not made a fence for him, and his house, and all his substance round about, and blessed the works of his hands, and his possession hath increased on earth? But stretch forth Thy hand a little," [2] visit him with trials, and then Thou shalt see if he will remain faithful to Thee. And so it is. Certain virtues that are practised in prosperity are not much to be wondered at. Many a one lives a chaste life with a wife who enjoys all the love of his heart; many a one gives alms, but he is so rich that he does not miss what he gives; many a one never gets angry, because he has no occasion for anger; many a one never nourishes hatred, because no one persecutes him. We must not imagine that these are great virtues. But to be contented and cheerful in the midst of poverty and persecutions, to rejoice at thus having an opportunity of becoming more like the poor and perse-

ful to God in time of trial surpasses all other good works in time of prosperity.

[1] Nonne et ethnici hoc faciunt?—Matt. v. 47.

[2] Numquid considerasti servum meum Job, quod non sit ei similis in terra, homo simplex et rectus, ac timens Deum et recedens a malo? Numquid Job frustra timet Deum? Nonne tu vallasti eum, ac domum ejus universamque substantiam per circuitum, operibus manuum ejus benedixisti, et possessio ejus crevit in terra? Sed extende paululum manum tuam.—Job i. 8–11.

cuted Christ; to be glad of contempt, shame, and disgrace, because we thus follow the despised Christ; to bear sickness and suffering willingly and thank God for having given us an opportunity of suffering with Our Lord, that is a virtue which makes men dear to God and the angels; it is a virtue which renders the greatest honor to God, to Christ our Redeemer. Unfounded therefore are the complaints of those who say that because they have to lie sick in bed they can do no good, as they cannot go to church, or hear sermons, or perform the usual devotions, etc. Ah, my good people, you do not know what you are talking about! You do not understand what doing good means! Only be patient in your illness, and satisfied with the will of God; thank Him in your hearts, if you cannot speak, for the pains and discomfort that your sickness causes; let your whole devotion consist in thinking now and then: Lord, Thy will be done! may the name of the Lord be blessed, and be assured that your resignation will give far more honor to God and do far more good to you than all your prayers and devotions and church-going when you are in good health. "It is more perfect," says St. Bonaventure, "to bear adversity patiently than to labor diligently in the performance of other good works."[1] With that firm resolution, "Lord, Thy will be done," man at once submits and gives to God all he has in and outside himself, his fortune, his goods, his health, his joy, his pleasure, all of which he places at the disposal of Providence, and is ready to give up at the call of God; and by the same determination he leaves in the hands of God his body, his soul, his understanding and will, which he most obediently submits in all things to the divine will; and thus he certainly practises a virtue that is in itself most perfect and excellent, and most pleasing to the Lord.

God boasts, so to speak, of having such servants.

Hear how God Himself boasts and vaunts, as it were, of such servants: "Hast thou considered My servant Job?" He asked Satan, when the latter appeared before Him a second time. For the second time thou hast wandered through the earth, and examined everything carefully; what wonder hast thou seen? "Hast thou considered My servant Job?" Mark how the Almighty does not ask if the evil spirit has seen how the kings and princes of earth lay down their crowns at the feet of the Divine Majesty, and adore the Lord as their sovereign Master. Nor does He ask him if he has seen the vast earth, covered with so

[1] Perfectius est adversa tolerare patienter, quam bonis operibus insudare.

many palaces, and filled with treasures and riches, which is yet
only the foot-stool of the Lord.   Nor if he has seen the birds of
the air, the beasts of the forest, and the other creatures that unceasingly praise their Creator.   No, the Lord did not boast of
such things; but to show the great honor and glory rendered Him,
it was enough for Him to say: "Hast thou considered my servant Job?"   Hast thou seen that there is none like him on earth,
"still keeping his innocence," [1] still remaining faithful to Me,
in spite of the frightful calamities with which I have allowed thee
to afflict him?   Hast thou seen how, in the midst of his trials, he
still blesses My name, as he did while in prosperity?   Is he not a
true and faithful servant?   Dost thou think there is anyone in
whom I can have greater pleasure and joy?   Imagine, my dear
brethren, that God can now say the same of us to Satan: hast thou
considered how things have been for many years on the banks of
the Rhine and the Moselle?   What calamities war has brought
on those countries?   How many have been carried off by sickness?   How many have been confined to bed by it?   How numbers have lost all their money through the heavy expenses they
were put to?   How many countries have been plundered?   How
many houses thrown down?   How many have thus been reduced
to beggary?   Hast thou considered how many of My servants of
Treves who suffered in the general calamities have still retained
their innocence, and still serve Me with love and zeal, and how
they continue to praise Me and bless My name?   What dost
thou think of those faithful servants of Mine?   Would it not,
my dear brethren, be a great honor and glory for the Almighty
God if He could speak thus of us?

But alas! I am afraid that Satan could say to Him of many: But He has
truly O Lord, I have considered all these things; I have seen not many o them.
how Thy servants of Treves have acted hitherto.   Thou didst
mean well with them; in visiting them with those trials, Thou
didst hope thereby to induce them to amend their lives, and
thus to give Thee more honor and glory; but what hast Thou
gained?   Are not those individuals, whom Thou, O Lord, knowest well, twenty times worse than before?   Have not they who
were formerly innocent and pious given themselves up to all
kinds of vice?   Hast Thou not seen who they are who indulge
in pride and vanity, in avarice and injustice, in wantonness and
impurity, in thieving and robbery, in cursing and swearing?

[1] Adhuc retinens innocentiam.—Job ii. 3.

This is the honor and glory Thou hast gained from the trials Thou hast sent them! My dear brethren, the all-seeing God, who knows the consciences of men, that are hidden from me, knows too whether Satan could say that to Him with truth.

Conclusion and exhortation to honor God in adversity.

Meanwhile I conclude with the words of the ancient Origen: "Let no one be so ignorant of the designs of God as to think that the trials He sends us are intended to injure us." [1] Let no one be so rash as to complain of God as a hard task-maker, because He sends us sufferings. Let no one be so foolish as to make his cross heavier by refusing to bear it patiently. If the cross brought us no other advantage but that of enabling us to further the honor and glory of our great God, should we not accept it with joy and thanksgiving as a glorious pledge from the hand of God, and like St. Paul boast of nothing but the cross of Our Lord Jesus Christ? St. John Chrysostom writing on those words to the Philippians, who were then suffering a grievous persecution: "Unto you it is given for Christ, not only to believe in Him, but also to suffer for Him," [2] asks why does St. Paul say, "unto you it is given"? Oh, answers St. Chrysostom, by those words he wished to remind us that suffering, and honoring God by it, is a special grace and gift of God; so that he considered it necessary to exhort the Philippians not to give way to vainglory on account of having to bear the cross. Therefore he wrote to them, "unto you it is given;" think of this, that you may not become proud; for you have not this gift from yourselves, but from the liberality of God, that you may further His glory by your suffering. [3] Come, my dear brethren, let us at least, as I have often exhorted you, bear our trials with patience and contentment for the honor of God; in any case we must suffer them; let us do so, then, with the consolation and firm hope that we shall one day be honored in the glorious resurrection, and shall be exalted to eternal joys in heaven by Him whom we have honored by suffering for a short time on earth. Give us Thy grace to this end, O Lord! Amen.

[1] Nemo igitur ita ineruditus sit divinæ disciplinæ, ut flagella divina perniciem putet.

[2] Vobis donatum est pro Christo, non solum ut in eum credatis, sed ut etiam pro illo patiamini.—Philipp. i. 29.

[3] Ne in eo extollantur, cum illud non habeant a se, sed a Deo.

SIXTY-SIXTH SERMON.

ON FIDELITY TO GOD IN JOY AND IN SORROW.

Subject.

To remain steadfast in virtue and in the love of God in sorrow as well as in joy, in adversity as well as in prosperity, constitutes the true virtue and piety of a Christian.—*Preached on the fourth Sunday after Easter.*

Text.

Quia hæc locutus sum vobis, tristitia implevit cor vestrum.—John xvi. 6.

" Because I have spoken these things to you sorrow hath filled your heart."

Introduction.

Such was the way in which Our Lord acted towards His disciples. Sometimes He filled them with joy and consolation, as when He showed them His glory on Mount Thabor; sometimes He caused them sorrow and trouble, as when He suffered a shameful death on Mount Calvary. Soon again He rejoiced them by appearing to them after the resurrection; and a short time after that He again filled them with sorrow when He left them and ascended into heaven. And so it is with us, too, in the world, my dear brethren, as daily experience teaches us. " There are mixtures prepared for us," [1] as Sinesius so well remarks. There is a constant alternation of sweetness and bitterness, prosperity and adversity. In the morning one is good-humored and cheerful, in the evening he is sad and melancholy; to-day he enjoys the society of a good friend, to-morrow he has to contend with a bitter enemy; this week he has the greatest happiness in his family, the next, one of his loved ones is taken away by death. This year, he says in cheerful tones, I have made a good deal of profit; the next year he sighs: oh how unfortunate I am! what fearful losses I have had! Now his cry is: God be praised! I am well and in good health; soon after you may hear him lamenting, and complaining of the pain he has to suffer. Now he exclaims: how fortunate that my plan succeeded so well! Alas, he cries out in a short time after, I know not what to do, or where to turn to

---

[1] Mixturæ pro nobis sunt.

for help! Thus the mixtures are prepared for us. Thus Divine Providence plays with us mortals, and mingles sour with sweet, prosperity with adversity. But what is the object of that change and alternation? It is, answers St. Bernard, to try us, and see whether we have a well-founded virtue, and whether we really love our God with our whole heart. This is a consolation for you, pious servants of God, who lead holy lives, and yet have many trials and crosses to bear. God sends them to you to try and to increase your virtue, as I shall now prove.

Plan of Discourse.

To remain steadfast in virtue and in the love of God in sorrow as well as in joy, in adversity as well as in prosperity, constitutes the true virtue and piety of a Christian. Such is the whole subject.

That we may all endeavor to possess such virtue, grant us Thy grace, O Teacher of truth; we ask it of Thee through the intercession of Mary and of our holy angels.

If man remained true to God either in prosperity or in adversity alone, his sincerity might be doubted: therefore God causes prosperity and adversity to alternate with each other.

When a man is always prosperous, and serves God faithfully, we might easily look on his virtue as somewhat suspicious, and say of him what Satan said of Job to the Lord: Thou art proud of Thy servant; but without reason! Thou hast surrounded him with blessings; why, then, should he not praise and bless Thee? But his praise is not sincere; it is only lip-service. On the other hand if a man has constantly to contend with suffering and adversity, and still remains devout and pious, even then we might have reason to suspect him, and to say: his devotion does not come from the heart; it is only forced; he prays to be freed from his miseries, or else since he can find no consolation on earth, he is compelled to seek it from God. Therefore to leave no room for doubt, God generally mingles sorrow with joy, prosperity with adversity, so as to come at the truth of the matter, and see what a man's virtue really is. If it remains constant and steadfast in both circumstances, then it is bound to be honest and sincere.

It is a great virtue to love God in adversity.

And in the first place, it is a beautiful proof of great virtue to love God and remain true to Him in the midst of crosses and trials. Therefore in many places in the holy Scriptures love is compared with gold, and adversity with fire. Thus Job says of himself: "He hath tried me as gold that passeth through the fire." [1] "Gold and silver are tried in the fire," says the wise

---

[1] Ipse probavit me quasi aurum, quod per ignem transit.—Job xxiii. 10.

Ecclesiasticus, "but acceptable men in the furnace of humiliation," [1] to see whether their piety is sincere or not. And in truth it is something wonderful to love one who deals harshly with us. "A friend in need is a friend indeed," says the old proverb; and if true friendship is proved in the time of necessity, how much more will not its sincerity be evident, if the very one by whom the need is caused is still loved?

Men are sometimes scandalized at this in their own minds. *And there are many who do not imagine it to be possible.* They are surprised to see a pious servant of God bending under the weight of many severe trials and miseries; as if they thought that God should not thus torture a soul that loves Him, or else that the soul itself was not acting wisely in remaining true to Him, and in praising and blessing Him in spite of the torments He inflicts on it. When Job was reduced to the direst poverty and had to sit on the dung-hill covered with sores, his only word was, "blessed be the name of the Lord;" but his wife mocked and jeered at him: "Dost thou still continue in thy simplicity?" she said; "bless God and die." [2] When the old Tobias was unfortunate, his wife too showed just as little sympathy for him: "It is evident," said she, "thy hope is come to nothing, and thy alms now appear;" [3] thy blindness should teach thee how vain is thy reliance on God, and thou shouldst now acknowledge that thy alms have been of little good to thee. But such people do not understand the benefit of adversity; and this very circumstance brings into still clearer light the great virtue of those who remain steadfast in the service of God in the time of trial; for being more enlightened they see that the sufferings that God sends them are nothing but proofs of His love, and real benefits, for which they therefore thank Him, and love Him all the more.

But if I have to speak out my mind on the matter, I agree *A still rarer virtue is it to serve God in prosperity.* with St. Augustine and St. Ambrose, that it is a far more difficult and rare thing to love God sincerely in the time of prosperity, when all our wishes are fulfilled, than when we have to suffer. How so? Although prosperity should impel a generous mind to sentiments of gratitude, although temporal goods, such as health, riches, honors, the esteem of men, and lawful pleasures are not evil in themselves, but rather opportunities given us to further the glory of God, and to help others; yet, on account

---

[1] In igne probatur aurum et argentum; homines vero receptibiles in camino humiliationis.—Ecclus. ii. 5.

[2] Adhuc tu permanes in simplicitate tua? Benedic Deo et morere.—Job ii. 9.

[3] Manifeste vana facta est spes tua, et eleemosynæ tuæ modo apparuerunt.—Tob. ii. 22.

of the corruption of our nature, they expose our virtue to far
greater dangers than trials and crosses do. Because the latter
draw the heart, as it were, violently from creatures, and force it
to turn to the Creator; while the former cause the heart and
mind to become attached to creatures and to neglect the Creator.
Adversity takes away from man many occasions of sin; but prosperity brings with it all that inflames our bad desires and leads
us into sin. It is, then, a great and difficult virtue to be prosperous, and yet not to allow our prosperity to get the upper hand;
to contend against it and not to be overcome in the struggle, as
St. Augustine says.[1] It is extremely difficult to be in an honorable position, and yet to be outwardly and inwardly humble; to
be rich, and yet to be poor in spirit; to have abundance of everything, and yet not to transgress the bounds of moderation; to be
in the midst of pleasures, and yet to keep one's senses in check
by mortification. It is a great virtue indeed to be pious in prosperity! "In fact," says St. Gregory, "it seems much easier to
bear adversity patiently than to avoid losing one's soul in prosperity."[2]

As men
themselves
acknowl-
edge.

The prudent and far-seeing emperor Galba, when giving instructions to Giso, whom he had designed to make his succes-
sor, added amongst others the following: you have not yet had
experience of all dangers; up to the present you have only had
adverse fortune to bear, and there is no great difficulty in that.
It is only when you ascend the throne that your trials will really
commence, for then you will have to show the world that you
are a brave and determined man: "prosperity proves our constancy much more than adversity; for miseries we bear, but we
are corrupted by good fortune."[3] The virtuous and heroic
Catharine, the wife of Henry VIII., king of England, who has
left behind her a reputation for the greatest patience and virtue,
when she was divorced by her impious husband and thrown into
prison, used to say: I do not wish for too great prosperity nor
too much suffering in this world; because each has its dangers,
temptations, and difficulties; but if I had to choose between them,
then should I prefer the greatest misery to the greatest good fortune; because while those who suffer are deprived of consolation,

---

[1] Magnæ virtutis est, cum felicitate luctari; magnæ felicitatis est, a felicitate non vinci.—
S. Aug. de verb. Dom. c. 13.

[2] Profecto facilius esse videtur adversam fortunam ferre, quam secundam conservare.

[3] Secundæ res acrioribus stimulis animum explorant; quia miseriæ tolerantur, felicitate
corrumpimur.

they who are in prosperity are nearly always blinded by their success and perverted. Mark those words, suffering Christians! You often sigh and wish to be freed from your domestic crosses. Would that I were in good health, you exclaim; would that I were not so poor and miserable; how zealously I should serve my God, and what good I should do my neighbor! My good friends, you do not know what you wish! It is not indeed impossible to be pious and virtuous in prosperity; but it is a rare and difficult thing. Truly it is a great virtue to love God in prosperity; but it is a far more certain virtue to love Him in adversity.

But without disputing any longer on this point, since men are wont to do wrong in both circumstances, the truth of my proposition is made evident at all events, namely, that the virtue of that man is certainly the greatest who, being proved in both ways, always remains faithful to God, so that he is neither elated by prosperity nor cast down by adversity; he serves his God as zealously when things go according to his wishes as when everything turns out a failure with him; like St. Paul he knows how to enjoy abundance and to suffer want with the same equanimity; whether he laughs with joy or weeps in sorrow, he is still true to his love for God; whether he is poor or rich, sick or healthy, despised or honored, sad or joyful; in a word whatever may be his circumstances, he is always the same with regard to his duty to God. There, says St. Bernard, you have a pattern of perfect and sincere virtue. For, one of that kind shows that he has a right appreciation of God and of created things; he proves that he esteems nothing outside of God; that he looks on God as his only true Good, with whom alone he is satisfied; that he does not desire temporal goods, health, comfort, pleasure, riches, honors, or the esteem of men, nor use them, unless in so far as they help him to offer to God an acceptable service according to the divine will and decree. Hence it is a matter of indifference to him whether he has those things or not, whether he gains or loses them. If God gives them to him, he accepts them with gratitude; but his whole heart and love still belong to God. If his health is taken from him by sickness, his joy by some trouble, his money by misfortune, his good name by disgrace, his pleasure by the death of some good friend, he is still satisfied with his God, and continues to serve Him with as much zeal as ever. And that is the way to keep the chief command-

Hence it i a sign of th sincerest virtue to love God both in pro perity and adversity.

ment of the law: " Thou shalt love the Lord thy God with thy whole heart, and with thy whole soul, and with thy whole mind." [1]   As St. Bernard says: Not to become perverted from the service of God by the caresses of prosperity, nor to be deterred from it by adversity, that is to love Him with our whole heart and soul and strength. [2]

As holy Job did. So it was with Job, who, when he was the richest and greatest man in all the East, was looked on by God as His most faithful servant, who had not his like upon earth, and when he lost his children, his property, and his wealth at once, and was stricken with a grievous ulcer from head to foot, abandoned and jeered at by his best friends, still remained faithful to God. " In all of these things," says the Scripture, "Job sinned not by his lips, nor spoke he any foolish thing against God." [3]   In all his troubles, not a word of sinful complaint escaped him; all he had to say was: " If we have received good things at the hand of God, why should we not receive evil?" [4]   "The Lord gave," and therefore I have always blessed His holy name; " the Lord hath taken away; as it hath pleased the Lord, so is it done: blessed be the name of the Lord." [5]

And the holy king, St. Louis. So it was with the saintly king Louis of France, who in the midst of royal honors and riches led a pious and holy life. He was once routed in battle by the Saracens, and taken prisoner; and what do you think he did, my dear brethren, when this great misfortune befell him? When he was brought to the room he was to occupy as a prisoner, he took his breviary into his hand, and without the least change of countenance, just as if he were in his own palace in Paris, began to read the office which he had not yet finished for the day.

And Seraphina Colonna, a noble lady. So it was (listen to this, you women) with Seraphina Colonna, as Mazzara writes in her life. She belonged to a rich and noble family, and although she was in the midst of worldly joys, yet showed from her earliest years that one can serve God by leading a holy life even in the greatest prosperity. But she was not

---

[1] Diliges Dominum Deum tuum ex toto corde tuo, et in tota anima tua, et in tota mente tua.—Matt. xxii. 37.

[2] Non abduci blanditiis, nec injuriis frangi ; toto corde, tota anima, tota virtute diligere est. —S. Bern. in Cant.

[3] In omnibus his non peccavit Job labiis suis, neque stultum quid contra Deum locutus est.—Job i. 22.

[4] Si bona suscepimus de manu Dei, mala quare non suscipiamus.—Ibid ii. 10.

[5] Dominus dedit ; Dominus abstulit ; sicut Domino placuit, ita factum est : sit nomen Domini benedictum.—Ibid i. 21.

long without the cross; she married a certain Count, a most wicked man, who treated her like a servant, compelled her to receive his concubine with every mark of respect, beat and abused her unmercifully, and at last put her away as an adulteress, and shut her up in a convent of poor Clares. Think of what this noble lady must have suffered from such treatment, while there are many who can not bear even a cross look from their husbands. Seraphina, what didst thou think of thy lot? Wert thou still satisfied with God, who sent thee such hard trials? Truly she was! Her heart and her love were centred in God as before; in the midst of her sore troubles her only prayer was: "God strengthen me, that I may bear all according to Thy will."[1]

I will relate for you still another example of fidelity to God in prosperity and adversity, which was exhibited to the world in the year 1703, and is recorded by Father Joseph Prola of our Society. Listen to this, you gentlemen! Charles of Carneato, Marquis of Bagnasco, who had imperial blood in his veins, was related to the greatest sovereigns of Europe, was the chief man at the court of Turin, Lieutenant-General of the army, Governor of many provinces and fortresses, and had been entrusted by the king with the administration of the affairs of the kingdom; in the midst of his good fortune, at the very summit of honors and dignities, in the greatest abundance of wealth and riches, this nobleman showed that one can be great in the eyes of the world, and at the same time in the sight of God. He was a model of all Christian virtues, so that he might well put to shame many a religious by his steadfast piety. He placed God and His holy law before all created things; and this was the only rule by which he managed all his affairs, submitting them and himself completely to the divine will. Do you wish to hear a proof of the genuineness and sincerity of his virtue? Mark, then, how he acted in the time of adversity. He was smitten by the hand of God almost like another Job. Seven of his sons died one after the other. Ah, what a sore blow for a father, and such a rich father! And yet he looked on with unchanged countenance and undisturbed peace of mind, as if he were not a whit concerned. His eighth son alone remained to him, as the heir of his name and the future hope of his family; but even he was carried off by a sudden death in the father's absence. Imagine how the father's heart was torn with grief! A priest, an

---

[1] Domine, comforta me, ut omnia possim.

intimate friend of his, visited him to console him; but when he saw no change or sign of sorrow in the countenance of the Marquis, he thought that perhaps the latter was hiding his grief so as not to allow it to appear outwardly, and therefore he exhorted him to indulge his sorrow for a time, and to relieve himself in that way. Charles turned to him and smiled; I have done what you suggest, he said; the words, "may the will of God be done," have completely assuaged my grief. But his troubles were not yet at an end. A grievous illness attacked him soon after and confined him to bed, causing him most fearful agony, and completely crippling him, so that he could not stir hand or foot; hot and poisonous humors coursed through his veins, torturing his whole body, and he was not able even to turn from one side to the other. For seven whole years he lay in this miserable state, suffering with the most heroic patience, and never letting a word of complaint escape his lips. "May the will of God be done," was his sole consolation during the whole time.

Most of us are quite the contrary and are as changeable as the moon in our love for God.

Ah, Christians, what do we think of this? Are we not forced to sigh deeply and to acknowledge that the virtue of those people was indeed rare, in prosperity as well as in adversity? So it is; they proved that they loved God with their whole heart and soul above all things and in all circumstances. But how is it with us in this respect? The Holy Ghost says by the Wise Man: " A holy man continueth in wisdom as the sun;"[1] he who loves God sincerely still continues to love, whether he is prosperous or the reverse; he is like the sun, that never changes its light, whether it is thrown on dung or on gold. But " a fool is changed as the moon."[2] Mark this simile. Astronomers tell us that when the moon shows her dark side to the earth, she throws all her light upwards towards heaven; on the other hand when her dark side is turned towards heaven, we enjoy all her light here on earth; thus she never sheds her light equally on heaven and on earth, but as her light is withdrawn from us it increases in heaven, and as it is withdrawn from heaven it increases on earth. " A fool is changed as the moon; " is it not so with the greater number of us, my dear brethren?

Many who serve God in adversity

When some find the star of their fortunes darkened by trials and calamities, so that they are deprived of all earthly joy and

---

[1] Homo sanctus in sapientia manet sicut sol.—Ecclus. xxvii. 12.
[2] Stultus sicut luna mutatur.—Ibid.

consolation, they send the rays of their love to heaven, they seek God and adore Him. But when the darkness vanishes, when their trials come to an end, and the full light of prosperity shines on them, oh, how they then withdraw their light from heaven! They forget their Creator; their love, which now attaches itself to creatures and temporal things, grows cold towards God and heavenly goods. Many a one living in lowly poverty, and working hard to support himself and his family, is truly humble, meek, merciful, modest, zealous in prayer, diligent in the performance of his morning and evening devotions, in frequenting the sacraments, in hearing sermons and in the practice of all the other virtues; but if fortune begins to smile on him, if he grows rich, or happens to be raised to some honorable position, then, humility, where art thou? Modesty, what has become of thee? Devotion, where hast thou vanished to? Ah, how soon those things are forgotten, and how quickly the usages of the world are learned, and its vanities and practices adopted! Nay, you will see many a one who after marriage fixes all his love on a creature, and hardly ever makes his appearance in church; as if he were one of the guests mentioned in the Gospel, who said: "I have married a wife, and therefore I cannot come."[1] "A fool is changed as the moon." So inconstant and fickle are we.

(margin: forget Him in prosperity.)

Others act in a way quite opposite to that. In the time of prosperity they are cheerful, and resigned to the will of God; they praise and bless Him, and say with joyful hearts: Lord, Thy will be done! But if they are visited by some affliction, if the husband or wife is attacked by illness, if a dear child dies, if they are disappointed of some legacy they hoped for, if they lose an important lawsuit, if they fail in their undertakings, if they are put to shame, or have some other trial to bear, then there is an end of their resignation and contentment. God is no longer pleasing to them. Their trouble and chagrin are so great that they cannot pray. O what a heavy cross! they exclaim. How have I deserved it from God? They think no more of their former prosperity and of the blessings that God bestowed on them so richly in preference to many others. "A fool is changed as the moon." Whence comes this inconstancy? Ah, from the want of true virtue and a sincere love of God. We have not yet given ourselves to Him without reserve; we do not love Him with our whole heart and soul and strength above all things. Other-

(margin: Others who love Him in prosperity abandon Him in adversity. Both are wanting in true virtue.)

---

[1] Uxorem duxi, et ideo non possum venire.—Luke xiv. 20.

wise we should be the same to Him in all circumstances, in prosperity and adversity, no matter what He does with us; so that if we were asked: what do you wish, what do you desire on earth? we should be able to answer with truth: I wish and desire nothing else but what God wills, and how God wills.

How to remain faithful to God in both circumstances. That is the difficulty, you think. And you are right. But we must endeavor to learn this difficult virtue, and we can learn it, if we frequently think of our last end, of the reason why we are on this earth, which is none other than to love God and be happy with Him forever. Therefore we must look on it as certain that all created goods, whatever be their names, such as riches, honors, pleasures, health, the love and friendship of men, are not real goods; and we must be fully convinced that all adverse circumstances, whatever they may be, such as sickness, natural sorrow, poverty, loss of good name, abandonment by men, have not the least particle of true evil in them; but that our true good, for which we have to strive, is the possession of God here on earth by grace, and hereafter in heaven by vision. This one supreme Good I can possess whether I am healthy or sick, poor or rich, joyful or sorrowful; therefore I have nothing on earth to fear, hope for, or love but God; and in all circumstances God must be the object of my greatest love and esteem. Let us keep this in mind in the daily alternations of joy and sorrow to which we are exposed, and accept those trifling changes from the hand of God, offering them up to Him, as I have explained more at length when treating of conformity to the will of God. Thus we shall gradually learn how to be the same towards God even in changes of greater importance. May God grant us the grace to do that! Amen.

See several sermons on the same subject in the first, third, fifth, and sixth parts.

ON A GOOD CONSCIENCE.

ON THE PEACE OF HEART THAT COMES FROM A GOOD CONSCIENCE.

Subject.

What a beautiful and consoling good this peace is, and how we are to seek and find it.—*Preached on the first Sunday after Epiphany.*

Text.

Ecce pater tuus et ego dolentes quærebamus te.—Luke ii. 48.

" Behold Thy father and I have sought Thee sorrowing."

Introduction.

And could such holy people be troubled and sad at heart? Mary and Joseph, whose souls were so enlightened and so united to the will of God, were they oppressed with sadness and anguish of mind? "Thy father and I have sought Thee sorrowing." Yes truly; but they had good reason for it; they had lost Jesus, the divine Child; had they not then cause to be troubled? The loss of Jesus was the only thing on earth that could disturb the peace of their hearts. My dear brethren, we are daily disturbed and uneasy at heart. Why? Is it because we have lost Jesus? Ah, if that were the reason of the sighs and tears of sinners, they would soon find peace again! But that is not generally the cause of our trouble. We must seek for it elsewhere. What is it, then? We have now so many trials and calamities to contend with; sickness threatens our health and life; wars deprive us of our goods and the usual means of subsistence; manifold troubles make life bitter to us. Ah, if I could now say to you with truth: be comforted! rejoice! we have nothing to fear; we shall be left in peace; all that before threatened us shall be removed; tranquillity shall be restored; would not that be good news for you? Now, I am not wanting in good wishes at least in your regard; and if you do your part, then you will experience in reality and attain that which will bring us most certainly to the enjoyment of peace.

Plan of Discourse.

Therefore at the beginning of the New Year I wish myself and all of you from my heart a constant peace of mind. What a beautiful and consoling good this peace is, and how we must seek and find it, I shall explain in the first part. My repeated wish in the second part shall be for this peace to remain with us in all circumstances. Peace be to you! is the compendium of the whole sermon.

Do Thou grant it to us by Thy grace, Christ Jesus, Author and Giver of true peace! We beg it of Thee through the intercession of Mary Thy Mother, and of our holy guardian angels.

In what peace of heart consists.

Yes, you think; but what is the good of your wishes? If wishing and desiring were of any avail, then we should have had peace long ago; in fact, there would never have been any war. God help us! we know too well what war is, and what it leaves behind. Too often have we had to learn that sad lesson. We all wish for peace, and seek it, and desire it. But vain are all our sighs, and wishes, and longings, as well as the means we use to realize them. We call out: "Peace, peace, and there was no peace."[1] We still suffer from the calamities of war. Thus you wish us a blessing that neither you can give us nor we with all our efforts can obtain. What you say is quite true, my dear brethren, if you mean every kind of peace; but what I wish you is the peace of the heart, peace with yourselves, which every man can have, even in the midst of the horrors of war; and it consists in this: that no matter what troubles, crosses, or trials come to us from exterior sources, we still keep the heart quiet and tranquil. This is what the angels announced at the birth of Our Lord: "And on earth peace to men of good will."[2] This is the peace that Christ left to His servants when He was sending forth His disciples as lambs in the midst of ravening wolves: "Peace I leave with you, My peace I give unto you."[3] It is the peace that St. Paul wishes the Philippians: "And the peace of God, which

---

[1] Pax, pax, et non erat pax.—Jerem. vi. 14.

[2] Et in terra pax hominibus bonæ voluntatis.—Luke ii. 14.

[3] Pacem relinquo vobis, pacem meam do vobis.—John xiv. 27.

surpasseth all understanding, keep your hearts and minds in Christ Jesus." [1]

Oh! what a beautiful good, to have peace with one's self, to be always and unchangeably contented and satisfied at heart! That is the best, nay, the only true good that man can enjoy on this earth. "There is no pleasure above the joy of the heart," [2] says the wise Ecclesiasticus. And in truth, how would it help me to happiness to have all the goods of the world, if I were discontented at heart? And how could it make me unhappy to be the poorest of men, if I am peaceful and contented at heart? Therefore whenever the Holy Scriptures speak of peace, they always assign the heart as its true dwelling-place. Thus Anna in her Canticle says: "My heart hath rejoiced." [3] And Ecclesiasticus: "My heart delighted." [4] And the Prophet David: "Thou hast given gladness in my heart." [5] The joy itself of the elect consists in inward joy and peace of heart, as the Prophet Isaias says: "Thus saith the Lord: Behold I will bring upon her as it were a river of peace, and as an overflowing torrent." [6]

This is the choicest good that man can enjoy on earth.

I acknowledge, says St. Augustine, that all men seek and desire this peace; "as there is no one who does not wish to rejoice so there is no one who does not wish to have peace." [7] That is, there is no one who does not wish to be contented, pleased, and satisfied at heart. Ask the soldier in the midst of the battle, the peasant in the field, the tradesman in his workshop, the merchant in his journeys by sea and land, what they seek by their labor; and they will all answer, contentment and peace of heart— that is the object of all my thoughts, desires, and cares. If I were not so poor, say some, if I were as rich as those others, I should be contented. If I were in as high a position, think others, as such-and-such a one, I should be contented. If there were nothing to prevent me from enjoying the love of that creature, I should be contented. Ah, my good people, you are wrong from the very start! "O ye sons of men," I may well exclaim with the Prophet David, "how long will you be dull of heart? Why do

But that peace is vainly sought for in transitory things. Shown by similes.

---

[1] Et pax Dei quæ exsuperat omnem sensum, custodiat corda vestra, et intelligentias vestras in Christo Jesu.—Philipp. iv. 7.

[2] Non est oblectamentum super cordis gaudium.—Ecclus. xxx. 16.

[3] Exultavit cor meum.—I. Kings ii. 2.

[4] Lætatum est cor meo.—Ecclus. li. 20.

[5] Dedisti lætitiam in corde meo.—Ps. iv. 7.

[6] Dicit Dominus : ecce ego declinabo super eum quasi fluviam pacis. et quasi torrentem inundantem.—Is. lxvi. 12.

[7] Sicuti nemo est qui gaudere nolit, ita nemo est qui nolit habere pacem.

you love vanity and seek after lying?"[1] Peace is not to be found where you are looking for it. The goods that you seek are external to yourselves; they cannot touch the heart or satisfy it interiorly. Get possession of all the riches and honors and pleasures of earth; what good will they do you, if you have to lie sick in bed? Will they give you peace? No. And why not? Because health, which is an interior good, is wanting to you; without it all outward things cannot bring you contentment. "When you say," writes St. Augustine, "I wish to live happily, you desire a good thing, but you cannot have it here."[2] When St. Maclovius was a youth he was singularly deceived in that matter. He had heard that there was somewhere on earth a fortunate island, in which no one had to work, or to suffer trials or contradictions. He believed the story to be true, and embarked in a ship to find the island. He came to one where he found a number of people with pale and haggard countenances. The air, he thought, must be very unhealthy here; this cannot be the place I am looking for. He sailed farther and came to another island, where he saw that the inhabitants were all healthy and strong of body, but they were clad in rags. The air is good here, he thought, but the poverty of the place is great; this is not the happy island. He went on farther and came to one that was full of riches, but hardly had he set foot on shore, when he beheld the inhabitants fighting with one another so fiercely that many were wounded, and some lost their lives. Truly, he thought, there is wealth enough here; but at the same time there is too much fighting and contention; this is not the happy island. Seven years did he spend in his search; but in one place he found too much heat; in another, piercing cold; in a third, fearful earthquakes; in a fourth, terrible storms. In one place he saw blind people, in another cripples; everywhere, sick and dead. Finally, after the lapse of seven years, his eyes were opened, and he saw that there is no place on earth where perfect peace and happiness can be found; therefore he resolved to leave all earthly things, to enter religion, by serving God zealously to seek true, heavenly, and eternal happiness; a resolution that he actually carried into effect. So it is; to no purpose do you seek in the world what you cannot find in it, nor expect from it. You place your happiness in earthly things, and say to

---

[1] Filii hominum, usquequo gravi corde? utquid diligitus venitatem et quæritis mendacium?—Ps. iv. 3.

[2] Quando dicis: beate vivere volo, bonem rem quæris, sed non hic.—S. Aug. in Ps. cxviii.

yourself: in that town a man can make his fortune and attain an honorable position, and lead an easy, comfortable life; there one can have no difficulty in getting on in the world. But go in thought to that very town, and see how things are there, and you will find a number of disappointed hopes, of heart-breaking failures; you will see those who were formerly the greatest of the land now plunged into the depths of misery; you will find wretchedness, suffering, and sickness even amongst those who are best off; you will see that neither honors nor riches can free men from trouble, persecution, danger, discomfort, and death; in all places you will come across rich and great men who lead very unhappy lives. It is true that the world esteems happy those who have an abundance of its goods and can live in magnificent style. "They have called the people happy that hath these things." [1] But they say not the truth, says the Lord. "O my people, they that call thee blessed, the same deceive thee, and destroy the way of thy steps." [2] Thus you only lose your time and labor in following up a shadow, instead of seeking the only true, supreme happiness, which you will certainly not find here; you betray yourself, and all those who pronounce you happy in the possession of worldly goods betray you also. No, quite different is the happiness you must seek in order to enjoy true peace. Nothing can fully satisfy the heart and mind but a genuine and permanent good, and it must be one that can content all the desires of the heart. But the honors, riches, and pleasures of the world are not goods of that kind; and therefore to no purpose do you seek for peace of heart in them.

There never was since the beginning of the world and there never will be till the end of it any one who found perfect satisfaction and contentment in such things. No matter how abundantly one may be provided with them, there still remains a want, which disturbs the peace of the heart. Achab was a great king in Israel; was he contented in the midst of his riches and treasures? Hear what the Scripture says of him: "Angry and fretting, . . . and casting himself upon his bed, he turned away his face to the wall and would eat no bread." [3] What was the matter with him? What distressed him to such an extent? *Shown by examples from Scripture.*

[1] Beatum dixerunt populum cui hæc sunt.—Ps. cxliii. 15.

[2] Popule meus, qui te beatum dicunt, ipsi te decipiunt, et viam gressuum tuorum dissipant.—Is. iii. 12.

[3] Indignans et frendens, . . . et projiciens se in lectulum suum, avertit faciem suam ad parietem, et non comedit panem.—III. Kings xxi. 4.

Naboth had a vineyard near the palace, and Achab wished to get possession of it in order to increase his gardens, but failed to do so. That was the sole cause of his discontent. And was it worth while to trouble himself so much about it? Was a piece of ground that he wanted able to disturb his heart and cause him such worry that he was inconsolable? What an extraordinary thing for a king, who received tribute from so many towns, who had so many magnificent palaces and buildings at his disposal, to be troubled because he could not get possession of a small piece of ground! So it is. Peace and quiet of heart do not consist in having an abundance of worldly goods and riches, but in being content even with a little. Aman, the favorite of king Assuerus, came home to his wife and dilated on the extent of his glory and honor: "And he declared to them the greatness of his riches, and with how great glory the king had advanced him above all his princes and servants."[1] Was he happy with all his honors? Not by any means! "And whereas I have all these things," he said with bitterness of heart, "I think I have nothing."[2] What was wanting to him? Mardochai alone refused to honor him, and that caused him so much pain that all his riches could give him no pleasure.

Confirmed by other examples. Ptolemy, king of Egypt, was once walking on the bank of the Nile, when he saw some laborers, who after having eaten their poor meal, which consisted of bread and water, began to laugh and joke with each other. The king could not restrain his sighs and tears at seeing how happy those poor and lowly people were. "Ah unhappy me!" he exclaimed, "that I cannot be one of them."[3] I, too, might enjoy myself if I were as contented as they. And, O great king, wouldst thou wish to change with one of those poor workmen in order to enjoy thyself? Thou wearest the crown and sceptre of a vast kingdom; many countries are subject to thy sway; many great lords wait on thee day and night; palaces, gardens, well-furnished tables and all imaginable delights are ready for thee at any moment! True, but of what good is that to me when my heart is not content? And it is not content; because the desire of possessing more kingdoms, the fear of my enemies, the doubtful fidelity of my servants, and unceasing cares leave me neither peace nor rest. Of what good

---

[1] Exposuit illis magnitudinem divitiarum suarum, et quanta eum gloria super omnes principes et servos suos rex elevasset.—Esth v. 11.

[2] Et cum hæc omnia habeam, nihil me habere puto.—Ibid. 13.

[3] Heu me infelicem, qui neque unus ex iis esse possum.

to me, then, are all my riches, as long as there is no peace or quiet of heart for me? Those poor people there are twenty times happier with their piece of dry bread and their drink of cold water than I am with all my treasures and my whole kingdom. Charles V., that great Roman emperor and king of Spain, makes the same confession with regard to himself. After having heroically despised the world so far as to abdicate his crown and retire into solitude, he acknowledged that the whole time while he was king and emperor he never enjoyed a single quarter of an hour of true peace and contentment of heart, such as he did enjoy after having left the world. To put the matter briefly; was there ever a man in the world who had more of its riches, honors, and pleasures than Solomon? Gold and silver were to him like the stones on the street, as we read in the Third Book of Kings: And he made silver to be as plentiful in Jerusalem as stones." [1] On account of his wonderful wisdom, kings and queens of other countries looked on him almost as a god. He himself describes the pleasures he enjoyed: "Whatsoever my eyes desired, I refused them not; and I withheld not my heart from enjoying every pleasure, and delighting itself in the things which I had prepared." [2] But was he contented and happy with it all? Hear what he says of it: "I saw in all things vanity and vexation of mind." [3] So true it is, my dear brethren, that all the exterior goods of the world, its honors, riches, and joys are not capable of contenting or filling the human heart. It is useless, then, to seek for peace of heart in such things.

Therefore, concludes St. Augustine, you must seek it in something better than all that the world can give or take away; in something better than yourself. And what will that be unless your Lord and God? [4] There is only one Good, and that is an infinite one which can satisfy your heart. "So great is the dignity of the human heart," continues the Saint, "that no good except the Supreme Good can satisfy it." [5] This Good we can all possess, if we wish, by keeping our consciences in the state of grace and free from sin. If I have a good conscience, then God is mine,

This peace is to be found in God alone, who is possessed by a good conscience.

[1] Fecitque ut tanta esset abundantia argenti in Jerusalem, quanta et lapidum.—III. Kings x. 27.

[2] Omnia quæ desideraverunt oculi mei, non negavi eis ; nec prohibui cor meum, quin omni voluptate frueretur, et oblectaret se in his quae præparaveram.—Eccles. ii. 10.

[3] Vidi in omnibus vanitatem et afflictionem animi.—Ibid. ii.

[4] Superest igitur, ut quæras quod sit melius. Quid erit obsecro, nisi Deus tuus?

[5] Cor humanum tantæ est dignitatis, ut nullum bonum præter summum bonum ei sufficere possit.

and with Him I have all that I can wish or desire. And God is so permanently and constantly mine that no angel in heaven no devil in hell, no man on earth, no joy or sorrow, can deprive me of Him, unless with my own consent; and He is mine with the assurance that, if I only keep my conscience pure, I shall possess Him for all eternity. O heart of man! what could content thee, if this cannot?

As the just know.
Away with your absurd ideas, children of the flesh and the world! You know nothing of this happiness, for you have too little experience of it! It is only those souls who seek and love God alone who understand what I mean; what peace, pleasure, and joy it brings to the heart to have a good conscience, and to think: God is my Friend; I am a friend and child of God; God pleases me and I please Him; God wills what He knows to be best for me, and I will all that He wills; God takes care of me, and all I need trouble about is to keep my conscience pure. If all temporal riches, consolations, and pleasures are taken from me by adversity; if my own natural inclinations oppose me to my great distress, and put difficulties in my way, I shall still remain undisturbed and peaceful at heart, resigned to God's will, and I shall be as rich as before in the possession of the Supreme Good. If death comes and carries me off in this state, in which I mean to persevere, then it will translate me to that place where I can enjoy my beloved Good for all eternity. So that, my dear brethren, if my conscience is like that, I have already attained that peace which the world cannot give, and, in the midst of the turmoil and tumult of the world, can with a smiling countenance say with the Prophet David: "The light of Thy countenance, O Lord, is signed upon us,"[1] and therefore, "Thou hast given gladness in my heart."[2] This joy of heart, this peace of a good conscience is what I wish you, not only for the coming year, but for all the years of your lives, as I shall explain further in the

Second Part.

This peace is wished to the clergy.
Peace be with you, Reverend members of the clergy! All the duties to which we are bound by our holy state require us to possess this peace constantly in a good conscience. For our work is to be always occupied with God, either singing psalms in choir, or praising and blessing God at home in the divine office,

---

[1] Signatum est super nos lumen vultus tui Domine.—Ps. iv. 7.

[2] Dedisti lætitiam in corde meo.—Ibid.

or celebrating daily the holy sacrifice in which God is the food
of our souls, and in which we offer Christ to the Eternal Father,
or furthering the divine honor by our innocent lives, our instructions, and our edifying example. What better means could we
have to secure the possession of the Supreme Good, and of peace
and contentment of heart? But who does not acknowledge
that, for that very reason, we are bound to use the utmost care
to keep our conscience pure? For, (O my God! what an abom-
ination that would be!) how could I have peace of heart, if I
take Thy precious flesh and blood into my hands at Thy altar;
if I look at them with my eyes, eat and drink them with my
mouth, while my conscience reproaches me saying: thy hands
are soiled, thy eyes unclean, thy mouth a foul sepulchre; thou
hast a grievous sin on thy conscience; thou hast lost thy God?
How could I have peace and contentment, if, while I am praising God in daily hymns and prayers, my conscience reproached
me saying: thy prayers and hymns do not please the Lord; thou
art an enemy of God! How could I have peace and contentment, if, while I try by my instructions to deter others from vice,
and lead them on to good, my conscience cries out to me; thou
thyself art not as thou shouldst be! thou triest to lead others to
heaven, and followest the broad road to hell! O my God, preserve me from that! Let us often remember the Offertory prayer:
" The priests offer bread and wine, and therefore they shall be
holy to their God. " If we try to acquire this holiness, we shall
be able to enjoy peace of heart.

Peace be with you, members of the laity! I acknowledge that To the laity.
your different duties and occupations often disturb your rest,
when you endeavor to perform them properly. All sorts of cares,
plans, and considerations pass daily through your minds; many
of your undertakings come to naught; frequently you are doomed
to disappointment in the execution of some pet scheme. But
all these disquieting influences are external; they cannot interfere with your peace of heart. What you should be specially
careful of is this: your duties give you many an opportunity of sul-
lying your consciences by injustice, want of charity towards your
neighbor, envy, hatred and anger against your opponents, pride
and contempt of your inferiors, acting on worldly policy through
human respect, or culpable ignorance; if you allow yourselves
to be deceived by the false maxims and principles of the perverse
world, if you do not keep God before your eyes, oh, then it is

all up with your consciences, with the friendship of God, with your peace of heart, and you will have nothing but strife and contention within and without. Therefore whatever you do, see first of all that your consciences are in good order. Impress deeply on your minds this truth: that our only and supreme good is God, and God alone, whom we can possess by grace here and by vision in heaven. Ask yourselves often: "What doth it profit a man, if he gain the whole world, and suffer the loss of his own soul?"[1] What will it help me to gain all the honors, riches, and pleasures of the world by my labor and diligence if I lose God, my supreme Good, by sin? No; I will so manage matters as to keep peace with God and myself! So be it then! Peace be with you!

To married people.

Peace be with you, married people! The most necessary thing in your state is peace and harmony with each other. If that is wanting, oh, then your state is a bitter one, a hell as bad as it can be made on this earth! Ah, perhaps some are now thinking, that is what we have to complain of! That drunken, passionate husband has not a kind word or look for me; he can only curse and abuse. That vain, idle wife loses her time paying useless visits, and allows the house to take care of itself; she spends more in dress than we can make in a year; the children are obstinate and disobedient; we cannot trust the servants; what we tell them to do, we must often do ourselves; how can we have peace and contentment under such circumstances? True, it is not an easy matter! But where do all these disorders come from? You are not at peace with God in your hearts; you have not a good conscience which is in all things conformable to the will of God. If you only endeavor to keep in the friendship of God, the evils you complain of will soon be remedied; the husband will love his wife, according to the words of St. Paul, as Christ loves the Church; the wife will obey her husband as her superior in all things that do not run counter to the divine law; parents will bring up their children carefully for heaven; children will love their parents, and show them due honor; masters and mistresses will give their servants good example; servants will be ready to obey the least sign of their masters with respect and willingness; men will bear one another's faults with meekness, and leave to God what they cannot change or

---

[1] Quid prodest homini, si mundum universum lucretur, animæ vero suæ detrimentum patiatur?—Matt. xvi. 26.

amend, patiently and resignedly bearing it; they will share in each other's joys and sorrows, and therefore all will enjoy peace and contentment, on which so much depends. That is the peace I wish you with all my heart.

Peace be with you, unmarried people! Many of you, who are still in the bloom of youth, seek peace, pleasure, and happiness in living according to the world, in dressing and adorning yourselves to please the eyes of others, in talking, amusing yourselves, going on parties of pleasure, dancing, and such things. But what a great mistake you are making! "Seek what you are seeking," says St. Augustine, "but there is no peace where you are looking for it."[1] True peace of heart is to be found nowhere but in a pure conscience united with God; in the follies you seek the conscience is often wounded. You yourselves must acknowledge, if your consciences are still tender and you have any desire of heaven left, that after having enjoyed those pleasures, either immediately afterwards, or when you are going to confession, you have nothing from them, but uneasiness, anxiety, bitterness of heart, not to speak of the loss of holy purity. Come, Christian sons and daughters, children of God, co-heirs with Jesus Christ! your hearts are created for far better things! It is God, and God alone whom you should love, Him should you possess by sanctifying grace, and in Him should you rejoice. Only try to please Him; clear out your hearts for Him, and avoid with the utmost care all that could offend Him in the least degree; then you will be able to rejoice even in solitude, and to say with truth: "I found Him whom my soul loveth."[2] I possess God, and with Him true peace and joy of heart.

To the unmarried.

Peace be with you, widows and orphans! Death has deprived you of husband or parents, and you are left alone without help or consolation. Be comforted! If you only have your supreme Good by a pure conscience, you have something that death cannot deprive you of; and as long as God is your Friend, what have you to fear, or what more can you desire? Think with the Prophet David: "My father and my mother have left me, but the Lord hath taken me up;"[3] my husband, my parents, have left me; but God is my Guardian, my Provider, my Helper, my Father and Mother. "The Lord ruleth me, and I shall want

To widows and orphans.

---

[1] Quærite quod quæritis ; sed non est requies ubi quæritis eam.
[2] Inveni quem diligit anima mea.—Cant. iii. 4.
[3] Pater meus et mater mea dereliquerunt me, Dominus autem assumpsit me.—Ps. xxvi. 10.

nothing." [1] What I am now about to say will in all probability concern the most of you too.

Peace be with you, troubled and afflicted Christians! You are of the number of those of whom Christ said to His disciples: "You shall lament and weep, but the world shall rejoice;" [2] in poverty and misery, in pains and sickness, in persecution and oppression, in hard work and fatigue, in much want and suffering you shall mingle your bread with your tears. All this is very hard and bitter to the natural inclination. I compassionate you; yet I cannot say that you are unhappy. But if in the midst of your trials you have not a good conscience, and have lost your God, then I could shed tears of blood through pity for you! Then indeed you would be miserable in every way, abandoned by God and man, by heaven and earth, and not expecting any consolation or alleviation in your troubles; miserable in time, miserable in eternity! But if we have to suffer here a short time in accordance with the divine decrees, why do you not seek for some consolation in your trials, and that, too, the best of all, which you can find in your God by having a good conscience and keeping Him as your Friend? If you have Him, then let the world go as it may; the best Good is yours; in Him alone you have more than enough to fill your hearts with peace and contentment even in the bitterest sufferings, and to give you the joy of the children of God, as we shall see in a future sermon, for if it is God's will, I intend speaking of this subject for some months to come.

Peace be with you, last of all, sinners! For you and you alone this wish is most necessary, because, as you are in the state of sin, you have lost peace altogether. No doubt, unless you are hardened in wickedness, you will acknowledge the truth of the words of the Prophet Jeremias: "Know thou and see that it is an evil and a bitter thing for thee to have left the Lord thy God." [3] "For who hath resisted Him, and hath had peace?" [4] Who could be contented and happy, knowing that God, who is present everywhere, is his enemy? No one. Come, then; delay no longer; return by true penance, and enjoy that peace which the merciful, though angry God offers you every moment; then you will see and experience what a great difference there is be-

---

[1] Dominus regit me, et nihil mihi deerit.—Ps. xxii. 1.

[2] Plorabitis et flebitis vos; mundus autem gaudebit.—John xvi. 20.

[3] Scito et vide quia malum et amarum est reliquisse te Dominum Deum tuum.—Jer. ii.19.

[4] Quis restitit ei, et pacem habuit?—Job ix. 4.

tween being a servant of God and a slave of the devil, and how sweet it is to enjoy peace of mind in a good conscience. Again do I wish you all, "the peace of God which surpasseth all understanding." May it "keep your hearts and minds in Christ Jesus."[1] May it remain with you all the years of your lives, until you enjoy it with the elect of God in the kingdom of heaven for all eternity. Peace be with you! Amen.

SIXTY-EIGHTH SERMON.

ON THE HAPPINESS OF A GOOD CONSCIENCE.

Subject.

The peace of heart in a good conscience is a continual, joyful marriage-feast for the human soul; therefore let him who wishes to taste this joy preserve peace of heart with his God in a good conscience.—*Preached on the second Sunday after Epiphany.*

Text.

Vocatus est autem et Jesus et discipuli ejus ad nuptias.—John ii. 2.

"And Jesus also was invited, and His disciples, to the marriage."

Introduction.

Truly, a happy marriage-feast at which Jesus is present, seated at table! Doubtless those people of Cana had learned by faith that Christ, their Guest, was the true God and Saviour of the world. Now I leave you to imagine, my dear brethren, what exuberant joy and gladness they must have felt in their hearts at the marriage-feast; and meanwhile I shall continue the subject I have commenced, and wish you peace for the New Year; that peace which cannot be found unless in the possession of God by a good conscience, as I have shown on the last occasion. And that peace cannot be disturbed save and except by sin alone, which drives God out of the conscience; therefore, to keep it constantly, all we need do is to avoid sin. The proof of this I reserve for another occasion, and meanwhile I now go on to show the great consolation, joy, and happiness which that peace always brings the human soul in all circumstances; and to keep to the marriage-feast, I say:

[1] Pax Dei quæ exsuperat omnem sensum, custodiat corda vestra et intelligentias vestras in Christo Jesu.—Philipp. iv. 7.

Plan of Discourse.

The peace of heart in a good conscience is a continual, joyful marriage-feast for the human soul; therefore let him who wishes to taste this joy preserve peace of heart with his God in a good conscience. Such is the whole subject of this sermon.

Merciful Virgin Mary, at whose intercession the guests at the feast were miraculously provided with wine by thy Son, obtain for us through the holy angels from that same Son of thine His helping grace that we may always keep our consciences pure, and so taste how sweet the Lord is to those who love Him and have Him as their Friend.

What constitutes the pleasure of a marriage-feast.

Many delicate viands skilfully prepared, choice wines, agreeable company, pleasant conversation, laughing and jollity, music and dancing: there you have the joys and pleasures of a marriage-feast. But many a guest, although he seems to enjoy himself, is at heart ill at ease. He whose stomach rejects the costly dishes and wines cannot have much pleasure in eating or drinking. If there be among the guests one who is unpopular, or one who is regarded with dislike, or, as is often the case, who is a disagreeable, quarrelsome fellow, the harmony of the feast is disturbed, and each one wishes he had remained at home. He who thinks of his secret domestic cross can have no joy in the conversation, music, or dancing; for while his lips laugh, his heart is weeping. And when the feast is over the pleasure goes with it, and all one can say of it is, I have enjoyed myself. Even the bride and the bridegroom sometimes find their happiness gone after a few weeks, or even a few days; their laughter is turned into weeping, and one or other of them begins to sigh: ah, would that I were as I was before! Many of the guests bring home with them an uneasy conscience, a melancholy, gloomy spirit, on account of the too great freedom allowed. So it is in the world; the joy it offers its friends is seldom an unadulterated one, never a perfect, true, and constant one.

That is all to be found by peace of heart in a good conscience.

Far different, more pleasant, and joyful is the marriage-feast promised by the Holy Ghost to those who keep the peace of heart in a good conscience. " A secure mind is like a continual feast," [1] He says by the wise Solomon in the Book of Proverbs, which is never interrupted or disturbed in its joy. But you say, how is that? For even a poor man can have a good conscience. Truly he can, and, as a general rule, he can keep it more easily

[1] Secura mens quasi juge convivium.—Prov. xv. 15.

in poverty and want than in riches and abundance. But what sort of a marriage-feast is that in which even a bit of bread is sometimes wanting? Where are the different dishes? the costly wines? the pleasant company? the agreeable music? the laughing and dancing, that go to make up a merry feast? Ah, answers St. Paul, you are wrong in your ideas of the matter: "The kingdom of God is not meat and drink." You must know that the kingdom of God consists in a pious soul and a good conscience, not in earthly follies and amusements: "But justice, and peace, and joy in the Holy Ghost." [1]

The consolations of the Holy Ghost, which are compared to sweet wine, are more salutary for the conscience, and delight it more, than all worldly food and drink, for they enliven, not the body, but the soul, and never cause it disgust, as the body feels when it is satiated with food. St. Teresa once visited a princess in Spain, who had a great esteem for her. The princess brought her round her palace and showed her the gold and silver tapestry, her rare diamonds and costly ornaments, and told her moreover how she daily enjoyed the most exquisite dainties at table, etc. Teresa, hearing of all this magnificence, began to laugh heartily and uncontrollably, and being asked the reason of her merriment, she said: Madam, I must laugh at the great esteem in which you hold such things; for I look on them as mere rubbish. If in one hand I held all the treasures of earth and in the other a single consolation of the Holy Ghost, such as God gives me to taste in my heart, I would trample the whole world under foot, rather than lose a moment of divine consolation. Well does the Prophet Isaias say of the servants of God: "They shall run and not be weary, they shall walk and not faint." [2]

The consolations of the Holy Ghost are the sweetest wine.

And experience shows this to be the case. The worldling, whose only thought is the care and adornment of the body, and who is not much concerned about the purity of the conscience, is annoyed at the piety of the priest who takes half an hour to say Mass; when the law of the Church drives him to assist at the holy sacrifice once a week, he finds the time too long, and can hardly wait for the end of Mass, or else he complains of the heat or the cold. If one of those children of the world happens to come to a sermon once in three months, oh! what sighs and moans he indulges in secretly, not through contrition of heart,

As experience shows.

[1] Non est enim regnum Dei esca et potus. Sed justitia, et pax, et gaudium in Spiritu Sancto.—Rom. xiv. 17.

[2] Currecnt et non laborabunt, ambulabunt, et non deficient.—Isa. xl. 31.

excited by what he hears; but through weariness at the sermon, which he does not care to listen to; he wishes it were at an end. Why? Because the precious consolation of the Holy Ghost is wanting to him; he has no appetite for the food of his soul, no relish for God and heavenly things.   On the other hand, consider those who rise early, summer and winter, and hear two or three Masses every morning, assist moreover at the usual devotions, and are diligent in hearing the word of God, besides being zealous in other good works of mercy, charity, and mortification.   They do it all with earnestness and fervor, with relish, pleasure and spiritual joy; they never find the time too long, but rather too short; neither heat nor cold, nor severe weather, nor standing, nor kneeling can deter them, whatever exterior difficulty they may experience.   It would require an act of violence to make them desist from their usual pious practices, or lessen them in the least.   What is the reason of the great difference between those two classes of people?   The grace, the consolation of the Holy Ghost, which the former are without; while the latter taste it in God in their souls; they find namely, what an agreeable food a good conscience is, and how sweet the Lord is to those who seek to please Him alone.   Comforted by this food, "they shall walk and not faint;" they serve God without ever feeling fatigued.

In a good conscience there is the most delightful intimacy with God.   Now, my dear brethren, you can easily understand what makes up that pleasant company in the feast that a good conscience prepares for the soul.   Ah, what more pleasant company, or agreeable presence, or delightful society can one have than that which God cultivates with the soul, and the soul with God? Truly, says St. Thomas of Aquin, God is present in all places and with all creatures; but He is present in a special manner by sanctifying grace with the soul that has a good conscience; that is, as one friend with another, or as the lover who is in the same house with the object of his affections.   "By sanctifying grace," says the holy Doctor, "the whole Trinity dwells in the mind, according to the words: "We will come to him, and will make our abode with him.' " [1]   Shut up a soul that loves God in a gloomy dungeon where it is alone day and night, and never sees a human being; still it will find pastime and consolation enough in the company of God, whenever its conscience suggests the

---

[1] Per gratiam gratum facientem, tota Trinitas inhabitat mentem, secundum illud : ad eum enviemus; et mansionem apud eum faciemus.—John xiv. 23.

thought: "My beloved to me and I to Him."[1] What better thing can I have or wish for on earth?

In that company we need not fear annoyance, quarrelling, or contradiction; we have not to weigh our words, as is the case in other company and in worldly gatherings; the more freely and intimately the soul deals with God, the more is He pleased, and the more consoling is He in return; and what perfects the joy and pleasure of this intimacy is the assurance of a good conscience, that one loves the other sincerely and is loved sincerely in return. Nothing is sweeter among the children of the world than love, which alleviates all trouble and sorrow; and consequently nothing is more agreeable than the society of the loved one, especially when there is a certainty that one's love is reciprocated. Now that certainty can rarely be had with regard to men. For instance, you may be really loved by the person to whom you have given your heart; but if you are not aware of that fact your joy is not increased thereby; and if you think the contrary, namely, that you are not loved, your anguish and melancholy increase in proportion to the violence of your passion. But if you believed that you are loved, when such is not really the case, you are happy indeed, but your happiness is founded on a false idea. Nothing of the kind have you to fear with God, if your conscience is pure; for he who loves God is assured that God loves him, as our faith teaches: "I love them that love Me."[2] The very love that the soul has for God is an effect of God's love for the soul: "My beloved to Me, and I to him." *[In this intimacy there is no fear of annoyance.]*

There is, then, no company in which there is more joy and pleasure than that in which God and the soul are together by a good conscience. "Truly," says St. Bernard, who speaks from experience, "that is the only true joy which comes from the Creator, and not from the creature. Compared with it all pleasure is sadness, all sweetness pain." Such too was the experience of St. Augustine. At first he thought it an impossibility to renounce the love and desire of creatures; but as soon as he found out how sweet it is to love God alone and to be loved by Him, oh, then he wept at his folly and blindness in ever allowing creatures to take possession of his heart. Ah, he exclaimed, why did I not begin to love Thee, my God, sooner? "Late have I loved Thee, O Beauty ever ancient, ever new! Late have I *[But it gives constant joy and pleasure.]*

[1] Dilectus meus mihi, et ego illi.—Cant. ii. 16.
[2] Ego diligentes me diligo.—Prov. viii. 17.

loved Thee! "¹ Too late have I learned, what I now know to be the truth, how sweet the Lord is, and how great the joy of being on friendly terms with Him!

What more do you want at the marriage-feast, my dear brethren? Music? Then you will find that, too, in a good conscience, says St. Bernard: "the hearing also is delighted by the sweet voice of the interior Consoler," ² which testifies to the soul that it is in the state of grace, a child of God, the joy of the angels, a comrade of the elect, an heir of the kingdom of heaven. That is the voice of which St. Paul writes to the Romans: "For the Spirit Himself giveth testimony to our spirit, that we are the sons of God. And if sons, heirs also; heirs indeed of God, and joint-heirs with Christ." ³ It is the voice of Christ saying to His just servants: "Be glad and rejoice, for your reward is very great in heaven." ⁴ Epicurus, that wicked and carnal man, used to give this lesson to his disciples. He who wishes to enjoy thoroughly the pleasures of the world and of the senses, must first be firmly convinced and persuaded that there is neither God nor hell. What did he mean by that? His meaning was, that a pleasure enjoyed with the fear of hell and of the divine vengeance before one's eyes is no pleasure at all, but rather a torment and a misery. From this I conclude, that if the fear of hell, with which God can punish men, is in itself enough to embitter all enjoyment, and to turn pleasure into pain; then who has not the fear of hell, possesses the greatest peace of heart, and that all the more when he is assured besides of eternal glory. This is what a good conscience says to us: I am now in a state in which I need not fear hell; I am in a state in which I have a sure pledge of eternal happiness, a pledge that I can keep as long as I will, and that no man can take from me! Now I can consider heaven as something that is really prepared for me, and belongs to me by right. Could more joyful notes than these possibly resound in the ears of the heart?

And what can follow such joyful music, but dancing at the marriage-feast? Not indeed the rapid moving of the feet in the midst of a laughing circle, but the exultation of the heart rejoicing in God, as the Blessed Virgin says of herself: " My spirit

---

¹ Sero te amavi, pulchritudo tam antiqua, tam nova! sero te amavi!

² Auditui quoque dat gaudium et lætitiam dulcissima vox consolatoris interni.

³ Ipse Spiritus testimonium reddit spiritui nostro, quod sumus filii Dei. Si autem filii, et hæredes : hæredes quidem Dei, cohæredes autem Christi.—Rom. viii. 16, 17.

⁴ Gaudete et exultate, quoniam merces vestra copiosa est in cœlis.—Matt. v. 12.

hath rejoiced in God my Saviour: " that is, according to the literal meaning of the words, " has leaped with joy." [1] To this the Prophet David encourages all faithful servants of God: " Serve ye the Lord with gladness. Come in before His presence with exceeding great joy, " [2] that is, with hearts leaping with joy.

See now, my dear brethren, how true are the words of the Holy Ghost: " A secure mind is like a continual feast: " a mind that is sure of itself and means well with God is like a joyous marriage festivity. Therefore the holy Fathers cannot find words enough to praise the happiness that comes from a good conscience. They call it, with St. Bernard, the temple of Solomon, who was the greatest of men, as far as riches, honors, and pleasures were concerned; a fruitful field, a garden of delights, an ark of the covenant between God and the souls of men, the court of God, the dwelling-place of the Holy Ghost; or with St. Augustine, a paradise of true delights; the soft couch of the heavenly Bridegroom, in which the soul reposes in God without fear or anxiety. Nay, St. Augustine goes farther; all earthly joys are too vile in his sight, and therefore he does not hesitate to compare peace of heart with the joys of heaven. Hear what he says, for there is hardly a doubt that he speaks from personal experience. " O sacred conscience! thou art still on earth, and yet thou dwellest in heaven! " All places on earth are a heaven to thee, on account of the consolation thou enjoyest in God! " Rejoice, O soul, that art adorned with a good conscience; rejoice with a heavenly joy," [3] of which thou hast already a great portion. That is what David said to the just long before Augustine's time: " Blessed are the undefiled in the way, who walk in the law of the Lord. " [4] Mark how he attributes happiness to them, not merely on account of the glory awaiting them in heaven, but because they are actually happy here below; " blessed are the undefiled in the way, " although they are still on the way to heaven, yet they are almost as good as happy already, on account of the foretaste of heavenly joys that a good conscience gives them. St. Jerome says of himself: A gloomy desert was my dwelling-place; long fasting had reduced me to skin and bone; my skin, dried up by the fierce rays of the burn-

(margin note:) Hence, a good conscience is a constant joyous marriage feast. Shown from the Fathers.

---

[1] Et exultavit spiritus meus in Deo salutari meo. —Luke i. 47.

[2] Servite Domino in lætitia. Introite in conspectu ejus in exultatione.—Ps. xcix. 2.

[3] O conscientia sancta, interra adhuc es, et in cœlis habitas ! Gaude anima, sancta conscientia decorata, gaude cœlesti gloria !

[4] Beati immaculati in via, qui ambulant in lege Domini.—Ps. cxviii. 1.

ing sun, was like that of a blackamoor; the bare earth was my
bed, a hard stone my pillow, when sleep overcame me against
my will; daily did the tears force themselves from my eyes, the
sighs from my heart, and yet in the midst of it all, when I
raised my eyes to heaven, I sometimes seemed to be among the
choirs of angels. [1] Surius writes of St. Onuphrius that when
at the point of death he spoke thus to Paphnutius, who had
come to visit him: For sixty years have been serving God in
this desert, and during that time I have not laid eyes on a
human being, until I saw you to-day; I have had no society,
but that of my God; I have suffered much, endured much; but I
have learned, too, " that the servants of Christ are never in want,
not only of the things that are necessary, but even of those that
serve for their pleasure." [2]

The world
with all its
pleasures
cannot give
us anything
like it.

Vain children of the world, bring all your pleasures together,
and say, if you can, that no joy is ever wanting to you! You
dare not, could not with truth make that boast. To make that
still clearer, go with me in thought, and consider those two great
men, one of whom sought happiness in the pleasures of the world,
on the broad road leading to hell, and the other in the consolations
of a good conscience on his narrow path to heaven: the emperor
Tiberius in the island of Capri, and St. Francis Xavier in the
island of Goa.   Ask Tiberius how he enjoyed himself and you will
hear him exclaiming: " May the gods punish me, if I do not die
every day " [3] with sorrow and melancholy. But is that really
the case, Tiberius? Are you really dying of melancholy? Yes,
I cannot conceal my disgust and weariness; daily does it seem
to me as if I must die! Think of this, my dear brethren; an
emperor, a monarch of the world, with the crown on his head,
the sceptre in his hand, seated on the greatest throne on earth,
surrounded by the highest nobles of the land who wait on him,
served by numerous vassals, feared and honored by foreign nations; and yet he says of himself, " I die every day! " The monarch whose treasury both land and sea are filling daily, sighs forth;
I must die every day! The monarch for whom new pleasures were
waiting daily, for whose sensual delight all imaginable kinds of
enjoyments were invented, cannot conceal the anguish of his

---

[1] Post cœlo inhærentes oculos nonnunquam videbar mihi interesse agminibus angelorum.

[2] Reipsa cognoveram, Christi servis nihil omnino, non modo quæ ad necessitatem, sed et
quae ad voluptatem faciunt unquam deesse.

[3] Dii me perdant, si non quotidie morior.

heart; he is compelled to cry out publicly: May the gods punish me, if I have not to die every day! Yet I readily believe him; for even pleasures and delights turn to bitterness when the conscience is in a bad state. "All his good fortune, his riches, honors, and pleasures, could not save Tiberius from the tortures of his own mind, nor keep him from confessing his misery," such are the words of the historian Tacitus.

Now turn your eyes to St. Francis Xavier. See how he pants, and cries out: "Enough, O Lord, enough!" Oh, what consolation, what joy, inundates my heart; cease, O Lord, or else I shall die of abundance; my heart is too small to hold the immense consolation Thou dost pour into it! Mark, my dear brethren, that Xavier is a stranger among heathens, without money, servants, house, home, or bed; and yet he is compelled to cry out, on account of the exceeding great joy of his heart: "Enough, O Lord!" Xavier, whose eyes were constantly shedding torrents of tears, whose mouth was shrivelled up with continual fasting, hunger, and thirst, whose loins were girded with hair-ropes, garnished with iron points, whose hands were armed with scourges and disciplines, who never allowed the least indulgence to his senses; Xavier cannot contain himself on account of the superabundant consolation he enjoys, and is forced to cry out: "Enough, O Lord!" So great is the difference between the joy of heart in God, which a good conscience brings, and the vain delights of the world and the flesh. It is true, then, that "A secure mind is like a continual feast;" a good conscience, content with God, is a joyful marriage-feast. *While the servants of God can hardly contain their joy.*

Christians, do you, too, wish to taste the happiness of this feast? Do you wish to have here on earth consolation, joy, and peace of heart? Then see that you are free from sin, have good consciences, and keep in the friendship of God. But I am afraid, many will think like Nathaniel, when Philip described to him the wonders wrought by Our Lord, and tried to persuade him to follow Christ. What? exclaimed Nathaniel; "can anything of good come from Nazareth?" If you do not believe me, answered Philip, "come and see."[1] Come and see Christ; hear His word; you will surely be so attracted by Him that you will not wish to leave Him. There are many who think like Nathaniel; when one speaks to them of the indescribable joy of a good conscience, they say: how can that be? it is impossible! Ah, I say *Exhortation and conclusion to keep the conscience pure, in order to taste that joy.*

---

[1] A Nazareth potest aliquid boni esse? veni, et vide.—John i. 46.

to them in the words of Philip, "come and see!" If you do not believe it, then put it to the proof; purify your consciences and that thoroughly; begin to serve your God faithfully with your whole hearts, and then you will see how sweet it is to serve Him, to love Him above all things, to be His friends, His children. But you must be in earnest about it; for many flatter themselves that they have good consciences; but they deceive themselves, for they wish to look on everything as lawful that suits their inclinations, and are not willing to do all that God requires of them. What wonder, then, that they do not experience this consolation and peace of heart? Come and see; act honestly with God for once; begin to love Him with your whole hearts. "Oh, taste and see that the Lord is sweet" [1] to them that love Him; then your own experience will force you to acknowledge, with St. Bernard, that the true and only joy of the heart comes from the Creator and not from the creature, and can be had even in the midst of the trials and calamities of life, as I shall show on next Sunday. For my part I hold with St. Augustine: "Let others choose what possessions they please;" [2] let them seek for joy and peace and temporal goods, in honors, in eating and drinking, in dancing and singing, in the love of creatures and sensual enjoyments; they will not find true peace, repose, and consolation of heart therein; I will remain faithful to my God; "Thou art my portion; Thee, O Lord, I have chosen for myself." [3] Thee alone will I love above all things and possess in a good conscience; with Thee alone I have enough; in Thee I find consolation, peace, repose, and joy of heart. Amen.

SIXTY-NINTH SERMON.

ON THE CONSOLATION THAT A GOOD CONSCIENCE BRINGS IN TRIALS.

Subject.

The peace of a good conscience in the possession of God is a true joy of heart, even in the midst of the trials and crosses of this life.—*Preached on the third Sunday after Epiphany.*

---

[1] Gustate et videte quoniam suavis est Dominus.—Ps. xxxiii. 9.

[2] Eligant sibi, qui volunt, quod possideant.

[3] Pars mea tu es, te mihi elegi.

Text.

Ego veniam et curabo eum.—Matt. viii. 7.
" I will come and heal him."

Introduction.

So quickly can Jesus alleviate the pains and sufferings of men.
His mere arrival and presence is enough to free them from all
their torments. The centurion in to-day's Gospel went to Him,
and said: " Lord, my servant lieth at home sick of the palsy,
and is grievously tormented." " I will come and heal him,"
was Our Lord's answer. My dear brethren, what do you think
would happen, if Christ were to appear amongst us in visible
form and go about helping the poor and infirm in their necessities? What complaints and lamentations He would hear, especially in the hard times we are now passing through? " He
is grievously tormented," they would exclaim. My husband,
my wife, my father, my mother, my child, my brother, sister,
friend, is lying at home sick. We have hardly a bit of bread in
the house, the poor would say; we know not where to turn, so
great is our misery. We have suffered such losses, others would
exclaim; we have so much unhappiness, discomfort, and uneasiness at home; what will become of us? While others again, with
tears in their eyes, would sigh forth: now I am completely desolate; I have no one to help me, I am oppressed on all sides!
Ah, what am I to do? Hearest Thou these complaints, dearest
Saviour? Ah, say then, " I will come and cure you!" I will help
you in your crosses and trials! Yes, suffering Christians! Be of
good heart! Christ is ready to come! Hear what He says to all:
" Come to Me, all you that labor and are burdened, and I will
refresh you." [1] Come to Me. " Take up My yoke upon you." [2]
Serve Me faithfully and constantly; keep in My friendship by a
good conscience; and then I shall not need to come to you, for
I shall be already in your hearts; and I will refresh you; I will
console and comfort you. See there, suffering Christians! the
surest means, if not of getting rid of your crosses, at least of being abundantly consoled and strengthened in the midst of them;
and that is, constant friendship and peace with God by a good
conscience, as I shall now show.

[1] Venite ad me omnes qui laboratis et onerati estis, et ego reficiam vos.—Matt. xi. 28.
[2] Tollite jugum meum super vos.—Ibid. 29.

Plan of Discourse.

The peace of a good conscience in the possession of God is a true joy of heart, even in the midst of the trials and crosses of this life. Such is the whole subject of this sermon. Sinners! Awaken at once! Just souls, only keep in the friendship of God, and you will find comfort and alleviation in your sufferings! Such shall be the conclusion.

To this end, give us thy light and grace, O merciful Saviour, through the intercession of Mary and of our holy angels.

Joy of heart can exist with pain of body and sense. We must carefully distinguish the joy and peace of the heart or mind from the joy and peace that come from outward things and from our natural inclinations. It is true that temporal crosses and trials are painful and disagreeable to man, for they torment, annoy, and disturb him. There is no doubt that the pains of illness hurt; and so does the loss of temporal goods, and poverty and want, and shame and disgrace, and the death of our dear friends. Therefore those things are called trials and crosses; their nature is to annoy, trouble, and hurt. But what do they annoy? What do they trouble and cause pain to in man? The sensitiveness of the body, the outward senses, the natural inclinations that are always trying to shun what is painful and disagreeable to them, they indeed are tormented; but that is not always the case with the heart, the spirit, the reasoning soul.

As we see in the servants of God. For instance, the servant of God, who wishes to go to heaven, takes the discipline in his hand, and scourges himself bravely; he feels the pain, his shoulders shrink from it, he bites his lips, and pants for breath, and sighs. Nay, he is sometimes filled with fear and dread when the time comes for him to scourge himself; and yet in spite of all that, the heart remains calm, peaceful, perfectly contented. He does it of his own free will, rejoices in it, and is filled with special consolation at the thought that he thereby renders to God a pleasing and meritorious service. Thus the heart can have peace and joy, while the body is writhing in pain, the mouth sighing, the eyes weeping. And if that were not the case, how could so many martyrs have been able to laugh and make merry in the midst of their cruel tortures? How could St. Paul have said with truth: " I am filled with comfort, I exceedingly abound with joy in all our tribulation " ? [1]

[1] Repletus sum consolatione, superabundo gaudio in omni tribulatione nostra.—II. Cor. vii. 4.

Now what does it signify for the body with its sinful appetites to suffer a little pain, as long as the heart is peaceful and contented? When an architect, says St. Augustine, is selecting the timber of a building, what does he take first into consideration? He sees a beam of wood that is somewhat worm-eaten and rotten; does he put it aside as useless? No; he pays little attention to outward appearance. He turns the beam over and over, and sees whether the inside is still sound; if it is, then the outward rottenness makes no matter; the beam is fit for use. In the same way it should make little matter to us if the outward man, that is, the senses and their enjoyment, is tormented and afflicted, as long as the heart, which is the proper dwelling-place of peace, is sound and contented; for then we can say with the Apostle: "I am filled with comfort."

And this inward peace and joy of heart even in the midst of trials and crosses is the work of a good conscience, as St. John Chrysostom says: "There is nothing so powerful in consoling the mind as a pure conscience, although we may be surrounded by hundreds of temptations."[1] And elsewhere he says: The poor man, who has great difficulty in getting a piece of bread to still the pangs of hunger, if he is at peace with God by a good conscience, is in truth more contented and happy at heart than the rich man who, in the midst of abundance, has a bad conscience. Nor can it be otherwise; for the promise made by Our Lord, when inviting the afflicted to come to Him, must be fulfilled: "Come to Me, all you that labor and are burdened, and I will refresh you." And how wilt Thou refresh them, O Lord? "Take up My yoke upon you," He says; that is, keep My law inviolably. A wonderful manner of giving refreshment and comfort, to bind new burdens on those who have already enough to bear! If Thou hadst said: come to Me and I will take from off your shoulders the burden of crosses and trials that you have to bear; that would be the right way to refresh and comfort. But now Thou sayest: "take up My yoke upon you;" yes! do that, "and you shall find rest to your souls." Mind, He does not say, to your bodies, but to your souls; meaning thereby, the bearing of My yoke, that is, the constant observance of My commandments, will make your souls peaceful and happy, al-

And this joy comes from a good conscience.

---

[1] Nihil est quod ad consolandos animos tantum momenti habeat, quantum conscientia pura, etiamsi alioqui sexcentæ nos tentationes circumsedeant.—S. Chrysos. hom. 63. in ad Cor.

though your bodies and their inclinations are borne down and oppressed with the heavy burden of calamity and misfortune.

From the possession of God.

The reason of this is clear; for he who bears the yoke of Christ with a conscience free from sin possesses the great God as his own property; that is, a Good in which all other goods are included; hence nothing that is necessary to his peace of mind and contentment can be wanting to such a soul. A man may be in bitter poverty; the body may have to suffer hunger and thirst; but the soul remains fully satiated with God, who is its food and drink. The body through want of clothing or fuel suffers cold; but the soul remains with God in peace and contentment, well provided with everything, for His grace serves it as the most precious clothing. The poor man has no money to give away; but his soul is rich enough in the possession of the Supreme Good, that no one can take from him. In the eyes of the world he may be mean and contemptible; but his soul with its good conscience is in high honor and esteem with God and the angels. His body may be weak and sickly; but his soul is always healthy and strong. His eyes shed tears through suffering; but his soul is peaceful in the possession of God; and he can think and say with the poor St. Francis: "My God and my all." A pious hermit being asked how he could be so happy and cheerful in the midst of such extreme poverty and want of the necessaries of life, in such solitude where he had not a single companion to console him, and in the practice of such austerities and penances, answered; Why do you wonder at that? I am in want of nothing; I have a treasure that surpasses all the riches of earth, in which I can find all I am in need of; if everything else is wanting to me, no one can take Christ from me; Him I keep in my conscience as my Friend and Property. Have I not reason, then, to be contented and cheerful? That is what Our Lord Himself says: "Take up My yoke upon you" if you labor and are heavily burdened, "and you shall find rest to your souls."

From which springs an ineffable consolation.

Now I know what the Prophet David means by those words: "Blessed is the man that feareth the Lord." Why? "Glory and wealth shall be in his house:"[1] But how can that be, if he is a poor man, who has hardly enough to eat? if he is abandoned and rejected by all men, persecuted, oppressed, and overwhelmed with all kinds of miseries? No matter; he is blessed if he fears the Lord, and "glory and wealth shall be in his house." What

[1] Beatus vir qui timet Dominum. Gloria et divitiæ in domo ejus.—Ps. cxi. 1, 3.

is that house? Perhaps he has not even a room in a house. And what sort of glory and wealth will it be! "His house," answers St. Augustine, "is his heart; his glory and wealth the indwelling divinity;"[1] and in that house he is richer, more glorious and happier, than great lords in their palaces, if they have not God in their hearts. The poor, sick, desolate, afflicted servants of God appear to the world to lead unhappy lives; but, continues St. Augustine, you do not consider the matter in the right light; you see only the outside, and are not aware of what passes in the heart and soul. "Ask not the eyes of the body, but the eyes of faith."[2] They will show you the truth, and teach you that "blessed is the nation whose God is the Lord,"[3] and that "the souls of the just are in the hand of God, and the torment of death shall not touch them."[4] But how are we to understand that? Are not all men in the hand of God? Does not Job say expressly: "In whose hand is the soul of every living thing, and the spirit of all flesh of man"?[5] True; but the souls of the just are in the hand of God in quite a special manner; for they are so comforted and protected by His grace that they cannot be touched by pain or torment, even when the body is suffering.

"In the sight of the unwise they seem to die; but they are in peace,"[6] the peace and quiet of a good conscience. Imagine, my dear brethren, that a furious ox, rushing madly through the market place, seizes hold of a man by the cloak; the latter lets go the cloak at once, and the ox tears it to pieces and tosses it on his horns; meanwhile the man escapes. Those who are looking on at the affair from the windows think it is the man who is being gored, and cry out: Oh, the poor fellow, he is torn in pieces! And yet the man is safe at home, rejoicing at his lucky escape. It is lucky for me, he thinks, that I got off so well with the loss of nothing but my cloak. So it is with the souls of the just in the eyes of the world; when they have sorrow, suffering, and trial to bear, they who look on from a distance, that is, who take only outward appearances into consideration, think: oh, what that poor man has to suffer! What an unfortunate fellow he is! It is a wonder that he is still alive! Thus, in the eyes of

The just in affliction seem most unhappy: in reality they are the happiest of all. Shown by a simile.

[1] Domus ejus, cor ejus, ubi Deo habitante opulentius habitat, etc.
[2] Nolite interrogare oculos carnis ; interrogate oculos fidei.
[3] Beata gens cujus Dominus Deus ejus.—Ps. xxxii. 12.
[4] Justorum animæ in manu Dei sunt, et non tanget illos tormentum mortis.—Wis. iii. 1.
[5] In cujus manu anima omnis viventis, et spiritus universæ carnis hominis.—Job xii. 10.
[6] Visi sunt oculis insipientium mori ; illi autem sunt in pace .—Wis. iii. 2. 3.

the foolish world, which does not consult the light of faith, it seems as if he must die of grief. But meanwhile he is quite peaceful and contented; it is only his body and its senses,—his mantle—that are torn to pieces and tortured; his heart and soul are full of calm and peace. It is no great matter, he thinks, if my flesh is tortured for a time, as long as I am at peace with God in my conscience. Nay, he rejoices at his sufferings, and says with David: "Thou hast cut my sack-cloth, and hast compassed me with gladness." [1]

Explained by another simile. If we see such a sorrowful, afflicted man, we should certainly think that his heart and mind are disturbed and filled with anguish; but he is like the sky above which is always clear and calm, no matter what clouds or storms may be in the atmosphere. In a thunderstorm the clouds gather together; it thunders and lightens as if the heavens were falling down. Ah, people exclaim, how disturbed the heavens are to-day! And yet they are calm and still; it is only the passing clouds that hide the sky, and belch forth the thunderstorm. If we could look beyond them into the sky itself, we should see that it is serene and clear as ever. So too is it with the soul of the just man, which the Scripture often compares to the heavens. "Hear, O ye heavens, the things I speak, " [2] cries out the Prophet. What heavens? asks St. Gregory. They have no ears? He means, answers the Saint, not the lifeless, but the reasoning heavens. "There is no doubt that the soul of the just man is a heaven, " in which are the throne and dwelling-place of God. [3] In the time of trial the just seem to be surrounded with a dark, gloomy cloud of sorrow; they sigh when they feel the weight of the cross; they shed tears, and they are often heard moaning and lamenting. Alas! we should think, that man is completely disturbed. But let no one be astonished at the tears and sighs; they are only the thunder-clouds passing by; the tears and lamentations break forth from natural sensitiveness; but meanwhile the heavens, the reasoning soul, are calm and quiet with God in the safety and repose of a good conscience. Nay, says St. Augustine, the tears and sighs of a good conscience, that are poured forth in time of trouble, are generally much sweeter and more comforting than the joys and pleasures of those who assist at a comedy. [4]

---

[1] Conscidisti saccum meum, et circumdedisti me lætitia.—Ps. xxix. 12.

[2] Audite cœli quæ loquor. –Deut. xxxii. 1.

[3] Cœlum est utique anima justi.

[4] Dulciores sunt lachrymæ orantium, quam gaudia theatrorum.

With reason does St. Paul say of himself and all friends of God who are in suffering: "As sorrowful, yet always rejoicing." [1] They seem to be sorrowful and afflicted, but in reality they are rejoiced at heart, and at peace with their own consciences.

We have a striking example of this in the three youths in the fiery furnace. The flames, as the holy Scripture says, ascended to the height of forty-nine cubits, and darting out of the furnace, killed the servants of the king who were standing by. The spectators thought (and who could have thought otherwise?) that the youths were already burnt to ashes; but on the contrary they walked about amidst the flames, as if they were in a flower-garden, singing the praises of God, and not a hair of their heads was injured. What a wonderful miracle, exclaims St. Zeno; "within there was an agreeable shade, without, the burning fire; within were hymns of praise, without, lamentation." [2] And whence did this joy, this feeling of security in the midst of the flames, come? "And the form of the Fourth is like the Son of God." [3] There was One with the three youths in the furnace whose appearance was as if He were the Son of God; He changed the fire into a cooling dew. Again; Moses had been for a long time on mount Sinai; the Israelites in the camp saw the mountain covered with smoke, surrounded with flames, and vomiting forth lightnings and thunders. They thought (and who could be surprised at them?) that their leader must be either stifled in the smoke, or struck by the lightning, or burned by the flames: "And the people seeing that Moses delayed to come down from the mount said: the man that brought us out of the land of Egypt, we know not what has befallen him." [4] Meanwhile Moses sat in the midst of the flashing lightnings as joyful as if he were in paradise, and was happy in being able to speak with God. Jonas was thrown into the sea, and in the sight of his companions was swallowed by a huge fish. Ah, said they, there cannot be the least hope for him now! The fish has devoured him! And yet Jonas was quite strong and healthy in the belly of the whale, and after he had repented of his disobedience was filled with hope and confidence in God by prayer. All these are figures of the soul which has a good con-

(marginal note: Shown by similes drawn from Scripture.*)*

[1] Quasi tristes, semper autem gaudentes.—II. Cor. vi. 10.
[2] Mira res; opacitas intus, incendium foris; intus hymnus canitur, foris ululatus auditur. —S. Zeno. Serm. iv. de Dan.
[3] Et species quarti similis filio Dei.—Dan. iii. 92.
[4] Videns autem populus, quod moram faceret descendendi de monte Moyses, dixit: huic viro qui nos eduxit de terra Egypti, ignoramus quid acciderit.—Exod. xxxii. 1.

science, and has to bear all kinds of trials and contradictions. In the eyes of men, who are wont to look only at what appears outwardly, they seem on the point of dying of sorrow and anguish: " In the sight of the unwise they seemed to die;" but inwardly in their hearts they are quite pleased with their God: " But they are in peace."

Such was the experience of the saints in Holy Writ. Which of us, my dear brethren, seeing Job covered with ulcers on the dung-hill, hearing him wailing out, " Have pity on me, have pity on me!" hearing him curse the night in which he was conceived, the day on which he was born, would not have thought that the weight of his grief had made him desperate? And yet he was the most patient man on earth, the most resigned to the will of God. His lamentations and maledictions were not the voice of the inward reason, but of his natural sensitiveness, which felt the torture of his afflictions. Inwardly he tasted how sweet the Lord is, and ceased not to praise Him with his usual hymn: " Blessed be the name of the Lord." Who seeing the Apostle St. Paul lying in chains, beaten with rods in public, cowering under the shower of stones that the people of the towns rained down on him, suffering shipwreck, in danger from murderers, from false brethren who proved traitors to him, from hunger and thirst, from cold and nakedness, in many tribulations and misfortunes that he describes at length, who would not think him the most miserable man on earth, and have a heart-felt pity for him? But what does he himself say about it? We have already heard his words: " I am filled with comfort, " he exclaims exultingly; "I exceedingly abound with joy in all our tribulation." While the world imagines that I must sink under such a sea of calamities, I am enjoying a delightful paradise: " Our glory is this, the testimony of our conscience;" [1] that alone makes every cross bearable, and sweetens every affliction.

In other just people of later times. Who seeing Wenceslaus, king of Bohemia, after the loss of his son and the defeat of his army, taken prisoner and thrown into a dungeon, would not think that such a great monarch, thus hurled into the depths of misery from the very pinnacle of fortune, would die of despair and grief? But hear what he himself said to one of his attendants, who with tearful eyes was commiserating his master's unhappy lot: " Cease weeping, and if you are wise, learn a new kind of happiness." In the midst of all my

[1] Gloria nostra hæc est, testimonium conscientiæ nostræ.—II. Cor. i. 12.

trials, my mind is always filled with joy and consolation; for when a man has once given his heart to God, although he is laden with chains and has to suffer hunger and privation, yet his repose, peace, and happiness cannot be disturbed.[1]

What would have been our thoughts, my dear brethren, had we been present and seen the holy martyrs of Christ laughing, exulting, and mocking their persecutors in the midst of their torments, and urging them as it were to still greater cruelties? If we had seen a St. Lawrence roasting on the gridiron, and heard him saying to the tyrant: "I am now roasted on this side; turn me over and eat"? If we had seen a St. Eulalia, a maiden thirteen years old, with her whole body torn to pieces and covered with blood, and heard her asking the tyrant to put salt into her wounds to increase her pain, and to make her flesh more palatable for his cruel taste? If we had seen a St. Theodore, torn by iron hooks, so that his ribs were laid bare, and heard him in the midst of his torments entoning a hymn of praise to God, and crying out with the Prophet David: "I will bless the Lord at all times: His praise shall be always in my mouth"?[2] And when thus mangled he was thrown into a furnace, he still continued his hymn of praise, nor did he cease until he was outwardly consumed by the fire, and inwardly by divine love. If we had seen those truly Christian brothers, Marcus and Marcellianus, nailed to a post, and heard them laughing at the judge who was urging them to apostatize, and saying to him: "Never did a banquet taste so sweet to us as what we now suffer for the love of Jesus Christ"?[3] If we had seen that brave Japanese of our Society, Leonard Chimura, who, when he heard that he was one of those Christians who were condemned to die by slow fire, leaped with joy, tenderly embraced his fellow-prisoners, congratulated them on their happiness, and sang the Canticle of Simeon by way of thanksgiving for such a great grace: "Now Thou dost dismiss Thy servant, O Lord, according to Thy word, in peace"?[4] Nay, his interior joy was so great that when he tried to sing other hymns of praise to God with his companions, he could not restrain his tears, and was obliged to interrupt his prayers in order to allow his joy to have free course. When he was led to

And in the martyrs, even when they were cruelly tortured.

---

[1] Pone lachrymis modum, et si sapis, novum agnosce genus prosperitatis. Etenim qui cor Deo sacravit, non deturbari potest de culmine felicitatis.

[2] Benedicam Dominum in omni tempore; semper laus ejus in ore meo?—Ps. xxxiii. 2.

[3] Nunquam tam jucunde epulati sumus, quam hæc libenter Jesu Christi causa perferimus?

[4] Nunc dimittis servum tuum Domine, secundum verbum tuum in pace.—Luke ii. 29.

the stake and saw the fire prepared for him, he laughed at it as if it were too weak; and when the cords that bound him were consumed by the heat, he bent down reverently to the burning coals, and taking them in his hand, heaped them on his head, to show that he looked on them and rejoiced in them as the sign of his glorious and eternal victory. Thus, just souls who are tried by suffering seem " as sorrowful," but at heart they are " always rejoicing; " " as chastised and not killed; " [1] although they suffer in their bodies, yet in the midst of their pains they experience the sweetest consolation. Yes, you say, but they were holy and perfect people; we poor, weak mortals experience quite the contrary; we cannot bear the weight of the cross with such satisfaction. Eh? If we could only ask all who have a good conscience, and mean well with God, how they feel at heart in tribulations, they would be able to speak to us of similar consolations; and if they prefer to say nothing, Salvianus answers in their stead: " Although to the ignorant they seem to be unhappy, yet they cannot be otherwise than happy, " [2] if they only remember that they possess God, and with Him all that they can desire.

The disturbance of the just does not last long.

I do not mean, my dear brethren, that peace of heart, even in those who have a good conscience, cannot be attacked or disturbed by any trial. No, such an imperturbable peace belongs only to the elect in heaven. It is not unusual for a just soul to be sometimes suddenly laden with such a heavy cross that at first it is filled with anguish and disturbed in mind; but that disturbance does not last long; all it need do is to recollect itself, and offer up a short prayer to God, beg for patience, or hearken to some inspiration of the Holy Ghost, or make a short reflection such as the following: this cross comes to me from the hand of God, who is my Friend and Father, who loves me, and whom I love. This one thought is enough, in spite of the agitation and disturbance suffered by the natural inclinations, to bring back complete calm, peace, and comfort to the heart, the spirit, and the reasoning soul, from which the words, " Lord, Thy will be done " banish all disquiet. On the other hand, one whose conscience is not in good order is so distracted by the least suffering that he cannot be consoled, unless the suffering is taken away from him. The slightest word of contradiction, a cross look, excites him, some business that does not go according to his idea, some ebul-

---

[1] Ut castigati et non mortificati.—II. Cor. vi. 10, 9.

[2] Quamvis ignorantibus videantur esse miseri, tamen non possunt esse aliud quam beati.

lition of passion that he cannot master; nay, the mere dread of misfortune, loss, or death, a dread which will never perhaps be realized, is enough to drive him out of his mind almost, prevents him from sleeping at night, and deprives him of all peace of heart. Do what you will to console him, all your efforts are to no purpose; he has no relish for spiritual and supernatural things. Thus every mental disquiet and trouble is for the just like a summer-shower, that passes in a few moments and leaves the sky as clear as it was before; but for the wicked it is like a lasting thunder-storm, that never clears off, as long as the trouble lasts. What is the cause of this difference? The latter shut out from their consciences God, who alone can give peace of heart and joy of soul; but the former find the true Consoler in their good consciences, and with Him peace and joy of heart.

Therefore it remains true, my dear brethren, that the peace of a good conscience is the true joy of the heart, even in the midst of the trials of this life. The words of the Holy Ghost must be true: " Whatsoever shall befall the just man, it shall not make him sad." [1] Poor, afflicted, sorrowing Christians, who have many heavy crosses to bear, hear Our Lord calling out to you: " Come to Me, all ye, and I will refresh you! Take up My yoke upon you, " serve Me with your whole hearts, and you shall find rest to your souls. But perhaps you have not a pure conscience? Alas, in that case you are miserable, wretched, unhappy indeed! Miserable inwardly and outwardly; outwardly, because you are weighed down by the heavy load of the cross; inwardly, from the gnawing worm of conscience, which torments and annoys you, so that you have no consolation or comfort to hope for. Ah, come, come back to your God! Even because you are so afflicted and miserable, throw yourselves humbly at the feet of the angry God, repent, confess your sins, purify your consciences, amend your sinful or slothful lives, and begin to love God with your whole hearts; and I promise you, in the name of the God of truth, that you shall find rest; your burden will be lightened, your cross sweetened, and you will find rest, peace, and joy for your souls! But you, just souls, who have a good conscience, you are in need of no other consolation than that which you receive from the testimony of your conscience that you are friends and dear children of God; continue to rejoice therein with all your hearts. But be careful to avoid those dangers and occasions in which you

Conclusion and exhortation to purify the conscience and enjoy the peace it will give.

---

[1] Non contristabit justum, quidquid ei acciderit.—Prov. xii. 21.

might lose that desirable peace. "Blessed is the man that feareth the Lord;" blessed is he that loveth the Lord. Blessed here
on earth, blessed hereafter in the eternal kingdom of heaven!
Amen.

SEVENTIETH SERMON.

ON THE PEACE OF A GOOD CONSCIENCE UNDER CALUMNY.

Subject.

Let people think and say of you what they will; if you have a
good name before God, that is, if you are innocent in conscience,
you can and should treat all they say with silent contempt.—
Preached on the feast of SS. Peter and Paul.

Text.

Quem dicunt homines esse Filium hominis?—Matt. xvi. 13.
" Whom do men say that the Son of man is?"

Introduction.

That is the powerful enemy that daunts the bravest, and often
keeps them from good and urges them to evil: "what do people
say?" If I do or omit this, or say that; what will they say of
me? what will they think of me? how will they look on me?
Thus, for the sake of people's talk, God and the Christian law
are often put in the background. Rash judgments, fault-finding, criticising, sarcasm, tale-bearing, condemning the actions of
others, and similar sins so much in vogue, constitute that dam-
nable vice which works so much mischief in a community, and is
generally so dreaded by all. In itself alone it is able to make an
honest man uneasy, impatient, and to cause the bitterest anger
and hatred. But people trouble themselves little as to what God
thinks and says of their actions. Christians! let others think
and say of you what they please; let them talk until they are
tired; do you act like our dear Saviour in to-day's Gospel. When
the disciples had told Him the different views that had been expressed with regard to Him, He asked at once, as if what people
said did not concern Him: " But who do you say that I am?"
As long as you have faith in Me, and hold Me for what I really
am, it is all I want. Christians! see only that you have a good
conscience, a good name with God; and then you need not mind

what people say of you; and you will find rest and peace, as I am now about to explain, for the comfort and consolation of those who have much to suffer from calumnious and evil tongues. I repeat, then:

Plan of Discourse.

Let people think and say of you what they will; if you have a good name before God, that is, if you are innocent in conscience, you can and should treat all they say with silent contempt. Such is the whole subject, to the end that we may all endeavor to lead Christian lives, and have pure consciences, according to the teaching and example of the princes of the Apostles, SS. Peter and Paul.

The former warns us in his first Epistle: "Having a good conscience: that whereas they speak evil of you, they may be ashamed who falsely accuse your good conversation in Christ." [1] And the latter boasts, writing to the Corinthians: "To me it is a very small thing to be judged by you;" [2] what men say of me does not trouble me in the least: "Our glory is this, the testimony of our conscience." [3] Great apostles! we expect through the intercession of Mary and our holy angels the grace to imitate you in this.

It is a great annoyance for one who wishes to lead a quiet life, especially when he is engaged in study, to have as his neighbor one who plies some noisy trade, and fills the place with din and tumult the whole day long. No matter how carefully the student closes his doors and windows, or shuts himself up in the highest room of the house, or how he gives way to impatience and murmuring, he cannot be at peace; his windows are shaken by the noise, the floor trembles, the walls even feel the effect of it, so that he cannot rest by day, nor sleep in the morning or evening; unless, indeed, he gets so used to the din that he does not mind it any more. If you have a house to let or to sell, no matter how well-built and comfortable it may be, you will not get half of what it is worth if there is a noisy neighbor living next door. Therefore in large and well-ordered towns, all tradesmen, such as weavers and tinmen, are appointed by the

They who criticise and pry into the actions of others are like noisy neighbors.

---

[1] Conscientiam habentes bonam, ut in eo quod detrahunt vobis, confundantur, quia calumniantur vestram bonam in Christo conversationem.—I. Pet. iii. 16.

[2] Mihi autem pro minimo est ut a vobis judicer.—I. Cor. iv. 3.

[3] Gloria nostra hæc est, testimonium conscientiæ nostræ.—II. Cor. i. 12.

magistrate a certain place to live in by themselves, where they can hammer as long as they like without disturbing others, since they all make noise in their workshops. Thus at all events the other streets are free from the annoyance.

And do great mischief in a community. Rash suspicions, false judgments, wicked and contumelious tongues, tale-bearers, and you who occupy yourselves in putting evil interpretations on the actions of others, I cannot compare you to anything better than these noisy neighbors! What they cause in a place with their innocent and honest trade (for it is not their fault that it is such a noisy one, and they must earn their bread), that you do wantonly and wickedly in a whole community, either through malice, or curiosity, or thoughtlessness. There is many a one who would willingly live in peace and union with God, and could easily do so, if it were not that you disturb his repose and peace. No one is so innocent and pious as to escape your rash judgments and injurious talk. Let one be as pure as Joseph, as devout as the mother of Samuel, as penitent as St. Peter, as zealous as St. Paul, as holy as Our Lord Himself, if that could be; yet he will find some evil-disposed person to bring suspicion on his purity, to attribute his piety to drunkenness, his tears to hypocrisy, his zeal to deceit, his holiness to witchcraft, as was the case with those holy persons whom I have mentioned. A single word from your wicked tongues is often enough to turn love into hatred, friendship into enmity, even between the most intimate friends and relations, brothers and sisters, children and parents, husbands and wives, who otherwise would live in the greatest harmony with each other. A single word of scorn or contempt, uttered through malice or levity against another's actions, is often enough to ruin the reputation and credit of the best and most honorable of men, and to take from him the repose, joy, consolation, and pleasure he before enjoyed. In God's name, why do you concern yourselves so much about the affairs of other people? Look to yourselves and your own souls, which you utterly neglect and ruin by your wicked tongues. Leave others in peace, and practise Christian charity; fear and love your God, before whom you incur a great responsibility. Think of the terrible judgment to come, when you will have to give an account, not of your neighbor's actions, but of your own. In such terms would I now wish to address you, if I had not done so already on a former occasion.

I pity you, just and pious souls, who have sometimes most to suffer from and are most torn to pieces by wicked tongues! What are you to do? What means can you make use of to free yourselves from them, and to live in peace and quiet? Shall we put them away to live by themselves in some remote quarter of the town, like the tinmen? But where could we find a magistrate clever enough to provide room for all those people? A whole town would not hold them; nay, the world itself would have to be turned into a street for their accommodation. Must you, then, leave your present homes, and go elsewhere to live? But where will you go to? You will have to seek long before finding a place in which you will be free from all evil tongues; so common is that vice amongst men, so few there are who are not addicted to it. Even those who in other respects make profession of leading holy lives are sometimes subject to this fault, inasmuch as they cannot keep their unruly tongues in order, and speak in company of what they have heard or seen without any regard to the harm they may do thereby. Will you murmur and grow impatient with those people, and return abuse for abuse, sarcasm for sarcasm, and run them down in order to protect your own good name? But how would that help you? Would it close their mouths? No, that would be altogether to no purpose; for instead of thus regaining your good name, their calumnies would only be made more public, and the bad things they say of you would only make a deeper impression in the minds of those who hear them and are ignorant of the truth. Instead of the one whom you might reduce to silence, you will only set on ten, twenty, or more like him to say still worse things of you and your actions. Just as if you threaten to strike a dog that barks at you in the street. Try it only once, and you will see that he will run away from you to his own house, as soon as he sees you picking up a stone or taking a stick in your hand; but all the dogs in the neighborhood will soon be brought together by his barking, and will attack you with still greater noise and tumult. If you had allowed the first dog to bark at you unnoticed, and had kept quietly on your way, you would have avoided all that row, and he would soon have got tired barking at you.

And this is the best defence against talkative tongues; namely, to let them say what they will, to keep silent, laugh at them, entreat their calumnies with contempt, and not do them the honor of taking the least notice of them. And that means you can

Marginal notes: No one is safe from them, because they are everywhere.

A good conscience alone enables us to despise their talk.

best employ if you have a good conscience, which does not reproach you with any sin. "What shall be given to thee," asks David, "or what shall be added to thee, to a deceitful tongue?"[1] That is, according to the interpretation of St. Augustine, what medicine or comfort shall be given thee when thou art attacked by wicked tongues? "Let your conscience be your comfort,"[2] answers the holy Doctor. Serve God sincerely, live uprightly, do your duty to the best of your ability; fulfil the obligations of a good Christian; and then you will find comfort enough in yourself, and you will even rejoice and be undisturbed in the midst of the barking of malicious tongues, and be as cheerful as if what they said did not concern you in the least.

Shown by a simile.

You will be like the spectator in a theatre, when a battle is represented on the stage. The pretended soldiers fight with each other, and brandish their weapons fiercely, now on this side, now on that; sometimes even they seem to threaten the spectators; and one could almost imagine that they are on the point of attacking every one, an illusion which is encouraged by the fact that many of them are carried off the stage apparently wounded. Meanwhile the spectator looks on quietly from his seat; he is not afraid of the fighting, but rather enjoys it. So, also, you can and will hear the bad things that are said of you on all sides, without being in the least disturbed, you will look on them smilingly as mere empty words that simply move the air, but cannot touch you, since you are free in conscience, and with St. Augustine you will be able to say: "Think of Augustine whatever you please, as long as my conscience does not accuse me before God."[3] What do I care for the judgments and opinions of men, since my conscience alone can make me good or wicked, condemn or absolve me?

A bad conscience must fear such people.

And in fact, my dear brethren, to go to the bottom of the matter, how is it that we have such pleasure in being well spoken of and honored by others, while we hate and shun the tattlers who try to run us down? Simply because on the one hand we wish and desire that whatever good we have, or think we have, should be made public; while on the other hand we are most careful in endeavoring to hide our faults and failings and whatever is contemptible in us; thus we fear that the faults we seek to hide should be brought to light by talkative tongues. If I

---

[1] Quid detur tibi, aut quid apponetur tibi ad linguam dolosam?

[2] Sit conscientia solatium.

[3] Senti de Augustino quidquid lubet; sola me in oculis Dei conscientia non accuset.

know in my conscience that I have nothing good in me, the outward praise of men cannot bring me joy or comfort; if I know in my conscience that I have nothing to be ashamed of, their blame cannot cause me reasonable fear or annoyance. If all those who know me praise me as a just and upright, chaste, and holy man, what consolation will that give me, if I am aware that I do not possess those virtues, and my conscience reproaches me saying: that is not true; you do not deserve that praise; you are unjust, unchaste, and wicked? If I have any sense of decency left, that praise should rather put me to shame and confusion.

A woman who knows or thinks that she is beautiful is very pleased to be admired by others; but if she knows that she is ugly, she fears nothing so much as to have her personal appearance spoken of. If you wish to put her to shame, all you need do is to praise her beauty. Why? Because she knows that she is not beautiful. If I feel that I am pleased when others praise me, although I do not deserve their praise, it is because I am rejoiced that the faults which I try to hide are still unknown to others; otherwise I must feel ashamed in my heart at not being so good as people give me credit for being. Just as a poor man who can with difficulty support himself and his family must feel a secret shame and bitterness of heart if some one who does not know him looks on him as a rich man. Ah, he thinks, if that were only true! Rich indeed! I wish I had bread enough to satisfy my hunger! Nay, the praise bestowed on me is more likely to fill me with a secret dread lest the truth should be found out, and then my shame would be all the greater. This, I repeat, is the chief reason why evil tongues are so hated and feared. We are in dread of anything like prying into our actions, lest people should find out something wrong in them, speak the truth about us, and make known what we are. He who has a bad conscience, says St. Chrysostom, is afraid of everything.[1] He thinks that every one who sees him has discovered his secret vices, and he easily suspects people of speaking ill of him; "nay, he fears that the walls have tongues and make known his hidden misdeeds."[2] The commandant of a garrison who knows that there is a traitor amongst his men is very attentive to all that passes inside and outside the walls; at the least noise he imagines that the enemy is attacking him; he fears everything because he knows that there is a traitor in the garrison.

(margin note: Shown by divers similes.)

[1] Omnia pavet.
[2] Ipsos lapides, tanquam vocem emittentes.

But a good conscience need not mind them.

Now if I have a good conscience, I have no reason for fear or anxiety, and can afford to pay little heed to what people say of me; for how could I reasonably dread losing my good name by such talk, when my conscience does not accuse me of anything that I should be ashamed of? If my conscience acquits me, I can look each one boldly in the face, say what I have to say, give praise or advice where I think it necessary, despise what is contemptible, and if my duty requires it, reprove what is faulty. He who knows that he is guilty cannot be so bold. If my conscience is good, I can let all my actions appear in public without fear, no matter how many wicked tongues surround me; although I keep silence, my actions will defend themselves, and show that the calumniators are lying. A good conscience, says the heathen Seneca, is not disturbed in the midst of a crowd; while a bad one makes us feel insecure even in the most hidden corner. Velleius tells us that when Livius Drusus wished to build a house, the architect promised to construct it so that no one could see from without what was done inside. No, said Livius, if you are so clever, rather build it in such a manner that every one can see what I do in it."[1] His meaning was: I intend so to live that, although it is not advisable to proclaim all my actions publicly, yet if they happen to be found out, I should have no reason to be ashamed of them.

For they cannot do him the least harm.

Oh, if all Christians lived in that way, there would soon be an end of prying intermeddlers and gossiping tongues; a small lane would soon be enough to hold them, or at all events there would be very few who would have reason to fear them! If I have a good conscience, as I said before, I can let people say of me what they will; I can afford to despise all calumnies and detractions, and to treat them as contemptuously as I do the dog that barks at me in the street; for they cannot make me other than I am, and consequently can do me no harm. What harm is done to the sun by reproaching it falsely with having dark spots? Does it hurt the rich man to be accused of being poor? All that talk will not cause the sun to lose a particle of its light, or the rich man to be a whit the poorer. The praise of others, says Thomas a Kempis in his golden book, does not make me better or holier than I really am; nor does their contempt make me worse. I am neither better nor worse than I am in the sight of God. If my conscience tells me that I am good and innocent, then I remain

[1] Ita compone domum meam, ut quiquid agam, ad omnibus perspici possit.

good and innocent, even if the whole world were full of envious tongues trying to run me down. If, then, I hear that wicked people are speaking ill of me, and saying things that I know to be false, why should I be disturbed thereat or give way to anger against them? What would I gain thereby? Would I thus make what is said of me more false than it is already? Who is angry at seeing dung come forth from a stable? Who is vexed because a dunghill gives forth a bad smell? Who troubles himself because, as he is passing by a lunatic asylum, the inmates jeer and laugh at him? If he is a sensible man he will laugh at them. Now from calumnious tongues nothing but filth and dung can come, and it should be a matter of indifference to me whether they vomit forth follies like the lunatics or falsehoods like the wicked. If I am wise I will laugh at them, and remain what my conscience tells me that I am.

Oh, what a beautiful thing it is to have a pure conscience in the sight of God; one that can be reproved with nothing bad unless through folly and falsehood on the part of the accusers; which is pleased and satisfied in itself and can rejoice in its own praise, without having to fear either the talk or the scorn of others! This is the boast of the Apostle St. Paul to the Corinthians: "To me it is a very small thing to be judged by you;" that is the least of my troubles; I pay not the slightest attention to the judgments and opinions of men regarding myself: "Our glory is this, the testimony of our conscience, that in simplicity of heart and sincerity of God, and not in carnal wisdom, but in the grace of God, we have conversed in this world." [1] I have not injured or troubled any one; the duties that God has laid on me I have fulfilled; now go and say, or think of me, what you will: "To me it is a very little thing to be judged by you;" that is the last thing I should think of troubling myself about. My conscience comforts and defends me; in that is my glory, which is not begged from the praise of men, but comes from myself; and no one can take it from me. "Our glory is this, the testimony of our conscience."

St. Paul consoles himself with his conscience, and laughs at all idle talk.

That is the wonderful example that Jesus Christ, Our Lord and Saviour, has left to all His followers and true Christians. If there ever was a holy and innocent man on earth it was Jesus Christ, innocence and holiness itself, in whom there was nothing

We must d the same, like Our Lord, who answered nothing to

[1] Gloria nostra hæc est, testimonium conscientiæ nostræ, in simplicitate cordis et sinceritate Dei, et non in sapientia carnali, sed in gratia Dei conversati sumus in hoc mundo. —II. Cor. i. 12.

the false
accusations
made
against
Him in His
absence.

that could be reproved or found fault with. Yet if ever there was any one in the world who had to suffer from evil, wicked, lying tongues, it was Our Lord. "He hath done all things well."[1] is the testimony given of Him by the people; nor could the all-knowing God do anything faulty. What He did was not only good in itself, but was also advantageous to all men as well. Countless were the numbers of the ignorant whom He instructed, the sick whom He healed, the dead whom He raised to life, the possessed whom He freed from the evil spirit: He "went about doing good and healing all."[2] But meanwhile, what was not said and thought of Him, I will not say by the envious Pharisees to whom His miracles were a thorn in the side, but by the common people and even those on whom He conferred so many benefits? "For some said: He is a good man. And others said: No."[3] "And there was much murmuring among the multitude concerning Him."[4] If He preached or wrought miracles, they said, "He seduceth the people."[5] He is seeking to gain their favor, and to make Himself a king over us. If He healed the sick on the Sabbath day, there were lying tongues ready to accuse Him of breaking the Sabbath. If He did His duty by reproving the hypocrisy of the Scribes, they said that He had no respect for authority. If He converted sinners, they accused Him of frequenting the company of the wicked. If He ate and drank with the people, they called Him a glutton and wine-drinker. If He fasted, they said that He had a devil. In a word, He did hardly anything that was not interpreted in a bad sense. O dear Lord, dost Thou not hear what they say of Thee? Truly He heard it; for although He was not always present in body, yet He was present by His Godhead and infinite wisdom. And what dost Thou say to it? Dost Thou suffer it? Canst Thou allow such imputations to be cast on Thy good name? Hast Thou no words or chastisements wherewith to inflict due punishment on those wicked people? Let them speak as they please, answers Our Lord: "I do always the things that please Him," My Father. Let people, then, think of Me as they will. Thus He continued calmly doing the will of His Father, and even conferring benefits on the ungrateful people who were calumniating Him.

[1] Bene omnia fecit.—Mark vii. 37.
[2] Pertransiit benefaciendo et sanando omnes.—Acts x. 38.
[3] Quidam enim dicebant: qui abonus est. Alii autem dicebant : non.—John vii. 12.
[4] Et murmur multum erat in turba deeo.—Ibid.
[5] Seducit turbas.—Ibid.
[6] Ego quae placita sunt ei facio semper.—Ibid. viii. 29.

And not merely behind His back did they speak thus of Him; a fault that is very common nowadays, when many are apt to say behind their neighbor's back what they dare not say to his face; they praise and flatter a man in his presence, but abuse and ridicule him when he is absent; but not always did they act thus towards Our Lord. Consider the accusation levelled at Him before Annas, Caiphas, and Pilate, when He was dragged to their tribunals, and how He was treated as a fool by Herod's whole army. What wilt Thou do now, O Lord? This is the time to speak; otherwise Thy honor and good name are gone! Defend Thyself; show that Thou art innocent! When Thou wert a boy of twelve, Thou wert able to reduce to silence the doctors in the temple; do the same now, and show that they accuse Thee falsely. "But Jesus held His peace." [1] He did not deign to answer a word; or else He merely referred them to His life and to the doctrine He preached in public. He knew well how true His own words were: "I always do the things that please Him." "Answerest Thou nothing to the things which these witness against Thee?" [2] said the judge to Him. "But Jesus held His peace." His works were a sufficient proof of His innocence, His conscience reassured Him, and therefore He kept silent, although His silence cost Him His life.

Ah, dearest Saviour! where are Thy Christians? How many canst Thou count who keep silent and remain undisturbed when others speak ill of them? Nor do I refer now to a calumny that brings with it the danger of certain public shame or death; for in such circumstances I dare not expect any one to hold his tongue. But when people hear that in ordinary common conversation they have been spoken badly of, how uneasy they become all at once! what hatred and anger fill their minds! how their color changes! what a storm of abuse, complaint, invective, cursing and swearing bursts forth from their lips, when they cannot otherwise revenge themselves! Christians, how is that? Are we not ashamed of ourselves, we who have such a great and holy Lord, who has given us such a very different example? Are we not put to shame by the Gospel of Christ, which prescribes very different rules for our conduct? Ah, I know why we are so easily excited by such things; we have not always a good conscience; there are few of whom it could be said with truth: "he hath done all

---

[1] Jesus autem tacebat.

[2] Nihil respondes ad ea, quæ isti adversum te testificantur ?—Matt. xxvi. 62, 63.

things well," he does his duty as a good Christian should. There are few who live so that their consciences can give them testimony, and say to them: I always do what is pleasing to God. Therefore it is not astonishing that so many fear and dread tattlers.

It is lawful to defend one's honor; but we must not regard common talk.

But, you object, if I have a good conscience, is that a reason for letting them run away with my character? How does it help me to lead a Christian life, if wicked tongues cry me down as other than what I am? Am I not allowed to protect my innocence? Truly you are; there is not the least doubt of that. But you must use proper means for that purpose. Not only is that lawful; it is even advisable and sometimes necessary when God's honor requires it, as was the case with Judith, when she came from the camp of Holofernes, and from the midst of a dissolute soldiery. To avert all suspicion, she affirmed on oath that her purity had not been tampered with. "As the Lord liveth, the Lord hath not suffered me, His handmaid, to be defiled."[1] The humble Job did the same when his friends falsely attributed the evils he was suffering to his sins: "My heart doth not reprehend me in all my life,"[2] he says. And St. Paul writes to the Corinthians, amongst whom there were some who despised his doctrine because he had not been sent by Christ as the other apostles: "For I suppose that I have done nothing less than the great apostles."[3] Christ Himself did the same when He acknowledged and proved in a case of necessity that He was the Son of God. But what I mean is, that a true Christian should not mind the ordinary back-biting and fault-finding of people, to which nearly every one is exposed, nor should he be the least disturbed by it, but lay far more stress on the importance of having a good conscience before God than on gaining praise from men.

Exhortation and resolution to serve God with a good conscience, and despise tattling tongues.

Let us, then, my dear brethren, carefully observe what St. Peter exhorts us to: "Having a good conscience, that whereas they speak evil of you, they may be ashamed who falsely accuse your good conversation in Christ." If, then, we have to suffer innocently from wicked tongues, we ought to rejoice that we are innocent; and since our conscience tells us that we are free from what we are accused of, we have rather reason to exult on account of the words of Our Lord in the Gospel of St. Matthew: "Blessed are ye

[1] Vivid autem ipse Dominus, quoniam non permisit me Dominus ancillam suam coinquinari.—Judith xiii. 20.

[2] Neque enim reprehendit me cor meum in omne vita mea.—Job xxvii. 6.

[3] Existimo enim nihil me minus fecisse a magnis apostolis.—II. Cor. xi. 5.

when they shall revile you, and persecute you, and speak all that is evil against you, untruly," [1] namely, when the accusations they level against you are false. We should rejoice and esteem ourselves happy in being able to suffer such things with Christ, who will take as offered to Himself all the insults and injuries inflicted on His servants: "As long as you did it to one of these My least brethren, you did it to Me." [2] He can and will protect our honor far better than we ourselves could, if we leave all vengeance to Him. "Revenge to Me: I will repay, saith the Lord." [3] Just as a father says to his child, who is always complaining that other children are threatening him and calling out after him, Be still, my child, and leave them to me; I will see that they do not hurt you; when I catch those naughty children alone I will show them how to behave to you, and then you can laugh at them. Such, too, is the promise that our heavenly Father makes us when our honor is attacked, and we are made the innocent objects of calumny. He Himself undertakes to be our defender; and if our good name suffers, He will see that it is restored, if not in this life, at all events on that great day when the Lord will come to disclose the thoughts of all hearts, and the words spoken by every tongue: "And then shall every man have praise from God." [4] Then will be disclosed all the false and rash judgments that have been uttered here, to the eternal shame of the wicked who spoke them and the undying glory of the innocent. Then will be made evident who had good sense, and who was foolish; who knew how to live, and who did not. Then we shall see what the opinions of worldlings are worth, who think it good manners to condemn those who do not conform to the vain usages of the world, and say of them, oh, they have no sense; they do not know how to live. But wait a little; on that day we shall find out who had the right idea of life,—he who followed the maxims of the world or he who lived according to the Gospel truths. Even now worldlings are not always looked on as sensible by prudent people. Be that as it may, in future I will hold with St. Paul: "To me it is a very small thing to be judged by you, or by any man's day." Let people think and say what they please; let them talk of and criticise me till they are tired; it makes

---

[1] Beati estis cum maledixerint vobis, et persecuti vos fuerint, et dixerint omne malum adversum vos mentientes.—Matt. v. 11.

[2] Quamdiu fecistis uni ex his fratribus meis minimis, mihi fecistis.—Ibid. xxv. 40.

[3] Mihi vindicta; ego retribuam, dicit Dominus.—Rom. xii. 19.

[4] Et tunc laus erit unicuique a Deo.—I. Cor. iv. 5.

no matter to me. My only care shall be to keep my conscience pure; and then if men do not praise me, I shall have my glory to myself in my own conscience. Again I repeat it; I will do courageously what is required of me by the Christian law, by the duties of my state, by my God and His commandments; I will love God and be always faithful to Him, and so will endeavor to have a good name with Him, and to grow daily in His grace and friendship. Amen.

SEVENTY-FIRST SERMON.

ON THE JOY OF A GOOD CONSCIENCE ON ACCOUNT OF ONE'S GOOD WORKS.

Subject.

He who has a good conscience that does not reproach him with any grievous sin, and tries honestly to serve God: 1st., does what is most pleasing to God when he rejoices on account of the peace and satisfaction of his good conscience, and of his good works; 2d., he derives great profit therefrom for his soul. —*Preached on the fourth Sunday after Epiphany.*

Text.

Quid timidæ estis modicæ fidei?—Matt. viii. 26.
" Why are you fearful, O ye of little faith? "

Introduction.

What? exclaimed Our Lord; must you be frightened and timid, you, My dear disciples, who love Me, and whom I have chosen out of love as My companions, in preference to so many others? And what have you to be afraid of, since I am in the boat with you? "Why are you fearful, O ye of little faith?" My dear brethren, the peace of heart in a good conscience, by which we have God as our Friend, and of which I have spoken in the preceding sermons, is a continual joyful marriage-feast for the human soul, and brings true joy of heart even in the midst of trials and calamities, as I have already shown. Now there are souls, and even pious souls, who are never content with themselves, and are either unable or unwilling to enjoy the peace and happiness of a good conscience. They are always filled with anguish, and think that they cannot flatter themselves with having a good conscience, or else if they have no reasonable grounds for doubting that they are in the state of grace, and they try to serve God as well as they can, they imagine that they dare not admit any sense of pleasure or satisfaction in their good conscience, or in the service they render to God; and in that they are misled by a false idea that it is more pleasing to God for them to attach no value to what they do for Him and more advantageous to their souls to be always in a state of fear and trembling when working out their salvation. What a strange idea that is! "Why are you fearful, O ye of little faith?" Ignorant souls! to-day I mean to convince you of quite the contrary.

Plan of Discourse.

First, that he who has a good conscience, which does not reproach him with grievous sin, and who tries to serve God honestly, does what is most pleasing to God when he rejoices in the peace and satisfaction of his good conscience and on account of his good works. In the second part I shall prove that he will derive great advantage for his soul therefrom. There you have the whole subject of this sermon. That joy is most pleasing to God: the first part. It is most useful to the soul: the second part. Therefore rejoice, pious Christians, and exult in that sweet repose of conscience, because you serve God: that shall be the conclusion, and moreover, as I chiefly intend, an encouragement to persevere zealously in the service of God.

Help me and all of us thereto, O God of love, whose yoke is sweet and whose burden light; we beg this of Thee through the intercession of Mary and of the holy angels.

The basis of my subject is that undoubted truth which I remember having partly proved on a former occasion; namely, that the Lord God is more pleased and satisfied with a cheerful, joyous service than with a sad and melancholy one, and with a confident, child-like love, than a slavish, anxious fear. Truly, as the joy with which a work enjoined is performed is a clear proof that it is done willingly, readily, and freely, so there is hardly a man in the world of such a stern and savage disposition as not to prefer a gay and cheerful countenance to a discontented, sour one. No master is so heartless as not to be more pleased with the servant who carries out his orders readily and willingly than with one who does his duty in a sad and melancholy way,

Earthly masters prefer cheerful servants to sad ones.

trembling with fear before his master. For the latter thus gets a bad name before the world; see, people exclaim, the servants in that house are always going about with long faces, they rarely laugh, and are often heard weeping; they are never cheerful, but always discontented. Their master must be a very hard-hearted man, who treats them badly. I should not like to be a servant of his.

Much more does God require us to serve Him cheerfully. How much more, then, must not that great, infinitely happy, most glorious God, who loves us as a father loves his children; who wishes us to call Him Father, and to honor Him as our Father; how much more must not He be disgusted and displeased with the man who serves Him with fear and anxiety as a hard task-master, as a stern Lord, and who performs all his good works with unwillingness, distrust, and fear, and prays to Him in sadness and bitterness of heart? "How could I please the Lord in the ceremonies, having a sorrowful heart?"[1] said Aaron to Moses, when he omitted eating the sacrifice on account of having lost his two sons. No, the Lord expects a cheerful service, a confiding obedience from his children. "The voice of rejoicing and of salvation is in the tabernacles of the just,"[2] says the Psalmist. The servants of God must not wait on their Lord with sadness and through compulsion, but with pleasure and satisfaction: "Not with sadness nor of necessity: for God loveth a cheerful giver."[3] He is pleased with the servant who obeys Him with joy and readiness. The holy Scriptures are full of exhortations that God gives His people to induce them to serve Him in that way. "Come in before His presence with exceeding great joy."[4] "Serve ye the Lord with gladness."[5] "Rejoice in the Lord always: again I say, rejoice,"[6] such is the repeated exhortation given by St. Paul. So that the whole world may see by your conduct what a good and generous God you serve. "I have joyfully offered all these things," says David, the man after God's own heart, when he had enumerated the treasures he had collected for the building of the temple. Whatever I have given to my God, small and mean though it is, I have given joyfully. And the Scripture says of the people of Israel: "And the people rejoiced when

[1] Quomodo potui placere Domino in cæremoniis mente lugubri?—Levit. x. 19.
[2] Vox exultationis et salutis in tabernaculis justorum.—Ps. cxvii. 15.
[3] Non ex tristitia aut ex necessitate; hilarem enim datorem diligit Deus.—II. Cor. ix. 7.
[4] Introite in conspectu ejus in exultatione.—Ps. xcix. 2.
[5] Servite Domino in lætitia.—Ibid.
[6] Gaudete in Domino semper; iterum dico gaudete.--Philipp. iv. 4.

they promised their offerings willingly: because they offered them to the Lord with all their heart." [1]   And again; " And they sacrificed on that day great sacrifices, and they rejoiced; their wives also and their children rejoiced, and the joy of Jerusalem was heard afar off." [2]

Since that is the case, my dear brethren, since God expects a cheerful service from us mortals, I leave it to yourselves to judge whether he does not fulfil that desire of the Almighty who, having a good conscience, which does not reasonably reproach him with grievous sin, enjoys the peace that comes therefrom, and always keeps up a holy cheerfulness and contentment, performing meanwhile the duties imposed on him by the law of God and his state of life, and rejoicing in the good works he does, because he has thereby satisfied the obligations of his state, rendered a pleasing service to the Lord, and merited as a reward the favor and grace of God.   Is not that man much more pleasing to God than one who, although he is in the state of grace, for some reason or other can never persuade himself that such is the case, and who, although he cannot say with certainty that he has on his conscience a mortal sin unrepented of, is always uneasy and anxious lest some hidden sin might be on his soul unknown to him; and that fear he yields to, in spite of the many good works he performs every day for God's sake, which however he tries to shut his eyes to and to depreciate; nor does he dare to hope for heaven on account of them, through some mistaken, erroneous idea of humility that he has?   How can a service of that kind be called cheerful?   Nor can it be called a proof of humility either; for it is nothing else but self-deceit and hallucination. and a deliberate robbing one's self of spiritual, heavenly, and divine consolation.   How can the Lord be pleased with that? I must be upright and honest with myself as well as with others. I am not allowed to speak ill of my neighbor, and must look on him as good and holy as long as I am not certain of the contrary.   Do I, then, owe less love to myself? Must I condemn myself as wicked, and be always in a state of fear and anxiety, although I do my best to lead a good life?   No; such a mode of action is wrong and sinful; it is culpable and should be repented of. For if I do a good act it is praiseworthy, and deserves spiritual

Marginal note: This desire is fulfilled better by one who rejoices in his good conscience and good works than by one who never dares to approve of anything he does.

---

[1] Lætus obtuli universa. Lætatusque est populus cum vota sponte promitteret; quia corde toto offerebant ea Domino.—I. Paral. xxix. 9, 17.

[2] Immolaverunt victimas magnas et lætati sunt; sed et uxores eorum, et liberi gavisi sunt, et audita est lætitia Jerusalem procul.—II. Esd. xii. 42.

joy. But how can I rejoice in the Lord, according to His express command, when I have done something to please Him, if I do not even rejoice that I am in the favor of God on account of the service I have rendered Him in the past? How can I find the peace and rest for my soul which the Lord promises to those who take up His yoke and serve Him, if I find fault with all I do, and condemn my actions as worthless; if I am dissatisfied with my own good works, and cannot find any reason for rejoicing on account of them? There is not a doubt that I should be glad of them, says St. Bernard; "when we rejoice in that way it is clear that we rejoice in the Lord." [1]

A lover is rejoiced at being able to gratify the object of his affection.

And, what makes this truth still more evident, experience teaches us that, when people love each other sincerely, they find the greatest happiness and sweetness in sharing in each other's joys and sorrows. The greater the love, the greater the joy at the good fortune of the loved one, not only when that fortune comes from friends and relatives, but especially when the lover is the author and cause of it, so that he can say: I have done that, I have given that pleasure to the person whom I love. And when the other sees that the benefit conferred is the source of joy to the giver, it must make that benefit much more acceptable, because it is then a proof of the sincerity of the love from which it proceeds.

So, too, should men rejoice at having pleased God.

If, then, I love my God, why should I not rejoice at having done a good work conformable to His will and law, and therefore agreeable and pleasing to Him? Could there be a greater joy for a poor mortal in this vale of tears than to please such a mighty Lord, and to think as Our Lord said of Himself: "I do always the things that please Him?" [2] What joy it must have been for David to hear king Saul say: "Behold thou pleasest the king, and all his servants love thee." [3] Urged on by those words he went at once to risk his life among the Philistines, of whom he slew two hundred, and brought the trophies of his victory to the king, to gain still more of his good opinion; but much more was David pleased to learn that he was dear to God and a man after God's own heart. What joy it is for a courtier to know that his sovereign is pleased with his services! It seems to him that he has had a wonderful stroke of good fortune if he succeeds even once in being so witty as to make his royal master laugh. Must

[1] Cum sic delectamur, plane delectamur in Domino.
[2] Ego quæ placita sunt ei facio semper.—John viii. 29.
[3] Ecce places regi, et omnes servi ejus diligunt te.—I. Kings xviii. 22.

not a soul then have far greater satisfaction when it can think that it has pleased and gratified the King of kings by its good works? O men of the world, think and judge of me as you wish; talk of my actions as you please; hate or love me as best suits your fancies; if I succeed in pleasing my God, I should be more than satisfied; I should rejoice at it above all. And I know that this very joy is agreeable to God. Hear what He Himself says to a pious soul by the wise Ecclesiastes: " Go, then, and eat thy bread with joy, and drink thy wine with gladness: because thy works please God." [1]

Further, can any of you, my dear brethren, deny that I do what is pleasing to God when I think with sorrow and contrition of the sins with which my conscience reproaches me for having offended against the divine law and provoked the anger of God? Is there any doubt that this sorrow is so agreeable to Him that, although He has not the least need of me, although I have first offended Him, miserable creature as I am, without any reason, yet in virtue of this repentance, even if it lasts only for a moment, provided it is perfect, He pardons at once all my sins, no matter how grievous they are, even if they surpass in number the hairs of my head? He makes me His friend, His child, forgets forever the insults I have offered Him, and prepares for me His favors and graces in this life, and a new degree of eternal glory in heaven. Why, then, should I not please God by rejoicing with peace and consolation of heart at the good works that my conscience tells me I have done, by which I have fulfilled the divine law and shown due respect and honor to God? For my part, I cannot see why one should not please God as much as the other, and bring me His grace and favor.

And as God is pleased at my sorrow for my past sins, so, too, is He pleased when I rejoice at my good works.

Again, it is an act of the most perfect virtue and excellent charity, as no one will deny, to rejoice and exult when we see that others honor and love God; to rejoice at the thought that the princes, kings, and emperors of the world bend the knee before the Supreme Lord and humbly adore Him; to rejoice in the thought that there are so many pious souls who honor God in the religious state with fasting, watching, praying, and singing; to rejoice at seeing that in a Christian town people generally lead Christian lives, bring up their children carefully in the fear of God, practise the works of mercy, avoid dangerous company and

It is an act of the love of God to rejoice when others serve Him.

---

[1] Vade ergo et comede in lætitia panem tuum, et bibe cum gaudio vinum tuum ; quia Deo placent opera tua.—Eccles. ix. 7.

the occasions of sin, maintain peace, union, and harmony with each other, show the utmost reverence in the churches, frequent the sacraments on Sundays and holy-days, and are diligent in hearing the word of God. Oh, would that I were so inflamed with Thy love, O God, that all this would fill me with a joy and sweetness equal to that Thy apostles and other servants of Thine experienced, who were often compelled thereby to shed tears of joy, and had, as it were, wings given them to enable them to go through the world, in the face of countless difficulties, instructing souls, encouraging them to Thy service, and thus inducing others to praise and bless Thy name! A joy of that kind can come from nothing but a real love and zeal for the honor and glory of God.

And it must also be one, to rejoice when we ourselves serve Him.

Now, my dear brethren, I ask any sensible man, if I cannot rejoice, and have not just reason for rejoicing, when I see that I myself have done something for the honor and glory of God? If I must be glad of the good works of others, because God is honored thereby, why should I not be glad of my own, since God is honored by them too? Must I take less interest in the honor I give to God than in that given Him by others? But that would be against all rules of sound reason, and contrary to the order of true charity. My underclothing is nearer to me than my cloak; I am nearer to myself than others are, and hence it would be contrary to order to rejoice in the good of another and not in my own. The end for which I have been sent into the world is to serve God, to avoid sin, and by doing good works to gain heaven. If I have hitherto kept this before my mind, if I find in the evening that I have not committed sin during the day, that I have fulfilled the duties of my state properly and with a good intention, that I have borne my daily crosses with patience and meekness, and have performed other good works: why then I will rejoice in the Lord in my heart, and be glad that I have served Him according to my duty; I will thank Him, and at the same time congratulate myself that He has deigned to use me as an instrument for His service, that He has helped me with His grace, that I have done something to please Him. I will say or think to myself: thank God! this day has been well spent; there is no grievous sin on my conscience; I have loved my God; I love Him still; I will continue to love Him; and if death should come to me this night, I am prepared for it; my conscience is good, and heaven will be my portion if I die. "In peace in the self-same I will sleep, and I will rest;"[1] with joy shall I lie down to rest, and sleep peacefully in honor of God. You see then, my dear brethren, that it is a praiseworthy thing and pleasing to God to be at peace with one's conscience and to rejoice on account of this peace and on account of one's good works. It is moreover a very useful thing for our souls, as I shall show in the

Second Part.

There are some of the opinion that this joy and self-congratulation on account of our good works is not beneficial to our souls, and that it would be better for us to be in constant fear with regard to our past and present, as well as our future state, to put out of our heads all thoughts of our good works, and even to look on them as faulty and imperfect; for thus we shall be urged to work out our salvation with more care and diligence, to accumulate a greater treasure of merits and to be more secure of saving our souls. But I am of quite the contrary opinion, and I maintain that by that satisfaction of conscience and joy at our good works the soul is rather encouraged and urged to do still more good and to be more active and zealous in the divine service; while the loss of this joy in the service of God makes it slow, sleepy, and troubled in the acquisition of virtue. I will tell you why.

That joy in our good works encourages to serve God: but sadness hinders the divine service.

You are teaching reading or writing to a little boy; the child is most diligent and does his best to make the letters according to the pattern shown him. Now stand beside him, and do nothing but shake your head and find fault, and tell him that he has done nothing but make mistakes. The poor child gets quite nervous, takes another piece of paper, begins to write again, and brings the same copy to you three, four, or five times; but you never have a word of praise for him; each time you tear up the paper and throw it away. How long do you think will that last? And what progress do you expect to make with your system of teaching? Do you think you will make the child more earnest and diligent? Not at all! You are altogether mistaken. The boy will lose heart at length, and despairing of ever being able to learn to write, will throw down pen and paper; or else if he is compelled to continue, he will do so with tears and lamentations, and without any hope of succeeding. If you wish to teach your scholar well and quickly, you must adopt another

Shown by a simile.

---

[1] In pace in idipsum dormiam et requiescam.—Ps. iv. 9.

plan.   Praise the child frequently, especially when he does his best; good! you must say; that is excellent; if you go on like that, you will soon be perfect.   Then you will see how joyfully and eagerly he will set to work; how he will steal the time for it, and fill page after page.   And that is quite natural, not only with children, but also with grown up, sensible people.   The shopkeeper in his business, the peasant at his work, will never be more diligent than when he sees that he is succeeding and doing well.   If that consolation is wanting; if he finds all his labor turning out profitless; oh, he says, why should I torment myself to no purpose?   Whatever I do, I cannot get on.   And so in despair he gives up the business or the work.

Hence the devil tries to discourage the pious.   So, too, it is with the affair of our salvation and the divine service.   St. Chrysostom, the prince of preachers, says that the crafty tempter is well aware of this, and that he conquers by sadness those whom he cannot ensnare in any other way. [1]   How does he manage that?   He tries to persuade souls that are otherwise desirous of salvation to look on all they do as useless, and to interpret all their own actions in a bad sense, to consider their devotions as no devotions at all, their piety as mere illusion, and always to condemn themselves as if they never did any good whatever, and that under the pretext of a false humility.   His object in that is to make them anxious and despairing, to take away their zeal in the divine service, and to drive them at last to grow careless and to seek consolation from creatures.   Thus they verify the words of David: " My soul hath slumbered through heaviness," [2] because they imagine that nothing in them is praiseworthy or faultless, and therefore that with all their labor they have done little or nothing for the salvation of their souls.

By that joy pious servants of God have always urged themselves on to greater zeal.   On the other hand, common sense tells us that as in worldly affairs success, besides the joy it gives, inspires us also with fresh courage to continue our efforts, so also in spiritual matters a peaceful conscience that rejoices in past efforts to serve God, gives us fresh zeal and courage, and thus pushes on the pious soul, like a miser who the more he has the more he wants, to a holy avarice and greed of multiplying good works and merits, and daily adding to its stock of spiritual treasures.   And that is especially the case with the divine service, which usually grows

---

[1] Dæmon quoscunque superat, per mœrorem superat.

[2] Dormitavit anima mea præ tædio.—Ps. cxviii. 28.

more sweet and agreeable the longer one perseveres in it. I take as witnesses of this all pious souls, even those who formerly lived in sin, but now serve God zealously. It was that joy that encouraged David, Ezechias, and especially St. Paul, who felt a great satisfaction in recounting at length the dangers and temptations that he had to undergo, the imprisonments, scourgings, persecution, and labor that he encountered for Christ's sake; in fact he publicly boasts of his good conscience: "Our glory is this, the testimony of our conscience."[1] And when he saw that he had done so much good did he cease to labor, and begin to grow lazy? No; that very joy gave fresh strength to his wearied body to undertake still greater and more difficult tasks to further the glory of God throughout the world. Mark how, although he had not forgotten that he had persecuted Jesus and His servants and committed many sins, he still boasts with joy: "Our glory is this, the testimony of our conscience." Hear this, you who never dare to rejoice in your purified conscience, because you were formerly guilty of grievous sin!

Moreover, this joy brings also this advantage to the Christian soul, that it avoids with the utmost care, not merely great sins and their occasions, but even deliberate venial sin, that it may keep its peace undisturbed, and avoid the least offence against God, in whom it is so well pleased. By that joy the soul offers its due meed of gratitude to God for the graces received, for it takes them with cheerful heart and countenance from the hands of God; while another receives indeed the same graces, but with fear and dread because it is pusillanimous. Nay, since the latter dares not look on any of its works as good, it can neither appreciate the benefits bestowed on it by God, nor be duly thankful for them. Now if I make a present to a man, I like to see him accept it with pleasure, and thus to show that he values it. That joy causes in the soul a constant child-like confidence in God, which is so often inculcated in the holy Scriptures. For the soul in all accidents, dangers, and temptations abandons itself to its dear Lord, flies to Him for protection, and speaks to Him thus trustfully: Lord, I have served Thee faithfully up to this, and I wish to continue faithful to Thee; Thou knowest that I desire to love Thee with my whole heart; behold I am now surrounded by my enemies, who are attacking me and trying to make me desert Thee. Do Thou defend and protect me, that

It adorns the soul with mar virtues.

---

[1] Gloria nostra hæc est, testimonium conscientiæ nostræ.—II. Cor. i. 12.

the hellish birds of prey may not overcome me! But how can I venture to speak thus to God, if I am afraid that I am not in His grace; if I neither know nor acknowledge that I have ever done anything pleasing to Him? No, child-like confidence cannot exist with a fearful and anxious mind, and therefore St. Paul warns the Thessalonians: " That you be not sorrowful, even as others who have no hope." [1]

With pa-
tience and
resignation
in trials. That joy preserves in the soul an inward repose, contentment, and patience in all the trials and crosses of this life; for it knows that such things come from the decrees of the Lord whom it serves, no matter what their immediate origin may be. Therefore it enjoys an incomparable peace when it remembers its good conscience and good works, which comfort it with the assurance that it stands well with God, and that although it has to suffer here yet it will one day rejoice with God in heaven on account of having served Him zealously. Poor souls! who do not know how to rejoice in the Lord, who think that you ought never regard your actions or the state of your conscience with satisfaction! Poor souls, I say again, how I pity you when the cross is laid on your shoulders! Where can you go for consolation? You find none in temporal joys; for they are taken from you by trials; nor in heaven, which you are afraid of, and despair of ever reaching; nor in God, for you cannot persuade yourselves to look on Him as your well-meaning Friend; nor in yourselves and your own conscience, which you always look on as bad, never as good. Thus you deprive yourselves of all the consolation which could help you to bear your crosses with patience.

A perfect
love of God. Finally, that joy causes in the soul the most excellent of virtues, the perfect love of God; for it is certain that a happy, cheerful mind is much more apt to feel the sweet affections of love than the doubting, timorous heart, which is distracted with all kinds of sad imaginings; and the soul must have a special love for the Spouse who treats it so intimately, and gives it such repose and consolation. Finally, from this comes perfect resignation to the will of God, with which it submits itself to His fatherly hands in life and death, that He may do with it as He pleases. For, as it is comforted by its good conscience, it has nothing to fear in life or death; and it lives and dies assured of eternal happiness, of which it has already had a foretaste in this world. Can any one doubt then, my dear brethren, that such

---

[1] Ut non contristemini sicut cœteri; qui spem non habent.—I. Thess. iv. 12.

repose and joy is desirable and agreeable, since it brings so many advantages to the soul, and makes the way to almost all the virtues easy and safe? I will prove in my next sermon that it can consist with true humility, when I shall explain some apparent objections drawn from the Scriptures and the holy Fathers.

Let the pious Christian rejoice, then, in his good conscience! Let him rejoice in life and death without fear, and humbly congratulate himself and thank the Almighty for the sins that have been forgiven him, for those that he has avoided, and for the faithful service he has rendered God! And when that consoling joy makes itself felt, let him not refuse to entertain it, but rather dilate his mind and heart, so as to receive still more of it; for as St. Bernard says, " when we rejoice thus, we evidently rejoice in the Lord." Let each one who is animated by that joy say to himself: oh, what a pleasant thing it is to have a good conscience! what a sweet, comforting thing it is to serve God faithfully! I will continue, then, to do my best to avoid sin, so that I may preserve my peace of conscience; I will continue to serve my God faithfully, to increase my stock of merits, so that, if I have no other joy in the world, I may at all events rejoice securely in the Lord in life and death.

Sinners, come, ah, come back! Hear the merciful Saviour crying out to you: " Take up My yoke upon you." He is most desirous of your salvation; do penance and cast from you the heavy burden of your sins, and you shall see what a great change for the better that will be. " You shall find rest to your souls;" I promise by My divine truth that you shall find rest, consolation, joy, and pleasure for your souls, and at last you will enjoy eternal rest with Me in heaven; " for My yoke is sweet, and My burden light." Come, ah, come back! Amen.

Marginal notes: Conclusion and exhortation to the just to rejoice thus in the Lord. To sinners to take up the sweet yoke of the Lord.

SEVENTY-SECOND SERMON.

ON THE LAWFULNESS OF JOY OF CONSCIENCE ON ACCOUNT. OF GOOD WORKS.

Subject.

Joy on account of our good works: 1. easily harmonizes with true Christian humility; 2. it easily harmonizes with the example of humility given us by holy servants of God.—*Preached on the fifth Sunday after Epiphany.*

Text.

Triticum autem congregate in horreum meum.—Matt. xiii. 30.
" But the wheat gather ye into my barn."

Introduction.

By the weeds are meant bad, by the wheat good, works.   And
how different their fate!   The weeds go into the fire, the wheat
into the barn.   What different expressions of countenance there
will be seen on the last day, when the wicked shall be sent to
hell on account of their evil deeds, and the good shall be invited
by their Judge to enter heaven on account of their good works,
trifling though they may have been!   Rejoice confidently in
the Lord, by anticipation, you faithful servants of the Lord,
who have a good conscience!   Rejoice on account of that
good conscience!   Rejoice on account of your good conscience, of
the faithful service you have rendered to God, and of the good
works that will one day be garnered into the granary of heaven!
That joy, as I have already shown, is most pleasing to God and
most beneficial to your souls; for God requires a cheerful service
from us, and that joy is the best encouragement to the soul to
continue serving God and practising virtue.   Now let us hear
what might be said against this.   That joy, by which we exult
in our good conscience and in our good works, seems to run
counter to the Christian virtue of humility, which is so necessary to all men, and by which we must have a mean opinion of
ourselves.   That is the first objection.   And it seems to run
counter to the example of the Saints, who followed an entirely
different plan; the second objection.   Both I shall answer in
this sermon.

Plan of Discourse.

*That joy harmonizes easily with true Christian humility: the
first point.   It harmonizes easily with the examples of humility
given us by the holy servants of God: the second point.*

Do Thou, O God of love, give, preserve, and increase in us zeal
in Thy service, through the intercession of Mary and of the holy
angels!

Joy on
account of
one's good
works seems
vainglory.

First, then, is it not presumption, secret vanity, and self-com-
placency to admire one's own good works, approve of them, think
them worthy of praise, take pleasure in them, rejoice at
them, and centre one's delight and satisfaction in them?   What

else is that but placing one's self in the proximate occasion of becoming proud and conceited, as if one had done extraordinarily great things? Is it not taking occasion from one's good works to become slothful in the divine service, like that rich man, mentioned in the Gospel of St. Luke, who said to himself: " Soul, thou hast much goods laid up for many years: take thy rest, eat, drink, and make good cheer "? [1] Would not a man be exposed to the same danger, who sets himself to consider the good works he has performed with a pure conscience during his life, and takes pleasure in them? Might not he, too, exclaim: My soul, behold thou art in a good state; thou hast done much good, and gathered many treasures for heaven with thy zeal? Rest now; make good cheer; thou hast labored enough, and canst now enjoy thyself?

Quite different to that was the conduct of pious and holy men who wished to save their souls and get to heaven after death! What a mean opinion they had of themselves and of all their actions! Although they avoided with the utmost care the least shadow of sin, yet they looked on themselves as poor sinners; nay, they both thought and proclaimed themselves to be the greatest sinners in the whole world. Perfect and wonderful were their virtuous works; yet, to judge from the history of their lives, they thought they had done nothing for heaven; even their holiest actions they examined with the utmost care, so far were they from looking on them as deserving of praise, and often did they find fault with them, although in reality there was nothing in them that could be condemned. Let us take only one example. What a holy man Job was! God himself says that he had no servant on earth like Job in sanctity, innocence, justice. What a virtuous man he was in prosperity! " I was clad with justice," he says of himself, "and I clothed myself with my judgment, as with a robe and a diadem. I was an eye to the blind, and a foot to the lame. I was the father of the poor. "[2] How patient he was in the most grievous misfortunes and sufferings of body and soul! How submissively he accepted those crosses from the hands of God, and in the midst of them praised and blessed his God with undisturbed mind! And yet what an opinion he had of himself! "I feared all my works," he said with humility. "If I would justify myself, my

For the saints judged and spoke most humbly and disparagingly of their good works.

---

[1] Anima, habes multa bona posita in annos plurimos ; requiesce, comede, bibe, epulare. —Luke xii. 19.

[2] Justitia indutus sum, et vestivi me, sicut vestimento et diademate judicio meo. Oculus fui cœco et pes claudo. Pater erum pauperum.—Job xxix. 14, 15, 16.

own mouth shall condemn me.   I, who although I should have
any just thing, would not answer, but would make supplication to
my Judge."[1] Thus even Job is afraid when he considers his works,
holy though they are; and shall I, a poor mortal, rejoice at my
trifling good works, although I have not done the thousandth
part of what he did?   Job dares not to speak to God of his justice;
and shall I flatter myself with the idea that I am leading a holy
life, and indulge in that thought with pleasure, satisfaction, and
joy?   Oh, no! let me only have a mean opinion of myself and be
always afraid!

But even
the most
humble re-
joiced on
account of
them.

I acknowledge, my dear brethren, that this objection is a
specious one, yet if we take it in the right sense it will not
militate against the truth that I have undertaken to defend,
namely, that we can and with reason must rejoice at the good
works of which our conscience says to us that they were performed
according to the will of God.   And to answer the first question;
if that joy were vanity, idle boasting, or presumption, then we
should have reason to accuse David, that man after God's own
heart, of being vain, boastful, and presumptuous; for in many of
the psalms, especially in the 118th, he recounts before God, to his
own great consolation, how he kept himself free from sin, and
observed the divine law.   " I walked in the innocence of my
heart," such are his own words, "in the midst of my house.   I did
not set before my eyes any unjust thing: I hated the workers of
iniquities.   Not to me did the perverse heart cleave: and the
malignant that turned aside from me I would not know.   The
man that in private detracted his neighbor, him did I persecute.
He that worketh pride shall not dwell in the midst of my house;
he that speaketh unjust things did not prosper before my eyes."[2]
" I have run in the way of Thy commandments;"[3] "I have lifted
up my hands to Thy commandments, which I loved: and I was
exercised in Thy justification;"[4]   " I entreated Thy face with all

---

[1] Verebar omnia opera mea.   Si justificare me voluero, os meum condemnabit me. Etiamsi habuero quippiam justum, non respondebo, sed meum judicem deprecabor.—Job ix.
28, 20, 15.

[2] Perambulabam in innocentia cordis mei, in medio domus meæ. Non proponebam ante
oculos meos rem injustam ; facientes prævaricationes odivi. Non adhæsit mihi cor pravum :
declinantem a me malignantem non cognoscebam ; det rahentom secreto proximo suo, hunc
persequebar.   Non habitabit in medio domus meæ, qui facit superbiam ; qui loquitur ini-
qua, non direxit in conspectu oculorum meorum.— Ps. c. 2, 5, 7.

[3] Viam mandatorum tuorum cucurri.—Ibid. cxviii. 32.

[4] Levavi manus meas ad mandata tua, quæ dilexi ; et exercebar in justificationibus tuis.
—Ibid. 48.

[5] Deprecatus sum faciem tuam in toto corde meo.—Ibid. 58..

[6] Media nocte surgebam ad confitendum tibi.—Ibid. 62.

my heart:"[5] "I rose at midnight to give praise to Thee;" and so on through numbers of verses. If that joy is vanity, then Ezechias, one of the holiest kings of Juda, could be accused of vainglory and presumption; for when he was at the point of death he spoke to God thus confidently: "I beseech Thee, O Lord, remember how I have walked before Thee in truth, and with a perfect heart, and have done that which is good in Thy sight;" a prayer that was so pleasing to God that He spared the king's life for fifteen years: "I have heard thy prayer, and I have seen thy tears," He said to him by Isaias; and therefore, "behold I will add to thy days fifteen years."[1] If that joy is vanity, then the holy Apostle St. Paul was a boastful, vain, presumptuous man; for the greatest joy of his life was in his conscience, as his own words to the Corinthians sufficiently prove: "Our glory is this, the testimony of our conscience."[2] And what was the testimony of his conscience? "That in simplicity of heart, ... and not in carnal wisdom, but in the grace of God, we have conversed in this world."[3] It was in that that he placed all his joy and glory. If that joy is vanity, then St. Hilarion committed a sin of vanity, boasting, and presumption at the end of his life, when he said to his soul as it was on the point of departing: Be of good heart; fear not; for seventy years thou hast been serving Christ. If that joy is vanity, then Job himself was vain and presumptuous, when his friends came to comfort him in his misery as he sat on the dung-hill, and attributed his calamities to his sins; for he told them how he had led an innocent life, and found his consolation in the thought of it: "If I shall be judged, I know that I shall be found just;"[4] and again: "My justification, which I have begun to hold, I will not forsake; for my heart doth not reprehend me in all my life."[5] Hear how he rejoices at the future reward in store for him; although I am now a man of sorrows and abandoned by all, "I know that my Redeemer liveth ... and in my flesh I shall see my God. Whom I myself shall see and my eyes shall behold; ...

---

[1] Obsecro Domine, memento quæso, quomodo ambulaverim coram te in veritate et in corde perfecto, et quod bonum est in oculis tuis fecerim. Audivi orationem tuam, et vidi lacrymas tuas ; ecce ego adjiciam super dies tuos quindecim annos.—Is. xxxviii. 3, 5.

[2] Gloria nostra hæc est, testimonium conscientiæ nostræ.—II. Cor. i. 12.

[3] Quod in simplicitate cordis, et non in sapientia carnali sed in gratia Dei conversati sumus in hoc mundo.—Ibid.

[4] Si fuero judicatus, scio quod justus inveniar.—Job xiii. 18.

[5] Justificationem meam quam cœpi tenere, non deseram ; neque enim reprehendit me cor meum in omni vita mea.--Ibid. xxvii. 6.

this my hope is laid up in my bosom. "[1]   But it would be the height of presumption to accuse those holy men and many others like them of vanity and boasting.

By this joy we can practise true humility.

It would indeed be vanity if one were to publish his good works, and the graces and gifts bestowed on his soul, in order to gain the praise and esteem of men, as the Pharisees did.   It would be self-conceit if one were to think himself better than others, or to despise them on account of his good works.   It would be presumption if I were to ascribe to myself and my own powers the good I do; for God is by His grace the Author and Cause of all the praiseworthy actions that I perform.   It would be presumption if I were to pretend, either to myself or to others, that my actions are so good and perfect that they could not be done better, and that the least fault or defect cannot be found in them.   A great deal indeed is required to attain such a pitch of perfection as that!   But to live in peace, consolation, and joy when our conscience tells us that we have hitherto avoided sin; to rejoice that we do nothing against God; to rejoice when we do good, because we thus fulfil our obligations, do the will of God, and please and honor Him thereby; to consider our good works and be glad on account of them, thus exciting ourselves to renewed zeal in the divine service, to greater patience in adversity, and to a firmer confidence in God and heaven; to consider our good works, and offer due thanks to God for them as for a great benefit; no one could look on that as vanity, or seeking for praise, and still less as presumption.   That is acting reasonably, sensibly, and judging of the matter as it really is in itself; that is truly rejoicing in the Lord.

Therefore the holy Fathers exhort us to it.

And to that the holy Fathers exhort us when we make our examen of conscience in the evening, a most useful practice and one deserving of the greatest praise.   Many are of the mistaken idea that the only object of the examen is to discover and bewail our sins; and therefore they say, what is the use of my making an examen?   I do not leave the house the whole day; I am always occupied with my studies or my business: I have done no wrong.   But if you have done no wrong,—and indeed the chief matter of the examen are the sins we have committed, that we may blot them out by repentance, so as to go to bed with a pure conscience,—yet have you done no good during the day, at all

[1] Scio quod redemptor meus vivit, et in carne mea videbo Deum meum. Quem visurus sum ego ipse, et oculi mei conspecturi sunt: reposita est hæc spes mea in sinu meo.—Job xix. 25, 26, 27.

events by offering your daily duties to God by the good intention? And if you had done nothing more than keep your conscience free from sin, thus preserving a most desirable peace of
heart in the friendship of God, that should also be made part of
the examen, that you may offer due thanks for it to God as for a
great and special benefit. Hear what St. John Chrysostom says
of this examen: "When you go to bed, say to yourself: we have
come to the end of another day, O my soul! What good or evil
have we done? And if you have done good, thank God; if you
have done evil, repent of it and do it no more." [1] And that is a
truly useful way of practising humility, acknowledging the divine benefits and thanking God for them as we know we ought.
"It is not the pride of a self-conceited man," says St. Augustine,
"but the confession of one who is not ungrateful, to acknowledge that you have received benefits, and that of yourself you
have nothing." [2] That is, in a word, to serve God with a cheerful, confident, child-like heart; to love Him with the whole heart,
rejoicing that His divine majesty has been well served, and that
something has been done for His sake. Nor does this joy in the
Lord militate against the examples of the saints, as I shall now
show in the second part, thus further explaining what I said in
the first about humility.

Second Part.

To say that the saints always condemmed and thought nothing of their good works is not true. We have already seen
proofs of that in those holy men of whom I have spoken in the
first part. It is quite true that in spite of their holy lives they
had a mean and low opinion of themselves, and they were perfectly right therein; it is the opinion we must all have of ourselves, remembering that everything that is good and praiseworthy in us comes from above from the generous hand of the
Lord. Although St. Paul rejoices in his good conscience and
in the works he performed for the glory of God, yet he humbly
acknowledges that it must all be ascribed, not to himself alone,
but to the grace of God working with him: "By the grace of
God I am what I am; and His grace in me hath not been void,

Margin note: No matter what good we do, we should never grow proud, but be always humble, like the saints: at the same time, how-ever we should re-joice in our good works.

---

[1] Quando in lectum veneris, dicito in corde tuo expendimus diem, o anima! Quid boni fecimus? aut quid mali operati sumus? Et si quid boni feceris, age Deo gratias: si quid mali, de cætero ne facias.

[2] Non est superbia elati, sed confessio non ingrati, et habere te cognoscere, et nihil ex te habere.

but I have labored more abudantly than all they: yet not I, but the grace of God with me. " [1]   It is one thing to have a good opinion of myself and another to take pleasure in and esteem my works when they are good and according to the will of God; and that distinction we must carefully observe; for while the latter joy is praiseworthy the former is altogether unjustifiable.

by a   The beggar who receives a large piece of bread or some other generous alms at your door is justly pleased with his good fortune, and rejoices at it; but would it not be a ridiculous thing for him to think much of himself on account of it?   If you had not been generous to him he would have died of hunger; and although he is so lucky to-day, who knows how things will be with him to-morrow?   Therefore let him eat what he has with joy, and trust to his good fortune to be as well off to-morrow; but he must not get self-conceited.   The laborer rejoices when his day's work is done, on account of the wages he has earned, but he does not know how long his strength will last, so as to enable him to work.   So, too, it is with us, my dear brethren.   We are all beggars and have to knock at the door of the great Lord of heaven, and humbly await from His mercy and generosity the graces and blessings we stand in need of.   " What hast thou that thou hast not received? " [2] asks St. Paul.   According to the Prophet Job, the days of man are like those of a hireling. [3]   We all serve the same Lord for an eternal reward.   Now, no matter how rich I may be in merits and good works, I am still a weak, inconstant mortal exposed to many dangers, and I know not what may happen to me to-day or to-morrow.   What I have gained to-day, I may lose to-morrow by sin; although I am now steadfast and serve God as I ought, some violent future temptation or occasion may completely overcome me, change my will, and turn me away from God, unless He helps me in a special manner; although when I do my best to serve Him I have a firm and child-like confidence that He will assist me in the future. Thus, I have no reason for forming a good opinion of myself. Therein consists the humility with which the saints judged their good works; and I must use the same humility in judging of mine; but it does not hinder or exclude a peaceful joy arising from my good conscience, a feeling of pleasure and exultation at

[1] Gratia Dei sum id quod sum, et gratia ejus in me vacua non fuit, sed abundantius illis omnibus laboravi: non ego autem, sed gratia Dei mecum.—I. Cor. xv. 10.

[2] Quid habes quod non accepisti?—I. Cor. iv. 7.

[3] Sicut mercenarii dies ejus.—Job xiv. 6.

the good works that I have performed with God's grace. For what is once well done according to the divine will remains good for all eternity. Even if I fall to-morrow and offend God by mortal sin, that sin will not destroy the good works of to-day, which will still be praiseworthy, and it will always remain true that I have done something which has pleased the Lord.

But the holy servants of God have always looked on themselves and publicly proclaimed themselves as sinners. That is true, and they were perfectly right; for we can and must look on ourselves as sinners, no matter what we are. Why? Because we can sin; because our corrupt nature always inclines us to sin; because we commit small sins at least nearly every day. If I have committed but one mortal sin in my life, I have still reason to think and say of myself, no matter how holy I may be, that I am the greatest sinner in the world, considering the great light and grace given to me, and the gifts bestowed on me so generously, in preference to so many others, by the Almighty. If even the vilest wretch had the graces, lights, and impulses to good which I enjoy, he would serve God much more zealously than I do; and St. Augustine says we must look on all the sins from which God preserves us as if we had been forgiven them.[1] Yet pious servants of God, who humbly acknowledged that truth, must still have been greatly rejoiced that they repented of and were forgiven their former sins; nor is there any doubt that they thanked, with joyful and loving hearts, the Divine Mercy, which bore with them so patiently, and did not permit them to die and be lost in the miserable state of sin, freeing them in time from the slavery of the devil and bringing them to the liberty of the children of God. Although St. Paul acknowledges and professes himself to be the greatest sinner in the world, as he writes to his disciple Timothy: "Christ Jesus came into this world to save sinners, of whom I am the chief;"[2] and again to the Corinthians: "For I am not worthy to be called an apostle, because I persecuted the Church of God,"[3] yet that consideration did not deprive him of the joy, peace, and glory resulting from his good conscience and from the services he rendered to God, as we have seen before.

In spite of all their good works the saints thought they did

Almost all of us must, like the saints. look on ourselves as great sinners: yet we should rejoice in our good works.

Like the

---

[1] Omnia peccata sic habenda sunt, tanquam dimittantur, a quibus Deus custodit, ne committantur.

[2] Christus Jesus venit in hunc mundum peccatores salvos facere, quorum primus ego sum. —1. Tim. i. 15.

[3] Non sum dignus vocari apostolus, quoniam persecutussum ecclesiam Dei.—I. Cor. xv. 9.

saints we must acknowledge that we do very little for heaven; still we must rejoice.

little or nothing for God and heaven. Quite true, and again quite right also; even St. Paul, who rejoiced so much in his good conscience, says: "The sufferings of this time are not worthy to be compared with the glory to come, that shall be revealed in us." [1] All imaginable trials that can afflict us in this life are not worthy of being named even, when compared to the glory that God has promised us as a reward for them. But is that a reason for not rejoicing at the trials we bear? Rather the contrary. For instance; there is a magnificent property worth fifty thousand thalers; the owner of it gives it to you for one florin, because he has a liking for you; now if you are asked what you paid for that property, oh, you exclaim, the price is not worth mentioning; it has cost me only a florin. Meanwhile you rejoice, and with good reason, at having gained possession of such a valuable property for so small a sum. Is not that the case? So, too, should it be with us. There is not a doubt that all our efforts, even if we were to labor without intermission till the last day, are very small, worthless, nay, nothing, compared to the reward we have to expect for them. Our labor lasts a very short time; our reward in heaven will be eternal. Our works of devotion proceed from a miserable creature, who even if he had no hope of eternal reward is bound by countless titles to perform them, to be ready to obey the least sign of the sovereign will of God, and to serve Him with all his strength; and Thou, O God, art so good and loving that Thou givest an eternal reward, an immense Good, Thy own self, for the little we can do to serve Thee! This is the thought which, as I said before, fills the mind of the dying just man with great consolation and joy. How little the good I have done! he thinks, and what an immense reward I shall receive for it! On account of it I am now about to enter into the eternal joy of my Lord! And the same thought, my dear brethren, should make us rejoice during this life, and give us all the more courage in the divine service; namely, that God requires so little from us for His eternal heaven, for His everlasting rewards. Should I not exult when I think: I have done some good, only a little, it is true; but it is what God required of me; it is what He wished me to do in order to reward me eternally for it?

Like the

Finally, it is true that holy people examined most strictly their

[1] Non sunt condignæ passiones hujus temporis ad futuram gloriam quæ revelabitur in nobis.—Rom. viii. 18.

works of devotion and piety, and often found fault with them; saints we must ex- but how? Did they look on all the good they did as evil and amine useless? By no means; that would have been great folly and strictly our good works, ignorance on their part. They carefully looked into their good and fear works to see whether they had performed them with due zeal, lest there diligence, attention, and with the right intention, and whether be some im- perhaps they had not been guilty of some negligence or fault in perfection in them. performing them. For instance; it is certain that prayer, by which we praise and honor God, is a most excellent, holy, and praiseworthy act of religion, and yet it often happens, even with the most pious, that during prayer, especially when it lasts long, some small fault or sin is committed either through weariness or sluggishness of mind or some half-voluntary distraction. There is no doubt that the works of charity and mercy are holy; yet it often happens that they are slightly faulty on account of human respect or vainglory. But are we, then, to condemn all such works, and say that they lose their holiness, that they are not good or useful, or that we have no reason to rejoice on account of them? If that were the case we should be badly off indeed, and could hardly hope ever to be able to do any good! For who has advanced to such a degree of perfection that he does everything in the most perfect manner, with the most perfect zeal, the most perfect intention, and avoids even the least fault? Must we say that a loaf of white bread, made of the finest flour, is worthless and unfit to eat, because through some slight carelessness on the baker's part it is a little burnt in one corner, or because it has here and there a grain of chaff in it, that got mixed with the meal in the mill? No; you would certainly not give such a loaf to the pigs; it is quite good in itself; scrape off the burnt part with a knife; pick out the chaff, and the rest of it will be perfectly clean and sweet.

Such was the manner in which holy people examined their vir- And that in order to tuous works, and noticed even the least fault that had crept into please God them; their object was not to condemn the work as worthless, for all the more. it remained substantially good in itself, holy and pleasing to Shown by a simile. God, but to repent of the faults found in it, and to avoid them in future. Just as a young woman acts before the glass. She looks at herself most carefully twenty times in succession, to see whether there might not still be some small spot or stain on her face; or whether the lace on her head-gear might not be better arranged. Why does she do that? Is it because she fears she is ugly? No, for she knows, or at all events thinks, that she is beautiful. Why, then, is she so careful about those small spots? Does she fear that they who might see them would condemn her as ugly on account of them? Not at all; but because she takes pleasure in her beauty, and cannot suffer the least thing that might be unbecoming to her; therefore she most carefully wipes away all spots and stains, that they may not mar her appearance. Such, too, I say, is the reason why holy souls that love God zealously are so strict in examining their good works; but their motive is much more sensible, useful, and holy than that of the young woman. They have a spiritual pleasure in presenting them stainless and perfect before the sight of God. in order that their joy may be the greater in proportion as they make themselves more pleasing to Him. This is what Job sought in his works, when he said: " I feared all my works; " not that he was afraid they were wicked and culpable, but that something might be wanting to their perfection. I was most careful not to do anything that might in the least displease the Lord. Otherwise he relied on his good conscience to such an extent, and was so consoled and rejoiced at the thought of his pious life, that this joy was the only comfort he had in his afflictions, as he himself says: " I know that my Redeemer liveth, whom I myself shall see, and my eyes shall behold; this my hope is laid up in my bosom," that is, in the depths of my heart and conscience.

Thus this joy is not contrary to the practice of holy people. Therefore, my dear brethren, the practice of sensible, pious, and holy people, instead of condemning, rather encourages the feeling of contentment, the consoling joy that we have in our good works and in the service we have rendered our Lord and God. I say sensible people; for I know well that there are some innocent souls who indeed live piously, but are always frightened and anxious, as if everything they do were bad. St. Gregory says of them, that they fear sin where there is no sin. The care they use in order to save their souls is most excellent and praiseworthy; but the fear and anguish to which they are given cannot be approved of; in that they show not piety, but rather ignorance and an innocent stupidity. Why should I be afraid of a dog, when there is none in sight? Why should I be afraid of evil in that which my conscience cannot condemn as evil? If I wish to act sensibly, I should fear what is to be feared; but I should also praise and approve of what is good and praiseworthy.

My dear brethren, let us be sorry that we have ever offended *Exhorta to seek joy in a good co science.* the good God by the sins that our conscience tells us that we have been guilty of in the past; let us fear offending God in future by even one sin; and let us endeavor during the present time to love God with our whole hearts, and to do His holy will in all things. Beyond that there is nothing to cause us either fear or anxiety. If we do that we can be always peaceful, satisfied, and joyful, even because we serve the Lord. Oh, would that all men sought their joy and pleasure herein, that is, in the divine service! They would certainly find more real satisfaction and pleasure than in all earthly amusements, which indeed enliven the body, but cannot give either rest or peace to the heart. In the service of God we shall then seek our pleasure, and once for all we shall make the resolution with holy Job: " My justification, which I have begun to hold, I will not forsake. " I will remain always faithful to my God, whom I have begun to serve; and so the divine promise will be certainly fulfilled in my regard: " You shall find rest to your souls." Amen.

SEVENTY-THIRD SERMON.

ON THE CONFORMITY OF JOY OF CONSCIENCE WITH THE INSPIRED WORD OF GOD.

Subject.

The joy of a good conscience on account of one's good works is not contrary to Holy Scripture.—*Preached on the sixth Sunday after Epiphany.*

Text.

Cum autem creverit majus est omnibus oleribus.—Matt. xiii. 32.
" But when it is grown up it is greater than all herbs."

Introduction.

The good works that we perform for God's sake may well be likened to the grain of mustard-seed; considered in themselves they are utterly insignificant, mean, and worthless; but when after a happy death, in the state of grace, we are able to produce them before our Judge, oh, to what glory and happiness they will increase in heaven! Therefore rejoice, I say again, faithful servants of God, who have performed such works in your lives.

I showed in the last sermon that a peaceful joy of that kind easily harmonizes with Christian humility and a mean opinion of one's self, and also with the example given us by the holy servants of God. There is still one thing that might disturb the repose and peace of conscience of the good Christian, and make that joy and self-congratulation on account of his good conscience and good works suspicious in his eyes: I mean the word of God, which no man can call into doubt. For on the one hand Christ Himself says to His disciples: "When you shall have done all these things that are commanded you, say: We are unprofitable servants."[1] And the Holy Ghost says by the wise Ecclesiasticus: "Be not without fear about sin forgiven;"[2] and St. Paul writes to the Philippians: "With fear and trembling work out your salvation."[3] By the first of these texts we are forbidden to rejoice at our good works; for if I am commanded to look on myself as a useless servant, even after having done everything to which the will of God and His law bind me, how could it be lawful or advisable for me to rejoice at having done the will of God, or to look on my good works and the service rendered God as good and praiseworthy? The second disturbs the sweet repose and peace of conscience; for if I must be afraid with regard to sins that are really forgiven,—and a good conscience is one that is free from sin,—how can I have any feeling of security in a good conscience? According to the third I must work out my salvation with fear and trembling; how can I then be joyful at heart? To tremble with fear and at the same time exult with joy, are two things that cannot possibly exist together. Such is the objection. But be not disturbed, pious Christians, who have a good conscience and serve God! I will now explain away those apparently terrible words to your consolation, as I find them interpreted by the holy Fathers and other authors.

Plan of Discourse.

The joy of a good conscience on account of one's good works is not contrary to Holy Scripture. Such is the whole subject of this instruction. The object of it is to encourage all to serve God steadfastly and joyously, and to be peaceful at heart.

Give us Thy light and grace to this end, O God of love, through the intercession of Mary and of the holy angels.   ·

[1] Cum feceritis omnia quæ præcepta sunt vobis, dicite: servi inutiles sumus.—Luke xvii. 10.

[2] De propitiato peccato noli esse sine metu.—Ecclus. v. 5.

[3] Cmmu tu et tremore vestram salutem operamini.—Philipp. ii.12.

So Our Lord says: "When you shall have done all these things that are commanded you, say: We are unprofitable servants"? How so, dear Lord? What is the meaning of "unprofitable servants"? Must we say that we are wicked servants? But he is not a wicked servant who does all that his master commands him. Hast Thou not said elsewhere: "You are My friends if you do the things that I command you."[1] Certainly Thou wilt not choose wicked servants for Thy friends? for Thou hast told us to avoid the wicked and shun their company. Must we then say and think that we are at all events not good servants, and that we do no good? But how then wilt Thou be able one day to say to me with truth, if I persevere to the end doing all that Thou requirest of me: "Well done, good and faithful servant, because thou hast been faithful over a few things, I will place thee over many things"?[2] Did Thy disciples do no good when they fulfilled all Thy commands? That cannot be; for Thou addest the words: "We are unprofitable servants; we have done that which we ought to do."[3] But if they did what they were bound to do, surely they did some good; for they could not be bound to do evil; therefore since they knew that they did what they were bound to do, they knew also that they did good, and must necessarily have formed a good opinion of it. My dear brethren, when we have obeyed the law of God we must not think, much less say, that we are wicked servants; nor should we think or say that we are not good servants; but we should say: "We are unprofitable servants." That word "unprofitable" can be explained in three ways.

First, we must remember that our holiest and most perfect works, considered in themselves as they proceed from us, and in their own nature, are worth nothing in the sight of God, nor in the least degree meritorious of a supernatural reward; for they must receive all their value from the merits of Christ, from sanctifying grace, by which they are raised above their nature, and receive, as it were, a sort of divine property; so that God in consideration of this value given them by Christ, accepts our works as good, and gives us His friendship and heaven as a reward for them. Perhaps you will understand it better by means of a simile. A prince promises or commands his

[Marginal note:] When we have done the will of God we are good, but unprofitable, servants.

[Marginal note:] First, because our works in themselves are worth nothing, but must get all their value from the merits of Christ. Shown by a simile.

---

[1] Vos amici mei estis, si feceritis quæ ego præcipio vobis ?—John xv. 14.

[2] Euge serve bone et fidelis, quia super pauca fuisti fidelis, super multa te constituam ?—Matt. xxv. 21.

[3] Quod debuimus facere, fecimus.—Ibid.

chamberlain to give all those who present a note signed by his own hand and sealed with his own seal a hundred thalers. Now I present my petition; the prince signs and seals it; it becomes as valuable to me at once as a hundred thalers; for that sum will certainly be paid me when I present the note to the proper authorities. Why? The note I bring is indeed nothing more than a worthless piece of paper in itself; but since it has the prince's seal and signature it becomes very valuable. So, too, it is with the good works that we perform in the state of sanctifying grace, which are so many notes that we present to God. In themselves they are not at all deserving of a supernatural reward; but Christ sets His seal to them by sanctifying grace, and our heavenly Father signs them, binding Himself to accept them as of great value, and to give us a rich reward for them, if we can produce them after death.

But that should not prevent us from rejoicing on account of our good works.

In that sense, my dear brethren, we can and must acknowledge that we are unprofitable servants, although we have done all that we were commanded to do, because of ourselves we have done nothing deserving of a supernatural reward. Yet, just as the poor man who has the note with the prince's signature rejoices at being able to show something worth so much money, although he knows that his own part in the work consists simply in bringing a worthless piece of paper; so, too, have I good reason to rejoice at my good works, which are deserving of the favor of God and a heavenly reward, although I must at the same time humbly confess that of myself and my own powers I have performed a vile and worthless action. Is not that clear enough?

Secondly, because God is not in need of our works.

In the second place, we must not consider ourselves as profitable servants of the Lord, although we have done all that He has commanded, in the sense that we thereby make a valuable present to God, further His interests notably, or bestow on Him some favor or grace, for which He is bound to thank us and to prove His gratitude. That such is the meaning of the words of Our Lord is clear from the whole passage. For in the same place He asks His disciples: "Doth he thank that servant for doing the things which he commanded him?" And He Himself answers: "I think not."[1] And then He continues: "So you also when you shall have done all those things that are commanded you, say: We are unprofitable servants: we have done that which we ought to do." He would indeed be a stupid

---

[1] Numquid gratiam habet servo illi, quia fecit quæ ei imperaverat? Non puto.—Luke xvii. 9, 10.

lout of a servant who would think he does his master a favor by waiting at table and handing round the dishes, and expect his master to thank him for that! He should wait a long time before being thanked for merely doing his duty; he is there to attend on his master, and he must be satisfied if he gets a box on the ear sometimes, instead of thanks. Much less should we poor mortals, when we do anything to please the great God, in whose presence the powers of heaven cover their faces with awe, ready to obey His least sign.—much less should we imagine that we have done great things; for as the Lord of the universe He has the right to demand our services when, where, and how He pleases, without giving us any reward therefor. And moreover He has not the least need of them, not like earthly masters, who would be in an evil plight if their servants abandoned them altogether. What does God want with my works? Whether I praise and serve Him or not will not in the least interfere with His happiness. Therefore I can and must look on myself as an unprofitable servant, who does nothing but what he already owes his Lord on countless titles. Nevertheless, just as a servant has reason to rejoice at having served his master faithfully, although he is bound to do so, so too, should I rejoice at having rendered due obedience to my God and fulfilled His will; and that all the more since that great Lord in the excess of His goodness deigns to receive me into His friendship on account of the services I render Him, to love me as a father loves his child, nay, as it were, to consider Himself bound in gratitude to continue to be favorable and generous to me, as I showed when speaking of gratitude to God.

St. Augustine gives another beautiful interpretation to the words of Our Lord. Unprofitable servants, he says, means here as much as servants without work; idle servants; we have no more work, because we have done what we were told to do. We are like the laborer who is hired by the day to work as he is ordered. When he comes in the morning his master says: take the axe and cut up the wood you see lying there. The man sets to work, and in two or three hours he has finished it. What must he do now? Is he to lie down and say to himself: I have done what I was told; or must he go away home? No; he is hired for the whole day; so he goes to the master and says: I have finished cutting the wood, what else am I to do? So, continues St. Augustine, Christ warns His disciples and all His

Thirdly, because after having performed a good work we have not yet done all that God requires of us.

servants, saying to them: when you have done all that you are
commanded to do, you must not imagine that you are to serve
Me no more, and that you can now idle away your time. No,
you are hired by your heavenly Master for the whole day; that
is, you must serve Him your whole lives long, and do His will,
if you wish to gain heaven. Therefore you must say: we are unprofitable servants; present yourselves before the Lord always
willing to obey Him; say to Him: we are now idle; we have done
what was commanded us; tell us now what more Thou desirest us
to do. So, my dear brethren, should we think when we have
performed some good work; what more can I do for God's sake?
During this day I have served God and kept His commandments:
"We are unprofitable servants;" to-morrow I will continue to
serve Him. Lay on me, O God, what commands Thou pleasest;
with Thy grace I am ready to obey Thee in all things! The
cross, the trial, is over; I have borne it for Thy sake with patience: "We are unprofitable servants;" if it pleases Thee
to send me another, I shall willingly accept it from Thy hand.
In this consists a man's readiness and faithfulness in serving
God, when he thus submits himself to the divine will in all
things. And this harmonizes excellently with true joy and consolation on account of good works; nay, to await new commands
from Our Lord in that way is a clear sign of a cheerful, well-
disposed mind, that is ready to do all that God wishes.

We must not be with-out fear on account of sin forgiven; that is we must fear to sin again.   "Be not without fear about sin forgiven;" those are the
other and far more severe words of the Holy Ghost. Yet why do
I call them severe? They are rather consoling words; for they
are to be understood either of past sins, or of future sins that
may still be committed. In the first case, why should I fear
that my sins are not forgiven? That would not be good advice;
for we cannot think without blasphemy that the Holy Ghost
contradicts Himself, since He speaks of forgiven sin. But if it
is forgiven, how could He wish me to fear that it is not? Must
I be afraid that I have offended God thereby? But there is no
reason to fear that; that was done when the sin was committed;
that is what I have repented of, and what I am still sorry for.
Must I fear that God will condemn me for it? Truly He can
punish me in purgatory, if I do not fully satisfy for it here, and
in that sense I have reason to fear on account of sin that is forgiven; but He will not and cannot condemn me to hell for it,
since He cannot break His word. If I were to sin again, and

to die without doing penance, I should be lost forever on account of this last sin, but should not have my sufferings increased in the least on account of my former forgiven sins, even if there were a hundred thousand of them; they are and remain blotted out for eternity. So that the text must be understood of sins that I might commit in future, and the meaning of it is: O sinner, thou hast experienced the goodness and mercy of God; He has pardoned thy grievous transgressions because thou hast humbled thyself before Him with contrite heart, and hast candidly confessed them; He will never think of those sins again; but do not therefore be without fear; do not live so carelessly as thou hast hitherto done; avoid sin with the utmost care, and do not imagine that thou canst make little of it, because it is so easy to obtain forgiveness from the divine mercy. This is clearly the meaning of those words, as appears from the context: "Say not: I have sinned, and what harm hath befallen me." [1] I have confessed my sins, and paid off my debts; now I can commence to contract fresh debts. I shall sin again, and again repent; and I shall find forgiveness again from the good and merciful God as easily as before (and alas! there are many who act on that plan, constantly alternating between sin and confession, confession and sin). But that will not do; for as Ecclesiasticus adds: " Be not without fear about sin forgiven, and add not sin upon sin. And say not: the mercy of the Lord is great, He will have mercy on the multitude of my sins; because easy as it is for the merciful God. to pardon, it is just as easy for Him to give free rein to His anger; His patience at last changes into wrath and indignation: " For mercy and wrath quickly come from Him, and His wrath looketh upon sinners." [2] Therefore we must be afraid on account of sin that we have repented of, not because it is not forgiven, or because we might be condemned to hell on account of it, but lest after having obtained pardon from the good God, we should again offend Him and provoke His anger. Such was the meaning of what Our Lord said to the sick man, whom He healed at the Pool of Bethsaida: " Behold thou art made whole: sin no more, lest some worse thing happen to thee." [3] And that is only right and just. It would indeed

---

[1] Ne dixeris: peccavi, et quid mihi accidit triste.—Ecclus. v. 4.

[2] De propitiato peccato noli esse sine metu, neque adjicias peccatum super peccatum. Et ne dicas: miseratio Domini magna est, multitudinis peccatorum meorum miserebitur. Misericordia enim et ira ab illo cito proximant, et in peccatores respicit ira illius.—Ibid. v.

[3] Ecce sanus factus es; jam noli peccare, ne deterius tibi aliquid contingat.—John. v. 14.

be a dishonorable thing to expect such peace and comfort of
heart from God that we might sin boldly and not fear despising Him after having once obtained pardon of our sins. But
this fear of offending God need not hinder me from enjoying the
comfort that arises from my repentance, by which I have blotted
out my former sins, and changed my bad conscience into a peaceful and good one. This fear does not hinder the child-like confidence with which I trust that the generous God will by His
grace prevent me from offending Him again; provided I only
have the firm determination to remain faithful to Him, to serve
Him as well as I can, and to avoid the dangers and occasions of
sin as far as lies in my power.

Even the frequent and sorrowful remembrance of our sins occasions joy and peace of heart.   But, you ask, when we remember our former manifold and
grievous sins, should we not then be troubled, anxious, and fear-
ful at the thought that we have so often lost heaven and deserved
the eternal fire of hell? How could peace and repose of conscience consist with that; especially since it is advisable, even
after having done penance, often to remember our sins and renew
our sorrow for them? Yes, my dear brethren, we should indeed
often remember them, and renew our sorrow for them; but how?
With a child-like sorrow proceeding from a loving heart, and
caused by the thought that we have abandoned and offended our
dear Father in heaven. There is a senseless, stupid way of
remembering our sins after they have been forgiven, which
brings with it nothing but disquiet, mistrust, low spirits, anxiety,
and unfounded doubts: and it is a suggestion from hell, where
there is no order, but eternal horror. No, the Spirit of God is
a gentle, sweet, consoling Spirit. The saints remember their
sins with sorrow, which neither disturbs nor discomforts them.
Nothing, says St. Augustine, who speaks from experience, is
sweeter to the penitent soul than tears of contrition, even when
they are shed frequently; for that consoling and penitent recollection causes.first, the soul joyfully to thank God for the grace of
repentance, by which it escaped eternal torments; secondly, it inspires the soul with a child-like confidence in the goodness and
mercy of God, that since it is now of good will, it will not be
lost forever; for He bore with it most patiently even while it was
rebellious and hostile to Him, and when He had every right to
condemn it to hell He so lovingly received it into his favor;
finally, the more the soul is penetrated with the knowledge of
having offended God, the more it is now determined to serve

Him most zealously in future. All this does not cause fear or anxiety, but rather true consolation and joy of heart.

Finally, a terrible thunder-bolt is launched from the pen of St. Paul: "With fear and trembling work out your salvation." Yet I cannot say that I am much frightened at it, when I consider how the same Apostle, as I have often told you already, placed all his joy and glory in his good conscience and good works, and rejoiced in them to such an extent that his heart was too small to contain the happiness he felt. Therefore he says openly before the world: "I am filled with comfort, I exceedingly abound with joy in all our tribulation." [1] Is it possible, I ask myself, that the vessel of election, St. Paul, did not work out his salvation? The mere suspicion of that would be a most wicked injury against the holy Apostle. And yet he did not always tremble with fear, but rather exulted with joy, and that, too, although he had been a great sinner and persecutor of the Church of Jesus Christ. Therefore I can work out my salvation, and at the same time rejoice in the Lord precisely because I am working out my salvation.

We can work out our salvation with fear, and yet rejoice in the Lord.

Little do the texts I have quoted frighten me, when I consider hundreds of other texts in the Holy Scriptures, which inspire me with courage and confidence, and exhort me to serve the Lord joyfully. And if we are to be always in dread about our past, our present, and our future life, when shall we ever begin to serve the Lord with joy, as He has commanded us? "Rejoice, ye just, in the Lord." [2] "Serve ye the Lord with gladness; come in before His presence with exceeding great joy." [3] And the Holy Ghost repeats the same exhortation in countless other places. Is it really thy wish, O great St. Paul, that we should always fear and tremble? Why then dost thou say to us: "Rejoice in the Lord always;" [4] never should your joy be interrupted? And that we may make no mistake about it, thou repeatest thy words: "Again I say, rejoice." [5] But that would be a miserable kind of joy, in the midst of which we must always be trembling with fear! If we must fear and tremble, how can the words of Our Lord be true: "Take up My yoke upon you,"—

For God exhorts us to this joy.

---

[1] Repletus sum consolatione, superabundo gaudio in omni tribulatione nostra.—II. Cor. vii. 4.

[2] Lætamini justi in Domino.—Ps. xcvi. 12.

[3] Servite Domino in lætitia; introite in conspectu ejus in exultatione.—Ibid. xcix. 2.

[4] Gaudete in Domino semper.—Philipp. iv. 4.

[5] Iterum dico gaudete.—Ibid.

what is to happen then? " And you shall find rest to your souls. " [1]
What is more apt to disturb rest than fear and anxiety? And how
could the words be true: " My yoke is sweet and My burden
light?" [2]   Thou shouldst rather have said, O Lord, that Thy
yoke is exceedingly heavy and intolerable, if we must always
tremble when bearing it! Eh? Weeping and gnashing of teeth
belong to the reprobate in hell, or to sinners during this life;
but not to the pious and now just servants of God, who try to
do His will. No; " Whatsoever shall befall the just man, it
shall not make him sad, " [3] such is the assurance given us by the
Holy Ghost. But how could that be true, if even one's good works
fail to console him, and make him tremble with fear? " But
glory and honor and peace to every one that worketh good, " [4]
such are again the words of St. Paul. And they agree with
those which the God of truth speaks by the Prophet Isaias:
" And My people shall sit in the beauty of peace, and in the
tabernacles of confidence, and in wealthy rest. " [5]   What sense
will those words have, O holy Apostle, if we must always fear
and tremble? But I think to myself again, the Holy Ghost cannot contradict Himself; God cannot say yes and no to the same
thing at the same time, nor can He command me to do two contradictory things together, such as to rejoice and fear, to be at
peace and to tremble for the same reason. So that the words of
St. Paul must evidently be interpreted in some other sense.

The mean-
ing of the
Apostle's
words about
fear and
trembling.

What then am I to fear? Why should I tremble? Perhaps
lest I might not be in the state of grace, although my conscience
does not accuse me of any grievous sin? Truly that is not the
meaning of St. Paul; quite the contrary, as is clear from his own
words: " With fear and trembling work out your salvation."
For he is addressing those who are really saving their souls; now
no one can do that who is in the state of mortal sin and at enmity with God; such a one rather works out his damnation;
therefore he is addressing those who are in the state of grace and
serve God. What does he wish them to fear? Is it that they
have not a good conscience, that they are . not serving God?
But that would render his exhortation ridiculous. It would be
as if I said to a stranger who asks me the way to Treves; You are

---

[1] Tollite jugum meum super vos, et invenietis requiem animabis vestris. —Matt. xi. 29.
[2] Jugum meum suave est et onus meum leve.—Ibid. 30.
[3] Non contristabit justum, quidquid ei acciderit.—Prov. xii. 21.
[4] Gloria autem et honor et pax omni operanti bonum.—Rom. ii. 10.
[5] Sedebit populus meus in pulchritudine pacis, et in tabernaculis fiduciæ, et in requie
opulenta.—Is. xxxii. 18.

on the right way and cannot go astray; but at the same time you must be afraid that you are not on the right way. The man would think I was making a fool of him. It would be a stupid thing for me to give a pitcher to a child to carry home, and say to him: take this pitcher with you; but while you are on the way, you must be always afraid that you have not got it.

It would be a sensible thing to say to the traveller: you are on the right way to Treves; keep on as you are going, but be careful not to lose the road, for there are by-paths here and there that are apt to mislead. It would be a sensible thing to say to the child, bring this pitcher home; but be careful; hold it tight in your hands that it may not fall and be broken; otherwise you will get into trouble when you reach home. This, my dear brethren, is what St. Paul, writing to the Philippians like a father who is anxious for their eternal welfare, and who knew that they were working out their salvation, means by his exhortation. He tells them to fear, not that they are not working out their salvation, but lest they should cease to work it out, lest they should stray from the path to heaven, on which they had been so happily walking, lest they should go astray amid dangers and temptations, and be led into mortal sin; therefore they must fly all occasions of sin with the utmost care, so as not to lose the precious treasure of sanctifying grace, which they were bearing about in frail vessels. *Namely, that we must take every care not to offend God again.*

Thus the fear is directed to the future, and not to the past or the present; and thus the two things harmonize admirably. For I can rejoice that I have hitherto kept the right road to heaven, that I am actually working out my salvation; and at the same time I can be cautious and fearful lest I should ever wander away from the right path. I rejoice in my heart that my conscience does not accuse me of any grievous sin; yet I will be most careful in future, and that through fear and anxiety lest I should sully my conscience by sin; I will tremble at the very shadow of sin. I rejoice at heart that I have hitherto served the God whom I love, and still continue to serve Him according to my duty; but at the same time I will use the utmost diligence to be faithful in His service for the remainder of my life. *Meanwhile we can still rejoice.*

Let us all make that resolution, my dear brethren; we will serve our God as long as there is a drop of blood in our veins; we will serve Him no matter how things go with us in the world. No good shall seem to us so great, no man so dear, no pleasure so sweet, *Conclusion to fear sin alone, and rejoice in the Lord.*

no sorrow so bitter, as to make us provoke our God to anger or leave the way of His commandments. The only thing we have to fear in life and death is sin: this fear shall keep us in all dangers and occasions of evil, and shall preserve the sweet repose of our conscience from being disturbed. And we will fear not only manifestly grievous sins, that would make God our enemy, but we shall also dread committing venial sin with full knowledge and consent, so as not to lessen our agreeable friendship with and child-like confidence in God. This resolution we shall renew every morning when making the good intention, and every evening when, in the examen of conscience, we find that we have kept our resolution during the day. Then we can and will rejoice in the Lord, because we are His dear children and friends, who have served Him faithfully during the day. Almighty, most merciful, and heavenly Father! look on this good will of Thy children, by which they give themselves to Thee body and soul, ready to do Thy will in all things. Thou knowest our weakness and inconstancy: Thou seest the many snares that our enemies lay on all sides to entrap our souls; but Thou wilt never abandon those who trust in Thee. Strengthen then by Thy powerful grace this resolution of ours, so that we may serve Thee, bearing Thy sweet yoke with peace of soul and joy of heart, until we come to Thee in eternal rest. Amen.

SEVENTY-FOURTH SERMON.

ON THE MARKS OF A GOOD CONSCIENCE.

Subject.

He who wishes to know whether he has a good conscience must ask his own conscience.—*Preached on Septuagesima Sunday.*

Text.

Voca operarios et redde illis mercedem.—Matt. xx. 8.
"Call the laborers and pay them their hire."

Introduction.

Quite right and just too; for, as Our Lord says elsewhere, "The laborer is worthy of his hire." [1] The only thing that sweetens the workman's toil is the hope of the wages he is to re-

---

[1] Dignus est operarius mercede sua. Luke x. 7.

ceive for it in the evening when his work is done.   As long as
we live, my dear brethren, we are hired to work for the great
Master; we are laborers, whose only end is to serve God, to love
God, to keep God's law, and to do His holy will in all things.
The wages we are to receive at evening, that is, at the end of
our lives, for this labor is eternal happiness in the kingdom of
heaven.   Oh, who will not work willingly for the short, uncertain time of this life to gain such a recompense!   Yet we have
such a good and generous God that He will not allow His faithful servants to wait till the end of their lives for their reward; but
in the midst of their labors, during this life, He gives them a
notable portion of the future rewards that await them, namely,
peace of heart, a sweet repose of conscience, and joy in and on
account of the work they are actually doing for Him, as we have
already seen in detail.   Yes, some will think; all that has been
said of a good conscience is indeed consoling and comforting for
those who have a good conscience; and I, too, would willingly rejoice in the Lord, if I only knew that I am in the state of grace,
that I really have a good conscience.   But who can tell me that?
That question, my dear brethren, I am now about to answer.

Plan of Discourse.

*He who wishes to know whether he really has a good conscience
must ask his own conscience about it; for that will certainly tell
him whether it is good or bad.   Such is the whole subject.*

Most blessed Virgin, Discoverer and Dispensatrix of all the
graces of God! obtain to-day from Thy Son, as Thou easily
canst, grace for those who have a bad conscience to change it
at once into a good one by true repentance; and for those
who have a good conscience that they may preserve its purity
and serve Thy Son and Thee in joy and peace of soul!   And do
you, O holy guardian angels, prepare the minds of your charges
for this grace!

The woman who is really anxious to know how she looks and *The looking-glass i*
whether she is neatly dressed or not finds nothing in the house *the surest*
so useful to her for that purpose as the looking-glass; for that *means of*
alone can tell her what her outward appearance is.   But could she *finding ou
whether*
not ask her maid or her children, and depend on what they say to *the face is*
her?   No; she would not be at all satisfied with their judgment *clean or
dirty.*
in the matter.   What does my maid know, she would say to herself, about what is becoming to me?   Her only experience in

matters of dress consists in putting on her cap in the morning, and that she can do even without a light. The children know still less; they have yet to learn how to dress and adorn themselves; so that what they might say is not deserving of attention. Even her own husband she distrusts most of all in the matter; for he looks on all questions of dress as mere nonsense, and only laughs when they are made the subject of conversation. She must then see how things stand with her own eyes; otherwise she will not be satisfied, but will always be uneasy lest some spot or stain should disfigure her face, or lest her dress might not be in proper order. And how can she find out that? The glass is her only resource; that is the judge who has to pronounce sentence on her appearance; that is the adviser whom she consults; in that she looks at herself for a quarter of an hour at a time; what it says to her she believes, and if it pronounces a favorable sentence she is quite satisfied.

One's conscience is a looking-glass, in which he can see if his soul is free from sin.

Forgive me, my dear brethren, for bringing forward such a frivolous simile in such a serious matter; but I know of no better way to represent the holy care and anxiety of a pious, devout soul, whose greatest and only desire is to please its God, to keep itself always pure in His sight, to be adorned with virtue and good works, and thus to come at last to God in heaven. Now, the greater the care taken for that purpose the greater sometimes is the trouble, anxiety, and doubting fear on the part of the soul, as to whether it is really pleasing to God or not; really beautiful in His sight; really in a good state of conscience, so that if death came it would be sure of salvation. But who can persuade the soul of that? Say what you will to console it; it will not believe you so firmly as to put aside all its fears. Preachers may remind it of the infallible word of God, telling all those to rejoice who serve the Lord, and that they who love God and avoid sin can put away all anguish, that God requires a cheerful service, etc. But all to no purpose! That is all very good, it says; but what does the preacher know of the state of my conscience? The confessor tells it, since he knows it so well, to be satisfied, not to be troubled about this or that; to look on its fears as only idle fancies; to be contented with knowing that it is on the way to heaven; to go on as it has begun, and rejoice in the Lord. But not even that suffices to restore peace and repose; the soul fears that perhaps it is in the same condition as the people of whom God speaks by the Prophet Isaias: "O my people, they that call thee blessed the same deceive thee." [1] What is to be done then? If you refuse to believe others, you must at least believe your own eyes. Go then to the glass and look at yourself, and see what you are like. Where am I to find the glass? Your own conscience is the glass, and a most faithful one, that will not deceive you; it will show you in clear colors the state of your soul, and tell you whether it is pure and beautiful or defiled and hideous in the sight of God.

St. Gregory Nazianzen calls the conscience a judge placed over men by the Almighty in His stead, to pronounce finally on their actions whether good or bad. Whatever the sentence of that judge may be, God ratifies it, and rejects as bad what the conscience condemns as bad and approves as good what it approves of. If I satisfy my conscience, I satisfy God; if my conscience accuses me, I am guilty before God. If my conscience does not accuse or condemn me, neither will God accuse, punish, or condemn me. Therefore in theology the conscience is called the rule and guide to be followed in judging between good and evil; and according to the unanimous teaching of all Catholic theologians, I am bound to follow and obey it in all my actions to such an extent that if I act against my conscience I act against God, nor can I do anything good or pleasing to God, however good or pleasing to Him the work may be in itself, unless my conscience first looks on it as good and pleasing to Him; nor can I commit sin, although in reality I do something forbidden by the law of God, unless my conscience knows and reminds me that I am doing wrong, or at least suggests to me a reasonable doubt regarding the legality of my act. Thus I actually sin by doing a work that is good in itself and has nothing whatever wrong in it if my conscience erroneously judges, or gives me reasonable cause to doubt that the act is unlawful; and I actually perform a good work, although what I do is really sinful, if my conscience assures me that the act is pleasing to God.

The conscience is the judge to decide between good and evil.

For instance, to tell a wilful lie, or take a man's life, or wilfully shorten it, is certainly forbidden by the law of God, and is never lawful under any circumstances; yet if an ignorant man thought in his conscience that it would be a good act, and according to his duty to tell a lie to save his fellow-man from death; that it would be a charitable thing for him to put a man out of pain by killing him, he would be bound in such a case to follow the dic-

And I am always bound to follow it. Shown by examples.

---

[1] Popule meus, qui te beatum dicunt, ipsi te decipiunt.—Is. iii. 12.

tates of his conscience. Our Father Vasquez writes that he once met with a peasant who used to toss dying people violently about from one side to the other, imagining that he would thus facilitate the escape of the soul from the body, and free the dying sooner from their agony; and of course looking on his act as one of pure charity. Again, it is well known that there was a Spaniard who used to steal little children from the turks, baptize them, and at once put them to death, so that they might not fall again into the hands of the Turks and lose their souls. He thought he was doing wonders for the honor of God and the salvation of souls in thus sending to heaven little children who would otherwise be lost forever. These people did not sin, but performed good actions. Why? Are not lying and murder forbidden by God? Yes, and therefore what they did was in itself sinful, but because their conscience did not condemn but rather approved of such actions, they were not guilty in the sight of God; nay, since their conscience told them that they were bound to act as they did, they would have sinned had they not followed its dictates. On the other hand, there are many who think it a sin to go out of their houses before having washed, to receive holy Communion without having cleaned their teeth, to eat their dinner on Good Friday, and so on; these things are not sins, but because they believe in their conscience that they are, they would be guilty of sin as often as they do them. So great is the authority and power that our conscience has received from God to pronounce final and infallible judgment on all our actions, and to decide whether they are good or bad. Therefore if I look at myself in my own conscience, and see therein, that in what I am doing I am free from sin, I can be quite certain that I am innocent in the sight of God, and, as far as that act is concerned, that I can rejoice in the Lord.

In what a good or bad conscience consists, as far as our present acts are concerned. Yes, you say; but now we are just as wise as before! What sort of a thing is the conscience? Is it a little man that sits in my brain or heart to tell me, when I ask him, how matters stand with my soul? But if it is a looking-glass, how am I to get hold of it, so as to see myself in it? That is a very practical question, my dear brethren. People speak so often of a good or a bad conscience; they appeal to it; they say: I cannot in conscience do that; it is against my conscience, and so on; but many of them do not know in what the conscience consists. I will tell you then in a few words. Your conscience is nothing else than the reasonable, candid judgment that you form of your own actions. And with regard to the act you are about to perform, if you judge or think without any doubt that the act is a lawful one, you do it with a good conscience, and it is a good act; but if you judge, or have reasonable doubt, that it is not lawful, then you do it with a bad conscience, and commit a sin, no matter what the act may be in itself, whether it is good or bad, lawful or unlawful.

From this it follows, first, that the conduct of those people is most unreasonable, who, after having done something about the lawfulness of which they had not the least doubt, are filled with fear and anguish afterwards because they happen to hear that it is a sin. Then it is all up with them! My God, they think, I have often done that and never confessed it! What shall I do? All my past confessions are bad! Nonsense! You cannot sin unless you know, or have a reasonable doubt, that what you are doing is sinful; but that knowledge or doubt, you had not at the time of the action. What is once done well and without sin cannot be made sinful by any knowledge gained afterwards. Why then should you worry yourself so much? If it was forbidden a thousand times, or was the worst sin that one could commit, ask your conscience what judgment it formed at the time, and if it says that there was no sin be quite at ease; you are not even bound to mention the act in confession, because it is not matter for absolution. And, on the other hand, we see how great is the error of those who, having done what they falsely thought sinful, and finding out afterwards that the act is lawful, congratulate themselves, saying; oh, I am glad of that! I need not confess it now, because it appears it is not a sin. But do not be so sure of that; the sin is already committed, because you thought at the time that you were doing wrong; so that it remains a sin, although you know better now; and you must confess it and repent of it.

(margin: From which many can see the mistakes they hitherto made.)

Thirdly, it follows that those parents and servants are very unwise who, to keep children in check or frighten them from evil, either tell them that things are sins which are no sins at all, or else make the sins greater than they are in reality. If the child throws away the bread after it has eaten the honey or butter, they cry out; you must not do that, or you will go to hell! Disobedience to parents or making a cross face is also condemned as a mortal sin. "Those naughty children who run about

(margin: Especially parents who make little children believe there is sin where there is no sin.)

in the streets will go to hell." "Be careful not to tell a lie, for a lie is a mortal sin;" and so on. That is not the way, O parents, to instruct children! You must not make them believe that there are sins where there are none; nor make sins greater than they really are; otherwise you teach them to do evil; for when they come to the use of reason, since what they have heard so often remains fixed in their memories, and they look on those actions as sins, when they do them they act against their conscience and thus commit sin, although the act itself is not sinful. You must have recourse to other means to keep them in check; threaten them with the rod when they do wrong, and if they do not amend beat them soundly in God's name; that is not so dangerous for them, and will do them far more good than that senseless manufacturing of sins.

How to know if our conscience is good with regard to past sins and our present state.

Now with regard to the conscience as far as the past is concerned (and it is of that I wish to speak chiefly to-day), whether I am now free from grievous sin, and in a good state with God, so that I can peacefully rejoice in it; that I have to learn from my own judgment with regard to my past and present life, whether it was wicked and still continues so, or was good and is still good; if I look at that judgment I shall certainly know whether I have a good or bad conscience in the sight of God. So says St. Thomas of Aquin, and almost all theologians agree with him. You have a bad conscience if, after diligent examination and with good reason, you judge on sufficient grounds and can say with truth: after having received holy baptism I sinned grievously when I came to the use of reason, when I was fully aware that what I did was a mortal sin; and if you can moreover say, with equal truth and good reason, that there is one of those mortal sins that you have not confessed, or not confessed properly. Or else if you can judge with good reason and say, with truth: I have now really a desire and wish to sin grievously against the law of God; or I am in doubt as to whether this or that is a mortal sin, and yet I do not intend to avoid it or amend my life in that respect. There you have a proof of a bad conscience, and if such is the case with you, believe me, you will not long have rest, if there is even a little of the fear of hell left in you, or a slight hope or desire of going to heaven. For therefrom comes the bitter sting, or, as it is called, the gnawing worm of conscience, which eats it away like a worm gnawing into an apple. The worm eats its way into the apple, until the latter loses its taste, color, and at last rots altogether; so does the bad conscience, that is, the bitter remembrance of his own deformity, act with the soul of man. I have sinned, he keeps on saying to himself; I have offended God! I have not yet made peace with God! I have in God a sworn enemy, in whose power I am completely! I have lost heaven forever! I am a child of damnation; I have trampled the blood of Jesus Christ under foot, and that, too, for some short-lived pleasure, some brutal lust, some trifling gain, or to please some mortal; a thing that I could have so easily avoided! If I die now, I shall go straight to hell! These and similar thoughts are the sharp teeth with which the heart of the sinner is torn, and as they force themselves on him against his will, and constantly recur to his mind, the unhappy man always has his own tormentor with him, so that he can have neither rest, nor peace, nor enjoyment. Such is the confession that king David makes with regard to himself after he had committed sin: " I know my iniquity: and my sin is always before me," [1] the thought of it prevents me from sleeping at night, and fills my life with bitterness: " There is no health in my flesh because of Thy wrath: there is no peace for my bones because of my sins." [2] True indeed are the words of St. Bernard: " There is no punishment greater than the torment of a bad conscience." [3] Now tell me, you who are so agitated by doubts as to the state of your soul, do you find your conscience uttering those bitter reproofs against you, and always tormenting you with the thought of grievous sins that you have not repented of? Can you with reason say: I have sinned mortally, and have not yet repented of and confessed my guilt, and so on? If not, if you cannot form such a judgment with truth, then you may be certain that you have not a bad conscience, and that so far as you are concerned your soul is not in a bad state.

On the other hand, if after due consideration you can say: as far as I know, I have never omitted a grievous sin in confession; as far as I know, I have prepared myself for confession always as well as I could; I have repented with my whole heart of my sins; I am still very sorry for having ever grievously offended my good God; if I had to live my life over again, I should never sin grievously. As far as I know, after that last mortal

How to know whether the conscience and soul are in a good state.

---

[1] Iniquitatem meam ego cognosco, et peccatum meum contra me est semper.—Ps. l. 5.

[2] Non est sanitas in carne mea a facie iræ tuæ : non est pax ossibus meis a facie peccatorum meorum.—Ibid. xxxvii. 4.

[3] Nulla pœna major est mala conscientia.

sin, I have never committed another. As far as I know, I have no ill-gotten goods and am not bound to restitution. I have hitherto tried to do the duties of my state according to the will and law of God; I am willing and am firmly resolved to do them in future as long as I live, and never to offend God by a mortal sin, even if I had to lose all I have in the world otherwise. If, I repeat, you can say that with truth, then you can be certain with a human certainty, which will not admit of any reasonable doubt, that you have a good conscience and are in the state of grace. "A pure conscience," says St. Isidore, "is one that does not justly accuse you of past sins, nor take an unlawful pleasure in present ones."[1] Mark the word, *justly;* for they who are plagued with scruples and unfounded fears have not just reason for their uneasiness, nor do they form judgments, but rather mere fancies and self-delusions on the point on which they are scrupulous. Nor do they often sin in those points, although they think the contrary. For such people there is no remedy but blind obedience to their confessor, whom they must obey as if he were an angel from heaven, nay, God Himself. Otherwise, says the pious Tauler, a man well experienced in spiritual things, " Let him who fears and flies mortal sin not doubt that God is with him."[2]

The first sign of being in the state of grace. This certainty becomes all the greater when you have good reason for believing, and can say to yourself, that for a long time, some months, for instance, you have avoided all mortal sin. "Show me the soul," says St. Bernard, "with whom Christ is present now, and has been for a long time, and I will not have the least doubt that that soul is a spouse of Christ."[3] For this is one of the surest signs of being in the friendship of God; since He does not so easily give to one who is in the state of sin those great, special, powerful graces which enable a weak mortal to avoid sinning grievously in the midst of so many dangers and temptations. Pearls are not thrown before swine; much less does God bestow special marks of His favor on His enemies. Hence, as the holy Fathers and all theologians teach, and as we know by experience, it is a most difficult thing for one who is actually in mortal sin to abstain from committing fresh sins for

---

[1] Conscientia munda est, quæ nec de præteritis juste accusatur, nec de præsentibus injuste delectatur.

[2] Non dubitet sibi adesse Deum, qui timet et cavet mortalia.

[3] Da mihi animam cui vivere Christus non tantum sit, sed et jam diu fuerit, non ambigo sponsum adesse.

any length of time. The first and chief advice to be given to a sinner is not to defer repentance, to free himself as soon as he can from the miserable state of sin, and recover the friendship of God; for the longer he remains in that state the farther away he goes from the grace of God and the more does he multiply sins. Hence, if you keep from grievous sin for a long time after having done penance, you have a good sign that you are in the grace of God.

Finally, do you not sometimes feel in your heart a fervent love of God, a desire to do something to please Him and to serve Him faithfully according to His holy will? Do you not feel an inward horror when you hear how recklessly men provoke God's anger? Are you not rejoiced to see people honoring Him publicly? Do you not experience an inward sorrow when in the examination of your conscience you find that you have wilfully committed even a venial sin? Are you not uneasy until you have confessed it? That is another sure sign that you are in the state of grace, and are beloved by God. The Lord Himself says: "I love them that love Me."[1] If I have committed even a hundred thousand million of sins, and make even for one moment an act of perfect charity, as David did when he said with a contrite heart: "I have sinned against the Lord,"[2] all my sins are at once forgiven, and I am again beloved by God. This is an undoubted fact, as theologians teach. "Oh," exclaims St. Bernard, full of joy and consolation, "I am not afraid, because I love."[3] Why so, great saint? Because I am thereby assured that God loves me; "if I love God I can as little doubt that I am loved by Him as I can that I love Him."[4] Now every one can find out all this of which I have spoken hitherto, and can find it out with the utmost certainty from his own conscience, if he asks it to pronounce on the matter. For I can and must know whether I have wilfully sinned, or wilfully concealed a sin in confession; whether I truly repent of my sins and detest them; whether I love God with my whole heart, and am resolved to remain faithful to Him for the rest of my life. And if any of you, my dear brethren (and I hope, or at least wish, that all of you may be in that happy state),—if any of you can reasonably and honestly form that judgment concerning himself, then I

The se{sign.

---

[1] Ego diligentes me diligo.—Prov. viii. 17.
[2] Peccavi Domino.—II. Kings xii. 13.
[3] Non timeo, quia amo.
[4] Ego vero amans amari me dubitari non possum, non plusquam amare.

congratulate him with all my heart; he is all right; he has a
good conscience; he is a friend, a dear child of God, and if he
were to die now he would inherit the kingdom of heaven.   Let
him rejoice then in the Lord; let him be peaceful and satisfied,
and thank the good God.   Only one word of warning I would
wish to say to him with the old Tobias: "Take heed thou
never consent to sin, nor transgress the commandments of the
Lord our God. "[1] If you are careful in that, there is no fear for
you.

Three
doubts
solved.   But, you say, wait a little!   You cannot say that there is no
cause for fear yet.   Why?   Although I may judge for certain
that I have no mortal sin on my soul, may I not be guilty of
one that I know not of?   And besides, although I think I have
confessed everything properly, perhaps I made a mistake?   Perhaps I have forgotten something, and have never yet confessed
it?   Perhaps I have not been careful enough with the examination of my conscience?   Perhaps I did not explain myself clearly enough? Is there any other "perhaps"?   Yes; perhaps I had
not a real interior sorrow?   Very good!   Perhaps the priest did
not absolve me properly?   That might be!   Perhaps I am not
validly baptized?   Perhaps!   But do put an end to your perhapses, or I shall never get done!   Such is the manner in which
many souls plague and torture themselves; as if holiness consisted in persuading themselves that they are no good at all; as
if they must find out the least thing that they are not infallibly
certain of, in order to disquiet themselves in the service of God!
To all your perhapses I will give a short answer founded on the
word of God.   As long as you cannot get farther than a perhaps,
with regard to grievous sin on your conscience, so long all
your fears are utterly groundless, and it would be foolish for you
to think seriously even for a moment of that perhaps.   If you
are sure, after you have done your best, humanly speaking, to
find out the truth, that there is a mortal sin on your soul which
you have not confessed, then confess it; you need not for that
purpose repeat all your former confessions.   If you are certain
that you have committed a grievous fault in examining your
conscience or in telling your sins, then examine and explain
yourself better now, if you can do so; if you cannot, then all you
need say is: I once committed a mortal sin knowingly, but I

---

[1] Cave ne aliquando peccato consentias, et prætermittas præcepta Dei Domini nostri.
—Tob. iv. 6.

did not examine my conscience carefully, or else, I did not explain myself properly, and now I have forgotten what it is. If you are sure that you had not sincere sorrow for your sins, then repent of and confess them now. If you are sure that the priest did not give you absolution properly, then go to another confessor, who knows more about his duty. If you are sure that you are not baptized, then have yourself baptized to-day, and then you need not make any confession of the sins of your past life. But if you are not sure of all this, (and you cannot reasonably be, as I suppose,) then do not annoy yourself any more about it; what your conscience does not reproach you with, God will not look on as a sin. Even if you have committed a grievous sin, which has escaped your memory, you are bound to nothing more than to tell it whenever you remember it.

Yes, but (what? are you not satisfied yet?)—but if I really committed a mortal sin, which I have never confessed, how can it be forgiven me? Will I not be lost on account of it? And that is exactly what I wish to avoid. I quite believe you; but people are not lost for such sins. You must know that one mortal sin is never forgiven without the others that are on the soul at the same time; therefore when I am validly absolved, I am freed from all my sins at once, whether I remember them or not, whether I confess them or not, even if there were a hundred of them. Supposing, too, that through some fault on your part or that of the priest, you were not validly absolved two or three times, or even oftener, suppose that you have frequently not had true sorrow for your sins; yet on one occasion at least you had a true sorrow especially when you made a general confession with all possible care; so that you have certainly been properly absolved once at least; how can you reasonably doubt then? When a man does his best, says the great theologian Suarez, goes often to confession, and tries to awaken a supernatural sorrow for his sins, it is humanly speaking impossible for him not to have now and then a true contrition, and not to be cleansed from his sins, if we must believe the divine promises. Therefore the true contrition you had, the one valid absolution you received, frees you completely from all your sins known and unknown. But, supposing further, in order to put a stop to your objections once for all, that you were never validly absolved, that you are not even baptized (though you cannot have any reasonable doubt on these points) ; if you only once make a perfect act of charity,

[marginal note:] Comfort for those who are plagued with such doubts.

you will be certainly placed in the state of grace thereby, for it includes the baptism of desire. What else do you want, to put you completely at ease? I think nothing will satisfy you short of taking actual possession of heaven! And when you do so, I should not object to go with you; but you must wait awhile yet; the time for that will come; only love God with your whole heart above all things, and you will be sure of being in a good state during life; continue to love Him till the end, and you will be sure of possessing Him in heaven.

Exhortation to those who have a good conscience, to rejoice in the Lord. Meanwhile enjoy in peace and quiet the heaven of consolation which a good conscience brings in this life. The heaven of consolation, I say; for what can a man have to fear in this life whose conscience gives him good testimony of himself? Has he not reason to rejoice, for no matter what happens to him he can always comfort himself with the thought: I am not conscious of any sin; I am a friend of God; I am loved by Him, and He takes more care of me than a father does of his child. What more can he wish or desire than the favor and friendship of the sovereign Lord? "I want nothing else," he may well say with contented mind, as the Patriarch Jacob said to his brother Esau, "but only to find favor, my Lord, in Thy sight,"[1] and my own conscience, which cannot deceive me, gives me testimony that I have found that. What has he to fear in death? For death has nothing terrible either in itself or in its circumstances, except a bad conscience, as I mean to show in a future sermon; while he has his good conscience to console him. Should he not rather rejoice at the thought of death? for it will transport him to the place of safety for which he has been sighing so long; and instead of the little he has to leave here, he will enter then into the joy of his Lord. True are thy words, St Bernard: "Nothing pleasanter, safer, or richer than a good conscience, it is safe during life, safe at the hour of death; and there is no more useful means of attaining future beatitude, no more certain pledge of it, than a good conscience."[2]

Exhortation to all to keep the conscience pure. All I have to say now, my dear brethren, to conclude this subject, is this. He who wishes to lead a quiet, peaceful, happy, and cheerful life, and to die a happy death, should take to heart the advice of the Wise Man: "With all watchfulness keep thy heart,

---

[1] Hoc uno tantum indigeo, ut inveniam gratiam in conspectu tuo, domine mi.—Gen. xxxiii. 15.

[2] Nihil est jucundius, nihil tutius, nihil ditius bona conscientia : futuræ beatitudinis non est utilius, remedium, nec certius testimonium bona conscientia.

because life issueth out from it."[1] O mortals! you are careful
in your duties and employments; you daily trouble yourselves
about many things, trying to avoid misfortune, and to attain
success; ah, whatever you do, whatever you omit, whatever be
your fears or hopes otherwise, be careful above all things to have
a good conscience in the sight of God, and never to injure it!
The glass is often your best adviser, when you wish to know
what your outward appearance is like; ah, do not allow the glass
of conscience to lie idle, but consider your soul therein, to see
how you are before God. Before undertaking anything that
seems even suspicious to you, before resolving in a doubtful
matter, take counsel first with your conscience, and see
what is most conducive to its repose; and that particularly
when the mind is disturbed by the tempest of unruly passions,
and is easily inclined to submit blindly to the dictates of the
senses. You will have many occasions of putting this into
practice; for instance, there I can get hold of some property, or
make some money. But wait; do not decide yet; ask yourself,
first, can I do this in conscience? There is an office, a post va-
cant, that I am anxious to get. Take the glass in your hand
again, and see what it says; ask it if you are capable of performing conscientiously the duties attached to the office. Here there
is an opportunity offered of enjoyment or amusement, which
captivates all my inclinations. But wait! Perhaps I will sully
my conscience thereby. There an agreeable company invites me
to laugh, dance, make merry. But I must not suffer myself to
be led astray; I must first see whether there is danger of offending God and defiling my conscience. And so on, in all circumstances. Then you must make a firm resolution and say to
yourself, What will it avail me to gain the whole world if I have
one mortal sin on my soul, and cannot be the friend of God?
If the glass shows you a spot on your face, you wash it off
at once; be as careful with regard to your conscience; do not
put off confession too long; examine your conscience every evening to see and repent at once of the faults you have committed.
There is no better or surer means of keeping the conscience always pure than the daily examen and frequent confession; for
it is almost impossible for one to commit many sins who often
repents of his sins and renews his resolution to avoid them.
" With all watchfulness keep thy heart."

---

[1] Omni custodia serva cor tuum, quia ex ipso vita procedit.—Prov. iv. 23.

Conclusion and resolution to purify the conscience daily.

Away then with the vain goods, honors, and pleasures of the world, in which I have hitherto fruitlessly sought happiness, rest and contentment of soul, and real joy of heart! I must acknowledge, with the wise Solomon, that in all these things I have found nothing but vanity and affliction of spirit. I have now learned something far better than all the world can teach me, and that is, always to rejoice with the true joy that consists in the Supreme Good; always to live in the true peace that the world cannot give; that peace which the angels announced to the shepherds: "On earth peace to men of good will."[1] That peace I find in my good conscience; if I have it, I can laugh at all earthly happiness and prosperity, and at all earthly misfortune and distress as well; for no matter how things go with me, I shall find comfort and consolation in God my Lord. Accursed sin, that hast hitherto robbed me of peace of conscience and the friendship of God, this very day I will expel thee by true sorrow and a good confession; nor will I ever again be so foolish as to take thee upon my soul, even if I gained the whole world thereby! I will take upon myself the sweet yoke of the Lord; bearing that, I will live and die; and then I can be certain of living and dying cheerfully, and of attaining to the possession of those heavenly joys of which I have a foretaste here in a good conscience. Amen.

Another Introduction to the same sermon for the Feast of the Annunciation of the Blessed Virgin.

Text.

Ait angelus ei; ne timeas Maria, invenisti enim gratiam apud Deum.—Luke i. 30.

"The angel said to her: Fear not, Mary, for thou hast found grace with God."

Introduction.

True it is that he has nothing to fear who has found grace with God. This belongs to thee in a special sense, O most blessed amongst all mere mortals, most holy Virgin and great Mother of my God! Yet in this thou wert not in need of the words of the angel to reassure thee; for thy own highly enlightened soul was well aware that from the first moment of its creation it was

---

[1] In terra pax hominibus bonæ voluntatis.—Luke ii. 14.

in the highest favor. Truly, thou hast found grace, not only for thyself, but for us also. To thee, after God, who was born of thee, we owe our best thanks that we have been again admitted to grace, for otherwise we should have been lost on account of the sin of our first parents. If we only knew that we are still in the state of grace! That it is alone, my dear brethren, which constitutes the happiness and joy of the soul that truly longs and has the firm determination to get to heaven. I know well, many a one says, that he who, after having received baptism, has a good conscience is in the grace of God; I know, too, that he who has a good conscience has nothing to fear either in life or death, but can always be happy and rejoice in the Lord. If only an angel were to come and tell me that I have a good conscience, then I would be perfectly satisfied, and I, too, would rejoice in the Lord! Now I cannot bring down an angel from heaven to comfort you with that good news; much less can I take the place of an angel. But this is a matter in which we do not require the ministry of an angel; for the conscience of each one tells him clearly enough how things stand with him, as I shall now explain.—*Continues as above.*

SEVENTY-FIFTH SERMON.

ON THE LOSS OF PEACE OF CONSCIENCE.

Subject.

The loss of God, whom sin alone drives out of the conscience, disturbs the peace of the human heart; therefore if we wish to preserve this peace constantly we must fear and shun sin alone. —*Preached on Sexagesima Sunday.*

Text.

Qui in corde bono et optimo audientes verbum retinent, et fructum afferunt in patientia.—Luke viii. 15.

" They who in a good and very good heart, hearing the word, keep it, and bring forth fruit in patience."

Introduction.

They are then faithful servants of God who keep the divine law in a good and very good heart, and bring forth fruit in patience; that is, in the cheerful contentment of heart which they have from their good conscience. My dear brethren, may peace of heart be and remain with you! Such is my repeated wish in your regard, and I beg of you, for the sake of your salvation, never to disturb or interrupt this peace, which is the source of true joy in this vale of tears! I beg of you never to disturb it, because no angel in heaven, no devil in hell, no man on earth, no trouble or sorrow, can take this peace from you, unless you yourselves give it up of your own free will; and that you can do only in one way, namely, by losing God through sin, as I shall now show.

Plan of Discourse.

The loss of God, whom sin alone drives out of the conscience, disturbs the peace of the human heart; therefore if we wish to preserve this peace constantly we must fear and shun sin alone. Such is the whole subject of this sermon.

Virgin Mother Mary, we beg of thee, by the sorrow that pierced thy heart when thou didst lose thy Son in Jerusalem, obtain for us from thy Son, by the intercession of the holy angels, His powerful grace, that we may never consent to mortal sin and thus lose our God; but if that misfortune should happen to us, that we may at once seek Him again by true sorrow and repentance.

All creatures are ill at ease, when they are out of their proper resting-place. For the human heart to have rest and peace it must necessarily be and remain in the place appointed for it as its centre. Such is the case, too, with other creatures: while they are in their proper resting-place they are quiet; but if they are removed from it only for a moment they betray by their uneasiness the suffering caused them by the violence done their inclination. Consider the elements: when fire is confined in the earth, so that it cannot escape into the air, which is its proper centre, with what dreadful violence it bursts through the hardest rocks! Whence come those fearful earthquakes, that sometimes destroy whole cities, and cause them to be swallowed up in the earth? From the air that is enclosed in the earth and compressed by water until it bursts forth to seek its own place. Try to prevent a river from flowing in its bed, and it will break through the strongest dam you can make. How it hurts you to knock your foot against a stone, or even to have the smallest vein in the hand or one of the fingers put out of its place; the whole hand or arm then becomes swollen and inflamed, nor does the pain cease until the vein or limb is restored to its proper place.

Seneca invites us to put this fact to ocular proof; there are certain animals, he says, such as the tortoise, that have very hard backs; if they are turned on their backs their distress is such as to excite our pity; they twist and contort themselves in every direction in their efforts to get out of the unnatural position in which they are. They put out their feet, bend their legs, knock their heads against the ground, and try to force their whole bodies upwards so as to get an impetus which will enable them to stand on their feet once more. If one plan fails, they have recourse to another, and that with the sole object of regaining a natural position; if they succeed in doing that, they are perfectly quiet and satisfied. What is the cause of their uneasiness, of the violent contortions they make? They are not beaten, nor tortured, nor in any way hurt by any one. All their uneasiness, answers Seneca, comes from the unnatural position in which they are.

What is the proper natural centre of the human heart? Nothing else but God alone. Just as the Creator has appointed the forests for beasts, the air for birds, the water for fishes, their orbits for the planets, the firmament for the stars, so has He kept the human soul for Himself alone. "Man," says St. Augustine, " is created to know the Supreme Good, and knowing, to love Him, loving, to possess Him."[1] Thus it is in the Lord God alone that the human heart can find true peace and repose, as I have already shown at length, so that I can now take this truth for granted. For if nothing in the world can give rest and peace to the heart but the possession of God in a good conscience, it follows as a matter of course that there is nothing in the wo.'d but the loss of God by a bad conscience which can interrupt and disturb this peace. And if the tortoise that is made to lie on its back, a hollow tooth, a sprained foot or arm, a stone thrown into the air, a man violently prostrated on the ground contrary to the erect and upright form of his body, has neither rest nor ease, how can we imagine that a perverse mind, with a natural inclination towards God, but turned away from Him, can find either pleasure or peace?

Now it is by grievous sin, and sin alone, that God is driven out of the conscience. As long as man is in the state of sanctifying grace he is united with God, and God with him, in the

God alone is the resting-place of the human heart, and no peace can be found outside of Him.

He who has a good conscience possesses God.

---

[1] Homo creatus est ut summum bonum intelligeret; intelligendo amaret, amando possderet.

bonds of the most perfect friendship and love; so that not only does he belong to God completely and entirely, but God completely and entirely belongs to him; and he can say to God with truth, in the words of the Prophet David: "I am Thine, save Thou me." [1]   And also: Thou art mine, O Lord! Thou belongest to me! Nay, says St. Thomas of Villanova, there is no good on earth that he can call his own as much as the Supreme Good. "O man!" says the saint, "thou lovest what is thine; thy clothes, thy house, thy money; love thy God, too, for nothing is as much thine as He." [2]   He is thy Protector, thy Supporter, thy Friend, thy Spouse, thy Father, thy life, thy only, infinite Good; the great immense God is wholly thine! What a happiness for thee, O man! Couldst thou well be richer than thou art? Couldst thou possess more than thou hast already, since thou hast thy God and with Him all things? O good conscience! what a precious treasure thou bringest to the soul! O state of grace! what a desirable, glorious, happy state thou art!

Mortal sin alone drives God out of the conscience. But if thou losest thyself so far as to consent to one mortal sin, though but in thought, oh, then a thousand times unhappy man! Now and not till now is that bond of friendship and property between thee and thy God completely broken! Thou hast lost thy God and with Him everything else! Thou mayest be poor and needy as far as the outward goods of this world are concerned; yet thou canst still say: I am Thine; Thou art mine! For poverty and want do not separate men from God. Thou mayest be weak and sickly, still canst thou say: I am Thine; Thou art mine, O God; for sickness does not separate thee from God. Thou mayest be the most despised, abandoned, persecuted man on the face of the earth, still canst thou say: I am Thine; Thou art mine, O God! For contempt, desolation, persecution, and all calamities whatever be their names, do not separate men from God. There is nothing in heaven, on earth, or under the earth that can take God away from thee except sin alone; sin is that wicked thief that robs thee of God, the Supreme Good, and of everything else with Him. Sin is a turning away from God, [3] say theologians, by which the friendship of God with man, and that of man with God is turned into a deadly enmity. "Call his name: Not My people," said the Lord to the Prophet Osee,

---

[1] Tuus sum ego, salvum me fac.—Ps. cxviii. 94.

[2] O homo, diligis vestem tuam, diligis domum tuam; dilige quoque Deum tuum; nihil enim ita tuum est, sicut Deus tuus.—Serm. iii. Dom. 17. p. Pent.

[3] Peccatum est aversio a Deo.

speaking of the Israelites who had sinned against Him; "for you are not My people, and I will not be yours."[1]

When the Israelites fell into idolatry while Moses was on the mountain, God said to him: "Get thee down, thy people hath sinned."[2] When they were in Egypt the Lord always spoke of them as His people: "Thus saith the Lord God: Let My people go;"[3] and at that time He said to Moses: "I will send thee that thou mayest bring forth My people."[4] But now He speaks in quite different terms of them: "Thy people hath sinned;" as if to say, as the Abbot Rupert remarks, "he who sins belongs to Me no longer."[5] On another occasion the people complained to the Prophet Isaias of the hard trials from which they had to suffer, and of the fruitlessness of their prayers for relief. Do you wish to know the reason of that, replied the Prophet? "The hand of the Lord is not shortened that it cannot save: "God is powerful enough to help you, neither is His ear heavy that it cannot hear" your sighs, and prayers and lamentations; "but your iniquities have divided between you and your God, and your sins have hid His face from you."[6] You have left Him and gone far from Him; not indeed, as St. Jerome remarks, that there is a place in the universe where God is not, and does not see you, but because you have turned your hearts and wills from Him by sin. God is present with the sinner everywhere but, so to speak, through necessity, which His omnipresence imposes on Him: for His heart and inclination are so separated from the sinner that, as theologians teach, He would not be in the same place with him if He had not to be present everywhere. Thus the unhappy man who is in mortal sin cannot say with truth: I am Thine, and Thou art mine! And how, asks St. Ambrose, could a slave say to any other than his master I am thine? Now as the sinner makes himself the bondsman of the devil and the slave of his own wicked passions, each and every one of his desires would come forward and contradict him, if he dared to say that he belongs to God. "Lust comes, and says,

[marginal note:] And separates Him completely from man. Shown from Scripture.

---

[1] Voca nomen ejus ; Non populus meus ; quia vos non populus meus, et ego non ero vester. —Osee, i. 9.

[2] Descende ; peccavit populus tuus.—Exod. xxxii. 7.

[3] Hæc dicit Dominus Deus : dimitte populum meum.—Ibid. ix. 13.

[4] Mittam te, ut educas populum meum.—Ibid. xxxii. 7.

[5] Qui peccato lapsus est, jam meus non est.

[6] Non est abbreviata manus Domini, ut salvare nequeat ; neque aggravata est auris ejus, ut non exaudiat ; sed iniquitates vestræ diviserunt inter vos et Deum vestrum, et peccata vestra absconderunt faciem ejus a vobis.—Is. lix. 1, 2.

thou art mine," continues the saint: "avarice comes and says: thou art mine," thou hast sold thyself to me for money; "ambition comes, and says, thou art mine," thou hast adopted my maxims. The devil comes, and says, thou art mine, I have thee under my yoke![1] Unhappy man, thou art done with God! Thou belongest to Him no longer!

Hence sin alone destroys peace of conscience, and turns it into sadness. Hence it is by sin alone that the conscience loses God: and therefore it is sin alone that ruins peace and repose of mind. How could it be otherwise, my dear brethren? Ah, to lose God, the Supreme Good, to wander away from God, the central point, to belong no more to God, what anguish, fear, and despair that thought must fill the mind with! "You are not My people and I will not be yours." I will no longer be your God! Alas, what a terrible thunder-bolt! Can any one hear those words without dying of fear and dread? That God is robbed of me is a matter of little importance, for He is not in need of me: He is all-sufficient to Himself, and His happiness cannot be increased. But that I should be robbed of my God; that my title, my name, should be that I am no longer in the number of His people, that is the greatest of all evils, miseries, and losses for me. No longer to have God as my Refuge, my Spouse, my Comfort, my Protector, my Father and Friend, what a terrible separation that is for me! I have lost God and with Him my right to heaven! I have lost God, and with Him the eternal joys of the elect! I have lost God, and with Him have lost myself! I have lost God, and with Him everything! With thoughts like those, which my conscience always suggests to me if I sin grievously, how could I have anything in my heart but sorrow and anguish?

Shown by a simile. Imagine, my dear brethren, that a great king has fallen in love with some person of lowly station, that he has raised her from the gutter, and placed her on his throne as his bride: how would it not grieve him to find out afterwards that she proved unfaithful to him! Away with you, worthless woman, he would cry out with indignation! Never let me see you again! Away with you! I cannot bear the sight of you! And what would be the woman's feelings? Where would she go to hide her shame? What anguish would fill her mind? And yet this is only a figure of what takes place in the human soul. By sanctifying grace it is raised to royal dignity, it becomes a spouse of the Almighty

---

[1] Venit libido, et dicit: meus es; venit avaritia, et dicit: meus es: venit ambitio, et dicit: meus es.

God, and is placed, as it were, on His throne; but when it commits a spiritual adultery by falling into mortal sin, it must hear its angry God cry out: Away with you! You belong to Me no more! I cannot bear the sight of you! I am no longer yours, nor are you Mine! We are completely separated!

Ah, how bitterly Saul complained to Samuel of this separation or rather expressed the despair it inspired him with! "I am in great distress," he said, "for the Philistines fight against me, and God is departed from me,"[1] which is the most terrible of all. Michas had given hospitality to some strangers, who stole his idols when they went away; as soon as he found out the theft, he hurried after them, crying out aloud and filling the air with his lamentations, as we read in the Book of Judges. "What aileth thee?" they said to him. "Why dost thou cry?" Ah, said he, "you have taken away my gods, which I have made me, and the priest, and all that I have, and do you say: What aileth thee?"[2] With my gods you have taken away my goods; have I then not reason to cry and lament? How troubled king David was day and night, when his conscience reproached him with having lost God! "My tears have been my bread day and night: whilst it is said to me daily: Where is thy God?"[3] O sinner, see about you, look into your heart; "where is thy God?" You have Him no longer. "God is departed from me," you can say with Saul. "You have taken away my God," you can say with Michas to the sins you have committed. Accursed avarice! wicked pride! wretched gluttony and drunkenness! wild desire of revenge! you have taken away my God and with Him everything! And do you think that while your conscience thus stings you it is possible for you to enjoy repose and peace of heart? No, that cannot be; for how could you have peace when you have lost the Good that is your centre point and proper resting-place, which a natural impulse always urges you to seek? Although, says St. Augustine, the soul leads a most wicked, godless life, yet it always seeks God even in the midst of its sins. You imagine, O man, that you seek earthly treasures and riches by your avarice and injustice, the delights of the flesh by your impurity, the pleasures of sense by your gluttony, and so on. But

Confirmed by examples.

---

[1] Coarctor nimis; siquidem Philistiim pugnant adversum me, et Deus recessit a me.—I. Kings xxviii. 15.

[2] Quid tibi vis? cur clamas? Deos meos quos feci tolistis, et sacerdotem et omnia quæ habeo, et dicitis quid tibi est?—Judges xviii. 23, 24.

[3] Fuerunt mihi lacrymæ meæ panes die ac nocte; dum dicitur mihi quotidie: ubi est Deus tuus?—Ps. xli. 4.

you are mistaken; the chief good you seek in all these things is your repose and contentment, your welfare and satisfaction; but since this repose, contentment, welfare, and satisfaction can be found only in God, you seek God without knowing that you do so; how then can you find rest when you seek God as the place of your rest, and at the same time lose Him by sin?

The heart is already disturbed at the first idea of sin. What do I say, lose Him? Before you got that far, when you were still thinking and deliberating as to whether you would do that sinful work, or not, even then rest and peace left your heart. I call all sinners to witness the truth of this. How did they feel when for the first time they began to yield to the allurements of some temptation or occasion, and to consent to grievous sin? What a fierce contest arose in their minds! The light of reason, faith, the Gospel law, the graces and illuminations received from God, the inspirations of their good angels represented to their minds the enormity and malice of sin, of the act they were about to accomplish; their conscience cried out: It is not lawful! you are on the point of making an enemy of God, who is looking at you, of losing your precious, immortal soul, of depriving yourself of heaven, of incurring the anger of God and the eternal torments of hell! Your own inborn sense of shame made you feel a repugnance to the vicious act. What a hard struggle the evil inclinations and desires had, before they succeeded in overcoming the influence of this light, this knowledge, and the outcries of conscience! Thus, in the midst of the contest, you determined with shame, confusion, and fear to gratify your evil desires and commit sin. Remarkable are the words in which the Psalmist portrays this struggle, when he says of the sinner: "He hath conceived sorrow, and brought forth iniquity."[1] One might think that David should rather have said: "He hath conceived iniquity and brought forth sorrow." For experience teaches that punishment follows the footsteps of crime. But no, answers St. Augustine; David had good reason for saying that it is enough to have the wish to sin to cause yourself anguish and sorrow; the first punishment of the bad will is the sin itself, which conceives sorrow, before it is itself completed and accomplished in act.

And feels still more pain when the sin is committed. Now, my dear brethren, if sin at its very first appearance can cause such painful anxiety to the heart, what will it not do when it is already committed; when the pleasure of it is past;

[1] Concepit dolorem, et peperit iniquitatem.—Ps. vii. 15.

when the satisfaction given to the evil inclinations has vanished; when the conscience cries out: wretched man, what hast thou done? It is now all up with thee! Thou art a hated enemy of God, a bond-slave of the devil, a child of reprobation; and if thou dost not repent of thy shameful act above every other evil in the world, and clearly confess it in the sacred tribunal to the priest, thou art lost forever! Alas, what bitter stabs those are for the heart! Could any one enjoy peace and contentment under such circumstances? No, no. "There is no peace to the wicked," saith the Lord, "who sees the heart and knows all that passes therein." The wicked are like the raging sea, which cannot rest, and the waves thereof cast up dirt and mire. "There is no peace to the wicked,"[1] saith the Lord God.

Ask our forefather Adam how he felt after having disobeyed the command of God. "Adàm and his wife hid themselves from the face of the Lord God, amidst the trees of Paradise."[2] What is the matter with you, Adam? God has not even spoken to you yet, much less inflicted any punishment on you! Why are you so fearful and anxious? The sin that he had on his conscience made him afraid. Ask the prophet Jonas how he felt after having gone to Tharsis in direct disobedience to the command of God. Hear how he accuses himself before the sailors in the ship, and blames himself for the storm that arose. "Take me up and cast me into the sea, and the sea shall be calm to you: for I know that for my sake this great tempest is come upon you."[3] But, Jonas, why do you thus lay the blame on yourself? None of the sailors has any suspicion of your guilt. Be quiet and say nothing about it! No, the sin on his conscience gives him neither peace nor rest. Ask Judas how he felt when he had betrayed his divine Master, and delivered Him into the hands of the Jews. Christ, having received his treacherous kiss, speaks to him with the greatest friendliness, and calls him friend: "Friend, whereto art thou come?"[4] Not one of the apostles had uttered a word of reproof against him, and yet he went off filled with sadness, fear, and melancholy, until he put an end to himself to get rid of the intolerable pain. Judas, what

As all sinners have experienced.

---

[1] Impii autem quasi mare fervens, quod quiescere non potest, et redundant fluctus ejus in conculcationem et lutum. Non est pax impiis, dicit Dominus Deus.—Is. lvii. 20, 21.

[2] Abscondit se Adam et uxor ejus a facie Domini Dei in medio ligni paradisi.—Gen. iii. 8.

[3] Tollite me et mittite in mare, et cessabit mare a vobis; scio enim ego, quoniam propter me tempestas hæc grandis venit super vos.—Jonas i. 12.

[4] Amice, ad quid venisti?—Matt. xxvi. 50.

is the cause of thy torment? Who is torturing thee? His own bad conscience was his executioner and tormentor. There is no room for peace in the heart of the sinner; no peace to the wicked.

And still continue to experience.

Sinner, whoever you are, have you fared any better in your unhappy state? Have you enjoyed peace and repose of heart after having lost God from your conscience? Do you now experience real joy? No, that cannot be, and even if you affirmed it a hundred times on oath, I should not believe you, unless the long-continued habit of sin has at last hardened your conscience and rendered you obdurate; otherwise you cannot have rest or peace. Laugh as you will with the lips, your heart is filled with anguish and sadness. Not without reason are you so afraid to go to church and hear a sermon; for you dread lest what you hear should stimulate your conscience to give you a fresh thrust to disquiet you anew. Not without reason do you seek to distract yourself by going into society, by eating, drinking, gambling and all kinds of amusements, so as to divert your mind somewhat and find a little relief from the melancholy that oppresses you on account of your unhappy state. But all your efforts in that direction must remain fruitless; for the words of the all-seeing God cannot deceive; "there is no peace to the wicked." Sin on the conscience and peace at heart are two things that cannot exist together.

Exhortation to fear sin worse than the devil. Shown by an example.

Therefore, my dear brethren, if we desire to preserve this repose and peace of heart, all we have to do is to keep our Supreme Good in a pure conscience. Nothing in the world have we to fear and avoid save sin alone, and that we must fear more than all the trials and calamities that can assail us, nay, more than the devil himself; for not even he can disturb our peace of heart. St. Antony writes of a woman who was given to all the vanities of the world and to an impure life, but whom the merciful God visited with sickness and bodily pain, in order to save her soul; for He permitted the demon to take possession of her and to give her no rest either by day or night. The unhappy woman, thus tortured by two demons, sin on her conscience and the evil spirit in her body, fled in her anguish to St. Dominic, who was then living. Acting on his exhortation and advice, she first began to chastise her flesh, and then to repent of her sins, so that at last she was freed from the demon. So far so good. For a whole year afterwards she enjoyed an indescribable consolation and perfect peace of heart; she discovered how much sweeter it is to have God as a friend in the midst of bodily mortifications than to lose Him by sin in the delights and pleasures of the flesh. But after a time she began to grow cold in the service of God; she omitted her devotional exercises one after the other, and was again plagued by the inordinate desires of her corrupt nature. Ah, said she to herself, shall I again abandon my God, whose favor and grace I have hitherto so peacefully enjoyed? She again disclosed her trouble to St. Dominic. The holy man asked her if she would be satisfied for the devil to take possession of her again. Yes, answered she; I resign myself completely to the will of God, and will be content with whatever He ordains for me; for I would rather be tormented in my body by the evil spirit, having the grace of God in my soul along with His peace, than lose my repose of conscience by committing such shameful sins. And as she wished so it happened to her; but a few days after, at the prayer of St. Dominic, she was again freed from the demon, whose tormenting presence had become to her the means of avoiding sin and preserving peace of heart, with God. So you see that one can have peace of heart, even with the devil in his body; but that is utterly impossible if there is mortal sin on the soul.

Ah, how comes it then, my dear brethren, that since we all so long for peace and contentment of mind we still have such little fear of the only disturber of our peace, that we daily commit sin? O my God, am I not mad and foolish to have sinned so often and renounced Thy friendship? What have I gained thereby? Has it ever done me the least good to have lost Thy grace and favor? No, I acknowledge that I have never had more troublous and melancholy days than those on which my conscience said to me: God no longer belongs to you. When the younger Tobias left home and went into a foreign land, how his mother sorrowed after him! How she wept and filled the whole house with her lamentations! O my son! my dear son! she exclaimed; why were we so thoughtless as to let thee leave us? Accursed be that money for the sake of which thou hast gone from us! With thee we have lost all! Thou art the staff of our old age, the comfort of our life, the hope of our family, our only joy in this world! "And when they were departed, his mother began to weep, and to say: Thou hast taken the staff of our old age, and sent him away from us. I wish the money for which thou

[margin note:] Repentance for past sins and resolution never again to drive God out of our conscience.

hast sent him had never been. For our poverty was sufficient
for us, that we might account it as riches, that we saw our son." [1]
Such are the words of the holy Scripture. O my God, my only
Good, might I have cried out with much more reason; ah, why
have I been so mad and foolish as to drive Thee out of my heart?
Accursed gain, that has caused me such loss! Accursed the
brutish pleasure, that has robbed me of the Supreme Good!
Would that I had never seen that person for whose sake I have
abandoned Thee! Would that I had lost the use of my limbs before going into that company in which I lost Thee from my conscience! Accursed sin, which has taken from me my God, and
with Him my rest, my consolation, my joy, my all! On the other
hand, have I ever had reason to complain as long as I had Thee as
my Friend? No, truly; more joyful hours I have never spent
than those in which my conscience said to me, after I had repented
of my sins: now God is again mine; I am again a friend and
dear child of God. And so I will always remain. Away with
all creatures and all the goods and pleasures of the world which
could take the Supreme Good from me! I have possession
of it again; I will hold it fast and not let it go for all eternity!
Rather let all the pains and troubles of life come upon me, as
long as I have peace of heart in the possession of God, than that
I should lose my God and my peace of mind to gain all the goods
of the world with sin disturbing my conscience. Join with me,
my dear brethren, in making this resolution, and may the peace
of God be in your hearts. Amen.

*On the Torment of a Bad Conscience: see the foregoing third
part. On the Comfort of a Good Conscience at the Hour of
Death: see the following fifth part.*

SEVENTY-SIXTH SERMON.
ON THE VALUE OF TIME.
Subject.

1st. What a treasure time is. 2d. The use that each one
should make of it, according to his state of life.—*Preached on
the feast of the Circumcision.*

-----

[1] Cumque profecti essent cœpit mater ejus flere et dicere: baculum senectutis nostræ tu-
listi, et transmisisti a nobis. Nunquam fuisset ipsa pecunia pro qua misisti eum! Suffici-
ebat enim nobis paupertas nostra, ut divitias computaremus hoc, quod videbamus filium
nostrum.—Tob. v. 23, 24, 25.

Postquam consummati sunt dies octo.—Luke ii. 21.
" And after eight days were accomplished."

Introduction.

So we are another year older, my dear brethren.   God be
praised and thanked!   But I know not whether I should wish
you another year of life or not; for I should like my wish to be
efficacious and to produce its effect, and as I cannot see into the
hidden decrees of God, I cannot say whether or not all who are
here present will see another year.   Moreover, I should like to
wish you something agreeable, but there are some who would
not be satisfied with one year; they would like to live longer.
And if I were to confine my wish to one happy day for you it
would be too little altogether.   Therefore I will not measure your
lives by days or years, but will act like those travellers who, when
they come to a place and have not an exact idea of the time, salute people by saying good day, instead of good morning, or evening, so as not to make a mistake, or, as the old Treves custom
has it, they say, " a good time to you."   This salute will hold
good for the day and the year both.   And such is my wish to you
now, instead of the usual New Year's greeting.   A good time to
you, my dear brethren; may the time that God has appointed
for each and every one of you to spend on this earth be a good
one.

Plan of Discourse.

*The value of this wish, that is, what a treasure time is, I shall
explain in the first part.   How each one should use it in his state
of life, I shall show in the second part.*

Christ Jesus, who art God from all eternity, and hast become
Man in time for our sake, teach us through the intercession of
Thy virginal Mother Mary and our holy guardian angels, and
impel us, at the same time, to use according to Thy holy will the
precious gift of time that we have received from Thy hands.

It seems to me, my dear brethren, that I already see on your Time is
faces signs of the discontent with which you receive my greeting. priceles
What a cold New Year's wish, you think; a good time to you! treasur
I might expect that much from my servant, if I had remained at
home!   A good time!   What is that worth?   I hear it a hundred times a day, when I meet people in the street.   True, my

greeting is no novelty for you; you hear it very often; but perhaps you have never yet realized what a beautiful one it is: what a precious, incomparable good it is that is thus wished to you. Alas that men should think so little of the precious gift of time! If I could by my wishes give you a bag of gold, would you not press eagerly forward to receive it, and run off home filled with pleasure at the thought of the agreeable burden you carry? If I could by my intercession obtain some great favor for you from your sovereign, would you not look on yourselves as being under a great obligation to me? If I could cure one of you of some grievous illness, would he not consider that he owes his life to me next to God? On the other hand, if I spent a few hours talking with him about useless topics to entertain him, he would not feel grateful to me; and yet a single quarter of an hour is of more value than all those other things; that single quarter of an hour he cannot make me any return for. Consider now briefly with me what time is; how great the gain which the good use of it brings; how great the loss which the waste of it entails, and then you will change your opinion, and with the heathen philosopher Seneca, who had only the light of reason to guide him, you will acknowledge that time is beyond price in value. "Whom can you show me," he asks, "who will put a price on time?"[1]

For we have not a moment of it in our power.   The world values a thing either because it is rare and costly or because it is useful or necessary to our comfort and support. Why do people value gold more than wood and stone? You cannot eat the one any more than the other. Because the latter are common, but the former is rare and difficult to get. If gold and silver were as common as the sand-stone in our mountains, the streets would be paved with it, and we should tread it under foot. Now what is more rare than time? For no one during his whole life has more of it in his possession than a single moment; since what is past is no longer mine, and what is to come is not in my power. This present little moment of time, in which I draw my breath, and which is past even while I speak to you of it, is all that I can call my own. What is dearer than time? Bring together all the treasures of the whole world; you can buy fields and lands with them: you can blind and pervert men with them: but if you offered the whole lot of them for a single quarter of an hour, who would be able to give it you? No one.

[1] Quem mihi dabis, qui aliquod tempori pretium ponat?

Go to the most powerful kings and emperors, in whose favor And no man ca give it us. and protection you trust, for whom you are ready to shed your blood and give your life; ask one of them for a short hour of life for your dying son, and you will get from him the same answer that the emperor Charles V. gave one of his courtiers. As you have perhaps already heard or read, the emperor on one occasion visited a courtier of his, whom he greatly esteemed and who was at the point of death, and asked him whether he could do anything for him. Yes, answered the sick man, there is one favor I should like very much to obtain from your majesty. What is it, said Charles; something for your family? No, said the sick man, it is for myself; I have served you, as you know, for such a long time; all I ask of you now is to prolong my life for a few hours that I may prepare for eternity. A few hours of life! exclaimed the emperor, shrugging his shoulders; I cannot do that for you! Whereupon the dying man began to weep. Unhappy man that I am, he said; I have spent so many hours, days, weeks, months, years in the service of a master who is not able to give me one hour, when I am so badly in want of it! And meanwhile I have neglected the service of God, who has promised me an eternal reward for a momentary service, and who would now have given it to me. Thus weeping and lamenting he breathed his last. Truly, he would have done better if he had begun in time to serve the Lord; for it is God alone who can make time and give it when, how, and to whomsoever He pleases. Powerful as earthly lords may be, they are not able to give any one a moment of time. "It is not for you to know the times or moments, which the Father hath put in His own power,"[1] said Our Lord to His disciples. Men cannot even know what is to happen in future time, much less dispose of that time according to their pleasure. God alone sells time. And for what price? Not for gold or silver: they cannot buy it. For what then? For nothing less than the life's blood of Jesus Christ, His Son. When our forefather sinned in paradise, he and we too with him, lost all right to do penance, and would not have had a single moment given us to find grace again, if the Son of God had not offered to suffer death for us. O good time, what a precious treasure thou art! What a great price was required to buy thee!

Another circumstance that makes a thing valuable is the use And be-

---

[1] Non est vestrum nosse tempora vel momenta, quœ Pater posuit in sua potestate.—Acts i. 7.

cause the good use of time brings a happy eternity.

and profit we can derive from it. Of what good would all your gold be to you if you did not use it or turn it to account? If you had heaps of it, what good would it be to you, if you could not get a piece of bread with it all? In spite of your riches, you should die of hunger. What profit does time bring us, my dear brethren, when it is good time and well used? When God gives you a moment, how much do you think you can gain in that short time? A hundred thalers? A thousand pistoles? That would be a great deal in your idea, and in that way you would become a rich man in a quarter of an hour. But after all, that is not worth speaking of. It would be quite too small an interest for such a great capital as a moment of valuable time! You must expect much more than that. What then can you gain with it. A whole earthly kingdom? Still too little! The whole world? Even if you gained that with all its riches and treasures, you would still have reason to sigh and complain that your time was wasted. No, everything that perishes with time is not worth time. Tell us, O holy Apostle St. Paul, what time is worth! " That which is at present momentary and light of our tribulation, worketh for us above measure exceedingly an eternal weight of glory. " [1] But what do I say? The possession and enjoyment of the infinite God Himself (and no greater good can be named than that) is the reward of a moment of well-spent time.

As the elect in heaven know.

I take as witnesses of this all those who are now happy in heaven. They will tell me that a momentary good thought, a word spoken in a second, a trifling work performed for the honor of God, a momentary act of patience and mortification, a short act of contrition for sin, a momentary act of the love of God, was the seed they sowed; an eternal crown of glory, an abundance of joys, an infinite God whom they possess forever, is the fruit that grew from it. Such, my dear brethren, is the profit we can make every moment of our lives, if we wish. Oh, what consolation and happiness for us! If the bliss of the elect could be disturbed by any feeling of regret, or an unsatisfied desire, there would be nowhere greater sorrow than in heaven; for the saints would grieve intensely that they lost even one moment of time while on earth by not spending it in the service of God; nowhere would there be greater dissatisfaction than in heaven, on account of the fervent desire that all the elect would feel to have still a little time given them, that they might suffer all imaginable tor-

[1] Id enim quod in præsenti est momentaneum et leve tribulationis nostræ supra modum in sublimitate æternum gloriæ pondus operatur in nobis.—II. Cor. iv. 17.

ments in order to add to their glory. Yes, holy souls, if you were not satisfied with God's will, if you were not in a place where envy may not enter, you would certainly begrudge us our good fortune in still having time to merit, or at least you would ardently wish to share in it, so as to increase your eternal joys! But what must you think of us, when you see how we permit that precious treasure to lie idle, or wilfully squander it, as if we had too much of it? Are you not amazed at our stupidity, in setting such small value on our precious time? Or rather do you not pity our blindness in abusing to our eternal ruin that with which we might purchase such great happiness? O Christians! what use do we make of our time? What have we done with the costly days and hours of the past year? How many are there not who have spent them in a wicked and impious manner? But it is not my intention to denounce sinners to-day, otherwise that waste of time would deserve serious reprobation. So much, my dear brethren, can time bring us in by way of profit, when we use it properly.

From this, too, we can see what a terrible loss and injury are caused by the loss and abuse of time; for the greater the profit we can make, the greater the loss when we fail to make it. Come forth out of your torments, ye reprobate and demons, and tell us what the loss of time has caused you! You are best fitted to be impartial witnesses in this case; for your loss is as great as the Good from which you are excluded for all eternity; as immense as the evil to which you are now condemned; as terrible as the fire which the anger of God has kindled for your eternal torment. If I could give back to one of you that day that you lost in gambling and drinking, that night which hid your impurity from the eyes of men, that morning which you spent in bed indulging in foul thoughts, that evening that you squandered away dancing in dangerous company; nay, if I could restore you one moment of that time, what would you do? Ah, you would get rid of an eternity of misery by a sorrowful confession of your sins, and in the same moment you would gain an eternity of happiness. No penance would be too severe, no austerity too great for you; no suffering so acute that you would not joyfully accept it. But, unhappy creatures! there is no hope for you; continue in your despair; there is no longer the least chance of your having an hour, a quarter of an hour, a moment of time; your sorrow and repentance are not of the least use to you.

The loss of time causes an eternal loss.

Even in the last moment of your life you might have escaped those torments; but now that is impossible; time is no more for you! O God of goodness! eternal praise and thanks be to Thee for giving me still the present time! What the damned in hell cannot do in all eternity with all their howling and weeping, that I can do by Thy grace at any moment by one tear of contrition, by one sigh, by perfect sorrow for my sins; I can appease Thy anger, and blot out a million of sins. What the elect in heaven cannot merit by all their perfect acts of the most perfect charity, that is, an increase of glory, that I can gain every moment by every good thought. See, my dear brethren, how precious the treasure is that I wish you to-day. Take that wish then, all of you, in the sense in which I make it. A good time to you all! as long as God will give it to you; but, at the same time, would to God that each one used this gift so as to profit by it! And this is the wish I desire to express in the

Second Part.

Wish and exhortation to use time well. It is my wish, I say; for that is all I can do; I cannot realize it. God expects you to do that; but He will not force you to do it; each one must do it for himself while he has time. How then is time to be used? For nothing else but the end for which we are created. A good time to you! but use it in praising and serving God. A good time to you! but employ it for the salvation of your souls. A good time to you! but use it only to gain heaven. A good time to you! but see that it is spent in doing your duty according to the will of God in your different states of life. If you neglect this, the great treasure is useless to you; days, months, and years will be lost; many a time will be a pleasant one for you, but it will be followed by a terrible, unhappy eternity.

To the clergy. A good time to you, reverend members of the clergy! The envious and ignorant world imagines that your time is too good; for, according to it, one must look amongst you for good, that is as the world understands the phrase, idle days; because you have not to ply a trade or business, or to undergo hard bodily labor to earn your daily bread, which comes to you without all that trouble from the inheritance of Jesus Christ. But how beautifully and profitably the time will be spent if you employ it as you ought in performing the duties of your state! St. Augustine defends you and me. *Nostrum otium,* he says, *magnum negotium est :* our apparent leisure is in reality a most important work. Our idleness, as the world calls it, is a great thing in the sight of God; our praying, singing, and praising God is a great work! The holy sacrifice we offer every day on the altar is a great work! The sighs and prayers that we send forth to God to appease His anger are a great work! The instructions, exhortations, and good example by which we endeavor to lead others on to holiness of life and zeal in the divine service, thus opening to them the door of heaven, are indeed a great work! To be holy at all times, in all places, at home as well as in church, holy at table and at the altar, holy when alone and in company, holy in prayer and study, holy in inward intention and outward work, holy in the secret mortification and chastisement of the flesh, holy in our decent amusements, in word, and in all our behavior, that indeed is a great work! That is our chief pastime; that is the principal business which God expects us to attend to. Go, said God to Moses in the Old Law, and much more would He use those words to us in the Law of grace; " Speak to the priests." And what was he to say to them? " They shall be holy to their God, and shall not profane His name; for they offer the burnt-offering of the Lord, and the bread of their God, and therefore they shall be holy."[1] Oh, would that we thus spent the time given us by God; what great profit it would bring us! Such is at all events my earnest wish; let us try to carry it into effect.

A good time to you, laymen! magistrates, public servants, law- To the laity.
yers, and all, whoever you may be, who have been called by God to look after the welfare of the community! You are looked on in quite a different light, for, as it seems, you have not good times enough; often you have to steal, as it were, what is necessary for your rest at night, if you attend as you ought to the duties of your state. You have indeed much to do, and you do a great deal, if you perform those duties well, that is, for the proper end, the honor and glory of God, and the salvation of your souls. But if you forget that good intention, all your labor is fruitless, and we might apply to you the words of St. Augustine in another sense: *vestrum negotium, magnum otium est;* your work seems great in the eyes of the world, but it is mere idleness in the sight of God. Without the good intention, you resemble that emperor who spent the day in catch-

[1] Loquere ad sacerdotes: Sancti erunt Deo suo, et non polluent nomen ejus ; incensum enim Domini et panes Dei sui offerunt, et ideo sanctierunt.—Levit. xxi. 1, 6.

ing flies; you are like candles that give light to others, but consume themselves while doing so; you are like channels that convey water to others, but keep none for themselves. Your days are passed in serving a master, in looking after your family affairs, in making money; but the most important business you neglect; your soul remains always poor, naked, and bare of merit. Ah, time is too precious for you to be thus lavish of it in favor of others! If you wish then to make a good use of it, I beg of you not to forget God and your souls in the midst of your labors. You can easily so arrange matters, if you wish, that you will be able to spare half an hour in the day to hear one Mass, and a quarter of an hour in the evening to examine your conscience and settle your accounts with God; you will not miss the week or the few days at least that you will spend in the year in making a spiritual retreat, a practice which, if not necessary, is at all events highly advantageous for those who are distracted with business during the year. And even if you suffered some temporal loss by attending to those things, you should not omit them on that account. " You give away money to buy bread, " says St. Augustine, " give it away then to purchase peace, " in order to attend to the important business of your souls and to set it to rights. " [1] That is the way to buy time, when we have not enough of it, as St. Paul warns us: " See therefore, brethren, how you walk circumspectly: not as unwise, but as wise: redeeming the time." [2] If a poor man comes to you now and then to ask you for help and good advice; if desolate widows and orphans have some law dispute to settle; if there is a question of furthering and protecting the cause of religion or the honor of God; if abuses have to be abolished or prevented; do not say, as some do: I have not time now; you must come again; I have something else to attend to; in a month's time I shall be more at leisure, etc. And meanwhile the poor man, who could have been helped in an hour, has to remain for a month without assistance, advice, or bread. Ah, be assured that a single work of Christian charity and mercy will be far more profitable to you, even in temporal things, than a whole week spent in attending to your usual seemingly most important business. Redeem the time; buy it in that way, and then you will do something really important.

---

[1] Quomodo perdis nummos ut emas tibi panes sic perde nummos, ut emas tibi quietem.

[2] Videte itaque fratres, quomodo caute ambuletis; non quasi insipientes, sed ut sapientes; redimentes tempus.—Ephes. v. 15. 16.

A good time to you, married people! Oh, what a good time you To married people. will have, if you employ it well in serving your God! Your Creator has given you a time excellently suited for the practice of almost all the Christian virtues, and you have occasions of practising them from morning till night. For the duty imposed on you by God is to look after your domestic concerns with Christian care; thus you have a time of submission and obedience to God. Your duty is to bring up your children from their tenderest years to a Christian life, to instruct them in the Christian doctrine and in divine truths, to inspire them with the fear and love of God, to keep them from sin and the occasions of sin, to reprove and correct them when they do wrong, to give them good example and thus lead them on to virtue (and the same, due proportion being observed, is to be said with regard to your servants); see what a beautiful time you have to practise zeal for souls, to act as preachers and catechists, and thus to further the honor and glory of God. Every day you have to bear different crosses, trials, and contradictions; see what a time you have for the exercise of Christian patience and fortitude. The servants are not as you wish; the husband or wife is troublesome; one or the other is in a bad temper; if peace and harmony are to be preserved, much has to be given and taken on both sides, and faults have to be mutually borne with; there you have a time for humility, meekness, and Christian mortification. Sometimes the business is a failure; losses and misfortunes make it difficult for you to provide for your children; you find it hard to keep them decently according to their station; there you have a time for confidence in the great Provider, for resignation to the will of God. The Christian law requires you to be honest and upright in your dealings; there you have a time for justice. Poor beggars come to your door for a piece of bread; there you have a time for practising charity, for feeding and clothing Our Lord in the persons of the hungry and the naked. In a word, there is nothing that cannot be made available to your salvation. Happy are you, if you only know how to make a good use of your time, and if you do not wilfully make a bad time of it by carelessness, idleness, impatience, and neglect of the good intention.

A good time to you, unmarried people! But you do not want To the unmarried. any such wish from me; for your time is the best of all, and as the Wise Man says, you are in the flower of your time. But how long will it last? Oh, you think perhaps, we need not bother about that yet! We are still young and have many years before us: " Come, therefore, and let us enjoy the good things that are present, and let us speedily use the creatures as in youth; let not the flower of the time pass by us; let us everywhere leave tokens of joy."[1] Let us enjoy the pleasant days as long as we have them; afterwards we shall have time to think of eternity and to lead pious and holy lives. Ah, be not too confident! You are still young, but are you sure that you will live to be old? A flower may be very beautiful, but it is easily broken, and easily withers. Imagine that on a table before you there are many glasses that have been placed there at different periods; some have been there for fifty, others for ten years, others were placed there yesterday; and some are more precious than the others. Which of the glasses do you think will be broken first? The oldest and worst? That you cannot say; for they are all equally frail, and one can be broken just as easily as another. Which then will be smashed the first? The one that is the first to be thrown on the ground; and that may happen to the newest and most precious, as well as to the oldest and most worthless. So it is with us mortals; we are all frail and weak vessels; this or that one has now been many years on earth, while you are still young and strong; but will he have a shorter time to live than you? Ah, who can say that? He, you must know, will be the first to die whom the divine decree shall first cast to the ground. Now since the decrees of Providence are unknown to us, the young are in just as great a state of uncertainty with regard to the duration of their lives as the old; and, they, too, must wait for the hour when the Lord shall come, and according to what Jesus Christ Himself says, that will be when we least expect: " At what hour you think not, the Son of man will come."[2] Therefore the wise Ecclesiasticus warns us: " Son, observe the time, and fly from evil."[3] My son, my daughter, let not a particle of that beautiful flower, your youth, pass by uselessly! Sometimes young people deliberate as to how they shall pass the time away; come, they say, let us go for a walk to pass the time; let us eat, drink, and make merry to pass the time; let us hold convivial gatherings, and sing, play, and dance to pass the time; a great part of their time is spent before

---

[1] Venite ergo et fruamur bonis quæ sunt et utamur creatura, tanquam in juventute celeriter: non prætereat nos flos temporis; ubiquæ relinquamus signa lætitiæ.—Wis. ii. 6, 7, 9.

[2] Qua hora non putatis, Filius hominis veniet.—Luke xii. 40.

[3] Fili, conserva tempus, et devita a malo.—Ecclus. iv. 23.

the looking-glass, and all to get rid of the time. Is that all you think of that precious treasure? Must the beautiful time, or even one hour of it, which the merciful God has given you to serve Him and save your souls, be thus passed idly, uselessly, and as it were murdered? Alas, the time of salvation is passing away, and no one thinks of it! "Observe the time," I repeat, "and fly from evil." My son, my daughter, make a good use of your time, and be on your guard against sin. Since your time is still the flower of time, God requires in a special manner that you should devote it to His service. This is the good time in which, with the prudent virgins, you have to lay in a supply of oil, that is, to practise real devotion, and adorn your souls with virtues; if you lose this time, your loss will be irreparable. The five foolish virgins were not admitted to the nuptials; why? They came too late, and not much too late either, for the door was not yet shut; yet even the little delay they made was the reason why the Lord said to them, I know you not. Therefore, make a good use of your time.

A good time to you, widows and orphans, afflicted and op- *To wido* pressed Christians! A good time to you again! Ah, you will *and orpt* perhaps say to me as old Tobias said to the angel Raphael, when *and the afflicted* the latter wished him joy: "So going in he saluted him, and said: Joy be to thee always." Alas, sighed Tobias; "What manner of joy shall be to me, who sit in darkness, and see not the light of heaven?"[1] Such, too, will be your thoughts. What are you saying to us about a good time, while we are wailing and weeping in distress and misery, so that a day seems to us as long as a year, and we are weary of life? We have not a joyful moment on earth! Your wish is indeed good; but it is a pity that it cannot be realized, so that we might have better and more joyful times. But I answer you in the words of the angel Raphael: "Be of good courage, thy cure from God is at hand."[2] Courage, afflicted souls! Even yours is a good and desirable time; an hour spent in bearing the cross of adversity can be more profitable for you than years of prosperity and abundance. Only resign yourselves humbly and patiently into the hands of your heavenly Father; and then you will always be able to give a cheerful answer to those who question you, like that beggar at

---

[1] Ingressus itaque salutavit eum, et dixit: gaudium tibi sit semper. Et ait Tobias: Quale gaudium mihi erit, qui in tenebris sedeo, et lumen cœli non video ?—Tob. v. 11. 12.

[2] Forti animo esto, in proximo enim est ut a Deo cureris.—Ibid. 13.

the church door. He was greeted once with the same wish that I now offer you. Thank you very much, he replied; but you must know that I have never had a bad or unhappy day in my life, because I have everything I desire or wish for. How is that, poor man? You have to sit there in the cold and wet, hungry and thirsty, with hardly a rag to cover you? True; but that is what I delight in. I desire nothing but what God wills; and since I am certain that without His will nothing can happen to me, I always have what I wish for. Courage then; your cure from God is at hand! This troublous time will not last long. "That which is at present momentary and light of our tribulation" will be followed, not by anything lasting only for a time, but by "an eternal weight of glory," which the faithful God has promised and is keeping for you.

To laborers and servants.

A good time to you, tradesmen, laborers, and servants! You often complain of being kept so hard at work by your employers and masters that you have no time to do good. But you have time enough, if you only wish to make a good use of it; and no one in the world but your own selves can prevent you from doing that. "Time alone," says St. Bernard, "is ours;"[1] not in the sense that we can dispose of it as we choose; but the time now bestowed on us by our Creator is really in our hands that we may employ it for the salvation of our souls. Money can be taken from you; you can be deprived partially or wholly of food and clothing; by the contract you have made with your master, you have in so far sold him your freedom that you must obey him, and do, not what you yourselves please, but what he commands. But the time given you to work out your salvation no master on earth can take from you, unless he deprives you of life by violence. It is true that your masters and mistresses can prevent you from going to church, or hearing Mass or a sermon, or saying long prayers; but your obedience to the will of your superiors even in this particular is making a good use of your time and serving God faithfully; for that and no other, as I have explained on a former occasion, is the character that God wishes you to represent in this life. Act your part well therein, as and because God wills; never forget the good intention in your daily labor; and, above all, be careful that your soul does not fall under the yoke of the devil by mortal sin. If you do that, your time will be meritoriously spent.

[1] Solum tempus nostrum est.

And finally, a good time to you, O sinners! You are most in need of a good time; for, as the Apostle says, your days are all evil and unhappy. [1] They are days which, on account of your wicked lives, serve you for no other purpose than to incur more and more the anger of God; days which serve to fan the flames of hell and increase your eternal punishment; days which the devil writes down in his book, to produce against you on that day when time shall be no more: "He hath called against me the time," [2] as the Prophet Jeremias says. All the days, weeks, months, and years that you will have spent in the state of sin shall be brought forward by your accusers before the judgment-seat, and shall condemn you; for the only use you make of your time is to prepare for yourselves an eternity of torments. O sinners, you still have time to escape that fate! "Yet a little while I am with you," said Our Lord to the Pharisees, and He says the same to you now; "You shall seek me, and shall not find me; and He continues: "You shall die in your sin." [3] What will you have left then? A body to be fuel for hell; a soul, a memory to be tortured with eternal despair on account of the loss of the time during which you might have done penance; but you will have no time any more, not a moment; you will have no God, except One who will punish you most severely and without mercy. May God save you from that fate! O Christians, now is the good time for you; do not hesitate; do not defer repentance!

I must conclude, my dear brethren, because the time for preaching is at an end for me for the present. I again wish each and every one of you from my heart a good time, exhorting you in the words of St. Paul: "Therefore, whilst we have time, let us work good;" [4] for of the time that we have already lived there remains nothing to us, and perhaps we have wasted a good part of that. Once for all, do not forget that the time we do not spend for God and our souls is lost forever. Oh, what a loss of graces and merits that implies! But as we cannot recall that time, let us try to make up for it by greater zeal; like the traveller who, having lost his way in a forest, walks all the faster in order to come back sooner on the right road and get to

---

[1] Dies mali sunt.—Ephes. v. 16.

[2] Vocavit adversum me tempus.—Jerem. i. 15.

[3] Adhuc modicum tempus vobiscum sum ; quæretis me et non invenietis. In peccato vestro moriemini.—John vii. 33, 34 ; (John vii. 33, 34 ; viii. 21.)

[4] Ergo dum tempus habemus, operemur bonum.—Gal. vi. 10.

his destination before night-fall. The time that will be granted to us in the future, is very short and uncertain, and will vanish like an arrow shot from a bow. Who knows whether the greater number of us who are now here present will not be in our graves before the end of another year? If an angel came from heaven and announced the hour of death to each one of us, saying: you have a year, or half a year, or a few months, or a few weeks, or three or four days to live; how would we act during the time remaining to us? Oh, how we would purify our consciences! How carefully we would avoid sin and the occasions of sin! How well we would perform the duties of our state! In a word, how zealously we would serve God! Why then do we not do so now, since we are not sure of one moment in the day? "Therefore, whilst we have time, let us work good."

Resolution to use the time well.

Yes, O my God! "And I said, now have I begun;" [1] such is my earnest resolution with Thy holy servant David. Now I will begin to serve Thee, and what I have not, alas, done hitherto, to love Thee sincerely with my whole heart. Now, I say; for to no purpose would I look back on the past time, from which nothing remains to me but bitter sorrow for having misused it. Accursed idleness, what a treasure thou hast robbed me of! Useless conversations and company, what precious hours you have made me squander, which I could and should have employed so profitably for God and my immortal soul! Ah, these complaints come too late! The beautiful time is gone! Vainly should I rely on the future time, for I cannot promise myself a single minute of it; therefore I will use all the more profitably what I have still in my power. I am resolved; now I have begun. O year that art now commencing! O month, O week, O day! perhaps thou art mine! But be the time allotted me long or short, what a precious gift it is, since eternity depends on it? Would I not be blind and foolish to lose any part of it? Heavenly Father, who hast created time by Thy almighty power! Christ Jesus, who hast redeemed it by Thy precious blood! Holy Ghost, who hast sanctified by Thy grace the good use of it! make me use it in future as beseems such a Creator, such a Redeemer, such a Sanctifier! On this day I offer Thee all the days and hours that still remain to me; on this day on which my Savior shed the first drops of His blood for me, offering them to Thee. And that offering I make Thee trusting in Thy help to carry

---

[1] Sic dixi; nunc cœpi.—Ps. lxxvii. 11.

out my good resolution, so that not a moment of the time remaining to me may be given to the vanities of the world, or the delights of the flesh, but that it may be all spent for Thy honor and glory, so that I may gain a happy eternity! This I wish you, too, my dear brethren, with all my heart, as well as a good time. Amen.

On making a Good Use of and Redeeming the Time, see the First Part.

END OF THE EIGHTH VOLUME.

To the greater honor and glory of God, of the most Blessed Virgin Mary, the Queen of heaven, and of all the holy guardian angels, and to the salvation of souls.

Index of Sermons

FOR ALL THE SUNDAYS OF THE YEAR.

Easter Sunday.

Sixth Sunday after Pentecost.

INDEX OF SERMONS

FOR THE PRINCIPAL FEASTS OF THE YEAR.

Alphabetical Index of Subjects.

—A.—

Adversity.

—C.—

Christ.

—V.—

Vainglory.

—W.—

Will of God.

—Z.—

Zeal.

PRINTED BY BENZIGER BROS. NEW YORK.

ImTheStory.com

Personalized Classic Books in many genre's

Unique gift for kids, partners, friends, colleagues

Customize:

- Character Names
- Upload your own front/back cover images (optional)
- Inscribe a personal message/dedication on the
    inside page (optional)

Customize many titles Including
- Alice in Wonderland
- Romeo and Juliet
- The Wizard of Oz
- A Christmas Carol
- Dracula
- Dr. Jekyll & Mr. Hyde
- And more...

Lightning Source UK Ltd.
Milton Keynes UK
UKHW021024240519
343267UK00012B/1146/P